A History of
the Hussite Revolution

A History of
the Hussite Revolution

HOWARD KAMINSKY

BERKELEY AND LOS ANGELES
University of California Press   1967

University of California Press
Berkeley and Los Angeles, California

Cambridge University Press
London, England

Copyright © 1967, by
The Regents of the University of California

Library of Congress Catalog Card Number: 67–12608
Printed in the United States of America

To My Mother

IN ACKNOWLEDGEMENT

I HAVE LONG looked forward to the pleasure I now enjoy, of formally expressing my gratitude to Professor James Lea Cate of the University of Chicago, who directed my graduate studies and has always provided guidance, support, and encouragement. Knowing that I could count on him for these things has been a great source of strength. Professor S. Harrison Thomson, now at the University of California in Los Angeles, has also been most generous with his help in many ways, quite apart from the service his own work has rendered to all students of Hussitism. My indebtedness to many other scholars working in this field is apparent in my footnotes, but here I should like to express my particular gratitude to Professor Emeritus František M. Bartoš of the Comenius Theological Faculty in Prague. No one today can write on the Hussites without relying at every turn on Professor Bartoš's massive corpus of books and articles; in addition he has been extraordinarily generous with his time, advice, and encouragement.

My studies have been supported by grants from the University of Washington, the Social Science Research Council, and the American Philosophical Society. Publication of the texts in Appendix 3 has been made possible by a grant from the University of Washington Graduate School Research Fund —Agnes Anderson Section.

I have received much assistance from the staffs of the libraries where I have worked: the University of Washington Library, the Prague National and University Library, the Archive of the President of the Republic in Prague, the Vatican Library, the Vatican Archive, the Bibliothèque Nationale in Paris, the British Museum, the Vienna Nationalbibliothek. In addition the Historical Institute of the Czechoslovakian Academy of Sciences in Prague has been most generous with its facilities. I particularly wish to thank its director, Academician Josef Macek, who has graciously helped me to get most of the photographs that I have used. Dr. Jiří Spěváček, of the Institute, has helped with others.

The maps in this volume have been drawn by Mrs. Alice Alden.

Finally I should like to express my gratitude to the community of scholars in the Department of History at the University of Washington, for the encouragement and stimulation of their society.

Howard Kaminsky

Seattle, Washington

CONTENTS

Illustrations follow p. 270

A Guide to the
Pronunciation of Czech Names
in the Text

All Czech words are accented on the first syllable. But vowels may be long no matter where they occur; such vowels are marked: (e.g.) á, ů.

Most consonants are pronounced more or less as in English, except for the following:

c	ts
č	*ch*urch
ch	(German) na*ch*
j	*y*et
ř	rzh (approximate)
š	*s*ure
ž	a*z*ure

In certain combinations, when "r" and "l" seem unpronounceable (e.g., Plzeň), they are pronounced as though they had a mute "e" in front of them.

Most vowels are pronounced as in, e.g., Italian. But:

ě	*y*et
ou	al*o*ne

Consonants are sometimes soft, as though followed by a (Czech) "j": such cases are indicated by a hook (ň) or an apostrophe (ď).

ABBREVIATIONS

AC   *Archiv český*
AÖG   *Archiv für österreichische Geschichte*
ČČH   *Český časopis historický*
ČČM   *Casopis českého musea*
Cechy   F. M. Bartoš, *Čechy v době husově*
ČKD   *Casopis katolického duchovenstva*
CMM   *Casopis matice moravské*
CsCH   *Ceskoslovenský časopis historický*
CSAV   Ceskoslovenská Akademie Věd
CSPSC   *Casopis společnosti přátel starožitností českých*
Do čtyř art.   F. M. Bartoš, *Do čtyř pražských artykulů* (1925)
Documenta   F. Palacký ed., *Documenta Mag. Joannis Hus vitam, doctrinam, causam . . . illustrantia*
FRB   *Fontes rerum bohemicarum*
Goll, Quellen   J. Goll, *Quellen und Untersuchungen zur Geschichte der Böhmischen Brüder*
Hardt, III   H. von der Hardt, ed., *Magnum oecumenicum Constantiense concilium*, III (*alias, Tomus III. Rerum concilii oecumenici Constantiensis*)
Heymann   F. Heymann, *John Žižka and the Hussite Revolution*
HI   R. Kalivoda, *Husitská ideologie*
Höfler   K. Höfler, ed., *Geschichtschreiber der husitischen Bewegung in Böhmen* (3 vols.)
HR, I   F. M. Bartoš, *Husitská revoluce*, I
JSH   *Jihočeský sborník historický*
KD   V. Novotný, ed., *M. Jana Husi Korespondence a dokumenty*
KJBB   J. Macek, ed., *Ktož jsú boží bojovníci*
Laurence   *Laurentii de Brzezowa Historia Hussitica*, ed. J. Goll, *FRB*, V
LCH   F. M. Bartoš, *Literární činnost M. Jana Husi*
LCJ   F. M. Bartoš, *Literární činnost M. Jakoubka ze Stříbra*

LCP	F. M. Bartoš, *Literární činnost M. Jana Rokycany, M. Jana*
LČPP	*Příbrama, M. Petra Payna* (the abbreviations refer to the cata-
LČR	logues of Příbram, Payne, and Rokycana, respectively)
LF	*Listy filologické*
MVGDB	*Mitteilungen des Vereins für Geschichte der Deutschen in Böhmen*
Mon. Conc.	F. Palacký and E. Birk, edd., *Monumenta conciliorum generalium*
Saec. XV., I	*saeculi Decimi Quinti*, I
Nejedlý	Z. Nejedlý, *Dějiny husitského zpěvu* (new edition in six vols.)
Nov.	V. Novotný, *M. Jan Hus, Zivot a dílo* (2 vols.)
OCA	("Old Czech Annalists") F. Palacký, ed., *Staří letopisowé čeští, Scriptores rerum Bohemicarum*, III
OCA-R	F. Šimek, ed., *Staré letopisy české z vratislavského rukopisu*
OC & N	H. Kaminsky et al., edd., *Master Nicholas of Dresden, The Old Color and the New, Transactions of the American Philosophical Society*, N.S., Vol. 55, Pt. 1
Palacký	F. Palacký, *Dějiny národu českého* (2d ed.)
SbH	*Sborník historický*
SKAW	*Sitzungsberichte der kaiserlichen Akademie der Wissenschaften in Wien*
ST	J. Sedlák, *Studie a texty k náboženským dějinám českým*
Tomek	V. Tomek, *Dějepis města Prahy*
TTE	J. Sedlák, ed., *Táborské traktáty eukaristické*
UB	F. Palacký, ed., *Urkundliche Beiträge zur Geschichte des Hussitenkriegs* (2 vols.)
VCA	*Věstník české Akademie*
VKČSN	*Věstník královské české Společnosti Nauk*

MANUSCRIPTS

Manuscript codices of the three main collections of Hussite sources are often cited by their signatures alone; these are characteristic in each case, e.g.:

> IV G 4 Prague National and University Library
> D 49 Prague Cathedral Chapter Library
> 4439 Vienna Nationalbibliothek

Codices of other collections are cited with full indications of their provenience.

John Hus's letters and documents, and the *Relatio* of Peter of Mladoňovice, are cited from Palacký's edition in the *Documenta*. Novotný's more scientific editions, in *KD* and *FRB*, VIII, are not as useful because in both cases the editorial language is Czech; the *Documenta* uses Latin for this purpose and also provides Latin translations of the Czech items. But Novotný's editions have been compared and used.

Bible quotations in the Latin sources are from the Vulgate, in the Czech sources from an Old-Czech translation of the Vulgate. When translating such quotations I have tried to use the corresponding passages in the King James Version, with such modifications as seemed necessary. In a number of cases the King James Version could not be used at all, and I have made my own translations.

The spelling of quotations from Latin sources reproduces that of the printed editions, when such exist. When I quote from unpublished sources I give the spelling of the manuscripts.

INTRODUCTION

THE HUSSITE MOVEMENT has often been praised or damned as a forerunner of the Reformation, as a step toward freedom of individual conscience, or as an early manifestation of nationalism; less often it has been judged as a movement toward democracy, or as a social revolution. Most of all, in modern times, it has been neglected, as a minor and somewhat exotic episode in what American textbooks call "the decline of the church." The Czech scholar, of course, does not have to worry about such neglect; secure in a century-long tradition of intensive study of Hussitism as the supreme moment of his nation's past, he can count on an interested audience for any contribution he cares to make. Outside Czechoslovakia, however, those interested in the Hussites often show a certain defensive pugnacity in presenting their work to the community of scholars—they must insist that the Hussites *were* important and are therefore worth studying, along with the more traditional subjects of late-medieval history.

It is in this spirit that the present author has written the lines that follow, designed to set forth his view that the Hussite movement was both a reformation and a revolution, in fact *the* revolution of the late Middle Ages, the history of which period cannot be properly understood if the Hussites are left out.

This view, like all others about the Hussites, has been stated before, but until recently it has been associated with anti-Hussite bias. It was more than a century ago that the German Catholic historian Constantin Höfler worked up his bitterly nationalistic attack on Hus and the Hussites as men whose hatred of the Germans led them to destroy the very foundations of civilized order.[1] In a few decades, Höfler observed, the Hussites played out the whole

---

[1] Höfler, I, pp. ix–xliv; III, pp. 5–144; see especially I, p. xiii.

tragedy that would be renewed a century later in Germany, and move out
from there to take its third form, the French Revolution, which transformed
both the Old World and the New into "what they now are, the world-
historical antithesis of the whole medieval order." The pages in which he
demonstrated this proposition are so venomous that they are no longer read,
but they may still be recommended as perhaps the best treatment of the
subject in "world-historical" terms, particularly now that the world has
changed its mind about revolutions, and now that the conflict between
Czech and German has been dwarfed by more momentous antagonisms.
Unfortunately, from about the middle of the last century, the foyer of
Hussite scholarship has been lodged in the sphere of Czech culture, and very
few "Western" scholars have penetrated that sphere. In fact, the West in the
twentieth century seems to have less knowledge of the Hussites than in the
nineteenth.[2] This is not only the result of the relative inaccessibility of works
written in Czech, for the Czech reappropriation of Hussitism has also meant
that the subject itself has been absorbed into the national interests of the
Czech people, and those few who have purveyed the findings of Czech
scholarship to the world at large have offered a Hussite movement of
seriously diminished and sometimes distorted proportions. The bad effects of
this situation are still with us, though the situation itself is changing. Not
only are more works being written about the Hussites by non-Czech scholars, but the Czechs themselves, under the inspiration or pressure of Marxism,
are setting their work within a broader framework, meaningful to even the
"bourgeois" scholars of the major countries. It may therefore be hoped that
the western world will once again see Hussitism as it was seen in its own
day, as a fundamental challenge to the old order, not only in Bohemia but in
Europe.

To talk of a Hussite revolution, however, is to raise a question that goes
beyond the particular subject. "The modern concept of revolution," it has
been argued, ". . . was unknown prior to the two great revolutions at the
end of the eighteenth century"—the American and the French. "For the fact
is that no revolution was ever made in the name of Christianity prior to the
modern age." Only in modern times, on this view, has there been a fusion of
the idea of freedom with the idea of novelty, "the notion that the course of
history suddenly begins anew"—and this fusion is regarded as central to the
concept of revolution.[3] Whether the definition is useful is one problem,
whether its historical claims are right is another; neither will be pursued
here, and the interested reader may be left to find his own answer to the

[2] F. Seibt, "Die Hussitenzeit als Kulturepoche," *Historische Zeitschrift,* CXCV, i
(1962), 21–62, especially p. 28.
[3] Hannah Arendt, *On Revolution* (London: Faber, 1963), pp. 19, 21, 27.

matter of fact in the pages that follow. But since these strictures may also be taken as examples of a more or less widespread modern concern for system and rigor in the treatment of revolution, it will be well to meet that concern, if not with argument, then at least with a clear statement of the position taken in this book. Briefly, revolution is seen here as coördinate with reformation: Hussitism is seen as beginning with a movement for reform, which then became a revolt; both then became wider and deeper, the reform passing into reformation, the revolt into revolution. At the same time the reformational aspirations, finding expression in political, social, and cultural revolution, were thereby intensified, and the two lines of Hussite development progressed together, in mutually reinforcing resonance. No single act can be taken as *the* revolution—not the utraquist revolt of 1414, nor the Prague insurrection of 1419, nor the pan-Hussite defiance of the Emperor Sigismund in 1420, nor, finally, the chiliast social revolution of that same year. Similarly it is impossible to take any single event as ending the revolution: neither the liquidation of the Pikarts in 1421, nor the murder of John Želivský in 1422, nor the defeat of Tabor at Lipany in 1434, nor the end of Prague-Tabor disputations in 1444. But when reformation and revolution are seen as two sides of a single process, then it is reasonable enough to begin the process with the conjunction of the two, in 1414 (with a possible claim for 1412), and to end it when the two had ceased to create novelty by their interaction—hence in about 1424, by which point the evolution of Taboritism was fulfilled. In this sense the Hussite Revolution is seen as beginning with the joint action of the groups that would later become its conservative and radical wings; but as the revolution and reformation were implemented to varying degrees in Prague and the provinces, they found their fullest expression in the Taborite movement. By the early 1420's, Prague had rejected revolution and had decided for a very incomplete reformation, in line with the program of John Hus before the radicalization of his movement in 1412. The full promise of Hussite aspirations was fulfilled only in the towns of the Taborite brotherhood.[4]

These considerations also determine the form of the present work, as a reconstruction of the reformational and revolutionary process, rather than a balanced narrative of events. Frederick Heymann's *John Žižka and the Hussite Revolution* offers just such a narrative, sound, accessible, and up to date;

[4] In his recent *Hussitica. Zur Struktur einer Revolution* (Köln: Böhlau, 1965), Ferdinand Seibt has argued for the importance of the Prague "revolution in the societal order of estates" as something much more than a mere conservative opposition to Taboritism, the revolutionary aspect of which he reduces to the brief phase of chiliast communism. Some of my reasons for disagreeing with him are apparent in the present work; for the rest, see my review of his book in *Speculum.*

the present work will often refer to it, in the spirit of a scholarly division of labor. Here the emphasis will be chiefly on ideas, programs, and doctrines, studied in their historical functions, as ideologies expressing the viewpoints of particular groups located in particular situations. This is not what is usually called a history of ideas, but rather—as suggested—a history of a process of development, reconstructed chronologically in as much detail as the sources allow. And the method is at least in principle one of textual analysis, designed to make the sources tell their own story—as they do when each item is correctly understood, dated, and associated with other items. It is a method that sometimes requires repetition and often involves the sacrifice of readability in favor of what some may regard as excessive density. In compensation, the sources themselves are usually much more interesting than anything written about them. Even those who do not accept the author's system of interpretation, which is admittedly sociological (in the German sense), will often find enough raw material to fuel a different engine of their own choice.

The author's Taborite understanding of Hussitism has much in common with the views set forth by Josef Macek, *Tábor v husitském revolučním hnutí,* and Robert Kalivoda, *Husitská ideologie,* but there are also many differences in the treatment of religion, in the evaluation of various tendencies among the Taborites, and in general approach—here problems of meaning are subordinated to the establishment of detailed facts. Both agreements and disagreements are indicated in some detail in the footnotes. On the other hand, the older Czech historians, especially František Palacký and Václav Tomek, are not cited as often as they might have been; where it has been necessary to summarize the findings of Czech scholarship, the most recent contributions have been cited as points of departure for those wishing to work further in the field. For similar reasons the footnote apparatus is in general rather elaborate, not only in the citation of sources and modern literature, but also in the sometimes digressive discussions of points that are important but do not belong in the text. This old-fashioned concept of the footnote leads at times to a certain clumsiness, and therefore requires an apology, but it is hoped that the results will be useful, both to specialists and to those interested in Hussitism but unfamiliar with Czech. The latter may also find useful the otherwise indefensible distinction between Czech and non-Czech works in the organization of the bibliography.

I

FROM REFORM TO REVOLT:
THE IDEOLOGICAL BACKGROUND

BEFORE there could be a Hussite reformation and revolution there had to be a Hussite revolt, a decision to defy the authority of the Roman church. It was not the decision of John Hus, or of his party as a whole, but of the party's radical wing, led by Master Jakoubek of Stříbro (Jacobellus de Misa), with the practical support of Master John of Jičín and the collaboration in theory and polemic of the German Master Nicholas of Dresden. These men and their followers among the students of Prague's university, as well as among the religiously awakened laity of the city, were responsible for an action that Hus himself did not wish and that failed for some time to win the approval of many of the most prominent leaders of the reform party: the introduction of communion in both kinds for the laity. This was begun in October, 1414, only a short time after Hus's departure for Constance on the eleventh of that month.[1] Thus, even before Hus could begin his hopeless task of trying to win over the Council of Constance to the ideas of the Czech reform program, a new issue had been created that would not merely prejudice his mission of reconciliation but make it irrelevant. And while Hus never ceased, in spite of everything, to maintain that his program was orthodox, and even carried this line to the point of repudiating some of the principles for which he had worked,[2] Jakoubek in Prague was claiming nothing less than that the universal church should accept instruction from himself in the correct way to give the sacrament of the Eucharist,

---

[1] F. M. Bartoš, "Počátky kalicha v Čechách," *Husitství a cizina* (Prague, 1931), pp. 86 f.; cf. *Čechy,* p. 398.
[2] See, below, *ad* n. 149.

on pain of damnation for all who continued to adhere to the orthodox practice of refusing the chalice to the laity. On 15 June 1415 the Council of Constance condemned utraquism—the doctrine that the laity should receive communion under the forms of both bread and wine, *sub utraque specie*—in the name of the whole church, and three weeks later the Council ordered John Hus's execution. Thus both paths, that of reconciliation and that of defiance, had led to the same place, the receiving end of the church's ban, all of which seems to show that Jakoubek, not Hus, had followed the right course.

But it was not so much a question of rightness as of the dynamics of the reform movement. Later, in the 1420's, when the Prague Hussite Master Laurence of Březová sought to validate his own movement by writing a history of it, he began not with the period of Hus's prominence, from 1402 to 1414, but with Jakoubek's introduction of communion in both kinds; John Hus made his appearance only as the holy man persecuted and then condemned by the evil prelates of the Council.[3] And, in fact, the Hussite movement that began in October of 1414, and ran its course of creativity for the next decade, was not merely or even essentially a continuation of the movement Hus had led. The men personally and ideologically closest to Hus soon lost their capacity for leadership, which passed to the radicals, led first by Master Jakoubek, then by the priests of Tabor, and although the radicals yielded to no one in their veneration of Hus the martyr, they did not draw their main inspiration from Hus the theoretician. Or if they did, it was not from Hus as he claimed he was—carefully and fundamentally orthodox in his writings—but from Hus as the Council of Constance judged him to have been: turbulent, seditious, subversive. One need not accept the Council's judgement, of course, but it would be reasonable to begin by crediting the Fathers of Constance with the ability to recognize a subversive when they saw one. At the same time, while Hus may have been wrong about himself, he would hardly have been completely wrong, nor would he have deliberately falsified his doctrine. All of which is to say that the figure of John Hus as leader of the Prague reform is ambiguous enough to pose a major historical problem, particularly when seen from the standpoint of Hussite history—the subject of the present work. For the same period of development that produced Hus's decision to submit his cause to the Council also produced Jakoubek's decision to defy the church. The dozen years of Hus's leadership must have contained the origins of both decisions—but in what forms, and in what sort of mutual relationship?

Taken in this sense, the problem of Hus points to a further problem, that

[3] Laurence, pp. 329 ff.

of defining the relationship of Hus's movement to its ideological and actual sources in the preceding century. For the decade or so before 1414 did not see the invention of any great novelties in the cause of reform; on the contrary, it was a time when the ideas, tendencies, and patterns of the immediate past were repeated, assimilated, and applied to new realities. The reform movement that took shape in Prague around the preaching of Conrad Waldhauser (d. 1369) and John Milič (d. 1374) survived into the 1380's and 1390's to produce the theoretical work of Matthew of Janov and, in 1391, to stimulate the founding of Bethlehem Chapel as a center for preaching in the Czech language. When John Hus was appointed to the pulpit of Bethlehem in 1402, he thereby took up a mission begun thirty or forty years earlier. But it was also in the 1390's that the Czech intelligentsia at the University of Prague began to receive, study, and succumb to first the philosophy then the theology of the English scholastic and reformer John Wyclif; Hus soon became the leading representative of this movement. Richly nourished by these powerful sources, the decade of reform over which he presided must be understood in the light of its past as well as in the light of what came later.

These are the considerations determining the form of both the present chapter and the one that follows. The decade of Hus's leadership and its fourteenth-century background will be treated here only as preliminary to the main subject of this study, the Hussite revolution. Attention will be focused on what was significant in the light of later developments; selection, abstraction, and analysis will take the place of chronological narrative. The result, it is hoped, will be at least a partial explanation of why the Hussite movement emerged and developed as it did, as a revolution localized in Bohemia but involving virtually all the elements making for change in late-medieval Europe.

THE RELIGIOUS MOVEMENT IN FOURTEENTH-CENTURY BOHEMIA

Charles IV of Bohemia, the son of John of Luxemburg and the Přemyslid heiress Elizabeth, succeeded his father as Bohemian king in 1346, only weeks after he had been awarded the crown of the Empire by the German electors, urged to this choice by Pope Clement VI. Well educated, conversant with the French culture that dominated the age, Charles resolved to make Bohemia an exemplar of that culture in both its material and its spiritual aspects. Prague, the capital of Bohemia, became the capital of the Empire as well, and Charles imported artists and architects to embellish the city with masterpieces of the late Gothic style. His court and, especially, his chancery became centers of art and learning, where some of the most prominent of

Europe's creative spirits could find welcome and support. In 1348, with the cooperation of the pope, Charles founded the first university in the Empire, at Prague; in consequence the city became a major center for philosophers and theologians. At the same time he promoted the construction of buildings and the introduction of viticulture and new types of fruit trees, among other useful works.[4] To make Prague not only great but holy, he sent far and wide for relics, none of which were too improbable for his taste; Prague thus became the repository for a fabulous collection of such treasures as the Virgin's milk, one of Jesus' diapers, and a nail of the Cross. Indulgences were granted to persons visiting the shrines. More usefully, perhaps, but in the same spirit of routine piety, Charles supported the cause of reform of the church. It was thanks to his father that Prague had been elevated to the rank of an archdiocese in 1344, but it was probably in reliance on Charles's support that Ernest of Pardubice, the first archbishop, felt able to commit himself to a struggle against the laxity prevailing in the lives of his higher clergy and indeed in the life of the church as an institution.[5] Not much reform was accomplished, in spite of abundant synodal legislation, but the spirit of reform on this level generated an atmosphere favorable to the cause.

Thus when Charles heard that in his absence the city had been visited by the preacher Conrad Waldhauser, an Austrian Augustinian canon, he invited Conrad to return and stay.[6] The invitation was accepted, and soon Prague's upper-class Germans were treated to sermons in their own language, criticizing their luxuries, their avarice, their pride, and their tepidity in religion. Rich people often like to hear such things. But Conrad also lashed out against the mendicant orders—not only against their simoniacal practices, like legacy hunting and receiving underage oblates for pay, but also against their basic theory of poverty, which he criticized along lines already developed in the much earlier polemics of the secular clergy against the Franciscans.[7] In his postil for the students of the University of Prague,

---

[4] See S. H. Thomson, "Learning at the Court of Charles IV," *Speculum,* XXV (1950), 1–20, with references to the literature; also K. Krofta, "Bohemia in the Fourteenth Century," chap. vi of *Cambridge Medieval History,* VII (1932).

[5] There is a useful summary account in Dom Paul De Vooght's *L'Hérésie de Jean Huss* (Louvain, 1960), pp. 5–7. For more detail see V. Novotný, *Náboženské hnutí české ve 14. a 15. století* (Prague, [1915]), pp. 3–56; J. Vyskočil, *Arnošt z Pardubic a jeho doba* (Prague. Vyšehrad, 1947), *passim.* The relationship between the Avignon papacy and the Bohemian church, very important in conditioning the development of the latter, has been carefully studied by J. Eršil, *Správní a finanční vztahy avignonského papežství k českým zemím ve třetí čtvrtině 14. století* (Rozpravy ČSAV, Vol. LXIX, No. 10, 1959), with a detailed summary in French on pp. 129–139.

[6] Novotný, *Náb. hnutí,* pp. 57 ff.; F. Loskot, *Konrad Waldhauser* (Prague, 1909), *passim.*

[7] Loskot, *op. cit.,* pp. 41–64; see also, below, notes 32, 51.

preached in Latin, he picked up these themes and dwelt also upon the vices and inadequacies of the ordinary clerics, who sought their own profit instead of attending to the care of the souls entrusted to them.[8] Thus Conrad was more than just a fashionable tickler of the rich, he was a downright odious enemy of the worldly beneficed clergy and the wealthy mendicant orders— the very groups that Archbishop Ernest's legislation was directed against. And in due course he received the tribute of their counterattack, in the shape of charges detailing the offensive things he was supposed to have said.[9] He survived the attack without much trouble, but the charges may be read as indications of what was in store for any preacher following in Conrad's steps; the pattern occurred again and again, until finally the scandalized prelates managed to procure the condemnation of John Hus.

There must have been a good number of Czech students who heard Conrad's Latin sermons, and at least some bilingual Czechs who listened to him in German, for Conrad's memory remained green among the Czech reformers well into the next century.[10] His most important success in this area was his effect on John Milič of Kroměříž, a Moravian who had come to Prague to pursue a career in the royal service.[11] He had indeed risen to some prominence in Charles's chancery, where he was exposed to the society of some extremely capable men and where he acquired a sense of European affairs that can be seen in his later work.[12] The normal source of income for chancery officials was an ecclesiastical benefice, and Milič came to acquire one, a rather good canonry in St. Vitus' Cathedral, but for reasons that are not clear he refused merely to draw his income—he insisted on working at it. Thus he left the chancery, took holy orders, and passed into the highest ranks of Bohemia's clergy. To judge from events he must even then have been undergoing a spiritual crisis, for he remained a canon only a very short

[8] F. Šimek (ed.), *Staročeské zpracování postily studentů svaté university pražské Konrada Waldhausera* (Prague, 1947), pp. xiii–xvi.

[9] Loskot, *op. cit.,* pp. 60–64; the charges and Waldhauser's responses are published in Höfler, II, 17–39.

[10] See the discussion in Loskot, *op. cit.,* pp. 118 ff., and Šimek, *op. cit.,* p. v, n. 3. The Czech translation of Conrad's Latin postil (above, n. 8) also attests to the reformer's influence on the Czechs; it dates from shortly after 1378 (p. xviii).

[11] F. Loskot, *Milič z Kroměříže* (Prague, 1911); Novotný, *Náb. hnutí,* pp. 65 ff. There is a good summary account in De Vooght, *L'Hérésie,* pp. 7–21.

[12] In addition to the works just cited, see F. M. Bartoš, "Miličovo obrácení," *Ze zápasů české reformace* (Prague: Kalich, 1959), pp. 7–17, and his "Dantova Monarchie, Cola di Rienzo, Petrarka a počátky reformace a humanismu u nás," *VKČSN* (1951), 22 pp., with a summary in French. Bartoš offers interesting evidence that the court of Charles IV may have brought Milič into contact with the reforming ideas of Rienzo and Petrarch, especially their critiques of papalism and their defense of the Franciscan ideal.

time; perhaps because of the impact of Waldhauser's preaching, perhaps for other reasons, he determined to renounce all his worldly honors, to become a poor preacher of God's word. He did so in the autumn of 1363 and about a year later, after a period of withdrawal, he began to preach in Prague. At first he spoke in Czech and, to the clerics, in Latin; later, after the death of Waldhauser (1369), he learned German and preached in that language too.

The late-medieval mind, oppressed by the sense that the old order was breaking up, escaping from any control by religious and moral norms that still claimed validity, often expressed its conviction of total crisis in apocalyptic terms, chiefly the imagery associated with the figure of the Antichrist. Totally evil, destined to appear in the Last Days to wage war on Christ, the Antichrist represented not merely this or that lapse from the Christian norm but the union of all the forces of perdition, including those in high places who were supposed to guard the Christian order but did not do so. Milič picked up this popular image, at first in a rather literal form: Antichrist was a definite person, his life and work the negation of Christ's, and he was to be found at the head of the evil world. Logically enough, Milič concluded that Antichrist was no other than the Emperor Charles IV, and in 1366 he pointed to that unfortunate ruler in the course of a sermon on the apocalyptic theme. Archbishop Ernest promptly confined him for a while, no doubt more to let the affair blow over than to punish the preacher, whom he respected; Milič, when he emerged, did not pursue the identification. Instead, in 1367, he went to Rome to present his more general views on the crisis of the day to Pope Urban V, due to move there from Avignon.[13] When Urban was delayed, Milič became impatient and decided to preach anyway, first intimating his intention in a notice tacked up on the doors of St. Peter's. Once again he saw the inside of a prison, this time through the agency of the Roman inquisition, but when the pope arrived, escorted by Charles IV, Milič was released. After a conversation with Urban, Milič returned to Prague, but soon after decided once again to go to Rome, in 1369. This time, however, he cut the trip short, perhaps after receiving the news of Waldhauser's death, and again took up his mission in Prague, where he preached from 1369 to 1374.

The works that Milič wrote for Urban V on the subject of Antichrist show the literal concept of the figure flanked by the more productive figurative one, with Antichrist standing for everyone opposed to Christ's order.[14] More

---

[13] F. M. Bartoš, "Miličův sermo de die novissimo," *Reformační sborník*, VIII (1946), 49–58.

[14] The Latin texts of Milič's letter to Pope Urban V and his *Prophecia et revelacio de Antichristo* (or *Libellus de Antichristo*) are published and discussed by F. Menčík, "Milič a dva jeho spisy z r. 1367," *VKČSN* (1890), pp. 309–336. The second work was

particularly, Milič was oppressed by the evils prevailing in the church, although he did not neglect to repeat the usual preacher's lament over sins in the secular order—pride, vanity, oppression of the poor, wars, disobedience to the church, usury, unjust tolls, lies, fornication, and false witness.[15] But nobody paid much attention to this sort of thing. It was different when Milič denounced simoniacal ordinations and consecrations, the violation of free elections by appointments procured through simony or the favor of princes, the prelates' luxury and concubinage, their wealth and pluralism, their practice of usury through the purchase of annuities.[16] He also followed Waldhauser in denouncing the privileges of the mendicant orders, who subverted ecclesiastical discipline by hearing confessions without the permission of the ordinary, sold indulgences, and used their special status to accumulate riches.[17] Nor did he spare the nuns who went about in society, danced, and fornicated. At the same time he had no use for heresy—under the title of Beguines and Beghards he denounced the subverters of order, and at all points he declared his submission to the papacy and his fervent desire that the pope take the measures needed to restore the purity of the church, preferably by calling a general council in Rome. "The church is laid waste by the negligence of her pastors"—that was his theme, and it implied not subversion but restoration of ecclesiastical authority.[18]

In Prague he pursued these same complaints, with the added snap that came from the instancing of particular cases. He constantly held up the image of apostolic poverty and purity to the rich prelates, who at one point complained, "From the time that you started preaching we have never known a moment's peace!"[19] We can sympathize with them when we learn how Milič wrote an admonitory letter to one prelate who had a special door made for his house, so that he could more conveniently bring in his women—when he heard the letter read, the prelate burst out that Milič was a sodomite.[20]

---

included by Matthew of Janov in his *Regulae veteris et novi testamenti*, ed. V. Kybal, III (Prague and Innsbruck, 1911), 368–381. Loskot, *Milič*, pp. 75 f., and following him De Vooght, *L'Hérésie*, p. 13, suppose that Pope Urban V persuaded Milič to give up his concept of the Antichrist as a particular person, in favor of a symbolic interpretation; it is not clear to me that the sources support this distinction. See Bartoš, "Miličův sermo," p. 49, n. 3, for a discussion of the dating. For the two interpretations of the Antichrist see H. Preuss, *Die Vorstellung vom Antikrist im späteren Mittelalter . . .* (Leipzig, 1906), pp. 25 f., 44 f.

[15] *Libellus de Antichristo*, in *Regulae*, III, 376.

[16] *Ibid.*, pp. 373 f.; letter to Urban V, in Menčík, *op. cit.*, pp. 318–325.

[17] *De Antichristo*, p. 374; letter to Urban, p. 322.

[18] Letter to Urban, pp. 322 f. and *passim; De Antichristo*, p. 380 (for a general council in Rome) and p. 373 ("The church is laid waste . . .").

[19] The anonymous *Vita Milicii*, in *FRB*, I, 424.

[20] *Ibid.*

Others called him a Beghard.[21] And in fact he did exhibit a certain extremism that might reasonably seem unwholesome to even a more or less virtuous worldly type. He repeatedly gave away his warm clothing to the poor, and himself went about in a simple tunic, which he piously never washed. His body was treated with even less respect—it was filthy and he beat himself with rods; he fasted, wore himself out with countless hours of daily preaching, and engaged in a whole battery of ascetic exercises.[22] His biographer does, to be sure, refer to his cheerful disposition, but he also reveals a certain somberness, a Gothic austerity of manner, that warns us against the otherwise irresistible temptation to see Milič as a kind of St. Francis of Assisi—the parallels are there, and they are meaningful, but the world was much younger in 1210 than it was in 1370, and the prelates whom Francis could win over with the message of the Gospels had become nothing but enjoyers of vested interests, ruthlessly determined to keep what they had. Then, too, although Milič prayed "ad modum crucis prostrat[us]," he never received the stigmata.[23]

With these reservations, however, we can note the more or less Franciscan style of Milič's practical, nondenunciatory efforts. He attracted a band of preachers who joined him in his poor life, dependent on alms, constantly working among the people. Increasing numbers of the laity also adhered to his movement, which thus began to take on a definite social form. This aspect of it was powerfully reinforced when Milič undertook to preach reform to the prostitutes of the city; here he was helped by Antichrist himself, for Charles IV gave him possession of one of Prague's leading brothels, known romantically as "Venice"; Milič acquired enough money to buy some of the adjacent properties and received others as gifts, and was thus able to set up an actual community. He gave it the new name of "Jerusalem," and devoted it in the first place to the housing and upkeep of the harlots he had converted—but his band of preachers also lived there. Subsequently Jerusalem was exempted from the parochial organization in which it originally lay and became a kind of independent parish, not unlike the orthodox Beguine parishes elsewhere in Europe.[24] The clergy were, of course, scandalized; they even called Milič a Beghard, and in 1373 a kind of united front of all the non-Miličian clergy of Prague met to prepare accusations against him. It was to clear himself of these charges that Milič once again had to leave

---

[21] *Ibid.;* cf., below, n. 57.

[22] *Vita Milicii,* pp. 414 f. and *passim.*

[23] *Ibid.,* p. 425. Milič's "hilarity" is attested, e.g., on pp. 421, 425; but for his austere manner, his avoidance of secular words of mirth, his refusal to smile or chat with people as he went his rounds, etc., see pp. 407 f., 409. For the comparison with St. Francis see, e.g., Loskot, *Milič,* p. 55.

[24] For all of this see, *ibid.,* pp. 82 ff., and Novotný, *Náb. hnutí,* pp. 74 f.

Prague, this time for Avignon, where he was well received, but where he died before his case could be disposed of.[25]

Patently inspired by self-interest, the charges of 1373 need not be taken at face value. Nonetheless they do show either what Milič's movement seemed to be or what it could be made to seem, and the difference here is not too great. His clerical followers perhaps did not wear a special habit, did not have a special rule, did not bear the title of "Order of the Apostolic Life"— but the charges to this effect would not have been possible if appearances had not supported them.[26] Since Milič denounced the Beghards and Beguines, it would be wrong to identify his movement with the heretics so designated, but, names aside, his community of pious men and women, some living in semiclaustration, others having constant recourse to Jerusalem, all engaged in meditations and good works, was not different from the typical *orthodox* Beguine community.[27] The emphasis on preaching was also typical here, as was another point common to many of the movements of lay piety—the emphasis on frequent, even daily reception of the Eucharist.[28] That such a group would cultivate an extremely ardent religious enthusiasm was only to be expected; that its feelings would constantly generate a hostile attitude toward the worldly clergy was inevitable, the more so since the Miličians saw the Prague prelates not as pillars of the church but as subverters of the true order, resisting the wholesome efforts of the archbishop (and hopefully the pope) to effect a reform.

Thus, although Milič never raised his voice against the jurisdiction of his actual superiors in the church, he never ceased to scourge the friars and the endowed clergy of Prague. Waldhauser had been bad enough, Milič was insupportable. When the news of his imprisonment in Rome came to Prague, the friars exultantly preached, "Ah, now Milič will be burned!"— and if it had been in their power they would certainly have made their dreams come true.[29] It is not surprising that when Milič died in Avignon his enemies exerted all their power to have Jerusalem suppressed, or that they

[25] Loskot, *Milič,* pp. 98 ff.

[26] See, *ibid.,* p. 87 for a discussion of this problem.

[27] See Ernest McDonnell, *The Beguines and Beghards in Medieval Culture* (New Brunswick, N.J.: Rutgers University Press, 1954), *passim.* The type of the Beguine parish, analogous to that of Milič's Jerusalem, is discussed on pp. 170 ff. For the heretical Beguines and Beghards—evidently the only kind recognized under the name by Milič—see pp. 475 ff.

[28] See, *ibid.,* pp. 305–319 for the general phenomenon of Beguine eucharistic devotion, including frequent communion. Many other sources could be cited—e.g., *The Book of the Poor in Spirit, by a Friend of God,* trans. C. F. Kelley (London: Longmans, Green, 1955), pp. 221 f., for a defense of frequent communion. The discussion in *Histoire de l'Eglise,* XIV, ii, ed. E. Delaruelle *et al.* (Bloud & Gay, 1964), 749, is inadequate.

[29] *Vita Milicii,* p. 413.

succeeded, in spite of the favor Milič had won in high places. Perhaps Jerusalem had depended too much on his charisma to survive his death. At any rate, it was given to the Cistercians as a college for their members at the University of Prague, and we can only imagine the monkish jokes that may have enlivened the no doubt un-Bernardian meals, when the brethren recalled what their college once had been. The former inmates and their sympathizers continued to form a kind of movement, under the protection of some leading figures in church and lay society, but much of the old dynamism must have been lost, for the Miličian clergy were thrust out of their positions, persecuted, and dispersed.

This was the situation when one of Milič's old disciples, Matthew of Janov, began to work in Prague. He had come under the reformer's spell in 1372, but had left to pursue his studies at the University of Paris, where he matriculated in 1373, became Master of Arts in 1376, then studied theology until 1381.[30] It may have been at Paris that he wrote the first draft of his work on the Antichrist, perhaps with his Miličian inspiration still warm,[31] but if that were the case he had brought coals to Newcastle. For some of the abuses that Milič had attacked as Antichristian had been attacked under the same title in Paris more than a century earlier, by William of St. Amour and his associates, and presumably this episode had not been forgotten. William's celebrated *De periculis novissimorum temporum,* directed against the mendicancy and the privileges of the friars, must have still been read in Paris, for Matthew found it there, along with other works of the same struggle, and he incorporated it whole in his own *magnum opus,* the *Regule veteris et novi testamenti.*[32] At the same time, other Parisian currents of thought may be presumed to have had some effect on Matthew, even though the literary proofs are lacking. The Great Schism broke out in 1378, during his studies, and from then on it was the University of Paris that produced the most celebrated formulations of conciliarism; moreover Matthew could hardly

[30] V. Kybal, *M. Matěj z Janova* (Prague, 1905), with full references to the older literature; also V. Kybal, "Étude sur les origines du mouvement Hussite en Bohême, Mathias de Janov," *Revue historique,* CIII (1910), 1–31, and De Vooght, *L'Hérésie,* pp. 21–35.

[31] Kybal, *M. Matěj,* p. 65, and his Introduction to *Regulae,* III, xii–xvii.

[32] *Regulae,* III, 243–332; this whole section is devoted to material by or about William. See also J. Sedlák, *M. Jan Hus* (Prague, 1915), p. 72, n. 1. The best recent discussion of the controversies between seculars and mendicants is Y. Congar's "Aspects ecclésiologiques de la querelle entre mendiants et séculiers dans la seconde moitié du XIIIᵉ siècle et le début du XIVᵉ," *Archives d'histoire doctrinale et littéraire du Moyen Âge,* XXVIII (1961), 35–151. See also P. McKeon, "The Status of the University of Paris as *Parens Scientiarum:* An Episode in the Development of Its Autonomy," *Speculum,* XXXIX (1964), 651–675.

the next few years not in Prague but in Paris. There, however, the university was in turmoil, pressed by the King of France to recognize the Avignon Pope Clement VII, but urged toward neutrality by those of its masters and scholars who came from lands of the Roman obedience, most notably the Empire. After first bravely proclaiming its neutrality, the university fell in line with French policy, in mid-1379; it was only in May of 1381 that the corporation recovered its independence and came out for neutrality and a council—a position that was then given up for the former one in January, 1383. But these last fluctuations did not affect Matthew of Janov; like many scholars of the English-German "nation" at the university, he left during the first Clementine period. From Paris he seems to have gone to Rome, in early 1381; on 1 April of that year he received another papal provision, an expectancy to a canonry in St. Vitus' Cathedral. At the same time he secured letters of recommendation from the University of Paris to King Wenceslas IV and the Archbishop of Prague, John of Jenštejn. By October, 1381, he was back in Prague, armed with what he hoped would be effective instruments with which to make a career. But they were not. The canons admitted him to membership, but he did not get an income-producing benefice, nor did his earlier papal provision lead to anything but litigation. He depended for his maintenance at first on his patron, the Milíčian prelate Vojtěch Raňkův (Albertus Ranconis), then on the favor of Archbishop John, also friendly to reform, who employed him in preaching and in hearing confessions, and who perhaps helped him, finally, to get a real benefice, a parish-living outside of Prague, which Matthew ran as a nonresident. But this came only in 1388, and the incomes from the parish were neither regular nor trouble free.[38] The wealth, prestige, and worldly brilliance that Milíč had voluntarily renounced were for Matthew the unattainable goals of a lifetime of inept careerism. But the careerist was also a Milíčian reformer, and the Prague in which he suffered his disappointments was also the theater of a continuing struggle between the Milíčians and the beneficed clergy.

The relationship between Matthew's frustrations and his reformism belongs to those mysteries of the heart and mind that the historian does best to avoid. But Matthew was enough of an intellectual not only to engage in self-analysis, but also to regard the results as worth the notice of his readers. There is a remarkable passage in the *Regule*—it is, indeed, the key to the whole work—in which he first describes the two paths, the strait and the broad, and shows how in his day the difference between them was not between obvious vice and obvious virtue, but between an apparently virtuous, "authentic" way that was praised by all, and the truly Christian way

[38] Kybal, *M. Matěj*, pp. 17–20.

have failed to feel the practical disadvantages of studying in the
obedience while hoping for a career in Bohemia, which was loyal
Furthermore, the Paris of Matthew's day can hardly have been int
the extraordinarily radical ideas it would generate in the 1390's,
supported the experiment of the French crown in withdrawing o
from the Avignonese pope. The ecclesiastical implications of th
amounted to a primitive but quite definite form of what would later
known as Gallicanism: the concept of the French church as a unity
unit of the French polity.[33] This idea itself was certainly in the air, a
Matthew had no use for it; more important in the present context v
the various theoretical justifications of it, which reached into every an
critical, antipapal, anti-Hildebrandine thought that the past two
centuries had accumulated. These radical ideas were not buried
manuscripts but lived in the talk and thought of the more sensitive
gians.[34] Matthew of Janov was certainly one of these, and we may
that when he returned to Prague in 1381 it was as a man able and
enrich the Milićian tradition with new ideas and, above all, new pers
acquired in France.

But while Matthew's *Regule* can be understood as having been insp
Milič, and indeed as constituting a systematization of Milič's ideas,[35]
also the product of the post-Milićian situation, in Prague and elsewhe
can Matthew's own career be neglected in this connection. Althou
South Bohemian family into which he was born about 1350 ranked
the gentry, little if any money was available to send its brilliant son tl
the higher schools: Matthew had to plead poverty to avoid paying his
Paris, and like others in his condition he looked to his education to
him success, in the shape of a church benefice.[36] But although he h
name put on the university's benefice roll sent to Pope Urban VI in 13
outbreak of the schism kept the roll from being delivered; mean
Matthew had in some other way, perhaps by a visit to Rome, secured a
provision, dated 11 May 1378, to some benefice in the gift of the F
archbishop or chapter.[37] Such provisions were essentially licenses to
litigation, and Matthew got no immediate benefit from his, since he

---

[33] *Histoire de l'Église,* XIV, i, 315 ff., offers good bibliographical notes, inc
systematic references to V. Martin, *Les origines du gallicanisme* (2 vols.; Paris,
Johannes Haller, *Papsttum und Kirchenreform,* (Berlin, 1903), I, 197–479,
indispensable.

[34] For all of this see Haller, *op. cit.,* pp. 331 ff.

[35] O. Odložilík, "The Chapel of Bethlehem in Prague," *Wiener Archiv für Gesc
des Slawentums und Osteuropas,* II (1956), 130 f.

[36] Kybal, "Étude," pp. 8 f., and *M. Matěj,* pp. 5–32.

[37] See n. 36; also Novotný, *Náb. hnutí,* pp. 146 f.

that was opposed as suspect and dangerous by the very "superiors and rectors" of the church; he then confesses that from "early youth right up to the present" he had "doubts about the choice between the two ways":[39]

> Whether to go after benefices and offices, pressing myself forward greedily and shamelessly, which I have usually done, or whether instead to go out of the camp and bear the poverty and reproaches suffered by Jesus Christ. Whether to seek a soft and quiet life in the present, living conformably and in peace with the multitude, or rather to cling to the faithful and holy evangelical truth.

In a word, whether to follow the example of Milič or whether to join "the great, the famous, the learned, those clothed in every appearance of holiness and wisdom."

> To this day [*usque modo*], I say, I have not been able to take a firm stand . . . and follow the divine spirit of Jesus . . . rather than the spirit of that infinite multitude who live well, wisely, and even devoutly, in peace and softness, who say they stand salubriously in Christ, serving him indeed with much diligence and endeavor, but in other respects show no mercy or charity. . . . And again I confess that to this day [*usque modo*] I have so wavered between these two that at one moment, seeing the beauty of the friends of this world, I have praised their diligence and strenuous service of Jesus Christ, and have blamed myself for not having imitated them as yet— and these thoughts usually came to me in the morning—and then in the very same hour I would be confused, I would turn my back on them and bewail what I had praised, once again seeing their systematic vanity, their great discrepancy from the virtue and truth of Jesus and from his words and deeds, which they zealously praised with their mouths alone.

The bad thing about these "friends of this world"—the prelates—was not just their "vain speech, gluttony, and drinking," not just their unevangelical way of life, but also their excuses: "We are only men; these things are the common practice of the great and learned." All of this was but the seduction of Satan, the allurement of the fornicating woman [*mulier fornicaria*] whom he had adorned so that she might lead astray those standing at the crossroads of the two paths of life. Matthew declared that he had learned from the crucified Jesus how to recognize that woman—and yet he had to confess that he had never been able to commit himself wholeheartedly to the narrow path.

Written near the end of his life, about 1392,[40] the passage points back to his

---

[39] *Regulae*, IV, 355-359; cf. IV, 97 f. Kybal's view (*M. Matěj*, p. 27) that Matthew had experienced a "complete conversion" is based on the second of the quoted passages, which seems to attest rather to a continued oscillation.

[40] Kybal, in *Regulae*, IV, xv.

youth, to the moment in 1372 when he decided to leave the society of John Milič and go off to Paris, to pursue the studies that would qualify him to become a prelate himself. For even then he must have had a good idea of the choice he was making—or rather the choice he kept trying to make. Back in Prague he still kept hammering away at the doors of the "soft life," but at the same time he formed part of the Milician movement, and his work as confessor and as preacher, a work that he never stopped of his own volition, must have kept him in contact with the pious laity who had formerly frequented Jerusalem. For a good while, under the benevolent auspices of Archibishop John of Jenštejn, Matthew could develop his program, fostering frequent communion, attacking the routinized and distracting elements of the cult, particularly the various aspects of the cult of saints, and preaching adherence to the simple faith of Jesus—the crucified Jesus and his Primitive Church.[41] But the enemy was still powerful; in 1388, after the theologians and lawyers of the University of Prague had condemned frequent communion, a Prague synod decreed that communion might be taken only once a month; the Milicians who disobeyed were persecuted.[42] Then in 1389 Matthew had to recant his own position in this matter and, in addition, his attacks on the excessive cult of saints and of holy images.[43] Removed from his priestly functions, he devoted himself to his writing; this, too, led him into some difficulties, but he was able to get by with promises of obedience, and he kept developing his original doctrine until his untimely death, on 30 November 1393. His purpose in writing what was to be his one great work, the *Regule*—in fact, a collection of treatises—was, of course, to promote the particular ideas of the Milician reform, but it was also to provide a theory that could hold these ideas together and justify them. Milič had not bothered about such a theory; he had preached a reform that aroused the hatred of the prelates, but his reaction to this hatred was one merely of patience and persistence. Matthew could see that more was necessary, he had the learning and training to meet the challenge, and in his own chronic ambivalence he felt a tension that could only be resolved by the work of writing.[44] He would not have been the last intellectual in Western history to make up for

[41] Kybal, *M. Matěj*, pp. 82–154, 207–291, offers an excellent guide to the relevant passages in the *Regulae*.

[42] *Ibid.*, p. 20; *Čechy*, p. 245.

[43] Kybal, *op. cit.*, p. 20; for the text of Matthew's revocation see *Documenta*, pp. 699 f.

[44] In *Regulae*, IV, 97 f., Matthew describes his spiritual wavering and the works he undertook to confirm his good resolutions: "scilicet cottidie ad wlgus predicando, continue confessiones audiendo et ista conscribendo cum magna solicitudine, in die et nocte." The first two were part of his job; the third can be seen as his more particular contribution, especially after his suspension from the other two functions.

weakness of character by scholarly exercises, to attempt a resolution in theory of an unresolved personal conflict.

His theory was itself rather ambiguous, at least in its formulations. "I love, hold, and confess," he wrote, "everything decreed, ordained, decided, and consecrated by my most holy mother, the Roman catholic church: that is, the lord pope, with his cardinals and other fellow bishops and holy fathers, right down to Pope Boniface IX [1389–1404]."[45] This seems clear enough, and Matthew's behavior when he was summoned before a church court did not contradict his professions; but his basic theme in the *Regule* was not the glory of the Roman church but rather the corruption of that body by the chilling of charity, the intense love of this world, the abundance of iniquity— Biblical phrases that are not so vacuous as they sound. In a general sense, he saw the evil of the day in hypocrisy, which he defined in great detail—but chiefly as complacence in external religious and moral goods, as well as in the good things of this world and of nature.[46] And it was about the year 1200, he wrote, that this sort of hypocrisy triumphed "in the Christian people and especially in the clergy, and above all in the Roman clergy"; it was then that charity grew cold, iniquity abounded, and "the church of Christ abounded in the greatest peace of this world, in riches and in glory." That was when the "magna mulier fornicaria" took her seat upon the scarlet beast, and Antichrist extended his swollen body throughout the church.[47] In modern textbooks this is usually called "the triumph of the medieval church in the pontificate of Innocent III," and so it was—that was Matthew's point. His target here was not moral sin as such, and certainly not the good things of this world as such, but rather the inclusion of the values of this world within the Christian church—that is, the Hildebrandine effort to dominate the world, and the resulting permeation of the church by the world. This secularized Christianity was the "mulier fornicaria," whom we have already encountered, in exactly the same sense, sitting at a crossroads in Matthew's own life. And the effect of the church's corruption in this sense was the destruction of her original unity, understood as the simplicity of the Primitive Church, by the "accidental multiplicity" produced by "human innovations": "The excessive

---

[45] *Regulae,* I, 172.

[46] *Ibid.,* pp. 172 ff. There are ten definitions of hypocrisy, the tenth containing what is common to the rest: "Item decimo collective ex precedentibus ypocrisis est omnis usus boni vel apparentis boni aut habitacio ipsius, qui facit hominem in seipso conplacere vel in hominibus in tantum, quod abducit a vera cordis humilitate et a spiritu contribulato et corde contrito in hac vita hominis et tempore dato ad penitendum, et obnubilat christianum ad pensandum et congnoscendum in veritate dona dei in se et sic extinguit gratitudinem eius ad Christum Jhesum" (p. 177). See also the fifth definition (p. 176).

[47] *Ibid.,* pp. 178 f.

multitude of traditions, doctrines, and mandates of carnal men is not useful but, rather, harmful, as when this excessive plurality occupies men's minds to the point where they become less solicitous about the divine precepts and sacraments."[48] But these evils in the church came from the world:

> Beasts indeed are infinitely many—or, rather, too many of them are wrapped up and fused together, in the one scarlet Beast who is full of the names of blasphemy, with seven horned heads [Rev. 17:3]. These are the modern hypocrites and fleshly Christians, who, after they have put together a law after the Mosaic model, out of infinite ceremonies, observances, mandates, and doctrines of men, lay "heavy burdens and grievous to be borne on men's shoulders" [Matt. 23:4], which neither they nor their fathers could bear [cf. Acts 15:10]. And so into the simplicity of the catholic faith and into the heavenly people they have introduced, as necessary for the kingdom of God, Greek rules, Aristotelic justice, Platonic sanctity, and gentile rites and honor: in such things they decree their justice; they preach and rely on such things for the salvation of souls; through them they glorify themselves before the people; from them they are enriched. . . . Therefore, with the great precepts of God cast into oblivion, as though abolished . . . , they solemnize their own recent inventions, guard over them, proclaim them and augment them, and magnify them among the simple and fleshly Christian people. . . . And by their multitude . . . the cross of Jesus Christ and the name of the crucified Jesus are now brought into disrepute and made as it were alien and void among Christians.[49]

Elsewhere Matthew testifies explicitly to this last point: to the prelates the cult of the poor, humble, suffering Jesus, Christ on the cross, seemed offensive if not downright heretical; they said it was "a shame and horror to Christians to hear such things about their God"—except perhaps once a year, on Good Friday.[50] Certainly the absorption of "Aristotelic justice" and all the other essentially pagan or secular values of this world into the Christian establishment and the Christian faith—this massive cultural enterprise could not be put under the patronage of Christ on the cross, at least not the agonizing crucified man portrayed in late Gothic art.

Matthew's reform program naturally flowed from his concept of the simplicity of the true church. The human inventions should be pruned away,

[48] *Ibid.*, p. 45. There are many similar passages; see especially II, 145: "O, quis igitur dabit ecclesie sancte, ut multiplicitas illa accidentalis et varia hominum seipsos amancium et fraternitatum scorsum conportancium moderna, superflua et nociva, destruatur!" In attacking accidental, human multiplicity, Matthew explicitly excepted the essential variety based on the diverse gifts of the Holy Spirit (II, 145 f.).

[49] *Ibid.*, I, 209 f.

[50] *Ibid.*, III, 125; for the general phenomenon of "devotion to the suffering Christ" see *Histoire de l'Église*, XIV, ii, 753–761.

the life of the clergy should be reformed, the true evangelical faith should be preached to the people, and the latter should find their perfect solidarity with the crucified Christ by frequent communion in the sacrament of the Eucharist. None of this was heresy. Both the authority and the sacramental functions of the church were recognized and even emphasized; what was attacked was on the one hand excrescences in the cult, on the other hand unwholesome developments in the institution, including the implementation of papalism. When the pope began to take all benefices into his hands and grant them out by his own provisions, when he began to give privileges to the friars and thereby erode the authority of ordinaries, when he caused the same evil by granting exemptions to local church corporations—that was when the evils began. This was exactly what William of St. Amour and his fellows had said in the middle of the thirteenth century, and Matthew explicitly associated his own critique with that of his predecessors at the University of Paris.[51] His ideal was the Primitive Church, but practically speaking, he was calling for a return to the pre-Hildebrandine system, before Antichrist had gained his control over the Roman institution. In principle his doctrine was not antipapal, only antipapalist, and while the line was sometimes hard to draw, he was helped by the Great Schism, which allowed him to attack at least one of the popes as Antichrist.[52] But he did not follow his theory into all of its potential ramifications by complementing his anti-Hildebrandinism with an exaltation of secular control over the church—as the Gallicans had done and were doing in France, and as Wyclif was doing in England. In fact, he condemned the undue exaltation of secular power, its essentially pagan character, as opposed to the way of Christ and as part of the dominion of Antichrist.[53] To him the locus of reform lay in the holy people, the community of the saints *within* the ecclesiastical establishment. By reestablishing the pure, simple church of Christ, this community could show how the work of Antichrist in the Roman church might be undone; here the

---

[51] *Regulae*, IV, 133: ". . . ego puto . . . illa omnia habuisse suum inicium, quando dominus apostolicus contraxit ad se omnia beneficia et officia ecclesie pro sua voluntate dispensanda, et incepit . . . conferre multa privilegia et exempciones ab obediencia infinitis personis . . . et subditis ordinarie aliorum, puta ut essent sibi soli subiecti." After developing the point he writes (p. 134), ". . . sicut reverendissimi et fidelissimi doctores et magistri in theologia Parisius ista dudum ante previderunt, predixerunt et limpide prescripserunt . . . ante annos CXXXVI."

[52] See the discussion and references in De Vooght, *L'Hérésie*, pp. 25 f.

[53] *Regulae*, II, 230 ff.; IV, 164 (secular government is the dominion of Antichrist); II, 227 f. ("The government of the kings of the earth is very similar to pagan government"); II, 229 (against the undue exaltation of the secular arm). See Kybal, *M. Matěj*, pp. 105 ff., and R. R. Betts, "Some Political Ideas of the Early Czech Reformers," *Slavonic and East European Review*, XXXI (1952), 20–35.

key emphasis was that placed on frequent communion, for the Eucharist was the common sacramental basis of both churches and the effects of frequent communion would be powerfully salutary.[54]

In this sense Matthew's theoretical work can be characterized as the ideology of the Beguine-type religious movement, a definition of such a movement's relationship, partly stable, partly dynamic, to the church at large. But this was just what the local chieftains of that church could not accept. To them the ideal of evangelical imitation belonged not in the world, in constant contact with the ecclesiastical establishment, but in the isolation of the cloister, and when the layman expressed a desire to turn from the world to the imitation of Jesus, he was told to go join a monastery.[55] Milič, for his part, had been tempted to do that, but had decided in favor of promoting his ideal among others, in the world;[56] this was, no doubt, a motive of many of his followers. Refusing to join an order, however, they were systematically vilified—the men were called Beghards, the women Beguines.[57] The terms had evidently come to be understood in Prague exclusively in their heretical sense, according to the Council of Vienne's condemnation of the Free Spirit movement, and it was in this sense that both Milič and Matthew rejected the charge.[58] But there were orthodox Beguines, and in any case the socioreligious reality was more important than this or that name. The reality existed in Prague, subject to relentless persecution, and Matthew of Janov made it his mission to serve the movement both by his priestly work and by his theoretical construction, which sought to do what Johannes Haller has called squaring the circle: to combine the ideal of pietism with that of the hierarchical church.[59] His fervor, his erudition, the

[54] Matthew's ecclesiology is treated by Kybal, *M. Matěj*, pp. 82 ff. There is a good summary in De Vooght, *L'Hérésie*, pp. 32–34.

[55] *Regulae*, IV, 395.

[56] *Vita Milicii*, p. 411.

[57] Matthew often complains of this—e.g., *Regulae*, IV, 138; V, 18; see the indices to the several volumes, *s.v. Beghardus*.

[58] The Council of Vienne's decrees on the subject, one of them referring to the Beguines and Beghards by name, appear in the Clementines, III, ix, 1, and V, iii, 3, ed. E. Friedberg, *Corpus iuris canonici*, II (Leipzig, 1881), cols. 1165 and 1183 f. McDonnell's discussion (*Beguines and Beghards,* pp. 521 ff.) is fundamental. In his rejection of the charge of Beghardism, Matthew explicitly identified the Beghards as the sect so named in the Clementines, and showed that the Free-Spirit contempt for the Eucharist was irreconcilable with his own movement's veneration of that sacrament (*Regulae*, V, 203). There were, however, houses of orthodox Beguines in Prague, and the movement was growing in Matthew's own day (Tomek, III, 233); its relation to the reform movement is not clear (see, *ibid.,* p. 440).

[59] Haller, *Papsttum und Kirchenreform*, I, 89.

broad range of his thought, which dealt with the local problem in European terms and defined the current situation in terms of the whole of Christian history—these traits would later make his *Regule* an inexhaustible treasury of inspiration for the Hussite left. But in his own day Matthew enjoyed only a limited success. The Milićian movement recovered some of its thrust, with the help of Matthew and other favorably disposed ecclesiastics and laymen, when Bethlehem Chapel was founded in 1391 as a center for preaching in Czech. Obviously a renewal of Milić's Jerusalem, the new foundation was not only well endowed but also well protected, its privileges secured in legal form and its relationship to the parochial organization fixed by permanent agreements.[60] Frequent communion had been suppressed, but zealous preaching was to take its place as the focal point of the religious movement. The idea that this movement might renew the church at large, however, did not have much success, for the vested interests were totally uncompromising and in a posture of permanent hostility. Only under different auspices and with a different theoretical emphasis could this idea be realized.

THE CONTRIBUTION OF JOHN WYCLIF

The English reformer John Wyclif became a Master of Arts at Oxford by 1360, and after a brief interlude went on to the study of theology, becoming a "Doctor" in 1371/72. At first, until 1373/74, he devoted himself to philosophy in the realist tradition that was still cultivated at Oxford, even though most of Europe's schools taught the *via moderna* of Ockhamite nominalism, or terminism. From about 1374 to his death in 1384 he produced his theological works, including both constructive and critical studies. Since he had a mind of the greatest brilliance and power, he impressed many of his associates and students—in fact he became the special pride of Oxford University, which sought to protect him even after most of its members had parted company with his increasingly radical ideas.[61] After he left the university, and after his death, his disciples continued to form a movement which won support from many of the laity, of all estates. Thus when Czechs began to frequent Oxford in significant numbers, after the Great Schism had made Paris less attractive, they came into contact with Wyclif's ideas, and the contacts were multiplied when, in 1382, Anne of Bohemia, the sister of

[60] The best discussion is in Odložilík, "The Chapel of Bethlehem."

[61] H. B. Workman's *John Wyclif: A Study of the English Medieval Church* (2 vols.; Oxford, 1926) remains the standard work, although important details are added by K. B. McFarlane, *John Wycliffe and the Beginnings of English Nonconformity* (London, 1952)—see, in particular, chap. i, "Wycliffe and Oxford," and pp. 97 f. See also J. A. Robson, *Wyclif and the Oxford Schools* (Cambridge, 1961).

Wenceslas IV, married King Richard II of England. It is worth noting here that in 1388 Master Vojtěch Raňkův founded a scholarship to support a Czech student at Oxford.[62] By about 1390 Wyclif's philosophical works had begun to reach Prague, where their philosophical realism found soil that had already been prepared by a Thomist revival among the Dominicans, whose Parisian college had been transferred to Prague in 1383 because of the schism.[63] At the same time, however, the increase in numbers and quality of the Czech members of the university, restricted to the Bohemian nation, was generating constant conflict over power and place with the Germans, dominant in the other three nations. Since Ockhamite nominalism was the doctrine of most of the Germans, the Czechs had an understandable inclination to embrace Wyclifism. It was not only opposed to nominalism: it had also the prestige of an import from the more advanced or at least more venerable scholarly circles of the west. John Hus was only one of the Czechs who, in the 1390's, earned money by copying Wyclif's works and in the process drank in his doctrines.[64] And when, around the turn of the century, Wyclif's theological works began to appear, chiefly through the agency of Master Jerome of Prague, they too aroused enthusiasm. Young Czech scholars began to go to England for the express purpose of finding and copying more of them.[65] By 1403, a year after Hus had begun his preaching career in Bethlehem Chapel, the Czech reception of Wyclifism was so marked that this corpus of doctrine could become *the* issue of Czech-German antagonism. In that year Master John Hübner, a German Master of Theology, presented a list of forty-five Wyclifite "articles" and requested the Prague diocesan authorities to condemn them. The latter submitted the list to the university, where a German majority furnished the votes for an official pronouncement that no member of the university might defend or teach the articles. The list was, to be sure, not a very accurate representation of Wyclif's system, but it included enough of both his philosophy and his theology to make the condemnation one of Wyclifism in general, an unmistakable repudiation of what had become the cause of the more progressive Czech academics.[66]

[62] For a general discussion of these contacts see R. R. Betts, "English and Czech Influences on the Hussite Movement," *Transactions of the Royal Historical Society,* 4th series, XXXI (1939), 71–102.

[63] *Čechy,* pp. 48, 261 f.

[64] F. M. Bartoš, "Hus a Viklef," *Husitství a cizina* (Prague, 1931), pp. 25, 29 f.

[65] Betts, "English and Czech Influences"; J. Loserth, "Über die Beziehungen zwischen englischen und böhmischen Wiclifiten in den beiden ersten Jahrzehnten des 15. Jahrhunderts," *Mitteilungen des Instituts für österreichische Geschichtsforschung,* XII (1891), 254–269.

[66] The text of the list and of the condemnation are in *Documenta,* pp. 327–331. Twenty-four of the articles were taken over from the condemnation by the Blackfriars

While the actual function of Wyclifism, as doctrine and as symbol, in the decade that followed these events can be best considered in the context of the following section, it will be in order here to consider what the English master had to offer his Bohemian disciples. Even here there can be no question of attempting a comprehensive account of his thought, but only an examination of those ideas that marked an advance over the Milič ian-Janovian doctrine, at least in the light of future events. The similarities between the two types of reformism were to be sure more extensive than the differences, a fact that undoubtedly explains much of Wyclif's initial popularity among the Czechs, but the differences were crucial. No contrast is more striking than that between the defensive passivity of the reform movement in the 1370's and 1380's, and its aggressive drive in the decade of Hus's leadership. Many factors made the difference, but there is no better way to formulate the contrast than by taking Matthew of Janov's doctrine as the dominant ideology of the first period, Wyclifism as that of the second.

In the matter of reform, all of Wyclif's critical and constructive points are, so to speak, the termini of a highly articulated system of ecclesiology, which itself can be understood only in contrast with other systems of the day. All of them proceeded from the common conviction that Jesus had founded a church to endure until the end of the world, and that this church, living the spiritual life he gave it, was his "mystical"—in plain language, "figurative"—body and as such was infallible (for its faith would never be destroyed) and immaculate (for Christ's institution could have no flaw). A *locus classicus* of this concept was Paul's Epistle to the Ephesians, 5:23–27: "For the husband is the head of the wife, even as Christ is the head of the church. . . . Husbands, love your wives, even as Christ also loved the church, and gave himself for it; That he might sanctify and cleanse it with the washing of water by the word, That he might present it to himself a glorious church, not having spot, or wrinkle, or any such thing; but that it should be holy and without blemish." This was the church against which the gates of hell would not prevail (Matt. 16:18)—a promise generally understood as referring to the church's invincibility by mortal sin and heresy.[67] But what organization here on earth could claim such traits? The papalist answer was that Jesus himself had instituted the church as an earthly organization, a body to be governed, and had entrusted its government to Peter; since Peter had exercised his

---

Synod of 1382; the other twenty-one were probably taken from another earlier condemnation: see L. Baudry, "A propos de G. d'Ockham et de Wiclef," *Archives d'histoire doctrinale et littéraire du moyen âge,* XIV (1939), 238–249. Cf. Workman, *op. cit.,* II, 266 ff., 416 f.; De Vooght, *L'Hérésie,* pp. 77–80; Nov., I, 108 ff.

[67] See the references in Brian Tierney, *Foundations of the Conciliar Theory* (Cambridge, 1955), p. 26, n. 1; see also Nicholas of Lyra's gloss quoted below, p. 27.

function as bishop of Rome, his successors in that episcopate, the popes, also succeeded to his rule over the whole church—like him, they were *ex officio* Vicars of Christ. And whatever might be their personal traits, they were *ex officio* sanctified by Peter's merits.[68] In this definite, jurisdictional sense the theory took shape as a result of the Hildebrandine revolution of the eleventh century, after which, as Gerhard Ladner has observed, "the terms *Ecclesia* and *Ecclesia Romana* . . . appear to coalesce into one concept comprising the Church both as an institution, that is, as an essentially clerical corporation, and as the community of all the faithful, the Body of Christ." [69] It was on the basis of this equivocation that the papalists, both lawyers and theologians, developed their extravagant notions:

> In the Decretalist writings the Pope was presented as a vice-gerent of God in the most literal sense, as the wielder of a *plenitudo potestatis* that set him above all human law and conferred on him absolute authority in every sphere of Church government. His very will, without any rational justification, was sufficient to establish a binding law, and even his unjust commands were to be obeyed for no one on earth could say to him, *cur ita facis?* . . . *De iure* the Pope possessed all the powers of Christ on earth.[70]

This was the pope in his quality as ruler of the world, not just as ruler of the clerical corporation; but even though the regular, bureaucratic routine of the latter body certainly represented a kind of limitation of papal absolutism, still, the drive to centralization of the church itself through papal provisions, exemptions, privileges, and jurisdiction had its legal basis precisely in the papalist doctrine of sovereignty.[71]

[68] Tierney, *op. cit.,* pp. 25–36, offers a useful discussion. See also. M. Wilks, *The Problem of Sovereignty in the Later Middle Ages* (Cambridge, 1963), *passim,* esp., for the pope as *ex officio* holy, p. 365 and the index, *s.v.* "Pope, *sanctus.*"

[69] G. Ladner, "Aspects of Medieval Thought on Church and State," *Review of Politics,* IX (1947), 410 f.

[70] Tierney, *op. cit.,* p. 88.

[71] See W. Ullmann, *The Growth of Papal Government in the Middle Ages* (London, 1955), pp. 276 ff., for papalism as the ideology of the whole medieval order. G. Barraclough offers a rather self consciously hard-headed view (*Papal Provisions* [Oxford, 1935], pp. 103 f.): the extreme formulations of papalist theory "are of little significance from the standpoint of administrative practice"; in studying the actual workings of the papal government within the church, "we should do well to forget" them. Not unrelated to this view is his interpretation of the development of the system of papal provisions as the result of a passive willingness of the popes to meet the requests of petitioners (pp. 162 f.). But in fact the system was closely connected with the elaboration of papalist theory—as is clear, e.g., in M. Pacaut, *Alexandre III* (Paris, 1956), p. 288 and *passim,* and may have had its origin in papal initiative, to provide incomes for the curialists; Professor Glenn Olsen, of Fordham University, has told me that his researches suggest this probability. See also J. Haller, *Das Papsttum, Idee und Wirklichkeit,* (Rowohlt, 1965; repr. of 1962 edition), III, 347, for a similar suggestion about Innocent III's use of reservations.

But just as the actual centralization met with bitter criticism in every generation of the high and later Middle Ages,[72] so the theories of papalism found many critics, even among the most important thinkers. Thus, to cite only a few examples, the Decretist Huguccio (d. 1210), commenting on the statement that the Roman church has "neither stain nor wrinkle," wrote: ". . . wherever there are good, faithful Christians, there is the Roman church; otherwise you will not find a Roman church in which there are not many stains and many wrinkles."[73] And the *glosa ordinaria* on the Decretum comments in a similar vein on the statement that the church cannot err: "What church cannot err? If the pope himself be meant, who is called the church,[74] then it must be said that the pope can err. The answer is that the congregation of the faithful is here called the church, and such a church cannot fail of being."[75] Even more forthright is the gloss of Nicholas of Lyra (d. 1340) on the scriptural text, "the gates of hell shall not prevail against her"; noting that "prevail" meant here to subvert from the true faith, he added: "Hence it is clear that the church does not exist in men by reason of ecclesiastical or secular power or office, for many princes and popes, as well as lower dignitaries, have been found to have apostatized from the faith. Therefore the church exists in those persons in whom there is true knowledge and confession of faith and truth."[76] The practical value of these distinctions was to associate with the Roman church *qua* congregation of the faithful those attributes of perfection so patently lacking in the Roman church *qua* clerical corporation, let alone *qua* papal Curia. As long as all these groupings were in fact associated in a single organism the attributes of the one could support the powers claimed by the other, through the kind of easy equivocation that was fundamental to medieval thought. Thus even those who rejected papalism in its baldest form could accept the idea of the pope as the ruler who exercised the prerogatives of the congregation of the faithful.

Still, the latter concept of ecclesiology did have a subversive potential, which came to light when the Great Schism, beginning in 1378, brought papalism to its *reductio ad absurdum*. For according to that theory there was no place for neutrality or even reserved obedience, and yet when there were two popes, each excommunicating the other, the Christian who gave his total

---

[72] For examples see Haller, *Papsttum und Kirchenreform, passim*, for the period after *ca.* 1300; Barraclough, *op. cit.*, pp. 4 ff., for some of the thirteenth-century complaints. It is suggested here only that the complaints existed, not that they were more important than the general acceptance of centralization.

[73] Quoted by Tierney, *op. cit.*, p. 41.

[74] For the meaning of *Papa=Ecclesia* see G. Post, *Studies in Medieval Legal Thought* (Princeton, 1964), pp. 352–354.

[75] *Glosa ordinaria in verbum* "novitatibus," *Decretum*, XXIV, q.1, c.9.

[76] *Postille, super* Matt. 16:18, *in verba,* "non prevalebunt adversus eam."

obedience to one might be committing himself totally to Antichrist—he could not be sure, and hence the divine promise of salvation seemed unreliable. Such was the observation of John Wyclif, who therefore concluded that it could not be "of the substance of faith to believe explicitly that either one of them was pope," and did not fail to draw the further conclusion: "Blessed be the God of Truth who has ordained this dissension, that the truth of this belief might shine forth!" [77] A more practical but equally radical lesson was pronounced by Matthew of Janov, ten years later: "I do not think this schism is damaging to the church of Jesus Christ, which abounds in his spirit, but rather it seems to be useful, that by it the kingdom of Antichrist may more speedily pass away"; for, he said, the schism was in the body of Antichrist, not in that of Christ.[78] What he meant was that the split in the clerical corporation, which he regarded as pervaded by Antichrist, did not affect the status of the true body of Christ, the holy community of the religious movement. But a comparable conclusion could also be drawn by more ecclesiastical thinkers, on the basis of the older distinction between the clerical corporation and the congregation of the faithful:

> It could never be admitted that the "seamless robe" had been rent apart, and if the hierarchical organization which should have manifested the intrinsic unity of the Church had become riven by inveterate schism, it was natural that well-intentioned churchmen should turn with new enthusiasm to the ancient doctrine of a unity inherent in the whole *congregatio fidelium,* a mystical unity that could never be compromised by the dissensions of Popes and prelates.[79]

It was on this basis that conciliar thought was developed into at once a means of ending the schism and an alternative to papalism in the governance of even a reunited church. In time the latter tendency of conciliar thought would be declared erroneous, a fact that only emphasizes the openness and indeed turbulence of the situation in the fourteenth century, when the intellectual community produced not only conciliarism but a whole series of

---

[77] The quotations are from *De potestate pape* (henceforth *DPP*), ed. J. Loserth (London, 1907), p. 248; see also p. 247, and *Responsiones ad XLIV conclusiones,* in *Opera Minora* (*OM*), ed. Loserth (London, 1913), p. 252. For Wyclif's doctrine of reserved obedience see *De civili dominio* (*DCD*), ed. Loserth (London, 1903), III, 44: "Certum videtur quod non est obediendum contra Christi mandatum sive consilium." This was against the ordinary scholastic view, that the *consilia* were optional (e.g., Thomas Aquinas, *Summa Theologica* (*ST*), I-II, q. 108, a. 4); hence Wyclif frequently understood as mandates what the canonists interpreted as (dispensable) *consilia*—e.g., *De ecclesia* (*DE*), ed. Loserth (London, 1886), p. 52.

[78] *Regulae,* II, 157 f.

[79] Tierney, *op. cit.,* p. 222.

doctrinal systems motivated by a desire to reconstruct an order whose crisis was apparent to all.[80] Wyclifism was only one of these efforts.

Like every Christian thinker, Wyclif began with the concept of the church as the immaculate Bride of Christ, or the perfect Body of Christ, and eventually ended up with an actual human organization, relevant to the problems that had spurred the work of theorizing in the first place. But he did not define the mystical body as the congregation of the faithful, for he objected that "no collectivity of Christians had wholly the same right faith," that "each time one of the faithful was born or died away, there would be a new catholic church," and that the true church, according to this definition, would include those only temporarily in a state of grace—the foreknown, who in the end would go to hell—and it would exclude those who were predestined to salvation but who might be temporarily erring in the faith.[81] To supply the stability he found lacking in the "congregation of the faithful" he turned to a definition based on God's omniscience, omnipotence, and invariability: the true church was the congregation of these predestined to salvation—past, present, and future.[82] Since no one could know God's decisions for himself or for others, men could have no certain knowledge of who was in the true church, who was not; but they could have an imperfect, approximate knowledge: "Those whom we see living according to the Law of God we deem to be sons of the Kingdom."[83] But this working rule was only for Christian convenience here on earth, it did not affect the actual constitution of the true church. There was a time, for example, when Judas Iscariot seemed to be a member of the true church, but in fact he never was—just as, conversely, Peter and Paul never ceased to be members, even when they were faithless.[84] Wyclif did not deny that the Roman church was the true church, for there was much venerable authority to that effect, but he insisted on his own definition of the Roman church:

> There are many laws and opinions of the saints about the pre-eminence of the Roman Church. But to understand these decrees of the holy doctors of

[80] See, *ibid.,* p. 240, for the dangerous implications of the conciliar *congregatio fidelium.* Wilks, *op. cit., passim,* offers up-to-date bibliographical notes on the explorations of fourteenth-century ecclesiology.

[81] *DE,* pp. 112 ff., 408 f.; cf. *DCD,* IV, 432, for a relevant authority from Augustine. Here and in the following discussion the reader is referred to my "Wyclifism as Ideology of Revolution," *Church History,* XXXII (1963), 57–74, for a more systematic discussion and for some Latin texts that are merely cited by page number in the following notes; in any case, the citations are only examples, the minimum necessary to support the argument.

[82] *DE,* p. 2.

[83] *DE,* p. 90, and, for the converse, p. 43. Cf. *De fide catholica, OM,* p. 116.

[84] *DE,* p. 114.

theology it is necessary to put aside the glosses of John de Deo, John Andree, John Monachus, and those like them [i.e., other canon lawyers], who are ignorant of logic, metaphysics, and the theological meaning of the saints.[85]

Wyclif was not the first theologian to reject the canonists' "ignorant" meddling with his discipline—Thomas Aquinas had expressed similar sentiments[86]—but with him the issue was one of fundamentals. The jurists founded their concepts of the church on law, on definable juridical functions, but to Wyclif the very word *jurisdiction* seemed "a poisonous term, smacking of pride, sloth, and greed, introduced by the devil's craft."[87] What he meant was that among the clergy, and between the clergy and the people, there was no place for rulership based on coercive power. Here he took up the formula pronounced by St. Bernard of Clairvaux: "This is the apostolic rule: domination is forbidden, service is commanded."[88] And like Bernard he contrasted the legacy of Peter with that of Constantine: as true leader of the Roman church the pope should imitate the love, humility, poverty, and suffering of Peter, for this was the only sort of primacy that Christ had founded. The rest had come in with the Donation of Constantine, for before then no one had claimed "to be Christ's vicar on earth, to have pre-eminent power in both spiritual and temporal things, and to be above all other bishops."[89] Insofar as he allowed for government within the clergy, Wyclif

---

[85] *DPP*, p. 250: "Multe sunt et leges et sanctorum sentencie de preeminencia Romane ecclesie. Sed ad intelligendum ista decreta sanctorum doctorum theologie oportet postponere glossas Johannis de Deo, Johannis Andree, Johannis Monachi et eis similium, qui logice, methaphisice, theologice sanctorum sentencie sunt ignari."

[86] In *ST*, II-II, q.88, a.11, Thomas gives his interpretation of a decretal and adds, "licet quidam juristae ignoranter contrarium dicant." The passage is quoted, along with a similar anti-legist passage from John of Paris, in J. Leclercq, *Jean de Paris et l'ecclésiologie du XIIIᵉ siècle* (Paris, 1942), p. 68, n. 11. See also Wyclif's *De officio regis* (*DOR*), ed. A. W. Pollard and C. Sayle (London, 1887) pp. 35 f., where an objectionable doctrine based on Innocent III's decretal "Solite" is blamed not on the pope but on "glosatores, sacre scripture et racionis ignari, [qui] textum papalem inficiant." The idea of the ignorance of the lawyers must have been a scholastic commonplace.

[87] *De ordine christiano*, *OM*, p. 136.

[88] *DPP*, p. 137. Paul De Vooght, "Du 'De Consideratione' de saint Bernard au 'De Potestate Papae' de Wiclif," *Irenikon*, XXV (1953), 114–132, has shown how effectively Wyclif used Bernard's criticisms of papal practice for the un-Bernardian purpose of rejecting the papal office in principle.

[89] Bernard's "In hiis successisti non Petro sed Constantino" is quoted several times by Wyclif—e.g., *DPP*, pp. 86 f. Here Wyclif was only one of many late-medieval writers who made the Bernardian contrast into a kind of *topos*—see G. Laehr, "Die Konstantinische Schenkung in der abendländischen Literatur des ausgehenden Mittelalters," *Quellen und Forschungen aus italienischen Archiven und Bibliotheken*, XXIII (1931–32), 120–181, esp. p. 129, n. 2. Wyclif's idea that it was Constantine who had established the papal jurisdictional primacy over the other bishops also appeared in other writers of

favored what he took to be the pre-Constantinian form of government by a college of equals (*per socios*)—hence government by mutual agreement, not by force or jurisdiction.[90]

But all of this concerned only the clergy. With the true church defined as the whole body of predestined, the distinction between clergy and laity lost its basic ecclesiological significance. Here Wyclif gave voice to perhaps the most powerful current in the religious life of the late Middle Ages, the claim to recognition of lay piety and spirituality. In the first part of the twelfth century, Hugh of St. Victor had formulated the older view in classical terms: the spiritual was the sphere of the soul, the secular the sphere of the body— hence the graded dichotomies: the clergy higher than the laity, bishops higher than princes, spiritual sword higher than material one, with the supreme directive function reserved to the spiritual powers. Usually accepted as a matter of course in the high Middle Ages, this scheme could not survive intact into the later centuries, when the laity and, indeed, the whole secular sphere had absorbed much of the spiritual. Thus Wyclif could argue that the two powers, though distinguishable, were not separate, for every Christian, cleric or lay, had spiritual power, as the means of sanctifying himself, while every secular activity had a spiritual significance, determined according to the Law of Christ—the Bible—which was the all-sufficient norm for all of human life.[91] On this basis Wyclif could proceed to his practical determination of the church as an earthly society. For the congregation of the predestined had three parts, the Church Triumphant in heaven, the Church Sleeping in Purgatory, and the Church Militant on earth, and the latter body was no mere concept or abstraction:

> It is false to say that the Church Militant is not circumscribed as to place, since it is a body having one place that circumscribes it, just as it has one faith, and thus it is an animated, rational body, for it is a sensible body, performing vital actions.[92]

As a political community, based on law and lordship, the Church Militant was simply human society, or specifically the realms and other units making up human society. But these were not exclusively populated by the predestined—the foreknown were also there, and in fact the two groups were mixed, the one indistinguishable from the other by human cognition. In

the time—Laehr, pp. 131 ff.; for Wyclif's position see, e.g., *Ad argumenta emuli veritatis, OM*, p. 262; *DE*, p. 352; *OM*, p. 133; see also the very full discussion in Laehr, pp. 140–148, with abundant references to the sources and literature. Hus followed Wyclif on this point; see his statement in *Documenta*, p. 211.

[90] *DPP*, p. 186; De Vooght, "Du 'De Consideratione,'" p. 128.

[91] *DPP*, pp. 7 ff.; p. 10.

[92] *DE*, p. 423.

more precise terms, the predestined were *of* the Church Militant, the fore-known were only *in* it, as fecal matter is in the body but not of it.[93] "The Church, while it is Militant, is stained and wrinkled" because of this admixture, with imperfections that would disappear on Judgement Day, as the Church Militant disappeared into the Church Triumphant.[94] Meanwhile the stains and wrinkles required the institutions of civil lordship or "dominion," which were granted by God to be used within the framework, also established by God, of civil society—the three orders or estates of clergy, secular powers, and commons.[95] Thus Wyclif's form of predestinarian ecclesiology, reinforced by his evangelical concept of the clerical corporation, ended in a representation of the real, human community of England and the other realms—the several "Churches Militant" (*militantes ecclesie*). Since the clergy might not use the imperfect coercive power of civil dominion, it could not govern the particular Church Militant to which it belonged, just as the pope could not govern the whole. Instead, Wyclif theorized, the supreme head of the Church was Christ, under whom the supreme heads of the Churches Militant were the actual secular rulers:

> It seems to me that reason dictates that the people set up a head for themselves, not just one genus of captains in political religion, but that each people take a single head for itself, as for example we English have one blessed king, to whom, according to the doctrine of the Gospel, . . . we must render secular obedience. And so it is with other greater or lesser realms, even up to the Empire.[96]

Thus in Wyclif's thought the terms church, realm, and commonwealth (*ecclesia, regnum, respublica*) are interchangeable.[97]

Thinking of the realm as the church, Wyclif sees the whole purpose of the realm's life in religious terms. The members of the various estates all live as vicars of Christ, that is, as Christians, but in their own specific ways—the commons by working and serving the others, the clergy by being exemplars of Christ's poor and humble way of life, the secular powers by "defending

---

[93] *De fide catholica, OM*, pp. 99, 112.

[94] *DE*, p. 418; *De servitute civili, OM*, p. 158.

[95] *DCD*, ed. R. Lane Poole (London, 1885), I, 196, and IV, 485 f.; *OM*, p. 154; *Dialogus*, ed. A. W. Pollard (London, 1886), pp. 2 ff.

[96] *DOR*, p. 249; for "militantes ecclesie" see *DE*, p. 424; for the prohibition of civil dominion to the clergy see *DCD*, IV, 440 f.—not even Christ could have it: *DCD*, III, 60 ff.

[97] Wyclif's terminology is discussed in detail by H. Fürstenau, *Johann von Wiclifs Lehren von der Einteilung der Kirche und von der Stellung der weltlichen Gewalt* (Berlin, 1900), pp. 8–19.

the Law of God by force," with "power regulated by reason." [98] Rulership is therefore both a secular and a spiritual function—the two are reduced to one. The king is "priest and pontiff of his realm," with a "spiritual and evangelical power" to "destroy vices and establish and augment virtues in himself and others." [99] Wyclif derives the political notion of virtue from Aristotle, of course, but he does not mean to distinguish it, in either a Thomistic or an Averroistic sense, from the strictly religious, salvationary virtues. For all depends on the Law of Christ:

> The Law of Christ, when perfectly executed, teaches most rightfully how every injustice must be extirpated from the commonwealth, and how those offending against the law should be chastised. . . . The Law of Christ teaches most completely how every sin should be destroyed and avoided; but since it is not possible that a commonwealth deteriorate except on account of sin, therefore if the justice [of the Law of Christ] be observed by every person, the commonwealth will prosper.[100]

Thus on the one hand, "there is no human law (*ius humanum*) except to the extent that it is founded in the divine law of God," but on the other hand, "human justice (*iura humana*) is included in divine justice, indeed it is the Law of God, insofar as it is useful and serviceable to the Law of God." [101] Human laws are to be sure imperfect, but so is everything else here on earth; in essence, what Wyclif is saying is that the laws of England are the Law of God. But if he insists that the secular powers defend the Law of God by force, he is thinking not merely of ordinary government but primarily of enforcing his own particular deduction from the Law of God, namely, that the pope should have no rights over the English church and that the clergy of the realm should have no civil right to lordship over persons or property. What they have is an evangelical right, if they fulfill their evangelical obligations, but the gospels do not allow them rule over people or actual ownership of property—only the enjoyment of property under the title of alms. And it is up to the king and the other secular lords to see to it that the clergy—their "almsmen"—live up to the obligations of the gospel.[102] There are some passages in which Wyclif seems to hold up the noncoercive

[98] *DE*, pp. 365 f. (the nature of the universal vicariate of Christ); *Dialogus*, pp. 2 f., and *DOR*, pp. 78 f. (the role of the secular powers).

[99] *DOR*, p. 152; Fürstenau, *op. cit.*, pp. 85 f.; *DPP*, p. 10. See also *DOR*, p. 44, where Wyclif rejects the idea "quod papa solum presit clericis et Cesar laicis"—in fact, he says, "uterque preest utrisque secundum disparem racionem."

[100] *DCD*, I, 432 and, for Aristotle's doctrine, 212.

[101] *DOR*, p. 73 (cf. Fürstenau, p. 78, n. 117); *DCD*, I, 349; for the sentence following see *DCD*, I, 435; *DOR*, pp. 55 f.

[102] *DE*, p. 341; *Dialogus*, pp. 79 f.

fellowship of the Primitive Church as a goal for all, and others in which he seems to envisage an even more radical return to a state of innocence,[103] but in practical terms what he offers is a powerful theory to justify the nationalization of the English church and the secularization of her property.

It would probably be pointless to ask if this was his ulterior goal from the first; the real point would be that he was certainly a sincere reformer, *Doctor evangelicus* as his followers called him, who felt that the Christian religion could be restored to its original purity only by a reconstruction of the church in accord with the contemporary realities both of power and of religious life. And this was his chief contribution to the Czech reformers. Matthew of Janov had not called for either the removal of lordship from the clergy or the leadership of the church by the secular powers, nor had he called for the corollary destruction of the juridical unity of the European church. On the contrary, he virtually presupposed a continuing tension between the ecclesiastical establishment and the religious movement, in a framework that could only be disadvantageous to the latter. Wyclif, however, envisaged an alliance between the evangelical ideal and the realities of secular power, including the latter's greedy anticlericalism. The theory, moreover, was presented in such detail, with such a superabundance of erudition, in an argumentative structure of such power and brilliance, that it could hardly fail to throw the more lightweight Janovian exposition into the background. At the same time, a crucial factor in the reception of Wyclifism was undoubtedly the emergence of the Czech university intelligentsia as leaders of the reform movement. Neither Waldhauser nor Milič had been a member of the University of Prague; Vojtěch Raňkův was, and so probably was Matthew of Janov, but their extra-university activities were of chief importance. Furthermore, the religious movement, although primarily a Czech affair, also included Germans as leaders and followers—the struggle over frequent communion, for example, involved such a leading German intellectual as Matthew of Cracow.[104] What happened in the 1390's was that the cause of reform was absorbed by the Czech masters and scholars, increasingly under the banner of the characteristically scholastic doctrine of Wyclif, and that the Czechs integrated this cause into their institutionalized struggle with the German masters over power and place in the university. The result

---

[103] *Trialogus,* ed. G. Lechler (Oxford, 1869), p. 310; *Dialogus,* p. 85; *OM,* p. 400. On the subject of Wyclif's theory of an ideal communism, which is not at issue in the present discussion, see Workman, *op. cit.,* I, 261 ff., and the recent article by Michael Wilks, "Predestination, Property, and Power: Wyclif's Theory of Dominion and Grace," *Studies in Church History,* II (1965), 220–236. The latter is a rather artful but also stimulating attempt to relate Wyclif's vocabulary of ideas to that of contemporary papalist writers.

[104] For all of this see Novotný, *Náb. hnutí,* pp. 96 ff., 236 ff.

was the transformation of the Milićian movement into what would soon become the movement led by Hus.

THE IDEOLOGICAL STRUCTURE OF HUS'S MOVEMENT

In his recently published *L'Hérésie de Jean Huss,* Dom Paul De Vooght has subjected Hus's case to a reexamination, from the point of view of enlightened, liberal Catholicism. Having carefully studied Hus's works and the charges brought against him both before and during the Council of Constance, De Vooght comes to the conclusion that many of the doctrines attributed to Hus were not heretical at all, many were not in fact what he had taught, and that his only real heresy was his denial of the divine institution of the papal headship of the church, a doctrine in which he was certainly not alone at the Council of Constance. "Il fut condamné à cause de sa doctrine sur l'Église par un concile qui professait sur le même point une doctrine sans doute pire." [105] In any case, De Vooght argues, Hus was not a great or adventurous theologian—his eminence lay elsewhere, in the field of moral reform. He did, to be sure, take up the ideas of John Wyclif, but almost always with the necessary additions or subtractions that would make them conformable to orthodoxy. [106] If the Fathers of the Council had been more decent, if they had been willing to converse with Hus in an atmosphere of good will, they would have seen that the man before them was no hardened heretic but, at the worst, a man guilty of lapses into bad taste, extravagant language, and poor judgement. [107] In an absolute sense, according to the transcendent canons of Catholic truth, Hus's trial was unfair, its verdict was unjustified, and his burning at the stake was "an inexpiable crime." [108] In form a historical study—and in its own way a good one, destined no doubt to become standard—De Vooght's monograph is really a work of doctrinal analysis, essentially the work that the Fathers of Constance should have done but did not. One reads it, one agrees with it, one even admires it, but in the end one is unsatisfied, for what the historian wants is not a careful demonstration that Hus should not have been burned, but a reasonable explanation —in a sense even a justification—of why he was. Were his writings really so orthodox? Was his Wyclifism really so moderate? Did he not in fact deserve to bear responsibility for the words and deeds of his more subversive follow-

---

[105] *L'Hérésie,* p. 481 and *passim.* See also De Vooght's "L'Ecclésiologie des adversaires de Huss au Concile de Constance," *Hussiana* (Louvain, 1960), pp. 186–208.

[106] *L'Hérésie,* pp. 85, 480, and *passim.*

[107] *Ibid.,* pp. 383 f., 386 f., 425, 473 f., 476 ("Avant tout, Huss n'avait pas le sens de l'opportunité").

[108] *Ibid.,* pp. 470–474.

ers? Was not his own work as preacher, organizer, and leader perhaps as seditious as his enemies claimed, on the basis not of his writings but of his actions and spoken words?

These problems have been bedeviled by the prejudices of modern scholars, not to mention those of both Hus's friends and enemies in his own day. It would take a whole book to straighten things out to the point, as yet unreached by modern scholarship, where the true figure of the historical Hus would begin to emerge. In the present context all that can be attempted is the definition of a series of limited truths, some of which will inevitably seem offensive to those who refuse to believe that the proto-Protestant martyr and national hero could, on occasion, be insincere, undiscriminating, opportunistic, and demagogic. And perhaps the best place to begin, after this unattractive preface, will be with the nature of Hus's Wyclifism. The difficulty here is that one can admit all the points made by the major scholarly opponents and still be faced by the original problem. Hus did copy whole pages and passages from the works of Wyclif into his own works (Loserth), but he would hardly have done so if the heritage of the Bohemian religious movement had not formed his thinking originally (Novotný, *et al.*); in any event he copied not slavishly but freely and creatively, disposing over the whole Wyclifite corpus with consummate skill (Sedlák), and converting the very difficult, often chaotic works of Wyclif into powerful, effective books (Bartoš); moreover, he took care to avoid Wyclif's outright heresies—like his rejection of transsubstantiation—and to make the verbal changes necessary to convert the quasi heresies into orthodox formulations (De Vooght).[109] But

---

[109] The basic picture of Hus's dependence on Wyclif, demonstrated by Johann Loserth in his *Hus und Wiclif* (1st ed., Prague and Leipzig, 1884; trans. M. J. Evans as *Wyclif and Hus* [London, 1884]; 2d ed., *Huss und Wiclif,* Munich and Berlin, 1925), has been strengthened by the even more expert work of Jan Sedlák, who has not only extended the evidence for more of Hus's Latin works (*ST,* I, 436–459; II, 179–196, 277–301, 478–527, 528–536), but has shown that several of the Czech works included large portions translated from Wyclif (*ST,* I, 170–247, 257–282, 305–311, and II, 355–368, 415–428). The facts are beyond question, even though it is possible to argue, as Václav Novotný has done in *Mistr Jan Hus: Život a dílo* (2 vols.; Prague, 1919–21), *passim,* that Hus's ideas were originally drawn from the native Bohemian reform movement—particularly from Matthew of Janov—but that he expressed these ideas in the keener formulations of Wyclif; cf. also Sedlák, *M. Jan Hus* (Prague, 1915), p. 72, n. 5. F. M. Bartoš has pointed out, moreover, that Wyclif's positive evaluation of the role of the state in achieving reform gave his doctrines an advantage over the native tradition, and that Wyclif's emphasis on the struggle against simony fitted in well with the contemporary current of European reform agitation and hence lent his works— otherwise very similar in tendency to Matthew of Janov's—a special value ("Hus a Viklef," *Husitství a cizina,* pp. 20–58). Finally, Sedlák has shown that Hus was no mere plagiarist but rather a skillful *user* of Wyclif's works, selecting for his own treatises

when all is said along these lines, one must still accept the basic point recently put by Robert Kalivoda: "Hus's doctrine in its final, ripened form is essentially identical with the doctrine of Wyclif." [110] The issue here is not one of technical heresy but of political significance, and it was put very well in 1414 by Hus's archenemy (and former friend) Stephen Páleč:

> [Hus] writes [in his *De ecclesia*] that "the dissension has arisen because priests of Christ have preached against the pestiferous crimes of the clergy." But this is not true, for long ago, when Hus was still in his father's loins, there were sound and weighty [*autentici et sollempnes*] preachers in the realm of Bohemia who preached against the simoniacal heresy and against . . . the avarice, sensuality, pride, and luxury of the clergy. But they did not mix the errors of Wyclif's Forty-five Articles into their sermons, and they taught the people to hold and believe what the Roman church held and believed . . . and therefore dissension did not arise among the clergy of Bohemia then as it has today. [111]

Although Hus did not remain in his father's loins beyond about 1370, Páleč's reference was most probably to the whole Miličian movement, and what he said was basically correct—there was dissension, to be sure, but it was always ended by the defeat or submission of the Miličians, who were handicapped by their refusal to reject the church's authority. Hus's party did not refuse, and that was Páleč's complaint.

At first, to be sure, the subversive implications of Wyclifism had not been so apparent. Nor, at first, had Hus been the leader of the Wyclifite faction—not in 1402, when he began to preach at Bethlehem, nor in the first years of struggle over Wyclifism at the university. At that time he was only one of the Wyclifites, who were led by Páleč and his future companion in renegacy, Stanislav of Znojmo. But apparent or not, the implications were there, and at a very early time some of the non-Wyclifite reformers, like Maurice

appropriate passages from several of the Englishman's, and composing works that were generally better organized and more effective than Wyclif's; and, of course, there were cases in which Hus did not use Wyclif at all (see, e.g., *ST*, II, 125–131). Still, when all is said and done, the fact remains that Hus differed from Wyclif chiefly in not taking over all of the latter's ideas; the ideas he did take over he neither changed nor deepened, nor did he add any new ideas of his own: these are the blunt conclusions of Kamil Krofta, in his review of Novotný's monograph, *ČČH*, XXIX (1923), 518 f., and now De Vooght has demonstrated essentially the same point in the whole of his *L'Hérésie*.

[110] *HI*, p. 159, and cf. the whole section on Hus, pp. 151–191. Kalivoda acknowledges Hus's verbal modifications of Wyclif's doctrine, but tends to regard these as inessential (e.g., p. 174); I agree with him, and on this basis I accept both his and De Vooght's interpretations, which are not as mutually exclusive as they seem.

[111] Páleč, *Tractatus de ecclesia*, ed. J. Sedlák, *M. Jan Hus* (Prague, 1915), p. 265*.

Rvačka and Andrew of Brod, saw what was happening and made their choice for Romanism, against Wyclifism.[112] There were many factors in play at that time, but certainly the ecclesiological one was basic, for the effect of Wyclif's doctrine was to deny the actual Roman church its title to institutional holiness, and hence to deny its final authority in matters of doctrine. Hus here followed Wyclif without significant variation. He held that the holy universal church was that formed by the grace of predestination; the ecclesiastical corporation, on the other hand, was composed only on the basis of "grace according to present righteousness" and its officials could claim the rights of their offices only so long as their virtuous lives convinced the people that the officials indeed enjoyed that grace.[113] If the people saw not virtue but sin and vice, they could be sure that their prelates were not of the church according to present righteousness, and they could reasonably doubt that they were of the church according to predestination; they were thus entitled to suppose that the prelates in question were "enemies of Jesus Christ." [114] The subversiveness of this doctrine is obvious, and Páleč did not neglect to explain it. The ecclesiastical institution, in his orthodox view, was composed by the grace of the sacraments, *gracia formaliter gratificans,* and was therefore holy, even if all its members were not of the predestined, for the grace came from Christ and the earthly church was a second mystical body of Christ, entitled to claim the objective authority of such a body regardless of the moral condition of the clergy.[115] Otherwise there could be no

[112] Maurice had once written a treatise advocating frequent communion (J. Fikerle, "Čechové na koncilu Kostnickém," *ČČH,* IX (1903), 250 f.) and had brought some of Wyclif's philosophical works back to Prague from Oxford (*Čechy,* p. 315). For his radicalism as a reformer at the Council of Constance see *HR,* I, 44 f. For Andrew of Brod's early reformism see, below, chap. iii, n. 54.

[113] *Magistri Johannis Hus, Tractatus de ecclesia,* ed. S. Harrison Thomson (Boulder, Colo., 1956), pp. 17, 99; cf. Wyclif, *De fide catholica, OM,* p. 114. See also, below, n. 114.

[114] Hus, *De ecclesia,* p. 38; Wyclif, *DE,* p. 43. Wilks, "Predestination, Property, and Power," pp. 224–226, argues that Wyclif (and, following him, Hus) did not attempt to determine for practical purposes whether a man was predestined or not. In fact, although both recognized that true certainty was impossible for men, the passages cited in this and the preceding note show that Wilks is wrong. Neither Wyclif nor Hus thought of predestinarian ecclesiology as a sort of *jeu d'esprit,* irrelevant to the practical problems of reform—problems of morality and obedience. Wyclif, indeed, made his position quite clear (*De fide catholica, OM,* p. 116): "Nec est racio quare ponenda foret predestinacionis gracia quin per idem ponenda esset virtus alia que est in predestinato radix vel minera ad virtutes alias adquiribiles et deperdibiles sibi accidentaliter inessentes." Also *DE,* pp. 90 f., esp.: "Illos autem quos videmus vivere secundum legem Dei reputamus esse filios regni." Ernst Troeltsch formulated the connection quite clearly in his *The Social Teaching of the Christian Churches,* trans. O. Wyon, (London, 1931), I, 360; it is a pity that he has gone out of fashion.

[115] Páleč, *De ecclesia,* in Sedlák, *op. cit.,* pp. 204* f.

authority, no discipline. And this was the crucial point, as one of Hus's future judges, Jean Gerson, saw quite clearly: to deny the jurisdictional power of anyone in a state of mortal sin was simply seditious, a threat to the stability of the polity of both church and state: "For political lordship on earth is not founded on the title of predestination or charity, for then it would be most uncertain and unstable, but it is stabilized on other foundations—according to ecclesiastical and civil laws." [116] In fact, both Wyclif and Hus refrained from emphasizing the application of the doctrine to secular lordship; their real interest was in breaking the effective jurisdictional power of the Roman church. For a pope to prove that he was really pope it was necessary that he exhibit the evangelical virtues of Christ and of Peter— but these excluded precisely the domination and power involved in jurisdiction.[117]

On this line of argument, which was not inseparably connected with predestinarianism, the model for a sound earthly church was to be sought in the actual community Christ had founded, the Primitive Church. This body had existed in its original condition for three centuries, until Pope Silvester I accepted the Donation of Constantine, on which occasion, according to Ranulph Higden's *Polychronicon,* an angel proclaimed that "poison has been poured into the church." [118] The disease spread until it infected the whole body; anticipating the modern emphasis on the crucial importance of the Hildebrandine reform, Wyclif placed the definitive victory of corruption in the eleventh century. Thenceforth few of the church's doctors would speak with the voice of evangelical truth, and from that time on the institutions and doctrines of the church as a juridical corporation, wealthy and powerful, were to be elaborated ever more decisively.[119] The Primitive Church now survived only as memory and tradition, its place in the real world having been usurped by something that could only be described as its opposite—not the church of Christ but the church of Antichrist.[120] Indeed one need only look at the Roman pope and compare his way of life with that of Christ to convince oneself of the antithesis.[121] Hus did not resist these ideas, but he tended to be more enthusiastic about praising the Primitive Church than

[116] *Documenta,* p. 528.

[117] Wyclif, *DPP,* pp. 43–62, 178; Hus, *De ecclesia,* pp. 70 f., 115.

[118] E.g., *DPP,* p. 198; *Trialogus,* pp. 309 f.; see Laehr, *op cit.,* pp. 140 ff. For Hus's ideas on the matter see, below, *ad* n. 156.

[119] Michael Hurley, S.J., " 'Scriptura sola': Wyclif and His Critics," *Traditio,* XVI (1960), 301.

[120] See the summary of Wyclif's views in Workman, *op. cit.,* II, 80–82, with references to the sources.

[121] Wyclif's fullest development of this antithesis is in the *De Christo et suo Adversario Antichristo,* ed. R. Buddensieg (Gotha, 1880); cf. *OM,* pp. 131, 136 f., 361 f.

in denouncing the popes as Antichrist. Still, the thrust of his doctrine was in this direction, and the effect of his powerful preaching against the vices of the clergy was certainly to whip up the hatred of the people, who for their part naturally tended to see things in the sharpest possible way. Accused of having preached that the pope was Antichrist, Hus responded that he had not said it—all he had said was that a pope who sold benefices, who was arrogant, greedy, and otherwise contrary to Christ in way of life, was Antichrist.[122] Accused of having preached that the Curia was the synagogue of Satan, Hus responded that he had not said it as a fact, but that he had heard it said by those returning from Rome.[123] And so on. Even if he had indeed been as cautious in his preaching as he later claimed, even if he had preserved sobriety in applying his own advice to speak according to the mood of the people [124]—still, the net effect of his impact must have been inflammatory, and his sermons must have worked to bring the people into the streets, in the potentially mutinous demonstrations that became more and more frequent in Prague from the middle of the decade on. The Primitive Church would have appeared as a kind of slogan, signifying everything good that the actual church lacked, and the figure of Antichrist must have become an all but palpable epitome of all who were loyal to the papal and Roman establishment. It was thanks above all to Hus's preaching and leadership that the intellectual leaders of the Wyclifite party enjoyed the enthusiastic support of the people, most of whom could hardly have understood the doctrinal complexities in question.

Furthermore, if Hus's own written works were at first rather anodyne, those of his more radical associates were not, and in the atmosphere of defiance that developed under Hus's practical leadership there emerged theoreticians and polemicists who did not hesitate to combine the most extreme ideas of Wyclif with the sensationalistic imagery of Matthew of Janov. The chief figure here was Master Jakoubek of Stříbro, about whom more will be said below, but he was not alone—in particular, he was joined by the German Hussite Master Nicholas of Dresden. One work of the latter, the "Tables of the Old and New Color," represents perhaps the highest stage of the passage of Wyclifism into propaganda, so stark and simple that it could be embodied in pictures to be carried in street demonstrations. As an expression of the radicalism of Hus's movement it is unsurpassed, and can be presented here in lieu of a more comprehensive treatment. In its final form

---

[122] *Documenta*, p. 170.

[123] *Ibid*.

[124] Some of Hus's notes to his sermons are quoted in Nov., II, 131, n. 4: "Tunc ultra, prout videbitur in populo, loquendum est contra ydolatriam"; "Hec est epistole sentencia. Et tunc secundum audienciam populi est amplius dilatanda."

dating from 1412 it consists of nine "tables"—*tabule*—or collections of authorities, selected to document the "old color"—the Primitive Church—and the "new color"—the modern, Roman church; or, as an alternate title puts it, "Christ's way of life opposed to Antichrist's way of life." [125] In most tables (1, 2, 3, 4, 6) the authorities for each side alternate; in others (5, 9) they are cumulative; in the rest (7, 8) they are arranged, with some editorial comment, in a form resembling a scholastic *questio*. In all cases, except probably the seventh and eighth tables, the authorities seem designed to appear on pictures illustrating their main themes. The pictures may or may not have been painted in a book edition, but they were, certainly, put on agitational placards, now unfortunately lost. But the titles survive, and they correspond in large measure with the pictures in the "Jena" and "Göttingen" codices, which preserve a much later Czech redaction of the work. In any case, the extraordinarily suggestive rhythm of the text, its antitheses alternating or accumulating, but always hammering away at their point, virtually forces the reader to imagine the original pictorial aspect of the work. And not only did a number of the antitheses correspond to those in Wyclif's work: the very idea of the pictures can perhaps be traced to Wyclif's urging, in his "On Christ and His Enemy Antichrist," that the reader should *see* the contrast between the apostolic and the papal writings.[126]

The first of the contrasts contains the meaning of the whole. Christ bearing his cross is labeled "The last among men" (Isa. 53:3)—*novissimus virorum*—and says, "If any man would come after me, let him take up his cross and follow me" (Matt. 16:24). Against this there is a picture of the pope riding a horse, with a fragmentary quotation from the Decretals (V, xxxiii, 23): "The Supreme Pontiff, employing the insignia of the apostolic office." The contrast is sharpened by the contraposition of "Christ, true God and true man" to "The Pope—a wondrous being, neither God nor man," the latter taken from John Andree's gloss on the preface to the Clementines. St. Bernard sums up in a passage taken partly from his *De Consideratione,* addressed to Pope Eugenius III: "Read the life of Christ from the womb of his mother to his death on the cross, and you will find only the marks of poverty. . . . In these things [*scil.,* pomp and worldliness] you are the successor of Constantine, not of Peter." Thus the pictorial contrast of Christ's humility and suffering with the pope's pomp and arrogance is given its theoretical meaning: as "the last among men" Christ provided the exemplar not only of the ordinary Christian's humility and suffering, but also of the proper way of life for the head of the church; the *conversacio* of the

---

[125] The reader is referred for what follows to the edition and translation in *OC&N*, pp. 38–65; see also the discussion on pp. 9 f.

[126] *De Christo et . . . Antichristo,* p. 50; the passage is quoted in *OC&N,* p. 10, n. 37.

pope, so remote from this exemplar, is rather the imitation of Caesar. As Wyclif had argued, the pope's official, jurisdictional position in the church was derived from the Donation of Constantine, not from the Petrine privilege.

The sequence indeed resumes in this vein with the second great contrast, fleshing out the first. Constantine is shown making his Donation—the text is quoted from the Decretum (XCVI. Dist., c. 14):

> We give to Blessed Silvester and his successors the palace of our Empire. We decree that they may ride horses decked out in caparisons and coverings of purest white, and we also confer upon them the various imperial ornaments and all the glory of our power, as well as giving them the estates that we possess and enriching them with various properties.

Opposite this we have Jesus saying, "The foxes have holes, and the birds of the sky have nests; but the Son of man does not have where to lay his head" (Matt. 8:20); with this there are the following:

> When Jesus therefore perceived that they would come and take him, to make him a king, he fled to a mountain himself alone (John 6:15). Man, who made me a judge or a divider over you? (Luke 12:14–15) They clothe him in purple and weave a crown of thorns and put it on him (Mark 15:17).

This is clear enough, but it is made to resonate down the centuries, the type repeating itself with specific bearing on the Petrine theory, by a third set of pictures. Lewis the Pious repeats and confirms the Donation (LXIII. Dist., c. 30):

> I, the Emperor Lewis, grant to you, Blessed Peter, and to your successors, the city of Rome with its duchy and suburbs and territories, in perpetuity, just as you have held them in your power and sway from our predecessors to the present, and have disposed over them.

But opposite him Peter hangs on his cross, saying (I Pet. 1:18–19):

> Knowing that you were not redeemed with corruptible things, gold and silver, from your futile way of living, but with precious blood, like that of a spotless lamb, the blood of Jesus Christ.

And Jesus stands by, pronouncing once more the law that he imposed on those who would be his disciples: "As for you, follow me. You will stretch out your hands and another will gird you and lead you where you do not wish to go" (John 21:22, 18). Here the first table ends, having not only stated the contrast between the two "colors," but having also applied it to particular features of each, the portrait of the Primitive Church suggesting the nature of a genuine reformation for modern times.

The second table pursues this point by a series of contrasts between the pope and Peter. The canons prohibiting the ordination of clerics who have neither benefices nor patrimonies [127] are forced to stand alongside Peter's dicta: "Gold and silver I have none" (Acts 3:6), "Behold we have forsaken all and followed you; what shall we have therefore?" (Matt. 19:27). Texts from both the Roman and canon law are cited as authorities to show how the church deliberately establishes its prelates in wealthy and multiple benefices, dispensing them from the prohibition against pluralism, but the dubious character of this practice is documented by a composite from the *glose ordinarie* on the Decretals (III, xxxiv, 5) and Decretum (XXXII. q. v, § 1):

> He who has received a dispensation shall have the exemption as far as the Church Militant is concerned, but with respect to God, in whose tribunal judge and witness are one, this allegation has no force. Nor can his conscience be changed by the pope, since the mind is not subject to coercion.[128]

Thus once more, but now in a narrower, more specific framework, the contrapositions point to the deformed character of the Roman church's institutions as against the divine law. It is then left to the third table to develop the argument by a more detailed attention to the subject of the

[127] Nicholas here attacks the church's theory rather than its practice, for in the later Middle Ages ordinations *sine titulo* were increasingly common. See J. Sedlák, "Nižší klerus v době Husově," *ST*, I, 283–304, for a discussion of the clerical proletariat of that period; he publishes a tractate, *De pluralitate beneficiorum*, that throws an interesting light on Nicholas's position. Cf. also Barraclough, *Papal Provisions*, p. 172, n. 1.

[128] Nicholas reworks and compresses the glosses to suit his needs, and since he does this in other places as well, it may be useful here to compare this text with the originals. The first point of departure is a letter from Innocent III to the Archbishop of Estergom, beginning: "Non est voti dicendus transgressor, qui quod vovit auctoritate sedis apostolicae distulit adimplere." The gloss on *adimplere* (*Decretales* [Lyons, 1613], col. 1280) comments: "Si iusta causa subest . . . , alias non est securus, quoad Deum, cum quo Papa dispensat, nisi subsit causa dispensandi. . . . Habebit tamen exceptionem quoad ecclesiam ille, cum quo sine causa dispensatum est . . . ; quoad Deum sibi allegatio non valebit, ubi iudicabitur eo teste quo iudice." The second passage rests on the preface to Question v of *Causa* XXXII, including the sentence: "Est enim virtus animi, quae violentiam non sentit. Corpori namque vis infertur, non animo." The gloss on *vis* (*Decretum* [Lyons, 1613], col. 1621) comments: "Absoluta, quae non potest animo inferri: sed conditionalis potest. . . . Vel dic, non potest inferri animo vis: verum est non consentienti." Since the discussion here has to do with the guilt or non-guilt of violated virgins, it is rather far-fetched to apply it to pluralists, who would have asked for their dispensations in any case. Nor does the first gloss really bear on the case, for it leaves open the question of whether or not the dispensation is for just cause. Thus Nicholas has transformed a typically legalistic exploration of possibilities into an unambiguous attack on papal dispensations.

church's law, again with pictures that state the issue in the most drastic form. First the pope appears on the scene, decreeing:

> A forger of papal letters is to be locked in prison for life, to live on the bread of pain and the water of sorrow (Decretals, V, xl, 27). Whoever does injury to the church or priesthood will be sentenced to death (XVII. q. lv, c. 29).

The eye then moved to a picture of Jesus being flagellated, with the following texts:

> I gave my body to the smiters and have not been rebellious (Isa. 50:5–6). You know not what manner of spirit you are. The Son of Man has come not to destroy lives but to save them (Luke 9:55–56). Pray for those who persecute you and slander you, and bless those who hate you (Matt. 5:44).

And lest the viewer succumb to the natural inclination to rest content with these precise and glaring contrasts, a text from Augustine (XII. Dist., c. 12) was set under the whole diptych, to relate the obvious message to the more general Hussite theory:

> Our religion which our Lord Jesus Christ wished to be free, with only the fewest of sacramental rites, is so oppressed by some with servile burdens that more bearable is the condition of the Jews, who are subjected not to human presumptions but to divine institutions.

If it be objected that Augustine's "sacramental rites" are something different from the judicial decrees under consideration, the answer would no doubt have to be that Nicholas of Dresden was simply following the theory of the Hildebrandine church, which saw its sacramental and judicial functions as a single homogeneous sphere of action. In any case, the table quickly returns to the question of jurisdiction, with a "doctor" portrayed uttering a little compendium of medieval papalism (Institutes, I, ii, 6; Decretum, XXXIII. q. iii, c. 11; Decretals, III, viii, 4):

> In those things which the pope desires, his will is sufficient reason. . . . Nor is there anyone who may say to him, why do you do thus? . . . According to our plenitude of power we are able to dispense, by law, from the requirements of the law.[129]

But the old color speaks in opposition:

> They bind heavy burdens and grievous to be borne, and lay them on men's shoulders; but they themselves will not move them with one of their fingers (Matt. 23:4). You shall not add to the word that I command you, nor shall you diminish from it. Cursed be he who does not persist in the works of this

---

[129] The collection of texts was undoubtedly taken by Nicholas from the *glosa ordinaria in verba* "Veri Dei vicem," *Decretales,* I, vii, 3 (Lyons, 1613), col. 217 (*q.v.*).

law, and who does not work to carry them out (Deut. 4:2, 27:26). I have come not to destroy the law but to fulfill it (Matt. 5:17). I do nothing of myself, but, as my father has taught me, I speak this (John 8:28).

And a text from Daniel (7:24–25) draws the lesson of the diptych: "He shall subdue kings and he shall speak words against the exalted and shall wear out the saints of the most High, and he shall think that he is able to change times and laws." "He" was of course the Beast, the Antichrist, here appearing as the type of the pope. The same attack on papal jurisdiction then continues in the third and fourth tables, the latter also offering material specifically discrediting the ecclesiastical status of the hierarchy, the monastic order, and the church's restriction of free preaching. Figures of canonists, monks, and the pope appear for the new color, and the fourth table concludes with a picture of three Jews, the scribes and pharisees, who seek to interfere with Jesus' mission (Luke 11:45, 53–54); they are a kind of middle term in the typological series running from the ancient Jews who slew the prophets (Acts 7:51), to the Jews of Jesus' own time who persecuted and killed him, on to the popes, who refuse to allow, without the evidence of special miracles, any preaching mission other than that authorized by the ecclesiastical institution (Decretals, V, vii, 12).

We now come to the fifth table, which breaks the rhythm of alternating pictures by offering a straightforward series of texts, first showing that simony is the greatest of all crimes and heresies in the church—the authorities are drawn not only from the Fathers but also from the legislation of the "modern" church—and then moving on to the sin of fornication as it affects the clerical function. The first subject was illustrated by two pictures, no doubt in sequence rather than contraposition, one of the Black Horseman of the Apocalypse carrying a balance, for the judging of heresy, the other of Christ driving the money-changers out of the Temple, as the type of battle against simony; the second subject seems to have had its type illustrated by Susanna and the elders—who were priests. The fifth table thus marks a break not only in the formal pattern of the work but also in its subject matter; it attacks not the constitution of the modern church but the abuses within it, the two major abuses that appear again and again in Hussite literature as somehow correlative characteristics of the opposing party.[130] Obviously there would not be any canonistic texts explicitly defending either simony or fornication: hence, no doubt, the difference in form between the fifth table and the first four.

The sixth table reverts to the scheme of contrapositions, this time attacking the precious vestments and other tegumental pomposities of the modern

---

[130] See, below, chap. iii, n. 76.

church; among the pictures is one of Constantine crowning the pope and clothing him in the imperial garments, thus suggesting what was said by Wyclif and later picked up by the Taborites, that the sacramental and official vestments of the Roman clergy had their origin, along with so many other evils, in the Donation of Constantine.[131] For the rest, the new color is represented by what seems to have been a procession of patriarchs and cardinals, all decked out in their canonically prescribed splendors, while the old color appears in pictures of Christ clothing Adam and Eve in animal skins, of Mary alongside the manger containing the infant Christ wrapped in rags, and of St. Martin, probably in the classic pose of dividing his cloak. Against the texts referring to the humble attire of John the Baptist and the apostles, and the dicta of such eminent castigators of clerical pomp as St. Jerome and St. Bernard, there are some typically medieval glosses:

> It is not to be pompously rejected, but rather defended, that doctors should go about elaborately and ornately gowned, that in them the dignity of the doctorate may be apparent. But students who wear the clothing fitting only for doctors are to be censured. (John Andree, gloss on *Liber Sextus,* V, vii, 6.)

> Clerics may wear costly clothing, according to local custom, in order to conform to the practice of those among whom they live, and so that the clerical estate not be cheapened. They may wear purple and silk, for the robe of the Lord was purple. (*Glosa ordinaria* on the Decretum, XXI. q. iv, c. 1.)

The last sentence, which raises very fundamental questions about the whole theory of imitation of the Primitive Church—more will be said on this later —is cleverly refuted by quotation of Nicholas of Lyra's glosses on John 19:2, showing that the purple robe put on Jesus by the soldiers was put on him in mockery—"for in this way fools were mocked in those times." But the argument does not stop here; in tables seven and eight the question of precious clothing, which seems to refer in general to the dress of the clergy rather than just to their liturgical or official vestments, is taken up in the rather incongruous form of a scholastic question, beginning with the citation of premised authorities, and then in turn citing and refuting seven arguments in favor of fine attire. The passage is a distinct weak spot in the work and may well have been an insertion, made, however, very early in the history of the "Tables" as a literary composition.

Once this section is out of the way, the "Tables" pick up much of their lost momentum. Tacked onto the eighth table is perhaps the most effective

---

[131] For the Taborite position, which will be discussed below, see Höfler, II, 555, a passage including the line, "doctor evangelicus [*scil.,* Wyclif] saepe in suis scriptis illas vestes vocat caesareas."

contraposition of all, the contrast between the "curia Cristi" and the papal Curia, figured, respectively, by a picture of Christ washing the disciples' feet and a picture of the pope having his feet kissed, the latter picture sarcastically entitled: "The Servant of the Servants of God, receiving kisses of his Blessed Feet." There was also a separate picture of the pope, embellished by a selection of currently circulating anti-Curial doggerel:

> Money is what the Curia likes best,
> It empties many a purse and chest.
> If you are stingy with your marks,
> Stay away from popes and patriarchs.
> But give them marks, and once their chests are filled,
> You will be absolved from the bondage of all your guilt.

> Someone wishes to enter. Who are you? Me. What do you want? To enter. Do you bring anything? No. Stay out! I do bring something. What? Enough. Enter! [132]

After some more of this, we move to the ninth and last table, which carried one picture, of the Antichrist, dressed in papal regalia and surrounded by whores; it was, no doubt, this picture that an anti-Hussite author of 1415 had in mind when he wrote, "They call the pope Antichrist and paint him in the papal crown and with the feet of an eagle." [133] The texts now do not alternate; they are all devoted to a single subject, the coming of the Antichrist, whose traits are defined by various biblical passages, culminating in II Thess. 2:4, 9–10: "So that he sits in the temple of God, showing himself as God. Whose coming is with all the seduction of unrighteousness in them that perish; because they have not received the love of truth," and Dan. 7:24–25: "He shall humble kings and think that he can change laws and times." The repetition of texts used earlier in the attack on papal pretensions helps to reinforce the identification of the pope with Antichrist; in any case, the sympathetic reader of the whole work cannot fail to get the point and to feel the aptness of the last table as both the logical and emotional outcome of

---

[132] One of the manuscripts has still another set of rhymes (quoted in *OC&N*, p. 61, apparatus); a slightly different version of them appears in one text of the well-known anti-simoniac tractate of 1404, *De squaloribus curie romane* (see Sedlák, *M. Jan Hus*, p. 32, n. 1), written by the one-time Prague professor Matthew of Cracow. The whole genre has recently been studied by John A. Yunck, "Economic Conservatism, Papal Finance, and the Medieval Satires on Rome," *Mediaeval Studies*, XXIII (1961), 334–351; he shows that the satires are best understood as attacks not on abuses but on the economic system of the Hildebrandine church.

[133] Hardt, III, 682. A picture in the "Jena Codex" (containing a later Czech version of the *Tabule*), fol. 35ᵛ, corresponds to both these descriptions; there is a photograph of it in *SbH*, V, 80.

the others. The pope, who first appeared riding a horse, as "the Supreme Pontiff, employing the insignia of the apostolic office," and who then exhibited himself in his various aspects as recipient of Caesar's Donation, wielder of cruel and arbitrary power, and bearer of the external signs of pomp and wealth, now stands finally revealed in the light of his own doctrine as Christ's opposite and enemy, a devil incarnate, the Supreme Antichrist. And if, according to orthodox theory, the pope was the head of the Roman church understood as a clerical corporation,[134] that institution was correspondingly regarded by the radical Hussites as the mystical body of Antichrist, in apocalyptic imagery as the Great Whore, "drunken with the blood of the saints," the image of Babylon, whose destruction is urged upon the faithful in the last days. And with Antichrist enthroned over the whole world, those days were imminent. "O Lord," Nicholas exclaims,[135] "will I live to see that blessed hour when the Whore of Revelations will be stripped bare and her flesh consumed by the fire of tribulation?"

Here we breathe the atmosphere of revolution, with evangelical love, humility, and suffering displaced by the fanatical hatred that so often forms their psychological correlate—as, indeed, it did when a Christian author composed the Book of Revelation and when the Christian people accepted that book as the final chapter of the New Testament.[136] And it is clear that

---

[134] There were many formulations of this idea; the most pertinent here would be that of the (anti-Hussite) doctors of the theological faculty at Prague in 1413: "Romanae ecclesiae papa est caput, corpus vero collegium cardinalium" (*Documenta,* p. 475). It was explicitly refuted not only by Hus (*ibid.,* p. 57) but by Nicholas (*Apologia,* in Hardt, III, 612), to the accompaniment of savage abuse of the papal institution. See also De Vooght, "L'Ecclésiologie catholique à Prague autour de 1400," *Hussiana,* pp. 102–160, esp. pp. 124 ff.

[135] In his exposition of the text, "Querite primum regnum Dei," MS IV G 15, fol. 124ʳ: "O domine, putasne inveniet me illa benedicta hora in qua sic meretrix apocaliptica denudaretur et carnes eius igne tribulacionum concremarentur?"

[136] The destinies of the Book of Revelation in church history are briefly treated by A. Harnack in his article, "Millennium," in the *Encyclopedia Britannica,* 11th ed. The subject is illuminated, fitfully but brilliantly, by D. H. Lawrence's study, *Apocalypse* (New York, 1932); some of his dicta are especially helpful in the present context. Thus (p. 12): "It is very nice, if you are poor and *not* humble—and the poor may be obsequious, but they are almost *never* truly humble in the Christian sense—to bring your grand enemies down to utter destruction and discomfiture, while you yourself rise up to grandeur. And nowhere does this happen so splendiferously as in Revelation." And (p. 13): "What we realise when we have read the precious book a few times is that John the Divine had on the face of it a grandiose scheme for wiping out and annihilating everybody who wasn't of the elect, the chosen people, in short, and of climbing up himself right on to the throne of God. With non-conformity, the chapel-people took over to themselves the Jewish idea of the chosen people [and of the] ultimate triumph and reign of the chosen people." The close psychological linkage

the anti-Romanism of Nicholas and his associates had its ground not in a scholarly determination that the contemporary church was unlike the Primitive Church, but in a general and comprehensive rejection of the Roman system, a kind of total alienation from the *status quo*. The point is best appreciated when we consider the "Tables of the Old and New Color" in the light of a Catholic polemic, part of an extensive refutation of Nicholas's whole program; the refutation is especially valuable because of its resolute acceptance of precisely the historical scheme used by Nicholas himself. Thus the author argues:

> It is proper for the church to have temporalities, without which spiritualities cannot long survive. And if anyone should allege the status of the Primitive Church, in which many abandoned all possessions and followed Christ the pauper, or if he should cite the evangelical dictum, "Whoever forsakes not all that he has, he cannot be my disciple" [Luke 14:33]—the answer to this is that one thing was reasonable and necessary in the propagation of the then nascent church, another thing however now, in the conservation of the church that has been strengthened and endowed with empire, kingdoms, and territories. For then it was impossible for Christians, living under the dominion of emperors and kings who were not yet Christian but rather sought to extirpate the faith of Christ, to keep their temporal goods. . . . Now, however, after emperors, kings, and territories have bowed their necks to the yoke of the faith, it would be utterly foolish to give up to the enemies of the faith the things necessary for the protection of the peace of the catholic religion. It is therefore obvious that in acquiring temporalities the church did not become defective [*non defecit*], but rather by their due use enjoys a happy increase.[137]

---

between evangelical idealism and apocalypticism has yet to be studied; Norman Cohn's *The Pursuit of the Millennium* (Fairlawn, N.J., 1957; 2d ed., New York, 1961) summarizes some of the currently available information about messianic movements, but its psychoanalytic system of interpretation moves away from the religious sphere, rather than more deeply into it.

[137] The first part is a treatise called, "Collecta et excerpta de summa Benedicti Abbatis Marsilie super capitulo, 'Firmiter credimus,' de summa trinitate et fide katholica." It refutes twenty-one points that together correspond more or less fully to the doctrines of Nicholas of Dresden (see chap. iii, below). A number of texts survive, including: MS British Museum, Arundel 458, fols. 107ʳ–147ᵛ; MS Padua, Library of St. John, Pluteo VII, fols. 190ʳ–249ʳ; MS Rome, Vatican Library, Ottob. Lat. 350, fols. 209ᵛ–236ʳ; MS Prague Capit. D 119, fols. 4ʳ–107ʳ; fragments are in MS Prague Capit. O 50, fols.143ʳ–144ʳ, and MS Prague Univ. I F 18, fols.227ʳ–232ʳ. The *incipit* is "Una est fidelium universalis ecclesia." For Benedict of Marseilles see the *Dictionaire de droit canonique,* II (1937), 761–765. Benedict D'Alignan, OFM, Bishop of Marseilles from 1229, died in 1267; his *magnum opus,* the "Tractatus fidei contra diversos errores," was begun in 1239. It consists of refutations of hundreds of "errors" drawn from many heresies; the whole is disposed according to the text of the decretal "Firmiter credimus"

History is thus understood in the light of religious sociology, the status of the Primitive Church corresponding to the status of the faith in society, and the author can observe that a similar status still exists in missionary areas.[138] Another treatise uses the same argument in a slightly different sense: "The apostles in the Primitive Church were more concerned with the conversion of the heathen to the faith of Christ than with the adornment of the church or with the form of devotion or with the adornment of the church's ministers."[139] Thus both the property and dominion of the church, and her sumptuous décor, are presented as the legitimate consequences of the Christianization of society.

In this light the Donation of Constantine remains a great turning point of church history, but becomes a thoroughly wholesome act. Nor, the author argues, was it in contradiction to the New Testament, which along with its examples of Christ's poverty, humility, and suffering, also contains documentation of his sovereignty, power, and triumph. "Christ not only died but was resurrected; he lives and rules. And the members of his mystical body not only provide examples of his suffering and humility, but also of his supreme power to judge and rule."[140] Naturally, having been sent to earth precisely to suffer, Jesus did not receive the donation of the Empire, nor were there any among the Palestinian mob, themselves subject to Rome, who could have given it; in the fullness of time, however, when the Emperor became a Christian, it was fitting that he gave the Empire to Christ, in the person of Christ's vicar, Pope Silvester. Thus "through Constantine the kingdom of this world became the kingdom of the Lord Jesus Christ."[141] And while

---

(Decretals, I, i, 1). Its popularity is attested by its survival in a great many manuscripts all over Europe, including several in Prague, but it has not yet been published. The "Collecta et excerpta" is, in fact, drawn from this work, but also contains much new material to meet the needs of anti-Hussite polemic; the tractate against the *Tabule* that follows it in some manuscripts is explicitly based on it, and there is no doubt that the two form a unity, although each sometimes appears by itself. K. Chytil, *Antikrist v naukách a umění středověku a husitské obrazné antithese* (Prague, 1918), pp. 237–247, prints the text of the latter tractate from MS O 50, fols. 133ʳ–137ᵛ, but inaccurately and with omissions; he ascribes it to Stephen of Páleč. Bartoš has ascribed the work to Páleč and Stanislav of Znojmo, working together (*ČČH*, XIX (1913), 507), but he does not seem to have studied it in detail. My discussion of both parts of the polemic is based on my use of several MSS. The passage quoted here appears in MS D 119, fols. 14ʳ–15ʳ. See also, below, chap. iii, *ad* notes 66, 67.

[138] Tractate against the *Tabule*, Chytil, *op. cit.*, p.239.

[139] The anonymous tractate beginning "Eloquenti viro," Hardt, III, 352 f.

[140] Tractate against the *Tabule*, MS Vatican Library, Ottob. Lat. 350, fol. 236ᵛ: "Cristus non solum mortuus est, sed et resurrexit et vivit et regnat. Ita et membra sui mistici corporis non solum preferunt paciencie sue et humilitatis exempla, verum eciam iudicii regiminis et excellencie potestatis."

[141] "Collecta et excerpta," MS D 119, f. 10ᵛ; Tractate against the *Tabule*, Chytil, *op. cit.*, p. 239. On the quoted words cf. Rev. 11:15.

Pope Silvester "succeeded to Christ in pontifical authority," he also "succeeded to Constantine, in imperial authority"—hence subsequent popes legitimately enjoyed both, and still "the church now called Roman had its beginning from Christ." [142]

Turning then to the Hussites' pictorial antitheses, the Catholic polemicist can refute them in general by developing the arguments already cited, sometimes with great effect. Thus in regard to the pictures of Jesus washing the disciples' feet and of the pope having his feet kissed, he observes that Christ on other occasions had his own feet kissed, as well as washed with Mary Magdalene's tears and dried with her hair: why then did the Hussites not paint a picture of Christ having his feet kissed, and against this a picture of the pope washing the cardinals' feet on Maundy Thursday? They could thus prove, by their own method, that the pope was Christ and Christ was Antichrist. [143] The answer, of course, was that the Hussites did not *want* to prove this: animated, as the author observed, "by one desire, to contradict," [144] they deliberately sought out contradictions between the Primitive and Roman churches and deliberately avoided reconciling them. Gratian in the twelfth century had worked to produce a "concord of discordant canons," but by the fifteenth century the time had come to undo his work and not merely accept but exult in the contradictions that the earlier age had tried to suppress.

Indeed the mood of contradiction had its origins in the religious movement of the preceding century. As Matthew of Janov had observed, in his own fashion, the "synthesis" of the high Middle Ages was a fraud, the doctrines and practices of high-medieval papalism were hypocrisy. And while the "Tables" of Nicholas of Dresden seem most obviously related to Wyclif's work, as noted above, they also corresponded to the attitudes and emotions of the religious movement that had found its spokesman in Matthew, and which continued its existence in the emerging Hussite movement.

[142] MS D 119, fol. 9ʳ–9ᵛ: "Sed quod obiciunt heretici, quod Silvester non successit Cristo sed Constantino, inducentes illud Mt. xx [25]: 'Scitis quia principes gencium dominantur eorum et qui maiores sunt potestatem exercent in eos; non ita erit inter vos': Respondetur quod per hoc ambicio fugienda innuitur, et Silvester Cristo successit in auctoritate pontificali, Constantino vero in auctoritate imperiali." And fol. 8ᵛ: "A Cristo igitur incepit ecclesia que modo Romana dicitur."

[143] Tractate against the *Tabule*, Chytil, *op. cit.*, p. 238.

[144] *Ibid.*, p. 241: ". . . solo contradicendi studio." The context is instructive: ". . . necesse est cum indagatione veritatis concordare diversitates scripturarum et jura contraria secundum exigentiam causarum, conditionum et temporum. Aliqua [*sic*] eciam rationabiliter convenit abrogare, unde et in hoc sanctos doctores plurimum laborasse conspicimus, unde Augustinus in ewangelistarum concordantiis et Gracianus in tocius decreti volumine, ubi et in prima rubrica dicit: 'Incipit discordantium canonum concordia,' et plurium doctorum apparatus in concordandis juribus. . . . Illi vero, qui huius fidei veritatem impugnant, solo contradicendi studio perdiderunt sensum."

The fact is clearest in the work of Nicholas' fellow radical, Master Jakoubek of Stříbro, who combined the Janovian and Wyclifian traditions, drawing what was most characteristic from each. In his public determination of the question, whether Antichrist had already come in person, Jakoubek composed his affirmative answer almost wholly from the work of Matthew of Janov (and left no doubt that the Antichrist was the pope),[145] and when he delivered a sermon against the corruption of the clergy he drew lavishly from the same source to construct a picture of the "sinful woman" given over to the delights of the world and the flesh.[146] But when he set about proposng ways of reform, he turned to Wyclif's *De officio regis* and argued that "clerics notoriously offending against the Law of the Lord . . . should be corrected by their kings, as their superiors, through the removal of their temporalities." "Every king," he wrote in the words of Wyclif, "rules his whole realm; every cleric of the king, every bishop or priest of the realm, is a part of the realm together with all that he possesses."[147] In this way the radical alienation of quasi-sectarian pietism found its constructive complement in the idea of the realm as salvationary community. Both points of view were represented in the radicals' willful refutation of high-medieval ideology.

It was as the patron of these subversive tendencies that John Hus was condemned and burned to death at Constance. Had the decision been left entirely to men like Pierre d'Ailly, the process might have found a happier solution, for Hus might have been given a chance to establish his own innocence; but, as he painfully observed in one of his letters, his capital enemies at the Council were his fellow Czechs, men like Páleč, who knew that whatever Hus might prove about the letter of his works, he in fact led a revolutionary movement.[148] Here nothing is more instructive than to analyze

---

[145] Most of the *questio*, pronounced in January 1412, "Utrum sicut ex scriptura plane constat Christum in plenitudine temporis personaliter advenisse, ita evidenter sit deducibile ex eadem antichristum in complemento seculi propria venire in persona," has been published by V. Kybal, "M. Matěj z Janova a M. Jakoubek ze Stříbra," *ČČH*, XI (1905), 22–37; parallel citations show the extent of the borrowing from Matthew of Janov. On p. 37 Kybal shows that although Jakoubek did not say that the Antichrist who had already come was the pope, his discussion of the matter left no doubt on the subject, and contemporaries so understood him.

[146] Jakoubek's sermon on the text, "Ecce mulier" (Luke 7:37), delivered 1409/1411 (*LČJ*, 19), has been published by Jan Sedlák (*ST*, II, 462–477), with indications of what has been taken from Matthew of Janov.

[147] The tractate "De paupertate cleri" (*incipit*, "Magne sanctitatis ille vir") has been published by Sedlák (*ST*, II, 449–462), with indications of what has been taken from Wyclif. Bartoš dates it 1407 (*LČJ*, No. 2), Sedlák 1411.

[148] See Hus's letters from Constance, most conveniently in *Documenta*, pp. 82 f., 90 ("Ipse Palecz omnium ductor"). The various charges brought against Hus by his Czech

Hus's attempts at Constance to vindicate his past, attempts motivated not by cowardice but by the perception, when the chips were down, that he was not prepared to repudiate the actual church as the body of Antichrist. Confronted in his prison cell with the famous list of Forty-five Articles, the list that his party had steadfastly refused to condemn in absolute terms, he responded to most of the articles, "non tenui nec teneo"—"I have not held it nor do I hold it"—and in most cases he was precisely or substantially correct, for he usually did not follow Wyclif's actual heresies and, in any case, the articles of the list were not always accurately drawn from Wyclif's works. But there were some articles that Hus had more or less clearly defended in the past, and to which his responses at Constance were rather odd; these are naturally the most revealing cases, and they are worth an examination.[149]

We may begin with perhaps the most far-reaching of all the articles, number 37: "The Roman church is the synagogue of Satan, and the pope is not the immediate and proximate vicar of Christ and the apostles." To this Hus responded: "I neither have held this nor do I hold it, for I have written the opposite in the treatise *De ecclesia*." Turning to this treatise, however, we find that although Hus did proclaim the perfect purity of the Roman church, he here explicitly defined "Roman church" as the congregation of the faithful, and observed that "this church cannot be understood to signify this or that pope with his cardinals"; in the same work, attacking the pluralism and simony of the cardinals, he compared them to "them which say they are Jews, and are not, but are the synagogue of Satan" (Rev: 2:9)—the context, moreover, brings the pope under this judgement, for Hus writes that "no one is truly the vicar of Christ . . . unless he follow him in way of life," and he notes that the pope does not do so.[150] To say that his response at Constance was not quite frank would hardly be unfair.

This impression is not contradicted by the responses to certain other articles. In the summer of 1412, when the controversy over Wyclifism had become very sharp, Hus had proclaimed that those who condemned the whole list of Forty-five Articles, without proof, were guilty of foolish presumption, and he had subjoined seven articles that he "did not dare to condemn, lest he contradict the truth."[151] The first of these was number

---

enemies turned not only on points of doctrine but also on his subversive words and acts over the past half-dozen years in Prague. See, e.g., *Documenta*, pp. 312 f., 153–173.

[149] The list of articles with Hus's responses has been published by Sedlák (*M. Jan Hus*, pp. 305*–310*) and discussed by him (*ibid.*, pp. 320 ff.). And see the discussion in Nov., II, 378 ff. Most recently Amadeo Molnár has offered a new and better edition, with a historical introduction, in his "Les réponses de Jean Huss aux quarante-cinq articles," *Recherches de Théologie ancienne et médiévale*, XXXI (1964), 85–99.

[150] Hus, *De ecclesia*, pp. 45 ff., 112–116.

[151] *KD*, pp. 123–125.

sixteen: "The temporal lords can, as they judge proper, take temporal goods away from habitually delinquent ecclesiastics"—these being, according to Hus, "clerics so stubbornly habituated and hardened to evil as obviously to be in mortal sin." In Constance, however, he wrote of this article: "I neither assert it nor deny it, for it can have a true sense"; thus the general principle was replaced by a case of possible exception. Also among the articles that he did not dare to condemn in 1412 was number eighteen, that "tithes are merely alms"; in Constance he "did not dare to deny or affirm it." In 1412 Hus had defended, among other articles of Wyclif,[152] the proposition that "any deacon or priest may preach the Word of God without the authorization of the apostolic see and of a catholic bishop" (No. 14 of the list); in Constance he responded that "this can have a true sense, namely, that in case of great need a priest or deacon would be permitted to preach without special licence." But the reservation had not been applied by Hus in 1412, nor had any reservation at all been applied by Nicholas of Dresden, who wrote to support Hus's position in that year.[153]

The articles treating of the church's endowment are even more instructive, although in a different way. Article thirty-two, "To enrich the clergy is against the rule of Christ," received the following response in Constance: "I have not held it nor do I hold it, for clerics may legitimately have riches as long as they do not abuse them"; the interesting point here is that Hus was right—he had not defended this article in 1412 but had left it to Jakoubek of Stříbro, who was less inclined to worry about its revolutionary implications.[154] And to article thirty-three, that "Pope Silvester and the Emperor Constantine erred in endowing the church," also defended by Jakoubek,[155] Hus responded in Constance: "I dare neither to assert it nor to deny it, for each could have sinned venially, the one in giving and the other in taking." In 1412, however, he did not dare to condemn it, observing: "Many legists hold this article, proving with great effect that the emperor did not have the right to diminish the empire for his successors." Thus on neither occasion was he willing to take a stand on substantive principle. Why did he not on these occasions say what he wrote in his Czech treatise *On Simony*, that "when Emperor Constantine first enriched the Roman bishop . . . a voice was heard from heaven saying, 'Today poison has been poured into the

---

[152] *LČH*, p. 67, No. 53.

[153] For Hus's attitude see Sedlák, *M. Jan Hus*, p. 321, and De Vooght, *L'Hérésie*, pp. 207–209. It is one of the few cases where De Vooght regards one of Hus's written works as clearly erroneous. For Nicholas of Dresden's still more radical position, in his *De quadruplici missione* (the text in *ST*, I, 95–117), see the references in *OC&N*, p. 29.

[154] *LČJ*, No. 28.

[155] *Loc. cit.*

Christian communion!' O how many souls have already died of that poison!" [156]

The answer would, no doubt, be that Hus had staked everything on a public hearing at the council, and that he did not wish to enter that hearing encumbered by either his own or his followers' doctrinal excesses of former years. What is at issue here is not Hus's integrity, but the historical problem, of how the pietistic religious movement of the fourteenth century, passing through the medium of Hus's leadership in the early fifteenth, emerged as the mutiny of 1414-1415 and the revolution of the following decade. Only part of the answer can be found in Hus's own theoretical work, which was important chiefly in promoting the more radical absorption of Wyclifism by others. The ideology of Hus encouraged others to revolt, but it led him to Constance—to submission and martyrdom. It was the ideology of men like Nicholas of Dresden and Jakoubek that actually justified schism with the Roman church, as the mystical body of Antichrist. Finally, apart from ideology, there was the movement itself—its turbulence, its passions, its permanent posture of contempt for ecclesiastical authority. Here Hus played a very clear part—not as academic theoretician but as preacher in Bethlehem Chapel, exercising a function of political leadership that bound him inseparably to the masses and kept him from any retreat in his successive encounters with the authority of his bishop and of his pope.

[156] *O svatokupectví,* trans. (in part) by M. Spinka in *Advocates of Reform* (London, 1953), p. 224; the treatise was written in 1413.

II

THE POLITICIANS AND THE RADICALS, 1409–1413

IN THE previous chapter an attempt was made to define and account
for the type of radical ideology that logically resulted in the utraquist revolt of 1414–1415. It now remains, still by way of introduction, to reconstruct the framework of ideas and actions within which radicalism actually
gained supremacy among the Hussites. Again the method will be one of analysis and abstraction rather than straight narrative; but the counterpart to radicalism will now be defined not as merely a different set of ideas, but as a
general mode of action that originated in the point of view of men whose
primary interests were not doctrinal but political. There were in fact two
approaches to reform in the period from 1409 on. One group of university
masters worked primarily in the area of practical politics—leading the Hussite faction at the university, representing the movement in its encounters
with the Roman hierarchy, and speaking for the cause at the royal court.
Another group was more concerned with matters of substance: its main
interest was in developing an adequate theoretical structure for the moral
agitation that was originally at the center of the Hussite program. Neither
group was perfectly homogeneous, neither was unconcerned with the main
interests of the other; but there was a real difference between them, and the
nature of Hus's leadership can best be characterized by observing that he
belonged to both. This is not to say that he was midway between conservatism and radicalism, for such a schematization emerged only after his death,
when the movement was committed to reformation and various groups of
Hussites disagreed on how far to go. Before 1415 things were much more
plastic, and if for the sake of convenience we reserve the name "radical" for
those holding a certain group of doctrines, it must be with the understanding

that the Hussite political leaders, who were not protagonists of these doc-trines, could be extremely radical in their own way. If they later formed a conservative party, interested chiefly in limiting the development of the reformation, this was not because they had always been timid or had suddenly grown old; it was because they had failed to turn the movement in the direction they favored and in consequence could no longer exercise positive leadership. Only by appreciating their failure can we understand the real meaning of the radical success.

THE POLITICIANS. JOHN JESENIC AND HIS WORK, TO 1411

A number of Hus's close associates in reform were specialists in the kind of political action that is often called politicking. Men like Christian of Prachatice, John Kardinál of Rejnštejn, Michael Čižek of Malenice, Mark of Hradec—all seemed to possess traits of character, or connections, that made them successful leaders in university circles, at the royal court, or in dealings with the church's hierarchy. Few of them had anything of their own to say about matters of doctrine, and one can only guess why they gave themselves to the cause of reform at all.[1] Personal ties with Hus and others, loyalty to the Czech cause, a certain capacity for moderate idealism—these were no doubt the main factors, the ideological reflex of which will be considered later. More immediately interesting here is the work of one of their fellows who did put his ideas into writing—the legal specialist John Jesenic. After the introduction of utraquism, which he opposed, he was to earn notoriety among the radicals for the intensity of his reactionary views; but in the earlier period he distinguished himself in the opposite way—no Hussite bore so heavy a burden of Romanist hostility. All of which suggests that he was a remarkable man whose career as a reformer requires careful appreciation.

A brilliant student who had very little money, he took first place on all his

---

[1] The problem is nicely illustrated by the behavior of Mark of Hradec and Christian of Prachatice at the Town Hall confrontation of 16 July 1412 (discussed below, in the section "The Radicals and the Beginnings of the Hussite Left"). Manfully refusing to condemn the list of Wyclifite articles that the king had ordered condemned, Mark held that some of the articles could be understood in both true and false senses; pressed for an example, however, he could think of nothing better than to observe that "Deus est" could mean "God eats." On the other hand, at the same meeting in the Town Hall, Christian of Prachatice calmly voted to condemn the articles, apparently without the slightest intention of leaving Hus's party. One can only wonder if these men saw the issue as much more than a conflict between "us" and "them."

major examinations but followed a somewhat irregular academic course.[2] He earned a baccalaureate in arts in 1397 (thus four years after Hus), but took the master's degree in arts only in 1408, a year after his baccalaureate in law. It was probably on the occasion of receiving the latter degree that he first engaged in public advocacy of Hussite principles. Charges made against him later were that on 25 September 1407, in the hall of the Law University, he defended the following propositions: (1) the unjust decision of a judge is neither valid nor to be feared; (2) Christ in the Eucharist is not to be honored otherwise than if and to the extent that the body of Christ is there; (3) Peter was not the prince of the apostles—he had the same power as the others, except that he was assigned to Rome; (4) the pope cannot grant a dispensation to a twice-married man to become a priest; (5) excommunication by someone in mortal sin is not valid.[3] Allowing for the inadequacy and possible distortion of our information, we can still recognize these ideas as Wyclifite commonplaces, except perhaps for point four, which seems more in line with the usual matter of legal scholarship.[4] In any case, whatever Jesenic actually did say on this occasion, and whatever others thought of his discourse—we have no information about either—he soon moved on to active participation in Hussite leadership. In 1408 when Masters Stanislav of Znojmo and Stephen of Páleč were imprisoned in Bologna while on their way to defend the orthodoxy of Wyclifism before the pope, Jesenic appeared with John Hus and the movement's elder statesman, Christian of Prachatice, in efforts to secure their release.[5] And when the struggle between Czechs and Germans at the University of Prague came to a head in 1408–1409 over the issue of Wyclifism, Jesenic found the fullest scope for both his practical and his theoretical abilities.

The struggle itself was not originally an ideological one; its roots lay rather in issues of power and place between the two nationalities at the university. Founded in 1348 by Charles IV, the University of Prague was

---

[2] Nov. I, 211 f., and now the definitive monograph by Jiří Kejř, *Husitský právník M. Jan z Jesenice* (Prague, 1965), pp. 5–11. There is a study of some aspects of Jesenic's work, with bibliographical notes, by Kejř, *Dvě studie o husitském právnictví*, Rozpravy ČSAV, LXIV, Řada SV, No. 5 (1954); cf. also his "O některých spisech M. Jana z Jesenice, "*LF*, XI, n.s. (1963), 77–81.

[3] Nov. I, 212 f.; Kejř, *Dvě studie*, pp. 35 f.

[4] Similar or related doctrines appear in the list of forty-five Wyclifite articles condemned in 1403: e.g., §§3, 11, 30; more precise parallels from Wyclif's actual works could easily be given. That Jesenic's fourth point was still being discussed in the law schools may seem strange; cf. W. Ullmann, *Medieval Papalism* (London, 1949), pp. 65 f.: "Innocent IV and with him all the canonists asserted that the pope had no power to admit anybody to holy orders who had lawfully been married twice."

[5] Nov. I, 288.

intended to be at once a focus of the international community of scholars and a school to train Bohemians for service to the realm.[6] Even the classic universities of Paris and Bologna served to fulfill such a training function, especially in the later Middle Ages, and local service was perhaps the prime goal in the new German foundations of the latter part of the fourteenth century.[7] But it took several decades before the numbers and quality of Czech scholars were comparable to those of the foreigners, and in the meantime the university had developed institutions that secured the privileged position of the latter. The four nations, in existence by about 1360, included only one for the Czechs; there were two for the Germans—the Bavarian and Saxon nations—and the Polish nation was actually dominated by Germans from Silesia.[8] Furthermore, the Germans acquired a virtual monopoly of places in the endowed masters' colleges. Since university affairs, including elections and exercise of the university's advowson in its estates, were directly or indirectly decided by vote of the nations—three to one against the Czechs— and since places in the masters' colleges were filled by cooptation, the Czechs were not able to secure the share in these things that their increasing numbers warranted. In 1384 there were sharp conflicts over places in the colleges, and only intervention by the Archbishop of Prague, the Chancellor of the University, could impose a settlement, in 1385: out of twelve positions, the Germans were to have six, the Czechs five, and the last would be rotated

---

[6] Charles IV's Bull of 7 April 1348 defines the purpose of the foundation: "ut fideles nostri regnicole, qui scienciarum fructus indesinenter esuriunt, per aliena mendicare suffragia non coacti, paratam in regno sibi mensam propinacionis inveniant, et quos ingeniorum nativa subtilitas ad consilia reddit conspicuos, literarum sciencia faciat eruditos. . . ." There are also other goals connected with the international aspect of the university (the Bull has been recently republished by Jiří Spěváček, ed., *Regesta diplomatica nec non epistolaria Bohemiae et Moraviae*, V, i (Prague: ČSAV, 1958), 170 f.). The present understanding of the quoted passage, namely that "ad consilia" modifies "eruditos" as well as "conspicuos," agrees with that of John Jesenic (*Documenta*, p. 358; see below) and that of F. M. Bartoš, "Příspěvky k dějinám karlovy university v době Husově a husitské," *SbH*, IV (1956), 34.

[7] See in general F. von Bezold, "Die ältesten deutschen Universitäten in ihrem Verhältnis zum Staat," *Historische Zeitschrift*, LXXX (1898), 436 ff., esp. p. 454. The point is also brought out in G. Ritter's *Die Heidelberger Universität*, I (Heidelberg, 1936), *passim;* e.g., p. 41: "If one observes to what a considerable extent, only a few years after the founding of the university [i.e., in 1386], the professors were used as envoys, councillors, and judicial officials of the Electoral Court, one will clearly see the inner connection of the founding of the university with Ruprecht's political endeavors."

[8] V. Tomek, *Geschichte der Prager Universität* (Prague, 1849), p. 8 f. and *passim*. Cf. J. Kejř, "Sporné otázky v bádání o dekretu kutnohorském," *Acta Universitatis Carolinae, Historia Univ. Carol. Pragensis*, III (1962), fasc. 1, 105–119, for a discussion of the ethnic composition of the *nationes*.

among the four nations.[9] Even this solution, which could be implemented only as the existing collegiate masters slowly died off, must have worked as a long-term source of irritation. Add to this the self-generating ardors of academic factionalism, and the bitterness of the struggle over Wyclifism is not hard to understand.

The struggle was in fact begun by the Germans, some of whom in 1403 prepared and secured the condemnation of the list of forty-five Wyclifite articles that was to become so important in the succeeding decade. Wyclif's eucharistic doctrine of remanence provided the outstanding issue, which came up again and again in the university and, thanks to the Germans' persistence, in the archbishop's court.[10] Then early in 1408, the controversy was raised to a new level; Ludolf Meistermann, a bachelor in the Theology Faculty, brought charges in Rome against the leader of Czech Wyclifism, Master Stanislav of Znojmo. Meistermann must have had the moral and material support of the other German leaders in Prague, but it is significant that he also consulted the masters of the University of Heidelberg, a number of whom had previously been at Prague; these gave him their fullest support.[11] The move was successful: Pope Gregory XII committed the case to Cardinal Francis of Bordeaux, who on 20 April 1408 pronounced his decision. No one might hold the Wyclifite doctrines in question (which included not only the eucharistic heresy but certain basic attacks on the Roman church's jurisdiction and even the philosophical doctrine of extreme realism[12]); no one might debate them; owners of Wyclif's works had to turn them in (or turn in accurate copies); Master Stanislav was to be cited to

---

[9] On the masters' colleges see Tomek, *op. cit.*, and Rostislav Nový, "Koleje mistrů pražské university do r. 1409," *Dekret kutnohorský a jeho místo v dějinách, Acta Univ. Carol.*, Philosophica et historica 2 (1959), 83–90.

[10] Nov. I, 103–205; Sedlák, *M. Jan Hus* (Prague, 1915), pp. 92–123.

[11] F. M. Bartoš, "V předvečer Kutnohorského dekretu," *ČČM*, CII (1928), 97–113; Bartoš, "Příspěvky" (as in n. 6), *SbH*, IV (1956), 33 ff.

[12] It will be useful to quote the passage *in extenso*, since it shows what Meistermann and the Cardinal regarded as the crucial points in early 1408: ". . . factum deducitur ad aures S.V. pro parte . . . Ludolfi Meisterman, . . . quod nonnulli . . . secuntur doctrinam pestiferam cuiusdam Johannis Wiclef, dicentis, quod si episcopus vel sacerdos existat in peccato mortali, non ordinat nec conficit nec baptizat; quod si papa prescitus et malus et per consequens membrum diaboli [est], non habet potestatem super fideles ab aliquo sibi datam nisi forte a cesare; quod nullus prelatus potest aliquem excommunicare, nisi prius sciat ipsum excommunicatum a deo; qui sic excommunicat, ex hoc fit hereticus vel excommunicatus; et quam plura enormia, que omnia continentur in tractatibus dicti Johannis Wiclef, quorum unus, ut dicitur, vocatur dyalogus et alter trialogus. Eciam . . . quam plures . . . docmatizant, quod eadem substancia sit deus, lapis, asinus et homo et quelibet res. . . ." The Cardinal then goes on to tell how Stanislav of Znojmo "dicere non erubuit, quod panis universalis manet in sacramento altaris post verba consecracionis prolata." The text in Bartoš, "V předvečer," pp. 107 f.

appear at the papal court.[13] Thus the conflict between the nations had the momentous result of bringing the Czech reform movement under the direct cognizance of Rome. This, in turn, helped to cause or provoke an equally momentous break between the reformers and Archbishop Zbyněk, who had previously been sympathetic to reform but who now began to show more and more energy in opposing the Wyclifites.[14] On 14 May 1408 Master Matthew of Knín, charged in the archiepiscopal court with belief in remanence, had to abjure the doctrine under humiliating conditions.[15] And on 24 May the Czech nation of the university, under pressure from the archbishop, had to issue an official declaration condemning the Forty-five Articles, in their heretical, erroneous, or scandalous senses—a qualification that allowed the Wyclifite members to join the rest.[16]

In the same month of May another factor was added to the situation, when a number of cardinals from both the Avignon and Roman courts renounced their obedience and invited Christendom to do likewise. The train of events set in motion by this action would eventually lead to reunification of the church; more immediately, from Wenceslas IV's point of view, it opened a possibility of reversing his deposition as King of the Romans, which had occurred in 1400 and had then been sanctioned by the Roman pope.[17] His successor as king, the Elector Ruprecht of the Rhenish Palatinate, of course clung to the Roman obedience, as did many of the German princes; for this reason the German masters of the University of Prague were reluctant to embrace neutrality—their future preferment in both state and church would become difficult if not impossible. Their attitude became an issue only at the end of 1408; meanwhile their anti-Wyclifite action, undertaken in close cooperation with Ruprecht's University of Heidelberg, must have seemed unfortunate to Wenceslas, for it put a blot on his realm's reputation for orthodoxy.[18] Furthermore, Archbishop Zbyněk also maintained his obedience to Rome, perhaps as a matter of personal honor, while the Czech Wyclifites, for both practical and idealistic reasons, could only welcome a policy of neutrality. The facts therefore dictated an alliance of king and reformers against the Roman pope, against the German masters, and against the archbishop; such an alliance could reverse the extremely unfavorable situation just described.

Perhaps the possibility was glimpsed as early as June 1408, for in this

---

[13] *Ibid.*, pp. 108–111.

[14] *Ibid.*, pp. 97–100; it should be noted that Bartoš's discovery of the Cardinal's decision has made possible a significantly better account of the events of early 1408.

[15] Nov. I, 217–220.

[16] Nov. I, 221 f.; Sedlák, *M. Jan Hus*, pp. 125 f.

[17] The best account is in Bartoš, *Čechy*, pp. 290 ff.

[18] Bartoš, "Příspěvky" (as in n. 6), pp. 36 f.

month Master Matthew of Knín, fresh from his humiliation in the archbishop's court, presented himself as a volunteer to conduct the quodlibetal
disputation regularly scheduled for January. It was extraordinary to volunteer for a duty so onerous that many masters preferred paying a fine to
fulfilling it, and it may be supposed that Matthew was encouraged if not put
up to it by his Wyclifite fellows.[19] As the only volunteer he had to be
accepted even though, as the Czech reformers had no doubt foreseen, the
Germans were offended. Indeed, when the time for the disputation was at
hand, leading German masters declared that they would suffer the penalties
prescribed for nonattendance rather than take part in an exercise presided over
by one suspect of heresy. Unfortunately for them, their threat to spoil the
quodlibet came at a time when King Wenceslas was on the brink of
declaring his neutrality in support of the cardinals who had called the
Council of Pisa; in fact, he was carrying on conversations with a Brabantine
and French embassy that had come to Prague for this and other purposes.
Probably for this reason, and to avoid a scandal, but perhaps also to oblige
the Czechs, Wenceslas commanded the Germans to attend and participate in
the quodlibet.[20] The point was then underlined by the most pugnacious
leader of the Wyclifites, Master Jerome of Prague, when he invited the
councillors of Prague's Old Town, who were royal officials, and the
members of the Brabantine-French embassy, to attend the quodlibet as
honored guests.[21] Jerome took advantage of their presence to deliver a
speech outside the order of the disputation, in which he bitterly criticized
the Germans for not wishing to attend, praised Matthew of Knín, and
denounced the luxury-loving, sensual, simoniacal plunderers of the poor,
the whited sepulchres who dared to suggest that the "sacrosanct Czech
nation" was tainted by heresy. He also praised the town councillors, who had
been honored by the king's appointment to protect the holy city of Prague,
and suggested that this duty extended to the protection of the Czech nation,
"the king's sincere friend." An extremely fervent defense of Wyclif's books
followed, and Jerome urged the youth to study them diligently; if they
found in them passages obscure to their immature minds, they should put
these aside for study at a future date.[22]

Such was the character of Matthew of Knín's quodlibet in the first week of

[19] Nov. I, 226 f. Jiří Kejř, "Struktura a průběh disputace de quolibet na pražské
universitě," *Acta Univ. Carol., Hist. Univ. Carol. Prag.,* I (1960), 17–42, offers an exact
description of the structure and course of the quodlibetal disputation at the University
of Prague. (There is an English summary on pp. 51–53.)

[20] Kejř, "Sporné otázky" (as in n. 8), pp. 85 ff.

[21] *Op. cit.*

[22] The text of Jerome's speech, in form a "Recommendacio arcium liberalium," has
been published in Höfler, II, 112–128, with a false attribution to John Hus.

January 1409. Greater events were yet to come, and quickly; but before considering them we can profitably examine, against this background, the *questio* composed for the occasion by John Jesenic: "Whether a judge who knows that the witnesses have given false evidence and that the accused is innocent, should condemn the latter." Dr. Jiří Kejř of Prague, who has recently edited and analyzed this work, has admirably brought out its true importance: the negative determination of Jesenic, so far from being the matter of course that an untutored modern might suppose, was in fact an attack on a central principle of the church's judicial system.[23] For according to canon law a judge *had to* accept the concordant testimony of two witnesses who rated as reliable according to stipulated criteria. Such testimony constituted full proof of a charge, and the judge was forced to pronounce sentence accordingly, no matter what his own conscience told him.[24] "The universalistic tendency of the medieval ecclesiastical system here pursued the same goal as the later centralism of the state administration and juridical system under absolutism: to liquidate the activities of courts that were independent of the one central and supreme power."[25] We are not surprised to learn, still from Kejř, that while this canonical regulation was approved by such a scholastic as Thomas Aquinas,[26] it was attacked by Wyclif, by Hus, and by other reformers including John Jesenic, who borrowed heavily from Wyclif's discussion in *De civili dominio*.[27] Nor did Nicholas of Dresden, himself a legist, fail to pick up the point in his *Tables of the Old and New Color*, where we find quoted the passage from the *glosa ordinaria* on the Decretals referred to by Jesenic: "Let the judge pronounce in the name of the Lord, according to the testimonies, and let him put his conscience aside."[28] Even allowing for the inner logic of the legal system, and for the ambiguity of the medieval-Latin "consciencia,"[29] we can

---

[23] Kejř, "Husitská kritika soudobé theorie soudních důkazů," in *Dvě studie*, pp. 19–52, the text on pp. 53–65. The canonistic rules of proof are discussed on pp. 21 f., with references to the canons and the literature.

[24] *Ibid.*, pp. 21 f.

[25] *Ibid.*, p. 20.

[26] *Ibid.*, p. 21.

[27] *Ibid.*, pp. 23 ff., 30 f.

[28] *OC&N*, Table IV §5. See also the discussion of the *Tables* in chap. i, above. For Jesenic's reference to the gloss see p. 61 of Kejř's edition (as in n. 23 above): "Leges scripture vel quecunque glose. . . ."

[29] According to DuCange, the word could mean either what "conscience" means in modern languages or *cognitio, monitum*. Thomas Aquinas provides the following definition: "[Conscientia] nominat ipsum actum, qui est applicatio cuiuscumque habitus vel cuiuscumque notitiae ad aliquem actum particularem" (*Qu. disp. de veritate*, Q. 17, a. 1).

easily understand how such a point of view would seem odious to religious reformers.

Thus Jesenic has no difficulty in finding his way, through *notabilia, conclusiones,* and *correlaria,* to the determination: "the question, as propounded, is false." [30] Without covering the full battery of his arguments, we can note some of his more interesting conclusions. The deposition of false witnesses, he asserts, proves nothing, neither making right [*ius*] nor removing it; similarly the unjust sentence of a pastor neither binds nor looses, and although it is to be feared should not be observed. [31] But a sentence pronounced according to the dictates of right reason—which Jesenic identifies with natural law, the Law of God, the Golden Rule—is just and valid, it binds and looses. [32] Thus no judge should give judgement according to the deposition of false witnesses; "every judge should give judgement according to the testimonies and proofs of his internal witnesses," namely his mind, reason, and conscience. [33] And if he knows the accused to be innocent, despite legally competent proof of the contrary, he should suffer any penalty, even death, rather than pronounce the sentence required by law. [34]

There is an obvious element of common sense in all of this; as Jesenic observed, "it is absurd that a judge who knows that testimony is false should judge in the same way as one who does not know it." [35] But it is common sense applied by a Wyclifite reformer, who does not fail to draw the practical conclusion that those whom bishops and judges declare to be excommunicated heretics are not necessarily so. [36] Jesenic shows no interest in a strictly legal line of thought that would suggest an alternate procedural system objective enough to protect individual rights, and elastic enough to allow for extraordinary perceptions of truth. Instead, he sets against the canonical system only the unmediated requirements of morality; that he does this with a considerable apparatus of canonistic argumentation does not alter the fact that he tends to reduce law to theology. [37] The subversive implications of his argument do not indeed escape him, and at the end of the *questio* he considers the appropriate objection:

> But it may be objected that if all judges had the conscience of theologians, in these times when the world is set in evil, with both witnesses and parties in a

[30] In Kejř's edition, p. 63.
[31] *Ibid.,* pp. 55, 58.
[32] *Ibid.,* p. 59.
[33] *Ibid.,* pp. 58 f.
[34] *Ibid.,* p. 64.
[35] In Kejř's edition, p. 63.
[36] *Ibid.,* p. 58.
[37] Kejř, *Dvě studie,* p. 5, comments on this: "For Hus and his pupils . . . the legal norm is transformed into a moral norm."

case cheating and deceiving their brothers in contentious litigation—that then legal judgements in this world would cease, and both commonwealth and laws would consequently perish; for the same act is a sin if done by a man with conscience [*i.e.,* ethical knowledge], but licit and not a sin if done by another who lacks this conscience.[38]

There is no distinction here between ecclesiastical and secular judgements— like Wyclif, Jesenic identifies *ecclesia* and *respublica*[39]—and the response to the objection sounds correspondingly radical:

The answer is that it would be expedient for all judges to be regulated so that they would not prefer human to divine laws. For the canonical sanctions have their origin from the divine law, as said in *De accusacionibus, "Qualiter et quando,"* II [Decretals, V, i, 24]. Then it would be necessary for the republic to return to an evangelical polity, with all things held in common; then, according to the Apostle's rule, we should be content with having food and clothing [I. Tim. 6:8], and we would follow the Lord's counsel, not rashly contending with anyone.[40]

This vision of a society different from that which requires a legal system is fully in line with the ideological aspirations of both Wyclifism and the Bohemian religious movement,[41] and in general it may be said that Hussitism knew no other ultimate ideal than that of *reducing* the world to the estate of the Primitive Church of the apostles. How far a given thinker really intended this at any given time is another matter; it would be naive to suppose that the most extreme position in a quodlibetal question was the author's considered program for practical action. Still, Jesenic's abrupt jump from questions of legal procedure to the lofty ideal of evangelical perfection is instructive *per se,* for the mode of thought that forestalls systematic, constructive discussion of a problem by invocation of an absolute ideal can usually be understood as a cover for something else. *A priori* we can surmise that the something else was Wyclif's political ecclesiology, which similarly attacked the church's jurisdictional authority by invoking Christ's law of

---

[38] *Ibid.,* p. 64.

[39] See the passages quoted just above and below; also the statement, "Omne, quod est legi divine contrarium, hoc est iniquum, ergo omne quod est iuri naturali contrarium, est iniquum; contra tenet, quia ius naturale in lege divina, puta in ewangelio, continetur, ut patet in principio Decreti. Ymmo constituciones *ecclesiastice vel seculares* [my emphasis], si iuri naturali contrarie probantur, penitus sunt excludende, sicut patet *Dis. X, In Principio"* (*ibid.,* p. 60). This last reference is to a decree of Nicholas I to the effect that the emperors' laws are not superior to church law; Jesenic has of course said something different. For Wyclif's doctrine see my "Wyclifism as Ideology of Revolution," *Church History,* XXXII (1963), 62.

[40] In Kejř, *Dvě studie,* p. 64.

[41] Bartoš, "Hus a Viklef." in *Husitství a cizina,* p. 37, n. 38.

poverty and humility; the powerless clergy were then put under the governance of the king, who ruled his realm—his section of the Church Militant—
in both spiritual and secular affairs. In fact, this was what Jesenic had in
mind.

We have already seen how political considerations in 1408 led King
Wenceslas into an alliance with the reformers, and how effectively royal
power was used to insure the success of Matthew of Knín's quodlibet in early
January of 1409. This unusual intervention in university affairs [42] was now
followed by one even more drastic. Wenceslas could no longer delay his
announcement of formal adherence to the Council of Pisa, and if his
archbishop would not agree with him, he had to have support from the
university. Representatives of each of the four nations were summoned to his
presence at Kutná Hora (Kuttenberg), where the German masters were
finally forced to make their refusal explicit; the Czechs of course indicated
their agreement with the king. Wenceslas's response was the Kutná Hora
Decree of 18 January, giving the Czech nation three votes "in all the
councils, judgements, examinations, elections, and all other acts and dispositions of the university"; the three German nations, referred to in the decree
simply as the *natio Teutonica,* would presumably have only one vote together, although this was not expressly stated.[43] It was a great victory for the
Czechs, and not only the reformers among them. Later, to be sure, when it
had become clear that the decree's chief effect was to deliver the university
over to Hussitism, to make it an instrument of the Czech reform movement
rather than an international scholarly corporation, some of the leading Czech
anti-Wyclifites joined the Germans in decrying it; at Constance, Master
Andrew of Brod even included in his accusations against Hus the charge
that the latter had procured the Kutná Hora Decree. Hus's response was that
he had indeed done so,[44] but with the counsel of Andrew of Brod, and he
went on to describe how both Andrew and the staunchly anti-Wyclifite

[42] Kejř, "Sporné otázky," p. 86.

[43] The text of the decree in *Documenta,* pp. 347 f.; that it gave the Germans one vote
among them appears from their supplication to the king, 6 February 1409, *ibid.,* p. 351.
A great deal has been written about the decree—it poses many still unsolved problems
of historical reconstruction and evaluation—but I list here only a few recent works,
which can serve as guides to the rest: J. Kejř, "Sporné otázky" (as in n. 8 above), pp.
83–119; *Dekret kutnohorský a jeho místo v dějinách* ("The Kutná Hora Decree and Its
Place in History"), a collection of essays (as in n. 9 above); F. Seibt, "Johannes Hus
und der Abzug der deutschen Studenten aus Prag 1409," *Archiv für Kulturgeschichte,*
XXXIX (1957), 63–80.

[44] Exactly what he did and when are not clear; see the critical discussion in Kejř,
"Sporné otázky," pp. 95–104; also F. M. Bartoš, "V předvečer Kutnohorského dekretu,"
ČČM, CII (1928), 102–107.

Master John Eliášův, a canon of the Cathedral Chapter, had come to his chamber on the day of the decree, when he was sick, and had rejoiced with him at the news.[45] Hus then told them, "See I am almost at the point of death; if I die, work diligently for the rights and freedom of our nation." In other words, the decree was to be regarded as only the beginning of a struggle; in fact, as Hus foresaw, the German masters were not prepared to acknowledge defeat, and the king's will was not so firm that it could not be changed. Manfully defying the immediate execution of the decree, the Germans tried to procure its reversal, while at the same time compacting with each other that if these efforts failed, they would leave Prague.[46] At times they seemed close to success, and the Czechs showed themselves willing to settle for much less than they had been granted; but in the end, for reasons that are not quite clear, the crown and the magistrates of Prague's Old Town enforced the Kutná Hora Decree in its original form,[47] and a large number of German masters and students—perhaps about a thousand of them—withdrew from Prague.[48] Many of them went to the new university at Leipzig, others went elsewhere; the University of Prague fell into the hands of the Czechs—the Wyclifites dominating the Arts Faculty, the Catholics ruling the Faculty of Theology.[49]

Near the end of February 1409, when the struggle over the Kutná Hora Decree was still going on, John Jesenic made his contribution in the shape of a legal brief defending the decree against German attacks. One of the most remarkable documents of Hussite political thought, the *Defensio mandati* combines a thoroughly Wyclifite framework of theory with an exultant play upon the facts of royal power as exercised within the legal community of Bohemia.[50] The decree itself had justified its favor to the Czech nation by noting that the king's love belonged first of all to those linked with him in a common destiny ("qui . . . nobis quadam sorte junguntur"), namely to the Czech or Bohemian nation, the "just heir of the realm"; it would be a perversion of due charity to love the foreigner more than the neighbor, and in any case the foreigner, the *natio Teutonica,* "had no share at all in the

---

[45] *Documenta,* p. 181.

[46] *Ibid.,* pp. 350–353.

[47] Bartoš, "Příspěvky" (as in n. 6 above), pp. 37–39.

[48] It is not clear just how many left and where they went; see Ivan Hlaváček, "Matriky Vídeňské a Krakovské university a dekret Kutnohorský," *Dekret Kutnohorský,* pp. 75–81.

[49] See below, the section on "The Crisis of Hus's Exile."

[50] The text in *Documenta,* pp. 355–363; for discussion and dating see J. Kejř, "Husitský právník v boji o dekret Kutnohorský," in *Dvě studie,* p. 3 f.; also Kejř, *Husitský právník,* pp. 15 ff. Seibt, "Johannes Hus" (as in n. 43 above), pp. 73–79, deals with Jesenic's role in the controversies over the Decree.

rights attaching to membership in the Bohemian realm" ("jure incolatus regni Bohemiae prorsus expers").[51] Jesenic used these considerations in his first paragraph, but in a Wyclifite translation:

> The most illustrious prince and lord, Lord Wenceslas, Ever-August King of the Romans and King of Bohemia, has dominion over the realm of Bohemia by the favor of divine grace. Therefore, according to the Law of God, the law of the canons, and the imperial law, it pertains primarily and chiefly to him to dispose over his realm and to provide for his subjects, over foreigners, with peace and special prerogatives. This is clear originally from the divine law and then from human law.[52]

Subsequent specifications all flow from this: thus the king has the right to regulate the university as he sees fit and to give special privileges to his subjects; the foreigners have the duty of obeying, with willing humility. But Wyclifism's powerful identification of the law of the land with the Law of God[53] allows Jesenic to deck out his rather coarse pragmatism with scriptural ornaments:

> The Bohemian nation should be the chief ruler of the other nations in the University of Prague. This appears from the similar case in the divine law. For it is the promise of the Lord: "If thou shalt hearken unto the commandments of the Lord thy God, which I command thee this day, . . . the Lord shall make thee the head, and not the tail; and thou shalt be above always, and not beneath." And again: "God will set thee on high above all nations of the earth." [Deut. 28:1,13.] If therefore God has made his obedient people the head, and set them above all nations, then similarly the King of Bohemia can, indeed should, make the Bohemian nation, which is his obedient people, the head and not the tail, that it may always be above and not beneath.[54]

These ideas are developed in several of their aspects, but always with the thrust in the same direction: each people should be supreme in its own land; the Bohemians should be on top in Bohemia; it is unnatural for foreigners to enjoy superiority over natives. Then, referring back to Charles IV's bull founding the university, Jesenic offers the above mentioned interpretation that the purpose of the institution was to train the Bohemians so they could be royal councillors; he argues, "first and foremost in the councils of the king should be the sons of the kingdom, who have a native inclination to seek the

---

[51] The significance of these concepts has been studied from the point of view of the history of law by Václav Vaněček, "Dekret Kutnohorský z hlediska dějin státu a práva," *Dekret Kutnohorský,* pp. 55–69.

[52] *Documenta,* p. 355.

[53] See above, chap. i, the section on "The Contribution of John Wyclif."

[54] *Documenta,* p. 356.

kingdom's welfare—but this is not the case with foreigners." [55] Why then should the Germans enjoy the lion's share of benefices and places in the endowed colleges? [56] The Germans had argued that the king should not change the customary arrangements embodied in the university's statutes, [57] but Jesenic replies that evil custom has no claim to validity. His authorities here are Augustine and Cyprian, and we are strongly reminded of other Hussite arguments against inveterate custom and in favor of truth—but where the others are concerned with religious reform, Jesenic deals with voting rights at the university. [58] And where the others rely purely upon the prerogatives of truth, Jesenic amplifies his proof that the Bohemians *should* have more votes with a simple appeal to political power: "it is the declaration and interpretation of the prince that makes a right [*jus facit*]"; but the Kutná Hora Decree has made a right for the Bohemian nation; why then should they not enjoy it? [59] The Bohemian nation does not make charges against the Germans; all it wants to do is gratefully enjoy the gift of three votes from the most serene prince. [60]

Jesenic had an opportunity to return to this matter in July 1409 after the Germans had left Prague, only to continue their anti-Czech agitation from abroad. At this time he determined a *questio*, "Whether a corrupted judge who decides in favor of the corrupting party sins more gravely than the corrupting party"; while its argument need not concern us here—except to note that it shows a strong dependence on Wyclif—the following passage deserves attention:

> Just as the Jews conspired against Christ and lyingly accused him before Pilate with false witnesses and criminous accusations . . . , so those modern conspirators [*scil.*, the German masters] have conspired not only against

[55] *Ibid.*, pp. 358, 361. Cf. Hus's similar confession, in response to accusations made against him at the Council of Constance: ". . . dixi et dico, quod Boemi in regno Boemiae secundum leges, imo secundum legem dei et secundum instinctum naturalem deberent esse primi in officiis in regno Boemiae, sicut et Francigenae in regno Franciae, et Teutonici in terris suis, ut Boemus sciret dirigere subditos suos et Teutonicus Teutonicos . . ." (*ibid.*, p. 177).

[56] Jesenic refers to the foreigners as "partes aliquot majores beneficiorum et collegiorum continue retinentes" (*ibid.*, p. 358); cf. Jerome of Prague's statement that the Germans monopolized the university's right of patronage in this period (R. R. Betts, "Jeronym Pražský, "*ČsČH*, V (1957), 203; the English version is not as detailed: "Jerome of Prague," *University of Birmingham Historical Journal*, I (1947), 51–91.

[57] *Documenta*, p. 351.

[58] *Ibid.*, p. 359; Jesenic's passages from Augustine and Cyprian are drawn from the *Decretum*'s section on the relationship between custom on the one hand, positive law and truth on the other, Dist. VIII, cc. 2, 6, 8.

[59] *Documenta*, p. 361.

[60] *Ibid.*, p. 360.

Christ but against the whole realm of Bohemia and our University of Prague. Not only have they lyingly accused her before the prince of the realm with false witness and criminous accusations, but they have treacherously defamed her to the extent of their ability in various kingdoms and provinces, with their writings and letters. They say: the Czechs [*Boemi*] are heretics, they are in error and deserving of death. But our prince and lord, not corrupted like Pilate by fear or their gifts, but like the most just King of the Romans, truly and ever August, knowing that they had committed those acts out of hatred, justly banished them and exiled them from his realms and domains.[61]

We have seen that the same man who had insisted that judges have the conscience of theologians was also capable of propounding a theory of right in which justice flowed from the mere will of the ruler. Now we see that Jesenic makes no distinction between the struggle of the nations at the university, the struggle over Wyclifite doctrines of reform, and the cause of the Bohemian realm. Even in its original form, Wyclifite theory had the great virtue of combining evangelical idealism with an acceptance of the facts of political life, the institutions of the realm;[62] in Jesenic's hands it proves that virtue in practice. The Czechs who have taken up the cause of the Law of God are identified with the national community loyal to King Wenceslas, the realm of Bohemia; it is a holy nation, as Jerome of Prague had said, comparable in its relationship with its king to Israel in its relationship to God, according to the figure used by Jesenic. The justice of the Czech reform movement based on God's Truth alternates with the justice of the Czech national community based on the *jus incolatus*—membership in a realm that has its traditional rights, secured by a king whose power to rule his people has no limit. There is room in this system for pure theory, but there is also room for the work of the politician, at all levels: organizing majorities in faculty meetings, cultivating good relations with prominent members of the royal court, appearing at that court to win the king's approval directly. The scanty sources allow us to see some of this work in connection with the procurement and defense of the Kutná Hora Decree— John Hus, Jerome of Prague, and John Jesenic seem to have been especially busy[63]—and this episode set the tone for future efforts and achievements by the political leaders of reform.

With the Germans gone, the main opponents of the reform party were the Catholic Czech masters, chiefly those of the Theology Faculty, Archbishop

---

[61] The *questio* has been published by Sedlák, *M. Jan Hus*, pp. 171*–181*, discussed and dated by Kejř, "Husitský právník," *Dvě studie*, pp. 4-12. The passage quoted here is on p. 180*.

[62] My "Wyclifism," p. 67.

[63] See the authors cited in notes 43 and 44 above.

Zbyněk, and certain prelates. The issues continued to be those memorialized in the list of Forty-five Articles, but there were shifts in emphasis. The question of remanence kept its vitality; the other key points are well summarized in this notice of a complaint sent by the archbishop to Pope Alexander V in the autumn of 1409, soon after Zbyněk had finally agreed to recognize the papal line instituted by the Council of Pisa:

> First [tell the pope] that all the dissension in the realm has its origin with the Wyclifites' articles. Second, the pope must be told above all how, under the leadership of the Wyclifites, the clergy has been brought to total disobedience of their ordinary [i.e., the archbishop]. For the Wyclifites openly contemn the church's censure, saying that ecclesiastical censures are nothing and that to rule the clergy pertains to the secular, not the episcopal power. In this way they have attracted many of the magnates to their erroneous opinions; indeed they are bringing the lord King Wenceslas to this point, that he seize the temporal property of the clergy and deprive them of it, as he is in fact doing.[64]

Wenceslas did not need any encouragement from the reformers to lay hands on church property—he had done it before, without them—nor was his hostility to the archbishop the fruit of Hus's agitation; the break had other causes, chiefly the dispute over transfer of obedience. Still, it is true that in 1409 the alliance between the crown and the reformers, which had worked so well for both sides in the matter of control over the university, continued in force, interfering with the archbishop's anti-Wyclifite program and encouraging the reformers to hold firm in spite of Zbyněk's efforts to force them to turn in their copies of Wyclif's works, and in spite of his excommunication of their leaders for disobeying this decree.[65] The archbishop was hampered, of course, by his long refusal to recognize his king's pope; and when members of the reform party appealed against his order to turn in Wyclif's works they were able to secure a hearing at the papal court. When Zbyněk finally did give his obedience to Pope Alexander V and, as we have seen, informed the latter of what was going on in Bohemia, it was too late to avoid his own personal citation to Rome to answer the charges against him.[66] But

---

[64] *Chronicon universitatis pragensis, FRB,* V, 570 f. There is different information about the complaint in a letter by Pope Alexander V, dated 20 December 1409 (the text in *Documenta,* pp. 374–376), but as Novotný suggests (Nov. I, 385, n. 1) the two sources can be combined. It is Alexander's letter that mentions the eucharistic problem. There is a discussion of these and the following events in De Vooght, *L'Hérésie de Jean Huss* (Louvain, 1960), pp. 119–162.

[65] Nov. I, 346 ff. The excommunication was pronounced during Lent.

[66] Nov. I, 386 f. For Zbyněk's recognition of Alexander V, on 2 September 1409, see *Documenta,* pp. 372 f.

his recognition of Alexander soon bore fruit; the pope changed his policy and decided to support Zbyněk's authority. In a papal decree of 20 December the archbishop was instructed to conduct an examination of Wyclif's works, to prohibit the erroneous doctrines in them, and to prohibit preaching in private chapels—this last a point directed against Hus's pulpit in Bethlehem Chapel.[67] The decree contained a clause forbidding any appeal against it, but as soon as it reached Bohemia, in March of 1410, John Hus did appeal, to a pope *melius informandum,* and Alexander actually did turn the appeal over to an auditor for action. But on 5 May Alexander died, to be succeeded by John XXIII, and after Zbyněk promulgated the anti-Hussite decree, on 16 June, the reformers on 25 June lodged a new appeal, to the new pope.[68]

This appeal was clearly the work of a clever lawyer, very probably John Jesenic.[69] It shows us the very instructive spectacle of the reform movement ignoring its principled rejection of the church's jurisdictional system in order to use that system for its own defense; the case reminds us that the canon law and its courts were not just means to enforce the church's will on its opponents, but rather a so-to-speak neutral mechanism limiting despotism by its mere existence, and available to all who could find the necessary legal talent and money. Thus the appeal of 25 June concentrated its fire on the impropriety of the archbishop's actions: he had flouted papal authority by taking action against those whose earlier appeal against him was still pending; he had procured Pope Alexander's decree by misrepresenting the facts; his own decree contained errors; with the death of Alexander V the mandate under which Zbyněk acted had expired. Since the condemnation of Wyclifite doctrine had been implemented by a burning of Wyclif's books, which had been requisitioned from members of the university, the appeal could also charge the archbishop with violating the papal privileges of that institution as well as with exceeding the just limits of his authority and acting with undue haste. Then, turning to the prohibition of preaching in private chapels, the appeal pointed to the royal and archiepiscopal privileges of Bethlehem Chapel, but also went on—in a striking passage of substantive rather than legalistic argument—to say that the preaching of the Word of God was enjoined by God's Law, the Gospel, and hence could not be prohibited.

[67] The text of Alexander's decree in *Documenta*, pp. 374–376. For his change of mind see Nov. I, 387–389; cf. Sedlák's different explanation in *M. Jan Hus*, p. 166. Kejř, *Husitský právník,* p. 29, suggests bribery.

[68] For Hus's first appeal see Nov. I, 390 f.; Sedlák, *M. Jan Hus,* pp. 167 f. For Zbyněk's action and the new appeal see Nov. I, 391 ff.; the texts in *Documenta,* pp. 378–396.

[69] Nov. I, 409 f.; Kejř, *Husitský právník,* pp. 33 f.

Although the appeal ended with a declaration of faith in the Apostolic See, the appellants had no intention of submitting to an unfavorable decision.[70] The primary battle was at home, against the archbishop and the prelates, and John Hus used the appeal itself both as an excuse to disobey the archbishop's injunction to stop preaching and as an instrument of propaganda. From the pulpit of Bethlehem Chapel he announced that he had undertaken the appeal; he read its text, and called out to his flock, "Will you stand with me?" They shouted that they would; Hus then, according to later charges against him, told them to gird on their swords and prepare for battle. We may believe him when he said, in his defense, that he had not meant this to be taken literally, but the words themselves are indicators of the mutinous atmosphere that he was generating.[71] The situation soon became even more tense when the archbishop excommunicated the appellants (on 18 July), and when Hus and some other masters conducted an ostentatious defense of Wyclif's condemned books in July and August.[72] At the end of August Hus was finally cited to Rome, and the pope confirmed the authority of the archbishop to act as he had done; but even this did not change matters, for Hus continued to function in Prague, entrusting his case in Rome to procurators—John Jesenic, Mark of Hradec, and Nicholas of Stojčín.[73] They left in December of 1410, fortified by interventions that had been made in Hus's behalf by King Wenceslas, Queen Sophia, a number of barons, and the governments of both Prague towns.[74] It is not surprising, in the light of all this, to find that when the pope himself excommunicated Hus in February of 1411 for nonappearance, the sentence, proclaimed in Prague on 15 March, only hurt the archbishop. In the streets and in their churches the people sang songs against him—"Soldiers of God prepare for battle. . . . Antichrist is on the march with his fiery furnace, giving birth to the arrogant clergy, whom he orders to prohibit preaching, to be lords of the world, and to scorn the apostles. How puffed up you've become, Zbyněk, to persecute priests and smother Christ's truth!" "The Hare," they sang, referring to Zbyněk's cognomen *Zajíc,* "dares to defy the Lion"—King Wenceslas: "Let the Lion rise up, destroy the clergy's mischief, promulgate the Law of Christ— let Hus teach you how!"[75] And in fact the king did set himself against the

[70] Novotný makes the same point, Nov. II, 249.

[71] *Documenta,* p. 405; cf. p. 281.

[72] The text of the excommunication in *Documenta,* pp. 397–399; for the defense of Wyclif's books see Nov. I, 417–429. The participants, along with Hus, were Masters Jakoubek of Stříbro, Simon of Tišnov, John of Jičín, Procop of Plzeň, and Zdislav of Zvířetice.

[73] Nov. I, 450 ff.

[74] *Loc. cit.;* the texts in *Documenta,* pp. 422–425.

[75] Text and discussion in Nejedlý, III, 442 f., 361 ff.

archbishop, even seizing the latter's estates, as countervalue for the books he had burnt. Zbyněk then, on 2 May, excommunicated the royal officials and councillors, and on 12 June imposed an interdict on Prague, which King Wenceslas simply commanded to be disobeyed. At this point the archbishop gave up: he had shot the last bolt in his armory of spiritual weapons, and the secular power was entirely at the disposal of his enemies. On 3 July he agreed with the university masters of Hus's party to submit their conflict to the judgement of the king and the royal councillors, a panel of whom then quickly pronounced an interim decision.[76] Zbyněk was to submit to the king and be reconciled; all interdicts and excommunications were to be withdrawn; he was to write to the pope that apart from the controversy now pending judgement he knew of no errors in Bohemia; all actions at the papal court by both sides were to be withdrawn. The king for his part would restore the clergy's incomes. As for the Wyclifites, their only obligations were to cancel their legal actions and to submit their cause, with the archbishop, to judgement by the king and council, which would be augmented for the purpose by prelates, masters and doctors, barons, and knights. In general, then, the decision was to restore the *status quo ante,* with royal judgement of the substantive issues. No good could come of this, from Zbyněk's point of view, and he refused to accept the consequences of his submission; in September of 1411 he fled Prague to seek refuge with King Sigismund of Hungary. En route he died, in Bratislava, on 28 September.

In 1409 the politicians of Hus's party had won control of the University of Prague; now, in 1411, they had taken a long step toward winning control over the Bohemian church. In actual fact, jurisdiction over that church had passed from the archbishop to the king; discipline could not be enforced, and the most fundamental questions of ecclesiology had escaped from the juridical control intended to insure their proper solution. Three hundred years of church history were being liquidated. It would be hard to imagine a more spectacular validation of the politicians' program, as set forth for example in Jesenic's *Defensio mandati*. The triumph, moreover, had not been won by the power of truth or by theological speculation; it rested on the politicians' preparation of a firm base in the university, on their careful cultivation of the king, his court, and the barons, and on an effective use of the procedural machinery provided by the Roman judicial system. Jesenic's role in all this was rather special; after he had undertaken to act as Hus's procurator at the papal court (where his two colleagues soon left him in full charge) he had to keep the process going as long as possible, and to find the right local advocates to win as favorable an opinion as possible from the successive

---

[76] Nov. I, 473–484; 490 ff.; the texts in *Documenta,* pp. 434–439.

judges appointed to handle the case. That he could hold up the final decision for over a year—Hus's excommunication was not fully implemented until September 1412, as we shall see—is evidence in part of his ability, in part of a mistake in judgement on the part of the pope, who treated the affair as merely one of several issues between himself and Wenceslas.[77] In any case, Jesenic's function as procurator ended when he was himself accused of heresy at the papal court and, in the first part of 1412, imprisoned; after he escaped he spent the better part of 1412 at the University of Bologna, picking up an LL.D. with incredible facility: by the end of the year he was back in Bohemia.[78] We shall return to him and the politicians in the final section of this chapter, after a detour by way of the radical wing of the reform party.

THE RADICALS AND THE BEGINNINGS OF THE
HUSSITE LEFT

On 8 September 1410 the English Lollard, Richard Wyche, wrote to John Hus and his party, noting their oppression by Antichrist and urging them to stand firm. At the end of the letter Wyche addressed himself in this vein particularly to Hus, and then saluted "all the faithful lovers of the Law of God . . . and especially Jakoubek, your helper in the work of the Gospel." [79] Czech Hussites must have informed Wyche of Archbishop Zbyněk's measures against Wyclif's doctrines and books, and of the prohibition of preaching in Bethlehem Chapel; they had evidently represented these actions in the most drastic terms and had given the Englishman the impression that, together with John Hus, the most notable reformer was Master Jakoubek of Stříbro. But however helpful Jakoubek may have been in "the work of the Gospel," and however much he shared with Hus in his hopes for a moral reform, his role in this period was much more than merely auxiliary. Unlike Hus and the politicians who combined a political Wyclifism with skillful politicking and legal maneuver within the framework of the Roman institution, Jakoubek eschewed all practical leadership except in his preaching, and his emotional, apocalyptical doctrine seemed almost designed to foreclose any possibility of dealing with the enemy. This was not because he was alien from the others: he was a friend and contemporary of Hus; he took his baccalaureate in arts in 1393, the same year Hus did, and his Master's degree in arts in 1397; like Hus he then taught in the Arts Faculty and studied

[77] Nov. I, 448 f., II, 55 ff.; see Kejř, *Husitský právník*, pp. 43–65, for Jesenic's role.
[78] Nov. II, 222 f.
[79] Nov. I, 457–460, for this and other letters from England and Scotland; cf. Sedlák, *M. Jan Hus*, p. 199 f.; the text in *KD*, pp. 75–79.

theology. He was not successful in finding a decent benefice; this failure was probably an effect rather than a cause, an effect of the same disposition of mind and spirit that kept him from taking any university office—in spite of the rotation system by which these offices were filled—and, until 1410, from filling any public role.[80] First and foremost he was an evangelical preacher, attacking the vices of the clergy and urging a moral reform in the spirit of Christ's poverty and humility; like Matthew of Janov, he favored a style of thought that moved from the basic evangelical ideal to a visualization of current reality in terms not of practical better-and-worse calculations, but of apocalyptic absolutes.[81] Men like Jesenic and the other politicians did not reject Jakoubek's ideals but they put their emphasis elsewhere.

Jakoubek's first official action for his party was, typically, doctrinal; he defended Wyclif's *De mandatis divinis* along with other Hussite spokesmen who defended other books of Wyclif in July and August of 1410, in protest against their burning by Archbishop Zbyněk.[82] The defense was in fact a *provocacio* to dispute, with only general references to the content of the book in question: "it contains the truth of evangelical life and doctrine"; it has been condemned as heretical but every faithful Christian is obliged to defend this truth unto death. Jakoubek then moved on to define the great secular battle of which the present case was only an episode:

> Therefore we have to join battle and *we wrestle not against flesh and blood* with a material sword, *but against principalities, against powers, against the rulers of the darkness* who have been introduced into the church, and *against spiritual wickedness in high places* in the church.[83]

The emphasized words are quoted from Ephesians 6:12; Jakoubek's additions show how Paul's general admonition to struggle against the satanic forces of evil was made into a specific order of the day for battle against the Roman hierarchy—further characterized as *gigantes gubernacula ecclesie occupantes,* and as those who "hold almost all the positions of rule in the church and govern everything." [84] At the heart of these evils lay the fact that "the carnal clergy and in consequence the laymen seduced by them have

---

[80] For these data see the sound but brief work of František Borecký, *Mistr Jakoubek ze Stříbra* (Prague: Kalich, 1945), p. 9 ff. There is an even briefer study by F. M. Bartoš, *M. Jakoubek ze Stříbra* (Prague, 1939). But perhaps the best appreciation of Jakoubek's early development is to be found in the series of essays published by Jan Sedlák under the title, "Husův pomocník v evangeliu," *ST,* I, 362–377; II, 302–316, 446–449; III, 24–38.

[81] *ST,* I, 364–368; one MS. of Matthew's *Regule* has Jakoubek's autograph notes (*ST,* I, p. i).

[82] *LČJ,* No. 21; the text in *ST,* II, 316–328. See n. 72 above.

[83] *ST,* II, 317.

[84] *ST,* II, 317, 325.

forgotten the humble, poor, and suffering life of our Lord Jesus Christ, so that now the house of God is deserted and desolated, for the holy spirit has fled from it." [85] The fervor of the true faith has been replaced by cold superficialities; the prelates are concerned only with the art of getting benefices; the "strait way of Christ . . . in which few walk" is rejected as antichristian, and "those who preach the poor and crucified Christ" as the model for the clergy are cruelly persecuted.[86] There is more material in the same vein, much of it drawn verbally from Matthew of Janov, but what has been quoted is enough to define Jakoubek's position. As Sedlák has observed,[87] it is already far beyond that of Hus and contains in itself all the germs of revolutionary theory.

The prime germ had probably appeared even earlier. In 1408 the Parisian Master Jacques de Nouvion was in Prague on a diplomatic mission, and during a dinner given him by the Czech masters he debated with them about the legitimacy of the church's endowment. This was of course one of the key questions raised by the Wyclifite theory common to all Hussites, but it had become actually significant as the reform movement worked out its close relationship with the crown, as described in the previous section. De Nouvion's later account of the debate, however, noted that some of his antagonists were operating with a concept of the church rather different in emphasis from the *ecclesia-regnum* equation—a concept that rejected the actual institution, led by corrupt prelates, in favor of a spiritual body, the church of the faithful, which did not err.[88] We will hardly be wrong if we identify these views with Jakoubek; his vigorous advocacy of an impoverished church had probably sparked the dispute in the first place,[89] but we also know that at about this time he was using Matthew of Janov to develop a more general theory of reform based on the idea of the church as a small group of holy men, the saints, persecuted by the majority, the church of Antichrist;[90] in the latter, leadership was based on office, but in the church of

[85] *ST*, II, 319.

[86] *ST*, II, 322.

[87] *ST*, II, 306 f.; see n. 94 below. The passages taken from Matthew of Janov are marked by Sedlák in the text.

[88] Sedlák, *M. Jan Hus*, p. 128 ff.; Nov. I, 244; the text in Sedlák, *Tractatus causam Mgri. J. Hus e parte catholica illustrantes*, I (Brno, 1914). See the discussion by De Vooght, *L'Hérésie*, pp. 89–92, and "L'ecclésiologie catholique . . . ," *Hussiana*, pp. 111–115.

[89] Sedlák, *M. Jan Hus*, p. 130.

[90] Sedlák, in *ST*, I, 368 ff. See, e.g., the sermon, *"Ecce mulier,"* *ST*, II, 462–477, which Bartoš dates probably in 1409 (*LČJ*, No. 19); also the sermon, *"Accipiebant spiritum sanctum"* of the same year, *ST*, I, 393–414, esp. p. 395. In both cases the lavish borrowings from Matthew of Janov are indicated by Sedlák in the text.

the saints it was based on virtue.[91] In this theory the apocalyptic or eschatological dimension associated with the imagery of Antichrist was closely tied to
the moral dimension provided by the evangelical ideal, the image of the
Primitive Church; perhaps the clearest statement of the linkage appears in
this passage from a sermon delivered in February 1412, but certainly based
on ideas that were in Jakoubek's mind much earlier:

> Now in this universal and perilous convulsion of the church the old darkness
> of sins and evil customs, excessively widespread, has covered the whole world
> among the Christian people. . . . And it is very hard for the faithful to
> discern which are the ways of the lord Jesus Christ and his saints, and which
> the evil ways of the serpent—the enemy or Antichrist. . . . And since now
> the ways of the Lord, consisting as they do in holiness of life, are so hidden,
> indeed in a sense choked over: let us therefore return to the beginnings, that
> is to the olden times of the church of Christ, and there contemplate with
> elevated mind the ancient ways of the Lord in his saints, and our ways of the
> present age that have been introduced by the work of Satan; so that the
> opposition between them may shine forth more clearly from the comparison.
> And finally let us compare the rule that the Apostle teaches us to observe,
> saying to the Philippians 3:17: "Brethren be imitators of me, and mark them
> who walk according to our pattern which you have." See how he brings us
> back to the beginnings of the church, to a consideration of the ancient ways
> of the lord Jesus Christ and his saints![92]

It was in fact at this time, in January of 1412, that Jakoubek pronounced his
scholastic determination that the pope, directly opposed to Christ in behavior
and action, was the supreme such opponent, hence the supreme Antichrist.[93]
But this was only one manifestation of the special nature of Jakoubek's
doctrine, which overlapped that of Hus in many points but was so different
from it in others. Jan Sedlák has pointed to the strongly sectarian flavor of
Jakoubek's ecclesiology, based on an idealization of humility and suffering
and smacking of a Waldensian type of religious outlook.[94] In a somewhat

---

[91] The clearest statement is in Jakoubek's quodlibetal question for January 1411,
"Utrum potest summus princeps . . . ," *ST*, II, 329: "Principatus ecclesiasticus fundatur
precipue in virtutum gradibus. . . ." But the point is more or less clear in other, earlier
works. Cf. Bartoš's notice of the sermon, "*Solliciti sitis*," which he dates in 1410 (*LČJ*,
No. 22.).

[92] *ST*, III, 38 f.

[93] *LČJ*, No. 25; see above, chap. i, n. 145.

[94] Since I accept Sedlák's formulation I offer it here in translation (*ST*, II, 306 f.):
"Jakoubek's pronouncement [*scil.*, in defense of Wyclif's *De mandatis divinis*] is much
more valuable than the others for an understanding of the Czech movement as of 1410.
Hus's dogmatic-polemical sermons on the church and its power show that the Master
was already settled in Wyclif's predestinarian concept of the church, and that the

different vein Vlastimil Kybal has also emphasized the contrast between the two types of ideology, Jakoubek's and Hus's:

> Jakoubek's view of Scripture as law is clearly a more individual one; it relies on the individual as fulfiller of the law more emphatically than on the whole or on the church as bearer of the law. This is a shading that links Jakoubek to Matthew of Janov and John Milíč but separates him from Hus, whose endeavor is to regulate the administration of the whole church by the law of Scripture.[95]

Something has already been said in the first chapter of the background and effect of these differences, and if we recur to them here it is because they are on the one hand extremely important, on the other hand quite hard to formulate in a definitive statement. Furthermore, Jakoubek's radicalism did not at first elicit the reaction we might have expected, and which would have given us more sources to define and date its development. His extremely forthright defense of Wyclif's doctrine of remanence in 1408–1409 was not even officially noticed by authority, although Hus, who did not embrace the doctrine, was more than once accused of doing so.[96] Similarly, Jakoubek's advocacy of disendowment of the church in 1407 attracted no attention from officialdom for over a year, and then the doctrine was imputed to the Wyclifite party in general: at this point it was not the doctrine so much as the actual agitation of the Wyclifites among the secular powers that aroused the archbishop's concern.[97] Even when Jakoubek said, in January of 1412, that the pope was the supreme Antichrist, he did not get an official reaction; not until a half-year later, when the Catholics were looking for a grievance,

---

movement had become schismatic. But Jakoubek sets alongside of this concept Janov's donatistic [*sic*] concept of the church of the saints, insignificant in numbers and persecuted by Antichrist, but which will win out in the end; he supplements the aggressive ideas of Wyclif with Janov's mysticism. The present church is entirely corrupted, ruled by Antichrist; the true church must fight against the other with spiritual arms, and meet persecution by the other with suffering and death. Where such ideas took firm root, there arose a religious sect, for which there could be no reconciliation with the Catholic Church. And in Hus's milieu this mysticism spreads, already colored by apocalyptic tones. Hus is not its leader, but his receptive nature succumbs to it: he too summons to spiritual warfare, and his mouth, too, occasionally pronounces the word Antichrist. . . . By 1410 the Czech movement is no longer purely Wyclifite, but intellectually and literarily dependent on the native reformer Matthew of Janov. And Jakoubek of Stříbro is no longer merely Hus's helper but fellow-creator of his structure—indeed in some points the creator whom Hus only helps."

[95] V. Kybal, *M. Jan Hus. Učení*, I, 135.

[96] Nov. I, 172 f. But cf. Bartoš, in *LČJ*, No. 1.

[97] Jakoubek's treatise is published in *ST*, II, 449–462; Sedlák dates it in 1411, but I follow Bartoš's dating in 1407, *LČJ*, No. 2. For the archbishop's concern in the autumn of 1409 see above, *ad* n. 64.

did they remember Jakoubek's position and complain about it.[98] This impassivity must have been due in part to Jakoubek's absence from the front line of the practical political action that hurt the Catholics more than his theories did; but it was perhaps also due to a Catholic reluctance to play into Hussite hands by engaging the reformers in a debate on the most fundamental questions of ecclesiology during a period when the Catholic authorities saw the main issue as one of church discipline. The substantive issues, as the Catholics saw them, were encapsulated in the list of Forty-five Articles in a form that met all the requirements of the church's juridical authority.

This situation changed in 1412, when the whole struggle for reform entered a new stage. By May of that year Pope John XXIII's bulls of indulgence—issued to finance his war against King Ladislas of Naples—were proclaimed in Prague, with the approval of King Wenceslas who received some of the money.[99] The commercializing of the indulgence was unusually bald, so much so that even some non-Hussites were openly critical, but John Hus led his party into outright opposition to the very doctrine involved.[100] Thus the alliance between reform and secular power was disrupted, and over an issue that could not be handled without opening the whole Pandora's box of Wyclifite doctrine. In the ensuing controversy the orthodox side was represented by the Czech masters of the Theology Faculty —the "doctors"—led by such long-time opponents of Hus as John Eliášův and Andrew of Brod, and by two new converts to Romanism, Stanislav of Znojmo and Stephen of Páleč. When they proved resolute enough to prevent the university from condemning the indulgences, as Hus had asked,[101] Hus scheduled a disputation on the matter for 17 June. Since the doctors did not attend, the meeting became a rally of the Wyclifite intelligentsia, who gave their full approval to Hus's *questio* which rejected the indulgences on broad doctrinal ground and culminated in a rejection of the pope himself as an antichrist—the point Jakoubek had made in January. The students, however, reserved their liveliest enthusiasm for Jerome of Prague who spoke in favor of Hus's determination, but then urged a protest march on the Town Hall. He was dissuaded by the rector, Mark of Hradec, but in the end more students accompanied Jerome to his lodgings than went with Hus.[102] The episode is instructive as proof that the open development

[98] Nov. II, 107 f.

[99] Bartoš, *Čechy*, p. 351 ff.; there is a more sympathetic interpretation of Wenceslas's attitude in Nov. II, 83–85.

[100] For the whole episode see the very full discussion in Nov. II, 61 ff.; cf. De Vooght, *L'Hérésie*, pp. 163 ff.

[101] Nov. II, 90 f.; Sedlák, *M. Jan Hus*, pp. 234–237.

[102] Nov. II, 93–97; Bartoš, *Čechy*, p. 355; for the text of Hus's *questio* see the notice in *LČH*, No. 52.

of reform doctrine could only have a radical tendency, both because the
theoretical foundations of reform were potentially radical, and because to
spell them out in a situation of stress naturally favored extreme positions
on the part of the intellectuals, direct action by the rank and file. These
tendencies necessarily favored leaders who, unlike Hus and the politicians,
were prepared to act even against the will of established authority.

Perhaps at the instigation of the doctors the royal court now intervened in
the controversy directly. Both sides were summoned to the king's presence at
Žebrák, at the end of June, and after hearing their positions the council
offered the impossible advice that they should work the thing out among
themselves.[103] The doctors at this point brought the whole issue into the open
by renewing the condemnation of Wyclif's Forty-five Articles, to which they
added prohibitions of the kind of agitation that Hus was carrying on; the
king for his part ordered that no one oppose the preaching of the indulgence
in the churches.[104] On 10 July, therefore, when there was another confrontation at Žebrák, the party of Hus could expect nothing good; in fact, the
king now confirmed the doctors' pronouncement against the Forty-five Articles and lent his authority to other prohibitions, including one against the
identification of the pope as Antichrist.[105] The break between the reformers
and the crown was now complete; all that remained was for the royal
government to kill its opponents. And so it happened: on the same day as
the action at Žebrák, three young followers of Hus—laymen—openly protested against the preaching of indulgences in the Prague churches; they
were imprisoned by the Prague magistrates and, despite assurances to Hus,
executed the next day on the king's order. Hus rightly held himself responsible for the youths' behavior, but the direct instigator was probably Jerome
of Prague; nor was it Hus who led the people in recovering the martyrs'
bodies and carrying them in solemn procession to Bethlehem Chapel; this
was the work of Master John of Jičín, a young man who had taken his
degree only in 1408, and who had taken part in the defense of Wyclif's books
in 1410, but who was not otherwise active as a theoretician. Later a key figure
in the utraquist revolt, and still later the only master to join the Taborites, he
now, like Jerome of Prague, represented a type of leadership distinct from
that of the politicians and that of the theologians like Jakoubek: we may
characterize this type as the activist correlate of Jakoubek's hortatory and
speculative radicalism. It was in any case not the kind of leadership offered
by John Hus, whose daily sermons in Bethlehem against the indulgences had
certainly inspired the three young men, but who did not preach a fiery

[103] Nov. II, 110 f.
[104] Nov. II, 113; Sedlák, *M. Jan Hus*, p. 242.
[105] *Loc. cit.;* the text in *Documenta*, pp. 451–457.

sermon over their bodies; nor indeed did he at that time say anything about them at all. Some thought he was afraid of the magistrates; more likely he was just being "responsible" according to the basic principle of previous Hussite policy, which rested everything on the alliance with the royal government.[106]

But a few days after this tragic episode, on 16 July, the Žebrák program was formally implemented at a meeting of magistrates, prelates, doctors, and university officials held in the Old Town Hall of Prague: the previous condemnations were repeated, and other points were added as a formula for pacification:

> 1. That no one may preach, dogmatize, or assert any error, and if some one should be found to have done so, that he first be disciplined by his ordinary, as an example to others, and further that he be banished from the realm by the lord king, and that he be in the lord king's disfavor.
>
> 2. That whoever may know someone to be a heretic or in error, and can prove it against him, that he denounce him to the diocesan or the diocesan officials, under penalty of excommunication.
>
> 3. Anyone who hereticates another or defames [*infamaverit*] him on account of any errors is to be compelled by the ordinary to prove his charges.
>
> 4. Let the diocesan prohibit any abuse of the [papal] bulls.[107]

Since with few exceptions the leaders of Hus's party did not attend the meeting, there was no final test of strength. Master Mark of Hradec, attending in his capacity as rector of the university, did have to respond to a direct question, whether he would obey the royal mandate and declare the Forty-five Articles to be erroneous, but he evaded a decision by saying that he would reject them in their erroneous sense, not in their true sense. Master Procop of Plzeň, a new master who would in time become a leader of the right wing, associated himself with Mark's position, as did Master Frederick Eppinge, a German ally of the Hussites about whom more will be said just below. Christian of Prachatice, the elder statesman of Hus's party, joined the Romanists in accepting the royal mandate; although he never wavered in his loyalty to the cause, his interest in and capacity for doctrinal exploration were minimal, and he evidently saw no alternative to submission to the crown.

The name of Frederick Eppinge leads us to another important development on the Hussite left, its reinforcement by the German teachers and

---

[106] Nov. II, 115–119, for the whole episode; for Jerome's role see Betts, "Jerome of Prague," p. 73, and Hardt, IV, 676.

[107] A notarized memoir of the proceedings is in *ST*, I, 55–65.

students of the "Dresden School."[108] This had begun as a secondary school in Dresden, but its teachers had enriched the basic curriculum in grammar and the other arts with the cultivation of an evangelical form of anti-Romanism that made use of both theological and canonistic materials. On 18 October 1411 Bishop Rudolph of Meissen, Dresden's diocesan, issued a decree forbidding the teaching of the Bible and *Decretum* in secondary schools, and soon after we find the group relocated in Prague, in a house "At the Black Rose" belonging to the Czech nation of the university. There is reason to believe that both the directors of the school, Masters Frederick Eppinge and Peter of Dresden, had been members of the University of Prague—perhaps they had left in 1409, perhaps earlier—and so had one of their leading pupils, John Drändorf; Master Nicholas of Dresden, who was to become the most important figure in the Dresden circle, had probably studied at Prague's Law University, if not also at the Arts Faculty.[109]

The precise nature of their reform doctrine is still a subject of scholarly investigation; while Nicholas eventually developed ideas that seem characteristically Waldensian, both his earlier work and the surviving work of Eppinge and Drändorf suggest not so much Waldensianism proper as a kind of generalized evangelical reformism, derivable and perhaps in fact derived from all of the sources current in Prague in the first decade of the century: Wyclifism, the ideas of Matthew of Janov, and the positions to be found in such works as the *Speculum aureum* and the *De squaloribus curie romane,* the latter written by the German master of Prague, Matthew of Cracow.[110] But whatever the sources, their doctrines were radical and militant. As we have seen, Eppinge was one of only three masters at the Town Hall meeting who refused to obey the royal command to condemn Wyclif's articles. Shortly afterward, in late July and early August, when John Hus decided to oppose this condemnation by a public defense of some of the articles, he had only two associates, Jakoubek of Stříbro and Frederick Eppinge.[111] The latter wrote a treatise, *Credo communionem sanctorum,* in defense of article eleven: "No prelate should excommunicate anyone unless he know that man

---

[108] For a detailed account of the Dresden School, with references to the modern literature, see my "Nicholas of Dresden and the Dresden School in Hussite Prague," *OC & N.* The most important modern works are J. Sedlák, *Mikuláš z Drážďan* (Brno, 1914), and F. M. Bartoš, "Vznik a počátky táborství," *Husitství a cizina* (Prague, 1931), pp. 113–153.

[109] My "Nicholas of Dresden," *ad* notes 26–34.

[110] Both of these works are discussed by J. Haller, *Papsttum und Kirchenreform* (Berlin, 1903), pp. 483–524; cf. Bartoš, *"Speculum aureum," VČA,* LIII (1944), 11–20 (that the author was the Pole, Paul Vladimiri). For Matthew of Cracow see Bartoš, *Čechy,* pp. 243 f., with references to the literature.

[111] Nov. II, 134 ff.

first to have been excommunicated by God. Otherwise, in excommunicating him, the prelate becomes a heretic or excommunicate himself." [112]

This subject would very soon become even more pressing than the issue of indulgences. It is noteworthy that Eppinge's discussion rested upon ecclesiological principles much like those of Jakoubek in their distinction between the church as an institution and the invisible communion of the saints—the judicial sentences of the former were at best merely declaratory of a man's standing with respect to the latter.[113] Unlike Wyclif, Eppinge defined the communion of the saints as the society of those who enjoyed spiritual goods on the basis of their individual capacities for goodness and love, capacities that could increase or decrease; Eppinge did not define this community as the corpus of those predestined to salvation.[114] Since his treatise was offered as a defense of a Wyclifite doctrine, his complete neglect of predestinarian ecclesiology cannot be regarded as less than significant, particularly since the ideas he did advance were so well in accord with the ecclesiological concepts of Jakoubek's radicalism, developing the idea of the church out of the principles of evangelical morality. Presdestinarianism was not incompatible with this approach—the two coexisted in Wyclif, Hus, and Jakoubek, for example—but important distinctions can be made on the basis of emphasis.

We are confirmed in these distinctions when we turn from Eppinge, who died in the latter part of 1412 or early 1413, to the man who apparently succeeded him as master in the Dresden School, Nicholas of Dresden.[115] His most valuable contribution to Hussitism was parallel to Jakoubek's, differing at first only in a peculiarly high degree of liveliness and emotional intensity, which later led him to go beyond Jakoubek into outright sectarian heresy. We have already seen how he set the churches of Christ and Antichrist against each other in the *Tables of the Old and New Color,* but it is worth recalling against the background of its time, the year 1412. This was the year

---

[112] The text in Hus's (?) *Tractatus responsivus,* ed. S. Harrison Thomson (Prague, 1927), pp. 103–133. Bartoš has argued that the author was Jakoubek: "M. J. Hussii tractatus responsivus," *ČČM,* CI (1927), 23–35.

[113] Using the canonistic distinction between minor and major excommunications, Eppinge argued that the minor kind, which excluded its object from taking the sacraments, was "proprie excommunicacio interior secundum se talis"—and it was incurred only by mortal sin (p. 108). The major excommunication was exterior—"et ista non auffert iusticiam vel virtutem, nec infert peccatum" (p. 110). This was the sentence that carried actual ecclesiastical penalties, but since, canonically, it was never pronounced except for contumacy, it did not include but only presupposed the truth of exclusion by sin from the communion of the saints (p. 117).

[114] *Ibid.,* pp. 104 f.

[115] Bartoš, "Vznik a počátky táborství," p. 132. For Nicholas see my study cited in n. 108 above.

when first Jakoubek, then Hus, publicly declared the Roman institution to be ruled by Antichrist; when anti-Roman demonstrations in the streets of Prague became more violent and frequent than ever before; when for the first time the reformers suffered serious persecution, even martyrdom, at the hands of an alliance between secular and ecclesiastical power. Moreover, it was the year when ideological conflict between reform and Romanism emerged in its full depth and breadth as an issue of polemic. All of these motifs are epitomized in the *Tables,* whose text and pictures can stand as at once a kind of encyclopedia of reform principles and a definition of the un-bridgeable gulf between the Roman institution and the new Hussite holy community that was taking on ever more solid outline in the minds of the aroused people.[116]

Indeed, the struggle over the indulgences was soon absorbed by the even more fundamental issues it had evoked. The doctrinal controversies now produced an abundance of literary work that would continue to distinguish Hussite history for the next decade. In August and September the Hussite defense of Wyclif's articles was answered in treatises written by Stanislav of Znojmo and Stephen of Páleč, who were in turn answered by Nicholas of Dresden in his *De quadruplici missione,* which moved from a defense of free preaching of the Word to a violent, apocalyptic attack on the church that sought to limit or forbid such preaching—the doctors of this church were doctors of Antichrist.[117] Meanwhile, on 4 September, the pope's "aggrava-tion" of Hus's excommunication—that is, its full implementation—arrived in Prague, to put an end to the sequence of procedural maneuvers that for two years and more had worked so well to delay precisely such a final judgement. By the end of the month the archbishop had placed an interdict on Prague because of Hus's presence there, and shortly after Hus went into what is called his "exile"; he appealed now from the pope to Jesus Christ, but this meant only that he refused to purge himself.[118] His followers were even more defiant: there were demonstrations in the streets, physical attacks on the clergy, and there even seems to have been talk of revolution.[119] Whether or not this was a real possibility cannot of course be known; certainly the

[116] See the discussion in chap. i, above.

[117] Sedlák, in *ST,* I, 79–85; against his argument, that Hus used this work in his defense of Wyclif in July 1412, see the arguments of Bartoš, "Studie k Husovi a jeho době," *ČČM,* LXXXIX (1915), 5 f., where it is shown that Nicholas's tractate is a reply to a sermon of Stephen of Páleč, delivered on 4 September 1412. The text of the tractate in *ST,* I, 95–117.

[118] Nov. II, 171 ff.; Sedlák, *M. Jan Hus,* p. 261.

[119] Nov. II, 190; for the turmoil in the streets see Höfler, I, 624; for the talk of revolution see just below. In the provinces, priests were actually killed at this time: see Sedlák, *M. Jan Hus,* p. 291, n. 4.

ideology for revolution was not lacking, and at least one source indicates a violence of temper on the left far in excess of the more ordinary sentiments of opposition already noticed. It shows not only a spirit of secession and alienation from the church, but a seditious attitude to the secular power as well.

The source is rather curious: it is a German text purporting to be a manifesto of "The Community of the Free Spirit of the Brotherhood of Christ"—that is, the Czech Wyclifites. Professor F. M. Bartoš, who discovered and first published it, has characterized it as a parody of authentic Czech manifestos that must have existed but are now lost; on the basis of internal evidence he convincingly dates the text in October/November 1412.[120] Bartoš's theory is that an anti-Hussite German author concocted a subversive manifesto that he could ascribe to the Czech Wyclifites and then use to turn the king against them; on this basis the text can be interpreted as a doubtless distorted but at least plausible reproduction of sentiments actually current among Hus's followers.[121] This explanation raises certain problems, and it must be said that the manifesto contains nothing that would positively prevent us from seeing it as a faithful translation of an authentic Hussite original; even the reference to the Free Spirit, which Bartoš understands as an attempt to smear the Hussites with the mud of an especially odious heresy, may be read much more generally, in terms of its biblical source; this must have been the referent of the phrase as used, for example, by Stanislav of Znojmo a few months later, in an attack on Hus and the Hussites: "He and his party regard themselves as evangelical clergy of the Free Spirit." [122]

---

[120] Bartoš published and discussed the text in his "Hus a jeho strana v osvětlení nepřátelského pamfletu z r. 1412," *Reformační sborník*, IV (1931), 3–8, the text on pp. 5–7. Unaware of this article, Dr. Ernst Werner of Leipzig published the text again, in his "Die Nachrichten über die böhmischen 'Adamiten' in religionshistorischer Sicht," in T. Büttner & E. Werner, *Circumcellionen und Adamiten* (Berlin: Akademie-Verlag, 1959), pp. 135–140, discussion on pp. 86 ff.; he regarded it as a German translation of an originally Czech manifesto of the Taborite chiliasts, and he dated it accordingly in 1420. The most notable product of the ensuing exchange of views between Bartoš and Werner was Bartoš's "Nový pramen k dějinám českého chiliasmu?" *Křesťanská revue* (1961), No. 2, *Theologická příloha*, pp. 10–16, in which the dating in 1412 is further supported by a very instructive discussion of the situation in that year. Werner has accepted Bartoš's conclusions: *Nachrichten über spätmittelalterliche Ketzer aus tschechoslovakischen Archiven und Bibliotheken* (Leipzig: Karl-Marx-Universität, 1963), p. 260.

[121] Bartoš "Nový pramen," pp. 13 f.

[122] Stanislav's tractate "Alma et venerabilis," one of many polemics generated by the synod of 6 February and its aftermath (see the section on "The Crisis of Hus's Exile," below), is published by J. Loserth, "Die Streitschriften und Unionsverhandlungen zwischen den Katholiken und Husiten in den Jahren 1412 und 1413," *AÖG*, LXXV

The problem deserves further study; meanwhile we may observe that the difference between a Hussite manifesto and a plausible fake is not so great, from the historian's point of view, as to destroy the value of the text when used indeterminately, as either the one or the other.

The manifesto begins with a striking denunciation of Wenceslas IV as an evil king, working to destroy those who hold to God's order—he is another Nero. In fact, he is no king: having fallen from divine grace, he has lost his right to the royal office and must now be regarded as at best an instrument, given power and used by God to inflict salutary chastisement on God's people. This is clearly Wyclif's doctrine that "dominion"—rightful title to lordship—is the effect of grace, and that loss of grace through sin makes the ruler a mere holder of power, a tyrant.[123] In line with his interpretation of the manifesto, Bartoš supposes that the author was deliberately recalling John Hus's defense in August of Wyclif's article fifteen, "Nullus est dominus civilis . . . dum est in peccato mortali," in order to show the king how dangerous the Wyclifites were, now that they were in opposition.[124] In any case, the subversive program of the manifesto is clear enough, and there follows its justification—the "long train of abuses," as a later manifesto would put it. These need only be touched upon here; they turn on the king's alleged exaltation of German "heretics" (i.e., Catholics) at the expense of both the material and spiritual interests of the Czechs. Hus, the blessed man who has resisted the pope-Antichrist and has opposed the selling of holy things, has been abused by these Germans. Conrad of Vechta, already taking over the archiepiscopal office from Albík of Uničov (who formally resigned it in November or December), is not only branded as a German but is also called a diabolic sorcerer who has seduced the king into believing the lies of Antichrist. There is also a reference to Jerome of Prague's narrow escape from his German persecutors in Vienna in 1410.[125] Among these persecutors

---

(1889), 361–413; the quoted passage is on p. 394: "ipse cum parte sua reputantes se clerum evangelicum de libero spiritu volunt omnia iudicare et a nemine iudicari." It probably refers to the well-known Pauline texts: I Cor. 2:15—"Spiritualis autem iudicat omnia, et ipse a nemine iudicatur"—and II Cor. 3:17—"ubi autem Spiritus Domini, ibi libertas." The name of the Brethren of the Free Spirit also derived, ultimately, from the vocabulary of these texts, but their more general use was not thereby foreclosed. John Hus indeed used the term "a priest of free spirit" as praise, for non-simoniacs: in his *On Simony*, trans. M. Spinka, in *Advocates of Reform*, (Philadelphia, 1953), p. 246; the Czech text, ed. K. J. Erben, *M. J. Husi Sebrané spisy české*, I (Prague, 1865), 436.

[123] See my "Wyclifism," p. 10 f.

[124] Bartoš, "Nový pramen," p. 12.

[125] For these events see *ibid.*; Jerome's process in Vienna has been discussed by Paul Bernard, "Jerome of Prague, Austria, and the Hussites," *Church History*, XXVII (1958), 3–22, esp. pp. 6–10.

was Duke Ernest of Carinthia, who now attends the German services in Týn Church in Prague, where nothing but Antichrist's lies are preached; at the same time he enjoys the constant society of whores, and thus scandalizes "the daughters and sons of God." This section ends with the dire prediction that the exaltation of the Germans will cause the ruin of the Christian faith and its upholders in Bohemia. The manifesto then concludes with a summons to battle against this unholy constellation of forces:

> And so, dear holy community in Bohemia, let us stand in the battle line with our head, Master Hus, and our leader, Master Jerome; and whoever will be a Christian, let him turn to us. Let everyone gird on his sword, let brother not spare brother, nor father spare son, nor son father, nor neighbor spare neighbor. But let all be killed, one after another, so that we, with your help, may sweep the German heretics, the merchants, usurers, and greedy clergy, from this world, and thus fulfil the dear command of God, according to the words of St. Paul: "Greed is the service of idols and the worshipper of idols" [cf. Col. 3:5]. All should kill so that we can make our hands holy in the blood of the accursed ones, as Moses shows us in his books; for what is written there is as an example to us.[126]

As Bartoš remarked in his original discussion of the manifesto, "When we read these lines we cannot help forgetting that we have before us a document of the year 1412, and we are moved to imagine that we are already in the midst of the violent revolt of 1420." [127] But he also noted that while the author no doubt exaggerated the call to violence, he probably did not need to add very much; we may observe that perhaps he added nothing. Already in 1410 John Hus had been accused of declaring to his flock in Bethlehem that "it would be necessary, as Moses commanded in the Old Law, that whoever wanted to defend the Law of God should gird on his sword and be ready"; the Dominican Master Peter of Uničov had publicly called this sermon a summons to the people to take their swords and strike their fathers and mothers dead.[128] And Jerome of Prague, whose preeminent position at this time is well reflected in the manifesto, had often moved in an atmosphere of physical violence,[129] even while developing a very strong messianic

---

[126] *Reformační sborník*, IV, 7.

[127] *Ibid.*, p. 5.

[128] Bartoš, "Nový pramen," p. 15; see above, *ad* n. 71. For Peter's statement see *Documenta*, p. 251.

[129] See R. R. Betts, "Jeronym Pražský," *ČsČH*, V (1957), 199–226, *passim;* for the English version see n. 56, above. Even across five centuries one can sense the adventurous, reckless, romantic, egotistical qualities that made Jerome fascinating to Poggio Bracciolini; eloquence and display of erudition were only expressions of these traits of character. As a leader of the Hussite party Jerome continually displayed the same traits in other ways: impulsiveness of action, exaggeration in discourse, etc. And there was

concept of the Czech nation as a holy community in opposition to the heretics, who were invariably Germans.[130] The manifesto's characterization of the pious Czechs as daughters and sons of God may well reflect these ideas —if indeed it does not merely correspond to John Hus's doctrine of the "communion of the saints";[131] in fact, one of his letters to Christian of Prachatice at this time calls the faithful "sons of God"—the phrase comes from Rom. 8:14—and in other ways, too, reminds us of the manifesto.[132] "I exhort you and your fellows," he wrote, ". . . to be ready for battle, for Antichrist's preludes have begun, and the fighting will follow at once." Hus in exile was indeed much closer to the radicals than Hus in Prague, and enough has been said of the radical concept of Antichrist to suggest that a progression from this concept and its related definition of the Hussites as the true church of Christ, to an actual summons to battle was by no means out of the question; in certain circles it must have been virtually inevitable. In his *De quadruplici missione,* written about the same time as the manifesto, Nicholas of Dresden described the Roman church thus: "She is the Great Whore, arrayed in purple and scarlet color, and decked with gold and precious stones and pearls, having a golden cup in her hand; Babylon, the great mother of fornications, who will be destroyed just as God destroyed Sodom and Gomorrah." [133] Against this stood the faithful, whose virtues and inspiration by God justified them in defying the Roman church and taking over that church's functions. When we recall that in the autumn of 1412 the Great Whore was fornicating with King Wenceslas IV—a union that had

---

also physical violence: On the streets of Prague, we are told, Jerome slapped around the Franciscan preacher Beneš of Boleslav (p. 214); weapons in hand, he chased preachers of indulgences out of a church (p. 215); he used a sword to round up three monks accused of exhibiting false relics, and turning over two to the town government, he kept the third prisoner in his house (p. 215); he led the people in demonstrations that smeared dirt and worse on crucifixes and other holy images (p. 217). And these are only examples. That Jerome was also involved in the 1412 propaganda against Ernest of Carinthia, as reflected in the manifesto, is strongly suggested by Jerome's statements at Constance (Mansi, XXVII, 845).

[130] Bartoš, "Nový pramen," p. 15; cf. the account of Jerome's speech at Knín's quodlibet, above.

[131] The doctrine is discussed by V. Kybal, *M. Jan Hus. Učení,* I, 225 ff., esp. p. 228, with a reference to Hus's *On Simony,* where we find, among other relevant passages, this: "All faithful Christians, fulfilling the commands of their father, Christ the savior, are sons of God. . . ." (*O svatokupectví,* in *Mistra Jana Husi, Sebrané spisy české,* ed. K. J. Erben, I (Prague, 1865), 431.

[132] *KD,* pp. 153 f.: "Quid [michi] infamia illata, que purgat et clarificat dei filios, humiliter tollerata, ut fulgeant sicut sol in regno patris sui. . . ." The last clause, from Matt. 13:43, also points to the chiliast ideology of 1420, at which time it was used in a more literal sense (see chap. vii, below).

[133] *ST,* I, 107.

already led to the killing of the three youths in Prague, venerated by the movement as martyrs—we can believe that the unparalleled bloodthirstiness of the manifesto was perhaps the genuine expression of sentiments cultivated by a significant group of radical Hussites. And at the moment such sentiments perhaps corresponded more closely to the realities of the situation than the more pacific disposition of the rest.

THE CRISIS OF HUS'S EXILE

After this sampling of the radicals' mood it comes as something of a disappointment to learn that the great confrontation with Antichrist did not in fact come off, that the threads of leadership were once again picked up by the politicians, on the basis of a new *modus vivendi* with the secular power.

Sometime in the autumn of 1412 John Jesenic returned to Prague, carrying his Doctorate in Laws from Bologna and a personal excommunication from Rome. He presumably did not arrive in time to counsel John Hus when the latter's excommunication was aggravated, nor would he have approved, as a lawyer, of Hus's final appeal, to Jesus Christ; [134] but after Hus had withdrawn to his "exile" Jesenic's hand became increasingly evident in the course of events. With the access of vigor and power to the enemy and a mutinous spirit on the Hussite left, there had emerged a situation that the politicians of the reform party could not master—we have only to remember Christian of Prachatice's submission to the doctors at the Town Hall meeting of 16 July—and the only hope lay in a new departure. Conferences of leading Hussites must have been held, and future events show that they decided to turn to their patrons among the nobility for the all-important access to secular power.[135] The tactic could succeed only if the king eventually came around, but this was not impossible; given the limitations of the situation, the Hussites could reasonably set as their goal the kind of stalemate imposed by the crown and submitted to by Archbishop Zbyněk in July of 1411. The reformers certainly understood that no settlement of the religious issues between them and the doctors was possible, but they, or at least the political leaders, still thought of the controversy as one lying within the Roman church and therefore capable of being debated in a suitable church forum. But such future developments presupposed a removal of the juridical disabilities that had been inflicted on Hus and others, a relief that at this

---

[134] Kejř, *Husitský právník*, p. 66.

[135] See *ibid.*, pp. 94–96, for a very instructive account of how closely John Jesenic, among others, depended on the pro-Hussian nobles for economic patronage. Bartoš, *Čechy*, p. 363, suggests that the turn to the nobility may have been arranged with Hus by his supporters in that estate.

point could come only from the kind of external peace that the crown might impose. The basic condition of such a peace—that both sides be prohibited from hereticating each other—had been imposed to the disadvantage of Zbyněk in July of 1411, and then to the disadvantage of the Hussites in July of 1412; all that was necessary was to revise the four-point formula of the latter settlement (quoted above) by changing the first and last points so as to leave the question of religious truth open.

The first step was to bring the matter under the official cognizance of the noble estate. One of this estate's institutional embodiments was the High Court (*Zemský soud*), whose next regular meeting was scheduled for the Ember Days beginning on 14 December. Hus appealed to this body.[136] He began by recalling the peace of 1411 between his party and the archbishop, thus elevating this precarious, ambiguous, and indeed unsuccessful arrangement to the status of a norm. In violation of this peace the Prague canons had pursued their legal process against Hus and procured his excommunication. He observed that the interdict and the citations of the reformers to Rome were in violation not only of God's Law but also of canon and imperial law. "Therefore, dear lords—heirs of the Kingdom of Bohemia—strive to make these abuses cease, that the word of God may enjoy freedom among the people of God." Hus was willing to appear before the masters, prelates, and the lords and submit to judgement, provided that his accusers also appeared; thus he refuted what he said was the only charge against him, that of disobedience. But he would not stop preaching in any case. He conceded that he had not gone to Rome when cited there, but noted that he had sent his procurators, who had themselves been imprisoned; had he gone he would have been dealt with similarly or worse. He closed his appeal with the hope that the nobles, together with the king and queen, would do what was good for the country.

Dr. Jesenic, who must have helped to draft this appeal,[137] now pronounced a full-scale "Defense of John Hus's Cause" at the university, on 18 December.[138] Canon lawyers recognized certain cases in which a sentence of excommunication was invalid, and Jesenic tried to show that Hus's excommunication fell into that category. Among other points: the excommunication by Archbishop Zbyněk had been invalid against a member of the University of Prague, which enjoyed papal privileges; the alleged cause of the present

[136] Nov. II, 223 ff.; the text in *KD*, pp. 157 f., and in *Documenta*, pp. 22 f., misdated 1411.

[137] Nov. II, 223.

[138] Nov. II, 224–226; cf. Sedlák, *M. Jan Hus*, pp. 269 f.; Kejř, *Husitský právník*, pp. 68 ff., offers the best discussion. The text is in *Historia et monumenta Joannis Hus*, I (Nürnberg, 1715), 408–419.

sentence, Hus's nonappearance, was false, since procurators had been sent and excuses given; the prelates' excommunication of all those associating with Hus was an invalid extension of the ban—it went beyond the mandate of the original sentence, and it failed to specify its victims by name, as canon law required. Such an invalid sentence—procured, Jesenic noted, by the bribes of Hus's enemies in Bohemia—could be legally set aside by a local bishop: that is, by Archbishop-elect Conrad, a royal courtier who had set his seal on the settlement of 1411 in favor of Hus's party.[139] The whole unjust process, so detrimental to the realm, should be stopped, and the Word of God be given the freedom due it. Thus far Jesenic's discourse, a copy of which was then given to Conrad. We do not know if this action had direct effects, nor do we know just what was done in Hus's behalf at the High Court; but we can surmise that these and no doubt other efforts were responsible for what actually did happen: King Wenceslas did change his stand and on 3 January 1413 ordered a synod of the clergy to meet "in order that the pestiferous dissension among the clergy of our realm . . . be removed and wholly extirpated." [140] Conrad's mandate to the same effect stated that it was issued at the order of the king and with the orally expressed support of the lords, barons, and nobles of the realm.[141] Nothing was said in either mandate about which side was presumed right; although Conrad did insert a phrase about dealing with the matter after taking the counsel of doctors of law and theology, the passage is so perfunctory as to be insignificant. When the synod met, on 6 February in Prague, both sides submitted their positions and programs.

The texts associated with this synod are very instructive. On the one extreme was the proposal of the theologians, that the dissident clergy of Bohemia be brought back to total unity with the Roman church, in doctrine and obedience.[142] On the other was a proposal advanced by Jakoubek of Stříbro, who predictably envisioned a kind of settlement that would have enforced Hussitism on the Bohemian church. The only way to true peace, he argued, was through the extirpation of clerical simony, fornication, wealth, and secular dominion. He proposed that Hus and his associates be faced with the other side's charges and allowed to defend themselves; if, however, this procedure did not lead to peace between the parties—and obviously it could not—then it should be understood that such external peace was not after all essential: the true peace of Christ, consisting in observance of his law, was all

---

[139] Nov. II, 228 f.

[140] Nov. II, 229 ff.; the text in *Documenta*, pp. 472 f.

[141] *Documenta*, pp. 473 f.

[142] *Ibid.*, pp. 475–480, and cf. Nov. II, 247, n. 1. For the course of events connected with the synod see Nov. II, 242 ff., and Sedlák, *M. Jan Hus*, pp. 271 ff.

that really mattered, and this sort of peace should be enforced, in the manner noted.[143] The future would be with Jakoubek but the present was against him; his program, undoubtedly representing the views of the doctrinaires of the left, was as unsuited as that of the doctors for the purpose of the synod, which had certainly not been called to make matters worse. The program that Hus lent his name to was not Jakoubek's but one that must have been worked out with the politicians of the party; it was based closely on the principles of the peace imposed by the crown in July 1411.[144] Any charges of heresy against Hus should be brought and proved, with the stipulation that those unable to prove their charges should themselves be punished; if no professor or cleric wished to make any charges, then official testimonials to Hus's orthodoxy should be obtained from them, and an embassy sent to the pope, at the clergy's expense, to remove the stigma of heresy from the realm of Bohemia. It was a proposal obviously designed to prevent a showdown in matters of substance, a tactical device to remove Hus's case from the Roman jurisdiction and bring it within the jurisdiction of the realm; Rome would then be informed of what had been done. The plan was justified by an appeal to the rights of the realm, and point two of the proposal was that "the realm of Bohemia should continue to enjoy the rights, liberties, and common customs that other realms and lands enjoy . . . , in all matters of approval, condemnation, and other matters, concerning the holy universal mother church." [145]

We have met these themes before in tracing the Hussite policy of alliance with the crown—there can indeed be little doubt that the plan just described was produced by the politicians; and the history of late-medieval Europe suggests that whatever may be said about the actual rights and liberties of "other realms" vis-à-vis Rome, there was at least a widespread conviction that the crown could be interposed in the jurisdictional channels leading from the national church to the papal court. The idea did exist in Bohemia and it was

---

[143] *Documenta,* pp. 493 f. I follow most other scholars against Novotný in placing this text in the present context: see Kejř, *Husitský právník,* p. 76, n. 10.

[144] *Documenta,* pp. 491 f. The first point was that the 1411 peace be accepted.

[145] The proposal has two headings, presumably from different MSS: (1) "Consilia et modi concordiae magistrorum pro parte M. Joannis Hus"; (2) "Articuli M. Joannis Hus cum sibi adhaerentibus, lecti in congregatione cleri in curia archiepiscopi" (*Documenta,* p. 491). These do not justify Novotný's statement that "the author was Hus himself" (Nov. II, 247), nor Sedlák's similar opinion (*M. Jan Hus,* p. 272). As both note, it was the proposal of Hus's party among the university masters, where it held the majority; the existence of Jakoubek's alternative proposal suggests that there might have been still others, and it may be guessed that this would not have been the case if Hus had from the first presented his own draft. If we must name an author for the proposal in question, the likeliest choice would be Jesenic; it shows his special gift for associating

not different from that expressed in the English statutes of *Praemunire*.[146] Having thoroughly absorbed Wyclif's doctrine, John Hus could even refer to King Wenceslas IV as "the first prelate" of the Bohemian clergy,[147] and this idea, too, would prove to have a brilliant future both in Bohemia and elsewhere. Indeed, only a few days before the synod of 6 February Hus had completed that masterpiece of applied Wyclifism, his Czech treatise *On Simony,* a blazing attack on all modes of exchanging spiritual for material goods—the "simoniacal heresy";[148] in this work he unhesitatingly followed Wyclif in calling for the most vigorous action by the laity to reform this basic perversion in the church. The people should withhold their tithes and other offerings from the simoniacs; the lords should use their rights of patronage to take up church property, the fuel feeding the fires of clerical avarice; the king should use his God-given power over his realm to rule the priests, who are part of that realm.[149] This was not unwelcome advice, and Hus could even claim that the king at least was actually carrying out the Wyclifite principle: Wenceslas did demand, in circumstances that are not clear, that the clergy give him its revenues due to be collected on St. George's Day (23 April) and, Hus observed, "that demand expressly approves the article on the taking away of temporalities." [150] The king who could do this could also impose a settlement of the religious controversies disturbing his realm.

Thus the Hussite proposal to the synod of 6 February corresponded not only to the interests and ideology of the Wyclifite party, but also to the

the Hussite cause with the rights of the Bohemian realm. For the principle of interposition, see below, chap. vi, *ad* n. 3.

[146] See below, p. 265.

[147] *KD*, p. 162.

[148] The edition has been cited in n. 131 above; there is an abridged English translation, with indications of borrowings from Wyclif, by Matthew Spinka in his *Advocates of Reform* (Philadelphia, 1953), pp. 196–278. For discussion see De Vooght, *L'Hérésie*, pp. 236 ff. On the simoniacal heresy see De Vooght, "La 'Simoniaca haeresis' de St. Thomas d'Aquin à Jean Huss," *Hussiana* (Louvain, 1960), pp. 379–399.

[149] In Spinka's translation, pp. 272 f. For Jakoubek's use of the same passage from Wyclif in exaltation of the royal power over the church, see above, chap. i, *ad* n. 147.

[150] *Documenta*, p. 501; cf. Novotný's notes on this text, Nov. II, 274, n. 1. The article Hus referred to was No. 16, quoted above, chap. i, *ad* n. 151. There are some interesting reactions to Hus's exploitation of Wenceslas's action: by Andrew of Brod ("Non sequitur: Iste fornicatur, ergo approbat fornicacionem licitam esse, iste bibit superflue, ergo approbat ebrietatem"—well-chosen examples for the case at hand!); by Stephen of Páleč (who apparently conceded that Wenceslas *was* practicing Wyclifism); and by Stanislav of Znojmo (who accounted for the king's action according to I Kings 8:46: "for there is no man that sinneth not"). All are printed in Loserth's work cited in n. 122 above, pp. 344, 358, 412 f., respectively.

thinking of the king. For this reason it was highly successful. The synod referred all the proposals to the king, who set up a special commission of four to effect a settlement, and it cannot have been by chance that the membership was sympathetic to the Hussites: Master Christian of Prachatice, rector of the university, and Master Zdeněk of Labouň were actually members of Hus's party; the royal physician Albík of Uničov, who had resigned the archbishopric of Prague, and the Protonotary of the Royal Chancery James of Dubá were the king's men, responsive to his will and to that of the royal council, which was generally pro-Hussite.[151] Shortly before Easter, which fell on 23 April, representatives of both sides were summoned before the commission: Doctors Stanislav of Znojmo, Peter of Znojmo, John Eliášův, and Stephen of Páleč, for the Theology Faculty, and Dr. John Jesenic, Master Jakoubek of Stříbro, and Master Simon of Tišnov for the Hussites. The positions were unchanged and there could be no hope of an agreement, but by a combination of pressure and deceit the doctors were induced to submit, along with their opponents, to a rule customary with royal commissions, namely, that they would accept the commission's decision, under penalty of a heavy fine and banishment.[152] The commission then decreed what was essentially the settlement of July 1411, and ordered the doctors to declare that there was no heresy in Bohemia, and to send this declaration to Rome.[153] The four doctors refused, and were in fact banished and their prebends confiscated. Although no real settlement was reached—the commission remained in existence into mid-June [154]—the vigorous action by the king at least paralyzed the process against Hus in Bohemia.

But it was a Pyrrhic victory for Hus: his intransigent attitude had contributed to the commission's failure; there was no settlement with Rome; and Wenceslas henceforth maintained a hostile attitude toward him that made a resumption of his work in Prague impossible.[155] He continued in his exile, chiefly in the South Bohemian castles of his supporters, with only intermittent visits to Prague. His preaching in this period seems to have been extremely radical,[156] and his literary work, especially the *De ecclesia*, finished in June of 1413, took on a classic quality as the application of Wyclifism to the most profound problems of a Bohemian reformation. The controversy

[151] Bartoš, *Čechy*, p. 365. For the commission's work see Nov. II, 272 ff., and Sedlák, *M. Jan Hus*, p. 276 ff. The basic source is the *Chronicon universitatis pragensis, FRB*, V, 575–579.

[152] Bartoš, *Čechy*, p. 366.

[153] *Ibid.*, p. 367.

[154] *Loc. cit.*

[155] *Ibid.*, p. 369.

[156] See, e.g., Nov. II, 334 f.

that had taken shape in connection with the synod of 6 February had had as one of its results an engagement of both sides in what was recognized as the basic question, the theory of the church; and the treatises of Stanislav of Znojmo and Stephen of Páleč on the one hand, of Hus on the other, brought a good deal of clarity to a problem that neither side had well understood.[157] From this time on, no intelligent man could suppose that the issues posed by the Czech reform movement were essentially ones of church discipline; what was at stake was nothing less than the nature of the church itself. The many manuscripts of Hus's *De ecclesia* show how important this work was to his followers; it is all the more significant that the questions it raised and the answers it gave corresponded very closely to the doctrine developed by the radicals in the previous period.[158] At this point the politicians of the party had become auxiliary. They would later have plenty of opportunity to exercise their special talent for securing the support of secular power, but meanwhile the situation they had so skillfully created tended to make a victory of radicalism all but inevitable.

[157] There is a good summary of the polemics, with references to the sources, in Sedlák, *M. Jan Hus,* pp. 282–288. Novotný's treatment (Nov. II, 266, 288 ff.) is hopelessly prejudiced against Hus's opponents. He is followed closely by M. Spinka, *John Hus' Concept of the Church* (Princeton, N.J.: Princeton University Press, 1966). See also De Vooght, *L'Hérésie,* pp. 263–281.

[158] The work is discussed in Sedlák, *loc. cit.;* Nov. II, 297 ff.; also in chap. i, above, with references to the recent edition by S. Harrison Thomson.

III

THE UTRAQUIST REVOLT, 1414–1415

IT SEEMS at first something of an anticlimax that the radicals who rejected the claims of the Roman ecclesiastical institution on so broad a front of doctrine, emotion, and action should have encapsulated their secession in the theory and practice of utraquism—giving communion to the laity in both kinds, bread and wine. The Roman church's shift from its own earlier utraquism to the practice of withholding the chalice had occurred around the twelfth century as a matter of ceremonial suitability, falling in the sphere of church law, not dogma or even doctrine.[1] By the fifteenth century the newer practice was universal, and no one before the Hussites seems to have felt that the laity were being deprived of anything important; orthodox theology defined each of the two elements as equivalent to the full body-and-blood combination, and few even of the Hussites were prepared to deny this.[2] Yet when the radical Hussite leaders began to offer both bread

---

[1] For a systematic account see D. Girgensohn, *Peter von Pulkau und die Wiedereinführung des Laienkelches* (Göttingen, 1964), pp. 82–120; see also Adrian Fortescue, *The Mass* (2d ed.; London, 1913, repr. 1953), pp. 376–381, with references to sources and Catholic scholarship. Withdrawal of the chalice came to have a more than ceremonial significance, as we shall see below in the section "The Utraquist Controversy," but this came later.

[2] The orthodox theory is summarized in the canonistic gloss quoted below, *ad* n. 17. William Durandus's *Rationale divinorum officiorum* (*ca.* 1270; Venice, 1568), IV, liv, 12–13, offers a clearer distinction between the modes of Christ's presence: "Etsi enim in hostia consecrata Christi sanguis sit, non tamen est ibi sacramentaliter eo quod panis corpus non sanguinem, et vinum sanguinem significat, et non corpus. . . . Sub altera tantum specie non est completum sacramentum, quo ad sacramentum vel signum. . . . Verumtamen cum unum sine reliquo nec sit nec unquam fuerit . . . , secundum hoc

and wine to their followers, they touched off a violent controversy that swallowed up even such apparently more important issues as the attack on the church's endowment, the identification of the pope as supreme Antichrist, and the defiance of ecclesiastical jurisdiction. From that time on the chalice stood as the symbol of the whole movement, the object of most anti-Hussite polemical literature, and the critical point distinguishing all Hussites, quasi-Catholics as well as violent sectarians, from the orthodox communion of the rest of Europe. Finally, at the Council of Basel, Hussite articles that were intrinsically more important than the chalice—free preaching of the Word of God, secular dominion over church property, the extirpation of public sins—proved so negotiable that they could be disposed of by massive Hussite concessions,[3] while the issue of the chalice alone kept its intractable core, in the end preventing a Calixtine reabsorption into the body of Catholicism. All of this seems paradoxical, but it can also be instructive. The historian cannot tell the objects of his solicitude that they were wrong: he must change his own mind and reform his thinking on the assumption that the lay chalice must have been fully as important as contemporaries thought it was. Not a quirk or an ornament, it must in fact have contained the essence of Hussitism.

ON THE ORIGINS OF UTRAQUISM

It has already been suggested, in the first chapter, that Jakoubek's introduction of communion in both kinds may be profitably contrasted with Hus's attempt at reconciliation in the Council of Constance. Utraquism indeed marked and to a considerable extent constituted a turning point in Hussite history; more specifically, it worked, even before Hus's death, to convert the

---

nunc Christi sanguine intra venas eius existente, unum sine reliquo propter unionem seu mistionem huiusmodi recipi non potest, quod tamen non est ratione sacramenti, vel signi quod idem est." Thus, considered as a *sign,* the Eucharist was incomplete without both elements—hence the priest's communion in both kinds; but considered as Christ's actual body and blood, each element contained both body and blood, even if ambiguously, and the lay communicant, taking only the bread, received both body and blood, although in different ways. Many sources could be cited to show that this was usually recognized by the Hussites; a good example is the following stanza of a utraquist song in Czech, "It is Christ's Institution": "Even though the whole Christ is under each of the species, still he is not superfluously given to the people in both kinds; but rather this is fitting, and very beneficial to the people—to do both, eat his body and drink his blood" (text in Nejedlý, VI, 259). But cf. n. 33, below.

[3] Mathilde Uhlirz, "Die Genesis der vier Prager Artikel," *SKAW,* CLXXV (1916), 21 f., offers a convenient comparison of the different texts of the Four Articles of Prague, (1) in their more or less original redaction of 1420/1421, (2) in the form submitted to the Council of Basel in the summer of 1433, and (3) in the final, mutually agreed-on form of the *Compactata* of November 1433.

reform-movement led by Hus into the Hussite movement. In recognition of this fact, no doubt, the Prague town secretary, Master Laurence of Březová, began his history of the Hussite parties and their wars with the introduction of communion in both kinds:

> In the year 1414 the venerable and most divine eucharistic communion in both kinds—that is, of bread and wine—to be given to the faithful laity, was begun in the noble and glorious city of Prague by that venerable and outstanding man, Master Jakoubek of Stříbro, Bachelor of Holy Theology, and by some others then helping him in this matter. It was first begun in the churches of St. Adalbert in the New Town, and St. Martin-in-the-Wall, St. Michael, and Bethlehem Chapel, in the Old Town.[4]

Notice that Laurence felt no need to account for the origin of the new practice, and neither in fact did most other Hussites until much later, well after the revolution had run its course. Perhaps in the 1430's the story arose that Jakoubek had gotten the idea from the Dresden masters, particularly Peter of Dresden. The explanation was taken up by Aeneas Sylvius Piccolomini in his *Historia Bohemica,* but the best modern scholarship rejects this tradition as an attempt to discredit utraquism by assigning it an external, German source.[5] Still later the Calixtine chronicler Bohuslav Bilejovský (d. 1555) attempted to give Hussitism a longer history by tracing utraquism back to the mission of Constantine and Methodius, who introduced the Byzantine practice of utraquism, which then never died out. This hypothesis, picked up by some later writers, enjoyed a revival in the nineteenth century, at which time it was definitely refuted.[6]

At present the only comparable attempt to find a discrete external cause is F. M. Bartoš's theory that Jerome of Prague brought back the idea of communion in both kinds when he returned at the beginning of 1414 from his trip to Lithuania and White Russia, where he had interested himself in the Orthodox rite.[7] It is a theory based on sound evidence for everything but the crucial point, where we must imagine excited conversations between

[4] *FRB,* V, 329 f. The subjects dealt with in the rest of this section are also discussed by Girgensohn, *op. cit.,* pp. 120–164.

[5] The best review of the sources and scholarly opinions is Bartoš's "Z vývoje legendy o Petrovi z Drážďan jako původci kalicha," *Husitství a cizina* (Prague, 1931), pp. 75–80. Josef Pekař, who accepts the Dresden theory, discusses some of the evidence in his *Žižka a jeho doba,* I, 10. The best study in a major language is H. Böhmer's "Magister Peter von Dresden," *Neues Archiv für Sächsische Geschichte und Altertumskunde,* XXXVI (1915), 212–231. And cf. M. Uhlirz, "Petrus von Dresden," *Zeitschrift des Vereins für Geschichte Mährens und Schlesiens,* XVIII (1914), 227–238.

[6] By J. Kalousek, *O historii kalicha v dobách předhusitských* (Prague, 1881).

[7] Bartoš, "Počátky kalicha v Čechách," *Husitství a cizina,* pp. 71–74; the argument is repeated with some additions in *Čechy,* pp. 395–399.

Jerome and his friends about the interesting mode of communion practiced by the Greek Church—which to be sure the Hussites did esteem, following Wyclif, as linked by an especially close tradition to the Primitive Church of the apostles.[8] But even if Bartoš were right, it would still be necessary for the historian to explain *why* Jerome's information had so profound an effect, and if Bartoš is wrong the task of explaining utraquism in terms of internal Hussite ideological development becomes all the more important. Only thus will we be able to bring ourselves to the outlook of the Hussites themselves, whose lack of interest in the question of origins must have stemmed from an unquestioned, perhaps even unrealized, assumption that the innovation was essentially part of their whole body of doctrine, rather than a foreign import.

Having said this, we can find almost complete satisfaction in the one notable passage where Jakoubek of Stříbro explained how he had come on the idea of the lay chalice. He had called it a revelation, and when his antagonist, Dr. Andrew of Brod, challenged him to prove it, he wrote:

> In general I shall term "revelation" a mode of knowledge coming from the scrutiny of the Law of the Lord [i.e., the Bible], and from the solid expositions and authorities of the ancient saints—such as Augustine, Cyprian, Bernard, Chrysostom, and others who followed them in the same sense. By this definition I can concede that I have a revelation, for I have knowledge from the Law and from authoritative writings, and this knowledge, newly acquired in this manner, can be generally called a revelation. For by it, in a certain way, the veil [*velamen*] of ignorance is lifted internally, according to the Psalm [119 (Vulg., 118), 18]: "Open thou [*Revela*] mine eyes, that I may behold wondrous things out of thy Law."[9]

What Jakoubek meant was merely that the flash of suddenly *seeing* the truth in theological texts that one has been studying—an experience we have all

---

[8] A statement of Jakoubek's in this sense is quoted by Bartoš, "Počátky kalicha," p. 73, n. 33. Later on Nicholas of Pelhřimov, Bishop of Tabor, appealed to the authority of the Greek Church to help support Tabor's rejection of Purgatory; he praised the Greek Church as "immediata apostolorum filia, . . . magistra per quam fides primitus ad nos descendit, . . . et per consequens in hoc est prae omni alia moderna excogitatione potius et securius imitanda pro eo quod ipsam immediate docuit Apostolus. . . ." (*Confession of 1431, in Waldensia,* ed. B. Lydius, I (Rotterdam, 1616), 183). For Wyclif's view see, e.g., *Supplementum Trialogi,* ed. G. Lechler, in *Trialogus* (Oxford, 1869), p. 446: ". . . Graecia a tempore suae conversionis per Paulum apostolum servavit nobis longe perfectius fidem Christi. . . ." Most recently Girgensohn, *Peter von Pulkau,* pp. 147 f., has rejected the "Greek" thesis on the grounds that the Greek Church's utraquism was practiced by intinction—the laity did not receive the chalice.

[9] Hardt, III, 566; cited by Bartoš, "Počátky kalicha," pp. 62 f. On Jakoubek's revelation see also Peter of Pulkau's *Pietatis inexpugnabilis,* in Girgensohn, *op. cit.,* pp. 219, 221.

had in less exalted contexts—may be called a revelation, a divine illumination. Today we just call it having an insight, or a new idea, but even so the event keeps enough of its mystery that we can appreciate Jakoubek's explanation without much difficulty. And we can guess from our own experience that if he suddenly had the new idea of utraquism, a whole line of thought must have led him to that point. In this sense the question of utraquist origins turns into the problem of relating utraquism to the main themes of Hussite radicalism up to 1414.

Thanks to the work of a number of scholars, especially Professor Bartoš, this problem can be set up in a fairly concrete form. It would of course be tempting to guess that the veil of ignorance in Jakoubek's mind was torn down at some moment when he was reading what would become the classic text of utraquist apologetics, John 6:53: "Except ye eat the flesh of the Son of man, and drink his blood, ye have no life in you." But this dictum was very well taken care of by the spiritual interpretation that it customarily received[10] and—more important—Bartoš has shown that we do not find it in Jakoubek's first utraquist explorations.[11] Instead, as early as 7 June 1414, we find a reference to the canon "Comperimus" of Pope Gelasius I (492–496):

> We have found that some, taking only the portion of the sacred bread, abstain from the chalice of the sacred blood. I do not know by what superstitious teaching they are bound; but certainly they should either take the sacraments complete or be denied the sacraments complete. For a division of one and the same mystery cannot flourish without great sacrilege.[12]

Thus, still according to Bartoš, Jakoubek's own evidence of what was on his mind in early 1414 suggests that we should look for the origin of the utraquist idea not in some new theological understanding of the sacrament itself—although this point must not be ignored—but in a historical realization that utraquism had been the universal custom of the early church, and that the current practice was a novelty.

Both the Wyclifite and native Bohemian traditions could have stimulated such a realization, and both possibilities have found their scholarly champions.[13] The advocate of Wyclif as the sole source of all Hussite doctrine

---

[10] This interpretation was a weapon used by almost all who attacked the lay chalice; for examples see the anti-Hussite anonymous treatise, *Eloquenti viro,* Hardt, III, 360; also Andrew of Brod's treatises against Jakoubek, Hardt, III, 398 f., 568, the last passage followed by Jakoubek's reply; also, another of the frequent Hussite refutations, Nicholas of Dresden's *Apologia,* Hardt, III, 632 f.

[11] Bartoš, "Počátky kalicha," pp. 84 ff.

[12] *Ibid.,* pp. 62 f., 84 ff.; the dated texts from Jakoubek's sermons are quoted on pp. 84 f. For "Comperimus" see the *Decretum, De cons.,* II. Dist., c. 12.

[13] The following discussion, although based on the works as cited, is indebted in the first place to Bartoš's "Počátky kalicha," pp. 61–71.

was of course Johann Loserth; for the origin of utraquism, however, the Wyclifite case was put by his disciple Mathilde Uhlirz, in a still valuable article, "Die Genesis der vier Prager Artikel." [14] Considering and refuting the alternative possibilities, Uhlirz first attacks the theological problem, arguing that Wyclif's doctrine of remanence, with its insistence that the substance of the bread and wine remained along with the accidents, was much more apt than the theory of transsubstantiation to inspire doubt as to whether the whole Christ, body and blood together, was contained in each of the elements, as orthodoxy declared. Or, as Bartoš puts it more precisely:

> Jakoubek, joining Wyclif in rejecting transsubstantiation, was thereby actually rejecting the dogmatic basis of communion in one kind, and was returning to the eucharistic doctrine that existed in the period when the [lay] chalice still survived. This doctrine assigned the second species, of wine, the function of spiritual nourishment (as the bread was held to be nourishment of the body), and found itself in sharp theoretical conflict with the universal church practice of communion in one kind. It can just about be said that Jakoubek, by his return to the chalice, only thought out what Wyclif had taken the first step toward.[15]

Bartoš goes on to say that this logical relationship must not be regarded as a causal one: Wyclif did not deduce utraquism from remanence, and there is no reason to think that Jakoubek did; all that can be said, presumably, is that the two theories fitted together. But even this is not as clear as Uhlirz and Bartoš suppose, for the orthodox theory of transsubstantiation could coexist with doubts about the integrity of the sacrament in each species. To show this, and also to help illuminate subsequent discussion, we may quote the *glossa ordinaria* on the Gelasian canon given above:

> *"For a division . . ."* This is understood of these external species. For it is impossible that the body of Christ be taken without the blood, and *vice versa.* For whether one takes the species of bread or the species of wine, he takes both; and they are here called two sacraments, but also one, on account of their single content. Indeed there is more than one sacrament there: the accidents of the bread are only the sacrament of Christ's body, the accidents of the wine only the sacrament of Christ's blood. For certainly the body and blood of Christ are under the species of the bread—nay the whole Christ is there; likewise under the species of the wine. But there is no double taking of the body and blood of Christ, nor is the one or the other taking superfluous: just as, if at the same meal I eat before drinking and after drinking, I am

---

[14] *SKAW,* CLXXV (1916), No. III; pp. 45–66 deal with utraquism (the second article). Though solid as far as it goes, Uhlirz's study is fatally crippled by her inattention to the basic works of Czech scholars.

[15] Bartoš, "Počátky kalicha," pp. 64 f.

still not said to eat twice. And communion is not taken superfluously when taken under both species; for the species of bread refers to the flesh, that of the wine to the soul, since wine is the sacrament of the blood, in which is the seat of the soul. And so it is taken under both species, to signify that Christ took on both—the flesh and the soul—and that both sorts of participation, in the soul and in the body, are valid. Therefore if communion were taken only under one species, this would mean that its value extended only to the viewing of the other.[16] But we do not concede this proposition: "The wine is transsubstantiated into the body of Christ." Nor this: "The bread is transsubstantiated into the blood." But rather the bread is only transsubstantiated into the flesh and the wine only into the blood; nevertheless, wherever the flesh is, there is the blood—but the flesh is there by transsubstantiation, and the blood by commixtion; just as the soul is there by union, not by transsubstantiation.[17]

One of the functions of a legal apparatus was to raise doubts in order to dispose of them, and it is no insult to the author of this gloss to observe that a sensitive reader of it, alert to theological problems, would not need any help from Wyclif to make him wonder about the relationship between the two parts of the sacrament. Furthermore, the gloss itself develops an argument for communion in both kinds, with the help of the very same older theory that Bartoš has associated with Wyclif's remanentist doctrine. Here, as in regard to the Gelasian decree, the commentator (John Teutonicus, d. 1246) was thinking only of the priest's communion,[18] but his words told their own story. We shall come back to this gloss later; meanwhile it serves to show that Wyclifite remanence was not necessary even as a logical correlate of utraquism, let alone as a cause.

But Uhlirz also advances a more substantial argument for Wyclif's influence:[19] "In the grounding of his demand [for the lay chalice] Jakoubek was led above all by Wyclif's doctrine of the unlimited authority of Holy Writ, whose commands might never be changed by the prescriptions of the Roman church." We are here pointed in the right direction, toward a historical rather than a primarily theological critique of the Roman practice, and certainly Wyclif's influence in this respect need not be belittled. But Jakou-

[16] "Unde si sub una tantum specie sumeretur, ad tuitionem alterius tantum valere significaretur [*scil.*, participatio?]."

[17] I use the edition of Lyons, 1613; the gloss, *in verba* "Quia divisio," is on coll. 1917–1918.

[18] See the gloss *in verba* "Aut integra," col. 1917: "Id est, integre: sub utraque enim specie Christus integre sumitur: et hoc intelligo de conficiente: nam infirmus, vel sanus in necessitate sine vino corpus sumere potest." The author evidently took it for granted that only the priest's communion was in question.

[19] Uhlirz, "Die Genesis," p. 61.

bek's appreciation of the difference between the Primitive and Roman churches was cultivated much less by Wyclifism than by the doctrines of Matthew of Janov, whose influence Uhlirz was not prepared to recognize.[20] In fact the Janovian theory, represented in modern scholarship chiefly by Vlastimil Kybal and Jan Sedlák, offers the most satisfying approach to the problem of utraquist origins. Kybal, who edited Matthew's *magnum opus* and wrote a monograph on his life and thought, was only incidentally concerned with this problem, but his formulations still deserve to be quoted at length:

> Janov knows only one question [in regard to the Eucharist]: whether frequent communion is permitted and advantageous to the laity. . . . For Matthew of Janov the chalice is an irrelevant question. . . . An external formality like communion from the chalice did not matter to Matthew in his propagation of frequent communion. . . .

> Nevertheless, it is impossible not to recognize an organic and developmental connection between the two symbols of the Bohemian religious movement in the fourteenth and fifteenth centuries. What frequent communion was to the followers of John Milíč in the fourteenth century, the chalice was to the Hussites and utraquists of the fifteenth. Both symbols accurately characterize the religious nature of their times. The original religious content and meaning of the idea of the chalice were, negatively, that of protest against the privileges of the clergy, especially the unworthy clergy; positively, that of return to the practice of primitive Christianity. . . . We find both of these tendencies also in the idea of frequent communion in the fourteenth century. The followers of Milíč, especially Matthew of Janov, worked for frequent communion by the laity in order to elevate the latter's moral and religious life according to the model of evangelical Christianity; and thereby they protested against the privileges of the unworthy clergy. This reforming aspect of the demand for frequent communion is quite obvious and undeniable in Matthew of Janov. . . .

> The historical value and fruitfulness of particular ideas lie in their capacity to adapt themselves to given conditions and needs. . . . The idea of frequent communion by the laity . . . satisfied the religious needs of the souls of that

[20] On p. 55 she mentions Kybal's views (see just below) but dismisses them without due discussion, perhaps because she used not his (Czech) monograph but his (French) summary of it (see above, chap. i, n. 30). Her conclusion: "Jacobell hat gewiss die Lehren Janows gekannt; aber gerade in diesen wichtigen Fragen [*scil.,* of the reduction of the clergy to their estate in the early church] lässt sich eine Abhängigkeit von Janow nicht erwiesen," is simply wrong. See the references to Kybal's work (1905) on Jakoubek's use of Janov (above, chap. i, n. 145) and to Sedlák's even more extensive proofs in his "Počátkové kalicha" (1911) (below), and in *ST,* I (1914) (above, chap. ii, n. 90). Uhlirz's article appeared in 1916, not too early for any of these.

time. . . . Its meaning and tendency were profoundly reformist, but its external form was ecclesiastical and as orthodox as possible. The priests were the only creators and distributors of this reforming medicine. Further development required that this thought be made concrete and that it be sharply and openly aimed against the priests. From this need flowed the idea of the chalice.[21]

These general judgements found a needed confirmation in the work of Sedlák, whose analysis of Jakoubek's first formal utraquist statement, his university *posicio* of October/November 1414, showed how much had been taken from Matthew of Janov's *Regule:*

> Jakoubek simply takes over as proofs for utraquism the authorities cited by Matthew for frequent communion, like: *Nisi manducaveritis . . .* [John 6:53], *Bibite ex hoc omnes* [Matt. 26:27], *Homo quidam fecit cenam magnam* [Luke 14:16], *Probet seipsum homo* [I Cor. 11:28], Pope Anacletus's decretal [*Decretum, De cons.,* II. dist., c. 10], etc. And he works them out using Janov's phraseology. Jakoubek's university *posicio* for communion in both kinds is the fruit of his study of the Parisian master's [*scil.,* Janov's] *Regule.*[22]

Sedlák offers a series of parallel quotations to show how Jakoubek operated, but these need not be reproduced here. Instead we can look at a text illustrating a somewhat different aspect of Kybal's theory—not Jakoubek's undeniable *use* of Janov, but his possible indebtedness to Janov for the utraquist idea itself; many Janovian passages could be cited, but the following was actually written out by a utraquist author as one of a series of authorities in behalf of the chalice:

> Master Matthew the Parisian: "There is no scripture, no reason, no usefulness, in the idea that one man can take the sacrament for another, or that the priest should consume the body of Christ for those who are present. For this sacrament has been instituted and given as food and drink [*in racione cibi et potus*]. . . . And so, just as actual [*veri*] food and drink cannot give pleasure or enjoyment to a man unless he personally and in fact [*in actu*] eats the food and drinks the drink, so also the case must be judged in regard to taking the sacrament of the altar."[23]

[21] Kybal, *M. Matěj z Janova* (Prague, 1905), pp. 315–317.
[22] Sedlák, "Počátkové kalicha," *ČKD,* LII (1911), 499.
[23] I use the text in MS UP, III G 28, f. 190ʳ–190ᵛ; the passage may be found in Matthew's *Regulae,* V, edd. V. Kybal and O. Odložilík (Prague, 1926), 274 f. The series of authorities of which the quoted passage is part appears in several MSS as an appendix to Nicholas of Dresden's utraquist sermon on *Nisi manducaveritis;* Sedlák mentions it in his "Počátkové kalicha" (1911), 789, and draws the same conclusions I do.

This was not an argument for the lay chalice, only for frequent communion by the laity; but without any distortion or important omission the words seem *obviously* to imply that the laity should take the chalice as well as the bread. Thus, not only was the meaning of frequent communion related to the meaning of utraquism, not only did the arguments for one serve the case for the other, but the demand for frequent communion could actually seem to be a demand for communion in both kinds. Jakoubek himself knew Matthew's work too well to be misled by such appearances, and as Bartoš has wisely observed, what seems obvious in retrospect was not so at the time; [24] but when we consider so hopeless a problem as that of intellectual origins— what conceivable source could give us a certain solution?—we are well advised to exclude no reasonable possibility. Matthew's words could easily have started a train of thought leading to an idea that Matthew had not had, [25] and if Jakoubek himself never cited Matthew as an authority for the lay chalice, his disciple and successor in Prague, John Rokycana, did so, quite explicitly. [26]

In any case, the opinions and texts that have just been canvassed suggest, among other things, that to understand the meaning of the utraquist innovation we must see it as an integral part of general Hussite development. Here we may refer to what has been said of the radicals and their work in the first two chapters, and recall that Jakoubek was not the only intellectual leader on the Hussite left; with him stood the important figure of Nicholas of Dresden. As already noted, some sources attribute the origin of Hussite utraquism to the Dresden masters, presumably including Nicholas, but insofar as these texts single out any individual it is Peter of Dresden who comes to the fore. [27] Still, Nicholas's name is not absent, [28] and the surviving literature of

---

[24] Bartoš, "Počátky kalicha," p. 65.

[25] This is also Sedlák's interpretation of Jakoubek's revelation, "Počátkové kalicha," (1911), 247 f.

[26] Kybal, *M. Matěj z Janova*, p. 2, with references to the sources. Also J. Prokeš, *M. Prokop z Plzně* (Prague, 1927), p. 26.

[27] See note 5 above. The undue importance attached to Peter of Dresden by historians has its source partly in the prominent role played by Peter in Aeneas Sylvius's account of the origins of utraquism, *Historia bohemica*, ch. xxxv.

[28] An anonymous account (in Höfler, III, 156 ff.) mentions his name along with Peter's as leader of the school in Dresden, where utraquism, among other heresies, was allegedly taught. Almost all scholars reject this information (e.g., Sedlák, *Mikuláš z Drázďan*, p. 2, n. 2; Bartoš, "Počátky kalicha," p. 67). Annalistic rhymes in Czech also talk of Nicholas along with Peter (but Peter "English"—i.e., Payne—not Peter of Dresden) as introducers of utraquism; here too, however, scholarly opinion has been reserved. The passage reads (*OCA*, p. 472): "That year the Dresden masters and bachelors lived . . . in Prague and had a college there: Master Peter and Master Nicholas, [that is, Peter] English and Nicholas Loripes. They had been expelled from

utraquist polemic shows that he played a very important role, infinitely more important than that of Peter; perhaps the sources naming the latter were in fact based, confusedly, on the preeminence of his colleague.[29] For one thing, Nicholas composed several powerful defenses of the lay chalice; in one of them, moreover, he explicitly indicated his membership in the circle of leaders:

> According to what [Jesus] himself instituted and practiced, and the Primi-
> tive Church after him, . . . we began to give the sacrament in both kinds, in
> his name, to all piously wishing them: not at our own whim, as the doctors
> [*scil.,* of the Council of Constance] claim, but according to the primitive
> institution of the son of God, and after long and mature preliminary
> deliberation with the masters and others who love the Law of Christ.[30]

That there was such a leading circle appears also from a corresponding passage in one of Jakoubek's works, where he replies to a charge of rashness and observes that the charge was directed against himself "and the others who are leading in this matter."[31] It is thus reasonable to ask whether Nicholas was not perhaps more than just a leader, but rather the originator of the idea. Again there is no way of proving one or another answer.

F. M. Bartoš makes the strongest case for Nicholas—to be sure, only to reject it. He observes that at the time when the idea of utraquism was emerging, in the first half of 1414, Nicholas was working on his *Puncta,* a rather disorganized discussion of many points, treated as was Nicholas's wont, by an accumulation of Biblical, canonistic, patristic, and medieval authorities, without much editorial matter.[32] Perhaps, suggests Bartoš,

---

Dresden for they had secretly given the Lord's blood. They began to advise Master Jičín to begin to give the Lord's blood, and he took this advice and persuaded Master Jakoubek and many other priests to join him. . . ."

[29] This is Bartoš's hypothesis, "Počátky kalicha," pp. 67 ff. Sedlák however attributes two utraquist tractates to Peter of Dresden ("Počátkové kalicha," *ČKD,* LIV (1913), 708–713), and if he is right, Peter must have in fact played a significant role among the pioneers of the lay chalice. But Bartoš offers more or less persuasive arguments for identifying the Peter in question with Peter Payne, who is actually named as author of one of the tractates by two MSS ("Počátky kalicha," pp. 89 f., 103 f.; *LČPP,* No. 1).

[30] The passage was cited by Sedlák, "Počátkové kalicha" (1913), 407; it appears in Nicholas's *Apologia,* Hardt, III, 616 (Von der Hardt's attribution of this work to Jakoubek is incorrect). In the same work Nicholas frequently refers to himself in the first person singular (e.g.: col. 620, "dico"; 628, "eligam," "scio"); so the "we" in the quoted passage must be understood as plural in meaning. For Nicholas's other utraquist works see the bibliography in *OC & N,* pp. 30 f.

[31] *Apud* Sedlák, *op. cit.,* p. 408.

[32] Bartoš, "Počátky kalicha," pp. 68–70; for the *Puncta* see *OC & N,* introduction and bibliography.

Nicholas's apparently haphazard order was really derived from Lombard's *Sentences,* followed loosely and selectively. Perhaps in working on this material Nicholas came to the part on the sacraments, set about compiling his authorities, and in so doing found Gelasius's canon, *"Comperimus,"* the utraquist implications of which he presumably grasped in the light of the whole tendency of the *Puncta,* to set the old church order against the new. Nicholas would then have stopped work on the *Puncta*—which remains unfinished—and rushed to tell Jakoubek the news. There is romance in this hypothesis but also a certain meatiness, for insofar as we are prepared to assign an important stimulatory role to the canonistic dossier in the period of utraquist origins, we are naturally led to think of Nicholas of Dresden, whose specialty, displayed so well in the *Tabule,* was precisely the use of *Decretum* and Decretals to develop the ideology of the two churches. We may add that Nicholas was also familiar with the glosses—more so than the other Hussites—and that the above quoted *glossa ordinaria* on *"Comperimus,"* with its discussion of the nonsuperfluity of communion in both kinds, was actually quoted in part by Nicholas, to show how Christ was not integral in only one of the sacramental elements.[33] Having said this, however, we have said all that there is to justify giving Nicholas credit for the idea of utraquism. Nothing has been proved but at least the substance of the problem has been illuminated, and we are pointed toward a further consideration of what utraquism really meant, in the context of radical Hussite doctrine.

THE UTRAQUIST CONTROVERSY

Although the preliminary discussions of the chalice by Hussite radical leaders must have brought out many possible objections, there is no evidence of open controversy until Jakoubek of Stříbro's university determination in October or November of 1414.[34] With the condemnation of the chalice by the Council of Constance on 15 June 1415 the controversy became much more

[33] *Apologia,* Hardt, III, 601 f. Nicholas here quoted only the last few sentences, from "But we do not concede . . ." to the end, with an interesting and unfortunately characteristic distortion: where the gloss reads ". . . panis tantum transsubstantiatur in carnem . . . ," Nicholas leaves out "transsubstantiatur." Another portion of the gloss is quoted *ibid.,* col. 605.

[34] Sedlák and Bartoš, the only considerable authorities, are in hopeless disagreement over the dating of utraquism and the sources therefor. The question will be taken up in the following section; meanwhile I note that in general I follow Bartoš, who regards Jakoubek's university *questio* (*LČJ,* No. 33) as the beginning of the written polemic ("Počátky kalicha," p. 86 f.). He dates it after Hus's departure for Constance, 11 October 1414, and dates the *practice* of communion in both kinds after the *questio.*

extensive and even violent; only a few weeks later, on 6 July, the Council had John Hus burnt at the stake, and the two issues were joined from then on in a mutually reinforcing union. The polemic continued to develop until 1417, when some of the most interesting treatises were written, but then lost much of its urgency; other problems supervened for both the Hussites and the Romanists.[35] Considered as a whole, from 1414 through 1417, the controversy forms a remarkable chapter in late-medieval intellectual history, comparable in breadth and depth to the earlier controversies over the legitimacy of the mendicant orders and the poverty of Christ. But surprisingly few scholars have done much with it; most of the treatises remain unpublished, and the only important collection of texts is still that of Hermann von der Hardt, in the third volume of his *Magnum Concilium Constantiense,* published in 1698.[36] Among Czech Hussitologues, only Jan Sedlák has attempted a systematic discussion of *all* the sources, and his frankly tentative effort, published a half-century ago, was not completed.[37] F. M. Bartoš has subjected some of the same material to a more critical review, but he covers only a small part of the extant sources.[38] In any case, neither Sedlák nor Bartoš has written a history of the controversy; both have been necessarily more concerned with problems of *Quellenkritik,* dating, and attribution than with the structure of the polemic.

Nor can such a history be attempted here—a whole volume would be needed, and more sources would have to be edited. What can be done here is to subject the polemical positions to a logical analysis, showing the major

[35] Sedlák, "Počátkové kalicha" (1911), p. 98, defines the "beginnings of the chalice" as lasting until 1420, and subdivides this period into three parts: (1) from the origins—at the end of 1413—to the prohibition by the Council of Constance, 15 June 1415; (2) from then to the University of Prague's declaration in favor of utraquism, 10 March 1417; (3) from then to the events of 1420: the formulation of the Four Articles and the beginning of the Hussite wars. His own study remained incomplete, and went only through stage two. If I here consider the arguments *pro* and *con* from 1414 to 1417 as composing a single debate, it is only for purposes of formal analysis; there remains a problem of *historical* periodization, which I attend to in the subsequent parts of this study.

[36] C. M. D. Crowther, "Le concile de Constance et l'édition de von der Hardt," *Revue d'histoire ecclésiastique,* LVII (1962), 409–445, offers a valuable discussion of Hardt's work, with bibliographical leads; he does not however deal with the materials that interest us here.

[37] Sedlák, "Počátkové kalicha," *ČKD,* LII (1911), 97–105, 244–250, 397–401, 496–501, 583–587, 703–708, 786–791; LIV (1913), 226–232, 275–278, 404–410, 465–470, 708–713; LV (1914), 75–84, 113–120, 315–322.

[38] Bartoš, "Počátky kalicha v Čechách," *ČČM,* XCVI (1922), 43–51, 157–173; XCVII (1923), 34–51; repr. in *Husitství a cizina,* pp. 59–112 (from which I cite it). The systematic study of the sources for the first year of the controversy is on pp. 80–107.

points at issue, the relationship between them, and—to some extent—the meaning of the controversy, both as an indicator of late-medieval thinking and as a factor in Hussite development. Thus far the best discussion of these matters has been Emile Amann's "Jacobel et les débuts de la controverse utraquiste"; [39] the context of the present work, however, should allow us to push the analysis somewhat further than Amann could go. At the same time, the discussion will be as brief as possible, covering only the major points and making no effort to draw all the treatises into the documentation; one example will often do duty where a half-dozen could be given.

The basic point at issue is perhaps the easiest to present. Had Jesus decreed communion in both kinds to be (1) the proper form of the sacrament and (2) necessary to salvation? [40] What he had actually done and said were of course not matters of doubt. The Synoptic Gospels agree—Matthew and Mark almost literally—that at the Last Supper,

> as they were eating, Jesus took bread, and blessed it, and broke it, and gave it to the disciples, and said, "Take, eat; this is my body." And he took the cup, and gave thanks, and gave it to them, saying, "Drink you all of it; for this is my blood of the new testament, which is shed for many for the remission of sins." [41]

This was the prime text quoted by the utraquists, in combination with John 6:53, "Except ye eat the flesh of the Son of man and drink his blood, ye have no life in you"; [42] together the two seemed to prove that Jesus had instituted communion in both kinds as necessary to salvation. The Catholics, however, argued against this conclusion, in several ways. First, the layman

[39] In *Miscellanea Francesco Ehrle*, I (Rome, 1924), 375–387. The work by Ivan Palmov, *Vopros o čaše v gusitskom dviženii* (St. Petersburg, 1881), has not been available to me; like Amann's essay, it is based on the sources printed in Hardt, III.

[40] Jean Gerson put the question so (Hardt, III, 773): ". . . illud, circa quod versatur difficultas, sicut in puncto, centro, vel cardine, est: Si communicatio talis sub utraque specie sit jussa generaliter a Christo sub debito salutis aeternae, et indispensabiliter ab homine." As an example of a sacrament necessary to salvation he cited baptism by water —no authority or custom could be introduced to the effect "ut certi homines non baptizarentur baptismo aquae." Since he undoubtedly recognized that in special cases men might be saved without the baptism of water—baptism of spirit and baptism of fire could do duty—his concept of necessity must be understood in a limited sense, not unlike Jakoubek's understanding of the necessity of the Eucharist in both kinds (below, *ad* nn. 51, 52).

[41] Matt. 26:26–28; Mark 14:22–24; cf. Luke 22:17–20.

[42] For examples of the utraquists' use of this combination as the primary authority see Hardt, III, 805 f. (a dossier sent to the Council of Constance and often ascribed to Jakoubek; Bartoš suggests Jesenic (*LČJ*, p. 69, No. 8)); also the dossier appended to the second Prague Article in 1420/1421, in Laurence of Březová's chronicle, *FRB*, V, 391 f. I. Cor. 10:16; 11:27,29, were also used as basic sources.

who received the body in the species of bread could be said to have also received the blood, for the real presence of Jesus was integral in each species.[43] Second, the text from John was to be understood as of spiritual communion—Jesus had said, "the words that I speak unto you, they are spirit" (John 6:63).[44] Indeed it was in this spiritual sense that the laity also received the blood.[45] And insofar as John 6:53 laid down a condition necessary to salvation it could not be understood of eucharistic communion, for this sacrament was not necessary to salvation.[46] Finally, these two lines of argument were supplemented by a Romanist interpretation of the Last Supper that differed sharply from the Hussite one. For one thing, the disciples were understood as a figure for the future clergy, and the gathering at the Last Supper was thus taken as a paradigm of the clerical corporation; since the priests did take communion in both kinds during the Roman mass, the institution of Jesus was preserved.[47] For another, it was noted that Jesus had instituted two things, a sacrifice and a sacrament of communion; his command, "This do in remembrance of me" (Luke 22:19), was obeyed by the Roman priest who offered up both the body and blood and consumed them both, while the sacrament was preserved by lay communion in only one kind, according to the arguments already noted.[48]

The Hussites did not deny that the complete Christ was present in each of the species, nor that John 6:53 was to be understood spiritually, but, as Jakoubek cogently argued, these points were not at issue. It did not follow that because Christ was wholly present in the consecrated bread, he therefore gave his blood sacramentally in that form; on the contrary, he explicitly gave himself sacramentally in two forms, as food in the bread and as drink in the

[43] E.g., the doctors of the Council of Constance, citing Thomas Aquinas (Hardt, III, 630): "qui communicat corpori, communicat sanguini, cum sub utraque specie totus Christus contineatur." The point appears in almost every anti-utraquist treatise.

[44] E.g., *loc. cit.;* also the treatise *Eloquenti viro* (*ibid.,* III, 360 f.); also Andrew of Brod, quoted by Jakoubek, *ibid.,* III, 419. No anti-utraquist treatise omits this point.

[45] E.g., Andrew of Brod, quoted by Jakoubek (Hardt, III, 540): "fidelis laicus et sine mortali peccato, sumens corpus Christi sacramentaliter sub forma panis, sumit spiritualiter sanguinem Christi."

[46] E.g., the treatise *Estote sine offensione,* Hardt, III, 699–702; also Jean Gerson, Hardt, III, 775.

[47] *Estote sine offensione,* Hardt, III, 708: "Etiam Christus exclusit septuaginta duos discipulos, in signum, quod laici non possunt hanc habere autoritatem offerre in altari. Quia tunc septuaginta duo discipuli gesserunt locum et vicem omnium fidelium laicorum futurae communitatis. Sed apostoli gesserunt vicem omnium sacerdotum in futurum fiendorum." See also Peter of Pulkau, *Pietatis inexpugnabilis,* ed. Girgensohn, *Peter von Pulkau,* p. 246.

[48] Hardt, III, 706 f. (". . . institutio Christi est principalissime oblatio sacerdotis in altari."); also 746 f.

wine.[49] As for the spiritual interpretation of John 6:53, it could not be used to justify denying the chalice to the laity without also justifying a denial of the bread;[50] moreover, although there were several possible forms of spiritual communion, there was one particular mode instituted by Jesus for the community of Christians here on earth—namely the Eucharist, in both kinds. Spiritual communion did not exclude sacramental communion: the pious Christian, receiving both consecrated elements, was taking communion spiritually as well as sacramentally, and such communion, if available, was indeed necessary to salvation.[51] If the priest refused the chalice the responsibility was his and the layman suffered no penalty; in a similar sense the sacrament itself was not necessary—a man could be saved without it if he had no chance to get it, but ordinarily it was available and the faithful Christian was required to take it.[52] Finally, the Hussites did not deny that the mass was a sacrifice: more interestingly perhaps, they ignored that issue, as indeed did most of the Catholic writers.[53] Given the extraordinary em-

[49] Jakoubek's treatise against Andrew of Brod, Hardt, III, 456–459. See above, n. 2.

[50] E.g., Nicholas of Dresden's sermon on *Nisi manducaveritis*, MS UP, IV G 15, fol. 210ᵛ: "Sic in presenti, [heretici glozant] scripturam presentem—'Nisi manducaveritis . . .'; quia transiit in diswetudinem, multipliciter impungnatur, ne populo detur calix consecratus, [dicunt quod calix datur] iam per comunionem spiritualem: non advertentes quod eadem racio concludit quo ad corpus Cristi, et quod Cristus hec verba dixit de comunio sacramentali, spirituali tamen non exclusa." For this work in general see Sedlák, "Počátkové kalicha" (1911), 786–789.

[51] Jakoubek vs. Andrew of Brod, Hardt, III, 425 f.: "Modus autem spiritualis proprie dictus in forma sacramentali duplici manducandi et bibendi corpus et sanguinem Christi, est, sumere verum corpus Christi in forma panis et bibere ejus sanguinem in forma vini." Also 433: "Concedam . . . quod illud verbum Salvatoris: *Nisi manducaveritis carnem filii hominis,* debet spiritualiter intelligi et non carnaliter, . . . sed non sic spiritualiter, quod non etiam sacramentaliter." And cf. the text quoted in the preceding note. Sedlák, "Počátkové kalicha" (1911), 497 f., shows that Jakoubek's theoretical discussion of spiritual and sacramental communion is taken largely from Matthew of Janov.

[52] Jakoubek vs. Andrew of Brod, Hardt, III, 433: ". . . si hoc sensibile sacramentum aufertur eis per sacerdotum negligentiam, et non in eis sed in sacerdotibus est defectus, tunc gratiosus et clementissimus Dominus et Pontifex Christus, ut confido, seipsum dat suis spiritualiter tantum ad fruendum." And: "Quia communitas laicalis, sine peccatis mortalibus vivens communiter in observatione mandatorum Dei, in sumtione integri sacramenti manducat spiritualiter corpus Christi, et debet sic manducare sub prima specie et bibere ejus sanguinem sub altera specie." This concept of the *ordinary* necessity of the sacrament of the Eucharist was refuted by Hus's successor in Bethlehem, Havlík, who opposed utraquism (Sedlák, "Počátkové kalicha" (1911), 39); also by the author of *Eloquenti viro,* Hardt, III, 363 f.

[53] Jakoubek's repeated failure to discuss the issue is noted by Sedlák, "Počátkové kalicha" (1911), 496, 586; (1913), 227. Nicholas also ignored the difference between mass and communion (*ibid.* (1911), 788). Some Catholic writers did draw attention to

phasis that the Janovian tradition placed on eucharistic communion as the key to regeneration of Christian life, it is not surprising that Jakoubek and Nicholas of Dresden were concerned exclusively with the sacramental aspect of the Eucharist; no doubt many of their Catholic opponents in Bohemia, partaking of that same tradition, agreed with them.[54]

In any case, the Hussites' ecclesiological use of the Last Supper opened up a field of argument that led directly away from an appreciation of the sacrificial aspect of the mass. The disciples were of course to be leaders of churches, bishops, but at the Supper, in relation to so great a shepherd as Jesus, they could stand only as his sheep; he gave them food, they took it. Thus, as Jakoubek declared, they stood for "the whole future church militant," whose head was Jesus,[55] and in the communion that he gave, they occupied the place of the future laity.[56] Otherwise there would be no man-

---

the significance of the distinction between sacrifice and communion (e.g., as noted above, n. 48; also Peter of Pulkau's *Pietatis inexpugnabilis* (May, 1415), ed. Girgensohn, *Peter von Pulkau*, pp. 234, 248; also, much later, the eucharistic treatise forming part of Peter of Pulkau's work against the Four Articles, MS VNB, 4293, fol. 66ᵛ–67ʳ; also the author of *Eloquenti viro*, Hardt, III, 368 f.); but in relation to its great theoretical importance, the distinction was hardly exploited.

[54] Stephen of Páleč had of course been a leader of the reform party before his conversion to Romanism. And Jakoubek himself recalled that Andrew of Brod had once been on the side of those who wanted to prune away excessive rituals and traditions: "Memini enim Doctorem remurmurasse contra institutionem multitudinis horarum, orationum vocalium psalmorum et multi cantus clamorosi, excessivi et superflui, quae sunt ad fastum secularium et avaritiam cleri adinventa, quibus carnales clerici et seducti laici plus innituntur, quam sequelae et legi Domini Jesu Christi" (Hardt, III, 527). This particular aspect of the reform was of Janovian inspiration, as was also the extreme emphasis placed on the cult of the Eucharist. Both Andrew and Stephen had undoubtedly drunk of these waters. See also above, chap. i, n. 112.

[55] Jakoubek vs. Andrew of Brod, Hardt, III, 442 f.: ". . . discipuli in coena Domini, adhuc nimis fragiles ad peccandum existentes, tunc gesserunt vicem et figuram totius communitatis futurae fidelium usque ad consummationem seculi, in suscipiendo corporis et sanguinis Christi sacramentum sub utraque specie." A corresponding passage in his *Posicio pro informacione monachi Petri (de Uničov)*, written two years later, in 1417, refers to the disciples as "gerent[es] in hoc vicem tocius future ecclesie militantis usque ad diem iudicii, sic quod in hoc et in comparacione ad tantum pastorem non habebant se ut pastores sed ut oves pascue eius, tenentes locum et vicem tocius communitatis ecclesie future" (MS VNB, 4488, fol. 97ᵛ; cf. *LCJ*, No. 46). As for the idea that Jesus was the proper head of the church militant, this apparently reasonable doctrine must be understood as a specific attack on the Romanist doctrine that the pope was head of the church on earth—e.g., in the treatise *Estote sine offensione*, Hardt, III, 659: "Multa enim membra unum corpus sunt, videlicet ipsa ecclesia Dei, cujus caput Vicarius Christi demonstratur"; see also n. 72 below.

[56] Jakoubek vs. Andrew of Brod, Hardt, III, 444: "Dominus Jesus per haec consecrationis verba alloquendo discipulos alloquebatur futuram plebem Christianorum. . . . Et

date here for any future lay communion, even in one kind.[57] In line with this interpretation, there was added another relevant consideration: Gelasius's canon "Comperimus" had indeed been glossed to make it refer only to the priests, but why should communion in only one kind be sacrilege for the priest but not sacrilege for the layman? "In the matter of communion [*racione comunicacionis*] the priest is not to be set higher than the layman, nor the other way around, but he is to be set higher whose devotion disposes him better."[58] At this point a Catholic could presumably argue that the *sacrifice* of the mass did give a special status to the priests' communion, but if the utraquists considered this question at all, they seem to have felt that the sacrifice was consummated by the communion of all.[59] In fact, Hussitism's single idea of reform was that all the faithful, clergy and laity, should follow Christ's law by imitating his virtues: it was a reform centered in the individual Christian, not in the ecclesiastical institution. For this reason the disciples at the Last Supper *had* to stand for the whole future church; as Jakoubek put it:

per consequens discipuli virtute illorum verborum sumentes eucharistiam utriusque speciei, figurabant in hoc, quod posterior plebs fidelis virtute eorundem verborum deberet eandem eucharistiam sumere sub utraque specie. Et hoc voco in proposito discipulos gerere vicem futurae plebis Christi." Thus they represented not only the whole future church (as in n. 55) but also the future *laity*.

[57] Hardt, III, 445: "Quod si discipuli tunc non gesserunt vicem futurae plebis in suscipiendo hoc divinissimum sacramentum sub utraque specie: Tunc per idem, nec gesserunt vicem populi ad suscipiendum tantum sub prima specie. Eo, quod non datur ratio diversitatis."

[58] Nicholas of Dresden, sermon on *Nisi manducaveritis,* MS UP, IV G 15, fol. 202[r]: "Rogo qua racione sacerdos in sumendo non integrum committeret sacrilegium et non laicus, cum racione comunicacionis non est sacerdos preferendus nec e converso, sed qui se melius per devocionem disponit" (Also quoted by Sedlák, "Počátkové kalicha" (1911), 787, n. 89). Cf. also Jakoubek vs Andrew of Brod, Hardt, III, 477: "sumtio sacramenti est ejusdem rationis in sacerdote et in laico, circumscripta confectione auctoritativa sacerdotali."

[59] Thus Nicholas of Dresden, sermon on *Nisi manducaveritis* (as above, fol. 203[r]): "Item si hoc esset tantum dictum apostolis, Bibite ex eo omnes, eadem racione solum ipsis esset dictum illud, Accipite et dividite inter vos. Et sic quantum ad plebem omnino cessaret comunio sacramentalis et per consequens iuge sacrificium, quod est anticristicum—Daniel. 12 [11]." Compare Matthew of Janov's complaint about lack of frequent communion (quoted by Sedlák, "Počátkové kalicha" (1911), 499): ". . . communitas plebis christiane cessavit hoc nostrum iuge sacrificium ymmolare . . . propter negligenciam vel crudelitatem quorundam ministrorum. . . ." More study would be needed to determine whether this concept of the sacrifice actually competed with the usual concept based on the priest's offering and consuming of the consecrated elements; meanwhile I offer these passages as possible indications of how Nicholas's and Jakoubek's minds were working.

Otherwise the evangelical law itself would not pertain to the Christian community—that is, if the disciples of Christ who received that law from the Lord had not held the place of the future community of the faithful.[60]

Utraquism was only one part of this law, a law that, binding upon all individual Christians, constituted them a community, the true church.

The utraquist controversy has thus led us back to the basic themes of Hussite ideology, in particular to the crucial concept of the Primitive Church as at once an inspirational ideal and a model for imitation. These themes were well developed before the introduction of the lay chalice and their appearance in utraquist polemics was certainly not accidental. Whether the cult of the Primitive Church actually generated the utraquist innovation in one way or another, or whether the case for the chalice, as argued by the radicals, necessarily disposed itself along their general ideological framework —the union between the two is clear enough. Still, the polemics surrounding the theory and practice of utraquism brought Hussite ideology to a new level of definition: its spokesmen found themselves forced to elaborate and justify their ideas, and they could focus their attacks not merely upon the Roman system but upon the specific body that had both condemned the lay chalice and killed John Hus—the Council of Constance, where all the sinful, simoniac, gluttonous, fornicating, luxurious, cruel, and powerful prelates were conveniently brought together in an all-too-visible society. Thus, for example, in defending the chalice against the Council's condemnation, Nicholas of Dresden had only to unleash his remarkable gift for imagery to produce the following picture:

> Suppose as a possibility that Christ and his Primitive Church, with their apostolic life and evangelical practice, were to come into the midst of the Council of Constance, and were to say to the multitudes there, as he said and taught at Capernaum: "Except you eat the flesh of the Son of man and drink his blood, you have no life in you." And suppose that he wished to perform the sacrament as he had instituted it. Do you think that he would be listened to and would have an opportunity for this, things being as they now are? It would go hard with him. Indeed those at the Council would probably not withdraw from him scandalized, as did those at Capernaum, but would hereticate and condemn him, according to their condemnation [of the lay chalice], saying that this was not their custom.[61]

[60] In the *Posicio pro Uničov,* MS VNB, 4488, fol. 98ʳ: "Alias enim nequaquam pertineret ad comunitatem cristianam lex ewangelica, nisi discipuli Cristi suscipientes eam a domino tenuissent vicem future comunitatis fidelium."

[61] In the *Apologia,* Hardt, III, 624 f.

Here, without any development in principle beyond the thought that had animated the *Tabule,* we have nevertheless passed from critique to challenge, simply because everything has been brought down to particulars.

Nicholas objected to the entirely honest way in which the Council's theologians had justified their condemnation of communion in both kinds. Some Catholic spokesmen, especially among the Czechs, had thought to dispose of the issue of the Primitive Church by arguing that communion in both kinds had never been the rule in that body: where attested in the Bible it was only as a local practice, at best tolerable for a time but eventually to be corrected.[62] This view was wrong, and the Council's doctors offered a sounder one, meeting the issue head-on:

> I. After the Supper Christ instituted and administered the sacrament of his most sacred body and blood in both kinds, bread and wine.
>
> II. This mode of institution and ministration notwithstanding, the church's laudable and approved custom has provided and provides, that this sacrament should not be prepared after dinner nor received then by the faithful, except in case of sickness or other urgency carrying threat of death.
>
> III. Although in the Primitive Church this sacrament was received by the faithful in both kinds, nevertheless, with equal or greater justification, to avoid certain dangers, the custom could be and has been introduced, that the sacrament should be taken in both kinds by those faithful who prepare it [*a fidelibus conficientibus*], and by the laity in the species of bread alone.
>
> IV. Since this custom has been introduced by the church, and with reasonable cause has been observed by the church for a very long time, it is to be held as a law, which may not be attacked or changed at will without the church's authority.[63]

If the doctors could thus readily concede the Hussites' point about the utraquism of the Primitive Church, it was because that church meant something different to either party. What it meant to the Catholics is expressed with exceptional clarity in the following passage from an anti-utraquist treatise, which for this reason is worth quoting at length:

> The Primitive Church is the rite, custom, and observance of the church of the faithful, concerning the faith, at the time of the apostles and of the other, seventy-two disciples, and of their followers, up to Pope Sylvester. What is

---

[62] Thus *Estote sine offensione,* Hardt, III, 747; also the treatise attributed to Andrew of Brod, Hardt, III, 404 f. For the same error in Andrew's major anti-utraquist work, still unpublished, see Sedlák, "Počátkové kalicha" (1911), 398.

[63] These are the "Conclusions" of the Council's theologians, published to justify the condemnation of communion in both kinds; Sedlák, *op. cit.* (1913), 404, supposes that the author was Jean Gerson. The text in Hardt, III, 586 ff.

called the modern church is the custom and observance of the church, concerning the faith, from Pope Sylvester's time to the present day. Or, in a more restricted sense of the word "modern," it is what has been in existence for a couple of hundred years. And the church of the past century is called modern, at least in referring this period to the observance of the faithful concerning the faith.

And here it must be understood that in the Primitive Church everything was done in a simpler and grosser way than in the modern church. For baptism was done with ordinary water, but now with holy water. And the divine office was performed more simply, as well as many other things; while in the modern church all things are done more worthily [*digniori modo*]. So also in the Primitive Church communion among the Corinthians was performed in both kinds; in the modern church, all things having been brought to a better form, it is given in one kind. For the apostles and the other followers omitted what the modern church has fulfilled. . . .[64]

Since, then, "the modern church is better than the primitive, at least in regard to its regimen and its ecclesiastical order"; "it is neither just nor holy to reduce the modern to the primitive." [65] We have already seen how this style of argument, also accepting the Donation of Constantine to Pope Sylvester as a turning point, was used to refute the premise of Nicholas of Dresden's *Tabule* and to justify the modern church's enjoyment of wealth and lands; [66] now it is used to refute utraquism. In both cases the argument must be understood as a reaction to the Hussite appeal to the Primitive Church during the utraquist controversy: utraquism could neither be defended nor refuted except by bringing in a wide range of fundamental ecclesiological issues.

But even the general Catholic position just illustrated presupposed something still more fundamental: an idea of progress derived from (1) a confident acceptance of the existing order of civilization, and (2) a reliance on the papalist theory that gave the pope full discretionary power to dispose the church as he wished.[67] The Catholic appeal to the church's custom must

---

[64] *Estote sine offensione,* Hardt, III, 693 f. See Appendix 1 for a discussion of authorship.

[65] *Estote,* Hardt, III, 713 f. Nejedlý, IV, 131 also calls attention to this and the preceding passages, as an instructive contrast to Jakoubek's esteem for the Primitive Church.

[66] Above, chap. i, *ad* n. 137 ff. In Appendix 1 I argue that the treatise cited in chap. i and *Estote sine offensione* were probably both the work of Stephen of Páleč.

[67] Thus the author of *Estote* associated his exaltation of the modern over the Primitive Church with the most extreme sort of papalism: "Papa est totius mundi Princeps" (Hardt, III, 672); the pope's behavior is not to be judged (672); it is not simony for him to take money for issuing bulls or confirming bishops (674); those who transgress the pope's decrees commit heavy sins (not just crimes) (697).

not be misread as a sign of conservatism; it meant that the church at any given time could decide what customs to keep and what to discard, and in the period we are considering this idea of the church's perfect freedom was pushed to an extreme, even beyond the point that would later be defined as the limit of orthodoxy. Thus it was declared by one writer that "the universal church can change not only the accidentals of the church but also the essentials, as it sees fit for the benefit of the faithful and the honor of God"—a view that the Catholic theologian Emile Amann has shown to be wrong.[68] The same self-confidence appears in Jean Gerson's anti-utraquist treatise, where he declares his amazement that doctors who are dead should *ipso facto* enjoy more esteem than the perfectly qualified living doctors of a great university.[69] One of Nicholas of Dresden's many objections to the Catholic theologians was just this, that "they follow modern realities rather than the Law of God, which for the most part they adapt to current realities and the customs of men, with their glosses and additions." [70]

Perhaps the main motive leading the radical Hussite theoreticians to reject this sort of glossing was that they felt so profound a sense of revulsion at current conditions that they could not conceive of a modern church whose authority could compare with that of the primitive one. As Jakoubek put it, "the contemporary [*novissima*] church should be the daughter of the holy mother Primitive Church, and so in this reasonable matter [of communion in both kinds] the daughter should obey, not contradict, her mother." History had brought no progress toward perfection; quite the contrary: the Primitive Church was closest to Jesus and was "regulated by his evangelical law more excellently and perfectly than the modern and contemporary church—for then the multitude of believers had one heart and one soul, but now these are perilous times . . . when charity grows cold and iniquity abounds." [71] One place where iniquity abounded was of course the Roman

---

[68] "Jacobel et les débuts . . ." (as in n. 39 above), p. 386, n. 3 f.—a contrast between the passage quoted (Hardt, III, 849) and a decree of the Council of Trent, Sess. XXI, cap. 2: "Declarat [synodus] hanc potestatem perpetuo in Ecclesia fuisse, ut in sacramentorum dispensatione, salva illorum substantia, ea statueret vel mutaret quae . . . expedire iudicaret."

[69] Hardt, III, 771 (He was not of course referring to the Fathers). For Jakoubek's rejection of the moderns see Hardt, III, 577 f.

[70] *Apologia,* Hardt, III, 602.

[71] *Posicio pro Uničov,* MS VNB 4488, fol. 97ᵛ: ". . . cum novissima ecclesia debeat esse filia sancte matris primitive ecclesie, videtur quod filia debeat in hoc racionabili obedire et non contradicere sue matri." And fol. 97ᵛ: "Cum ergo in primitiva ecclesia sancte et racionabiliter agebatur in hoc secundum ordinacionem prudentissimam et saluberrimam institucionem summi legislatoris, domini Ihesu Cristi, et primitiva ecclesia excellencius ac perfeccius regebatur ewangelica Cristi ordinacione, quando multitudinis

ecclesiastical institution itself, and nothing that the Hussites had said on this subject in the previous decade was omitted from their works in favor of the lay chalice. Nicholas of Dresden was especially zealous here, copying out whole sections from his *Tabule, Consuetudo et ritus, De quadruplici missione,* and *Puncta,* and adding to them, to show that the church was so radically corrupt, rotten, and diseased that its custom counted for worse than nothing, particularly when asserted against the custom of the Primitive Church.[72] Why indeed had communion in both kinds been allowed to fall

credencium erat cor unum et anima una, quam moderni [*sic*] et novissima ecclesia in hiis temporibus periculosis . . . : sequitur quod comunitas plebium fidelium pocius debet amplecti modum comunicandi . . . primitive ecclesie . . . quam modum moderne ecclesie . . . in hiis novissimis et periculosis temporibus quando karitas refriguit et superhabundavit iniquitas. . . ." Needless to say, this style of thought was inspired directly by Matthew of Janov. It will be useful here to reproduce two parallel passages from Jakoubek's university *posicio* and Matthew's *Regule,* respectively; they are quoted by Sedlák, "Počátkové kalicha" (1911), 499. Jakoubek is speaking of utraquism, Matthew of frequent communion:

Jakoubek: "Quamvis ergo communitates ecclesie bibere sacramentaliter de calice sanguinem Christi est contra consuetudinem vel desuetudinem modernorum malam, provenientem ex refrigescencia caritatis, tamen non est contra consuetudinem laudabilem primitive ecclesie. Ideo si debet sancta ecclesia resurgere et reformari instar primitive ecclesie, tunc necesse erit communiter ecclesie ruinas et sepes i.e. consuetudines sanctas ecclesie primitive redire et reformari.

Matthew: ". . . nec est contra consuetudinem ecclesie primitive . . . sed contra dissuetudinem multorum vel multitudinis in praesenti, in quibus habundavit iniquitas et refriguit caritas. . . . Quapropter si debet adhuc sancta ecclesia resurgere et reformari . . . tunc necesse erit ex consequenti ipsius ruinas et sepes i.e. sanctas consuetudines ipsius redire et reformari. [Ed. Kybal, Vol. V, 82 f., and slightly altered from Sedlák's quotation.]

An even sharper and more specific Hussite argument in favor of the Primitive Church is reproduced for refutation in *Estote sine offensione,* Hardt, III, 713: "Videtur quibusdam, quod justum et sanctum esset, modernam ecclesiam reducere ad primitivam, sic: Qualis observatio et consuetudo fuit in primitiva ecclesia, quod talis observatio et consuetudo fieri debeat in moderna ecclesia. Exemplum: Sicut in primitiva ecclesia sub utraque specie laicales communicabantur, sic etiam in moderna ecclesia deberent. Et probant sic: Quia in primitiva ecclesia omnia in meliori statu et ordinatione et dispositione fuerunt quam sunt in moderna ecclesia. Nam in primitiva nulla erat simonia, nulla avaritia cleri, quemadmodum in moderna ecclesia sunt. In primitiva ecclesia erant homines de bona vita, multi sancti, multa miracula. Non erat plenitudo praebendarum, quae avaritiam causant. Praelati non erant luxuriosi, gulosi, crapulosi, sicut sunt in moderna ecclesia. Igitur justum et sanctum esset, modernam ecclesiam reducere ad primitivam, si haec omnia mala vitari debeant, hominum pro salute."

[72] The high point here is in Nicholas's *Apologia,* Hardt, III, 612–615, where he reacts against the Council's argument that since communion in one kind was a custom of the church it should be kept. He notes that according to the treatises *de ecclesia* of Stanislav of Znojmo and Stephen of Páleč, the Roman church had the pope for its head and life-

into disuse? For the same reason that frequent communion was no longer practiced: the priests were lazy and indifferent, interested mainly in getting through the motions of the divine service as quickly as possible, and therefore discouraging frequent communicants and not bothering to give the chalice in any case.[73] The Council of Constance, which defended this corrupt practice, was "a congregation of Babylon, the Synagogue of Satan";[74] its doctors were doctors of Antichrist;[75] it was a gang of simoniacs and fornicators, who condemned John Hus to death because he had attacked their sins.[76] Thus Jakoubek could write:

> And if it is objected that "the church has long held to communion in only one kind"—then I ask: "What church? The one in Constance, infected by

giving element, and that the College of Cardinals was his mystical body. He goes on to observe, "Et in ista acceptione communiter accipiunt moderni ecclesiam, cum loquuntur de ecclesia Romana. Similiter et Doctores sic videntur accipere, cum in conclusionibus eorum dicunt, consuetudinem Ecclesiae servandam, et contra observationes ipsius et statuta non esse attentandum." Having established this, he offers as indication of the custom of *this* church a very long passage composed of sections from the *Speculum aureum* (see above, chap. ii, n. 110) detailing the total depravity of the Roman Curia, blinded from head to toe by errors, and filled with the poison thereof, with which it inebriates almost all parts of the world, and so on. Comparison with the text of the *Speculum* (as published by E. Brown, *Fasciculus rerum expetendarum et fugiendarum*, II (*Appendix*) (London, 1690), 63 ff.) shows that although Nicholas had to use his talents for artful omission and actual distortion, particularly where the original assumed the desirability of benefices and the validity of canon law, still, the main thrust of this violent but nonheretical work fitted in perfectly with Nicholas's polemical needs.

[73] Thus Jakoubek's university *posicio,* speaking of the falling away from communion in both kinds: ". . . ex negligencia et cupiditate cleri magna facta est iniuria communitatibus": quoted by Sedlák, "Počátkové kalicha" (1911), 499, where it is paralleled by a passage from Matthew of Janov on frequent communion (quoted in part above, n. 59). Nicholas of Dresden offers a similar judgement in his sermon on *Nisi manducaveritis,* MS UP, IV G 15, fol. 203ʳ: "Et sunt hii qui magis diligunt ocium hic quam laborare pro ewangelii implecione et gracie proximi augmentacione, qui forsan vel raro minimam scintillam divine gracie que in hoc sacramento tribuitur habuerunt, sed quadam indulta conswetudine et quasi perfunctorie res agatur, ad illud accedunt et sic inanes et sine gracia recedunt, non ut accedant sed ut recedant festinantes, non ex affectu devocionis sed ex defectu divini fervoris, et ideo fideles laicos, . . . ex fervore divine caritatis cupientes accedere, repellunt, et ipsis totum ac perfectum sacramentum denegant." The "totum . . . sacramentum" was of course communion in both kinds.

[74] Nicholas's *De iuramento,* quoted by Sedlák, *Mikuláš z Drážďan,* p. 40, n. 2.

[75] Nicholas, *Apologia,* Hardt, III, 599 f., and cf. 595 f.

[76] The point is made in Jakoubek's Czech treatise against the Council of Constance (*LČJ,* No. 42; quoted by Sedlák, "Počátkové kalicha" (1913), 410). The passage is strongly reminiscent of Table V of Nicholas's *Tabule*—the same two vices, simony and fornication, are emphasized together, and just as Table V uses Susanna and the elders as a case in point, so Jakoubek charges that Hus was condemned by false witnesses against him "like those against Susanna."

the simoniacal heresy? Or perhaps the one described in Apocalypse xvii, which sits upon the waters and on the many-headed and horned beast?"[77]

In this way the Roman church, currently represented by the Council, was declared to be not only wrong but heretical, and the faithful were released from their duty to obey it.[78]

In his anti-utraquist treatise Jean Gerson made the apt observation that the advocates of communion in both kinds, damning their opponents as heretics, evidently "thought that the church as a whole existed only among themselves."[79] "One is stupefied," he wrote, "at their horrendous presumption." We who have approached the utraquist polemic *via* the general ideological positions of Hussite radicalism will be less surprised: in one way or another the radicals had defined the true church as the community of faithful Christians, those obedient to Christ's Law, and the effect of utraquism was to transform this abstract or at best imprecise criterion into one that left little room for doubt. Communion in both kinds was part of Christ's Law, and the priests who gave it, together with the laity who took it, were thereby constituted as a truly Christian community. In this sense the utraquist revolt, both as theory and as practice, imposed a duty to construct an alternative church. Such a church had existed before, *de facto*, in the reforming clerics and the men and women who frequented their sermons—especially in Hus's Bethlehem Chapel. It would be a great mistake, for example, to attach less than the greatest importance to the action of the three young men against indulgences, and to the tragic sequel that provided the *de facto* Hussite church with its first martyrs, who were venerated as such.[80] What utraquism contributed was a more rigorous definition, a more public aspect, and a certain quality of personal commitment as one made the great decision to

---

[77] *Posicio pro Uničov*, MS VNB, 4488, fol. 101ᵛ: "Et si obicitur: ecclesia diu tenuit sub una tantum—Que rogo ecclesia, an symoniaca heresi infecta in Constancia vel alia, de qua Apok. xvii, que sedit super aquas et bestiam capitatam et cornutam?"

[78] The point is implicit in most utraquist tractates—cf. Nicholas of Dresden's sermon on *Nisi manducaveritis*, MS UP, IV G 15, fol. 212ᵛ: ". . . subditi non tenentur prelatis obedire in quantum deviant a Cristo, quia lex superioris per inferiorem tolli non potest. . . ."

[79] Hardt, III, 774.

[80] Sedlák, *M. Jan Hus*, p. 244. That the three youths were in fact venerated appears from the text in *Documenta*, p. 638; their memory remained green along with a select group of other martyrs—cf. the reference to them in John Želivský's sermon for 23 July 1419, MS UP, V G 3, fol. 19ᵛ: ". . . ex malicia occidere est homicidium. . . . Sic nunc factum est in Constancia, ergo omnes homicide qui consenserunt ad mortem Mr. Joh. Huss, Jeronymi. Et ad mortem laicorum qui sunt decolati in antiqua Civitate Pragensi. Et qui sunt in Holomucz combusti." The psychological importance of this lively memory must have been very great.

take (or, for the clergy, to give) communion in both kinds. These elements in turn required a theoretical expression—or as the Hussites said, foundation —at any rate, a definition of the relationship of the new visible community to the Roman church, to the Primitive Church, and to the mystical body of Christ. It would take a decade before all the answers were in, but almost all the intellectual guide lines of that decade were marked out in the utraquist controversy.

To a considerable extent the principles of utraquist ecclesiology and its criticism of the Roman institution were merely reassertions of the Wyclifite and Janovian ideals already canvassed in the preceding chapters. It would be tedious to repeat them at length, but it must be understood that they *were* repeated by the Hussites, at length and often, in association with the defense of the chalice. The Roman church had begun its corruption with the Donation of Constantine in the pontificate of Pope Sylvester I (314–335). Subsequently Antichrist had extended his rule to the point that after the first thousand years of church history he had won; the suppression of the lay chalice was declared to have been part of this process.[81] The Roman church's

---

[81] The historical element in this chronological structure is still too much a projection of ecclesiology to be taken precisely at face value. What is relevant here is that these ideas of periodization, derived from Wyclif and Matthew of Janov (see above, chap. i), came up again in the utraquist controversy. Thus when Andrew of Brod challenged Jakoubek to specify how long communion in both kinds had been observed in the Primitive Church, and just when "our church" began to change it, Jakoubek could on the one hand protest that he was no historical scholar (". . . non est meum nosse tempora et momenta determinate et distincte usque ad ultimum . . ." (Hardt, III, 506)), on the other hand offer a festoon of Janovian rhetoric as a general response: ". . . remitto Doctorem ad scrutandum scripturas. Quando coepit videri abominatio desolationis, . . . et quando coepit stare in loco sancto: Quando incepit superabundare iniquitas et refrigescere charitas . . . [etc., etc.] . . . : Tunc incepit auferri a plebium multitudine juge sacrificium, secundum hunc modum communicandi . . . sub utraque specie. . . . Legat Doctor scripturas divinas, ut mysteria intelligat, quando per mille annos regnarunt sancti in ecclesia, et quando et quomodo post mille annos solutus est sathanas de carcere suo, quando exivit et seduxit gentes. . . . Et ex illis perpendat Doctor, quando nimia hypocrisis redundavit in populo Christiano, et maxime in clero, et super modum in clero Romano, cum ecclesia summa pace hujusmodi divitiis et gloria coepit abundare" (Hardt, III, 505 f.). Jakoubek goes on to advise Andrew to investigate the "priorum temporum gesta" "in annalibus"—there, with God's help, he will find the answer. In his Postil of 1413–1414 (*LČJ*, No. 95) he used the Donation in a different scheme: "Trecentis enim annis regebantur lege dei, sed quando post mille annos dotata est ecclesia ["now that the church has been endowed for a thousand years"], statim vix quis invenitur sanctus in officio illo" (quoted by Nejedlý, IV, 128, n. 110). Finally, it is noteworthy that Andrew of Brod's anti-utraquist work deliberately picked up the issue of Jakoubek's earlier (1412) identification of the pope with Antichrist; Jakoubek restated his position in the treatise against Andrew of Brod, Hardt, III, 516 ff.

corruption was exhibited by the sins and crimes of its prelates—the very ones who condemned the lay chalice.[82] The Roman church's own spokesmen had admitted that the church could err, that papal jurisdiction did not extend to what had been established in the early church, that the true church—indeed the true "Roman church"—was the congregation of the faithful, not the corporation of office-holders: why then should the prelates' condemnation of the chalice be heeded? [83] The Law of Christ and the Primitive Church perfectly governed by that Law were the absolute standards by which all such matters were to be judged—Christ had commanded communion in both kinds, and the Primitive Church had faithfully practiced it. All of this was more than a repetition. Even more sharply than in the controversies of early 1413, the two sides were drawn up in battle formation along the very lines marked out by the *Tabule* in 1412, and if on the earlier occasion Jakoubek of Stříbro had frankly conceded that the external peace of this world might have to be shattered in favor of the true peace coming from fidelity to Christ's Law, now he proclaimed the same principle even more frankly, more positively, and more authoritatively.[84] In February 1413 his proposal for true peace had been bypassed by the political leaders of his party, but in 1414–1415 his declarations were those of a man who himself held leadership and intended to use it. What he aimed at was nothing less

[82] This is one of Nicholas of Dresden's main points in his *Apologia*, e.g., Hardt, III, 612 ff. See also Jakoubek against Andrew of Brod, Hardt, III, 490 f.

[83] A favorite proof that the church could err was Innocent III's acknowledgement that error was indeed possible in matters of excommunication (Decretals, V, xxxix, 28); Jakoubek uses it, e.g., in the treatise against Andrew of Brod, Hardt, III, 490 f.: "confitetur enim ibi papa de sua ecclesia, quod saepe fallit et fallitur, *etiam* de excommunicatione et absolutione" (I emphasize Jakoubek's tendentious phrasing). There were also many canonistic explorations of the limits of papal power to judge and dispense, and Nicholas frequently exploited these for his own purposes: e.g., in the *Puncta*, MS. UP, IV G 15, fol. 24ʳ: "Est . . . omnium doctorum generalis sentencia quod papa non potest tollere vel dispensare contra ea que generalibus maxime quattuor principalibus conciliis sunt diffinita" (with a reference to Gregory the Great's dictum, *Decretum*, XV. dist., c. 2). The definition of the true church as the congregation of the faithful, according to the *Glossa ordinaria* on the *Decretum* and Nicholas of Lira (they are quoted above, chap. i), was used by Nicholas in his *Apologia*, Hardt, III, 610, 611, 615 f., to defend the lay chalice by undercutting the authority of the current ecclesiastical institution.

[84] Thus in his treatise against Andrew of Brod, Hardt, III, 512 f.: "Observare sic legem evangelii ad salutem electorum et Dei beneplacitum, hoc in se non turbat charitatem, sed magis eam pacificat et auget. . . . Sed aestimo, quod simulata pax in divitiis, deliciis et gloria seculi et mundana confoederatione, turbatur per hoc occasionaliter. . . . Pacem malorum rumpendam dixit Salvator: *Non veni pacem mittere sed gladium*. Veritas enim evangelica de communione utriusque speciei, sicut et aliae veritates, dividit electos a reprobis, secundum disparem vitam et dispares voluntates."

than a resurrection of the religious life of the Primitive Church. "They call us innovators," he said in a sermon of this period, "but in fact it is the old faith . . . that we preach and recall to memory." [85] Or to pick up a telling formulation of Nicholas of Dresden, the Hussite faithful were those "who felt themselves to be in the estate of the Primitive Church." [86] And again Jakoubek: "The man born of baptism should love the holy church of the ancient saints, should have recourse to it in all his perils and find his consolation there, and should be nourished by the documents of the ancients. . . . This is what it means to be born in the spirit." [87]

One effect of utraquism was to encourage such attitudes and feelings among the laity. The Catholic writers indeed pointed to what they considered a baleful consequence of giving the layman the same communion as the priest: the former would think that "the layman's worthiness was as great as the priest's" in this matter. [88] They would ask, "What difference is there between us and the priests?" And then, urged by their rashness—and in the case of the women, by their special proclivity to evil—they would want to take active part in the mass, reading the collects and scriptural portions, and perhaps even taking the priest's very office away from him. [89] Jakoubek rejected this nightmare as illogical, [90] but he did not deny that there was an issue between the two sides on this point of lay worthiness; there was indeed no difference between laity and clergy in regard to taking communion. [91] In a more general context he conceded that many of the church's traditions and customs in its religious services should indeed be pruned away, to promote lay piety. [92] Perhaps even more notably, Jakoubek defended translations of the Bible and of the liturgy into the language of the people. Jean Gerson had attacked the utraquists for insisting on the "naked words" of Scripture, and not accepting the authoritative interpretation of the church; he went on to say that the Beghards and Waldensians had grown from this very root, and indeed many of these heretics were laymen who had translations of the Bible in their vernacular. [93] Jakoubek replied with proofs that the Bible might be translated into every tongue; he referred in particular to the former papal

[85] The Postil of 1413–1414, *LČJ*, No. 95, quoted by Nejedlý, IV, 128, n. 110.

[86] In his sermon on *Querite primum regnum Dei*, MS UP, IV G 15, fol. 131ʳ: "Si igitur homo sentit in statu primitive ecclesie, communicet frequenter." Nicholas does not develop this point, which is no doubt more interesting to us than it was to him; what it shows is the *premise* of a great deal of what he did say about reform.

[87] Postil of 1413–1414, Nejedlý, IV, 128, n. 110.

[88] Jean Gerson, Hardt, III, 778.

[89] Andrew of Brod, quoted in Jakoubek's treatise against him, Hardt, III, 524 f.

[90] *Loc. cit.*

[91] See n. 58 above.

[92] Hardt, III, 527 f.

[93] Hardt, III, 770.

sanction of the Slavonic Bible and the Slavonic liturgy.[94] Nor, in this period, did he reject the idea of a spiritual continuity between the sectarian heretics and himself; without naming the Waldensians he nevertheless referred to them, according to one legendary version of their history, as the faithful who had withdrawn from the church when Sylvester had accepted Constantine's Donation—their followers still survived, in hiding.[95] Nicholas of Dresden went even further, and coupled his defense of the lay chalice with a resolute espousal of certain sectarian doctrines, particularly the denial of Purgatory, that can only be defined as Waldensianist.[96] Thus while utraquist practice worked to bring a new religious community into open existence, the polemics centering around that practice led to an ever clearer definition of the future Hussite church in Janovian terms, as essentially a congregation of the faithful, both laity and clergy, who stood in direct subordination to Jesus Christ, obeyed his Law alone, and thereby reincarnated the Primitive Church.

The importance of the controversy was thus very great. Everything earlier passed into it, everything later came out of it. It even absorbed John Hus's martyrdom, not merely as a source of emotional intensity or as a proof of the Council's degeneracy, but also as a symbol inseparable from the symbol of the chalice. Together the two became a shield for a wide range of radical ideas, including many that were held only on the extreme left and would eventually split Hussite ranks as one tendency after another separated out of the original united front. All these matters will be discussed below; meanwhile we may observe that the Hussite context was not the only one, and that the utraquist controversy also had its significance for the church at large. Amann called it the beginning of "polemical" and "historical," as against "scholastic," theology.[97] Whether he was right may be doubted; certainly there was plenty of both polemical and historical theology in the much

---

[94] In his treatise replying to Gerson, *LČJ*, No. 47, MS Capit., D 51, fol. 173ᵛ–174ʳ: ". . . addit adversarius caudam pestiferam: Quod videlicet orti sunt et cottidie crescunt multi errores Beghardorum et Pauperum de Lugduno et multorum similium, quorum multi sunt layci habentes in suo volgari translacionem biblie in grande preiudicium et scandalum catholice veritatis. Istud additum est expresse erroneum et sacre scripture contrarium. . . . [there follow authorities, from which:] . . . liquet evidenter quod translacio biblie quasi ad omnia genera et ydiomata linguarum racionabiliter est inscripta. . . . Ceterum, ex ordinacione ecclesie Slavi in ydiomate cum Boemis ut plurimum concordantes non solum scripturam sacram in suo ydiomate permissi sunt habere, ymmo eciam divina in lingua sua peragunt per orbem universum."

[95] Quoted by Bartoš, "Vznik a počátky táborství," *Husitství a cizina*, p. 138, n. 75; the passage was in a sermon dated 8 September 1415 (*LČJ*, No. 55). Bartoš also quotes the following from Jakoubek's postil of spring 1416 (*LČJ*, No. 96): "O quanti sunt in ducentis annis fideles Christi combusti non propter errorem, sed domini evangelium!"

[96] See my introduction to *OC & N;* also below, chap. iv.

[97] "Jacobel et les débuts" (as in n. 39 above), pp. 376, 380.

earlier disputes over the mendicants' privileges and the poverty of Christ. In fact those earlier passages of arms made many of the same anti-Roman and anti-papalist points that have just been studied,[98] and it may even be suggested that we have here a case not merely of anticipation but of actual paternity. One has only to observe that Matthew of Janov, who had studied and taught at Paris, incorporated into his *Regule* the complete text of William of St. Amour's *De periculis novissimorum temporum,* a treatise originally designed to serve the interests of the secular masters against the mendicants at the University of Paris, but which went far enough beyond its immediate purpose that it could rank as a treatise *de Antichristo.*[99] Moreover, insofar as the utraquist polemic turned into an ecclesiological controversy, its Biblical and patristic dossiers were remarkably similar to those developed in the earlier struggles, to say nothing of those in the works of Marsilius of Padua, William of Ockham, and the other fourteenth-century figures who bridged the gap. But to say this is only to emphasize the importance of the utraquist controversy, as part of the main stream of religious thought in the later Middle Ages; it may be conjectured that when historians of that subject begin to study the tractates for and against the lay chalice,[100] they will find many sources of much-needed illumination.

THE UTRAQUIST VICTORY

In the radical form given it by Jakoubek and Nicholas, utraquism forced the reform movement into a new stage of hardening and definition that

[98] Yves Congar, "Aspects ecclésiologiques de la querelle entre mendiants et séculiers dans la seconde moitié du XIII° siècle et le début du XIV°," *Archives d'histoire doctrinale et littéraire du Moyen Âge,* XXVIII (1961), 35–151, provides a systematic study with full bibliographical leads to sources and scholarship. On pp. 52 f., 63, he summarizes the key ideas of the seculars on the drastic limits to be placed on papal power. For the bibliography of the controversies over poverty and the poverty of Christ, see the recent work of M. D. Lambert, *Franciscan Poverty* (London: SPCK, 1961).

[99] Matthew of Janov, *Regulae,* III, 252–314, 315–331; in his introduction (pp. 249–251) Matthew says the work "openly and nakedly reveals the Antichrist."

[100] It may be useful to conclude this section with a note on which of the treatises in Hardt, III would be most rewarding to scholars who are not especially interested in the Hussite movement. On the Hussite side the most systematic exploration of all aspects of the controversy is in Jakoubek's treatise against Andrew of Brod (416–585); the best presentation of the case for the chalice (and against its critics) as an expression of extreme radical Hussite ideology is Nicholas of Dresden's *Apologia* (591–657). On the Catholic side the most far-ranging and interesting work is *Estote sine offensione* (658–762); the more famous *Eloquenti viro* (338–391) is similarly broad but perhaps not as deep. All these works were written in 1415; for a lapidary digest of the main issues, refined by the acid of controversy, Jean Gerson's work, written in mid-1417 (765–780), should not be missed. In fact, it would be a good item to begin with— everything is made crystal-clear in very few words.

could not fail either to arouse resistance or, in the end, to exclude certain former members. Both of the radical leaders had previously said many things that the less doctrinaire masters could hardly have espoused with enthusiasm, but there had not been any need for inchoate disagreements to be actualized —all were together against the German party at the university and against the corrupt or misguided hierarchy, all were together in the cause of Master John Hus and under his leadership. If Jakoubek and Nicholas had merely advocated communion in both kinds as a desirable practice, justified by the usage of the Primitive Church, this situation would not have changed. Instead, the radicals insisted that the lay chalice was not only desirable and in accord with the Primitive Church, but also necessary to salvation, according to the literal sense of John 6:53—"Except ye eat . . ."—and on this basis they poured *all* of their doctrines into it. When therefore they put utraquism into practice, as they could not avoid doing, they thereby said to all Hussites: Accept *our* concept of reform, or else!

Hus himself had obviously foreseen the dissension that this step would cause, for we are told that before he left for Constance he asked Jakoubek to hold off: "Go slow with it, Kubo," he said, "and when, God willing, I return, I'll help you faithfully." [101] The fact was that Hus did not then or ever after agree that the lay chalice was necessary to salvation: why not then postpone its introduction until the more basic tasks he hoped to accomplish at the Council would be disposed of? But Jakoubek regarded nothing as more basic than communion in both kinds, and soon after Hus's departure on 11 October 1414, the former delivered his university *posicio* in favor of that communion as necessary to salvation. Perhaps also, as Bartoš argues, a condemnation of the lay chalice by a Prague synod on 18 October forced his hand.[102] Soon after, at any rate, the radicals proceeded to give the chalice to the laity in some of Prague's churches, among them Bethlehem Chapel; [103]

[101] Hus's words were reported later by John Rokycana; they are quoted in Nov. II, 352. "Jakoubek" was of course a diminutive of "Jakub," = "James"; Hus used another diminutive form, (in the vocative) "Kubo."

[102] "Počátky kalicha," p. 87 f. The anonymous report printed by Höfler, III, 156, says the practice of utraquism was begun "contra prohibitionem Conradi Archiepiscopi Pragensis et aliorum praelatorum. . . ."

[103] See the passage from Laurence of Březová quoted above, *ad* n. 4. The Old Czech Annalists mention only the church of St. Martin-in-the-Wall (*OCA*, p. 20); their account shows that the step was taken after Jakoubek's *posicio*. Cf. Höfler, III, 156 f., and *OCA-R*, p. 14, for more details. On the whole matter of dating see Bartoš, "Počátky kalicha," p. 86, n. 12; Sedlák, the other chief authority, dates Jakoubek's *posicio* in May/June 1414 (*M. Jan Hus* (Prague, 1915), p. 303), and the practice of communion in both kinds at the end of April 1414 (*M. Jan Hus*, p. 301; "Počátkové kalicha," (1911), 99 f.). If I here follow Bartoš it is chiefly because his scheme seems to be the product of a more critical analysis of the sources; there can be nothing even approaching certainty, however, until more scholars have subjected the unpublished treatises to close study.

what this step meant appears when we read the sermon on *Nisi manducaveritis* that Nicholas of Dresden preached in early November: all the radical positions were inextricably associated with the new doctrine of communion.[104]

But the radicals' effort to impose their ideology on the movement did not succeed without a struggle, and it is noteworthy that the spokesman for the opposition was Hus's own *locum tenens* as preacher in Bethlehem, the priest Havlík. He seems to have begun by opposing Jakoubek at the university, but without being able to engage the Arts Faculty in this theological issue, he could only appeal to the rector to hold a hearing. As for himself, he wrote, "I do not think I have erred, err, or will err when I teach the people to believe that it suffices for salvation if they take communion worthily in one kind." It was true that Jakoubek had already decided the contrary, but he manfully declared, "My faith is not based on one master." Let the rector convoke all the masters to decide on the issue; Havlík would then stand by this decision.[105] Perhaps he knew that there was no chance such a meeting would be called, for the University of Prague was far from united in Jakoubek's support; a strong party continued to oppose the necessity of the lay chalice for well over a year, and the official university declaration in its favor did not come until 10 March 1417.[106] No doubt in response to this opposition by his colleagues Jakoubek wrote to Hus in Constance, asking for a statement; he must have hoped that his friend would now support his own stand. If so he was disappointed. Sometime in November Hus wrote what would be his definitive word on the subject, a positive determination of the question, "Whether it is useful [*Utrum expediat*] for the faithful laity to take the blood of Christ under the species of wine"; his conclusion that the lay chalice was indeed both permissible and useful [*licet et expedit*] was certainly closer to Jakoubek than was Havlík's opposition, but only accidentally so, inasmuch as Hus in Constance did not have to cope with the aggressive radical *action* that had forced Havlík to the wall. Agreeing that Christ had instituted the sacrament in both kinds and that the Primitive Church had kept it so, he did not move on to the literal interpretation of John 6:53, nor did he

[104] See the references to this sermon in the notes to the preceding section. I follow Bartoš (as cited in n. 103) for the date; Sedlák dates the sermon on 7 June 1414 (*M. Jan Hus*, p. 304, n. 4).

[105] The text is published by Sedlák, "Počátkové kalicha" (1914), 320–322, and attributed to Peter of Uničov in 1417; I agree with Bartoš ("Počátky kalicha," p. 94) that Havlík in 1414 is more likely.

[106] See below, *ad* nn. 128–134. For the background of the university's declaration see J. Kejř, "Deklarace pražské university z 10. března 1417 o přijímání pod obojí a její historické pozadí," *SbH*, VIII (1961), 133–154; also my "Hussite Radicalism and the Origins of Tabor 1415–1418," *Medievalia et Humanistica*, X (1956), 121 and *passim*.

even mention this text; like other theologians of the time, he understood its practical significance in the spiritual sense alone.[107] Thus his whole approach to the problem of utraquism was very different from what Jakoubek's had become, and Hus's *questio* could easily justify the *anti*-utraquism of those who thought that communion in both kinds, however defensible in principle, ought not to be put into practice at that time. The theologians of the Council who later condemned the practice also acknowledged its use in the Primitive Church, and we have seen how little that consideration alone meant to the Romanist spokesmen.

By the end of 1414 the split between radicals and anti-radicals, the latter appealing to Hus's authority, had become so serious that the master himself, by now in prison, had to be asked for help. On 4 January 1415 his patron and supporter at Constance, Lord John of Chlum, wrote him:

> We ask you in all earnestness [*intime*] that if you see fit you write down what are your reasonings and final intentions regarding the communion of the chalice, so that your words may be shown to our friends at the right time. For there is still a degree of dissension among the brethren [*quia fratrum adhuc aliqualis est scissio*] and many are agitated on account of this issue, referring to you and your decision, according to certain writings of yours.[108]

Given the political urgency of this request, it is impossible not to read Hus's reply as a deliberate refusal to espouse the radical cause: "As for the sacrament of the chalice," he wrote, "you have the work I wrote in Constance, in which the reasonings may be found, and I do not know what else to say but that the gospel and Paul's epistle [*scil.,* I. Cor. 11:23,26] are directly to the point, and that it was held to in the Primitive Church."[109] And he added a practical suggestion that, as Sedlák has observed, proves his complete dissociation from the radical mutiny: "If it can be done, try to get at least permission, by a bull, for the chalice to be given to those who ask for it out of their devotion, in suitable circumstances."

In this spirit of moderation, indeed of reconciliation with the church, the preacher Havlík developed his own anti-radical position, not only in sermons

---

[107] Sedlák, "Počátkové kalicha" (1911), 790 f. Neither Novotný (Nov. II, 367 ff.) nor Bartoš ("Počátky kalicha," p. 86) does proper justice to the actual import of Hus's *questio* in relation to Jakoubek's position; I follow Sedlák. For the *questio* see *LČH,* p. 91, No. 85. It is interesting that Andrew of Brod actually cited Hus's spiritual interpretation of John 6:53 against Jakoubek (Sedlák, *op. cit.,* p. 104), and that Laurence of Březová, p. 333, was obviously unable to regard Hus's *questio* as clearly encouraging to the utraquists.

[108] *Documenta,* p. 85 f.; *KD,* p. 238 f.

[109] *Documenta,* p. 91 f.; *KD,* p. 239 ff.; cf. Sedlák, "Počátkové kalicha" (1911), 790 f.

but in at least one treatise, *Asserunt quidam,* probably to be dated in the first half of 1415, where he directly refuted Jakoubek's utraquist treatise, *Magna cena sacramentalis.*[110] Against the latter's standard argument, that Christ had commanded communion in both kinds as necessary to salvation, Havlík held that the eucharistic sacrament itself was not necessary—only *spiritual* communion was, and this could be consummated without the sacrament.[111] Furthermore, the emphasis on the external act of drinking from the chalice would encourage the utraquists to think that merely by so doing they were pleasing to God, when in fact no man should presume this, particularly in so solemn a matter as the sacrament of the altar.[112] Without certain proof, therefore, of the necessity of communion in both kinds, it was safer to follow established custom; thus, while not necessarily attacking the lay chalice itself as a possible valid mode of communion, Havlík declared that the radicals' insistence on immediate implementation of their reform was as yet unjustified. Uncertainty was what he sought to prove: "I write these words but I am ready to receive better information. . . . It is very serious business to decide such things and abruptly adhere to them—far better piously to admit one's ignorance. . . ."[113] The radicals who replied to this treatise[114] could hardly find its counsel congenial, but they recognized that Havlík was not after all a reactionary. "It may yet be hoped that he will be converted to God . . . ," wrote Peter Payne, "for he has not thus far spoken against the chalice, as some have done, but he only confesses his ignorance; perhaps he will recover his estate and, as he has done on other occasions, promote the

---

[110] See Sedlák, "Počátkové kalicha" (1911), 706–708, for a summary of *Asserunt quidam* (which is attributed to Havlík in one manuscript) and a discussion of its relation to Jakoubek's *Magna cena* (for which see *LČJ,* No. 37). Neither is published. Bartoš also offers some information about *Asserunt quidam,* in "Počátky kalicha," pp. 99–102; there, and also on p. 93 f., he seeks to show Havlík's authorship of another work, an anti-utraquist portion added to a quodlibetal *questio* on the trinity, but since his own opinions seem subsequently to have changed, the matter need not be taken up here. I discuss the *questio* in the next chapter, where I also give the bibliographic references.

[111] Sedlák, "Počátkové kalicha" (1911), p. 707.

[112] Bartoš, "Počátky kalicha," p. 101: ". . . sine dubio scit se digne accipere et scit se deo placere per hoc factum et per consequens scit se dignum amore et non odio; quod est expresse contra scripturam utriusque testamenti."

[113] Sedlák, "Počátkové kalicha" (1911), p. 708.

[114] Two replies are extant, one by Nicholas of Dresden and the other by the English Wyclifite Peter Payne; both are summarized by Sedlák, "Počátkové kalicha" (1913), 468–470, 708–711. He attributes the second to Peter of Dresden, on the grounds that Payne, whom two manuscripts name as author, was not yet in Prague; Bartoš, however, makes a good case in favor of Payne's presence in late 1414 ("Počátky kalicha," p. 103 f.; cf. *LČPP,* No. 1).

cause of the Lord." [115] But why should Havlík have deserted his position, in principle so close to that of his master, John Hus,[116] in order to please the radicals? If Havlík was willing to entrust the externals of religious observance to the authority of the church—and specifically of the pope [117]—he was only repeating the principle expressed by Hus himself, who advised his followers to ask for a papal (or conciliar) bull that would allow communion in both kinds on an optional basis.

This proposal, so ludicrously out of tune with radical attitudes toward both the chalice and the modern church, would come into its own much later, at the Council of Basel, when the utraquist issue was settled in exactly this way, after intensive study of the original positions, including that of

[115] Quoted by Bartoš, "Počátky kalicha," p. 100: "Adhuc, ut speratur, non est impossibile ipsum converti ad deum, cum in consciencia sua viderit, quod erravit. Non tamen dixit adhuc, ut quidam dicunt, contra istam materiam, sed fatetur semper suam ignoranciam, quin possit suum statum recuperare et ut alias domini promovere causam." Sedlák also quotes this passage, slightly differently, on p. 710, n. 145, and on the same page offers other quotations to show that the writer regarded Havlík as more than just another enemy: "Meo amico occasionaliter, sed tamen veritatis adversario ignoranter"; "secum caritativam luctam inire cupio, quousque unus nostrum casum arripiat altero non cadente aut si deus hoc concesserit, quod simul stemus in veritate, quam Christus instituit, tamquam pugiles dei."

[116] Havlík's relationship to Hus was a close one, as can be seen from the letters Hus wrote to him or about him: e.g., *KD*, pp. 137, 278, 294, 323, 337. In one of the last letters, written on 27 June 1415, Hus urged his associates at the University of Prague: "Rogo, diligatis Bethleem et Gallum [i.e., Havlík] constituite in locum mei, quia spero, quod dominus cum eo est" (p. 323). But one manuscript of a letter that Hus wrote on 19 January 1415 has a note to the effect that it was read out by Havlík from the pulpit in Bethlehem, and that Havlík held up the torn piece of paper and said: "Ha, ha, Hussi již sě papiru nedostává"—"*Ha, ha,* Hus is running out of paper" (*KD*, p. 244). Novotný regarded this as a bit of nasty sarcasm (*KD*, p. 254, n. 4), and Bartoš seems of the same opinion ("Počátky kalicha," pp. 99, 103), holding that the episode must have marked the end of Havlík's career in Bethlehem and as a Hussite. It is inconceivable to me that such an interpretation can be true: whatever may have been the feeling between Havlík and the utraquist radicals, he could not possibly have regarded the imprisoned Hus, who after all did not support Jakoubek's views on the lay chalice, with such spite. Palacký (*Documenta*, p. 255) was certainly right when he translated "Ha, ha" as "Heu heu" ("Alas"); this is exactly the meaning of the phrase as used in the "Complaint of the Czech Crown" written in June 1420; the context is a lament for the Hussites killed by the royalists in 1419–1420 ("Žaloba koruny české," in *Hustitské skladby budyšínského rukopisu*, ed. J. Daňhelka (Prague, 1952), p. 25).

[117] The point is not perfectly clear in *Asserunt quidam*, but that Havlík did think along these lines is a necessary inference from the theory expounded in that treatise, and it is also obvious from Payne's mockery, evidently based on what Havlík had said in his sermons or personal discourse: "Si dominus suus papa cras diceret una cum suo concilio generali cleri assertive, quod illa conclusio est vera, ubi tunc essent sua correlaria?" (quoted by Bartoš, "Počátky kalicha," p. 103, n. 70).

Hus.[118] But a great deal had to happen on both sides before such a solution was possible; now, in 1415, the Council of Constance was entirely indisposed to conciliation with Hussitism, and reports that began to reach it of what was going on in Bohemia did nothing to change its mood. Some of these reports were no doubt confected—for example, that cobblers heard confessions and administered the Eucharist—but others seem to have described only the inevitable consequences of radical utraquism: the Lord's blood was carried around on the streets in flasks, and the priestly offices of the non-utraquist clergy were being rejected in the most violent terms. Certainly the anti-Hussite Bishop John Železný of Litomyšl was not lying when he told the Council on 16 May 1415 that "the followers of this sect give communion to the laity of both sexes in both kinds, bread and wine, in various cities, villages, and places of the realm, and they constantly teach and insist that communion must be given in this way." [119] As one chronicler reported, "Many of the simple priests adhered to them [*scil.,* the utraquist leaders] and went about through the whole land, giving communion to the people in both kinds and asserting in their sermons that the old priests were thieves of the sacrament." [120] There is evidence that this phrase, "thieves of the sacrament," became a kind of slogan: [121] it expressed the radical viewpoint in its simplest form, and it suggests that although various radicals kept up their end of the intra-Hussite polemic, chiefly by writing treatises against Havlík,[122] the battle of words was being bypassed as utraquist *practice* spread both in Prague and in other parts of the realm. And there is evidence from both sides to show that the implementation of communion in both kinds was working to detach the people from their ordinary priests and to form them into new congregations—in other words, a new church was being organized in *de facto* secession from the established one.[123] Thus when the Council of Constance

[118] For references and apt quotations see Jaroslav Prokeš, *M. Prokop z Plzně*, p. 192, n. 76.

[119] *Documenta,* p. 259; Železný was responding to a complaint by the Bohemian and Polish lords at the Council of Constance, about the allegedly false reports made (by him) to the Council (*ibid.,* pp. 257 f.). He denied having said that cobblers heard confessions and administered the Eucharist, but insisted on the truth of several other reports and showed that, in addition, the abuses they described were inevitable or likely. Laurence, pp. 333 f., emphasizes the influence of the reports on the Council.

[120] *Chronicon universitatis pragensis, FRB,* V, 580.

[121] Thus, for example, the extremists around Ústí in 1415 said to the people: "omnes sacerdotes usque huc fuerunt fures, quia sanguinem Jesu Christi vobis non dederunt" (*Documenta,* p. 637; see the next chapter).

[122] Two are extant (above, n. 114) and it is therefore likely that still more were written.

[123] The subject will be discussed in some detail in the following chapter. Meanwhile these texts will serve as examples: (1) In his sermon on *Nisi manducaveritis* (Novem-

issued its official condemnation and prohibition of communion in both kinds, on 15 June, this inevitable step probably served only to strengthen the radical position against both the moderate Hussites and the Romanists in Bohemia.[124]

For if there were those in the reform party who continued to insist that the lay chalice was either undesirable or superfluous, they now found themselves ranged with the Council, a body that had by now clearly shown itself to be hostile to the Czech reform, whose leader indeed still suffered in the noisome cell where the Council was confining him until it could dispose of him altogether. And from this cell Hus did not fail to use his last opportunity to help his party. Commending the reform in general to his patrons at Constance, Lords Wenceslas of Dubá and John of Chlum, he included a strong passage denouncing the Council's decree:

> O what madness, to condemn as erroneous the Gospel of Christ, the Epistle of Paul, which he said he received not from man but from Christ, and the acts of Christ and of his apostles and of other saints! To condemn, that is, communion with the Lord's cup, instituted for all faithful adults. See how they call it an error, namely that it is permissible for the faithful laity to drink of the Lord's chalice. . . . O St. Paul! You say to all the faithful: "As often as you eat this bread and drink this cup, you do show the Lord's death till he come" [I Cor. 11:26]—that is, until Judgement Day. . . . And behold: now it is said that the custom of the Roman Church is in opposition to it.[125]

Hus still did not go beyond his original theoretical position, but the Council's condemnation had *ipso facto* pushed him into practical identification with Jakoubek's stand: the custom of the Primitive Church should be imitated, and to condemn it in favor of the modern custom was madness. In

---

ber 1414), Nicholas of Dresden held that "quando proprius sacerdos non vult dare [*scil.*, calicem], potest ab alio recipi" (MS UP, IV G 15, fol. 212ᵛ). (2) The anonymous anti-utraquist treatise *Eloquenti viro* upbraided its anonymous addressee: "Insuper praedicas, quod quilibet homo, quando vult, cui vult, ubi vult, potest confiteri et communicare, non advertens suum plebanum, forte avarum, superbum, luxuriosum, simoniacum, etc." (Hardt, III, 378; cf. also 414).

[124] As we have seen, moderates like Hus and Havlík had been able to urge, against the radicals' mutinous implementation of communion in both kinds, that *permission* be sought from the Council of Constance; after 15 June this line was no longer open. Much later, in 1433, John Rokycana said that the Hussites "had been about to go" [*eramus in proposito eundi*] to the Council of Constance to explain their reasons and authorities for utraquism, but gave up the plan when they learned of the Council's hasty decree against them [*sed audita celeri sentencia contra nos . . .*] (quoted in J. Prokeš, *M. Prokop z Plzně,* n. 71 on p. 192). He may of course have been inventing this might-have-been for his own polemical advantage, but if he was right, then certainly the Council's decree must be seen as a crushing blow to the Hussite moderates.

[125] *Documenta,* p. 125 f.; *KD,* p. 289.

other words, whereas before the condemnation, Hus's position was objectively allied to anti-utraquism, now it had the opposite tendency. In this sense he now, on 21 June, addressed himself to Havlík, whom he urged "not to resist the sacrament of the Lord's chalice." Christ had instituted it himself and had confirmed it through Paul; against it there stood no scripture "but only custom, which I think grew up out of negligence." He concluded: "I ask for the sake of God that you stop attacking Master Jakoubek, lest there be schism among the faithful." [126] This was of course the very schism that had existed since Jakoubek's first public action for the chalice and which Hus's own position had helped to support, but now the master felt it had to come to an end. And when the same Council that had condemned the chalice also condemned John Hus, and had him killed on 6 July, there was no longer any room for Havlík's stand; since he still refused to accept utraquism he was forced out of Bethlehem and passed from the scene of history.[127]

Although no other Hussite seems to have opposed the chalice the way Havlík did, in sermons, disputes, and treatises, the "many" whom John of Chlum's letter referred to as being agitated by utraquism, and as using Hus's *questio* for their authority, must have included other leaders. As we have seen, the doctrine that communion in both kinds was necessary to salvation, and the practice of such communion based on that doctrine, were extensions of the whole ideology of radicalism. It would be inconceivable that the politicians of the party, whose approach to problems of reform was so different from Jakoubek's, would have held still for what amounted to the latter's taking over of the Hussite movement. We have direct testimony from John Želivský preaching in 1419, that precisely the leading politician, John Jesenic, was the first to oppose the lay chalice,[128] and we may suppose that his associates joined him in opposition. Those who like him later resisted the doctrine of infant communion, which was only a direct consequence of the

---

[126] *Documenta,* p. 128; *KD,* p. 294 f.

[127] All the scholars agree that Havlík left Bethlehem after Hus's death and that it was Jakoubek who received the appointment (from the masters of the Czech Nation, who held the advowson) that Hus had requested for Havlík, namely as first preacher. No one cites any sources for either event; the only one I know is the Taborite statement of 1431, that Jakoubek "primum post M. Ioannem . . . cathedram in Bethlehem recepit" (in B. Lydius, *Waldensia,* I (Rotterdam, 1616), 299).

[128] Quoted from Želivský's still unpublished cycle of sermons, in MS UP V G 3, by J. Truhlář, "Husitská kázání z let 1416–1418," *VČA,* VIII (1899), 288: ". . . Gessenicz doctor . . . primus fuit contra communionem calicis, sed in infirmitate fuit conversus. . . ." By 1419, to be sure, Jesenic had become so repugnant to the radicals that they were probably ready to accuse him of every possible crime, but otherwise there is no reason to think that this particular accusation was untrue.

radical doctrine that the Eucharist was necessary to salvation,[129] may be confidently set down as originally either anti-utraquists *tout court,* or as exponents of the moderate view put forth by Hus: these were, in addition to Jesenic, Masters Simon of Tišnov, Simon of Rokycany, and perhaps John Kardinál of Rejnštejn.[130]

Throughout 1415 and 1416 these men and no doubt others were powerful enough in the university to prevent that body from pronouncing in favor of the chalice as necessary, and when Hussite communities asked for guidance in these years of turbulent reform, the university could only reply with varying degrees of restraint. Thus in 1416 it told the magistrates of Louny that "all of us are not yet in agreement on this matter, for some hold that the long-practiced custom should not be opposed, while others, the greater number [*alii autem et plures*], infer, from the gospel of the Lord Jesus Christ, from the epistles of St. Paul, and from the rite of the Primitive Church, that this custom should give way to the truth." [131] At the same time, the university could agree that the lay chalice was not heretical nor opposed to any point of scripture, a formulation that constitutes the crux of another letter, to the magistrates and community of the town of Příbram.[132] Individ-

---

[129] More will be said on this below; for the present see Jakoubek of Stříbro's treatise against Andrew of Brod, Hardt, III, 421, 431 f., for passages showing how the question emerged from the radical utraquist interpretation of John 6:53. The important testimony of Pseudo-Dionysius, that every sacrament is incomplete without communion, was cited by Nicholas of Dresden in his treatise against Havlík in the summer of 1415 (see Sedlák, "Počátkové kalicha" [1913], 469).

[130] Jesenic and Simon of Tišnov were the most active opponents of infant communion; see Bartoš, "Roztržka v husitské straně r. 1417," *Do čtyř pražských artikulů* (Prague, 1925), p. 68 f.; also *LČJ*, Nos. 71, 72 (text in *Documenta*, pp. 674 f.). Some years later Simon wrote that although he had indeed given communion in both kinds, he "had never held that it was necessary for salvation" (MS 4314, fol. 153ᵛ). Simon of Rokycana, active among the Hussite politicians (see e.g. below, *ad* n. 138) and mentioned in rather select company as one of the "friends of truth" to whom Hus sent greetings from Constance on 16 June 1415 (*Documenta*, p. 120; *KD*, p. 278), was probably the Master Simon who was burnt to death by the Hussite armies in 1421; one of his companions in martyrdom was Master Laurence of Nimburk, who probably left the Hussite ranks because of utraquism and clerical disendowment (Tomek, IV, 91 f., 137; cf. Höfler, I, 83)—Simon must have left for similar reasons. As for John Kardinál, his vigorous leadership of the conservatives in 1417 suggests that he must have opposed infant communion in that year; cf. O. Odložilík, "Z počátků husitství na Moravě," *ČMM*, XLIX (1925), 122.

[131] The text is published by Sedlák, "Počátkové kalicha" (1914), 115.

[132] *Loc. cit.* and, for the text of the letter to Příbram, Bartoš, *Do čtyř art.,* p. 13, n. 43. For the dating of both in 1416 see, e.g., Kejř, "Deklarace pražské university," p. 135, n. 7. That the university received requests for guidance from *many* towns appears in a later but reliable report (*Mon. Conc. Saec. XV.,* I, 386): "Requisita . . . universitas a pluribus huius regni magistratibus et communitatibus. . . ."

ual masters in favor of the chalice as necessary could of course offer their own guidance in more forthright terms,[133] but it is important to observe that there were two distinct approaches to the matter, in effect Hus's and Jakoubek's, coexisting among the intellectual leaders for several years after the issue had arisen. Indeed, not even the official university declaration for the chalice, on 10 March 1417, accepted Jakoubek's formulation in any clear words; instead, with intricately elephantine style, it pushed Hus's phraseology to the most extreme point that it could reach.[134] The important thing of course is that the differences in theory, destined to become issues of actual controversy in the struggle over infant communion, made no difference in the period after the Council's condemnation: in fact utraquism was being extended, and in fact even the nonradicals did not fight it. Utraquism had won.

THE ORGANIZATION OF THE HUSSITE NOBILITY

If the first year of the struggle for the chalice saw the political leaders of Hussitism playing the role of ineffective opposition, the same period also saw them engaged in a totally different role, much more in line with their past and much more successful. In respect to utraquism they figured as conservatives, with all the inevitable disadvantages of such a position in a period of revolutionary thrust, but in their other role, as organizers of the nobility in the interests of Hus and Hussitism, they were even more radical, in their nondoctrinal way, than they had been before. Eventually the two lines of radical action would merge, as the religious community based on communion in both kinds became an established church under the patronage of the Hussite feudality, but in this period they were distinct and even competitive. To those engaged in the day-to-day work of organizing, arranging, maneuvering, and negotiating, all in the interest of John Hus's cause at Constance, the utraquist revolt could only seem at best a dangerous distraction, at

[133] As the letter to Louny said, "plures ex nobis practicam calicis domini astruentes quid in hoc senciant, quomodo vos de hoc in parte non latere concipimus, caritatem vestram in brevi clarius edocebunt." Some such action may well be represented by the letter to Příbram, which was sent not by the university (as was the letter to Louny), but by the rector of the university, John Kardinál, and "a majority of the masters" [*maiorque pluralitas magistrorum*].

[134] The text of the declaration in Czech is in *AČ*, III, 203–205; in Latin, Hardt, III, 761–766. There is no assertion that the lay chalice is necessary to salvation, but only a very vigorous justification of utraquism in tacit defiance of the Council of Constance—which is indeed referred to only for its admission that utraquism was practiced in the Primitive Church. The language is more convoluted than even the most ornamental chancery style of the time, which is saying a good deal, and it must have been the work of a committee set up to make sure that no clear-cut sentence would get in.

worst an action guaranteed to help the enemy brand the reform with the mark of heresy.

This stage of the politicians' activity begins with Emperor Sigismund's request that Hus bring his case to the projected Council. Lords John of Chlum and Wenceslas of Dubá, who were to become Hus's protectors in Constance, had distinguished themselves in Sigismund's service, and it was they who conveyed the Emperor's request to Hus in the Spring of 1414.[135] After some negotiation on the conditions under which Hus would comply— he demanded a safe-conduct [136] and guarantees of an open hearing—he decided to do so, and at once set about making the necessary preparations. First, he needed official testimonials to his faith, so that when he left the safety of Bohemia it would not be in the vulnerable condition of one suspected of heresy.[137] On 26 August he publicly challenged all who would accuse him of heresy to do so before the Archbishop of Prague, and on the following day John Jesenic, along with other masters—Simon of Tišnov, Simon of Rokycany, Procop of Plzeň, Nicholas of Stojčín, John Příbram [138]— and with various lay Hussites, tried to gain entry to the archbishop's palace, as Hus's representatives. When they failed—a synod of the clergy was going on at the time—Jesenic procured a notarial statement of the fact for future use.[139] At the same time the resident inquisitor, Bishop Nicholas of Nezero, evidently quite unsuited to his office, issued testimonials that he knew John Hus well and that the latter was blameless in life, pure in doctrine: Nicholas knew of no heresy in John Hus.[140] It was now the turn of the King, Queen, and the leading officials of the court to be asked to declare that Hus had indeed publicly presented himself to all who would accuse him of unortho-

[135] Nov. II, 338 ff. Bartoš, *Čechy*, p. 374 ff., offers a fresh interpretation of the events connected with Hus's presence at the Council, but since the purpose of the present section is only to outline the facts, these will be taken from Novotný's standard work. See also Kejř, *Husitský právník*, pp. 85–98.

[136] Much has been written on the nature of Hus's safe-conduct, chiefly on the question of whether it guaranteed only a safe trip to Constance or complete immunity not only for the journey but also for the stay at the Council and the trip back even in the event of an adverse judgement. Novotný believes the latter; see Nov. II, 344 f. for his view and a bibliographical note on the scholarship. Bartoš, *Čechy*, p. 384 argues that Hus knew he was going to his death and that his only real concern was for a guaranteed open hearing—the safe-conduct was thus only a minor means to this end. These and other opinions are reviewed by M. Spinka, *John Hus' Concept of the Church*, pp. 329–337.

[137] *Documenta*, p. 66 f.; *KD*, pp. 192–195; Nov. II, 347 f.

[138] At this time Procop of Plzeň and John Příbram probably belonged to Jakoubek's party; they later became arch-conservatives. The other masters in the group were leading "politicians."

[139] *Documenta*, pp. 240–241; Nov. II, 348.

[140] *Documenta*, pp. 239, 242 f.; Nov. II, 348.

doxy, that no one had taken up the challenge, and that the archbishop had not let Hus or his spokesmen into the palace—now Hus would go to Constance for the same sort of exposure.[141] And on 1 September he formally notified Sigismund that he would indeed go.[142]

Still other preparations followed. On 18 September Master John Příbram obtained from the rector of the University of Prague a notarized copy of the act of 1409 by which the university had incorporated the Kutná Hora Decree into its statutes; Hus would now have evidence with which to meet anticipated charges from the German émigrés that he alone had procured the decree.[143] At the same time he himself assembled copies of earlier accusations against him and annotated them to indicate either that they were false or that the statements they accused him of having made could be understood in an acceptable sense.[144] He also wrote some new works to develop certain of his doctrinal positions that he wished to bring before the Council.[145] Finally, in October, he requested the barons meeting in the High Court [*Zemský soud*] to secure a statement from Archbishop Conrad as to whether the latter knew of any heresy in John Hus. Conrad obliged by saying that he did not, although he observed that it was not he but the pope who had conducted judicial proceedings against Hus: let Hus answer to the pope. On 7 October several of the leading barons—Lords Čeněk of Vartemberk, Boček of Kunštát, and William of Vartemberk—wrote a letter to Sigismund in which Conrad's answer was set forth, and they urged the Emperor to make sure that Hus got an open hearing and was "not furtively abused, to the dishonor of our nationality and of the Bohemian land."[146] Only after all these preliminaries did Hus set out for the Council, on 11 October, in the company of an escort led by Lords Wenceslas of Dubá and Henry Lacembok, also John of Chlum and the latter's secretary, Master Peter of Mladoňovice, and, as representative of the University of Prague, Master John Kardinál.

It is not hard to imagine the councils of war, plans, démarches, confidential conversations, comings and goings, that all of these actions involved, nor

---

[141] *Documenta*, p. 68 f.; Nov. II, 348 f.

[142] *Documenta*, pp. 69–71; Nov. II, 346 f.

[143] Nov. II, 349.

[144] *Documenta*, pp. 164–185; Nov. II, 349 f. John Jesenic was instrumental in collecting these documents and, according to Bartoš, *Čechy*, p. 385, n. 3, it was he who composed the *Ordo procedendi* (*Documenta*, pp. 188–193), an interestingly tendentious history of Hus's whole case, to be used at the Council.

[145] Nov. II, 350; the most notable of these new works was the Wyclifian *questio*, "Utrum lex Jesu Christi . . . per se sufficit ad regimen ecclesie militantis" (*LČH*, p. 89, No. 82). The positive determination of the question provided the basic doctrine for the general reform of the European church that Hus evidently hoped to promote at the Council of Constance.

[146] *Documenta*, p. 531 f.

will anyone fail to perceive in them the direct continuation of earlier Hussite efforts to ally the reform with the secular powers, to identify the cause of reform with the Czech national cause, and to present the issues of reform as in some significant way falling within the competence of the secular government of the realm. The Council, of course, was not impressed by any of Hus's preparations, which prevented neither his imprisonment, his physical abuse, his unfair process, his condemnation, nor his execution. Already disposed to recognize the subversiveness of Hus's program, the Fathers of Constance made themselves the instrument of vengeance for Hus's enemies, chiefly the Czech Romanist academicians, who provided the agitation, and the Prague prelates, who sent a stream of money to finance the process.[147] But the engagement of his supporters in planned action for him continued to bear fruit, in the shape of a whole series of démarches and protests by the Czech and Moravian nobility at home and in Constance. The same themes appear again and again: Hus was a good Christian, he had gone to Constance freely, the accusations against him and the Bohemian nation were false, his imprisonment violated Sigismund's safe-conduct, he must have a fair and open hearing. On the basis of these texts, it may be confidently supposed that no matter who was doing the protesting, the same circle of Hussite political leaders was at work, organizing action and drafting statements.[148] Their hand is especially evident in the greatest of all interventions when on 12 May two hundred and fifty barons and nobles of Bohemia and Moravia, meeting for the purpose in Prague, attached their seals to a letter addressed to Sigismund. Nothing of substance was added to what had been said before, but the act itself represented something new, by associating so many of the nobility in a firm declaration that no matter what had been said against Hus at the Council, he was a man of impeccable virtue, entirely guiltless, a faithful preacher of God's Truth; Sigismund was urged to honor his safe-conduct and procure Hus's release and return home, for the sake of God's Truth, the Emperor's reputation, and the peace and honor of the

---

[147] The nature of the Council's proceedings against Hus cannot be discussed here; see in general P. De Vooght, *L'Hérésie de Jean Huss* (Louvain, 1960), pp. 289–481. The financial contributions of the prelates are mentioned in a number of sources—e.g., Laurence, pp. 338 f.; *OCA-R*, pp. 12, 14. The basic source, Peter of Mladoňovice's account, has been translated into English most recently by M. Spinka, *John Hus at the Council of Constance* (New York: Columbia University Press, 1965). Although highly tendentious, it is true in its facts.

[148] Novotný, *Hus v Kostnici a česká šlechta* (Prague, 1915), provides the best systematic account of all these actions. The similarity of language and content among the texts, often the result of deliberate plagiarism, is obvious enough not to need proof —see, notably, the texts in *Documenta*, Nos. 63, 65, 73, 74, 75. Novotný, p. 20, supposes that all of the protests originating among the Czechs at Constance were composed by Master Peter of Mladoňovice. In Bohemia the action on Hus's behalf was probably led by John Jesenic (Bartoš, *Do čtyř art.*, p. 5).

Bohemian realm.[149] There is evidence that this impressive declaration was coordinated with a démarche in Hus's behalf by the Czech and Polish nobility in Constance,[150] and again we must try to imagine the enormous if unattested effort that such organization required. To those involved in this enterprise, the furor connected with the beginnings of utraquism must have seemed somewhat beside the point. At the same time, however, the posture of defiance that the radical utraquists were developing vis-à-vis the Council was not very different from the position set forth in the protests that we have just considered, nor indeed from the position implicit in Hus's previous dealings with church authority: that authority was in fact rejected, although verbally recognized, and the single principle of fidelity to the Law of God was set up as a kind of all-purpose response to every demand for obedience on the part of the ecclesiastical institution.

Historically, the main importance of the politicians' organization of the nobility in behalf of Hus was precisely that while it failed to prevent the latter's martyrdom, it laid the foundations for the interposition of secular authority that would safeguard the Bohemian reformation from future suppression by the Council or the papacy. Under the slogan, "the Law of God," many lines of reform, including utraquism, could be pursued with more or less freedom. Hus himself had promoted this development, and in a prophetic letter to Lords Wenceslas of Dubá and John of Chlum, written shortly before his death, he commended the cause of reform to the protection of the Bohemian feudality:

> I beseech you by the bowels of Christ to flee evil priests but love good ones, according to their works, and, together with other faithful barons and lords, to the extent of your power, not to permit these good priests to be oppressed. It is indeed for this that God has set you over others. I believe that there will be a great persecution in the Kingdom of Bohemia of those who faithfully serve God, if God does not intervene through the secular lords, whom he has enlightened more than the spiritual ones in his Law.[151]

By moving at once from this passage to a passionate defense of the lay chalice (quoted above), Hus left no doubt that the good priests whom he asked the lords to defend were those who gave communion in both kinds. After fifty years of trying, the prelates of Prague had finally brought one of their enemies to his death, but this one knew how to fight back; the prelates would pay for their victory by losing everything—not to the old religious movement but to the new one, prepared by Hus: the "diabolic fraternity of nobles, knights, burghers, and peasants." [152]

---

[149] The text in Czech in *Documenta*, pp. 550–552, with a Latin translation by Palacký.
[150] Novotný, *Hus v Kostnici*, pp. 23–27.
[151] *Documenta*, pp. 125 f.
[152] Andrew of Brod, *Tractatus de origine Hussitarum*, Höfler, II, 349.

IV

THE ESTABLISHMENT
OF HUSSITISM AND THE CRISIS
OF THE HUSSITE LEFT, 1415–1416

THE HUSSITE LEAGUE

WITH the Council's condemnation of utraquism, on 15 June, and the martyrdom of John Hus, on 6 July, there began a new period of Hussite history, in which the development of radical ideology marched hand in hand with the organization of a Hussite society in Bohemia and Moravia. At the same time the Catholic forces, led by Bishop John Železný of Litomyšl, were also being consolidated out of the wreckage of what had been a single Bohemian church and, together with the leadership of international Catholicism, were passing to a posture of combat that would eventually find its proper expression in the anti-Hussite crusades. Part of this pattern had indeed come into being even before Hus's death. On 29 June 1415 the German townsmen of Olomouc in Moravia burned to death two lay preachers of "John Hus's errors"; [1] one of them, named John, had been a student at the University of Prague, the Hussite masters of which promptly protested to the Hussite Lord Lacek of Kravař, the royal Captain of Moravia. Calling John a "true and faithful protagonist of the Law of God," the masters applied the same designation to Lacek and appealed to him in that capacity, as well as on the basis of his Czech nationality—"strenuous defender of the good name of our race [*gentis*]"; the Olomouc citizens, as

---

[1] According to the account of Wenceslas of Jihlava, ed. J. Loserth, *MVGDB*, XIX (1881), 88.

Germans, were "patent enemies of our nationality [*linguae*]" and their action tended "to the confusion of our university—nay rather to the indelible besmirching of our Bohemian and Moravian race and of the whole Slavic nationality." [2] There was not much that Lacek could do to the offending citizens, but their action provoked its own punishment. Not only were the Olomouc martyrs remembered as such, along with the three youths killed in 1412, John Hus, and later Jerome of Prague, [3] but the combination, Germans-townsmen-Catholics, naturally helped to reinforce its counterpart: Czechs-nobility-Hussites. All that was needed to insure the future of Hussitism, as the university masters envisaged it, was a development of their long-prepared coalition with the nobility to the point of programmatic defense of the reform.

There was more than the Olomouc episode to suggest the need for such a defense. On 11 July 1415 Bishop John Železný wrote from Constance to Archbishop Conrad of Prague:

> This holy council is even now deliberating on how to carry through, quickly and effectively, measures against the adherents and supporters of this condemned heresy, with all the rigor prescribed by the law. I, however, with some of my other colleagues, have intervened with my prayers as best I could, asking that before those measures were taken, the holy council should send ahead . . . exhortatory, friendly, and benign letters [urging a return of the heretics to the church]. [4]

Later in July general letters were in fact sent by the Council to the nobility of Bohemia, Moravia, and Silesia, the Prague diocesan clergy, and the town governments of Prague, reviewing the whole process against Hus, emphasizing the Council's patience and Hus's stubbornness, and urging the addressees to oppose Hussitism, to move King Wenceslas IV to do so more actively, and to exclude Hussite agitators from their towns and domains. [5] In this correspondence there was perhaps a certain touch of benignity from the Council's

---

[2] *Documenta*, pp. 561 f.

[3] See above, chap. iii, n. 80. There are also references in Jakoubek's Postil of 1415–1416 (*LČJ*, No. 96), MS. UP, VIII E 3, fol. 70ᵛ ("Cur igitur Magister Johannes Hus et duo in Olomucz sunt combusti nisi quia veritas prosternitur et anticristus in malicia sua prosperatur?"), and in his Bethlehem sermon of c. 1417 on the Hussite martyrs, *FRB*, VIII, 241 f.

[4] *Documenta*, pp. 566 f.

[5] *Documenta*, pp. 568–572.. The text for Moravia in J. Loserth, "Beiträge zur Geschichte der Husitischen Bewegung," *AÖG*, LXXXII (1895), 376; that for Wrocław in J. Cochlaeus, *Historiae Hussitarum Libri XII* (Mainz, 1549), pp. 120 f.

point of view, but the situation itself required stronger measures. At the end of August the benign period was ended, when Bishop John Železný was appointed by the Council as special legate, with great discretionary powers of citation, excommunication, interdict, deprivation of benefice, inhabilitation for future benefice-holding, and revocation of fiefs held from the church by heretical laymen. These powers were explicitly declared to supersede existing constitutions of the church in Bohemia and Moravia.[6] All in all, the Council's provisions indicated a determined effort to destroy Hussitism, the kind of effort that the church authorities of Bohemia should have been making for at least the past five years; since now it might be supposed that the King, who had let Hus be sacrificed, would range himself with the church, there was reason to fear the worst.

It is against this background that we must understand the new action of the Hussite nobility, in other respects a clear continuation of their earlier interventions on Hus's behalf.[7] Meeting in Prague on 2 September, about a month before the regular Diet, fifty-eight Hussite barons and nobles of Bohemia and Moravia issued a protest against Hus's execution that amounted to a formal defiance of the Council of Constance.[8] The letter of protest praised Hus's life, lived "piously and gently in Christ," asserted that his doctrine was catholic and free of error or heresy, and charged that the Council's condemnation, which brought so much infamy to the realm, was baseless: "John Hus confessed to no crime, nor was he legitimately and properly convicted of any, nor were any errors or heresies cited and demonstrated against him." The Council had declared itself to be inspired by the Holy Spirit; the barons meaningfully declared that they "did not know what spirit" had moved the Council to condemn such a man. Anyone who said errors were teeming in Bohemia and Moravia and had infected the Christian population of the realm—in other words, anyone carrying out the Council's policy against Hussitism—was a foul liar and traitor. The nobles would appeal to a future pope; meanwhile they defiantly promised "to defend and protect, to the point of shedding our blood, the Law of our lord Jesus Christ and its devout, humble, and constant preachers, disregarding all human statutes to the contrary." The letter was circulated in various regions of

---

[6] *Documenta,* pp. 574–577.

[7] Cf. Bartoš, "Vznik a osudy protestu proti Husovi upálení," *JSH,* XXII (1953), 50–60, esp. pp. 53–55. The treatment in *HR,* I, 15 ff., does not supersede this article.

[8] The text in *Documenta,* pp. 580–584; also in V. Novotný, *Hus v Kostnici a česká šlechta* (Prague, 1915). Most modern scholars agree that the meeting of the Hussite nobility that issued the protest was not part of the regular Diet (e.g., Bartoš, *Do čtyř art.,* pp. 4 f.; Pekař, *ČČH,* XXI (1915), 400). F. Palacký had said that it was (III, i, 237 f.) and he is followed here by Heymann, pp. 57 f.

Bohemia and Moravia to be furnished with the seals of the Hussite nobility; 452 names in all were on the eight copies delivered to the Council.[9]

Three days later, on 5 September, all but three of the original fifty-eight who had issued the letter took the logical step of implementing its threats: they compacted to form a Hussite League under the presidency of three barons, Lord Čeněk of Vartemberk, the supreme Burgrave of Prague, Lord Lacek of Krava027y, the Captain of Moravia, and Lord Boček of Kunštát and Poděbrady.[10] The pact was to last for six years, and it included provisions for joint action and enforcement; it also provided for sending the letter of 2 September and for appealing to a future legitimate pope, whose decision would be obeyed "as long as it not be against God and his Law." The heart of the pact, however, was formed by the following provisions:

> We shall command that on all our domains and properties the Word of God be freely preached and heard . . . without hindrance. If any priest at all should come and ask in the name of God to be allowed to preach the Word of God according to Holy Scripture, he is to be allowed to do so.
>
> And if that priest who has preached should be accused of some improper error, he should be cited for this before the bishop under whom he serves, in Bohemia or in Moravia; and if it be publicly proved against him, by Holy Scripture, that he has preached any errors, let the bishop correct him and punish him publicly, as is proper, and we undertake not to allow that priest to preach any more on our domains.
>
> But if any bishop should seek, on the basis of any accusations, to punish any priest improperly, privately, and without demonstration on the basis of Holy

---

[9] The consensus of modern scholarship is that the 452 surviving names, grouped in the eight copies we know about, represent all the signatories: this was the opinion of Novotný in his edition cited in n. 8, and he defended it successfully, against J. Pekař's critical review (cited in n. 8), in his "K protestnímu listu české šlechty z dne 2. září 1415," *ČSPSČ*, XXIII (1915). The researches of A. Sedláček, "Úvahy o osobách v stížných listech l. 1415 psaných," *ČČH*, XXIII (1917), 85–109, 310–352 (and cf. *ČSPSČ*, XXX), have succeeded in locating most of the names and in thereby making possible a precise determination of which regions of Bohemia and Moravia had a significant number or even a preponderance of Hussite nobility. Bartoš's "Vznik a osudy protestu" (above, n. 7) discusses these matters and cites the scholarly literature. It is worth noting, however, that not every signatory was necessarily a Hussite: a formula found by Sedlák in a MS of the Olomouc Chapter Library has the nobleman A affirming that some years ago he had handed over his seal to B, "propter commune bonum, prout idem B asserebat," and that B used it on the letter of protest, even though A was always opposed to Wyclifism (*ST*, III, 86–89). Whatever we make of this—and it may have been only a formula for mendacity—we will not neglect the probability that a good number of the signatories must have simply followed the lead of the stronger men of the region.

[10] The text in *Documenta*, pp. 590–593.

Scripture, then we should not give over such priests or allow them to be summoned before that bishop, but rather before the rector, doctors, and masters of Holy Scripture of the University of Prague, and these should be judges according to the institutions of God and his Holy Scriptures.

We have also agreed to enjoin all our clergy whom we have under us not to accept any excommunications from anyone except those bishops under whom we live in Bohemia and Moravia; for we are glad to be obedient to their proper citations and excommunications.

But if any of those bishops under whom we live should seek to oppress us or our clergy by improper excommunications or by force, because of the Word of God or his Law, or for some cause that pertains to a secular court in the first instance, we shall not obey them or accept them, but shall oppose them and help each other in the matter, so that we should not be oppressed by them.

And if anyone should seek to oppress us with any other, foreign excommunications, and should invoke the secular arm in connection with the issuing of them, we ought and wish to be of assistance to each other in this matter too, so that we may not be oppressed; for we wish to be obedient only to the excommunications and citations of our own bishops.

These points are clear enough in themselves, but the system they add up to requires some explanation. We will not of course suppose that the compacting barons themselves invented this system; the text of their pact must have been prepared by their collaborators among the political leaders of university Hussitism (who on 11 September would issue their own declaration in praise of John Hus and Jerome of Prague),[11] and the League must be understood in its relationship to the protest of 2 September and thereby to the whole movement of protests and interventions by the feudality in Hus's behalf. This movement in turn had its source in both the practical and theoretical orientations of the period beginning in 1408. The political ecclesiology of Wyclif had defined the body politic of the realm as an *ecclesia,* an autonomous section of the Church Militant, and had seen the secular powers of the realm as also the rulers of the church.[12] Applied to actualities, this program meant that the institutional structure of the Bohemian church was to be detached from its juridical membership in the European institution; it would continue to work, but within the realm and subject to the judicial instances of the realm. The purpose of such a national church-state combina-

---

[11] Bartoš, *Do čtyř art.,* p. 5, agrees with Novotný that in Bohemia the guiding spirit of all the interventions for Hus was John Jesenic, and holds that he "obviously" wrote both the text of the protest and the compact of the League. For the University's declaration see *FRB,* VIII, 228–230.

[12] See above, chap. i, the section on "The Contribution of John Wyclif."

tion was to promote the Law of God by the preaching of God's Word. Thus far the theory. But if we now consider the practical experience of the years in question we find that it conformed precisely to this theory. The main interests of Hus and his associates had been to get control of the university, to secure the power and freedom to carry on reform agitation among the people, and to protect themselves from the jurisdictional power of their ordinaries. From 1408 through 1411, an alliance with King Wenceslas and the royal court had not only delivered the university to the Hussites but had forced the archbishop to agree to submit the whole case against them to judgement by the crown rather than by the pope. In 1412, when the issue of indulgences alienated the King from Hus, the reformers turned to the barons and *their* most effective institution, the High Court [*Zemský soud*], and this tactic, along with the continued cultivation of the Hussite members of the royal court, had produced the stalemate of 1413. In all these cases the Hussite appeal had always been to the "rights of the realm," and the various actions arranged by the politicians had always taken the form of interposition of the secular power between Hus and Rome; the archiepiscopal jurisdiction was allowed to operate, but only as a mechanism in the national structure; in practice, when the Hussites were successful, this condition meant that the archbishop could not take the proper steps against the Hussite heresy. The Hussite League of 1415 is essentially the translation of these basic principles into a positive program, the distilled essence of political Hussitism.

Ideally, to be sure, the defense of reform should have been undertaken by the king, as the "first prelate" of the *ecclesia Bohemica*,[13] but ever since 1412, when the issue of indulgences had caused a break between Wenceslas and Hus, the reformers had been unable to count on more than, at best, the king's passivity. Wenceslas had allowed Hus to be drawn to Constance— perhaps indeed he had forced him to go [14]—and had done nothing in his behalf in all the months of imprisonment and trial; from the latter part of 1412 on, the only effective support Hus enjoyed from the secular power came from the nobility. Here he and his associates could take advantage of an aspect of Bohemian institutional development that had a history of its own: ever since the baronial estate had emerged as such, in the thirteenth century, its institutions, chiefly the Diet and the High Court, had stood as a countervailing power to the institutions representing the direct government of the realm by the crown.[15] Those developments in England and France that would eventually secure a drastic diminution of baronial autonomy were

[13] See above, chap. ii, n. 147.
[14] See the account in Bartoš, *Čechy*, pp. 374 ff.
[15] *Ibid.*, pp. 113 ff.

never matched in medieval Bohemia; efforts by Charles IV in that direction were frustrated by baronial resistance, and Wenceslas could not take them up again. In fact, he was twice imprisoned by groups of his barons who on one occasion, in 1402, enjoyed the help of Sigismund, then King of Hungary. Thus the Hussite League of 5 September 1415, although by no means an open defiance of the king, necessarily implied a recrudescence of the old opposition, and when on 1 October 1415 a group of Catholic barons joined with Archbishop Conrad to oppose Hussitism, the unity of the realm suffered an additional reverse.[16] Parts of Moravia and, roughly, the eastern half of Bohemia were controlled by the Hussite feudality—the lesser nobles following the local barons—and the rest by the Catholics; although the latter were led by some of the same lords who had conspired to capture the king in 1402,[17] they now enjoyed at least his passive support, so that hundreds of royal officials and dependents were kept out of the Hussite camp.[18]

If King Wenceslas took any steps to control the situation they are not attested by surviving sources; instead, Emperor Sigismund comes to the fore, in the incongruous role of his brother's defender: since Wenceslas had no children, Sigismund was next in line to the Bohemian crown, and he did not hide his personal interest in preserving that crown's authority. In letters to both the Hussite and Catholic lords, in March of 1416, he bewailed the division of the realm into parties that had no other reason for existence than that "some held with Hus's side and some did not." [19] The pact of the Hussites, he declared, was "against the dignity of our dear brother, for no lord in the land ought to arrange or set up any league apart from the king's will"; [20] although he welcomed the decision of the non-Hussites to stand with the church,[21] he knew enough about the nature of these barons, having formerly intrigued with them himself, to realize that their league was of a piece with the other one.[22] Conflict between the two would diminish royal

---

[16] *Documenta,* pp. 601 f.; cf. Bartoš, *Do čtyř art.,* p. 6.

[17] Bartoš, *Do čtyř art.,* p. 7. Wenceslas's enemies among the barons in 1402 are named in *OCA-R,* p. 5; at least three appear in the Catholic League of 1415—see Palacký, III, i, 241.

[18] Bartoš, *Do čtyř art.,* pp. 6 f., and for more details, his "Vznik a osudy protestu," pp. 57 f.

[19] *Documenta,* pp. 610, 620.

[20] *Documenta,* p. 610.

[21] *Documenta,* pp. 613 f.

[22] Sigismund wrote two letters to the orthodox barons, one (21 March 1416; *Documenta,* pp. 613 f.) approving their resolve to stand by the Church, the other (30 March; *Documenta,* pp. 619–621) criticizing the division of the land into hostile leagues. For details see *HR,* I, 35, n. 51. Bartoš interprets the first as Sigismund's real and confidential message, the second as his public position (*Do čtyř art.,* p. 10). But it is possible to take each letter at something like its face value: Sigismund was certainly

power, devastate the realm, and open the way for Bohemia's ever-hostile neighbors to invade her. Expressing what was probably sincere regret that Hus's case had turned out so tragically, he informed the Hussite barons that, given the state of affairs at the Council, nothing could have been done to save Hus, nor would further defiance of the Council have any good effect. The Hussite protest of 2 September had aroused the Council's wrath, and if the barons were not careful they would find themselves the object of a crusade, and that would certainly be bad for the realm.[23] "Let the priests," he wrote, "discipline themselves, as they know how to do: they have their hierarchy and Holy Scriptures which they understand; it is not fitting for us laymen to delve into this."[24]

Meanwhile the Council of Constance was reacting in its own way to the situation created by the Hussite League. It had foreseen some such development as early as July 1415, when it had taken care to write to the Bohemians to justify its treatment of Hus and to forestall any defense of the latter's cause;[25] now, in March of 1416, it could only express its horror over the defiance of its authority. Indeed, the eight copies of the protest of 2 September must have caused a sensation when they arrived at the Council, each liberally festooned with pendent seals at the bottom and all around, a total of 452; the Council called it a *horrendum . . . et ridiculosum spectaculum;*[26] the one original that still survives certainly has a curious appearance, quite apart from the horrendous implication of its content.[27] It is noteworthy that the Council, like Sigismund, felt it necessary to insist on its remarkable

---

glad that some of the barons stood by the Church, but he was also disturbed at the prospect of a civil war in Bohemia. His aim, amply attested in the sources (*Documenta,* pp. 652 ff.; cf. Bartoš, *loc. cit.*), was to solve the Bohemian problem by his own offices as mediator between the parties and between Wenceslas and the Council.

[23] *Documenta,* pp. 610 f. In the corresponding letter to the Catholic barons Sigismund adds the point that he personally is distressed "because we are the just and legitimate heir of the Bohemian Crown" (*Documenta,* p. 620).

[24] *Documenta,* p. 611.

[25] Above, n. 5. There is a reference in the letter to those "qui . . . hanc nostram sententiam . . . quoquomodo impugnare tentaverint, ac in eadem damnatissima haeresi perstiterint, aut in ea persistentes juverint quomodolibet vel defenderint. . . ."

[26] *Documenta,* p. 616: The Hussite barons "quosdam libellos famosos, pelles scil. grandes suis calumniis jurgiisque plena(s) turpiter transscripserunt, quas in congregatione nostra . . . non erubuerunt facere publice praesentari; et earum pellium margines in gyrum circum circa suorum appensorum sigillorum . . . stupenda et ridiculosa praeoccupat multitudo, quae nedum horrendum, sed et ridiculosum spectaculum intuentibus praestant."

[27] It now belongs to the University of Edinburgh; the names of those whose seals are still attached to the parchment are printed in *Documenta,* p. 585 f., from a different source. Cf. Bartoš, "Vznik a osudy protestu," pp. 51 f., 59 f., for interesting details about the MS and the way it may have taken to Edinburgh. A photograph of it is printed in Novotný, *Hus v Kostnici,* with a study of the seals by A. Masák.

benevolence to John Hus in terms that today have their own aroma of the ridiculous: "Even though both divine and human laws decree that a heretic should respond to questioning from a prison cell, and in fetters—nevertheless we more than once gave him a public hearing . . . and not only was he given an opportunity for conversion, but, that his obstinate malice might be overcome, he was urgently besought, with superabundant instruction in the catholic truth, . . . to return to the bosom of the church." [28] Such passages show how remote the Council was from any understanding of the Bohemian temper; in any case, they eventually give way to nastier lines in which the fathers pronounce their single practical program for dealing with the religio-political mutiny of half a nation: the orthodox should "further the glory of God by the effective destruction of his enemies." [29] As for the protesting barons and knights, the Council decided to cite each of them to appear before it for judgement.[30] Fortunately they were well prepared, ideologically, to bear up under such attack. Not only did they enjoy the righteous conviction that it was they who were defending the honor of the realm, which the Council and Sigismund had besmirched; they also believed what years of diligent cultivation of their estate by John Hus and others had taught them, namely, that Christ's Truth urgently required a kind of reform that only they could provide and protect. Since this kind of reform involved the secularization of the church's estates, perhaps a third of the cultivated land,[31] self-interest confirmed the lesson that idealism had taught.

Here we come to a problem that leads us to the center of the situation created by the baronial defiance of the Council. Did the nobles who compacted to defend the Law of God have as their real motive the desire to get their hands on the church's estates? Catholic writers, beginning with such contemporary critics as Andrew of Brod and Stephen of Dolany, have never been reluctant to say yes—at least not until the challenges of our own century forced Catholic scholars to see that anti-Romanism might not always have had its source in vice. Now, paradoxically, it is the Marxist scholars who take up the charge—most notably, in the present case, Josef Macek, whose lavish use of the Catholic sources in this connection tells its own story, which we shall gloss in our footnotes.[32] But certainly a man like Andrew of Brod

[28] *Documenta*, p. 617.

[29] *Documenta*, p. 618: ". . . et dei gloriam in hostium suorum exterminio efficaciter prosequantur. . . ."

[30] The Council made its decision on 24 February 1416, and the citations were published in various cities in May and June. See the texts in Hardt, IV, 829–852; I draw these data from Palacký, III, i, 257.

[31] J. Macek, *Tábor v husitském revolučním hnutí,* I (2d ed.; Prague, 1956), 59.

[32] Since Macek sees the Hussite movement as essentially a class struggle, there is no place in his account for the Hussitism of the Hussite barons. The protest of 2 September 1415 cannot be ignored, but it is explained as an action organized by the *lower* nobility,

deserves to be heard, for some of his observations, in his anti-Hussite work of about 1421, are deep enough to be instructive. Thus:[33]

> This was the evil reasoning . . . of the magnates: "See, the burghers [*cives*] now surpass us in wealth, the clergy are swollen with possessions, the king enjoys vast treasures and lands. It would be the counsel of wisdom to move the burghers against the king, if he should be unwilling to embrace their sect. In this way we shall prosper no matter what happens, and divide up among ourselves the temporal goods of either the burghers or the clergy, at no cost to us. For if the Lord King sides with the burghers and accepts their dogmas, then indeed, since it is the burghers' will that the clergy not possess temporal property, that property will certainly be given to us. But if the king does not go along with them, there will be passages of arms, wars will sweep from one end of the land to the other, and military stipends will not be skimpy— indeed they will be lavish, and thus knights and fighting men will at least be enriched. Moreover, those temporal properties that adjoin our forts and castles will fall under our permanent rule." This was the secret hidden in the quiver of some, but not all, of the magnates.[34]

If then a sizable portion of the nobility chose to follow the path of plunder, it was because they envied the wealth of the other classes; "they themselves had squandered their own property in gluttony, pomposity, and luxury, and they sought to recoup their fortunes by rapine."[35] Their ancestors had been generous providers for the church, but as generation had followed generation, liberality had given way first to a certain tepidity, then to self-indulgent stinginess, then to occasional spoliation of church property, and finally to the self-destructive posture of the Hussite nobility, whose rebellion against the

---

whose 391 names far outweighed the only 58 names of the barons (I, 178). In fact, although there could hardly have failed to be more of the lower than of the upper nobility in any mass action of the noble estate, the protest was undoubtedly organized by a few *barons,* in conjunction with the Hussite masters of the University. The fact is quite clear when we note the baronial organization of the Hussite League of 5 September 1415, an event that Macek does not even mention! But he does mention the Catholic League of 1 October (I, 178), although with the questionable statement, that King Wenceslas opposed it (I, 176). Instead of the Hussite League of the barons, Macek offers the case of a local compact between three lesser noblemen, in 1417 (I, 178; from Bartoš, *Do čtyř art.,* p. 18, n. 62). In fact, this is a valuable datum, but only when understood in the light of the baronial league, which the compact of 1417 clearly intended to implement.

[33] Höfler, II, 347. For Andrew himself and his treatise, *De origine Hussitarum,* see Pekař, *Žižka a jeho doba,* I, 32–36.

[34] This sentence, "Hoc erat absconsum latibulum in quorundam, non tamen omnium, pharetra magnatorum" (*loc. cit.*), is translated by Macek in just the opposite sense: ". . . ne některých, nýbrž *všech* . . ."—"not of some but of *all*" (I, 80).

[35] Höfler, II, 348.

church had led them into "a monstrous league with burghers and peasants." [36] It is clear from this that Andrew of Brod's religious critique was not
devoid of socio-historical solidity, and everything that has been written about
the crisis of the late-medieval feudality can be usefully borne in mind at this
point.[37] But as he himself conceded, not all the nobles of Bohemia and
Moravia were guided by such calculations, and according to his own analysis,
any particular baron might have sought his material advantage on either
side; indeed those who stood by Catholicism were recompensed by church
property, either given to them in pledge of payment or simply taken over by
them in the general turmoil.[38] By the end of the Hussite wars both parties of
the nobility had proved to be winners.[39] Thus, without denying that the
Hussite doctrines justifying secularization of church property must have
been very attractive to the nobles who formed the Hussite League, we must
also make room for more complex motives.

Here it may be suggested that the best point of departure would be the
formulation in the compact of the League: "our clergy whom we have under
us." This or that lord might have had either a solid or a superficial understanding of what was implied by the "Law of God" and the "Word of God,"
the free preaching of both of which the League guaranteed, but all had a
very clear idea of the *ius patronatus* that they had been exercising all along,

[36] *Ibid.*, p. 349.

[37] Macek, who regards the social and economic factors as primary, devotes a good deal
of very useful study to "the crisis of feudalism in the fourteenth and fifteenth centuries"
(I, chap. ii, 39–54) and to "the social and economic situation in pre-Hussite Bohemia at
the beginning of the fifteenth century" (I, chap. iii, 55–126). For a more detailed study
of the socio-economic position of the feudal landlords in pre-Hussite times, see F. Graus,
Dějiny venkovského lidu v Čechách v době předhusitské, II (Prague, 1957). Graus has
also advanced an interpretation of the crisis of the feudal order as rooted in the
transition to a money economy: see his "Krise feudalismu v 14. století," *SbH,* I (1953),
65–121, with French summary on pp. 250–252; there is an abridged German version,
"Die erste Krise des Feudalismus," *Zeitschrift für Geschichtswissenschaft,* III (1955),
552–592. But the scholarly discussion of the nature of fourteenth-century social and
economic developments is still going on, and it cannot now be said that there is real
agreement on even the most basic generalizations.

[38] For examples of Sigismund's pledges of church property to Catholic barons see
Palacký, III, i, 410. Tomek, III, 595, gives an example of outright seizure: on 1
November 1415 the Catholic lords John of Opočno and Otto of Bergov attacked and
captured the monastery of Opatovice and dispersed the monks. This was just one month
after Otto had helped to form the Catholic League. Macek, I, 182, discusses the incident
as an example simply of the greed common to all the nobles.

[39] When in 1455 Aeneas Sylvius wished to prove the desirability of negotiating with
the Hussites, he could argue that their secularization of church property should not be
made an issue—the Catholic lords too, he noted, had taken such property. See my "Pius
Aeneas among the Taborites," *Church History,* XXVIII (1959), 299.

as a matter of routine, within the Bohemian church. By the fifteenth century, of course, the "liberty of the church" had been institutionalized to the point where the rights of secular patrons amounted to little more than the right of advowson—that is, of presentation of their candidates to church livings; but here as elsewhere the practical tendency of Wyclifite reformism revivified the older situation.[40] Reform was deduced in theory from the Law of God, but in practice, since it sought to undo the institutional work of what may be called for convenience the Hildebrandine reform, it appealed to those elements that Hildebrandinism had not been able to master or destroy. The nobility's right of patronage was one such element, and it is not too much to say that the ecclesiastical structure actually envisaged by the Hussite masters of the university and their allies among the nobility rested not upon the ideal of the Primitive Church, but on the *ius patronatus,* understood in a very broad sense. Some of the most effective works of Wyclif including the doctrine under discussion were translated into Czech by John Hus and Jakoubek, no doubt for the purpose of instructing the secular powers,[41] and the Wyclifite concept of the patron's rights was pronounced very clearly by Hus in his Czech work *On Simony:*

> . . . advowson [*podacie = patronatus*] is not a church, an altar, or any material thing, but it is a spiritual power, and the lord who has that power can and ought to see to it, that all remains well with the alms [*scil.,* the endowment] originally given for the glory of God. Therefore the holder of the advowson is called in Latin, *patronus*—that is, father, or defender; for as a faithful father he should take diligent care that all goes well, spiritually, with the church, the altar, the chapel, or the alms-endowment.

> A man is a patron . . . on account of three things, the ground, the building, and the endowment. . . . But these three things entail for the patron three

[40] See my "Wyclifism," pp. 63 f., 67 f. It should be noted that the special rights of the lay patrons over churches were not denied by even the most authoritative canonistic collections and glosses of the thirteenth and fourteenth centuries—see, e.g., the texts Wyclif cites in his *De Simonia,* eds. Herzberg-Fränkel and M. Dziewicki (London, 1898), pp. 34–36.

[41] For Hus's lost translation of Wyclif's *Trialogus* see *LČH,* p. 123. Stephen of Dolany, in his *Epistolae ad Hussitas* (1417), wrote of Hus's translation: ". . . transcriptum Wikleff Trialogum maledictionis olim Marchioni Judoco [*scil.,* Margrave Jošt of Moravia], et aliis viris notabilibus; aliis autem laicis et mulieribus translatum Bohemice pro magno munere transmisit," ed. B. Pez, *Thesaurus anecdotorum novissimus,* IV, ii (Augsburg, 1723), col. 527. For Jakoubek's translation of the *Dialogus* see *LČJ,* No. 103 (where the work is dated *ca.* 1415). In late 1417 or in 1418 the Council of Constance's conditions for "reducing" Bohemia to obedience included the demand "quod tractatus Johannis Wikleff translati in vulgari per Johannem Hus et per Jacobellum . . . reponantur ad manus legati vel ordinati [ordinarii?] . . . et comburantur" (Höfler, II, 241).

other things: honor, responsibility, and profit. Honor from the people and the priest, for they should hold him in esteem; responsibility, because he must exercise care in granting the benefice to a good priest, so that the spiritual ministration be well cared for, and also that he not become proud; and profit, which consists in the eternal reward, unless he lose it. He also is entitled to material profit, so that if he should become so impoverished as to be unable to provide a suitable livelihood for himself or his children, it would then be proper that he receive aid from the church property. . . .[42]

Similar points were also developed by Nicholas of Dresden, in his own fashion, by recourse to the *Decretum* and the glosses thereon: the descendants of the man who endowed a church have the right to keep watch on the priest, and even to use force in correcting the priest, under certain conditions, a right also conceded more generally to the secular powers by Pope Urban II. "Wherever ecclesiastical power fails," Nicholas summarizes, "recourse is always had to the secular arm."[43] We have already seen that both Hus and Jakoubek used Wyclif to justify the reforming mission of the secular powers, including the latter's right to take away church property from delinquent priests; such ideas were not only remembered but repeated in the period now under discussion, not only in the form of theoretical disquisitions,[44] but also

[42] *O svatokupectví*, ed. K. J. Erben, *Mistra Jana Husi sebrané spisy české*, I (Prague, 1865), 449 f.; I follow M. Spinka's translation in his *Advocates of Reform* (London, 1953), p. 258, but I have reworded certain passages. Hus's formulations are taken, with much reworking and composition, from Wyclif's *De simonia*, pp. 34 f.

[43] *Puncta*, MS UP, IV G 15, fol. 15ʳ sqq., the quoted passage on fol. 16ʳ, where Nicholas cites the *glossa ordinaria* on "Per seculares," in XVII. Dist., c. 4, and adds: "Hic habes quod ubicumque deficit ecclesiastica potestas, semper recurritur ad brachium seculari." It may be of use to give his other canonistic authorities in this discussion: XVI. q. vii, c. 31; XXIII. q. v, c. 20 (and the gloss on "laici habent"); XXXII. Dist., c. 10 (and the gloss on "Consenserint"); XL. Dist., c. 6 (and the gloss on "a fide devius"). There is a corresponding discussion in Nicholas's sermon on *Querite primum regnum Dei*, MS UP, IV G 15, fols. 111ᵛ–112ʳ, and, on fol. 124ʳ, after an attack on the heresy of simony, Nicholas writes: "Et ideo domini temporales iuste et catholice auferrant et auferrent ab huius [modi] anticristis et maximis hereticis possessiones temporales, et in usus pauperum et defensionem legis dei converterent"—an evident echo of Wyclifite doctrine (see above, chap. i, *ad* n. 151).

[44] So for example Jakoubek's polemical treatise of 1415 against Andrew of Brod included a presentation of Wyclif's doctrine, that the clergy should lead more perfect lives than the secular estates and should therefore renounce temporal dominion. Using Wyclif's words he defined four possible relations of the clergy to temporalities: the best (1) was to be entirely dependent on the laity's alms for necessary food and clothing, but (2) the receipt of regularized tithes and offerings was also admissible, if less laudable, while still worse was (3) the possession of estates and the like by title of alms; (4) actual ownership of these by civil dominion was downright pagan. The passage is in Hardt, III, 437 ff.; it is drawn from Wyclif's *De vaticinacione*, in *Opera minora*, p. 171 f.

in direct advice to the king and barons.[45] The expanded concept of patronage represented the same idea, arrived at, so to speak, from below, and thereby endowed with the enormous advantage that facts always have over theories. At the same time facts and theories worked together. The clerical estate ought to imitate Jesus and the apostles in evangelical poverty and evangelical preaching, to say nothing of evangelical morality; on this basis the complex of potential rights clustered around the lords' status as patrons could be activated.

If then the Hussite League represented a fulfillment of the program of political Hussitism, it also stood as the foundation for a reconstruction of the

---

Bartoš observes that Jakoubek had used the same formulation in a sermon of 20 March 1414 (see *LČJ*, No. 58), and used it again in 1415 in a *responsum* "de censibus ecclesie" addressed to a questioner who, we may guess, was engaged in the actual work of carrying through a reformation (MS UP, III G 28, fols. 227ᵛ-228ᵛ; *LČJ*, No. 58). The allegedly milder position taken by Jakoubek in another, perhaps later *responsum* (*LČJ*, No. 67; cf. No. 58 and also J. Pekař, "Nový Bartoš," *ČČH*, XXXII (1926), 350) does to be sure correspond in general to only the second and third positions defined above—as we shall see, only the Taborites tried to put the first into practice—but the important point is that in all three of the permissible positions the clergy are allowed only enough for sustenance, and that on the basis of their pastoral work: thus in any case most of the church's property could be legitimately taken away, and civil dominion over the rest would also belong to the secular powers. The same Wyclifite doctrine, linked however with Matthew of Janov's ideology of the simplified church, was pronounced at the Quodlibet of January 1416 by Peter of Benešov (MS III G 8, fols. 104ʳ-110ᵛ; see J. Prokeš, "Kvodlibet Šimona z Tišnova r. 1416," *ČMM*, XLV (1921), 25-51; cf. *HR*, I, 21, n. 15).

[45] Jakoubek's translation of Wyclif's *Dialogus* can be regarded as an example of such direct advice, particularly since it included a number of changes designed to make the work more popular, as well as adaptations of Wyclif's remarks about England to the Czech situation (see the remarks of M. Svoboda, the editor, in *Mistra Jakoubka ze Stříbra Překlad Viklefova Dialogu* (Prague, 1909), p. xxi). But since the natural vehicle for advice to take the church's property would have been conversation rather than the written word, we must rely chiefly on the anti-Hussite sources: thus an anonymous poet of c. 1417 wrote: "they flatter the secular lords and give them bad advice. . . . They whisper to the lords to take the priests' property away and leave only the tonsure. . . ." ("Všichni poslúchajte," in *Výbor z literatury české*, II, ed. K. J. Erben (Prague, 1868), 243 f.; quoted by Macek, I, 181). The anonymous "Slyšte všickni staří i vy děti" has similar passages—e.g., "They say, 'O King, it is no sin to take away whatever the priests have!'" (ed. V. Nebeský, *ČČM*, XXVI (1852), 141 ff., lines 437-438). And in Stephen of Dolany's *Epistolae ad Hussitas* (see n. 41), col. 596, there is this passage: ". . . publice praedicastis et odiosissime affirmastis, quod Dominus Rex Wenceslaus, . . . si nullam aliam occasionem suae perditionis haberet, hoc solum sufficeret ad suam damnationem, quod possessiones Ecclesiasticas non auferat Clero circum circa." Many other examples could be cited; see, e.g., Jakoubek's sermon for 21 March 1416: "The secular arm should take goods away from heretics and evil people, and give them to the good" (*Betlemská kázání* (Prague, 1951), p. 69).

Bohemian Church: a restoration of the extensive ecclesiastical powers enjoyed by the secular lords in pre-Hildebrandine days, but now understood in the light of the evangelical reform movement produced by the religious development of the later Middle Ages. If we now ask whether the lords' motives were pure or not, we can reduce the question to its proper insignificance: no man's motives are pure, the complex of idealism and self-interest in any man's mind is perfectly impenetrable, and every great work of historical construction moves along by enlisting *all* the sources of energy available in the human material, which is of course tainted by sin. The Catholics naturally reacted to the construction of a Hussite church by protesting when they were hurt, hence we have a list of complaints showing the negative side of the phenomenon: seizure of church property, intrusion of unentitled priests into parish livings, destruction of the episcopal power, contempt of church censures, and violent hands laid on the orthodox clergy.[46] The already-mentioned letter of the Council of Constance to the orthodox barons of Bohemia, dated 27 March 1416, may be quoted as a summary of such complaints:

> We think it is no secret to your lordships that the boldness and number of these perverse people is steadily increasing. Alas, the unbridled pride and impiety of the impious ones is ever growing, to the point that through them ecclesiastical censure is being dissolved and the authority of the canons is being sapped. The fear of God is put aside, and the very divine offices are profaned; many other nefarious and absurd things, repugnant to the Catholic faith, are, as we learn from common report, being publicly preached, with damnable audacity, against God and the saints and the holy mother Church. Priests, both regular and secular, are being despoiled, driven away from their benefices, injured, killed, and horribly treated, against the liberty of the church. Those who try to flee the society of the heretics or who do not wish to adhere to them suffer many injuries and offenses from them. . . .[47]

The Hussite chronicler, Master Laurence of Březová, must have been referring to the same realities when he wrote:

> After the death of John Hus the perverse clergy of Bohemia and Moravia, who had procured his condemnation by contributing money and by various other means, and who had consented to his death, were by just judgement of God afflicted increasingly every day, by having their property taken away by laymen, by being ejected from their places and offices, and even by being made to suffer physical violence.[48]

[46] The sources just cited teem with references to these actions, about which more will be said, in detail, below.

[47] *Documenta*, p. 618.

[48] *FRB*, V, 338 f.

In other words, the Hussite League was working. Although we have almost no information about which lords confiscated which estates, or which Hussite priests were obtruded into which parishes,[49] we can be sure that 1416 was a year of considerable achievement in both respects.

The martyrdom of Jerome of Prague, on 30 May of that year, must have stimulated this work, nor could either the Council or the domestic Catholics do anything to stop it. By the end of the year the Council could only turn to Sigismund, with a strong plea that he act to correct the unwholesome situation caused by the shameful sloth of his brother.[50] The heretics were stronger than ever, the Council wrote, and their pride had become so inflated that their program was "much more detestable than previously." Under the protection of the Hussite nobility the Wyclifites were exalting the memory of John Hus and Jerome of Prague into a holy cult, were giving communion in both kinds and proclaiming that such communion was necessary to salvation. The clergy were being despoiled "in villages and towns, not only in their incomes but in their movable property"; the Catholic priests were being injured and even killed; the faithful clergy were being expelled from their benefices and Wyclifites intruded. "Certain barons," moreover, "have defamed this holy Council with their letters, and have leagued together to prohibit the clergy subject to them from receiving the mandates of this holy Council, and many of them have despoiled and expelled their parish priests who have obeyed the mandates of the holy Council." The Wyclifite revolution was continuing.

Finally it remains to observe that the prosperity of the reform under the patronage of the Hussite feudality was more than matched by its success in Prague, under somewhat different conditions. Ever since the autumn of 1414 there had been open religious conflict in the city because of the lay chalice, with the people divided into two parties, each with its own mode of

---

[49] From the middle of 1417 on, as will be seen, there were many illegal installations of Hussite priests that we know about; for the previous period, however, we can only speculate, on the basis of Catholic complaints, that many non-Hussite priests were driven out and their places taken, perhaps without formal illegal installation, by Hussites. See, e.g., the anti-Hussite rhymes in *OCA,* p. 474: "Lords Lacek of Moravia, Peter of Strážnice, Heralt of Skala, and John of Tovačov brought in Wyclifite priests to Moravia, to give the Lord's blood, and the bishops of Moravia complained bitterly of them." The one brought in by John of Tovačov was Master Simon of Tišnov, sometime in 1416 (O. Odložilík, "Z počátků husitství na Moravě," *ČMM,* XLIX (1925), 53). It may be that in addition some of the seventeen or so priests called "occupatores" of various Moravian churches by Bishop John Železný on 5 February 1418 had been brought in during 1415 or 1416 (*ibid.,* pp. 117 f.; B. Bretholz, "Die Übergabe Mährens an Herzog Albrecht V von Österreich, im Jahre 1423," *AÖG,* LXXX (1894), 334 f.).

[50] *Documenta,* pp. 647–651. The dating in the end of 1416 is Palacký's; Bartoš, *Do čtyř art.,* p. 11, n. 35, dates it in May 1416, for reasons that are not clear to me.

communion, its own priests, its own churches. Moreover, within the Hussite party there were controversies between the radical utraquists and the others. The turmoil was so intense that on 12 April 1415 the town councillors, no doubt at the king's orders, formally prohibited mutual heretication [51]—a device that, as we have seen, was the king's standard response to religious dissension. But any effect that this action might have had was certainly nullified in June and July, when the Council prohibited the lay chalice, condemned Hus to death, and immediately proceeded to organize anti-Hussite action within the realm. On 5 September 1415, moreover, the authorities of the Prague diocese implemented the Council's condemnation of utraquism with one of their own, perhaps a renewal of action taken a year earlier.[52] Noting that some were in fact taking communion in both kinds, the letter commanded the parish clergy to make the Council's prohibition known to their flocks, to agitate against the practice themselves, and to threaten the defiant with excommunication. Indeed, the attitude of the Catholic clergy in Prague became so militantly hostile that the Hussite community met on 16 September and addressed a complaint to the magistrates, that the decree of 12 April was being violated.[53] Two days later, however, the diocesan authorities pushed their campaign even further, by condemning the itinerant preachers who were stirring the people up with attacks on the orthodox clergy and preaching without the permission of anyone, not even the local priests. Such preachers were to be kept out of churches and, if insistent, formally excommunicated.[54] The Hussite League had been designed to deal with this sort of repression, and if the condemnations had any effect at all, it must have been in the parishes controlled by as yet uncommitted powers, and in the city of Prague, where the contending parties were still maneuvering for the initiative. Both the archbishop and the king, the two powers who together controlled the city, in theory, gave their allegiance to the Catholic party and to the Catholic League that was organized on 1 October, but neither man was much good at anything and their personal ineptitude was reinforced by circumstances: Conrad was a royal servant and never forgot it,[55] while the king was surrounded by courtiers who were for the most part Hussite. Thus in spite of ecclesiastical pronouncements against the reform, and in spite of a formal opposition to

[51] *Documenta*, pp. 604–606.

[52] *Documenta*, pp. 595 f.

[53] *Documenta*, pp. 604–606.

[54] *Documenta*, pp. 600 f.

[55] See, for example, Conrad's own declaration to Wenceslas, *Documenta*, p. 630. Conrad had been a member of the royal council from 1398 on, had served as Mintmaster, then as Subchamberlain, before becoming Bishop of Olomouc, in 1408; see Bartoš, *Čechy*, p. 470.

utraquism that earned both king and archbishop a bad reputation in Hussite circles,[56] the political situation in the capital city was by no means hopeless: the Hussite politicians could maneuver and the radicals could preach and practice utraquism in relative peace.

This balance was upset, however, when John Železný returned from Constance, sometime in October.[57] We do not know whether he took up residence in his own city of Litomyšl or elsewhere, but it seems clear that he plunged immediately into the vortex of conflict, partly because his own estates were suffering from depredations by the surrounding Hussite feudality,[58] partly because he seems to have been personally under attack—according to one report, he could not even leave his residence,[59] and partly because his mandate from the Council and his own desires combined to prescribe a course of militant action. Although by no means unconcerned with the doctrinal deviations of the radicals, or with the problems posed by utraquism, he naturally supposed that the first necessity was to limit and if possible diminish the power of the Hussite League. He therefore refrained from publishing the anti-utraquist decree of the Council and the disciplinary measures with which he was empowered to implement it—they were published only on 29 October 1416.[60] Instead he prevailed upon King Wenceslas to summon a meeting of the leading nobles of the realm, to hear Železný's report of the mission the Council had assigned him; the king called such a meeting for 11 November, and the one surviving source shows that Lord Čeněk of Vartemberk was particularly enjoined to attend.[61] There is no evidence that the meeting was held, but we do know that Čeněk had a personal talk with Archbishop Conrad in Prague, probably at about this time, and that the Hussite urged a kind of settlement that the political leaders of the party had always promoted: namely the enforcement of peace, without a change in the *status quo*.[62]

---

[56] See Laurence of Březová's testimony, *FRB*, V, 329.

[57] Bartoš, *Do čtyř art.*, p. 7.

[58] Palacký, III, i, 236.

[59] *Ibid.*, p. 243 (quoting Dietrich of Niem, in Hardt, II, 425).

[60] The text in J. Loserth, "Beiträge," *AÖG*, LXXXII (1895), 378–381. The document carries its own dating: "Datum et actum Luthomissl anno domini 1416 indiccione IX die XXIX mensis Octobris." Bartoš supposes that this dating is incorrect, and that Železný actually published the decree on 29 October 1415 (*Do čtyř art.*, p. 12, n. 40), but it is not clear why he thinks this; there is no discrepancy, as he seems to say, between the indiction-number and the calendar date in the document.

[61] *Documenta*, pp. 602 f. The letter is dated 31 October.

[62] *Documenta*, pp. 536 f. The text is a letter from Conrad to Čeněk, dated 6 March; Palacký suggests 1415, but internal evidence (e.g., "sanguinis effusio exspectatur"; references to nobles who look to Čeněk ("vestri ob respectum . . .") and who "ecclesias et personas ecclesiasticas invadentes et blasphemiam committentes, in vilipendiam

As for Conrad, the last thing he had looked for when he bought his office was an opportunity for martyrdom; his inclination was always to treat the disturbances in his province as something that the pope or the Council should deal with; [63] if he now proceeded to an energetic defense of the faith, we may assume that here too the powerful hand of John Železný had been at work. What Conrad did was to enforce an interdict on Prague, at the beginning of November—not because the altars of the city's churches were being daily dishonored by communion in both kinds, not because such violent anti-Romanists as Jakoubek of Stříbro and Nicholas of Dresden were daily pouring forth their notoriously heretical doctrines, not because the University of Prague had recently (on 11 September) pronounced in favor of the condemned heretic John Hus—not for any of these reasons, but because John Jesenic, whose original excommunication in 1412 had been aggravated and reaggravated over the years, was residing in the city. [64] Since Jesenic had probably been the leading figure in the organization of the Hussite nobility during the past year, the interdict must be interpreted as another effort to deal with the problem of Hussitism by attacking the Hussite League. If Lord Čeněk and the others had yielded to pressure, if the king had felt strong enough to take real repressive action, if Jesenic and the other masters had given up their political activity—then perhaps the policy might have succeeded in liquidating the reform itself. But in fact none of these things

censurae ecclesiasticae nefanda et scandalosa committere praesumpserunt") makes so early a date almost impossible. On the other hand, a reference to Patriarch Wenceslas of Antioch as (*de facto*) bishop of Olomouc rules out a later date than 1416, for he died on 12 September of that year. Hence Conrad's letter must be dated 6 March 1416, and the personal talk it mentions would most probably have taken place in the autumn of 1415, when Čeněk had emerged as leader of the Hussite League.

[63] It will be recalled that when Hus's supporters had asked Conrad in October of 1415 for a testimonial to the master's orthodoxy, Conrad had observed that the issue was between Hus and the pope (above, chap. iii, *ad* n. 146)—a remarkable statement for Hus's ordinary to make. A year later he was still trying to play it safe: at the end of 1416 Sigismund informed the Council that when King Wenceslas allegedly invoked the archbishop's jurisdiction over John Jesenic, whose presence in Prague was responsible for the interdict upon that city, Jesenic said that he would take his law before the archbishop, but "archiepiscopus se excusat propter praesentiam hujus sacri concilii, ad cujus examen et judicium hujusmodi negotium pertinere dicit, cupiens esse non martyr sed confessor" (*Documenta*, p. 653).

[64] Laurence of Březová, *FRB*, V, 341 f.: "Item anno eodem [1415] circa festum Omnium sanctorum [1. Nov.] et anno domini MCCCCXVI currente ante festum Purificacionis [2. Feb.] factum est interdictum in Praga." The *Chronicon universitatis pragensis, FRB*, V, 580, mentions only the later date, but adds the cause: "propter Magistrum Jessenicz." Cf. also *Documenta*, pp. 606–608. Kejř, *Husitský právník*, p. 99, n. 15, shows that even earlier there had been an interdict on Prague, on account of Jesenic; what Conrad did on 1 November was probably to renew or sharpen the ban.

happened, and the course of events will show that John Železný might have been better advised to have concentrated his fire on the religious front, and to have moved against the radicals, not the politicians, of the Hussite party.

For the response to the interdict was nothing less than a radical revolution, on the religious level. With the orthodox clergy dutifully refraining from administering all the sacraments except baptism,[65] the churches silent and empty, the priests and preachers of the Hussite party could move in and take over. "There was freedom in all the churches and monasteries for all the priests who adhered to Master John Hus and who promoted communion . . . in both kinds, daily to celebrate the divine rites and preach the Word of God." And, "many of the Prague clergy, especially the prelates and monks, were thrown out of the places that belonged to them, and replaced by priests who favored utraquist communion and Master John Hus, King Wenceslas of Bohemia permitting this at the urging of some of his counsellors." Since of the legitimate parish priests only one, Christian of Prachatice, was a Hussite, the turnover was quite drastic.[66] It was accomplished and accompanied, moreover, by forceful direct action on the part of the Hussite people of Prague, who had been accustomed to display their sentiments and power in the streets of the city during the previous years of religious controversy.[67] This time, however, the people were joined, protected, and perhaps led by several of King Wenceslas's favorite courtiers, especially John Sádlo, and by the magistrates of Prague, no doubt under royal orders.[68] In these circumstances violence produced lasting effects: the Catholics were henceforth able to provide for their people only in suburban churches, outside the bounds of the interdict, and the king's unwillingness to defend the Catholics' rights seems to have had as one result the lifting of the interdict by Conrad—in other words a recognition of the new situation's stability.[69] To be sure, when informed, no doubt by Železný, that this

---

[65] A complaint of the "Prague Community" to the town councillors about the effects of the interdict mentions noncelebration of mass, nonperformance of burial services, etc., but says nothing about refusal to baptize. Cf., however, the later evidence of *Mon. conc. saec. XV.*, I, 415.

[66] Laurence, pp. 341 f.; *Chronicon universitatis pragensis, FRB*, V, 580.

[67] Tomek, III, 593 f.

[68] The guilty courtiers and magistrates were later cited for judgement before the Council of Constance and then Pope Martin V; see the text and explanation offered by V. Novotný, "Monitorium Patriarcha Konstantinopolského Jana . . . z R. 1418," *VČA*, XXIV (1915), 1–16. John Sádlo's prominent role is reflected in this text and is otherwise attested by Laurence of Březová, *FRB*, V, 515.

[69] A later agreement between Conrad and the university (*Doc.*, p. 646) includes a remark to the effect that "propter priorem resumtionem divinorum et violationem interdicti praefatus D. Archiepiscopus fuit et est personaliter ad Constantiam citatus." It would seem likely that the second date given in the sources cited in n. 64 was in fact the date when Conrad *re*-imposed the interdict, after he had prematurely lifted it.

accommodation was unacceptable, Conrad reimposed the interdict, shortly before 2 February 1416; the net effect of his vacillation was to make him seem a friend of heresy, and the Council of Constance accordingly issued a citation against him. But none of this seriously affected the radical victory, which even spread to other royal towns of the realm, the utraquists taking the churches away from the Catholics and depriving the latter of their incomes.[70]

In one way or another, by seigneurial establishment or radical seizure, a sizable portion of the Bohemian church organization thus passed into Hussite hands, and in a situation of successful expansion there was no cause for dissent between the two wings. It is true that utraquism had been a point of controversy and that the Hussite League had not even mentioned it, but by the end of 1416 the lay chalice was accepted by all who stood for the cause of Hus.[71] There were other points of difference between Jakoubek's party and the rest, but these would certainly have been moderated under the stabilizing influence exerted by the ecclesiastical institution that now provided all Hussites with a common home. If this did not happen, if instead the development of radicalism continued even more rapidly than before, to the point of causing incipient and then full-grown schisms between radicals and conservatives, and between more and less extreme wings of the radical party itself, one reason is that the lines of action just canvassed were flanked by a third development, the eruption of a kind of sectarian extremism at various points in the provinces. At first appearing to both the conservative and radical masters of Prague as a series of difficulties and challenges, the extremist movement would eventually transform the whole inner development of Hussitism, bring about new alignments of the parties, and cause a continuation of both reformation and revolution far beyond anything foreseeable in 1415. Virtually everything that follows in these pages is concerned with this cycle of transformations.

SECTARIAN EXTREMISM IN THE PROVINCES

In 1415–1417, the same period that saw the beginnings of a seigneurial Hussite establishment and the radical coup in Prague, the struggle for control of the Bohemian and Moravian church was also pursued on another front, that of direct local action by radicals in the provinces. Rightly seeing this action as one of the main roots of later Taborism, historians have spent much effort trying to determine the essential nature of what was going on:

[70] Bartoš, *Do čtyř art.*, p. 8, citing texts in *Documenta*, pp. 642 f.

[71] As we shall see, the decisive actions of the national Hussite party in the first half of 1417 presuppose the common ground of utraquism.

Was it simply the application of Jakoubek's doctrines to particular cases? Or must we also reckon with the ideas of Nicholas of Dresden? Or was it a quasi-independent application and extension of Wyclifism? Or an upsurge of long-extant but previously hidden Waldensianism? Or a manifestation of the class war? Each possibility has found its adherents, and the resulting controversies—some of which go back to the Hussite period itself—have produced light as well as heat; nor is there any reason to think that the problem can be further illuminated except by further argument, which will appear below in due course. But first of all we must look at the evidence, systematically and in detail.

One of the more useful of King Wenceslas's courtiers, Wenceslas Králík of Buřenic, Patriarch of Antioch, also held the less prestigious but more profitable see of Olomouc in Moravia—not of course as bishop but as "permanent commendator." When he died on 12 September 1416 the local canons at once voted for Bishop John Železný of Litomyšl to succeed him, and then postulated John's appointment from the Council of Constance.[72] King Wenceslas, however, wished the post to go to one of his men, Aleš of Březí, a canon of the Vyšehrad church in Prague, and the nonresident canons of Olomouc met in Prague to make this election; Aleš was at once consecrated and confirmed by Archbishop Conrad. None of this was unfamiliar or even abnormal in the late-medieval church, but the ensuing struggle was quickly complicated by issues of Hussitism. While Aleš was not a Hussite, he represented a royal government that had shown considerable indifference to the heresy; John Železný was the most effective persecutor in the realm and, as we have seen, the Germans of Olomouc had their own tradition of ruthless piety. Hence the canons of John's party, addressing a letter on his behalf to the Council of Constance, found it advisable to dwell upon the progress that Hussitism had made, to the great peril of the church; their report, composed at the end of 1416, has passages that are indeed exceptionally informative:

> [1] When the heretical pravity of the Wyclifites and the Hussites spread in
> the Margravate of Moravia and in the diocese of Olomouc, it was held and

[72] For Králík's career see Bartoš, *Čechy*, p. 469. The canons' letter has been published twice, by B. Bretholz, "Die Übergabe Mährens an Herzog Albrecht V. von Österreich, im Jahre 1423," *AÖG*, LXXX (1894), 312–316, and by J. Loserth, "Beiträge zur Geschichte der Husitischen Bewegung V.," *AÖG*, LXXXII (1895), 386–391. The background is discussed by Bretholz and in more detail by O. Odložilík, "Z počátků husitství na Moravě," *ČMM*, XLIX (1925); 45 ff. The Council confirmed John Železný as Bishop of Olomouc on 14 December 1416, so the letter could not have been written much later than that; the *terminus a quo* is provided by its reference to a mass celebrated on Advent Sunday—hence 29 November 1416. I have supplied the numbers for the translated paragraphs below.

defended by many barons, nobles, and knights, and by some commoners. Through this heretical pravity the catholic faith has been and is now most seriously threatened; the sacraments of the church have been turned into virtual jokes by the said Wyclifites and Hussites; the keys of the church and ecclesiastical censures have been derided by them; obedience to the Roman church and the Apostolic See, as well as to other bishops and prelates, has been wholly removed by them. As a result of all this the church of Olomouc is grievously oppressed in many ways and with excessive cruelty, together with the canons and clergy of the diocese.

[2] And, descending to particulars, certain lay barons maintain priests from whom they take communion in both sacramental species of the Body of Christ, in contempt of the Holy Council of Constance and the Apostolic See and the Roman church.

[3] Certain priests before the elevation or consecration of the Body of Christ break the oblate into three parts and only elevate one to the people. Certain ones baptize children in fish-ponds, others in rivers, even when there is no imminent danger of death. Others, excommunicated by canons and by men, and interdicted, celebrate mass in fields and on casks, in barns and on no consecrated altar. Others do not say the canonical hours but go right on into the divine office. Nor do they hear any confessions, but rather preach to the laity that they are not required to confess.

[4] Others hold services in churches, before many people, for John Hus and Jerome of Prague, condemned public heretics, as though for deceased faithful Christians. Others celebrate festivities for them and sing the *Gaudeamus* and other songs, as though for martyrs, comparing them in merits and sufferings to Saint Laurence the martyr, and preferring them to Saint Peter and other saints.

The letter then complains that Catholic parish priests were being expelled from their livings, despoiled of their incomes and crops, denied tithes, and thus in any case forced to abandon their parishes for want of subsistence. Some priests indeed were being held captive, tortured, killed. And all this was the work of the Hussite patrons of the local churches.

It is useful to learn from paragraphs one and two, and perhaps also four, that by the end of 1416 the program of the Hussite League was not only being extensively implemented, but that, as we would expect, the nobility's Hussitism now also included utraquism and the cult of Hus. Even the violence used against Catholic incumbents can perhaps be understood as merely the consequence of the seigneurial establishment. But paragraph three tells a new story. The odd business with the breaking of the eucharistic bread is not, to be sure, attested in other sources, and it is not clear what its significance was; it may have been a unique occurrence, for the letter says that a certain priest John did these things in a mass celebrated in Olomouc

Cathedral on Advent Sunday (29 November) 1416. Perhaps the canons gave a distorted version of a somewhat similar incident reported in more detail by Stephen of Dolany in his *Epistolae ad Hussitas*.[73] In any case, greater interest attaches to the other practices mentioned in the paragraph: certain priests baptized in ordinary water, celebrated mass outside of churches, omitted canonical hours, and rejected auricular confession. These were probably not the chaplains or parish priests of the Hussite nobility, for they would have had no need to celebrate mass in barns; as Stephen of Dolany wrote, on the basis no doubt of the same Moravian experience, the Hussites gave communion in stables or barns when they could not get into the regular churches.[74] Furthermore, the language of the letter itself separates the priests of paragraph three from those of paragraph two.[75] We must infer that certain Hussites who were *not* installed in livings under the patronage of the nobility were organizing their own congregations at the expense of the Roman parish priests, and that they did not hesitate when necessary to dispense with such externals as holy water and consecrated altars, as well as with the preparatory canonical hours. Since, as we shall see in the following section, Jakoubek of Stříbro had authorized such deviations as well as the rejection of compulsory auricular confession,[76] we may guess that the Hussites in question were his followers, benefiting no doubt from the protection

[73] Ed. B. Pez, *Thesaurus anecdotorum novissimus*, col. 596 f.: in 1417 a certain priest came to celebrate mass in Olomouc Cathedral; after the elevation he broke one of the three parts of the host into enough pieces to give communion to himself and his two assistants, to whom he also gave the chalice. He was then arrested, interrogated, and released. I would suggest the possibility that there was only one incident, which took place as Stephen described it, but on the day given by the Olomouc canons.

[74] *Ibid.*, col. 579 f.: "ubi per fideles clauduntur vobis Ecclesiae, facitis hoc [*scil.*, utraquist communion] in stabulis vel horreis."

[75] The passage in paragraphs two and three beginning "certain lay barons" reads thus: ". . . quidam barones laici tenent presbyteros, a quibus communicant sub utraque specie . . . , quidam ante elevacionem corporis Christi sive consecrationem frangunt oblatam. . . ." The second "quidam" is grammatically parallel to the "quidam barones" but in fact it must refer to priests; and yet the structure does not allow us to suppose the "presbyteros" already mentioned. Such deceptive language suggests a desire to deceive on the part of an author who yet retained some scruples. It should also be noted that insofar as we can identify the priests who enjoyed the patronage of the Moravian Hussite barons, we can see that they were not doctrinal radicals at all; the two known names are those of Master Sigismund of Jistebnice, chaplain to Lord Lacek of Kravaři, and Master Simon of Tišnov, who held a living from Lord John of Tovačov (Odložilík, *op. cit.*, pp. 117, 53).

[76] In his *Sermo de confessione* (*LČJ*, No. 53) of May, 1414, Jakoubek had argued that the only true and necessary confession was to God alone. Secret confession to a priest was recommended only when the priest was suitable, and it was not "de necessitate salutis, et specialiter in levibus peccatis" (MS D 53, fol. 183^r, 187^r).

of the Hussite nobility but working directly among the people. One can only try to imagine the radicalizing effect of the actual situation created by this activity.

Another report, also dating from 1416, offers much more information and at the same time takes us to the heartland of provincial extremism, South Bohemia. In fact, it takes us to the very place, Kozí Hradek, where Hus had earlier found refuge and popular support: "They miss me very much," he had written, "in the region where I preached: in the towns, in villages, in fields, at castles and around the castles, and in the woods under a linden tree at the castle called Kozí Hradek." [77] There is a late and hostile, but reassuringly circumstantial account to the same effect, in a rhymed Czech chronicle:

> In the year 1413 [*sic pro* 1412] Master John Hus was expelled from Prague because of his excommunication. He performed divine services and preached at Kozí Hradek, in a barn, and many came to his preaching from Ústí. For he inveighed against the pope, bishops, and canons, and constantly heaped abuse on the spiritual order. Here the priest Věněk began to baptize children in a fish-pond and to slander the chrism and holy oil and holy water. Afterward Master Hus returned to Prague and the king ordered him to appear at the Council of Constance, and he never returned from there.

Here the radical preaching of Hus seems somehow connected with the extreme radicalism of Věněk, who must have functioned as the leader of a group of Hussite activists.[78] Eager to know more about them, we cannot

---

[77] *Jan Hus. Sebrané spisy české*, p. 241.

[78] The quoted passage in *OCA*, p. 471 f. The rhymed chronicle just cited is uniquely valuable for its details but it is not trustworthy in its implications of cause and effect, or even of close chronological sequence. Thus it is literally impossible to say when Věněk began his work or whether there was any connection between it and Hus's preaching. Věněk indeed appears in another passage of the same chronicle immediately after the one just quoted: "Then there was quarreling among the priests in Prague, and they gave out the Lord's Blood. Master Jakoubek was the first to do this, at St. Michael's, and then the practice spread from there to Ústí. At Ústí it caused quarreling, priests driving each other out of the church. They stayed at Joha the baker's for almost a year. Pytel the clothier was a rich man of the town, and he took care of them: Jičín, Věněk, Peter the Tall, Antoš, Peter of Ústí, Pšenička, Kaniš, Bydlín, and other priests were boarded there. They did as they saw fit, thereby dividing the city into three factions, and they were never at peace among themselves, and they deprived many people of their lives. And thereby they destroyed the city, laying it waste." Scholars have taken the passage to refer to the immediate consequences of the spread of utraquism from Prague to South Bohemian Ústí, but as I have shown elsewhere ("Hussite Radicalism . . . ," p. 110, n. 2), the formation of the Ústí group and its internal difficulties must be referred to the years 1418–1419; hence the three previous years, after the introduction of the lay chalice in *ca.* 1415, are simply unaccounted for. Indeed they are suppressed by the chronicle's telescoping of events. Thus it would be improper to rest any important constructions

avoid attaching a special importance to the text that we shall now consider, an anonymous account of radical activities "in the castle of Kozí Hradek and around the castle and in the town of Ústí-nad-Lužnicí"; the author was apparently a local Catholic, who wrote a colorful but bad Latin, interspersed with Czech phrases. It is so basic that it must be quoted in full; the originally Czech phrases are here underlined:

> First that in the castle of Kozí Hradek and under the castle and in Ústí it has been preached and is being preached, that consecrations of ecclesiastical vestments and sacramental objects are vain, and that with any kind of covering of cloth, clothes, or robes, a priest can officiate and give communion to the people on the ground or on a table or on a cask. And that the bishops, whom those preachers call *locusts* and *coxcombs,* have invented all these consecrations of vestments, sacramental objects, altars, and churches, from avarice. They say that a simple priest can do all those things, arguing from the major premise that because the simple priest can make the Body of Christ he can do the other things all the more. With this they give communion to the people without mass, making the sacrament with only some prayers being said.
>
> Also they preach that baptism and the solemnities of the mass and all other things can be performed and celebrated outside the church. And thus they officiate in barns and baptize in *fish-ponds.* They say that the stone church, in which those evil *concubinaries* officiate, is a den of thieves, and they say that the images there are in vain. And on Good Friday they said to the people that they were adoring an idol, and they sought to prove it by saying that the *concubinaries* and *monks* do not begin or finish the mass.[79] And on that day they celebrated two complete masses in a barn near Kozí Hradek, and then said contemptuously, *"Today the concubinaries and monks will play with dolls and blocks of wood."* The common people, hearing this, derided and even blasphemed the praiseworthy way, withdrawing from obedience.
>
> Also there has been preaching by simple laymen, and these preachers have heard confessions in the houses of the city. Afterward they baptized the son of a layman called Krampeř outside the church in flowing water, in contempt of the church. This layman had been whipped in a town of the lord of Řečic

---

upon the chronicle's details. (For an accessible discussion of this source see H. Böhmer, "Magister Peter von Dresden," *Neues Archiv für Sächsische Geschichte und Altertumskunde,* XXXVI (1915), pp. 216 f., where it is dated in 1474.)

[79] The Good Friday in question would have been either 31 March 1415 or 19 April 1416. In the mass for that day the priest does not consecrate the Eucharist but uses a consecrated host left over from the previous day; he himself takes communion in only one kind, since the wine is not consecrated. In 1417 the radical John Čapek, then a partisan of Jakoubek of Stříbro but later to become a priest of Tabor, criticized the incomplete Good Friday mass just as the radicals around Kozí did—see the discussion in Nejedlý, IV, 161 ff.; cf. Bartoš, "Kněz Jan Čapek," *SbH,* V (1957), 32–36.

because of erroneous preaching; and he still holds now that every priest who does not hold with Hus is evil and cannot make the Eucharist. And so from those sermons many of the laity bring women to the church after childbirth, and similarly wives, in contempt of the church.

Also they say that all priests up to now have been thieves, because they have not given you the blood of Jesus Christ. Instructing the people they speak thus: if a concubinary in giving you the body of Christ says, "Do you believe that the body of Christ is here?" you should say, "I believe it"; if he goes on to ask, "Do you also believe that the blood of Christ is there?" you should say, "I do not believe it"—the reason being that Christ gave communion in both kinds and if Christ had seen no difference between those two, he would not have offered communion in both kinds, and therefore etc.

Also they say that it is better to gamble one's money away on dice than offer it to evil prelates, and they call everyone evil who does not hold with Hus. Both he who has renounced the truth and he who gives tithes sin mortally. And they add that Hus was of more benefit to the Catholic church and did more miracles than St. Peter or St. Paul, because they did miracles corporally, but Hus spiritually.

Also laymen wishing in time of pestilence to have the priests march in procession at a funeral, and having then been instructed by them, have rejected bell-ringing, offertories, and offerings for the dead, and have themselves carried away their dead, singing the song, *"We Christians of True Faith,"* and bearing a staff for a cross; putting the bodies in the graves, they blessed them, saying *"I commend you to God Jesus Christ with papal power, for I can do as much as an archbishop,"* etc. And they add that it is better to lie under a gibbet than to lie dead in a cemetery of *concubinaries* and *monks;* and that it is better to go a hundred miles to a good priest than to stay and hear the masses of the others, the reason being that the latter cannot make the Eucharist, and therefore any layman can take what they offer and wipe his backside with it, etc.[80]

This sort of violently abusive, even filthy anti-Roman propaganda, carried on among people who were obviously in the process of seceding from the established church, points toward the actual use of physical violence; another item of evidence, this time for radical action in nearby Písek and its surroundings, shows that such violence was in fact used. The text is a judicial citation, prepared in Constance in 1418 on the order of Pope Martin V, of five priests and twenty-seven laymen who had been accused by the vicar of Heřman and parochial administrator of Písek, one John, of having in 1416, forced their way under arms into his church and parish house, where they

[80] *Documenta,* pp. 636–638. I accept Palacký's suggested date of 1416, even against the strong argument for 1415 in Holinka, *Sektářství v Čechách před revolucí husitskou* (Bratislava, 1929), p. 271. The difference is not important for the present purpose.

despoiled him of the rents, tithes, monies, and various goods that were there; they also imprisoned and tortured his assistant, a cleric named Čapek. Apparently—the text is damaged—they tried to lay violent hands on John himself.[81] All of this, we read, did serious damage to John and to the privilege and liberty of the clergy, but, what was worse, the intruders did not blush to celebrate masses in Czech, in villages, ordinary rooms, and barns, and they venerated John Hus and Jerome of Prague as saints. Fragmentary passages in the damaged text suggest that they were also accused of having given communion in both kinds to the laity and of having baptized with ordinary water.[82] There is not much detail about any of this, but there is enough to nourish the imagination, and to suggest that the spiritual battle against Antichrist, when worked out in terms of real people and real situations, must have tended to become a real battle, a clash of arms. We do not know much about the laymen: they are indeed named, ten of them identified as artisans of one sort or another, but we do not know if they were well off or poor; nor can we tell whether the other seventeen, sometimes identified as from this or that local village, were indeed of the peasantry, or whether they were townsmen who had kept the names of their places of origin.[83] Fortunately more can be said about the priests; two were only named, but the other three were described as holding parishes, and two of these, Jaroslav of Lažiště and Vojtěch of Chelčice, appear subsequently in the sources as active Hussites.[84] We can thus infer that the radical movement,

[81] The text, surviving on a single parchment sheet in the Prague Cathedral Chapter Archive, is published by J. Macek, "K počátkům táborství v Písku," *JSH*, XXII (1953), 119–124; the dating in 1416 is in the citation.

[82] The beginning and end of the following passage are missing, but it almost certainly refers to utraquist communion: ". . . utriusque sexus hominibus indifferenter contra ritum et consuetudinem Romane ecclesie ac determinacionem [cardinalium] sacri con-[sistorii] . . ."; instead of the bracketed words supplied by Macek we might conjecture "[concilii] sacri con[stantiensis]" (*ibid.*, p. 120). The passage on baptism is represented by only one surviving word, "baptizare" (*loc. cit.*), which however would hardly have appeared at all unless some deviation were being described.

[83] Of the artisans one is called a "rich cloth-cutter" (*dives pannicida*), and most of the others were in the cloth industry. Macek supposes that those identified as from villages indeed belonged to the rural population (*ibid.*, p. 113; *Tábor*, I, 188).

[84] For Jaroslav see *Documenta*, p. 694 (to be discussed below, in chap. v). Vojtěch (*Albertus*) was martyred as a utraquist by the Germans of Budějovice in July 1420 and Laurence of Březová, informing us of the fact (*FRB*, V, 366) goes out of his way to insist that Vojtěch did not approve of Taborite violence. But I agree with F. M. Bartoš, *Petr Chelčický* (Prague, 1958), p. 13, that Vojtěch must have been the predecessor of Peter Chelčický as leader of the Chelčice brethren, and since we know from Peter's works that he subscribed to the extremely radical Waldensianist doctrines of pre-chiliast Tabor, we can assume the same of Vojtěch.

with its creation of new congregational units, was not the work merely of those preachers who did not enjoy parochial livings; rather the social existence of the movement, outside of the established church organization, was itself the effect of radical doctrines that could appeal even to clerics who held parishes, and—here one can only guess—even to laymen who enjoyed the security of a definite craft.[85] In any case, the text just discussed prepares us to find radical reform passing over into mutinous action, of a kind that had indeed appeared before, and we will not be surprised if we find evidence that the doctrines themselves might become revolutionary—that is, sectarian, genuinely heretical.

This sort of situation is indeed attested by the final item in this review of the sources, a letter from the Prague conservative, Master Christian of Prachatice, to the radical preacher Wenceslas Koranda, formerly one of the eager young radicals of Prague and now—the letter was written in early 1417 —leader of a group of extremists in the provinces.[86] The more general import of Christian's letter will be discussed in a subsequent section, but it contains some details about Koranda's extremism that are of special interest here:

> . . . the evil Devil, who could not break up our movement [*congregationis*] by citations, excommunications, interdicts, and heretications, has sown tares in the grain: he has torn some loose from the concord and consensus of the brethren and has made them go against the masters' counsels and writings, even though these are true. And alas, some . . . have spurned the frequent fraternal admonitions of the masters; they follow their own opinion and that of unlearned men and women who, under the appearance of piety, often wound the hearts of many of the innocent—they argue that there is no Purgatory, that there should be no prayers for the dead, that the suffrages of the saints should not be sought, that the *Salve regina* not be sung, that dubious relics of the saints should be thrown out on dung-heaps and their

[85] In addition to the Písek evidence that artisans, including at least one who was well off, were involved in radical action, see the evidence for Ústí quoted above, n. 78.

[86] *Documenta,* pp. 633–636; for the dating in early 1417 (against Palacký's conjecture of 1416, which no one now accepts) see below, chap. v. Palacký's text is printed from a copy made by the nineteenth-century archivist Antonín Boček and bears a heading to the effect that the letter was written by Christian to Koranda, "pro tunc praedicatori in Plzna." It is not clear who supplied the heading—the original copyist, Boček, or Palacký —and although no one has questioned it, there is also no reason to trust it. The author was to be sure quite probably Master Christian, and the recipient was certainly Koranda (he is named in the text), but the statement locating the latter in Plzeň may have been based on the fact that he probably came from there and was certainly active there in 1419, In the period we are now considering, however, he may have been working in South Bohemia, where a source from the latter half of 1417 seems to locate him (*Documenta,* p. 694; see below).

images burnt, and that there should be no practice of ceremonies and ecclesiastical rites invented by man, but that in all things there should be conformity to the rites of the Primitive Church.

And now public report about you has reached our ears and resounds through
all Prague and indeed through the realm of Bohemia: how by your preaching
you have gotten images of the saints to be basely thrown out of churches;
how you give communion in both kinds to infants who have neither the
ability to swallow nor knowledge at all; how you despise all ecclesiastical
rites, [even those] not contrary to Scriptures, and do not allow them to be
observed by yourself or by others. . . .

On all sides we see our pseudo-priests, drunk, sensual, and scandalous beyond
measure, who want to seem to be doing something new and under this
hypocrisy empty the purses of widows, preach poverty but themselves cloak
the ignominy of poverty by a certain unveiled hypocrisy, wish to have the
income of a church but to enjoy all things without labor. And if the people
have not given them enough they forsake the threshed-out granaries and go
to other, fatter churches; then, with stuffed wallets, they leave, saying, "We
must now go evangelize other people."

Allowing for the natural differences between the previously examined reports, all originating with offended Catholics, and this monitory letter from a
Hussite to one of the brethren, we have no difficulty in imagining Koranda
leading a group similar to those around Kozí Hradek and Písek. But what
are we to make of the charge that Koranda and his associates were following
the opinion of "unlearned men and women"—that is, laity—in denying the
existence of Purgatory, attacking the cult of saints and their images, and
seeking to reestablish the pure simplicity of the Primitive Church and its
rites?

In reviewing the other situations of local extremism we have noted two
elements: a militantly sectarian mode of existence and a body of doctrine and
practice that could be explained as resulting from the application of Jakoubek's theories to reality. Certain ideas, like Krampeř's doctrine that an evil
priest had no sacramental power, went beyond Jakoubek's teachings, to be
sure, but such ideas can be reasonably understood as intensifications or
simplifications of what the master had said. Much the same can be said for a
good deal of what Koranda was accused of: Jakoubek believed in getting rid
of images, in giving communion to infants, in drastically limiting the cult of
saints, and in pruning away many rites of post-Primitive invention. But he
did not reject the doctrine of Purgatory—on the contrary, he vigorously supported it against those who denied it.[87] On the other hand, rejection of Purga-

[87] *LČJ*, Nos. 63 and 64; see also the next section.

tory was perhaps the most notorious of the doctrines held by the Waldensians, and since these sectarians also held almost all of the doctrines of Jakoubek's radicalism, we must consider the possibility that the unlearned men and women who influenced Koranda were indeed of the Waldensian sect.

This point leads directly to the further possibility, that perhaps the *other* situations of local extremism had been generated not by the preaching of Jakoubek's ideas by his disciples, but by the emergence of sectarian groups that had already existed underground, and needed only the stimulation and relative security offered by Hussitism to come to the surface, no longer as passive but as active sectarians. On this view the later doctrines of Tabor, which clearly derived from the extremist situations of 1415–1417, can be understood as rooted in the Waldensian heresy. Such indeed was the view of certain older German scholars, notably Wilhelm Preger and Hermann Haupt; it was extensively refuted by Johann Loserth, in favor of his own theory of Wyclifite origins.[88] In more recent times the Waldensian hypoth-

---

[88] W. Preger, "Uber das Verhältnis der Taboriten zu den Waldesiern des 14. Jahrhunderts," *Abhandlungen der königlichen Bayerischen Akademie der Wissenschaften,* Hist. Cl., XVIII (1889), 1–111, shows the correspondence between Taborite and Waldensian doctrines on the basis of an extensive and solid documentation; it is still very instructive. H. Haupt, *Waldensertum und Inquisition im südöstlichen Deutschland* (Freiburg im Br., 1890; originally in the *Deutsche Zeitschrift für Geschichtswissenschaft,* I (1889), 285–330, III (1890), 337–411, from which I cite it, according to the volume numbers), studies the actual history of his subject and incidentally notes the ties and parallels to Taboritism. Both works appeared after J. Loserth's *Hus und Wiclif* (1884), which conclusively proves Hus's extraordinary debt to Wyclif for not only his ideas but a good many of his words; Loserth also noted that Hus's associates and followers were similarly indebted, and he developed the point for Taboritism in his reviews of Preger's and Haupt's works, in the *Göttingische gelehrte Anzeiger* (1889), No. 12, 475–504; (1891), No. 4, 140–152. A number of subsequent articles pursue the same aim. Since in fact Wyclif's encyclopedic anti-Romanism did include most of the doctrines that distinguished radical Hussitism, and since from 1420 on the Taborite theoreticians did defend their beliefs with the help of Wyclif's works, Loserth's argument has considerable force. Its limitations stem from his curious concept of historical explanation, implicit for example in his question, "Why pursue the phantom of Waldensianism when it is so easy to demonstrate the genesis of these doctrines from the writings of Wyclif?" (*Göttingische gelehrte Anzeiger* (1889), 501 f.). But it is just the matter of genesis that cannot be easily explained, and certainly there is no need to insist on a *single* explanation. Haupt, for example, was quite willing not only to recognize in Hussitism the existence of a Wyclifite radicalism alongside that of the Waldensians, but also to see the special strength of Hussitism precisely in the combination of the two (*op. cit.,* III, 388 f.). Here we may quote the synthesizing formulation of Jaroslav Goll: "Both currents could exist alongside each other and strengthen one another, the Wyclifite taking shape among the theologians, and the Waldensian originating among the people" (*Quellen,* II, 41). This dictum does not solve the problem but it defines in advance the first stage of the controversy.

esis has been taken up by Czech scholars—Josef Pekař, Václav Chaloupccký, and, most effectively, Rudolf Holinka[89]—only to be again rejected, both by F. M. Bartoš[90] and by Josef Macek.[91] The latter's Marxist reconstruction, rejecting doctrinal in favor of social origins, has however been resisted by other Marxists of one hopes equal orthodoxy: Robert Kalivoda and Ernst Werner.[92] All of these conflicting theories are, in the words of the classic

[89] Pekař, *Žižka a jeho doba*, I, chap. i and *passim*. V. Chaloupecký, "K dějinám Valdenských v Čechách před hnutím husitským," *ČČH*, XXXI (1925), 376. Holinka, *Sektářství*, pp. 160 ff.

[90] Bartoš, "Vznik Táborství a Valdenští," *JSH*, III (1930), 38–48 (a critique of Holinka). On pp. 41–47 Bartoš tries to disqualify one by one all of the main points of evidence introduced by Holinka, and he sums up his own views thus (p. 47): "We can say that it is not only possible to elucidate the origins of Taboritism on the basis of Wyclifism, completely and down to the last detail, but that in the present stage of our knowledge this is the most likely explanation of its origins." In his "Počátky táborství a pražské jeho ohnisko z let 1414–1417," *Do čtyř art.* (1925), pp. 45–63, Bartoš had offered a full-scale critical discussion of the Waldensian problem and had suggested that insofar as specifically Waldensian elements—and particularly the denial of Purgatory—were demonstrable in 1414–1417, they had their origins in *Prague* radical circles, specifically in the work of Nicholas of Dresden. There is an obvious discrepancy here, and it would be fair to say that Bartoš's hypotheses are not solidly or even clearly worked out (cf. Pekař, IV, 191 f. for a similar judgement); on the other hand, his critical observations are often cogent.

[91] Macek, *Tábor*, I, 158–160, and *passim*. Macek's argument is that popular sectarian heresy was an ideological manifestation of the class struggle, and that the doctrinal definitions and labels provided by the Catholic authorities who dealt with heretics are not of decisive importance. "The very term 'valdensis' in the contemporary sources (chiefly to be found in inquisitional materials) is pretty much identical with the general designation 'hereticus,' 'scismaticus,' and it designates a man of the lowest social classes (especially a peasant) who rebels against the feudal order and the Catholic Church" (pp. 158 f.). Therefore when we hear of Waldensians in this or that place we can infer only that there were such rebels—not that one particular organized sect was involved. In other words, no amount of testimony for the existence of Waldensians in Bohemia would prove that that particular sect was in fact there. Macek has since modified his views: "Chiliasmus ve svetových dějinách," *ČsČH*, XII (1964), 860–863.

[92] R. Kalivoda, *Husitská ideologie* (Prague, 1961), pp. 292–316 and *passim*. In a long note on pp. 401–404 he deals critically with the various scholarly positions, including Macek's "one-sided sociologism." The East-German scholar Ernst Werner discusses the evidence in his *Nachrichten über spätmittelalterliche Ketzer aus tschechoslovakischen Archiven und Bibliotheken*, Beilage zur Wissenschaftlichen Zeitschrift der Karl-Marx-Universität Leipzig, Gesellschafts- und Sprachwissenschaftliche Reihe, XII (1963), Heft 1, pp. 215–250, and although he refers to Macek's "healthy reaction to the old bourgeois historiography" (p. 235), he clearly agrees with Holinka on the one hand, Kalivoda on the other, that there were Waldensians in pre-Hussite Bohemia, that it is meaningful to use the specific term "Waldensian," and that the parallels between Waldensian doctrines and early-Hussite extremism are "too obvious to allow us to speak of coincidences" (p. 245).

dictum, true in what they affirm, false in what they deny, and the following pages have been written in the light of this principle.

The "Waldensian problem" that has just been posed breaks down naturally into several partial problems. Was there significant Waldensian activity in Bohemia before the Hussite movement? If so, did preexisting Bohemian Waldensians actually influence the Hussite radicals? And, moving in another direction, does the analysis of early-extremist and Taborite doctrines show that these doctrines must have been derived from Waldensian sources? And if so, can the Waldensian sources be identified otherwise than as the doctrines of local sectarians—specifically, can they not perhaps be found in the writings of Master Nicholas of Dresden? Much has been written about all of these questions and the relevant literature will be cited where appropriate, but the basic work that guides most of the following discussion is R. Holinka's *Sectarianism in Bohemia before the Hussite Revolution* (1929), which is naturally strongest for the first question but also deals with the others.[93] It is clear from Holinka's review of the sources and literature that by at least the late 1330's Waldensianism flourished among the German settlers in parts of South Bohemia, and this point has only been confirmed by documents turned up since Holinka's time.[94] Papal letters and inquisitional records show that the heresy affected especially the domains of Lord Ulrich of Jindřichův Hradec (Neuhaus, Nova Domus), and we hear of an actual Waldensian insurrection in two of his villages, Velký Bednarec and Malý Bednarec.[95] Later evidence is more fragmentary, but it points in the same direction. Thus when a contemporary inquisitional record notes that in 1377 the burgrave of Kozí Hradek—an area we have already become familiar with—was ordered to give up Henzl and Konrad of Bednarec, whom he had taken from the inquisitor, it suggests that the movement had not only persisted but even spread—from Bednarec to the Kozí Hradek region.[96]

[93] Holinka's presentation of the major items of evidence for pre-Hussite Waldensianism in Bohemia is extraordinarily full, but is essentially similar to that of Haupt, *Waldensertum und Inquisition*, which most readers will find more accessible. Still more convenient is the good English summary of the sources and literature in S. H. Thomson's "Pre-Hussite Heresy in Bohemia," *English Historical Review*, XLVIII (1933), 23–42, which I therefore cite by preference in the footnotes that follow. The relevant portions of Holinka are pp. 147–158 (the relationship between Waldensianism and early Hussitism) and pp. 160 ff. (the Waldensian origins of Tabor).

[94] See especially I. Hlaváček, "Inkvisice v Čechách ve 30. letech 14. století," *ČsČH*, V (1957), 526–538, with the text—a fragmentary record of inquisitional interrogations in 1337—on pp. 535–538. In addition to confirming the evidence for South Bohemian Waldensianism, this text also tells of heretics—at least some of whom seem to have been Waldensians—in several other places: Žatec, Prague, Hradec Králové, etc.

[95] Thomson, *op. cit.*, pp. 35 f.

[96] Chaloupecký, "K dějinám Valdenských," p. 376.

There is also some indication that the city of Písek may have been a center of Waldensian activity in the 1360's; here our confirmation comes from the charge made in 1381 that for two generations the family of a certain Johlín of Písek had been heretics.[97] The fact that a Prague provincial synod in 1381 mentioned Waldensian activity for the first time in a synodal statute suggests that the heresy had become a problem for church authorities,[98] and other pieces of evidence indeed picture Bohemia as, by the end of the fourteenth century, a leading center and breeding ground for the heresy in Central Europe.[99] Thus an anonymous statement of the 1390's says that the Waldensians "were formerly flourishing in Austria, now in Bohemia," [100] and in the same period there is evidence that at least the inquisitors operating over a wide area of East-Central Europe were drawn from Bohemia—a fact that may possibly mean something.[101] In 1404 the Bohemian Augustinian canon Johlín of Vodňany wrote that the Waldensians were "alas multiplying considerably," [102] and rather earlier we learn from the Prague Archbishop John of Jenštejn, writing against Bishop Peter of Olomouc, that the Waldensians had prospered so much in the latter's diocese that it would have been difficult and even dangerous to proceed against them.[103] In Prague at any rate such dangers were overcome: in the late fourteenth century there were actual burnings of heretics in the capital; we know that they were Germans, but we do not know exactly what their heresy was.[104]

[97] Thomson, *op. cit.*, pp. 39 f.

[98] *Ibid.*, p. 41.

[99] Holinka, *Sektářství v Čechách*, p. 123.

[100] *Ibid.*, p. 135.

[101] Such was the suggestion of Haupt, but Bartoš, "Počátky táborství," p. 49, argues that the inquisitors were chosen from Bohemia because no other Central European country had inquisitors at that time.

[102] Cited by Holinka, p. 133, n. 441. But R. Říčan, "Johlín z Vodňan, křižovník kláštera zderazského," *VKČSN* (1929), pp. 116 f., argues that Johlín's testimony is not very reliable, for when he wanted to give the characteristic doctrines of the Waldensian sect he used not his own observation but a standard inquisitional list (the one cited below, n. 106). Thus his whole testimony about the Waldensians would be a stereotype. This line of argument is not obviously cogent, and I think it is in fact mistaken.

[103] Thomson, "Pre-Hussite Heresy in Bohemia," p. 41.

[104] At Matthew of Knín's Quodlibet in 1409, Jerome of Prague recalled that in the memory of those present some men of other nations had been brought to Prague and burnt as heretics; none of them, he said, was a "pure Bohemian"—i.e., presumably, a Czech (Höfler, II, 122: ". . . nullum autem purum Boemum audistis vos neque patres vestri cum suis antecedentibus patribus vel semel ob haeresim fuisse combustum."). More important evidence is provided by *OCA-R*, p. 29 (quoted below, chap. vii, *ad* n. 122). Although the context clearly suggests that the martyrs were Free-Spirit Beghards of some sort, their localization around Jindřichův Hradec leads us to suppose that they

This is clearly a very mixed bag of evidence, but some of it at least is quite solid—only a quibbler would refuse to concede that an underground movement, known almost exclusively from the actions and statements of its opponents, must be presumed to have existed even in the silent years between such actions and statements. It is true that one may suppose that a given inquisitional action may have succeeded in wiping out a given heretical group, but the probabilities are that for every heretic who was arrested there must have been some who escaped.[105] Thus we will hardly go wrong if we assume that at the time utraquism and the cult of Hus were preached in the provinces—and above all in South Bohemia—there were on hand sectarian heretics of the Waldensian type. But can we say more than this? Here we may profitably pause and consider just what these heretics believed; only after doing so can we take up the problem of their possible influence on the Hussite left.

There are of course many Catholic sources for Waldensian doctrine, but one of them is especially relevant: it is a list of "articles" compiled by Peter Zwicker or Martin of Prague, along with various other compositions written after their wide-ranging tour of duty as inquisitors in German and Bohemian lands in the 1390's. Holinka has noted the importance of the text as one that enjoyed a certain popularity; it and its related material were also developed in some redactions with special relevance to Bohemia and Prague.[106] A selection of these articles follows:

[1] Confessions are heard among them by men who have been neither sent by the church nor ordained.

[2] They deny Purgatory.

[3] They say that masses for the dead, vigils, offerings, and all other sorts of testaments made for the remedy of souls, have been invented by the avarice of priests.

[4] They do not believe in the suffrages of the Blessed Virgin, nor consequently of any of the saints. . . . Therefore they do not observe saints' vigils nor celebrate their days, nor do they make offerings or kiss relics. . . .

[5] They say that Christians are idolaters because of images of saints and the sign of the crucifix. . . .

---

may in fact have belonged to the Waldensian movement that we know had flourished there a couple of generations before. Waldensian-Free-Spirit syncretism was not unknown in 14th century Central Europe—see, e.g., the text quoted below, n. 112.

[105] For the contrary view see Bartoš, "Počátky táborství," pp. 48 f.

[106] Holinka, *Sektářství v Čechách*, pp. 176–179 (the numbering is mine). For another redaction see Döllinger, *Beiträge zur Sektengeschichte des Mittelalters*, II (Munich, 1890), 335–343. E. Werner, *Nachrichten*, offers the fullest discussion of the various manuscripts of the list.

[6] They say that there is absolutely no use or value in the things blessed by bishops and priests in churches—the church itself, the baptismal font, other water, candles, palms, ashes, plants, or anything else of the sort.

[7] They say that ordinations of clergy and consecrations of churches are an infamy and an error, and that the clergy have invented them for the sake of gain.

[8] They call superstition all of the equipment of bishops—the chasubles, gloves, mitre, rings.

[9] They disapprove of church-buildings, altars, towers, bells, organs, and other adornments of the church.

[10] They say that ecclesiastical song and the reading of canonical hours are the barking of dogs.

[11] They reject and abuse all ecclesiastical vestments and the rites of Christians.

[12] They say that no prayers should be said—not the Ave Maria, nor the psalms, nor other prayers—except the Lord's Prayer. . . .

[13] They say that all words read in the mass and all the preparations bearing on it are a mistake, except for the words of consecration of the sacrament.

[14] They do not believe at all in indulgences, pilgrimages, and dedications of churches.

[15] They do not care about church funerals and burial in cemeteries . . . and they say that it is more useful to be laid to rest in other places than in those. . . .

[16] They say that the pope, cardinals, and bishops do not have greater authority than simple priests.

[17] They say that the pope is the chief of all heresiarchs, and therefore the cardinals, archbishops, bishops, emperors, kings, dukes, princes, all magistrates both spiritual and temporal, as well as priests—all are to be damned. . . .

[18] They pay no attention to anything that the highest pontiffs and ordinaries decree must be kept and held to in the church.

[19] They care nothing for the sentences of the holy doctors—except insofar as these support their sect—but observe only the New Testament, literally.

[20] They reject all orders of religion, both of monks and of nuns, saying that they are empty and superfluous.

To say that the men and women who held such beliefs were profoundly alienated from the medieval social and religious order would hardly go beyond this evidence, but the point is worth insisting upon, and other Waldensian views support it. The Waldensians, we are told, say that their sect "is the true and only Catholic faith, outside of which no one can be saved." [107] "They call us Christians, among themselves, 'dye fremden,' and themselves 'die kunden' "—that is, those in the group. When they pray, they ask "that God give us Christians . . . evils and reverses to suffer, so that we may meanwhile forget them and stop persecuting them." Although by no means a simple movement of the poor against the rich, the sect's doctrines naturally resonated with the attitudes and feelings of those who were poor and who suffered, and in one list of articles we find the report: "They say that there is no Purgatory, for when man lives here in poverty, that is his purgatory." [108] The rich and powerful Roman church was thus *ipso facto* damned "because from the time of Pope Silvester it received, held, and sought possessions." [109] Holding that to swear any oath at all was a mortal sin, as was all killing, even of the worst criminals, the Waldensians undercut the civil order no less radically than they did the institution of the church. In sum, the sect lived in complete secession from the consensus that kept the surrounding society together. At the same time there is much evidence to show that for at least a century before the Hussite revolt Central European Waldensians were occasionally capable of passing over to violent action. We have already noted the insurrection on the Jindřichův Hradec domains, but this was only one case. In the light of the incident in the Písek area in 1416— discussed above—it is illuminating to learn that in nearby Wolfern, near Steier, the Waldensians set fire to the parish house and burnt the pastor and his servant to death, probably in reaction to a death sentence passed on the heretics by the inquisitor Peter Zwicker.[110] Indeed, a whole list of similar cases has been compiled by Hermann Haupt,[111] and it would only be burdensome to extend the documentation here. Such violence, in apparent contradiction of the point about not killing, may be interpreted as a kind of dialectical conversion from passivity to activity, both based in the same objective alienation from society, or it may be ascribed to "contamination" of pure Waldensianism by Free Spirit tendencies—and there is evidence for this, too.[112] We thus have every reason to think that by 1415 there were

---

[107] Holinka, *loc. cit.* Kalivoda, *HI,* presents the social import of Waldensian sectarianism very effectively; he notes that although clearly opposed to the medieval order, it remained sectarian, for it did not raise the question of eliminating that order (p. 260).

[108] Döllinger, II, 614.

[109] *Ibid.,* II, 306.

[110] Haupt, *Waldensertum und Inquisition,* III, 372 f.

[111] *Ibid.,* III, 302–311 and *passim.*

[112] In Döllinger, II, 363 f., there is a list of articles held by heretics in Augsburg in 1393. All were typically and unmistakably Waldensian, except for No. 14: Some believed their sect would last secretly until a future judgement, but then, after the coming of Elijah and Enoch, openly; at which latter time the sect would include all the

Waldensian groups in South Bohemia who were doctrinally, socially, and emotionally apt not only to receive the Hussite message but to take it up, extend it, and make it the ideology of a revolutionary sectarian movement.

But did this in fact happen? This is the crucial question, and strictly speaking it cannot be answered, for we have no direct or unimpeachable evidence for the affirmative. On the other hand, the negative is not very well supported either. Few scholars have been convinced by F. M. Bartoš's radical critique of the evidence for pre-Hussite Waldensianism, or by his corollary arguments that by 1415 there were few if any Waldensians still on hand in South Bohemia.[113] His further point, that since the South Bohemian Waldensians were in any case Germans, they were unable to influence the Czech Hussite radicals, seems even less valid. We know that Bohemian Czechs and Germans could communicate with each other and in some cases even cooperate in the work of reform;[114] also, extreme radical Hussitism itself can be taken as the answer to Bartoš's objection: "For Waldensianism to spread to the Czech elements there was necessary . . . the translation of Waldensianism into Czech; there are not the slightest traces of any such thing."[115] Furthermore, although it is true that there is no documentary evidence of *Czech* Waldensianism before 1415, there is some for the later period—by about 1421, the list of Waldensian "errors" discussed above was used by an anonymous author as the basis for a new redaction that clearly betrays the Czech character of the heretics it describes. The German terms in the original are replaced by Latin; St. Wenceslas is added to the list of saints whom the Waldensians contemned; the Latin articles are extended by *volkstümliche* phrases in Czech.[116] This new redaction is too late to prove pre-Hussite Czech Waldensianism, but it supports the hypothesis that radical Hussite preaching from 1415 on stimulated the emergence of Waldensian

---

generations of those who had belonged to it. I read this tenet as the abbreviated form of an apocalyptic millenarian hope; for the relationship between such a hope and the use of violence against outsiders, see the discussion of Taborite chiliast warfare, in chap. vii below.

[113] See n. 105 above.

[114] The primary case of German-Czech collaboration would be that of the Dresdeners and Czech Hussites in Prague; here, to be sure, the language of intercourse might have been Latin. But we know that John Hus and Jerome of Prague spoke German and so did some of the Hussite leaders at the Council of Basel, for they were asked not to preach publicly in that language; in fact a substantial dossier of evidence for Hussite bilingualism could be easily compiled. As for the common laity, we know that today in areas of mixed nationality, many ordinary men and women have a workable smattering of a second language, and such must have been the case in pre-Hussite Bohemia. The large number of German loan-words in Old Czech confirms the point.

[115] Bartoš, "Počátky táborství," p. 50.

[116] Höfler, I, 503–505.

sectarians; if the latter were indeed Germans, they soon passed their ideas on to their Czech associates. Finally we may note that there is abundant later testimony to the effect that the Taborites were disciples of the Waldensians, in regard variously to their denial of Purgatory, rejection of the cult of saints, rejection of auricular confession, and rejection of post-Biblical authority.[117] Although these charges were perhaps based on nothing more than a recognition of doctrinal similarities, coupled with a lively awareness of Waldensianism and, no doubt, a desire to be abusive—still, the testimony is there, and it does not weaken the Waldensian hypothesis.

In questions of this sort, where final proof or disproof is beyond reach, the historian's last word is usually the same as his first. Czechs who begin by resisting the idea of any German influences on their great national enterprise will find that the evidence for Waldensian penetration is inadequate. Roman Catholics or other anti-Hussites rejoice in the thought that the reformation was rooted in sectarian heresy, and their pleasure is shared by Protestants of German nationality. Scholars well trained in the great positivistic tradition have no patience with concatenations of circumstantial or merely probable evidence, while those who like the image of a powerful secret underground of heresy will gratefully accept all data pointing in that direction. And so it goes. Since historical explanation does not demand a single cause for a single effect, we can perhaps rest content with the relatively modest notion that a significant Waldensian penetration of extreme-radical Hussitism was certainly possible and, given the natural tendencies of contiguous groups to influence each other, likely. More ambitiously, we may guess that the intensely passionate anti-Roman hatred and alienation that we have noted in the extremist situations of 1415–1417 were perhaps the specific contribution of heretics who had cultivated just those emotions and attitudes during generations of withdrawal and suffering. But this is only a socio-psychological guess, and in any case it marks the extreme limit of inference, the point at which we must end the present line of study in favor of one moving in the opposite direction. We must now turn back to Prague, to consider in some detail what has only been mentioned above: namely, the relationship between the extreme radical doctrines we have seen emerging in the provinces and the radicalism cultivated in the milieu of Jakoubek of Stříbro and Nicholas of Dresden—the milieu in which preachers like Koranda were formed. If thus far we have emphasized the gap between Prague and

---

[117] The numerous passages have been collected by Chaloupecký, "K dějinám Valdenských," p. 377, n. 4, and even more extensively by Holinka, *Sektářství v Čechách,* pp. 164 ff. Unfortunately the best testimony, John Příbram's "Velint, nolint . . . ad suos praeceptores pauperes de Lugduno redire coguntur," is not to be found where Chaloupecký locates it (Höfler, II, 568), nor have I been able to find it anywhere else.

provincial radicalism, we can now ask whether that gap was indeed so wide as to represent a break in continuity between the original Prague reform movement and the national reformation that it generated.

JAKOUBEK AND THE
RADICAL PARTY, 1415–1416

As Hussitism sank its roots in various parts of the realm and in various ways, the Prague University masters were faced with new problems of leadership. The politicians, who worked with the nobility, did not have to do more than stick to the Wyclifite ideology that had proved its utility, but the radicals around Master Jakoubek were in a much more difficult position. Apart from having to work out various doctrinal or practical matters of pan-Hussite significance, they had also to cope with the new needs and orientations of those disciples who had moved out to work in the provinces, where both the logic of facts and the influence of preexisting sectarian heresy drove them into the paths of extremism. Eventually the two wings of the radical movement would break apart, so that by 1420 Jakoubek was ranged with the other masters against the Taborites, while the latter were referring to Prague as Babylon of the Apocalypse. But, as Master John Příbram pointed out at that time, it had been the very city of Prague that had once taught the Taborites to know the truth,[118] and it would be a great mistake for us to anticipate the later break in our study of the situation of 1415–1417. In these years there were, to be sure, signs of a split, but there were also movements in the contrary direction, toward preservation and restoration of radical-Hussite unity; we must try to reconstruct what happened on the basis of both tendencies. The problem is basic but also very difficult and even delicate, the more so because it has rarely been systematically investigated.

Insofar as it *has* been studied it has usually been formulated as one turning on the character of Jakoubek himself, as a man and as a mind, and successive historians have presented a whole gallery of diverse and sometimes mutually exclusive Jakoubeks. To Zdeněk Nejedlý, whose chapter on the reformer marks the beginning of serious study, Jakoubek was a dry, abstract, doctrinaire intellectual, whose radicalism was the result chiefly of the tendency of such a man to push every idea to its logical conclusions. He was not a *popular* leader, like Hus, and he lacked the normal human feeling for worldly joys, including the aesthetic ones. Since he therefore regarded most

---

[118] John Příbram, *Contra articulos picardorum,* MS 4749, fol. 71ᵛ: "Quod autem scribentes et docentes vocaverunt eam Babilon, . . . recte mentiti sunt"—Prague is really Jerusalem, the city "que huiusmodi pseudo sompniatores veritatem noscere docuit et in omni ingenio preter falsum fovit et educavit."

of the sensuous and popular elements of the Roman liturgy—Nejedlý's study was primarily concerned with this subject—as at best superfluous, more often distracting, he criticized Roman customs but did not always reject them out of hand; his disciples, however, had a better developed feeling for art and therefore felt those customs to be positively pernicious: hence they insisted on abolishing what Jakoubek could find reasons for tolerating. It was their practice that opened a breach between Jakoubek's theories and reality, and led to an estrangement between the leader and his followers.[119] This is an ingenious explanation, including many elements that seem sound and have been accepted here; it has also found other recent adherents, most notably Josef Macek.

But if Jakoubek was indeed a doctrinaire he was far from dry, and what has been said in the preceding pages has perhaps been enough to suggest that there was in his makeup a rich vein of religious enthusiasm, the expression of a personality full of emotional ardor. It is also worth noting that he was not even the usual type of academic: he led a life that even his enemies conceded to be holy, and his quiet, humble spirit duly impressed those who knew him.[120] Thus Nejedlý's picture must be modified, chiefly on the basis of the Jakoubek portrayed by Jan Sedlák, who was in his day uniquely familiar with the large body of still unpublished works left by his subject, and who more than anyone else succeeded in showing, in detail, how the mystical, apocalyptical style of thought cultivated by Matthew of Janov passed over into Jakoubek's writings, composed as these often were of long quotations from his predecessor.[121] Unfortunately Sedlák could not push his studies beyond about 1415, and thus did not provide a definitive answer to the problem of the relationship between Jakoubek and the Taborites, but his work did suggest that much of the Taborites' hostility to the Roman system could well have come directly from their master. He also provided the first significant study of Nicholas of Dresden, a man who worked with Jakoubek for several years but then went beyond the latter to develop a number of doctrines similar to those of the Waldensian heresy.[122] Thus it could be argued that where Jakoubek's influence left off, that of Nicholas began, and in fact the Taborite doctrinal system did turn out to be remarkably close to that of the Dresdener. On this basis Josef Pekař projected his view of the

---

[119] Nejedlý, IV, i, chap. 1 (pp. 87–147), esp. pp. 87–94.

[120] See Pekař, *Žižka,* I, 1, n. 2, for references to the sources, including Aeneas Sylvius Piccolomini's characterization in the *Historia Bohemiae,* chap. xxxv: ". . . Jacobellus . . . , litterarum doctrina, et morum praestantia juxta clarus."

[121] See the references to Sedlák's studies above, chap. ii, n. 80, and *passim* in the section on "The Radicals and the Beginnings of the Hussite Left."

[122] J. Sedlák, *Mikuláš z Drážďan* (Brno, 1914), *passim* and p. 53; also *ST,* II, 124.

matter, akin to Sedlák's but with a greater emphasis on the differences between Jakoubek and Nicholas. The former, according to Pekař, reached the height of his militancy in 1411–1415, probably under the influence of Nicholas, a more genuinely radical and original spirit; in fact Jakoubek was really a sober, realistic type, who reverted to character when the days of his collaboration with Nicholas were over, and when the emergence of proto-Taboritism drove him, along with other Prague masters, into a conservative position. At the same time Pekař also stressed the probable influence of *popular* sectarian Waldensianism upon the radicals in the provinces, who could for precisely this reason find Nicholas's doctrines so congenial.[123]

Some of the other Jakoubeks pictured by scholars are less convincing. Thus Vlastimil Kybal's attempt to show that Jakoubek was more conservative of the church's tradition than John Hus [124] may be dismissed as an example of how even the most erudite scholar can go wrong when he does not go beyond the words of his sources: if Hus did not spend much time praising the customs and traditions of the Primitive Church, as Jakoubek did, this was not because he held to the norm of Scripture alone—Kybal's thesis—but because he really accepted most of the Roman customs and traditions in matters of liturgy.[125] And to suppose that Jakoubek's norm of the Primitive Church actually restrained his religious innovations is to suppose his idea of that norm to have been much more detailed, not to say rigid, than it was. In another sense Josef Macek has offered a conservative Jakoubek, but it too carries little conviction beyond the points it shares with Nejedlý and Pekař. To say that Hus had a revolutionary ideology that Jakoubek failed to fulfill is simply to leave the evidence behind, and to characterize Jakoubek as "the typical spokesman of the wavering and indecisive Prague bourgeoisie" does little more than translate the problem into Marxist categories. In any case, although Macek concedes that "Jakoubek still maintained a generally progressive position in the years 1417–1418," he cannot tell us why, nor can he account consistently for what happened after those years, except to bring in the *deus ex machina* of fluctuating class interests.[126]

It remains finally to consider the Jakoubek that F. M. Bartoš has drawn, on the basis of a greater knowledge of his subject's work, published and in

[123] Pekař, I, chap. i, esp. pp. 12 ff., 17. See also pp. 3 f., for Pekař's position vis-à-vis Nejedlý.

[124] Kybal discusses Jakoubek chiefly on pp. 130–144 of his *M. Jan Hus*, II, *Učení*, i; other references are to be found *passim*. His interpretations are criticized by Pekař, I, 3, n. 2.

[125] Thus, e.g., Sedlák, *ST*, II, 134: "With regard to the liturgical life of the church Hus was a completely conservative Catholic."

[126] Macek, *Tábor*, I, 164 and n. 112, 192, 194.

manuscript, than anyone has yet had. In a special brochure criticizing Nejedlý's work, Bartoš as early as 1915 managed to prove that on point after point, where Nejedlý had associated Jakoubek with a conservative position, the reformer had actually held radical views—for example, approving of the mass in Czech and of church songs in Czech.[127] In other works [128] Bartoš developed the same views, showing that Jakoubek approved of the simplification of the mass, of the removal of images, of the destruction of superfluous churches and of course cloisters, of the doctrine of clerical poverty, of the confiscation of church property in the public interest—in short, of many drastic reforms that could be derived from the principle of a return to the Primitive Church. Unlike the other university masters, who condemned the more extreme practices of the provincial radicals, Jakoubek expressed his occasional disapproval by kindly admonitions, and remained in very close contact with his disciples working in the country. When the break did come, in 1420, with Tabor's creation of a new form of divine service to replace even the most simplified Prague form of the Roman mass, and with Tabor's secession from the universal church by her creation of a separate clerical organization under an elected bishop—then Jakoubek emerged as an anti-Taborite, in company with the other Prague masters. But he still kept in contact with Tabor, and still maintained a critique that was far from the blind condemnations offered by the others; in fact, he differed from Tabor hardly at all in matters of abstract doctrine, but chiefly in the matter of whether this or that reform was opportune. "There are many truths," he wrote in early 1414, "that should not be pronounced in their own time, because hearts are not disposed for them; but at another time, when hearts are more ready to receive those truths, then they should be pronounced." [129] This, Bartoš suggests, is "the key to an understanding of the complex relationship between Jakoubek and Tabor." And he notes that in time the priests of Tabor came somewhat closer to their former teacher and learned, in their own difficulties with other Hussite parties, to appreciate his tolerance of diversity.

It is characteristic of Bartoš's work, at least in the view of the present

[127] Bartoš, *Kniha Zd. Nejedlého o husitské písni a bohoslužbě* (Prague, 1915), pp. 18 f.

[128] Especially his "Táboři a duchovní jejich otec" ("The Taborites and Their Spiritual Father"), *JSH*, II (1929), 75–83—the source for the rest of this paragraph. In many subsequent works Bartoš offers the same basic conceptions.

[129] Quoted *ibid.*, p. 81, from Jakoubek's postil of 1413–1414, *LČJ*, No. 95. The Latin reads: "Multe sunt veritates que propter indisposicionem cordium tempore suo non sunt dicende, sed alio tempore, cum illa magis erunt apta ad suscepcionem illarum veritatum, tunc debent dici." Cf. Thomas Aquinas, *Summa Theologica*, II-II, Q. xl, a. 3: ". . . etiam in doctrina sacra multa sunt occultanda, maxime infidelibus, ne irrideant. . . ."

writer, that it often expresses a fundamentally sound position in a manner
that fails to convince. His great enemy Josef Pekař suffered from the
opposite defect. Thus if the following pages develop a view of Jakoubek that
has much in common with Bartoš's, it is because a more or less independent
(although unfortunately more limited) study of the sources has forced that
view on the writer. At the same time Bartoš does not offer more than a few
passing references to the situational realities of 1415–1417 that determined the
development of the Hussite left, and probably for this reason does not give a
satisfactory explanation of why the Taborites a few years later found themselves in schism with their erstwhile teacher; it is along these lines that the
present study claims whatever new value it may have. The problem is not
one of culling significant statements from the sources but of arranging the
source data in their proper relationship to each other within the given
situation and along the axis of time; ideas are historically meaningful only
when treated so. In particular, it is essential to keep the scope of the inquiry
broad enough to include, along with Jakoubek's doctrines, those of the
Waldensians and of Nicholas of Dresden, and along with all doctrines, the
sociological, psychological, political, and economic realities that determined
what actually developed out of the potentialities of the various doctrinal
systems. These are lofty aims; fortunately they can be realized by the
relatively simple device of following the facts in as much detail as the sources
allow.

* * * * *

Perhaps the central point in the present context is that from 1415 on,
Jakoubek functioned not as an academic intellectual but as the leader of a
party and, at times, as a leader of the national reformation. In this capacity
he could be as harsh as was necessary—even John Hus had to complain of
the anguish he suffered in his prison cell when he heard the *respon-
sionem . . . duram* addressed to him by Jakoubek on one occasion. Certainly in the matter of utraquism, which so many of the masters regarded as
at the most a permissible practice, Jakoubek was very strict, calling for the
enforcement of the lay chalice as the only practical way to implement the
theory that it was necessary to salvation.[130] He can indeed be seen developing
precisely this point, within the Wyclifite framework of ideas about the

---

[130] For the letter to Hus see *KD*, pp. 244–245. The hard line appears several times in
Jakoubek's Czech sermons for 1416, *Mistr Jakoubek ze Stříbra, Betlemská kázání z
roku 1416* (Prague, 1951), pp. 51 ("And whoever speaks or acts against it [*scil.*,
utraquism], let him be accursed to us in his words and deeds."), 62 ("The Christians
who will not come to this holy supper of the Body and Blood of Christ . . . will be cast
out from the communities of the good."), 104.

proper religious function of secular power. It was probably at the quodlibet of January 1416, or perhaps in some sort of loose connection with the ceremony, that some non-utraquist reformer—possibly Havlík—pronounced a *questio* [131] in which he pleaded for the right to disagree "with some of my senior masters . . . and especially with my reverend master Jakoubek, in whose humility and patience I trust." After all, he argued, he was entitled to propound his position "as probable, in the scholastic manner," according to the principles of "academic freedom"—which, however, certain "iniquitous brethren" were trying to suppress. Taking essentially the same position we have already seen in our consideration of Havlík's *Asserunt quidam,* the author urged that since there was no proof that utraquism was necessary, the best course would be to bring the issue before the supreme head of the church—evidently the pope whom the Council of Constance would elect—in order that problems of truth within the church might be solved not by secular coercion (*non per coaccionem secularem*) but by ecclesiastical censure: thus the church's liberty would be preserved. Hus, too, had suggested recourse to the supreme constituted authority within the church, but by 1416 such a suggestion had become downright counterrevolutionary, and the line of thought that led to it had to be not merely refuted but suppressed.

Thus Jakoubek responded with none of the patience and humility his opponent had hoped for: his *questio* was a positive determination of "Whether a priest who will not minister the body of Christ to the people in both kinds is a seducer and a heretic." [132] The arguments for the necessity of

---

[131] The work is actually a treatise on utraquism attached to a quodlibetal question on the trinity; it is discussed by Sedlák, "Počátkové kalicha" (1911), 99 ff., who attributes it to Peter of Uničov and assigns it to the (cancelled) quodlibet of January 1414—in line with Sedlák's very early dating of the beginnings of utraquism. Bartoš has offered more than one alternative identification of the work (see esp. his "Nové světlo do Husova rektorátu na Karlově universitě, *JSH,* XI (1938), 9, n. 38), but all previous speculations have been largely invalidated by B. Ryba's "Kvodlibet Šimona z Tišnova," *LF,* LXXII (1948), 177–186, which identifies a quodlibet manual containing the title of our question as that used by Simon of Tišnov in January 1416. Without study of the manuscript material I would not venture to guess whether or not the utraquist treatise in question was actually pronounced at that Quodlibet (or just tacked on later to the actual, trinitarian question, as Bartoš supposes), nor can I say whether or not Havlík was indeed the author, as Bartoš has said. Taken together with Jakoubek of Stříbro's question, *Utrum sacerdos nolens,* discussed below, the work does seem to imply a fairly well-developed stage of the utraquist controversy, one in which arguments were being replaced by force, and such a situation points to the period after the massive Hussite take-over of Prague churches, in early November 1415. All my quotations from the work are drawn from Sedlák's discussion of it and from Bartoš, *Husitství a cizina,* pp. 99 ff.

[132] "Utrum sacerdos nolens populo ministrare corpus Cristi sub duplici specie est seductor et hereticus" (*LČJ,* No. 45); I have used the text in MS D 48, pp. 442–500, and

the lay chalice are set forth in all of their exhausting detail, but they are now accompanied by other, grimly practical determinations. Obviously replying to the opponent's call for judgement by the church courts, Jakoubek argued that a heretic was not just a theologian who had been convicted by the church: rather "everyone who stubbornly defends what is contrary to the gospel of . . . Jesus, either scholastically or practically (*sive . . . scolastice sive practice*), incurs the stain of heretical pravity." But to deny communion in both kinds and resist it even merely as a matter of probability, in disputations (*probabilibus disputacionibus*), is heresy of this sort—a point made earlier by Nicholas of Dresden [133]—and Jakoubek meaningfully observed that he included not only those who preached sermons against utraquism but also those who attacked it in the schools.[134] Logically he should now have passed directly to an appeal to the secular power to suppress such heresy, but he perhaps felt that this would be too raw; instead he developed the point rather circuitously,[135] in a discussion of what had become a Hussite commonplace: the heresy *par excellence* was simony, and church law itself provided that this heresy should be suppressed by joint

-----

compared that in D 53, pp. 188–216 (both MSS are paged). The discussion that follows brings out the passages that lead me to regard the question as a direct reply to the one described just above.

[133] Sermon on *Querite primum regnum dei,* MS IV G 15, fols. 107ᵛ–108ʳ: a heretic is not only one "male senciens de articulis fidei vel sacramentis ecclesie," but rather "omnes homines pertinaciter fideles Cristi verbo, facto, aut scripto ab huiusmodi ewangelica veritate [*scil.,* utraquism] et apostolorum ceterorumque fidelium primitive ecclesie praxi . . . retrahentes sive impedientes."

[134] "Communiter errant qui putant non alium esse hereticum nisi speculatum theologum" (p. 453). "Omnis pertinaciter deffendens contrarium ewangelio nostri Ihesu, sive hoc fuerit scolastice sive practice, incurrit maculam heretice pravitatis. Et patet ulterius quod ministracionem vel sumpcionem calicis sacramentalis sub specie vini populo cristiano secundum ewangelicam tradicionem observandam negare, vel ei pertinaciter obsistere, et eam impugnare et persequi, verbo et opere, consiliis, perswasionibus, probabilibus disputacionibus, publice vel private, scolastice sive practice, cum pertinacia, est incurrere maculam heretice pravitatis. Scolastice dico propter inpugnantes in scolis vel in sermonibus ewangelicam tradicionem de communione calicis sacramentalis sub specie vini ministranda . . . —caveant sibi tales ne propter ista sint heretici in veritate coram deo et sanctis eius!" (p. 456). "Ex quo videtur quod sacerdos nolens . . . [etc.] . . . est hereticus" (p. 457).

[135] The transitional passage is very interesting: "Modo vero tantum cecamur ceremoniis quod credimus hominem non esse hereticum excommunicatum et dampnatum nisi in facie ecclesie probatus fuerit esse talis vere sive pretense, nec absolutum, catholicum, vel salvatum nisi hoc fuerit in facie ecclesie approbatum. Et patet opinio heretica contra ewangelicam paupertatem et suorum dicencium quod Cristus non fuit pauperrimus sed civilis et proprietarius, et sic communiter [D 53, p. 201: consequenter] quod licet religiosis et episcopis, prelatis esse dominos proprietarios erga suos proximos" (p. 459).

action of the ecclesiastical and secular powers. But what if the clergy were unwilling?

> If then the secular lords should help the clergy in coercing heretics, it follows that this office pertains to the lords when the clergy defects from it. Nor is there any doubt that all the characteristics of heresy are fulfilled in the simoniacs, and let there be no pretense that they need not be guarded against as heretics before the church has proclaimed them to be such, for heretical deeds give clearer certainty of heresy than the false writings or words of a malevolent or ignorant prelate.[136]

Now firmly rooted in the canons, at least as the relevant dossier had been developed by Nicholas of Dresden, Jakoubek could return to the priest who refused to give communion in both kinds: he was indeed a heretic;[137] and since the proper treatment of heretics had just been outlined, the point was made. It remains for us to observe that if the Roman church had shared Jakoubek's contempt for procedural safeguards—or indeed for any formal procedure—the Hussite heresy might well have been suppressed several years before the utraquist revolt had begun.

Even though Jakoubek was willing to invoke the Wyclifite principles of the Hussite League, he was not primarily interested in the national-political approach represented by that organization. For one thing, he knew very well that many of the Hussite nobility had their own reasons for supporting reform—"to enjoy an increase of earthly goods," as he put it in a sermon of 15 March 1416[138]—and for another, he saw that the success or failure of

---

[136] "Si ergo secundum leges humanas seculares domini debent iuvare clericos ad cohercendum hereticos, sequitur quod quoad illos, in deffectu cleri, spectat istud officium. Nec est dubium quin tota descripcio heresis impletur in symoniacis, nec est fingendum quod non debet caveri tamquam hereticus antequam ecclesia ipsum denunciaverit esse talem, quia facta heretica dant planiorem fidem de heresi quam scripta fallacia vel verba invidi vel ignari prelati" (p. 460).

[137] For Nicholas's dossier see above, n. 43. Cf. also Jakoubek's Wyclifite formulation in his Czech sermon for 21 March 1416: "Sometimes someone gets an office or an income from people, but according to God he has no right to it; for those who are in mortal sins have no divine right over what they rule. . . . And therefore St. Augustine says that the secular arm should take property away from heretics and evil people and give it to the good" (*Betlemská kázání*, pp. 69 f.). Jakoubek allowed for the possibility that there might be plenty of priests giving communion in both kinds, and thus any particular priest might usefully devote himself to other pastoral duties (p. 442, p. 462), but a priest who refused to give both kinds "ex odio et contemptu," "hereticus videtur esse et sic seductor" (p. 462). Havlík may have been actually persecuted under this principle—see the text in Höfler, I, 623.

[138] Quoted by Bartoš, *Do čtyř art.*, p. 26, n. 92, from the postil described in *LČJ*, No. 96: "Domini convenientes et ceteri congregaciones suas facientes solum instant, ut habeant profectum in rebus terrenis."

religious reform depended on what was done in each congregation. One of his hopes for utraquism was that "this evangelical mode of communion would unite . . . the people with the priests in pious affection and . . . in mutual love," [139] and in one of his replies to a request for guidance from his followers he defined the practical aspects of such a union:

> All and single, joined as one, rich and poor, should press for holy Christian union with one another and with Christ in Christ's gospel and its observance, so that, with God's help, they may live together in harmony. But there are two kinds of union: one kind is the union of the evil and hypocrites . . . in the transgression of the evangelical law. This sort of peaceful union Christ came to destroy and cut apart with the sword. . . . The second kind is union in Christ, a holy union consisting in observance of his evangelical law. . . . And to consolidate this union in the towns and communities the evangelical priests should by virtue of their office destroy all mortal sins by preaching the gospel, and what they cannot accomplish by words, the magistrates (*scabini*) should do with the power granted to them by God. That is, they should root out, destroy, and eradicate all irregularities (*deordinaciones*) and sins—cases of fornication, adultery, usury, avarice, and other things introduced against the gospel of Jesus Christ: so that the Lord God and Christ may be their Lord and they be his people, and that he may dwell with them forever, giving them his peace. . . .[140]

This was what Jakoubek had advocated back in early 1413: smash the worldly peace of the evil ones and enforce observance of God's Law—but then his rather unrealistic advice was addressed to the King and Archbishop; it was in any case not taken up by Hus, Jesenic, and the rest as their policy.

---

[139] A passage in *Utrum sacerdos nolens,* MS D 48, p. 492: "Item iste modus ewangelicus uniret et confederaret in affeccione pia plebem cum sacerdotibus, et econtra, in mutua dileccione. . . ."

[140] *De quibusdam punctis (LČJ,* No. 70), MS VIII E 7, fol. 105ʳ: "Quod omnes et singuli simul in unum, dives et pauper, instant pro unione sancta cristiana adinvicem et ad Cristum in ewangelio Cristi et in eius observancia, ut deo faciente habitent quasi unius moris in domo [*cf.* Ps. 67:7]. Ubi est notandum de duplici unitate vel unione: quedam enim est unio malorum et ippocritarum . . . in transgressione ewangelice legis. Istam unionem cum pace venit Cristus destruere et gladium [*sic*] ad scindendam eam. . . . Secunda unio in Cristo est sancta, in observancia sue ewangelice legis consistens. . . . Et pro ista unione in civitatibus et communitatibus firmanda, ewangelici sacerdotes ex suo officio debent ewangelisando omnia peccata mortalia destruere et quod ipsi verbo non possunt facere debent scabini potestate a deo sibi concessa, omnes deordinaciones et peccata, scilicet fornicaciones, adulteria, usuram, avariciam, destruere, et alia contra ewangelium Ihesu Cristi introducta evellere et eradicare, ut dominus deus et Cristus sit eis in dominum et ipsi sint sibi in populum suum et habitet cum eis in seculum, dando eis suam pacem." The relationship between the priests' preaching and the magistrates' power is that set forth by Isidore of Seville (*Decretum,* XXIII, c. 20) and often used by Wyclif (see my "Wyclifism," p. 63 and n. 45).

Now the social framework is different and the matter can be treated in perfectly realistic terms—in fact, it is now the conservatives who are the impractical ones, as will appear more than once.

In the same *responsum* Jakoubek further described the methods of institutionalizing the "holy Christian union":

> There is need for serpentine prudence and dovelike simplicity in the towns and communities, so that they have evangelical priests of Christ in whom the spirit of Jesus dwells, priests who preach by word, by example, and by good life, who light the way to evangelical truth and kindle the flame of love of the Lord in the Christian people. Only so are holy unity and union consolidated in the communities, nor should the communities lightly accept any priests at all, who are not yet proven in life and morals, for such unknown priests may be pseudo and thus break, prevent, and weaken this union. But let inquiry be made with great diligence about their lives, and whether they are proven in Christ's doctrine and life. . . .
>
> It is better to have a few good and holy priests . . . than many useless, scandalous, blind, ignorant, and avaricious ones, who would do little or nothing good for the people's spiritual edification. Therefore altarists and chantry-priests, living in idleness on permanent rent-incomes, should not be multiplied, but the community with its magistrates (*cum scabinis*), or the other secular powers (*vel alii seculares*), should have all alms in their hands and in their power, so that if the priests should in some cases stray from the path of truth, then the magistrates and others can deprive them, take the means of support away from them, and thereby support others who are better and more useful to the community. By this system the [unfit] priests will not be able to cite in court or excommunicate or otherwise be vexatious on account of their deprivation.[141]

---

[141] *De quibusdam punctis,* fol. 105^v: "Eciam [oportet] prudencia serpentina cum simplicitate columbina in civitatibus et communitatibus, quod habeant sacerdotes Cristi ewangelicos quos inhabitat spiritus Ihesu, qui predicant verbo et exemplo et bona vita, qui illuminant ad ewangelicam veritatem et accendunt ad amorem domini in populis cristianis. Talibus enim firmatur unitas et unio sancta in communitatibus, nec ita leviter debent ad se communitates suscipere quoscumque sacerdotes nondum probatos in moribus et vita, quia tales sacerdotes incogniti possunt esse pseudo et sic scindere unionem prefatam, impedire et debilitare eam. Sed debent inquirere cum magna diligencia de eorum vita et scrutari, an sint probati in doctrina Cristi et vita." And fol. 106^r: "Melius ergo habere paucos, bonos, et sanctos sacerdotes . . . quam multos inutiles, scandalosos, cecos, ignaros, avaros, qui modicum vel nichil boni facerent in populo quo ad spiritualem edificacionem. Ideo non sunt multiplicandi altariste, capellani ociose annuatim de censu viventes perpetuo, sed communitas cum scabinis vel alii seculares omnem elemosinam habeant in manibus et in potestate sua, ut si sacerdotes in casu exhorbitarent a via veritatis, quod possent eos alienare et necessaria subtrahere et aliis melioribus et communitati utilioribus ministrare, ne pro eorum ablacione possint citare, excommunicare, vel aliter vexare."

This blueprint for a *congregational* establishment of the reform, with the secular magistrates in charge of selecting, disciplining, and supporting the clergy, harmonized in theory with the more general, national establishment envisaged by the Hussite League, but it is clear that the two lines of attack involved two different patterns of emphasis and could readily lead in practice to conflicts about church polity if nothing else.

What the quoted passages show is that Jakoubek in 1415–1417 looked forward to a reformed Bohemia that would be a mosaic of reformed congregations, each under local secular control—whether by the feudality or by the magistrates and people of the towns. Furthermore, he quite obviously envisaged and accepted a serious conflict at the local level as the old superfluous clergy were thrown out, as the church's endowment was secularized (as "alms"), and as the new congregations took shape in the context of a necessarily passionate battle against moral laxity and common sins. Nor did he lay undue stress on legitimacy of leadership. If his ideal was action under the magistrates, he was also prepared to sanction the leadership of the reforming priests themselves, to abolish abuses that were positively harmful. Writing, for example, about the Romanist clergy's collection of hearth-taxes (*fumalia*), he declared that "this is not founded in the Law of God, but is rather a plundering of the poor, sanctioned by ancient custom"; it was, in fact, simply evil. When the people as a whole did not recognize this, however, then "the few good and simple faithful, considering their insufficient strength," might have to submit to force, "humbly tolerate this rapine and suffer such unbearable burdens." But, "if the simple poor can safely resist this or any other spoliations by Antichrist, without detriment or damage to their salvation, then let them resist in the name of the Lord, together with their good priests, and with serpentine prudence." [142] The circumstances under which such a battle against Antichrist would take place can only have been those with which we became familiar in the preceding section—the people split into two camps, a black-and-white antithesis between Romanists and Hussites, violently abusive anti-Roman propaganda,

---

[142] *De fumalibus, imaginibus, censibus ecclesie* (*LČJ*, No. 58), MS III G 28, fol. 225ʳ: "Amice in Cristo Ihesu diligende, de censu fumalium bene dicis, quod non fundatur in lege dei, sed est iam ex antiquata conswetudine pauperum spoliacio." "Sed quia universus populus istam et alias versucias anticristi non cognoscit, et . . . valde debilis est populus sceleratus ad opponendum se anticristo, ideo fideles simplices boni et pauci, considerantes insufficienciam suam, iam quasi compulsi et vexati excommunicacionibus fictis vel aliis comminacionibus, dum coguntur talia tributa dare symoniacis, oportet eos humiliter talem violenciam tollerare, et pati talia onera importabilia." But ". . . nunc simplices pauperes, si possunt comodose huiusmodi anticristi spoliacioni, vel quibuscumque aliis, sine dispendio salutis vel dampno resistere, resistant in nomine domini, una cum bonis sacerdotibus, cum prudencia serpentina."

and perhaps even violent action. It is not surprising to find that in such situations those doctrinal positions seemed most relevant that were most absolute, most extreme, least weakened by the qualifications that Jakoubek felt obliged to make in his capacity as scholastic theologian and leader of a national movement.

These considerations can help explain Jakoubek's relationship to the provincial radicals as well as his own doctrinal positions in this period. At times he urged extremely radical reforms and stood by those who carried them out, while on other occasions he found it either necessary or desirable to defend existing practice against attacks from the left; most often, however, he pronounced in favor of what may be defined as basic Catholicism, drastically simplified and purified according to the ideals of Matthew of Janov, or in other words, according to the norm of an idealized Primitive Church. Thus when he was asked for advice on how to deal with the myriad rites and customs of contemporary Roman observance, he offered this Janovian rule:

> If there are praiseworthy rites or customs in churches, introduced by the apostles and the Primitive Church . . . to promote and not hinder the divine cult due to the most divine sacrament [of the Eucharist], they should be observed even if they are not explicitly expressed in the evangelical law. . . . Customs or rites introduced afterward, when charity was growing cold, can also be observed without sin, to avoid scandalizing the weak, if they do not hinder the observance of the law of Christ and of his cult but rather promote it, and if the people do not esteem them as the gospel, nor fix their hopes for salvation on them, nor practice any superstitions in connection with them. But if there are too many superfluous rites and an excessive number of traditions, impeding evangelical observance . . . then I judge that these should be pruned away at opportune times and in opportune places.[143]

---

[143] *De quibusdam punctis*, MS VIII E 7, fol. 104ʳ–104ᵛ: "Si qui sunt in ecclesiis ritus vel consuetudines laudabiles ab apostolis et primitiva ecclesia . . . introducte ad promovendum et non impediendum cultum hunc debitum et divinum ad ipsum divinissimum sacramentum, debent observari licet expresse in lege ewangelica non exprimantur. . . . Consuetudines vel ritus posterius refrigescente caritate introducti, si non impediunt observanciam legis Cristi et sui cultus sed magis promovent, nec eos appreciant ut ewangelium, nec in illis spem // salutis reponunt, neque per hec superstitiones aliquas exercent, possunt licite observari sine peccato quandoque, ad evitandum scandalum pusillorum. Si autem sunt nimis multi ritus superflui et excessiva multitudo tradicionum impediens observanciam ewangelicam . . . , puto quod sint tempore et loco oportunis resecanda." The originals of Jakoubek's phrases are to be found everywhere in Matthew of Janov's *Regule,* although as far as I know the quoted passage as a whole is not there. For its doctrine see e.g. *Regule,* I, 45 ff. And for a parallel but milder treatment see Jakoubek's utraquist tractate against Andrew of Brod, in mid-1415 (Hardt, III, 526–529).

We have just seen that he did not shrink from applying this formula to justify a revolt against the collection of hearth-taxes by the clergy, and there is good evidence that he also applied it to abolish all forms of what the Hussites called simony—that is, not so much the buying and selling of church offices, but the charging of money for such priestly functions as absolution, anointing with holy oil, the churching of women after childbirth, the blessing of eggs, grain, palms, horses' reins, and pilgrims' wallets, aspersion with holy water. In some cases, as in absolution, the only evil was the charging of fees, but more often the practices themselves were regarded as superfluous—as indeed invented for the very purpose of making money—and they were abolished.[144] Furthermore, he never faltered in his opposition to one of the most important single post-Primitive accretions, the cult of holy images and the practices associated with it. Again and again Jakoubek repeated Matthew of Janov's strictures against the superfluity of statues and pictures, their excessive decoration, the people's superstitious reliance on the power of the images themselves, and their effect in distracting people from the only true cult, that "of the most divine body and blood of Jesus Christ." He did not say flatly that all images were to be destroyed but his formula for action, taken directly from Matthew of Janov, pointed in this direction:

> As soon as one image is more revered than other ones in the church, or when more people visit it with candles and genuflexions and other unwholesome acts, then it should be swiftly cast out of the temple as a stumbling block to the people.[145]

Other passages in his work make it clear that he regarded such unwholesome acts as the rule when images were present, and in fact his radical disciples understood him in this sense when they went ahead and got rid of all images. Thus when in early 1417 the more conservative masters criticized

[144] See, e.g., the *De fumalibus,* fol. 225ᵛ: "Et idem judicium de aliis exaccionibus prelatorum, archidiaconorum, decanorum, vel quorumcumque aliorum ducum cecorum et cupidorum adinventis." For the particular cases that Jakoubek opposed, see Nicholas of Pelhřimov's testimony quoted below, *ad* n. 165. The custom of charging for absolution was prevalent enough to draw the attack of reformers—e.g., Doctor Heinrich of Bitterfeld, of the Prague Theological Faculty, who determined a question on the subject in 1404 (excerpts in Bartoš, *JSH,* VIII (1937), 30).

[145] "Quam cito una ymago amplius reveretur quam alie ymagines in templo, vel cum habet concursum ampliorem plebis cum candelis et genuflexionibus, vel aliis inordinatis modis, mox est de templo eicienda tamquam offendiculum populi"—the passage (fol. 227ᵛ) is from a section, *De ymaginibus* (fols. 225ᵛ–227ᵛ), in the same *responsum* that contains the *De fumalibus* discussed above. It is copied from Matthew of Janov's *Regule,* from the unpublished Bk. V: see V. Kybal, *M. Matěj z Janova* (Prague, 1905), p. 134, n. 1. The same passage was also used by Nicholas of Dresden in *his* work on images, *De ymaginibus,* MS Mikulov, II 123, fols. 171ᵛ–172ᵛ.

the provincial radicals for their categorical iconoclasm, Jakoubek deliberately repeated his condemnation of images,[146] clearly as a sign of solidarity with his followers. And when, several years later, he vigorously dissociated himself from the Taborites on a series of points where they had claimed his authority, he did not, even then, condemn their destruction of images—his silence on the point shows that he agreed with them.[147]

Less clear but even more instructive are his discussions of the mass itself, particularly in his *De ceremoniis,* written perhaps as early as 1415.[148] His declared purpose here was to show that a priest might say mass in the home of a sick man—even one not rich enough to have his own chapel and chaplain—and his method was to define the mass in terms of its four essentials: the proper material of bread and wine, a duly ordained priest, the correct words of institution, and the priest's true intention of consecrating.[149] The Roman mass of course included a great many other things—the *Kyrie,* prefaces, *Introit, Agnus Dei,* and other parts of the canon, the consecrated altar, vestments, vessels, and other parts of the décor: these, Jakoubek showed, were only "accidentals," added by this or that pope; they were human inventions and as such, however suitable or useful, could be omitted in cases of necessity.[150] He did to be sure describe the modern rite as a "laudable custom"; [151] but those who had attended to his distinctions in the matter of customs could recall how tenuous, conditional, and reluctant was his acceptance of even laudable customs that had been introduced in the post-Primitive period, when charity had grown cold. And when they began to follow his particular arguments in the *De ceremoniis,* they could hardly fail to draw conclusions that went far beyond the words themselves. Consider, for example, the effect of this argument: Christ and the apostles had often and ordinarily (*pluries et communiter*) consecrated and administered the sacrament outside of churches, without special altars, and without special vestments, and this rite had then been followed by the saints of the Primitive Church. "Therefore by the same reason it is even now quite possible that

---

[146] The *posicio de imaginibus* of 31 January 1417; *LČJ*, No. 69. It is discussed and extensively quoted in Nejedlý, IV, 105 ff. The action of the conservative masters is discussed below.

[147] The reference is to Jakoubek's *Apologia contra Taboritas; LČJ*, No. 101. It is printed in *ST*, II, 161–164. Sedlák and Bartoš both dated it 1428, but Bartoš has since changed his mind twice, first choosing 1421 (*JSH*, II (1929), 83 f.), then 1426 (*JSH*, IX (1936), 29–34).

[148] *LČJ*, No. 59; the text in *ST*, II, 145–149 (Part I), 149–160.

[149] *ST*, II, 146.

[150] *Ibid.*, pp. 146, 150. Jakoubek calls the four elements variously—*essencialia, substancialia, necessaria* (pp. 152, 146, 150).

[151] *Ibid.*, p. 152.

priests of Christ, moved by the same spirit as the saints of old, and by the same charity," should consecrate the sacrament and give it "to the sick or to others" without the customary vestments, outside consecrated churches, and without church altars, when "the other, more fitting (*conveniencior*) mode cannot be observed." [152] Could any radical who had been exposed to the driving propaganda of the *Tables of the Old and New Color,* and who still vibrated to the strident polemics of the utraquist controversy, now suppose that Christ's simple rite should be reserved only for exceptional cases of necessity? Could he indeed fail to understand Jakoubek's "conveniencior" as meaning merely "more conventional"? Searching for the right form of liturgy for the new utraquist church, how could such a radical avoid interpreting Jakoubek's words in the light of the formula repeated over and over in the utraquist polemics:

> The most certain and secure thing for the Christian to hold in all cases is what our Jesus himself instituted and did and wanted his Primitive Church to do, and thus, together with his church, showed posterity that it should be done and ordered it to be done. [153]

In fact, as we have seen in the case of the Kozí Hradek extremists, the "accidentals" of the Roman mass *were* rejected both in theory and in practice, [154] precisely in line with the *De ceremoniis.* It is hard to avoid inferring both that the extremist preachers had learned their lesson from Jakoubek and that the latter had *meant* to teach them just that lesson.

Indeed, Jakoubek went out of his way in that treatise to draw all sorts of issues into his curiously flirtatious scheme of radical possibilities. Thus he argued that the mass had originally been celebrated in Hebrew, then in Greek, then in Latin—always "for the benefit of the faithful"—and for the same reason it had once been authorized in Slavonic: if then the faithful wished it, and since the same benefits would probably result, the mass could be celebrated in Czech, or at least the Gospel and Epistle could be read in that language, for the people would be more edified by what they could understand than by "hearing Latin and understanding nothing." None of this seems to bear on the matter of saying mass for the sick, but Jakoubek drags it in anyway, by noting that if a Czech mass could be justified by the "necessity" just described, then certainly mass could be celebrated in homes

---

[152] *Ibid.,* p. 153.

[153] *Utrum sacerdos nolens,* MS D 48, pp. 490–491; many other similar passages could be cited—see, e.g., above, chap. iii, *ad* n. 71.

[154] See the text quoted above, in the section on "Sectarian Extremism in the Provinces"; also Nejedlý, IV, 148–176.

when necessary without the usual vestments and other accidentals.[155] Similarly he argued that wooden chalices could be used, as in the early days of the church, "if the gold and silver ones have been taken away and distributed to the poor or otherwise used for the benefit of the commonwealth (*reipublice*)." [156] Further, the special consecration of churches, altars, and cemeteries had been instituted by Pope Silvester I and could now be omitted in time of necessity.[157] The use of the "Kiss of Peace" plaque in the mass as substitute for communion, the reservation to bishops of the function of dedicating churches, the celebration of dedication-day festivities, a series of other specifications about the liturgy—of all these Jakoubek exclaimed:

> See what a great variety of papal decrees there has been in the course of time, decrees that many deem must be observed, just like the gospel, as necessary. But the faithful should know that although these and many others be observed by ancient custom, nevertheless they can be reasonably changed, in time of necessity, under the proper circumstances.[158]

Again, noting that a year after the death of Jesus, the Apostle Peter had "celebrated the first mass, saying only the *Pater noster*," Jakoubek commented that this short form had been left by Peter as an example to posterity; the rest of the liturgy had been "instituted by men for the décor of the mass (*pro decore misse*)" and could be changed or omitted.[159] Much of the argumentation of the *De ceremoniis* depends on such historical reconstructions, and it is quite instructive to observe how this style of theological argument, extensively used in the utraquist polemic, can be made to bear so heavy a burden of reform: the chronicle of Martinus Polonus, the *Flores temporum,* the *Polychronicon* of Ranulph Higden—all are put under contribution to fill out a detailed picture of the progressive human inventions and papal decrees that had taken the church away from its primitive condition.[160]

---

[155] *ST*, II, 154.
[156] *Ibid.*, p. 156.
[157] *Loc. cit.*
[158] *Ibid.*, p. 157.
[159] *Ibid.*, p. 159.
[160] The just quoted item about Peter's mass was taken by Jakoubek from the "cronica Martimiani," i.e., the *Chronicon pontificum et imperatorum*, composed in 1277 by Martinus Polonus (Potthast, I, 771); see the edition in *MGH, SS*, XXII, 408. The extensive material in this work on which pope decreed what was compiled from earlier compilations, and itself served as a source for later chronicles. The *Flores temporum* (Potthast, I, 451 f.) has similar items; unfortunately the edition in *MGH, SS*, XXIV, omits the material before the eighth century. The *Polichronicon* of Ranulph Higden ("Cestrensis") was known to the Hussites only insofar as Wyclif quoted it,

If we now recall the complaint of Master Christian of Prachatice about the extremists led by Wenceslas Koranda—they say "that there should be no practice of ceremonies and ecclesiastical rites invented by man, but that in all things there should be conformity to the rites of the Primitive Church"—we infer that some responsibility for their beliefs belongs to Master Jakoubek. The same can be said for most of the extremist theory and practice surveyed in the preceding section, particularly if we bear in mind not only Jakoubek's doctrines but also his prescriptions for action—and similarly, not only extremist doctrines but also the circumstances in which the preachers and laity were carrying on their anti-Roman agitation. The parallels in thought and even expression could be extended well beyond the range covered above.[161]

But it is not just a matter of parallels. The leaders of provincial extremism in 1415–1417 later became leaders of the Taborite movement, which Jakoubek opposed, and in the course of their controversies with him and the other masters, the Taborites had more than one opportunity to reflect on how different things had once been. In 1420, when the argument concerned Tabor's rejection of the Roman mass and vestments, Tabor's spokesman, Bishop Nicholas of Pelhřimov, justified his rite by copious quotations from Jakoubek's *De ceremoniis,* which he assigned to the period when Jakoubek "once thought the same as we do."[162] And when Jakoubek objected that to reject the "accidentals" of the mass would give scandal to many, Nicholas could recall that his opponent "frequently used to say that it was better to let

which he did often; it too contained much of the material here under discussion, and it may be guessed that it was from Wyclif that the Hussites learned to use history to back up their critique of the Roman church. At the same time, Jakoubek's immediate source here was probably Nicholas of Dresden, who in several of his works developed a historical dossier from the chronicles just cited (see Bartoš, "Vznik a počátky táborství," *Husitství a cizina,* p. 133).

[161] Thus, for example, the Anonymous Account of extremism at Kozí Hradek (quoted in full above, in the section on "Sectarian Extremism in the Provinces") tells us that the extremists said, "Today the concubinaries and monks will play with dolls (*lútky*) and blocks of wood." And Jakoubek, in his Postil of *ca.* 1414 (*LČJ*, No. 95; quoted by Nejedlý, IV, 112), wrote: "Sacerdotes . . . nunc introducunt imagines et auro ossa circumdant *jako lútky* ("like dolls")." Elsewhere Jakoubek used the same derisive word for "monks"—"kuklikones"—as did the Kozí Hradek Hussites (Nejedlý, IV, 122). And when we read that the latter, on Good Friday, told the people they were adoring an idol, we can compare Jakoubek's complaint (Nejedlý, IV, 112) that men showed more devotion to images than to the Body of Christ, "et hoc ostenditur feria sexta magna, quando homines plus ructuant, dum crucifixus elevatur, quam dum corpus Christi elevatur." And the Kozí Hradek rejection of various funeral ceremonies can easily be read as an application of Jakoubek's ideas, assembled by Nejedlý, IV, 122 f.

[162] Höfler, II, 489, 499: "qui quondam in hac materia nobiscum idem sentiens"; "quamdiu in ista materia nobiscum idem sensit." See also pp. 488–502, 545–574, *passim,* and Sedlák's discussion in *ST,* II, 135–143.

scandal arise than to abandon the truth." [163] In fact, in the *De ceremoniis* itself, Jakoubek had considered the objection, that many would be scandalized by his proposed method of bringing the Eucharist to the poor; his response was: "It is scandal to the Pharisees, when they take it in bad part." [164] Nicholas then continued, in a passage of irony as beautiful as it is valuable:

> He says it is evil of us that we not give up a truth founded in Christ, because it is an occasion of scandal to those who take it in bad part, but he doesn't impute evil to himself when many fall away and are scandalized by him, because of his defense of human traditions and refusal to assent to the truth. Moreover, if he would avoid any scandal at all, even one arising from truth taken in bad part, led him and the others stop giving communion in both kinds, let him practice the cult of images in church, let him church women for money, bless eggs, oats, palms, horses' reins, pilgrims' purses, let him sprinkle cemeteries with holy water, and let him resume the many other practices that against custom he has caused to be omitted! For many take these omissions in bad part and are scandalized by them.[165]

And when in 1431, two years after Jakoubek's death, Master John Rokycana produced what he claimed was the former's explicit dissociation of himself from the Taborites, Nicholas commented:

> If he has excused himself well, then it will be well with him, but the character of these excuses will be clear to those who know [*expertis*], those who many years ago used to hear his sermons, when he was preaching in the church of St. Michael and afterward in Bethlehem, when he first received that pulpit after Master John [Hus] of good memory. It is not for us to judge, how he then thought about those points and how afterward he turned to another position. . . . [166]

Putting all of this together, we get a very clear picture of the young students who followed Hus, who responded to the radical reform agitation of Jakoubek, took part in the strenuous events of the years just before Hus's departure for Constance, then supported Jakoubek and Nicholas of Dresden in the great utraquist reform, and then went out to preach the cause of Hus and the lay chalice in the provinces, particularly in South Bohemia. We can imagine these men applying Jakoubek's ideas, keeping in touch with him, no doubt responding to his leadership, but at the same time being led by circumstances and the radical temper of the laity, as well as by their own inclinations, to

---

[163] Höfler, II, 495.

[164] *ST*, II, 160.

[165] Höfler, II, 496.

[166] The Taborite Confession of 1431, ed. B. Lydius, *Waldensia*, I (Rotterdam, 1616), 293 f.

develop a sectarian psychology that would eventually cause a break with even the most radical doctrines of Prague. Later on, looking back, they would naturally believe that it was not they who had moved off to the left, but Jakoubek who had turned to the right.

In fact, the matter was more complex. It is now time for us to turn to the other side of Jakoubek's activity in the years 1415–1417, and to try to understand how he functioned as not merely a leader of radicalism but a statesman, so to speak, of the national reformation. His colleagues on the right, those masters whom we have previously called the politicians and who can now be accurately labeled as conservatives, were also statesmen, but their constructive capacity in this period was entirely exhausted by the program of the Hussite League, which they implemented, intensified, or revived, according to circumstances and opportunity. Jakoubek undertook the much more difficult task of promoting a genuine reformation, up to and in one or two cases somewhat beyond the limits of what the national coalition would accept. Thus, for example, he did not stop with his remarks about the legitimacy and desirability of a Czech mass; even though he did not otherwise reject the "accidentals" of the Roman mass, he encouraged his disciple John Čapek to translate the whole Roman liturgy into Czech, and this rite in time became standard in the non-Taborite regions of Hussite Bohemia.[167] Similarly, utraquism became standard practice thanks to Jakoubek's continuing agitation, and we have seen how ready he was to depend on the secular powers to enforce it. And his concept of moral reform, both in the clergy and in the laity, included the idea that it was the solemn obligation of the magistrates and secular lords to impose such reform by force if necessary; here he differed from medieval orthodoxy only in having a somewhat longer list of things to be suppressed.[168]

Within the framework of this kind of leadership he inevitably had to face the duty of imposing limits on his more radical followers. He must have relied a great deal on talk, for which we naturally have very little evidence; but he also composed written *responsa,* replies to requests for guidance from his followers outside of Prague, and some of these texts—no doubt only a small fraction—still survive. Their value has already been exploited in the preceding pages, when it was a question of showing not merely what

[167] For sources and references see Bartoš, "Z politické literatury doby husitské. 2. Kněz Jan Čapek," *SbH,* V (1957), 34–36. See also above, chap. iii, n. 94.

[168] The sins of fornication, adultery, usury, and avarice specified in the passage quoted above, *ad* n. 140, do not exhaust the targets of Jakoubek's puritanism; see Nejedlý, IV, 87–147 *passim,* for a good survey of the sources, especially for Jakoubek's hatred of singing and dancing. The duty of secular power to suppress such sins is set forth frequently by all Hussite writers—their theory here was nothing unusual even if their practice was notably strict.

Jakoubek believed but what he actually formulated as policy; in this sense the *responsa* are more valuable than his more abundant treatises and sermons of this period. Moreover, their very existence documents the important point urged by Bartoš and repeated here: that Jakoubek functioned not merely as a teacher and intellectual, but also as a party leader, hence as a man whose involvement in the problems posed by the leftward movement of the reformation was direct, continuous, and functional.

One such problem was the relationship between the Hussites and the Romanist clergy. Both Wyclif and, following him, Hus had declared that a pastor who did not validate his leadership by his virtuous works was not entitled to either the allegiance or the obedience of his flock; he certainly did not enjoy the grace of "present righteousness," and as for the grace of predestination, he might have it but there was no reason for any human to think so.[169] The radical theoreticians went even further: the lesson of such works as the *Tables of the Old and New Color* was that there were only two kinds of priests, those of Christ and those of Antichrist, and the latter included not merely those lacking in personal virtue but *all* who identified themselves with the Roman, papal institution. In this spirit Jakoubek issued the *responsum* already quoted above, instructing the Hussites to choose useful priests and get rid of not only those who were bad but those who were superfluous; and in the consideration of badness he did not distinguish between the patent viciousness of simony and the much more questionable defect of non-utraquism. In this practical context the issue of Donatism—whether evil priests had sacramental powers—was rather academic, for although both Jakoubek and Nicholas of Dresden argued that evil priests were not useful, and supported these arguments with weighty patristic dossiers, their point was that such priests should be boycotted, not that they lacked magical powers.[170] But it must have been all but impossible to preserve this distinction when trying to organize the people against Roman incumbents, and it will be recalled that one of the complaints of the Anonymous Account of extremism around Kozí Hrádek was that the layman Krampeř said "that every priest not holding with Hus is evil, and that such a priest cannot

[169] See above, chap. i.

[170] Nicholas of Dresden's dossiers appear in his *Puncta*, MS IV G 15, fols. 17ʳ sqq., and his *Querite, ibid.*, fol. 112ʳ. See my introduction to *OC & N*, n. 68, for references and quotations. The closest he came to Donatism was the argument, well based on authorities, that a priest who had acquired his consecration by simony had not in fact been validly consecrated and hence was no priest to begin with; see Nicholas's sermon on *Nisi manducaveritis*, MS IV G 15, fol. 202ᵛ: "Et quid sit de symoniacis, qui lepram recipiunt in ordinacione et ma勒diccionem, secundum Ambrosium [*Decretum*, I. q. i, c. 14], an conficiant vel non, relinquo iudicio superiorum meorum, sed utique nichil dat quod non habet."

consecrate the Eucharist [*nec . . . potest conficere*]." Nor was he the only
one, as we learn from one of Jakoubek's *responsa,* addressed to a provincial
correspondent who had sent him a text of a sermon that someone had
preached, to the effect that "evil priests who sin mortally are all, universally,
generally, and always, lacking in the power to consecrate the Eucharist for the
the faithful people." [171] The preacher had insisted that the laity who resorted
to such a priest shared in his sin, and that the evil priest deserved to be
deprived of his priesthood because he had broken the law of Jesus Christ.[172]

There is much evidence to show that the Donatist issue kept its liveliness
throughout this period and indeed much later—in the 1420's it was revived
by the Taborite priest Markolt, a Prague bachelor of arts and no doubt one
of Jakoubek's former disciples.[173] Having been led almost to the point of this
doctrine by the violent anti-Roman propaganda of Jakoubek and Nicholas of
Dresden, the young radical preachers carrying through the reformation
could hardly have seen much point in insisting that even the worst priest still
kept his power.[174] If it is correct to suppose that Waldensian sectarians were
among those with whom the preachers worked, then the Donatism of that
heresy must be supposed to have reinforced the logic of the situation.[175] But

---

[171] The text survives in MS IV H 17, fols. 181^r–183^v, fols. 188^r–189^v; its author is not
named but is obviously Jakoubek—this is also the judgement of F. M. Bartoš,
M. Jakoubek ze Stříbra (Prague, 1939), p. 19. In the text on fol. 189^r is a reference to
"illud publice predicatum, scilicet quod mali sacerdotes mortaliter peccantes universaliter et generaliter omnes numquam possint conficere eukaristiam plebibus fidelibus."

[172] *Ibid.,* fol. 188^r, where Jakoubek responds to the preacher's argument, namely
"quod decreta prohibent astare missis concubinariorum," and to the authorities cited
therefor: "Sed ex hoc non oportet sequi hoc et verificari semper et universaliter pro
omnibus fidelibus. . . ." And fol. 188^v—the preacher had said "quod prelati propter
tradiciones suas possunt aliquem privare a sacerdocio, quare autem non magis esset
dignus privacione qui non servat legem domini nostri Ihesu Cristi."

[173] Höfler, II, 589 ff.

[174] On this point the Anonymous Account of the Kozí Hradek situation tells its own
story—there was obviously no room in Hussite agitation for any arguments that were
not *against* the Roman clergy. Cf. also Stephen of Dolany's interesting remarks, dating
from the latter part of 1417: "Dum enim vestri ex se ipsis praedicatores praecipui in
fastu castrorum, in latibulis villarum et sepium, non missi sed propriis voluntatibus
commissi per fas et nefas, praecipue et pene solo omni studio in confusionem et
contemptum Cleri Romanae Ecclesiae . . . in propriam gloriam impudenter praedi-
cant; et in his non locum, non tempus, sed nec personarum conditionem observant"
(*Epistolae ad Hussitas,* ed. B. Pez, *Thesaurus anecdotorum novissimus,* col. 518).

[175] Some at least of the Waldensians believed that "omnis sanctus est sacerdos Christi"
(Holinka, *Sektářství v Čechách,* p. 138, n. 466; Preger, "Ueber das Verhältnis der
Taboriten," p. 75, n. 5), and it was perhaps as a corollary of this notion that some of the
Waldensian groups (the Italo-German branch) denied that bad priests had sacramental
powers (Preger, p. 89).

this was just the sort of thing that Jakoubek could not tolerate, in his capacity of national leadership, and so we find him in his *responsum* pronouncing all the classic criticisms of Donatist heresy: by virtue of his office even the evil priest can validly administer sacraments and preach God's word to others, albeit to his own damnation; God can work through unworthy instruments; God can accept the sacrifice offered by a bad priest in behalf of good laymen. He even added a perverse twist of Wyclifism: one who is predestined may spend a good part of his life without the grace of present righteousness; therefore a predestined priest, no matter how grave a sinner, may well retain the grace of the priestly office. Although Jakoubek himself had for years been categorically denouncing the Romanist clergy as fornicators, concubinaries, and simoniacs, he now said that even though it was indeed possible that a man who was not a priest in the sight of God might hold priestly office, still "it is extremely difficult to say this about any particular person without a special revelation. . . . And to attempt to make such a judgement generally about each and every evil priest seems presumptuous and most dangerous." For no one can say who is predestined and who is not, without special revelation.[176] Those scholars who try to derive facts from doctrines may well pause for instruction by this spectacle of how the very Wyclifite doctrine that had helped to destroy confidence in the Roman Church could now be used, in the interest of the Hussite Church, to refute the subversive excesses of sectarianism.

Even more instructive is the issue attested by another *responsum,* which shows that some radicals in the provinces were preaching that any priest who continued to hold a parish house or other properties attached to his church was a "priest of Pharaoh"—a term of abuse derived perhaps from Origen.[177] Here the issue was entirely practical, with no reference to the difficult

---

[176] MS IV H 17, fol. 182ᵛ: ". . . licet posset contigere propter peccata populi ypocritam regnare et infidelem subdole sine dei vocacione vel humana ingerere se ad nomen sive pretensum sacerdocium apparens; hoc tamen tangere distincte difficilimum est de quoquam sine speciali revelacione. Et hoc generaliter de singulis malis sacerdotibus iudicare videtur esse presumptuosum et periculosissimum attemptare." The Wyclifite twist appears especially on fol. 189ʳ-189ᵛ: "Ex quo patet quod sicud sine revelacione non potest sciri certitudinaliter quis tam malus sit sacerdos quod non sit predestinatus ad vitam eternam, sic non potest sciri communiter quis propter gravitatem sui peccati finaliter privatur sacerdocio. Et si quantumcumque predestinato peccante graviter adhuc in eo remanet gracia predestinacionis, que est maxima graciarum, cur non in predestinato sacerdote quantumcumque graviter peccante non remaneret gracia sacerdotalis officii? Divinare autem de unoquoque an sit predestinatus ad vitam eternam vel prescitus ad dampnacionem, nemo vestrum scit sine speciali revelacione."

[177] The source is Jakoubek's reply to an otherwise unknown follower, Sopušek, who must have written in to ask for advice or perhaps complain about extremist propaganda; the work is listed in *LČJ,* No. 67, and survives in MS 4937, fol. 141ʳ. The only

question of God's secret judgement, and Jakoubek's way of dealing with it can be made to bear a heavy burden of sociological interpretation. His general theory was clear enough—it was in fact pure Wyclif—and we have seen it formulated in the *responsum* advising the secular authorities to support good priests and get rid of bad ones. Under the Roman system the clergy held civil, legal title to moneys, lands, and lordships over persons, and Wyclif's doctrine called for this title of civil dominion to be removed in favor of evangelical dominion—that is, possession of goods by title of alms, with of course no lordship over persons. But there were several ways in which evangelical dominion might be practiced, and Jakoubek on a number of occasions repeated Wyclif's very words to define the three permissible modes of possession, in descending order of desirability. The best way was for the clergy to imitate the status of Christ and the apostles, by receiving only food, clothing, and other necessities from the laity—this mode, if applied, would restore the order and peace of the Primitive Church. But it was also legitimate for the clergy to receive tithes, offerings, and private gifts—always as alms—and to divide this income into the canonical four parts, one for the priests, one for auxiliary clerics, one for the poor, one for repairs to the churches: "but in this status there lies some considerable peril, through possible sophistry." Even worse, indeed just barely permissible, was a third mode, by which the clergy would receive not only offerings and so forth, but also lands, rent-incomes, and estates (*dominia laicalia*), still however as alms.[178] Thus even though Jakoubek's own theory left no doubt that the way to realize the goal of radical Hussitism—reduction to the estate of the Primitive Church—was to enforce the first mode of clerical possession, he could with some consistency defend the other modes, and this is what he chose to do in the *responsum* under consideration here. If, he wrote, there

---

identification of the offending viewpoint appears in this sentence of Jakoubek's: "Nec dicendus est quisquam sacerdos pharonis ex hoc quod predicto titulo dispensacionis vel elemosine aut aliquo alio ewangelico pertinenti eidem, bona . . . habeat fortune, sicut domum et cuncta alia sibi necessaria aut utilia ad salutem." Elsewhere the "bona" are characterized as "ecclesie collata." The phrase "sacerdos pharonis" is not perhaps much to go on, but it leads in interesting directions. Nicholas of Dresden, in his *Puncta,* had written "Et dicit Origenes . . . : Vis scire quid intersit inter sacerdotes dei et sacerdotes pharaonis? Pharao terras concedit sacerdotibus suis; dominus autem sacerdotibus suis partem non concedit in terra, sed dicit eis: Ego sum pars vestra . . ." (MS IV G 15, fol. 8ᵛ). And when John Příbram later refuted Taborite doctrines, in 1420–1421, he commented that "ante annum" the Taborites had been ardent in praise of Matthew of Janov, Chrysostom, and Origen (Höfler, II, 531). Thus even though we cannot move from these juxtaposed texts to a knowledge of what happened, we can reconstruct at least some of the connotations of the radical cliché.

[178] See above, n. 44, for references to the sources.

were no superfluity or civil dominion, then "modern clerics faithfully working for the people's salvation" could legitimately hold property attached to a
church, "like a house or other necessary or useful things," and if there were
no defect otherwise, such a priest was not a priest of Pharaoh but "a true
priest of our lord Jesus Christ." [179]

Since Jakoubek would hardly have pronounced this formula for the sake
of the Romanist clergy, we must suppose that he was thinking of priests who
were loyal to Hus's memory and who gave communion in both kinds, but
who also held regular parish livings, even if without civil title. In other
words, what he was saying to the extreme radicals was this: I have nothing
but praise for you if you wish to imitate the status of the Primitive Church,
and indeed I wish everyone would, but in fact many do not and these, too,
are parts of the Hussite reform and we must accept them. His pronouncement on the Donatist issue could no doubt be interpreted in a similar sense,
but there a genuine question of theological doctrine was involved, together
with the political question, and although Jakoubek's scruples were politically
convenient they may also have been quite sincere. In the matter of clerical
poverty, however, everything is perfectly clear. By accepting the Hussite
establishment that had been effected by some members of the nobility and by
some town magistrates, Jakoubek necessarily set limits on the development
of his own radical program, which could not be allowed to embrace extreme
positions intolerable to the national consensus. Nor could the radicals seek to
impose their program on the other Hussites, least of all on those relatively
conservative circles associated with the Hussite feudality, whose support in
the nation and at the royal court was of crucial importance in these years. In
fact the real question, from the point of view of most of the university
masters, was how much scope could be allowed to radical theory and practice
among the people whom the radicals led. Although the more conservative
masters had their own ideas about the matter, the major burden of exploration, adjustment, compromise, and even withdrawal had to be borne by the
one master who combined the two functions of partisan and national leadership. Later the Taborites would look back on this period as one during
which Jakoubek began to move away from the truth he had once preached,

[179] MS 4937, fol. 141^r: "Tenendum est et docendum, quod bona ecclesie collata,
circumscripta . . . circa eadem omni superfluitate, haberi possunt licite et cum modera-
mine a modernis clericis fideliter pro salute populi laborantibus. Cum hoc tamen quod
dominium civile seu proprietas eorundem secularibus pertineat, et non clerico, cui ex
lege dei non licet civiliter aut proprietarie, sed elemosine aut dispensacionis titulo bona
habere fortune. . . . Nec dicendus est quisquam sacerdos pharonis . . . [as in n.
177] . . . ad salutem. Sed est talis quilibet si non aliunde assit defectus sacerdos verus
nostri domini Ihesu Cristi."

but a fairer judgement would be this: in a time when he faced enormous pressure from the center and the right, Jakoubek still managed to salvage a very respectable portion of the almost sectarian radicalism that he personally believed in. Whether it was enough is another question, and we may also ask whether he did not perhaps pay too high a price in the shape of his followers' disillusionment and his own inconsistency. These questions lead to another line of Hussite development, centering in the figure of Nicholas of Dresden and the Waldensianist doctrines that he developed in defiance of those practical calculations that controlled his Czech associate.

NICHOLOS OF DRESDEN AND HIS DOCTRINES, 1415–1416

Up to about September or October of 1415 the career of Nicholas of Dresden as radical ideologue was fully contained within the general framework of Hussite radicalism. Specializing in the anti-Romanist use of canonistic materials, and endowed more richly than Jakoubek with liveliness and imagination, Nicholas made a valuable contribution to the popular agitation of 1412–1413 and to the utraquist enterprise of 1414–1415; at the same time he did not advance ideas that moved significantly beyond Jakoubek's, and the two seem by all evidence to have been close associates, perhaps even literary collaborators.[180] But rather suddenly, in the autumn of 1415, this situation changed; the two men found themselves holding different ideas, and Jakoubek and the other Czech masters attempted to isolate Nicholas, to counter his influence, and eventually to force him out of Prague. Probably by 1417, certainly by 1419, Nicholas died a martyr's death in Meissen, the same sort of destiny that lay in wait for several other Germans of the Dresden School.[181] Since the main evidence for this split in the Hussite left comes from the treatises of the two parties, with virtually no information about details or particular events, we can only guess about the underlying causes and hence about the nature of what was going on; what is known shows that at the very least a drastic realignment of ideas and tendencies was taking place. Nicholas was moving toward a development of Hussite radicalism into a sectarian religion of the Waldensian type, while Jakoubek not only refused to go along but vigorously fought the new ideas. The question of why these things happened remains open.

[180] See, e.g., *OC & N*, p. 16, n. 84, and see above, chap. iii, n. 30 and *passim*.

[181] See Bartoš, "Vznik a počátky táborství," *Husitství a cizina*, pp. 141 f.: in 1417 a refutation of Nicholas's *De purgatorio* referred to the esteem in which he was held for his strict life and martyr's death. In 1419 John Želivský referred to a "Nicholas, priest of Christ," who had died in Meissen, evidently as a martyr. For the Dresden School as a "School for Martyrs" see H. Böhmer, "Magister Peter von Dresden" (as cited above, chap. iii, n. 5), p. 228.

One answer has been offered by Jan Sedlák, the first to study the corpus of Nicholas's works, which then as now were for the most part unpublished. He noted that Nicholas held certain positions characteristic of Waldensianism, such as the absolute prohibition of oath-swearing and of killing, the denial of Purgatory, the rejection of the Roman hierarchy, the belief that even laymen and women might legitimately preach. Adding these to the many points at which Nicholas's more ordinary Hussite radicalism overlapped the Waldensian faith, Sedlák supposed that the Dresdener was in fact a Waldensian who for a time succeeded in radicalizing Hussitism far beyond the Wyclifite doctrine of Hus, but who was then rejected by all but the most extreme radicals, those who eventually became the priests of Tabor.[182] But F. M. Bartoš, the only other scholar with an equal knowledge of the sources, has argued convincingly in favor of a more complex interpretation: up to 1414–1415 Nicholas was only a radical Hussite, nourished chiefly by Wyclifism, and his Waldensianism does not appear until after that time.[183] For reasons too detailed to be fully discussed here,[184] Bartoš's periodization seems more or less sound: even though sectarian views do appear before 1414,[185] the main body of what Nicholas wrote in his early period was in harmony with common Hussite radicalism, while Jakoubek's own development, even before the appearance of Nicholas on the Prague scene, had reached a point that the latter did not really surpass until the second half of 1415.[186] At the same time it is hard to accept Bartoš's rather fanciful explanation for the shift—the advent of the English Wyclifite Peter Payne, who came to Prague in 1414, allegedly bringing information about the German Waldensians whom he had visited en route. Nicholas, a German, would then have formed the idea of bringing Hussitism into line with Waldensianism in order to effect a union with his heretical countrymen.[187] Bartoš may well be right in dating Peter Payne's arrival in 1414, and it is probably true that Payne then refused to swear the oath required for his admission to the University of Prague; but there is no other reason to think that he had anything to say

[182] See the summary, with references, in my "Nicholas of Dresden and the Dresden School in Hussite Prague," the introduction to *OC & N, ad* n. 76. (Since this essay covers much of the material of the present section, but in more detail, I shall refer to it in the following set of notes, rather than reproduce the documentation itself.)

[183] *OC & N, ad* n. 78.

[184] *OC & N, ad.* nn. 79–88.

[185] Most notably the defense of preaching by laymen and women, in the *De quadruplici missione,* ed. Sedlák, *ST,* I, 95–117. See *OC & N, ad* n. 85.

[186] *OC & N, ad* nn. 82, 83. See also the first few paragraphs of chap. ii, the section on "The Radicals and the Beginnings of the Hussite Left."

[187] Bartoš, "Vznik a počátky táborství," pp. 142–146; cf. Pekař's critical note, *Žižka,* IV, 191. See also above, chap. iii, n. 114.

about the German Waldensians, or that he said it to Nicholas, or that Nicholas formed the bold idea Bartoš attributes to him. These are possibilities, no more, and since they cannot be proved we must look for other explanations of a more fundamental sort.

Here the most obvious consideration also seems the most illuminating. From the second half of 1415 on, Jakoubek was not only opposed to Nicholas of Dresden, he was also concerned to limit the extremism of his own followers working in the provinces. If we were right in interpreting this concern as the result of Jakoubek's determination to maintain the national union of all Hussite forces, then a similar interpretation should hold for his polemics against Nicholas. Similarly, the latter's development toward sectarianism can be readily understood in the light of his position as a German, at one with the Czechs in the general program of reform, but excluded from the national enterprise in which Czech university masters collaborated with the barons of the Hussite League and the magistrates of the Hussite towns. Any trained intellectual could participate on terms of absolute equality in the work of anti-Roman theorizing and agitation, but once the reform passed out of the university and the streets of Prague, once the cult of the chalice and of John Hus began to create a Hussite nation, and once the new faith was taken up by a large section of the urban classes and the nobility in the form of a religious establishment—then the men of the Dresden School were inevitably pushed to the periphery of events.

The issue here was a very concrete one; the analysis of Jakoubek's works in the previous section has shown that his main concern from 1415 on was twofold—on the one hand to provide leadership for a radical reformation, on the other hand to prevent that reformation from implementing the ultimate ideals that his own works either expressed or implied. From the disingenuous ambiguities of his *De ceremoniis* to his remarkably supple doctrine of evangelical poverty, his practical leadership was always mindful of the fact that there were many Hussites who were not radicals, and we can safely infer what he must have had in his mind: the kind of Hussitism represented by the more conservative masters, burghers, and barons had to be accepted as a valid part of the general Hussite consensus. If then Nicholas, free of so heavy a burden of leadership, did not imitate Jakoubek's prudence, but rather pushed what had been their common radical doctrine to the sectarian extremes it actually implied, we need not look any further for an explanation. At the same time we are free to speculate that perhaps the new position of the Dresden School, outside the mainstream, contributed to this leftward tendency in a positive way, by providing an objectively sectarian standpoint. And nothing prevents us from supposing that Nicholas may indeed have felt the specific attraction of Waldensian doctrines, with which he was certainly familiar, either from his German experience, from knowledge available in Prague, or from the Waldensian sectarianism that had probably penetrated the Hussite movement in certain parts of Bohemia. In this sense we can also accept some part of Bartoš's hypothesis: the crucial fact *was* Nicholas's German nationality, and he may have felt some bond of common destiny with the German Waldensians. And we can understand why those Czech radicals who were themselves inclined to break out of Jakoubek's restrictions would find a prime source of inspiration in Nicholas of Dresden, particularly after the emergence of Tabor had made any possibility of genuine consensus a thing of the past. Thus, as Sedlák discovered, the Taborites were able to make good use of Nicholas's works when they had to defend similar ideas in opposition to the Prague masters.[188]

When we now try to reconstruct the nature of Nicholas's "Waldensian" development we immediately feel the great disadvantage of having to deal with unpublished works. It is hard to date such sources with accuracy, particularly since the usual evidence for dating is internal, and it is hard to establish interrelationships without ready access to printed, annotated texts. But if we focus our attention on the two unquestionably most important works of this period, the cycle of sermons on *Querite primum regnum dei* and the *Dialogus de purgatorio,* we find that they seem to have been composed at about the same time, September or October of 1415, along with some less important treatises—the second redaction of the *De iuramento* and a *De imaginibus.*[189] It may be significant that we do *not* have any major utraquist work in this period; what seems to have been the last and most brilliant of Nicholas's many defenses of the lay chalice, the *Apologia,* was probably written in July or August of 1415.[190] Thus the break between his pan-Hussite activity and his sectarian development comes just when we would expect it, in the light of our sociological hypothesis: after the formation of the Hussite League, on 5 September 1415. By that time the Hussite left, ideologically active for several years, had created more than enough radical doctrine to supply even the most enthusiastic reformers; the problems now were how to apply this doctrine and how to keep it within due limits— problems that Jakoubek was uniquely disposed to handle. But if the national

[188] Sedlák, *Mikuláš z Drázdăn* (Brno, 1914), p. 45, showing the Taborite Nicholas of Pelhřimov's use of the *De purgatorio*. See also *OC & N,* n. 152.

[189] See the bibliography of Nicholas's works, *OC & N;* the dating is discussed by Sedlák, *op. cit.,* pp. 31 ff., and *ST,* III, i, 91. An edition of the *Querite* by Jana Nechutová will be published shortly.

[190] Sedlák, *Mikuláš,* p. 29.

Hussite movement no longer needed the special talent or outlook of Nicholas, he was still not inclined to relapse into passivity. Others might work out the problems of reform in terms of political calculations, he remained true to his vision of total regeneration. Thus he exclaimed in the *Querite:*

> O Lord God, grant me that I see the renovation of your holy church! Anxious, alas, in heart, with what voice can I speak? What pen suffices to describe, what mode of eloquence to explain, the disease raging among the Christian people and bringing death to their souls? Their hearts cannot be reached. See everywhere, infinite schisms, heresies, and errors! Now alas the secular rulers of Christendom are occupied with their own dissensions, weighed down by greed, blinded by sensual indulgence, hemmed in by other vices—they do not pay attention to the great corruption of the church of Christ, but rather protect, promote, and even foster priests who are simoniac, heretic, and greedy, hateful to God and useless to prince and people. You then, Christ Jesus, see the affliction of your people whom you have redeemed with your blood! [191]

And it was in the *Querite* that he gave vent to his passionate, apocalyptic hatred of the propertied Roman church: "O Lord, will I live to see that blessed hour when the Whore of Revelations will be stripped bare and her flesh consumed by the fire of tribulation?" [192] There is nothing here that deviates from the ideas or feelings long cultivated by radical Hussitism in general, but we can understand that the author of these lines would naturally tend to push his doctrines to their maximum point of anti-Roman intensity, and that he would not moderate his ideas to suit the less ardent temper of those who by late 1415 had become the Hussite majority.

By the same token, however, it would be mistaken to look for some sharp break between Nicholas's "Waldensian" doctrine and the common corpus of radical Hussitism. Even the *Querite,* which Sedlák has characterized as a masterpiece of systematic Waldensianism,[193] contains a great deal of material that had done service before, often more than once, in Nicholas's somewhat less extreme works, such as the *Puncta* of about 1414. Most notably, there is the same canonistic dossier to justify the secularization of ecclesiastical property by the secular powers and the latter's right to discipline evil priests.[194] Indeed Nicholas appeals directly to the secular patrons to throw out simoniacs and install other priests, a proposal strikingly similar to Jakoubek's contemporary recommendations, quoted in the preceding sec-

---

[191] MS IV G 15, fol. 116ʳ; the Latin is quoted by Sedlák, *op. cit.,* p. 34.
[192] MS IV G 15, fol. 124ʳ, quoted by Sedlák, *op. cit.,* p. 35.
[193] *Op. cit.,* pp. 38 f.
[194] See above, n. 43.

tion.[195] All of this is very far from Waldensianism, with its alienation from all established power. Furthermore, it is in the *Querite* that we find Nicholas's one explicit mention of Jakoubek's work; that the *questio* he refers to was in fact the work of John Hus merely emphasizes the Dresdener's invocation of Jakoubek's name.[196] And although there are several points in the *Querite* where Nicholas's position seems in some respects more extreme than Jakoubek's, the discrepancy may be merely a matter of style or circumstance. Nicholas liked to work by accumulating and arranging authorities, with his own summations rather terse and therefore sharp, while Jakoubek indulged himself in a wordy, often repetitive style that no doubt expressed both his need to obfuscate and his basic tendency to explore all the subdivisions, modalities, and shadings of any given topic; in consequence, no possible exception or qualification was left unmentioned. Thus although Nicholas rejected the cult of images and the swearing of oaths *in toto* while Jakoubek made certain specific exceptions in both cases—the possible spiritual benefit of contemplating a crucifix, promises of matrimony and of feudal fidelity—still there is no doubt that the two men held substantially identical views.[197] Similarly, when Nicholas condemned human traditions in the *Querite* he did so in the same terms used by Jakoubek, but he did not bother to make the latter's distinction between traditions that had to be rejected and those that might be tolerated to avoid scandal.[198] Nicholas had no interest in

[195] MS IV G 15, fol. 115^v: ". . . discedite servitores symoniacorum, vosque promotores ad hoc instate . . . ut huiusmodi removeantur et alii canonice et propter deum instituantur." The "canonice" must of course be understood in Nicholas's own terms.

[196] MS IV G 15, fol. 121^r; cf. Sedlák, *op. cit.,* p. 35, n. 1.

[197] *OC & N, ad* n. 90. In the *Posicio de imaginibus* of 31 January 1417 Jakoubek said: "Ex istis tamen omnibus non sequitur quod nullomodo in templis cristianorum possit esse aliqua ymago vel quod nullus umquam fidelium per ymaginem aliquam talem crucifixi possit moveri ad memorandum de Cristi amara passione et morte" (MS IV G 14, fol. 259^v; the context is clearer in III G 28, fol. 200^r). But this concession was only *pro forma,* and Jakoubek's real view appears in his remarkable formulation (fol. 262^r): "Quod si alique auctoritates videntur sonare quod adorentur remota reverencia, etsi aliqua talis esset, non est dicenda laycis. Sicut quelibet creatura aliquomodo, quia habet esse in deo et a deo et habet in se divinum trinitatis vestigium, ut sic est veneranda, sed tamen laycis simplicibus non dicitur quod eas adorent." Here we see a radical application of the principle of guile quoted below, *ad* n. 234.

[198] MS IV G 15, fols. 133^v–134^r: "Hic applica de tradicionibus inutilibus et legem dei onerantibus, paparum, collegiorum monachorum, sacerdotum, et de ritibus superfluis et ornatibus et aliis ceremoniis missarum, et locionibus et rasuris exterioribus, cum quibus // communiter se plus occupant hodie et deo servire credunt [MS: credere] quam cum lege. . . . Cum tamen quilibet cristianus deberet credere firmiter quod si viveret ut sanctus Petrus ceterique sancti in mandatis et lege dei, quod salvaretur sicut

avoiding what Jakoubek himself, in a more radical moment, referred to as "scandal to the Pharisees." In these and other like points, the real difference between the two doctrines was that Jakoubek's could coexist with more conservative beliefs while Nicholas's could not.

Having said this, we must still recognize that a number of positions taken by Nicholas probably did go beyond Jakoubek's self-imposed boundaries. Thus the assertion of the Kozí Hradek extremists, that a simple priest can do anything a bishop can do because he who can consecrate the Eucharist can certainly consecrate lesser things—this assertion also appears in the *Querite,* with a well-developed patristic dossier that had also served Nicholas in his earlier *Customs and Rites of the Primitive and Modern Churches,* where however the explicit lesson was not formulated.[199] In the *Querite* it was: "a duly ordained priest can absolve from any sin," including those legally reserved to the bishops, and ordinary priests can bless and consecrate in all cases, including the reserved ones. He did not go on to say that the episcopal office was useless, but the conclusion was not hard to draw, and in any case what he did say went beyond Jakoubek's views.[200] Similarly, I do not know

isti, dimissis istis superfluis tradicionibus que vel legi dei contrariantur, vel adminus legem dei impediunt, vel onerant, quia interim quod quis se occupat illis tradicionibus, vel impeditur in lege dei vel semiplene se occupat in ea, et sic non potest esse toto corde, tota anima, tota mente, totis viribus, occupatus in lege dei, propter istas superfluas tradiciones hominum."

[199] See the edition of the *Consuetudo et ritus* in *OC & N,* Part I, §§ 21–28, and the *Querite,* MS IV G 15, fols. 127ʳ sqq. A key text was Jerome's paragraph beginning "Olim idem presbiter, qui et episcopus," *Decretum,* XCV. Dist., c. 5. Then in c. 6 there was Jerome's "Si presbiter Cristum consecrat, cum in altario dei sacramenta benedicit, benedicere populum non debet, qui Cristum consecrare non metuit?" It appears in the *Consuetudo,* Part III, § 24, and in the *Querite,* fol. 127ʳ. The *Consuetudo* has almost no "editorial" opinion, but the *Querite* does: "Quo . . . ausu audent moderni episcopi inhibere sacerdotibus benedicere populum?" (fol. 127ᵛ). "Sacerdos rite ordinatus a quocumque peccato absolvere potest" (fols. 127ᵛ–128ʳ). "Quos autem iam dicunt casus episcopales, pocius seduccionales et predales; sicut annus eorum iubileus pocius annus spolii et depredacionis et seduccionis, quia tunc maxime spoliant et seducunt homines" (fol. 128ʳ).

[200] The standard medieval theory was that the distinction between bishops and priests went back to Christ's own institution of twelve apostles and seventy-two disciples, respectively; for a rundown of the tradition see Yves Congar, "Aspects ecclésiologiques de la querelle entre mendiants et séculiers . . . ," *Archives d'histoire doctrinale et littéraire du Moyen Age,* XXVIII (1961), 60 ff. Jakoubek accepted this idea without apparent question—for example, in his sermon for 6 March 1416: "Lord Christ commanded [monitory preaching] to the apostles and lesser disciples, whose successors are the bishops and priests" (*Betlemská kázání z roku 1416,* p. 29). In the *Consuetudo et ritus,* Part I, §§ 21–24, Nicholas includes this formula but also quotes other texts that call it into question or reduce its significance—most notably Jerome (XCV. Dist., c. 5), "Once priest and bishop were one" (n. 199 above). Given the Hussites' drastic

that Jakoubek ever pronounced the principle, asserted by the Waldensians and later by the Taborites, and more than once by Nicholas, that the Church Fathers were to be believed only insofar as they agreed with the Bible, or more particularly the New Testament.[201] In this matter a great deal depended on formulas but even more on how they were applied, and Jakoubek did not hesitate to resort to patristic authority for what he could not find in the gospels but nevertheless needed—most notably a defense of killing.[202] He held to the classic principle that the "Four Doctors"—Ambrose, Jerome, Augustine, Gregory—could be given full trust when they all agreed on a particular point.[203]

The question of killing was indeed an important one from the standpoint of Hussite sociology, for those who held to the perfectionism of the Sermon on the Mount as the norm for all could hardly develop their religious faith into the ideology of a nominally Christian society. Jakoubek had to do this but neither the Waldensians nor Nicholas of Dresden did—they were free to be pure; hence Nicholas could insist that the commandments of the Sermon on the Mount were indeed commandments, not "counsels" as the Roman tradition had it. Following Pseudo-Chrysostom he defined six: not to anger,

---

reduction of episcopal powers, as in the compact of the Hussite League, the basic question was that of ordination through apostolic succession; here Jakoubek and the other Praguers held to the Catholic principle. Nicholas did not pronounce on the point.

[201] After quoting a homily of Chrysostom in the *Querite,* Nicholas exclaims (fol. 137ʳ-137ᵛ): "Quam pulchre concordant hec dicta doctorum cum ewangelio, et ergo amplectanda." Nor did he shrink from rejecting patristic authority when the agreement with the gospel was not evident: e.g., he rejected Augustine's sanctioning of oaths (fol. 138ᵛ). See also below, n. 205.

[202] See below, chap. ix, *ad* n. 18.

[203] In his anti-utraquist treatise of 1417, Jean Gerson began by defining the rules for interpretation and application of Holy Writ; his aim was to show the necessity not only of authoritative interpretation by the Fathers but also of equally authoritative interpretation by the living doctors of great universities (Hardt, III, 765–772). Responding to this treatise, Jakoubek had to develop his own rules for interpretation, which he limited very severely. But he did give as his fourth (and last) rule: "Quatuor sancti doctores ecclesie universalis, scilicet Ieronimus, Ambrosius, Augustinus, et Gregorius, et alii, qui sunt prediti ingenio, exercitati studio, humiles iudicio, immunes ab affectato vicio, proprius et autencius exponunt et interpretantur sacram scripturam, precipue ubi in idem consenciunt, quam mille moderni expositores et tractatores ambicione seculi et veneno ecclesie [*!*] ac symoniaca heresi infecti. Ipsi enim non solum modernis expositoribus sed et romanis pontificibus in sacrarum scripturarum exposicionibus preponuntur." (MS D 51, fol. 168ᵛ.) This was a radical position, in context, but it could also become a conservative one, and when it was thus used the Taborites rejected it, with admirable crispness: "Si doctores quatuor in aliqua materia fidei unanimiter loquuntur erronee, tunc ipsi unanimiter errant, et hoc est valde possibile" (Höfler, II, 578).

not to lust, not to put away one's wife except on account of fornication, not to swear at all, not to resist evil, and to pray for and do good to one's enemies.[204] And in another passage he explicitly denied the legitimacy of any killing, and observed that "any writing of the doctors that seems to legitimize killing on the basis of the common evangelical law is either contrary to Scripture or points back to the righteousness of 'them of old time.'"[205] Jakoubek could not afford this purism, although he probably would have liked to; instead he necessarily followed Wyclif's doctrine, that the secular powers have the duty of defending the evangelical law by force, against criminals and external enemies.[206]

Conceivably none of these differences between the two radicals necessarily created a schism between them, but their cumulative effect must have led in that direction. And when they were joined by a genuinely theological disagreement a showdown could not be avoided. Already in the *Querite* Nicholas implicitly justified the rejection of Purgatory, a point that he went on to develop explicitly and at length in his *Dialogus de purgatorio*.[207] Why

---

[204] *Querite*, MS IV G 15, fol. 135ᵛ (cf. Matt. 5:19 ff.). Nicholas introduces the passage thus: "Ecce quomodo hic iste doctor manens circa textum qui dicit 'mandatis istis' non dicit 'consiliis,' sicut alii multi dicunt 'consilia.' Ymmo sunt sex Cristi mandata. . . ."

[205] *Ibid.*, fol. 137ᵛ, after extensive use of Pseudo-Chrysostom: "Aliqua igitur scriptura doctorum per quam videtur fore licitum occidere de communi lege ewangelica, vel est priori contraria vel ad iusticiam antiquorum reducens." For the last phrase see Matt. 5:20, 21, 27, 33. The principle is applied to reject the authority of Nicholas of Lyra, in a set of glosses on Lyra's postil on the New Testament; the glosses are either by Nicholas or by someone whose ideas were identical to his. The passage reads: "O bone Lira! Quomodo tu liras quod dicis, quod licitum est homini, qui tenet locum iusticie, publice interficere hominem, cum non advertisti sentenciam Christi, qui dicit: 'Quicunque solverit unum de mandatis istis minimis' etc." (in A. Neumann, "Glossy v Drändorfově postile," *Hlídka*, XLI (1924), 464).

[206] See *OC & N*, *ad* n. 91, and see below, chap. ix, *ad* n. 18. In his Czech sermon for 15 March 1416 Jakoubek repeated the standard medieval doctrine that the secular lords have a right to their incomes because they defend their people against injustice and defend the faith. "And it is their particular duty to defend the Law of God." (*Betlemská kázání z roku 1416*, p. 54.) It was only later on, after the question of whether a *Hussite* might kill had been raised with great urgency, that Jakoubek took a more reluctant line, but even then his conclusions were usually the same.

[207] In the light of the *De purgatorio* the following passage of the *Querite* takes on a heretical significance that its actual words do not quite have: (MS IV G 15, fol. 106ʳ): "debet quilibet bene facere dum vivit ante mortem suam, et non se committere pueris suis, uxori, amicis, sive avaris, luxuriosis, immundis, et symoniacis sacerdotibus . . . , quia per illum modum multi se ipsos negligunt et dampnant animas suas in eternum." He also quotes a passage from Augustine that seems to deny Purgatory: ". . . qui in hac vita non fecit [penitenciam] habebit quidem penitenciam in futuro seculo de malis suis, sed indulgenciam in conspectu dei non inveniet . . ." (*ibid.*). That it was Nicholas who first publicly raised the question of Purgatory seems probable from the

he did so is unclear; we can only guess whether the emergence of actual Waldensian heresy on the Hussite left had perhaps forced an open discussion, or whether the application of standard Hussite views about the unwholesomeness of excessive works for the dead had perhaps led to questions about the doctrine that justified such works in principle. In any case, it may be supposed that Nicholas knew his principled rejection of Purgatory would lead to open schism among the radicals, and that he was prepared to accept this result, even though he must have foreseen that the outcome would not be favorable to himself. As we shall see, his work was not merely a technical theological discussion of its nominal subject, but rather an extraordinarily profound examination of the very meaning of the Christian religion in both its salvationary and sociological functions. It could only have proceeded from a spirit so anxious and aroused that it could dismiss the ordinary considerations of prudence as irrelevant.

Its main body cast in the form of a dialogue between *V* and *M*—probably *Veritas* and *Mendacium* [208]—the work opens with a preliminary discussion of the practical question, are prayers for the dead of any use? The answer is no, because the house of Christ has only three stories, Hell, Earth, and Heaven, and those who have died are either in Hell, where prayers will not help them, or in Heaven, where they have no need of prayers; the authority here is Nicholas's favorite, the Pseudo-Chrysostom's *Opus imperfectum in Matthaeum*.[209] Some, to be sure, hold that there are four stories, with Purgatory between Earth and Heaven, but they are wrong, not least because the religious consequences of such a belief run counter to the teaching of the gospels:

> Neither the prophets, nor Christ with his apostles, nor the saints who immediately followed them, taught explicitly that we should pray for the dead, but rather carefully taught the people to live without sin and to be holy. Wherefore the Savior in his Sermon on the Mount taught his disciples and others of the crowd . . . about the strait gate and the broad way, saying (Matt. 7 [13–14]): "Enter ye in at the strait gate: for wide is the gate, and broad is the way, that leadeth to destruction, and many there be which go in thereat. How strait is the gate, and narrow the way, which leadeth unto life, and few there be that find it." Whence the saints had great confidence of being immediately saved, because they led a holy life in the present world; and so, undoubtedly, if men were to live well in the manner of the saints, they would reach the Fatherland [*patriam:* Heaven] immediately after death.

---

sequence of the sources: see *LČJ,* No. 63, and Bartoš, "Vznik a počátky táborství," pp. 139 ff.

[208] *OC & N,* n. 98a. I use the text in MS III G 8, fols. 36ʳ–66ʳ.

[209] In Migne, *PG,* LVI, 817.

For who does not know that the most secure way to life is to live as Christ and his apostles taught? [210]

This is certainly the heart and soul of Nicholas's whole approach to religious life, and no one can read any considerable part of Jakoubek's work without sensing that he too would have approved of these words: in doing so, however, he would be agreeing not only with Nicholas but with John Hus, whose sermon on *Dixit Martha ad Iesum,* preached on 3 November 1411,[211] contained everything in the quoted paragraph except the scriptural quotation. But what appears as one paragraph in Nicholas's work is actually a mosaic of four separate passages from different parts of Hus's sermon. Elsewhere in the *De purgatorio* the pattern of borrowing is even more intricate, so much so that one must infer that Nicholas went to a great deal of trouble *in order to* use Hus's words.[212] Since, moreover, Hus had not said anything that Nicholas could not easily have said for himself, the further inference is unavoidable: Nicholas used Hus in order to present his own rejection of works for the dead and of Purgatory as essentially the teaching of the master, whose recent martyrdom had given him saintlike status among all Hussites, from left to right. It is true that Hus's *Dixit Martha* explicitly accepted the doctrine of Purgatory and the utility of works for the dead presumed to be there, but in his typical fashion he combined this basic orthodoxy [213] with a savage criticism of the kind of religiosity that depended on such works, to say nothing of the priests who grew rich from charging for memorial masses. Perhaps for this reason Nicholas did not label his borrowed passages; it was left to Jan Sedlák to discover an indebtedness that Hussite contemporaries must have recognized at once.[214]

Nicholas's *modus operandi* becomes even more curious as the dialogue progresses. *V* will not accept the doctrine of Purgatory without scriptural proofs, and in rather contrived fashion his position is compared with the University of Prague's demand, in 1412, for scriptural proofs before it would agree to condemn the Forty-five Articles of John Wyclif; the episode is described in the very words used by John Hus, three years earlier.[215] Later, toward the end of the dialogue, the Romanist *M* chooses a procurator—actually an inquisitor—to carry on his cause, and *V* in turn chooses his own

[210] MS III G 8, fol. 36ʳ.

[211] *OC & N,* n. 96.

[212] *OC & N,* n. 97, n. 81, and *ad* n. 106.

[213] See on this point P. De Vooght, "La doctrine et les sources du sermon Dixit Martha ad Jesum," *Hussiana* (Louvain, 1960), pp. 365–378.

[214] *Mikuláš z Drázdăn,* pp. 46–48, but with a false theory that it was Hus who copied from Nicholas (see *OC & N, passim*).

[215] MS III G 8, fol. 47ᵛ; see Novotný, II, 125, n. 3.

procurator—Master John Hus.[216] A point of the other side is refuted by a duly acknowledged passage from Hus's attack on John XXIII's indulgences, and *M*'s procurator, at a loss for arguments, replies by having Hus cited to the Council of Constance.[217] A brief account follows of what happened to Hus there, with his martyrdom thus literarily transformed into a consequence of his defense of *V*. Nor is this all. *V* has chosen Hus as procurator because, he says, he himself is needed back home to give communion in both kinds and to administer the other sacraments; then, reflecting on Hus's death, he says that he is not surprised that the Council has done this to a saint of God, when it did not fear to condemn what it itself recognized as Christ's own institution, the lay chalice. *V* then prophesies that the people will do God's will not only in the matter of utraquism, but "in every truth inspired by the spirit of God." [218] Thus only two or three months after Hus's death, the martyr replaced the actual man, the symbol of evangelical anti-Romanism suppressed the living teacher, and the man who had always tried to avoid doctrinal extremities that would have separated him from the Roman church was transmuted into the patron saint of endless sectarian innovations. We have already seen that the same sort of thing was happening in South Bohemia, where the extremists went considerably beyond Hus's teachings but at the same time drew the line between good and bad priests according to the attitude taken to Master John Hus.

All of this is not to say that Nicholas was some species of liar, for however true Hus remained to orthodox doctrine, he supplied his German follower with a great deal of material that led in the other direction. Thus, for example, both these passages spoken by *V* are put together from Hus:

> I wonder why it is that men of modern times are so concerned with suffrages for the dead, when in the whole of canonical scripture the Spirit of the Lord has not expressly taught these things. . . .
>
> I cannot see any other cause why men of modern times are so concerned with suffrages for the dead, than men's evil life and, as a result, their lack of confidence. For this is why men have little confidence that they will enter the Fatherland immediately after death—because they live evilly in their present life. And the cause of this is seduction by the priests, which stems from avarice: the priests do not imitate the prophets, Christ, and the apostles, and carefully teach the people to live well, but they teach them to make abundant offerings, and set before them the hope of blessedness and speedy liberation from Purgatory.[219]

[216] MS III G 8, fol. 64ʳ sq.
[217] *Ibid.*
[218] *Ibid.*, fol. 65ᵛ.
[219] *Ibid.*, fol. 38ʳ, 38ᵛ; *OC & N*, nn. 104, 105.

Sometimes, to be sure, Nicholas must use cunning to omit unacceptable acknowledgements of Purgatory and the like, or to transpose arguments that Hus used in an unsuitable order,[220] but in the last analysis Nicholas remains true to what was obviously Hus's main point. While conceding the existence of Purgatory, Hus had no interest in developing its cultic implications; quite the reverse: he wanted to reduce the prayers and works predicated on Purgatory's existence to a minimum in order to foster a religious life based on the imitation of Christ. His attacks on the institution of thirty masses for the dead were as savage as any heretic could desire; he insisted that Christ's sacrifice was enough to redeem all, while in any case no soul could receive more help after death than it had earned in life.[221] In this sense Hus's belief in Purgatory can be regarded as a piece of excess baggage, whose only function in his religious system was to create embarrassment. If then Nicholas, by suppressing that belief, betrays Hus, it is in order to reveal Hus's truth.

But there is more to the *De purgatorio* than this. Here, more eloquently and profoundly than in any other of his works, Nicholas develops the idea of an evangelical religious life as one not only of virtue but of tribulation, in imitation of Christ's goodness but also of his suffering. The true Christian is tried by fire here on earth, "the elect are punished in this world that they may not be punished in the next," and—relying on the Pseudo-Chrysostom— Nicholas shows that the church is never to be free of tribulation, or the just of the baptism of fire.[222] The rationalizations of the orthodox in favor of Purgatory as a kind of bookkeeping device, to make sure that every sin is fully atoned for, are dismissed partly by these arguments, partly by rationalizations on the other side, and partly by a faith that embraces the mystery of divine judgement: grace can supply man's wants, God's election is beyond human comprehension.[223] The Romanists want "to assimilate God and his works to human works and to creatures," but grace is a free gift, not determined by human calculations of justice.[224] And there is always the central point: Christ's teaching about the two paths and the harsh corollary, that "more will perish than will be saved." [225] The very purpose of Purgatory was to provide for those who did *not* live up to Christian teachings, those

---

[220] See for example, *OC & N, ad* n. 106.

[221] *OC & N,* nn. 107, 108.

[222] MS III G 8, fols. 48ᵛ–51ᵛ.

[223] *Ibid.,* fol. 53ʳ.

[224] *Ibid.,* fols. 52ʳ sqq., fol. 58ᵛ ("Contra illos enim volentes deum in factis suis assimilare operibus humanis et creaturis. . . .").

[225] *OC & N,* n. 121.

who were neither very good nor very bad;[226] but this accommodation, so useful to a universal ecclesiastical institution based on either orthodox or schismatic Catholicism, is rejected by Nicholas in favor of his sectarian concept of the true church as the small band of those who follow the evangelical commandments of perfection in their full rigor.

Such a band would naturally be as small in Hussite Bohemia as in any other sector of Christendom. Virtuous talk is very cheap in anti-Roman polemics, and ideas similar to the ones just summarized can be found in the works of Hus, Jakoubek, and others; but there can be no mistake about what Nicholas was doing in the *De purgatorio,* addressed as it clearly was to other Hussites, indeed other radicals, rather than to the Romanists or the neutrals. He was saying that true fidelity to Hus's cause and to the ideal of the Primitive Church demanded not the establishment of a national church but rather a permanent posture of rejection of the world. As much as he favored such external reforms as secularization of church property, he did not fail to insist on the more important point: "It does not do much for salvation to give up those external things that we possess unless we give up and deny our very selves."[227] Whether he had a clear idea of the kind of religious community that could realize his teachings may be doubted, for the purity he sought could never be institutionalized.[228] The concrete issue was a more modest one: there should be no concessions in either theory or practice to the religious requirements of the lukewarm, of those whose Hussitism was merely a matter of external adherence to the chalice and the memory of Hus. And if he pronounced Waldensianist ideas beyond the original core of Hussite radicalism, he must have been motivated by the logic of his struggle —only continual development of the sectarian implications of the cult of the Primitive Church could serve to counter the powerful enterprise of accommodation to which Jakoubek had committed himself. We shall probably

---

[226] *OC & N,* nn. 122, 123 (Augustine had distinguished a middle class of "non valde mali" (*Sentences,* IV, xlv, 2, and *Decretum,* XIII. q. ii, c. 23); Hus picked this up as "non valde boni, nec valde mali, sed medii"; cf. also Innocent III's decretal, in *Decretales,* III, xli, 6).

[227] *Querite,* MS IV G 15, fol. 124ʳ: "parum est ad salutem relinquere exteriora illa que possidemus, nisi relinquamus et abnegemus nosmetipsos."

[228] Extremely interesting in this context is the gloss (very possibly by Nicholas) on Lyra (see n. 205 above). Lyra wrote: "Propria igitur beatitudo dicitur paupertas spiritus. Racione enim exteriorum bonorum, que sunt divicie et honores, unde se habet homo modo humano et communi, quando non querit talia ultra gradum sui meriti, sed secundum condecenciam sui status. . . ." The gloss on this classically medieval bit of distortion reads: "Nescio, quid denotat cum statu, non placet multum." (Neumann, "Glossy v Drändorfově postile," p. 460.)

never know the source of Nicholas's Waldensianist doctrines, nor can we do more than guess how much if any influence they had on the extreme radicals of 1415–1417 or the Taborites of 1419. However, if we assume that in a rather close-knit religious movement like that of the Hussites doctrinal correspondences could not have been accidental, we can appreciate the radical crisis of 1415–1417 as Jakoubek probably saw it—a *single* crisis, the practical sectarianism of the extremists in the provinces resonating with the ideological leadership provided in Prague by Nicholas of Dresden, and the two components together forming a deadly challenge to the national-political program to which the Hussite leadership had been committed since at least 1408.

No wonder, then, that Jakoubek very quickly replied to the *De purgatorio,* in a highly suitable context, the traditional commemorative sermon of the anniversary of the death of Charles IV, 29 November 1415.[229] Nothing is more instructive than to read this sermon immediately after reading Nicholas's work. For one thing, Jakoubek begins by putting the case against Purgatory, with many of the same authorities and arguments used by Nicholas. He carefully reproduces the argument that there are only two paths, and that Purgatory after death would seem superfluous for those who have followed the strait path of suffering on earth,[230] and he cites many authorities for this position, including the text of Matthew 7:13–14 (quoted above) and passages from Cyprian, Chrysostom, and Jerome. Then however he proceeds to the opposite side, with II Maccabees 12:42–44 (which both Hus and Nicholas had deprecated as of the Apocrypha[231]), Matthew 5:26 ("Thou shalt by no means come out thence, till thou has paid the uttermost farthing"), and a few texts from Augustine and Gregory. These authorities are fewer than those against Purgatory, they are on the whole not as old, and they are much less powerful; if Jakoubek still refused to agree with Nicholas it was undoubtedly because of the usual rational argument that some of those slated for salvation—the *salvandi*—might not be fully purged before their death. Nicholas, of course, had dealt with this argument—the *salvandi* would be purged by suffering on earth or by God's grace; the real point, obviously, was that Jakoubek chose to follow the Romanists in defining the body of the *salvandi* broadly enough to accommodate the spiritual mediocrities. At the same time he said that even though Purgatory existed, the faithful should behave as if it did not, placing no emphasis on works for the dead and, themselves, trying to lead the virtuous lives that would make it unnecessary

[229] *LČJ*, No. 63; see *OC & N*, n. 126. I use the text in MS 4524, fols. 39ʳ–45ʳ.
[230] *OC & N*, n. 127.
[231] *OC & N, ad* nn. 104, 105.

for them to pass through Purgatory.[232] Thus he, too, believed in the religion of the strait way, but he refused to make it the basis of a religious sociology— his sociological framework was the existing order of society, not a revived Primitive Church in the form of a necessarily heretical sect. If we may believe Peter Chelčický, Jakoubek was even prepared to admit, under no doubt pointed questioning, that a Christian was not bound by faith to believe in Purgatory as in other articles of faith, and on another occasion he defined Purgatory not as palpable torment but as the soul's shame at recognition of its stains.[233] In this matter he was obviously less than frank. Here we may recall his dictum about the need to keep certain truths under cover when times were not opportune, and we may add the remarkable revelation made much later by his leading Prague disciple, Master John Rokycana: when Jakoubek was on his death bed he said to those attending him, "You should have two sets of books, one set for your own contemplation—and do not take these to the people—and another set for the information of the people." [234] We may even attach some weight to the argument of Master John Příbram, writing in late 1420 against Tabor's rejection of the Roman liturgy and vestments, a rejection justified in part by the authority of Jakoubek's *De ceremoniis* of about 1415. Příbram argued that this work was not a treatise, as the Taborites alleged, but only a collection of authorities for and against, and that in any case the Taborites had gotten it by fraud, through the agency of one of the brethren.[235] The work as we know it was by no means the neutral repertory that Příbram claimed it to be, but perhaps Jakoubek had indeed meant to keep it secret, as a book not to be taken to the people because it contained ideas unsuitable for the realities of the time. This interpretation would fit in with both Příbram's testimony and with everything that has been said about Jakoubek's line of action, in this and the preceding sections.

The controversy that we have been tracing through the polemical literature must have been pursued on many fronts now hopelessly lost from view, and with important effects that we can reconstruct only hypothetically. The immediate result was that Nicholas could no longer function in Prague; according to John Želivský in 1419 the university masters forced him out— they gave him "poison"—and we can suppose that he left in 1416, preached his doctrines in Meissen, and quickly found martyrdom there. None of this could have been pleasant for Jakoubek but it was certainly what he wanted;

---

[232] *OC & N,* nn. 128, 129.
[233] See Bartoš, "Vznik a počátky táborství," p. 140.
[234] *OC & N,* n. 132.
[235] Höfler, II, 532, 544 f. Cf. Sedlák's judgement, *ST,* II, 136 f.

henceforth, until the emergence of Tabor, he was the only productive theoretician on the Hussite left. As we shall see in the next chapter, he made good use of this circumstance to provide genuine radical leadership within the framework of the national establishment, thereby achieving successes that in a sense justified the purge he had carried through. On the other hand, the schism produced by Nicholas's agitation could not be healed, it could only be partially bridged, and in addition to the Dresden School itself, which remained in existence for several years, there were Czech radicals—like John Želivský, John Čapek, and John Jičín—who remained loyal to doctrines similar to those of Nicholas and perhaps derived from him. Furthermore, the period 1415–1416 saw the emergence of extremism in the provinces, again with doctrines much like Nicholas's. All of these developments were relatively inevitable, beyond Jakoubek's capacity to control. But by the same token we may guess that if the final open schism on the left did not come until 1419, rather than immediately in 1416–1417, much of the credit belongs to Jakoubek's harsh and resolute line, coupled with the new opportunities that he more than any other single master helped to make possible in the course of 1417. It is to this new chapter of Hussite history that we now turn.

V

NATIONAL CONSOLIDATION
OF THE REFORM, 1417-1418

REACTION AND RESISTANCE IN PRAGUE

THE POLITICAL LEADERS of the Hussite movement had scored many successes in the years following the Kutná Hora Decree of 1409, but by the second half of 1416 they could hardly have felt inclined to pause and congratulate themselves. The apparently endless development of Hussite doctrine, exclusively the work of the radicals, had long since passed beyond the limits of the politicians' national Wyclifism, and the controversies on the left actually threatened to tear apart any national establishment that the politicians might create. Even without this threat there was reason for worry. The Hussite League still did not include all or even most of the Bohemian feudality; real power in many of the towns lay with anti-Hussite burghers and magistrates, very often Germans; King Wenceslas was by no means committed to the reform; and the Hussites' possession of parish churches in Prague and several other places was still only *de facto*—having been won by direct action, it lacked the stability of legitimate title. None of these disadvantages was necessarily fatal, but they imposed a critical handicap on the political leadership in its confrontation of the greatest threat of all—the vigorous, implacable hostility of the Council of Constance. Never even considering the possibility of a settlement less than total restoration of the *status quo ante,* the Council thus denied the Hussite leadership the essential condition for the latter's concept of reformation— recognition of a reformed Bohemian church as a legitimate member of the Roman communion. The extreme radicals were ready to do without such recognition, the others were not; as long as it was withheld even the most fundamental reformation in Bohemia would seem to be built on the sands of self-defined schism.

It is easy to lose sight of this consideration in retrospect, and it is correspondingly important to insist upon it: although the implementation of reform necessarily took place within a particular socio-political framework, the Hussite idea was conceived in Latin, not Czech, and it was an idea of what the European church should be. In the age of the Schism and the Councils this program was much less fantastic than it may seem today; in any case, the Hussite masters held to it and although they were capable of extremely vigorous action in behalf of the reformed Bohemian Church, they always suffered from the self-imposed disability of Socrates in Athens and Hus in Constance—convinced of their right, they still recognized the legitimacy of the institution that condemned them. Not that they were willing to abide by an unfavorable verdict—here they wisely refused to follow Hus— but rather that in the mode, extent, and timing of their reformational activity, they always had reference to the preferability of accommodation over open mutiny. Since, however, the Council was not interested in an accommodation, the Hussites had to secure their own defense, even while trying to keep their case open, an effort that in turn required them to make their position in Bohemia as solid as possible. Here everything depended on the secular powers—specifically on the alliance with the Hussite nobility and on at least the neutralization of the King by his pro-Hussite courtiers. If either or both of these conditions threatened to change, the university masters could only have one policy, namely to forestall the threat. Thus although the reform had flourished beyond what might reasonably have been predicted, its future could never be regarded as safe. If the Council of Constance could bring effective pressure to bear on either the Hussite nobility or the King, the cause of Hussitism would be in danger.

We have already seen how sharply the Council reacted to the Hussite nobility's protest of 2 September 1415, against the burning of John Hus; each of the 452 protesters was personally cited to the Council's tribunal. The citations were of course only a first step in a legal process that would ultimately have to rely on secular power in Bohemia and Moravia; in itself the process could accomplish nothing, and in fact the Hussite feudality went right ahead with its work of secularization and other anti-Roman action.[1]

---

[1] The citations issued in March 1416 were ignored, and on 4 September 1416 the Council decided to cite the protesters again, rather than push the process forward; at the same time the affair was turned over to the direction of Patriarch John of Constantinople (see V. Novotný, "Monitorium Patriarcha Konstantinopolského Jana na uchvatitele církevního majetku v Čechách," *VČA*, XXIV (1915), pp. 3 f.; cf. *HR*, I, 33). John seems to have let the matter lapse, perhaps at the request of the Emperor Sigismund, made later in 1416 (*Documenta*, p. 653; cf. Bartoš, *Do čtyř art.*, p. 11, n. 35).

Somewhat later the Council began a similar process against some of King Wenceslas's courtiers and some of the Prague magistrates, presumably because of their support of the violence and depredations following the interdict of early November 1415; again the judicial proceedings had no apparent effect in Bohemia.[2] However, when Archbishop Conrad lifted the interdict, probably in the last part of 1415, only to reimpose it in early 1416, he got into serious trouble with the Council; not only was he personally cited, at about the same time as the Hussite nobility, but as an ecclesiastic he was forced to heed the citation, at least by using procurators and undertaking the heavy expenses of self-defense. Anxious only to avoid trouble, he had not shown any energy in opposing Hussitism—it was this that the Council objected to—but now, although he still conducted himself as essentially a royal servant, he had a personal interest in suppressing the heresy in his diocese.[3]

By about the middle of 1416, Conrad was joined in his anxiety by the King himself. Wenceslas was neither for nor against the reform, but he had to do something: there was talk at the Council about citing him and his queen, and even more ominous talk of an invasion of the realm.[4] Perhaps in the spring of 1416, perhaps in the fall, the Council actually requested Emperor Sigismund to undertake such action, or any other steps that would be suitable; although Sigismund refused, claiming that people would think he only wanted to get his hands on his brother's realm, the threat was there. In fact, Wenceslas himself had sent a mission to Sigismund, asking for help in his difficulties and in particular requesting a meeting of the two; since the Council depended to a considerable degree on the Emperor's support, Wenceslas no doubt thought that the latter could arrange matters satisfactorily.[5]

---

[2] The process mentioned may have begun when the one against the protesting noblemen was dropped; a review of the whole case dated 18 March 1418, has been published by V. Novotný, *op. cit.*, with a historical introduction. The eight courtiers and eleven burghers named in the citation were charged with spoliation of the clergy's property and incomes, under cover of Wyclif's (and of course Hus's) familiar principle, "quod domini temporales possunt ad arbitrium suum auferre bona temporalia clericis delinquentibus" (pp. 8 f.).

[3] The agitation at the Council of Constance and threat of a citation against Conrad are reported in a letter of *ca.* April 1416 (*Documenta*, pp. 622 f.); apparently the threat was made good. In a letter to the king on 19 July 1416 Conrad mentioned a mission that had been sent to the Council, obviously on account of his citation, and in a document of late 1416 we read that "propter priorem resumtionem divinorum et violationem interdicti . . . D. Archiepiscopus fuit et est personaliter ad Constantiam citatus; super qua citatione die hodierna disputatur"; the whole thing had so far cost Conrad 400 sixties of Prague groschen (*Documenta*, p. 646). Cf. Tomek, III, 601 f.

[4] For the Council's efforts to organize intervention see Bartoš, *Do čtyř art.*, p. 11, n. 36, and *Documenta*, p. 651.

[5] All of this information comes from the exchange between the envoys of the Council and the Emperor Sigismund, *Documenta*, pp. 647–654. Palacký's dating—in Novem-

At the least, he may have hoped that the mere act of requesting intervention would ease the situation. But it was his indecision that had brought down the Council's anger—as its envoys complained to Sigismund, King Wenceslas behaved as though the suppression of Hussite excesses was not his affair, he let everything go its own way, and his toleration of the evils laid him open to the suspicion of actually favoring them.[6] Shown this indictment,[7] and perhaps chastened by Sigismund's resolute anti-Hussitism, the King must have realized that some action was required. And he could only have been confirmed in this idea when Bishop John Železný of Litomyšl, the Council's special legate for anti-Hussite action in Bohemia, finally published the Council's decree against utraquism, on 29 October 1416. Having waited to do so for over a year—the decree had been issued on 15 June 1415—Železný must have chosen his time with some deliberation, and we may therefore suppose that his declared intention of taking judicial action against every utraquist in the realm really constituted a threat to the Hussite establishment.[8]

If indeed we consider Železný's measures as the Bohemian focal point of the international anti-Hussite constellation that the Council was trying to organize, we can understand why King Wenceslas, hitherto tolerant of utraquism, should now have resolved to limit and if possible suppress the innovation. Master Jakoubek of Stříbro, to be sure, rushed to the king's aid, but all he could offer was one of his gems of doctrinal rectitude: Utraquism was not heresy but truth; for the king to foster and defend utraquist priests was therefore not to favor heretics; if you want to find heretics look at the evil-living simoniac prelates—these are the ones the king should act against.[9] Wenceslas understandably ignored such advice; instead, sometime at the end of 1416, he forced the University of Prague, the chief organ of Hussite ecclesiastical leadership, to conform to his new policy of Catholic restoration. The masters resisted, at least to the point of trying to bargain, but in the end Master John Kardinál, rector of the university, had to agree with Archbishop Conrad on a virtual restoration of the *status quo ante*.[10] Church

---

ber–December 1416—seems reasonable; Bartoš's dating in late May 1416 (*Do čtyř art.*, p. 11, n. 35) is unlikely—see Kejř, *Husitský právník*, p. 103, n. 44.

[6] *Documenta*, p. 651.

[7] *Ibid.*, p. 652.

[8] Železný's decree is published by J. Loserth, "Beiträge zur Geschichte der Husitischen Bewegung," *AÖG*, LXXXII (1895), 378–381; it includes the Council's decree against utraquism, Železný's summons to obey it, and a precise delineation of the procedure to be followed against the contumacious. See also above, chap. iv, *ad* n. 60.

[9] The brief "Defense of King Wenceslas" (*LČJ*, No. 57) is published in abridged form by J. Sedlák, "Počátkové kalicha," *ČKD*, LV (1914), 117–119.

[10] *Documenta*, pp. 645–647; the agreement was reached *post diversos tractatus*. For

property was to be restored; the expelled Catholic priests were to be reinstated; the archiepiscopal authority was to be fully recognized; Doctor John Jesenic, because of whom the interdict had originally been placed on Prague, was to leave the city. Only utraquism was not surrendered—Conrad urged that it be stopped, in obedience to the Council's decree, but Kardinál wanted it to be allowed in certain Prague churches, pending the decision of a future pope. The last phrase, like its counterpart in both previous and subsequent Hussite declarations, was of course merely a device to keep the matter open.[11] Royal decrees of 2 December 1416 promulgated this settlement, including the limited toleration of utraquism, and commanded that neither side hereticate the other.[12]

If fully implemented these decrees would have marked the beginning of the end for Hussitism, for even though the compromise on utraquism fell far short of what John Železný or the Council would have wished, the general Catholic restoration would certainly have made possible a future complete suppression of the lay chalice. But the Hussites had submitted only *pro forma*. Thus when the Prague Cathedral Chapter was informed that the matters at issue had been corrected, and was accordingly requested to resume services, the canons refused; for, as they pointed out, church property was still in the hands of those who had taken it (and some royal courtiers were named); certain clerics were still suffering injury; the churches had still not been restored to their rightful rectors; John Jesenic was frequently glimpsed in the city. Indeed there were other people under even heavier excommunication than Jesenic, as well as "innumerable" people who had been defying the interdict and who would certainly cause trouble if services were resumed.[13] Archbishop Conrad, who had already felt the consequences of a premature lifting of the interdict, also refused to follow the king's wish.[14]

One defect of the king's policy was that it sought to bring about great changes with inadequate means. A real restoration would have required the steady, ruthless application of force, in the first place against the people of Prague. The Hussite people, still flocking to Bethlehem Chapel and other

---

the background of this and related episodes see Tomek, III, 600 ff.; also the recent discussion by J. Kejř, "Deklarace pražské university z 10. března 1417 o přijímání pod obojí a její historické pozadí," *SbH*, VIII (1961) 133–154. Cf. *HR*, I, 35 f.

[11] Thus in September 1415 the Hussite barons who defied the Council of Constance declared they would submit their cause to a future pope (*Documenta*, p. 592); in 1419 the utraquist nobility sought to appeal from the pope to a future council (*AČ*, III, 207).

[12] The decree for Prague, dated only 1416, is in Loserth, *op. cit.*, pp. 375 f.; the very similar one for Beroun, dated 2 December, in *Documenta*, pp. 644 f. See Kejř, *Husitský právník*, p. 104, n. 48, for the dating.

[13] *Documenta*, pp. 606–608.

[14] *Ibid.*, p. 607 (according to the canons' report).

centers of radical preaching, were in no mood to give up their gains. Nor did
their chief spiritual leader, Master Jakoubek, neglect to attack the royal
decree of 2 December in his sermons; pretending that the king had been
brought to his policy by bad advice and misinformation, Jakoubek urged his
flock not to comply.[15] As we have just seen from the testimony of the Prague
canons, no one else complied either, not even the more conservative masters.
Acting from either prudence or ineptitude, King Wenceslas seems to have let
the matter rest in this unsatisfactory condition; his new policy had been
enough to call the previous situation into question, but no more than that,
and if the Catholics wanted more they would have to accomplish it themselves, without royal leadership, without the help of the town magistrates,
who were royal officials, and apparently without any significant basis of
popular support. On the other hand, the university, which still maintained
its institutional freedoms and was still sensitive to the obligations of its
international status, might offer a theater of Catholic action; in fact, the
quodlibetal disputations scheduled to begin on 3 January 1417 had been
entrusted to the direction of the Catholic Master Procop of Kladruby.[16] In
sharp contrast to the Hussite quodlibets of preceding years, Procop's contained a great preponderance of purely philosophical and theological questions, with very few concerning issues that might lend themselves to reformist agitation. Given the superior strength of the Hussite masters at the
university, Procop's selection of questions was probably intended to accomplish the most that could be done by the Catholic minority, namely, to
prevent the exercises from being used as a platform for Hussite propaganda.[17] Even here, however, he was not entirely successful, for at least one
master, the conservative Hussite Simon of Tišnov, managed to use a relatively unpromising question of scholastic philosophy to develop a sharp
attack on the Prague interdict.[18]

Perhaps a clearer measure of Catholic impotence at this time was an
apparently parodistic *questio,* displayed in various places in Prague on the
eve of the disputation: "Whether it is permitted to the masters of the
University of Prague to define and approve what the authority of the whole
world condemns." Allegedly formulated by the "magistri de Constancia"—
that is, the university masters who were at the Council, and probably the
work of Master Peter of Uničov, who had just come back from Constance,

[15] Passages from the sermons are quoted by Bartoš, "Sborník husitského kazatele asi z
r. 1415," *VČA,* LVII (1948), 15–33; I follow Kejř, "Deklarace," pp. 138 f.

[16] J. Kejř, "Quodlibet M. Prokopa z Kladrub z r. 1417," *Acta Universitatis Carolinae,
Philosophica et historica,* II (1958), 27–48.

[17] Thus Kejř, "Deklarace," p. 139.

[18] *Ibid.,* p. 140.

the question was not of course actually debated—it was a scholastic equivalent to chalking a slogan on a wall.[19] Insofar as it had any dimension of
practical significance, this was not at the university, and certainly not at
Procop of Kladruby's bloodless quodlibet, but rather in connection with an
action taken by Archbishop Conrad on 10 January, the promulgation for his
diocese of the Council of Constance's anti-utraquist decree, proclaimed for
the realm as a whole by John Železný a few months before.[20] Like Železný,
Conrad surrounded the decree with the usual executive and procedural
formulas, so that there was no doubt that his action was not merely one of
publication but rather one aimed at nothing less than a purge of utraquist
priests from the Bohemian church. The policy could not be applied where
the secular powers were either Hussite or neutral, but at least a beginning
could be made in other areas, and care could be taken to insure that no
utraquist or "Wyclifite" was ordained or confirmed in a benefice.[21] The
sharp division between Hussite and Catholic clergy that existed in Prague, as
a result of the interdict, would now be extended to the realm as a whole;
future Hussite gains would have to be made not within the established
church, as previously, but against it. Nor did Conrad fail to move against the
university: on 20 January 1417, after several days of argument and in
defiance of the royal will, he refused, as chancellor of the university, to allow
the regular examinations for the master's degree.[22]

The whole sequence of abortive and inconclusive anti-Hussite actions,
together with the harder line now followed by the church, had a remarkable
effect upon the university masters, whose policy for the past few years had
been to preserve as much as possible of the appearance of normality, in the
sound realization that the line between appearance and substance was neither sharp nor fixed. If Hussites could take over the churches of Bohemia,
they would eventually control the Bohemian church, and by so doing they
would present King Wenceslas with a *fait accompli*—it was the only way to
deal with him. Then the Hussite realm, under the leadership of its king,

---

[19] For the text and identification see J. Sedlák, *Několik textů z doby husitské*, I
(Brno, 1912), 39–41.

[20] The text in J. Loserth, "Beiträge," pp. 382 f.

[21] Conrad issued the decree as Archbishop of the Prague province and addressed it to
the archdeacon of the Prague diocese. (There were several archdeacons, for various
regions—perhaps our text is merely one of several originals.) Within nine days the
latter official was to communicate the text to his rural deans, who in turn, within
twenty days, were to convoke their parish priests and notify them. The deans were then
to begin looking for violators, whose names they would pass on to the archbishop. This
mechanism, if carried through, would take care of utraquists already in the church
structure; for the preventive measures see below, *ad* nn. 52–54.

[22] Tomek, III, 609 f. For the background see *HR*, I, 32, n. 41.

could hope for European acceptance of an unalterable situation. Utraquism was of course something of an embarrassment, for it drew an uncomfortably conspicuous line between Hussites and Romanists, and for this reason the majority of Hussite masters were reluctant to accept it; having come to accept it, they were similarly reluctant to proclaim it as official doctrine—by the beginning of 1417 they still had not done so. But now everything was different. With King Wenceslas submitting to pressure from the Council of Constance and the Emperor Sigismund, with John Železný and even Archbishop Conrad working actively to isolate or expel Hussites and moving to destroy the university's status, it must have been obvious to all that a new posture was required, one of consolidation, self-help, and readiness for even rebellious action. The radical preachers who worked directly with the people were already in such a posture, but most of the masters—the conservatives, the politicians of the party—could interpret the new situation only within the framework of their alliance with the Hussite nobility. That alliance had to be strengthened and put to work.

The great difficulty here was that the past two years of radical and extremist development had made the Hussite party something different from the great cause that the nobles had embraced in September of 1415. It is easy to imagine a baron listening appreciatively to a rousing "evangelical" sermon, full of anticlerical abuse, and still easier to imagine him piously confiscating the lands of an adjoining monastery, or the endowment of "his" parish church; the picture is only enhanced if we add a sequence showing the lord expelling a Romanist priest, perhaps with physical violence, and installing a Hussite, in contempt of the canons. That such a lord should feel a stir of emotion at the memory of the martyred John Hus was only to be expected, and when the lay chalice had become a symbolic epitome of the whole reform movement, the lords accepted it too, apparently without much strain. But what would be the attitude of such a Hussite if his priest cast off the Roman vestments, smashed the statues of the saints and their altars, dumped relics on the dungheap, and reduced the sacred mass to Czech hymns and prayers, and communion? And what if the priest told him that the usual prayers for the lord's ancestors were not to be offered because there was no Purgatory and the prayers did no good? A few barons might have accepted all this, glad perhaps of the shorter, cheaper, and understandable ritual, but most would undoubtedly have felt shocked in the presence of such subversion, and disquieted by the lack of visible evidence that the religion was working for them.[23] Thus when in early 1417 Master Christian of Prachatice wrote to the extremist Wenceslas Koranda to protest against the

[23] There is support for this statement in what immediately follows. See also below, chap. x, n. 171.

latter's doctrines and practices, he included the information that "some of our sedulous promotors of the evangelical truth before the king have been very downcast by the things I have just written about, and they say that they no longer wish to involve themselves on our account, but rather wish to live like others, in peace of mind."[24] And, "the things that are daily done by our people not only do not induce enemies of the truth to accept it, but repel our most powerful friends and promoters of the truth. In fact, Lord Čeněk [of Vartemberk] at a recent meeting of our senior masters harshly accused our priests who have disregarded the advice, both oral and written, of the masters and follow their own minds." Some of the written advice referred to survives—it will be discussed below—but there must have been a good deal more; in fact, there must have been a considerable period of time in which the university masters observed the growth of sectarianism on the left and sought to limit it, with no appreciable effect beyond the creation of controversy and ill-will. "How the enemies of the truth rejoice," Master Christian wrote Koranda, "when they sense that we do not agree with each other and when they hear of our discord!" This discord, together with the nobility's disillusionment because of extremist irregularities, thus posed a serious problem for the masters at the beginning of 1417.

The problem could be attacked in the first place only by an attempt to suppress extremism, and this in fact is what the masters did, on 25 January 1417. Sometimes interpreted as an attempt to appease the Archbishop (who had just prohibited the master's examinations), or as a device of the conservative Hussites to show how basically orthodox they were,[25] the masters' action seems rather to have been the first step in a new policy of movement designed to meet the challenges of the previous months. We do not know enough of the background to be sure, but the surviving sources allow us to guess what common sense would in any case suggest: that when the masters considered issuing a condemnation of extremism, there must have been several suggested drafts. Perhaps the original proposal was this protocol submitted by John Jesenic:

[24] *Documenta*, pp. 634 f. (see above, chap. iv, *ad* n. 86). For the dating see below, *ad* nn. 36 and 37.

[25] According to Bartoš (*Do čtyř art.*, pp. 12 f.; *HR*, I, 36) the action described in these paragraphs was an effort inspired by Jesenic, to save the chalice by sacrificing the radical and Waldensian doctrines of Nicholas of Dresden; thereby the university would appear to be standing in the moderate center rather than off on the left, and would be offering its help against elements the Catholics too regarded as dangerous. Kejř, "Deklarace," p. 143, interprets the masters' action as a continuation of the policy of retreat that they had begun with John Kardinál's concessions to Conrad in late 1416; at the same time he also interprets it as a result of collaboration with the Hussite nobility.

The conclusions of Jesenic, which he submitted on the day of the conversion of St. Paul [25 January] 1417. . . . (1) That there is Purgatory. (2) That suffrages are of help to those in Purgatory. (3) That images should be adored, venerated, and be the subject of cults. (4) That the pope can be adored and the knee can be bent to him, nor are those thus acting idolaters. (5) That councils are to be believed in. (6) That customs of churches are not to be contradicted. (7) That those who kiss images are not idolaters. (8) That images should even be adorned for the increase of devotion, because beautiful images are more moving than ugly ones. (9) That images are not to be destroyed in any way on account of human abuses.[26]

Since we know from Jakoubek of Stříbro's previous and subsequent pronouncements that he disagreed wholly or partly with all but the first two of these proposals, we may guess that he and his adherents held out against Jesenic's stand, which would certainly have destroyed Hussite unity beyond repair. Unfortunately it is not clear that all arguments were in fact heard; what seems to have happened was that the majority of Hussite masters, those ready to agree on something that would be reasonably conservative, met away from the university, in the parish house of Christian of Prachatice's church, St. Michael's in the Old Town.[27] There they unanimously voted for a declaration that included the following essential passages:

> It has come to our hearing, by frequent accounts and repeated complaints, how some men from various communities . . . rashly hold and seek to show that there is no Purgatory, and that consequently there should be no praying or almsgiving for the dead. They also hold that images should not be kept in the church—indeed they assert, albeit falsely, that it is against the law of God to have images of Christ and of the saints. Moreover they hold that blessings of salt and of water and of the baptismal font, and the blessings long observed on Sundays and in the whole world of Christendom, along with other blessings of the church confirmed and approved by the holy fathers and the Christian religion—that these blessings smack of error, according to their fond but also false imaginings. Hence they seek and struggle to overthrow and utterly destroy these blessings, along with other laudable ceremonies of churches. . . .

[26] Discovered by F. M. Bartoš and printed in *Do čtyř art.*, p. 13, n. 45. I have reprinted the original Latin in my "Hussite Radicalism," p. 118. Kejř, *Husitský právník*, pp. 109 f., explains Jesenic's extreme conservatism as a result of his close political and economic ties to the Hussite nobility, and his reliance on their continued Hussitism to protect him from persecution by the Roman church.

[27] It is not clear whether they went there at first or only as a reaction to Jesenic's protocol: the latter is entitled "Conclusiones Jesenic, quas posuit . . . in lectorio ordinariarum," which last Kejř understands as referring to the university ("Deklarace," p. 142). I do not know what the last word means.

Wishing unanimously to check these many and other unfounded temerities, we exhort all of you . . . that together with the holy mother Church, with us and with the holy doctors, you hold and confess that there is a fire of Purgatory after this life and lasting till the final Day of Judgement. Also that you firmly maintain that suffrages for the dead should be offered—such as prayers, fasts, alms, masses for the dead, and other works of piety. Also that you not allow yourselves to do away with images of the Crucified and of his saints; with blessings of the holy font, of salt and of water, of palms, of fires, of grains, eggs, cheeses, and other paschal things; with thurification, aspersion, bell-ringing, the kiss of peace, and all ceremonies whatsoever that have long been kept in the holy church of God and that agree with the law of God. . . .

We also request that if any sort of dogmatizers of these errors should come to you with their false opinions, wishing to dogmatize against this our present judgement, that you deny them a free hearing so long as they have not shown their opinion to be just, before us.[28]

Bearing in mind the fact that Jesenic's extremely terse protocol naturally sounds more drastic than the more detailed declaration, we can still attach significance to the substantial differences between them: where Jesenic was evidently prepared to recognize the authority of the pope and of the Council of Constance, the majority of masters said nothing about either; instead they pronounced a norm quoted from a text of St. Augustine's, in the *Decretum* —"According to the canons of the saints, in matters about which divine Scripture decrees nothing definite, the custom of the people of God and the institutes of our predecessors are to be held for law." [29] Otherwise the declaration was quite severe, even arrogant, in its formulations, and we may assume that the unanimity it expressed had been achieved by the exclusion of the minority who stood with Jakoubek, who of course had no desire to condemn the rejection of images, miscellaneous blessings, and the ceremonies mentioned in the text. In fact, on 31 January Jakoubek publicly pronounced a *Posicio de imaginibus* in which all the themes that he and Nicholas of Dresden had developed in their struggle against the cult of images and of saints were repeated, in very sharp form.[30] On the other hand, here as

---

[28] The text in *Documenta*, pp. 654–656; it includes the date and place, and has this heading: "Universis Christi fidelibus, ad quos praesentium tenor pervenerit: Joannes Cardinalis, magister in artibus et baccalaureus in decretis, rector coetusque magistrorum ad hoc praesertim vocatorum universitatis studii Pragensis unanimis: salutem. . . ." Palacký lists two surviving MSS; there is another in MS XII F 30, fols. 37ᵛ-38ʳ.

[29] *Decretum*, XI. Dist., c. 7.

[30] *LČJ*, No. 69; parts of the *posicio* are printed in Nejedlý, IV, 105 ff. It contains little or nothing that Jakoubek had not already been saying for years; the very fact that he repeated his old ideas on 31 January is significant.

always in this period he was more interested in practical reform than in theoretical absolutism; although he disagreed with the more conservative masters' idea of what Hussite religious life should be, he accepted the basic point of the university's doctrinal authority within the framework of a national reformation. Indeed, he had been waging his own war against the theoretical sectarianism of Nicholas of Dresden and the practical sectarianism of the provincial extremists. In this context he had long since pronounced his own defense of Purgatory against Nicholas, in a moderate, even hesitant style.[31] Like the other masters, however, he was less inclined to be respectful when dealing with heretical practice—the Waldensianist sectarianism in the provinces—and in a second defense of Purgatory, perhaps written at the time we are now considering, he expressed himself in terms very similar to those of the more conservative masters:

> A universal Purgatory of souls is expounded by the church and by the holy doctors, with no exceptions, who base themselves faithfully on Holy Writ. But with charity growing cold and iniquity abounding, with pseudo-prophets being multiplied and even increasingly so in these perilous times, the spirits of certain men given to mortal things, puffed up in their own opinions and phantasies, concoct novelties and reject and despise the old, the fixed, the proven, and the solid. And this to the point that not only do they refute and spurn the pronouncements of the more recent and modern saints, but . . . they hold as nothing the saints of the Primitive Church, the disciples contemporary with Christ, and the rite of our mother, the Primitive Church. Thus without the help of solid scripture or the support of any deductive reasoning, with no confirmation at all, . . . they dare to say and assert that the fire of Purgatory after this life does not exist and that there should be no prayers for the souls of the faithful who depart from this world.[32]

This passage represents more than mere disagreement: it documents Jakoubek's outrage at the disruptive effect of those tendencies that flouted the principles of Hussite scholastic authority—something that Nicholas of Dresden had not done. This point of view, in harmony with that of the other

---

[31] See above, chap. iv, *ad* n. 229 ff.

[32] The text of this treatise *De purgatorio* has been published by C. G. F. Walch, *Monimenta medii aevi*, III (Göttingen, 1759), 3–25; the quoted passage is on pp. 3 f. Bartoš (*LČJ*, No. 64) dates the work shortly after the sermon on Purgatory that Jakoubek preached against Nicholas of Dresden, on 29 November 1415, but there is no reason to think this; on the contrary, the differences between the two works suggest that they were written in different circumstances. The sermon against Nicholas gives strong authorities against Purgatory as well as for it, and Jakoubek's conclusion comes only after evident hesitation; the later treatise however consists of little but authorities for Purgatory—there are none for it, and, as evident from the quoted paragraph, there is no hesitation in Jakoubek's own mind.

masters, was perhaps more important than the question of whether this or that ceremony was justified. For such a question could always be explored and argued with the opposing party, on university ground, and it was not impossible that the opponents would eventually be convinced by the force of truth, or, failing this, that the more radical congregations could in time proceed with *de facto* reforms even while the questions of principle were still being debated. In fact, we know that such a debate was taking place in the matter of infant communion. Since the utraquist polemic had drawn attention to the principle that the Eucharist was necessary to salvation, the idea that it should be given to infants and children as well as to adults could hardly escape consideration, and it was probably in 1416 that Jakoubek began to develop the doctrine.[33] By January of 1417 it was being discussed in university circles so vigorously that it could not be treated in the declaration of 25 January, although we can be fairly sure that the extremists against whom that declaration was aimed were indeed advocating infant communion.[34] The disputes would go on through 1417, but meanwhile Jakoubek and his party had every reason to respect the university forum as the arena in which they could hope to win a favorable authoritative decision. For all of these reasons we may suppose that Jakoubek's opposition to the declaration of 25 January was that of a faithful, law-abiding minority *within* the body of masters.

It was therefore possible for the conservative authors of that declaration to

[33] In a consideration of this matter F. M. Bartoš, "Roztržka v husitské straně r. 1417," *Do čtyř art.*, pp. 68 f., notes that the issue of infant communion came up in 1415, in Jakoubek's polemic with Andrew of Brod, but that "unfavorable circumstances" pushed it into oblivion until 1417; the mention of it in Christian of Prachatice's letter to Koranda suggests that at that time it was an unheard-of novelty. Actually it came up several times, as a logical possibility, in the utraquist controversy (see Hardt, III, 366, 406 f., 421, 431 f.), and a key text, the Pseudo-Dionysius's statement that every sacrament is incomplete without communion, appeared in Nicholas of Dresden's defense of utraquism against Havlík (Sedlák, "Počátkové kalicha," *ČKD*, LIV (1913), 469). On the other hand, I find little in Christian's letter to support Bartoš's inference—on the contrary, since Christian talks of authorities pro and con, we can assume the matter had been argued before the letter was written—hence that the issue was in the open in the second half of 1416. How it came up then is another matter—we do not know. If Bartoš is correct in regarding Jakoubek's treatment of the question in his *De quibusdam punctis* (*LČJ*, No. 70) as the beginning of the polemic, then we might suppose that the original impetus came from the radicals outside Prague, for this work was a *responsum* to their questions (see above, chap. iv, the section entitled "Jakoubek of Stříbro and the Radical Party, 1415–1416," *passim*). But this particular portion of the *responsum* may have circulated as an independent tractate—see below, n. 106.

[34] Indeed the report was that they were practicing it; thus Christian writes Koranda: "Nunc de te publica vox . . . insonuit . . . qualiter . . . infantulos . . . communices . . . " (*Documenta*, p. 634).

bring it before the university as a whole. Although we do not know why they did so, we may guess that it was because the action of 25 January had been that of a caucus, albeit one that included Master John Kardinál and was therefore able to provide its manifesto with the Rector's seal; but the doctrinal authority of the university could be properly exercised only by a full meeting of all the masters. Furthermore, Jakoubek's ostentatious action of 31 January must have made the conservatives realize that they could ignore his party only at their own peril. And indeed his party was not ignored: perhaps as a result of discussion, or perhaps merely in anticipation of radical objections, the version of the masters' pronouncement that issued from the full university meeting, on 7 February, struck a new note of moderation, at least in its language.[35] We no longer read that the Devil, under the pretext of piety, had caused intra-Hussite dissension by bringing some to despise the truth and assert that there was no Purgatory, and so forth. Instead, as the formula of 7 February put it, in language reminiscent of Jakoubek's, the world was growing old, the end of the ages was coming, and in these perilous times some men were curiously scrutinizing novelties, so that "recently some questions have come up"—namely whether there was Purgatory, among other questions. This note is carried through consistently and in detail, to the point that the image of vicious, diabolical heretics suggested by the formulations of 25 January is entirely replaced by the image of sincere but misguided doubters who in their uncertainties have asked the masters for counsel. The masters of 25 January wished to "check temerities" while those of 7 February wanted to "check the division" among the people; on the former occasion the masters feared lest their silence "allow any and all the free faculty of erring," but two weeks later they feared lest because of their silence "the controversies would most harmfully become worse." And instead of exhorting the recipients of the letter to believe this, believe that— all in the imperative mood—the masters now calmly declared the desirability of the old beliefs and customs in the passive periphrastic.

Furthermore, there was some attempt on 7 February to provide reasons for the conservative position, and in the matter of Purgatory there was also added an earnest request to all the faithful, that they be so studious in correcting their defects that they not have to suffer the pain of Purgatory. (Again the formula was Jakoubek's.) Although there was the same clause

---

[35] The text in Loserth, "Beiträge," pp. 57 f., and (apparently better) in *Mon. conc. saec. XV*, I, 385 f. (Both have the date 7 February; for some reason a tradition has taken root among Czech scholars that Loserth's text is dated 9 February—it is not [see, e.g., Kejř, "Deklarace," p. 145].) The letter was issued "in plena congregacione magistrorum universitatis sub sigillo." A third Latin text, in MS O 39, fol. 121ʳ, is unpublished; it bears the no doubt erroneous date of 1418. There is a Czech translation in *AČ*, VI, 36 f. For the note of moderation see n. 109 below.

about refusing to allow anyone holding the condemned beliefs to teach them, until he should have proved his opinion to be just, on 7 February the proof could be made not only "before us"—*coram nobis*—but alternatively "before those whose business it is"—*aut coram hiis quibus interest*. The import of the added phrase is not clear, but it is not impossible that it was a way of exonerating the university in case it should be necessary to tolerate future deviations within the framework of Hussite unity. The difference between the two redactions seems clear enough to support a structure of inference: without changing the substance of their condemnation, the masters altered its tone drastically enough to change what had been a simple, blunt antiradical attack into a lofty, official, almost impartial *responsum* to sincere doubts that had arisen in Hussite ranks. Although they still could not secure the active support of Jakoubek's party—the 7 February text dropped the reference to unanimous consent—they could at least win the defeated minority's acceptance of the new redaction as the official university position.

If we now ask why the conservative masters—the political leaders—did not fully meet Jakoubek's position and confine their declaration to those points of *sectarian* radicalism that he also opposed, omitting the defense of images, ceremonies, and blessings—a defense that could hardly have changed radical theory or practice—we can seek the answer most reasonably in considerations of political necessity. Faced with the urgent task of solidifying their alliance with the Hussite nobility, the masters had to condemn what the nobles would not tolerate. Here Master Christian of Prachatice's letter to Wenceslas Koranda offers our best guide, particularly in the following passage (part of which has already been quoted):

> Lord Čeněk [of Vartemberk] at a recent meeting of our senior masters harshly accused our priests who disregard the advice, both oral and written, of the masters and follow their own minds. He concluded with the masters that he would order the masters' letter on ecclesiastical rites to be followed on his domains in every respect.[36]

There may have been several meetings that we do not know about, but since the letter in question clearly had the character of a public declaration, and since we have several surviving copies of the 25 January letter but none of any other that was issued by a meeting of the "senior masters," the easiest hypothesis would be that Lord Čeněk in fact attended the 25 January meeting. Furthermore, the phraseology and content of Christian's letter to Koranda clearly reflect the declaration of that meeting,[37] which moreover

[36] *Documenta*, p. 635.
[37] Thus, e.g., both begin by blaming the extremist beliefs on the Devil, who, failing to tear the Hussites away from Christ's truth, resorted to fostering schism, *sub specie* (or

was held in the parish house of Christian's church. The reactionary policy newly pursued with such relative vigor by the king and the archbishop, and above all the latter's condemnation of utraquism on 10 January, forced the masters and the lords to take stock of their cause: ready to defend Hussitism in general, the chalice in particular, they naturally did not want to pursue this dangerous course with the burden of also defending doctrines and practices that they themselves regarded as indefensible.

They seem to have agreed with each other on what these practices were—with one exception: Christian writes that "in the second place" Čeněk went on to tell the masters "that under no circumstances would he permit infants to be given communion immediately after baptism." [38] We know that the most conservative masters agreed with Čeněk on this point—men like John Jesenic and Simon of Tišnov [39]—but the others either did not, or were not sure enough on the point to deal with it in their declaration. Typical of these was the moderate position expressed by Christian to Koranda, who had been reported to have given communion to infants; urging the political wisdom of refraining from the practice—"both the king and all our people" should follow Čeněk's policy "if we wish the good of the realm"—Christian still left the door open for possible acceptance of the novelty:

> Although there are some authorities for it . . . and some directly opposed, it would be good and useful not to leap immediately to the other, the uncustomary side, but only after frequent prior conference with learned men as to whether it is expedient to promulgate these novelties thus or otherwise. As for me, I do not dare rashly to define what position in this matter would be more acceptable to God, but I humbly desire all to labor so, that without questioning the main point about communion, we may try to agree on the other issues that have come up. And I urge this on you too, if you wish the prosperity of our side.[40]

This is not the only reference in the letter to "the main point about communion" or to the idea that "our side" is facing a crisis because of

---

praetextu) pietatis. There is also the same reference to what was been *heard* by the masters about what was going on, and the same emphasis on the fact that the extremists were following their *own* opinions. For the similarity in content, see the quoted passages; above, chap. iv, the section on "Sectarian Extremism in the Provinces," and in this chapter *ad* n. 28.

[38] *Documenta*, p. 635.

[39] According to John Želivský, preaching in 1419, Jesenic was the first to attack infant communion and he was joined by Simon of Tišnov (quoted by J. Truhlář, "Husitská kázání z let 1416–1418," *VČA*, VIII (1899), 288). For their work see Kejř, *Husitský právník*, p. 111.

[40] *Documenta*, pp. 635 f.

extremist excesses, which have been associated with utraquist preaching.[41] If we read Christian's letter as a prime source for the background of the masters' antiradical action, we have no difficulty seeing the latter in its true light, not as a movement away from Hussitism, nor even in its basic sense a significant movement toward the right, but rather as a resolute attempt to consolidate Hussite ranks in order to defend the reform against both national and international reaction.

In this sense the conservative action of late January and early February can be related to what followed in the next few months, both at the university and among the Hussite feudality. Having staked out a claim to doctrinal leadership, the masters understandably went on to validate this claim by taking a step that they must have deliberately postponed during the previous year: the issuing of a declaration in favor of utraquist communion. In a sense it was a declaration of war, and for this reason it was not taken as long as there was hope that the Catholics would remain inactive while the Hussites scored successes. But the new Catholic militancy, culminating in the publication of the Council of Constance's anti-utraquist decrees, required a corresponding Hussite action, and after the way had been prepared by the consolidating activity we have just been considering, there was no reason for further delay. The first step was to break the opposition of the leading antiutraquists at the university, one of whom was currently Dean of the Arts Faculty, Master Nicholas of Pavlíkov.[42] According to an anti-Hussite source he announced a public disputation on the question of utraquism and determined against the novelty, but the Hussites kept up a filibuster of heckling objections to the point that Nicholas, unable even to take time out to rest, was defeated: in several days of determining and responding he had gotten through only half of his *questio,* and the Hussites went about saying that he had been unable to answer their objections. We will never know if this version is true, but it does not matter; the main thing is that Nicholas and his associates were unable to block the newly resolute majority.

Another, parallel episode is much better documented. Master Peter of Uničov, whom we have just seen displaying a sarcastically anti-utraquist *questio*-title at various places in Prague on the eve of the 3 January quodlibet,

---

[41] *Ibid.,* p. 635: "Non deducto principali evangelico puncto, ceterum alias novitates non fundatas attentamus, prout cum eisdem verbum annuntiant. Ex omni parte enim insurgunt nostri pseudosacerdotes. . . ." And, "Mihi enim constat, quanta audivi, quantaque scio, quae quotidie fiunt per nostros, quod non solum inimicos veritatis ad acceptandam veritatem (non) alliciunt, sed quod amicos fortissimos nobis et promotores veritatis repellunt." For what follows see n. 83 below.

[42] For what follows see Höfler, III, 157 f. The episode is not dated but it would fall logically into this period. Nicholas was Dean of the Arts Faculty from 15 October 1416 to 17 April 1417 (Tomek, V, 232).

was a well-known leader of the Romanist party even before that episode. John Hus in Constance had called him one of his chief enemies, and Peter boasted of this accolade,[43] which indeed he had earned and continued to earn by agitating against Hus's heresy in Prague, at the University of Bologna, at the Council of Constance, and in various other places.[44] A master in Prague's Theology Faculty, he was also a Dominican friar, preaching in his order's church of St. Clement in Prague. There Nicholas of Dresden or one of Nicholas's disciples heard him preach that "Christ did not prohibit the pope from fighting,"[45] perhaps a reference to John XXIII's crusade against Ladislas of Naples. He also said many other things abusive of Hussitism. He branded Hus's followers as typical pale-faced heretics, as blasphemers who drunkenly guzzled their utraquist Eucharist, and he said they were "devilish ones who beat people, carried long swords, and killed people without any fear."[46] Unlike other heretics, who had previously been burned in neighboring regions, the Hussites were exceptionally damaging because "they knew how to defend their heresy with the false exposition and glossing of Scriptures." Dedicated to such a high pitch of odious militancy, Peter would have been well advised to stay at Constance; once back in Prague he could hardly avoid falling victim to the new program of Hussite action. And so it happened. The masters who were preparing to come out formally in favor of utraquism could not tolerate a leading opponent like Peter, and both conservatives and radicals joined against him;[47] with the help of the secular powers they imprisoned him in the Old Town Hall, where he was allegedly tormented and tortured and even threatened with death unless he would recant.[48] At about the same time Master John of Hradec, who had probably been involved in the original administration of utraquist commun-

---

[43] The information comes from the account of Hus's cause in Constance written by Peter of Mladoňovice, *Documenta*, pp. 251–253. It had been Peter of Uničov who had accused Hus of inciting his audience to violence in Prague.

[44] This is according to his recantation; see below, n. 50.

[45] A. Neumann, "Glossy v Drändorfově postile," *Hlídka*, XLI (1924), 460. According to Tomek, V, 209, Peter was preacher at St. Clement's from 1414 to 1417, but he had been preaching from at least 1410, and in 1412, the year of John XXIII's indulgences and crusade, he was a *praedicator Theotunicorum*: see Sedlák, "Počátkové kalicha," *ČKD*, LV (1914), 315 f.

[46] See below, n. 50.

[47] His final recantation was made at a gathering presided over by the conservative Master Simon of Rokycany (Höfler, II, 62), and it was acknowledged by the university as a body (Loserth, "Beiträge," pp. 58 f.). At the same time Jakoubek wrote a utraquist treatise, *Posicio pro informacione monachi M. Petri* (*LČJ*, No. 46, MS 4488, fols. 97ʳ–101ʳ).

[48] The incident is perhaps best described in Tomek, III, 613 f. There are many sources: Höfler, II, 62; "Slyšte všickni staří i vy děti" (below, n. 98), lines 187 ff.; Stephen of Páleč in Höfler, II, 317 f. (Sedlák, *op. cit.*, pp. 318 f.).

ion but who had subsequently moved to the other side, was also subjected to physical coercion when he attempted to propound an anti-utraquist *posicio* at the University.[49]

Against this background the masters could proceed to issue their declaration in favor of the chalice, on 10 March 1417. Although they still shrank from the radical position that utraquist communion was necessary to salvation, they made up for this moderation by using very vigorous language, in a lofty, congested style clearly designed to mask the differences in this matter between radicals and conservatives. The significance of the declaration as a rejection of the authority of the Council of Constance was balanced by a deliberate reference to the Council's own admission, that communion in both kinds had been the practice of the Primitive Church. In fact, although the masters *had* to make their pronouncement, for the reasons outlined above, they were aware of the disadvantages it entailed in the way of deepening the split between the Hussites and the universal church. At least they could comfort themselves with the spectacle of Peter of Uničov brought to his knees. On 13 March, after what must have been a stubborn struggle, Peter signed a recantation which he then read out in the university's main hall, the Carolinum, in the presence of the masters and students and many of the laity, including Prague's magistrates and members of the royal court.[50] The recantation summarized all the damage Peter had done in his lively career of anti-Hussitism, and then went on to declare that in fact utraquism was Christ's own institution, that everyone in Bohemia was praiseworthy in life and true in faith, that especially the masters of the university were so, always teaching the truth, hating heresies, and offering obedience to the holy Roman church in all proper things. Please forgive me, Peter asked his audience and the king, please impose a penance on me, and if I ever repeat my errors do not believe me. He also declared that John Hus and Jerome of Prague were free of error. The recantation was ordered to be copied many times in Czech, German, and Latin, and the many surviving texts show that it was regarded as quite important in spite of what everyone must have known, that its protestations of having been made freely were false. "My son was dead and now lives again," wrote the university in a disgustingly hypocritical acknowledgement of Peter's conversion,[51] and, in fact, although there were still some non-utraquist masters on the scene, they had no power

---

[49] Höfler, II, 317 f.; cf. Tomek, III, 614. A Bachelor of Arts, Stanislav of Rudžice, may also have been coerced into recanting anti-utraquism: see the reference in Loserth, *op. cit.,* p. 59, n. 1.

[50] The Latin text is published in J. Loserth, *Hus und Wiclif* (Leipzig, 1884), p. 296; I have used the Czech text in MS XI E 3, fols. 96ʳ–97ᵛ (the German text follows on fols. 98ʳ–99ᵛ).

[51] In Loserth, "Beiträge," pp. 58 f.; see Luke 15:24.

to make trouble. Now for the first time the university could claim to be living up to its task of providing Hussite ecclesiastical leadership, although at the cost of its academic integrity.

THE UNIVERSITY, THE NOBILITY, AND THE RADICALS

In thus committing themselves to revolt against the Council and the Bohemian hierarchy, the university masters must have been executing a plan that had been agreed upon with Lord Čeněk of Vartemberk at the 25 January meeting, a plan that however bold must have represented the only response suitable to the situation at that time. John Jesenic had, to be sure, suggested another response—submit to the Council and acknowledge papal authority; but the other conservative masters and the leading Hussite barons, motivated no doubt by a mixture of political prudence and religious idealism, and foreseeing how unacceptable would be the consequences of Jesenic's program, had chosen to consolidate the movement internally and construct a Hussite church in opposition to the Catholic one in Bohemia. Here an enormous role had to be assigned to the feudality, for unless the battle of words and ideas at the university were backed up by real changes in the nation at large the new policy could hardly affect the institutionalized strength of the Catholic establishment. And indeed the crisis itself dictated the terms of its solution, for at the same time that the Catholic forces were pushing toward an ideological showdown on the matter of utraquism, they were also inaugurating a purge of the Bohemian church. By September 1416, if not before, it was ecclesiastical policy to refuse ordination to "Wyclifite" candidates,[52] and when John Železný promulgated the Council's anti-utraquist decree on 29 October 1416 he included definite provisions for the canonical citation of all violators, just as Archbishop Conrad did when he promulgated the decree on 10 January 1417. On 3 March 1417 we find the first evidence of administrative action to deprive Hussite priests of their benefices, action that was carried on more and more energetically in the following months.[53] In continuation of this policy, but also perhaps in reaction to the university's utraquist declaration of 10 March, the church

---

[52] This provision was included in the oath Aleš of Březí had to swear when he was ordained Bishop of Olomouc by Archbishop Conrad in September 1416 (the text in Loserth, "Beiträge," pp. 90–92). There is no evidence that this policy was actually being carried out at that time in the Prague diocese, but it certainly must have been in the period now under discussion.

[53] *Libri confirmationum ad beneficia ecclesiastica Pragensem per archidiocesim,* VII, ed. J. Emler (Prague, 1886), 220. Subsequent cases appear on pp. 223 (2 April 1417), 233 (5 July), and then later on pp. 246, 247, 249, 252 f., 266.

authorities began refusing to confirm benefices to priests who would not swear an oath against the Forty-five Articles of Wyclif and against utraquism; the first reference, on 8 April 1417, is to "the usual oaths to be taken from newly instituted parish priests." [54]

The more militant and radical Hussite clerics could hardly have worried too much about any of this, for they did their work not primarily by administering a utraquist parish but by agitation carried on outside of or against the parochial structure. We have seen something of the form of this agitation in the preceding chapter, but it must have been even more widespread than the sources for sectarian extremism say; simply administering utraquist communion to those wishing it might lead a convinced Hussite to ignore parish boundaries or even to leave his own parish to work elsewhere, supporting himself "evangelically" by the alms of the devoted people. From the point of view of the Catholic hierarchy such a priest was not only a heretic, he was a violator of ecclesiastical order and a neglecter of the souls officially committed to his care. [55] The more conservative Hussites, whose ideal was a regularized establishment similar to the Catholic one, would also disapprove of itinerant evangelists, particularly when the latter preached extreme radical doctrines. Add to this the probability that a number of clerical misfits, failures, and opportunists must have found the radical movement extremely attractive, for all the obvious reasons, and we can understand another dimension to the concern of the university masters, a dimension expressed quite sharply in Christian of Prachatice's letter to Wenceslas Koranda, quoted in the preceding chapter: "On all sides we see our pseudo-priests, drunk, sensual, and scandalous beyond measure. . . ." The whole paragraph is instructive; written by a man who had good sources of

---

[54] *Ibid.,* VII, 224: a newly confirmed priest John "juravit, quod omnia contenta in juramentis a plebanis de novo instituendis recipi consuetis tenebit et observabit." There are many references to the oaths from then on, *passim,* and in a confirmation of 1 July (p. 232) we learn what they were: "Juravit ibidem articulos Wicleff et non communicare sub utraque specie." In early 1418 the references to the oath fade away, no doubt because the Hussite-Catholic split had become so definite as to make special mention of the oath superfluous.

[55] John Železný took action, probably in 1416, against a priest of the Prague diocese, John, who had entered a parish of the Litomyšl diocese, where "homines quam plures . . . utriusque sexus colligendo et congregando sub utraque specie communicavit . . ." (*ST,* III, i, 96). And the *Libri confirmationum,* VII, 233, tell of a parish priest Maršík of Muta, who on 5 July 1417 was deprived of a living in Domaslav to which he had been recently presented. He had, the authorities complained, "per diversas ecclesias dioc. Prag. discurrens nonnullos errores predicando seminavit contra prohibicionem d. nostri archiepiscopi, . . . sacramentum sub utraque specie ministrando." The decision came only at the end of a judicial process, which had included a citation of Maršík to appear on a certain day—thus the action must have been begun several weeks earlier.

information, it allows us to take similar Catholic accusations at something like face value: the Hussites "work hard to get rich parishes and neglect poor churches; they stay as long as they can find what to take, then they run away." [56] The radical Master Jakoubek was also concerned about pseudo-priests, "not yet proven in life and morals," [57] who might find their way into Hussite communities. Such priests had to be guarded against but, more important, the conditions under which they flourished had to be changed, even while the more "regular" Hussite clergy had to be secured against Catholic action. This combination of requirements dictated another great enterprise of the Hussite party.

Here the leading figure was Lord Čeněk of Vartemberk, fulfilling what must have been his share of the plans agreed on at the 25 January meeting. He began by taking prisoner the Augustinian friar Herman, titular Bishop of Nicopolis and suffragan of the Prague Archdiocese,[58] whom he forced to ordain a number of candidates for the priesthood in Čeněk's castle of Lipnic, on 6 March 1417.[59] The ceremonies were attended by at least one of the senior masters, perhaps in order to make sure that all of the legal forms were observed. There can be little doubt, moreover, that by and large the new priests were men whose progress to holy orders had merely been interrupted by the religious conflict,[60] and who were as suitable as the priests of the

---

[56] Ed. J. Feifalik, "Untersuchungen über altböhmische Vers- und Reimkunst," *SKAW*, XXIX (1858), 326.

[57] See above, chap. iv, *ad* n. 141.

[58] Herman is listed by C. Eubel, *Hierarchia catholica medii aevi*, I (2d ed.; Münster, 1913), 365. He was a Swabian and a Master of Theology. For his literary work see J. Kadlec, "Die Bibel im mittelalterlichen Böhmen," *Archives d'histoire doctr. et litt. du Moyen Age*, XXXI (1965), 103. His see, to which he was named on 1 September 1413 by John XXIII, was presumably in Palestine, although there are other Nicopolises.

[59] *OCA*, p. 43; Laurence of Březová, pp. 425, 447; also in several other sources.

[60] The Lipnic candidates are referred to as *scolares* (*Chronicon Procopii notarii Pragensis*, Höfler, I, 71 f.) and as "Subdeacons, deacons, etc." (*Documenta*, p. 737). Laurence of Březová says that they were "those whom the Archbishop would not consecrate" (p. 447). The invitation was probably extended to the Czech students at the university, and to the Germans at the Dresden School. The only more or less detailed account of what took place is in the confessions of Bartholomew Rautenstock (J. Döllinger, *Beiträge zur Sektengeschichte des Mittelalters*, II (Munich, 1890), 628 f.), who fell into the hands of the Catholics at Nürnberg and, under interrogation, told how he had been a student of Masters Peter and Nicholas of Dresden in Prague, how when Bishop Herman had been captured some of the students at the Dresden School were asked to take holy orders at his hands, and how in connection with his ordination the usual *littere formate* (*Ein Format und Brief*) were written for him. But, he also said, he was asked to pay money—no doubt the standard notary's fee (see John Hus, "On Simony," trans. M. Spinka, *Advocates of Reform*, p. 244)—and to swear an oath. He refused and reminded those in charge (*den Gewaltigen*) that they had brought him there; accordingly one of these, a Doctor, paid for him.

Catholic side. Still, in the nature of the case, they were the younger clerics of the movement, students rather than teachers at the university or elsewhere, and perhaps for this reason they were a radical group. We know that two students in the Dresden School, John Drändorf and Bartholomew Rautenstock, passed through Herman's hands at this time, and so probably did others—all no doubt as radical as these two, who variously rejected Purgatory, oaths, images, and ceremonies.[61] Among the Czechs John Čapek, Jakoubek's associate and author of the Czech mass, was very probably ordained at Lipnic,[62] along with many other students who, later sources unanimously assure us, were to form the main body of the Taborite clergy.[63] Some, like Čapek, had undoubtedly been loyal to Jakoubek's program even in the controversies on the left, but they were certainly not more conservative than their master and could have had little more sympathy than he did for the conservative condemnation of radicalism. Yet it was the conservative coalition of masters and lords that had brought about the Lipnic ordinations.

Nor was this all. Now well provided with Hussite priests, the nobility could proceed to install them in livings more extensively and systematically than had been done before. We have already seen that the formation of the Hussite League had been followed by such action, in some cases legally, in others by force; but however much the Catholics protested, there was no formal break between the two faiths within the ecclesiastical institution: Hussite patrons continued to make legal presentations that were acknowledged and confirmed by the diocesan authorities. But shortly after Lipnic, on 15 March, Archbishop Conrad condemned the act, deposed Herman from his office, and annulled his actions. And from mid-1417 on, the *Libri confirmationum* of the Prague diocese at least suggest—this invaluable record has not been properly analyzed by Czech scholars—that recognition was with-

---

[61] For Rautenstock and the others, see the preceding note. When John Drändorf fell into the hands of the Catholics at Worms in 1425 he confessed that he had been ordained by Herman; the text of his whole process is published by J. E. Kapp, *Kleine Nachlese einiger . . . Urkunden,* III (Leipzig, 1730), 33–60, see esp. pp. 38 f. Rautenstock confessed to not believing in the cult of saints, in images, or in Purgatory, and as we have seen, he refused to swear an oath. Drändorf confessed to a wide range of Wyclifite beliefs, but also indicated his rejection of oaths and of the ceremonies of the mass; there is no mention of Purgatory, but perhaps our information is incomplete.

[62] F. M. Bartoš, "Z politické literatury doby husitské. 2. Kněz Jan Čapek," *SbH,* V (1957), 37 f., identifies Čapek as the man referred to by the town books of Prague in 1417 as a *scolar* and in 1418 as a *presbyter*—Bartoš's further hypothesis, that in between the two entries Čapek had become a priest at Lipnic, seems irresistible.

[63] Laurence of Březová, pp. 425, 447 ("almost all" and "many," respectively, of the priests of Tabor had been ordained at Lipnic). *OCA,* p. 43 ("many"). John Příbram, "Život kněží táborských," *KJBB,* p. 283 ("many").

drawn from Hussite patronage and, increasingly, from Hussite patrons.[64] This policy was obviously in line with the Catholic reaction that we have already traced, but it was also provoked by the new Hussite program of presentations. Again the leading figure was Čeněk of Vartemberk, a great lord in his own right but a still greater one in his capacity as guardian of the young Lord Ulrich of Rožmberk, the greatest feudatory in South Bohemia.[65] On 17 June 1417 Lord Čeněk, acting in this latter capacity, summoned the priests holding Rožmberk livings to a meeting at which they were offered the choice of either giving communion in both kinds or turning over their parishes to priests who would.[66] The threat was carried out in many cases, although not in all, and a similar policy was carried out on Čeněk's own domains, and no doubt elsewhere as well.[67] Archbishop Conrad himself

[64] Conrad's decree is published in John Cochlaeus, *Historiae Hussitarum Libri XII* (Mainz, 1549), p. 169. According to the *Libri confirmationum,* the sequence of Lord Čeněk of Vartemberk's officially recognized presentations (made either in his own right or as guardian of Ulrich of Rožmberk) begins on 12 January 1407 (VI, 197) and goes on right through 1415 and 1416, despite his position as head of the Hussite League. The last one is dated 28 December 1417, but since it comes right after one dated 18 December 1416 and is clearly in the 1416 sequence (VII, 214), I assume the date 1417 is an error. Čeněk does to be sure continue to figure in the *Libri* through 1417 and even into 1418, but not as making new presentations—only as consenting to exchanges ("permutations") of benefices (pp. 214, 215, 220, 227, 232, 255). Whether they had anything to do with Hussitism is not known—the practice of permutation itself was a standard one, and the *Libri* never tell why a given exchange was carried out.

[65] The guardianship was arranged on 14 August 1412, after the death of Lord Henry of Rožmberk on 28 July; it ended, probably, on 13 January 1418, when Ulrich became fifteen years old. For details see B. Rynešová, ed., *Listář a listinář Oldřicha z Rožmberka,* I (Prague, 1929), iii–iv.

[66] *OCA,* pp. 23 f.; *OCA-R,* p. 17. The priests who did not wish to give communion in both kinds were told that they would have "to exchange their parishes" with utraquist priests or, if unwilling to do this, they would be deprived of their parishes. If we take this at face value we would have to suppose that Čeněk did not intend in the first place to carry through a simple purge, but wherever possible to use the customary mechanism of permutations to obtain the vacancies he wanted. One case seems to show this policy in action: on 11 April 1415 Čeněk had presented one John to the parish in Velešín (*Lib. conf.,* VII, 150); on 20 July 1417, however, John appears (p. 235) as "olim cappellano in Welessin," to be presented to the parish of Drachov, vacant because its holder, one Příbik, had had to resign, "ex tenore sentencie diffinitive." Příbik was evidently a Hussite, John a Catholic. In fact, according to *OCA,* pp. 23 f., Čeněk installed Sova in Velešín as part of the turnover of 17 June—no doubt at the expense of John.

[67] For Čeněk's domains see the *Chronicon Procopii,* Höfler, I, 71 f. The more general range of the new policy, as one of the Hussite League, is suggested by a fortunately preserved pact of three petty noblemen, in 1417, to defend the chalice and their own utraquist priests against both ecclesiastical and secular authorities (cited by Bartoš, *Do čtyř art.,* p. 18, n. 62).

wrote a vigorous protest to Čeněk,[68] while Emperor Sigismund, writing to the Bohemian nobility on 4 September 1417, complained that in spite of promises from the king and certain barons that the injuries to the clergy in Bohemia would cease, the situation had in fact become worse:

> Again scandals even more cruel have ensued, and now depredations more serious than before are committed against the clergy everywhere in the realm. Incomes are taken away; the divine services are profaned, and the obedient clergy are compelled to profane them; those who have been excommunicated and interdicted are tolerated and protected in contempt of the keys of the church; rectors of parish churches and other beneficed clergy are disgracefully expelled from their benefices by the power and ferocity of laymen. Indeed some of these clergymen have been hurt and are imprisoned by laymen; they are cruelly tortured and payments are forced out of them. Horrible to say, moreover, Catholic preachers and also certain masters preaching and teaching the Catholic faith are forced by tortures, torments, and Neronic persecution to abjure the Catholic faith that they have preached and taught. Further, frivolous declarations, against the determination and decrees of the holy mother church and of this holy council, especially in the matter of communion in both kinds, are rashly promulgated, and some Catholics are frequently forced by the secular arm to take such communion in both kinds.[69]

In tone quite similar to several complaints of the previous two years, this one is more particular in its references to the university's declaration for utraquism, the forced recantation of Peter of Uničov, and such "scandals even more cruel" as the Rožmberk turnover of 17 June. Inevitably, as the Hussites themselves must have foreseen, the measures necessary to safeguard their cause produced even more of the Catholic outrage that had made those measures necessary in the first place.

The matter is complicated by another line of action pursued by the Hussite nobility in the same period. Still in close collaboration with the university— whose rector from 23 April was the nobleman Master Zdislav of Zvířetice[70] —the barons decided to send the Council of Constance a dossier of "authorities" in behalf of utraquism. The decision was made at the Diet of June 1417,[71] so it was probably not part of the program of action agreed on at the

---

[68] The text is published by Bartoš, *JSH*, XVIII (1949), 93; I interpret it as a simple protest against the violation of the archbishop's anti-utraquist decree of 10 January 1417, not as a reference to a new, synodal prohibition of the chalice after the Rožmberk turnover.

[69] *Documenta*, pp. 659–663.

[70] Bartoš has called attention to the significance of this fact: "Hus jako student a profesor Karlovy University," *Acta Universitatis Carolinae, Phil.-hist.*, II (1958), 20–22.

[71] The most detailed account is in J. Prokeš, *M. Prokop z Plzně* (Prague, 1927), p. 31 ff.; for the dossier see Hardt, III, 805–827.

beginning of the year; if it had been, the dossier would no doubt have been
sent soon after the university's utraquist declaration of 10 March. Perhaps it
was an attempt to forestall some decisive intervention by the Council and
Sigismund, with whom King Wenceslas had arranged a meeting in May,[72]
or perhaps it was a concession to those barons who were uncomfortable at
the thought that they had embraced a definitely condemned doctrine. In any
case the authorities, collected from earlier works chiefly by Jakoubek,[73] were
very quickly refuted, most notably by Jean Gerson writing *raptim* on 20
August and calling for an end to words and a beginning to armed anti-
utraquist action;[74] his short treatise was eventually answered by Jakoubek,
again at the request of the Hussite nobility, on 2 December 1417.[75] The
exchange thus produced a delay of sorts, and perhaps this was what the
Hussites wanted, but otherwise the episode bore no fruit. In fact, in the
summer or autumn of 1417, the Council took a step that the university's
official utraquism had made inevitable: it formally suspended the university
in all of its functions.[76] But the new exchange of treatises on utraquism does
serve to show more clearly what would otherwise have to be inferred as a
hypothesis: at a time when the most important developments within the
Hussite movement were connected with doctrinal explorations and controversies on the left, the pan-Hussite program agreed on by the university and

---

[72] *Do čtyř art.*, p. 16 f. The meeting did not take place.

[73] Bartoš, *loc. cit.*, accepts the testimony of one manuscript of the dossier, attributing
it to John Jesenic. Kejř, "O některých spisech M. Jana z Jesenice," *LF*, LXXXVI (1963),
86 f., adds another MS. testimony and regards the question as solved. The material,
however, goes back chiefly to the works of Jakoubek and Nicholas of Dresden, and it
seems unlikely that Jesenic, who was originally an anti-utraquist, could have had much
to do with it, except as a politician working with the nobility to arrange things; hence
his name was associated with the work not as compiler but as expediter—this is the
sense of the MS. attribution quoted by Bartoš and again by Kejř.

[74] Hardt, III, 765–780.

[75] *LČJ*, No. 47; the treatise begins (MS D 51, fol. 167ʳ): "Quamvis quidam magnifici
et nobiles cristianissimi regni Boemie et marchionatus Moravie, magnates, barones,
nobiles, et proceres pro lege divina devotissime et ferventer zelantes, tot sanctarum
scripturarum solidissima fulcimenta et sanctorum doctorum ac Romanorum pontificum
plurima et preclara decreta et documenta pro materia venerabilis sacramenti eukaristie
sub utraque specie panis et vini fideli populo laicali ministranda, transmiserint et
porrexerint Concilio Constanciensi: Attamen . . . surrepsit Irregularis scriptor [*scil.*,
Jean Gerson]. . . ." And Jakoubek writes: "Ad premissorum dominorum, magnatum,
baronum, et nobilium monicionem specialem . . . presentibus compendiose duxi respondendum. . . ."

[76] Most scholars date the suspension much earlier, at the end of 1416 or in January
1417, but Kejř's argument for the later dating ("Deklarace," pp. 152–154) seems
perfectly cogent. Bartoš, *HR*, I, 32, n. 41, argues that the Council considered but
did not finally decree the suspension.

the barons deliberately focused on one issue, that of the lay chalice. By emphasizing the chalice and forcing its acceptance wherever possible, in utter defiance of the Catholic authorities, the political leaders of Hussitism could avert their eyes from the radicalism that their official statements of January and February had condemned but had not liquidated.

The way in which this strange but not unrealistic policy worked appears most strikingly in the Rožmberk turnover, engineered by Čeněk as a purely utraquist action.[77] Sometime in the second half of 1417 an anonymous Catholic priest, quite possibly one expelled from a Rožmberk parish—he was very well informed about the turnover and other South Bohemian matters— composed a set of Latin "Sermones ad Bohemos," [78] including one addressed to Lord Čeněk, whom he apostrophized thus:

Nobilis domine Čenko	Noble Lord Čeněk,
tua prudentia en quo	behold your prudence
ad praesens evanuit,	is now vanished,
quod rumoribus frivolis	for to frivolous reports
et hominibus malivolis	and to malevolent men
tam subito annuit	it has so suddenly consented.

He then named the malevolent men: the first of them was Olešák, a turbulent drifter, who went about in villages and towns leading this group with him—Vácha, Koranda, Mníšek, Jaroslav of Laziště, Nicholas of Ujezdec, Ambrose, Pater, Rohlík, Sigismund of Chotišan, Čapek, Franěk, Petriolus, Abraham, Lupus, and Otík. These men "wounded the souls of the poor and defrauded the people"; addressing Čeněk, the author wrote, "they are the apostles of your law for they hope to be exalted by you," and, "you have been elected captain, . . . and in a pagan manner you practice tyranny, your satellites agreeing with you and praising you; you expel the legitimate parish priests and replace them with profane ones, who dispense

---

[77] The chalice was the only point at issue, according to *OCA*, p. 23 f.

[78] The text is printed in *Documenta*, pp. 687–698, with the suggested date of 1418. The *terminus a quo* would be 17 June 1417, the date of the Rožmberk turnover, which is referred to (p. 695). The *terminus ante quem* can be fixed in two ways: (1) The verses refer to the imminent end of Čeněk's term as guardian of Ulrich of Rožmberk, whose fifteenth birthday we know came on 13 January 1418. (2) The verses refer only to the Council of Constance, in a context where they would also have mentioned the pope if there had been one (p. 691); Martin V was elected on 11 November 1417, and the news certainly reached Bohemia before the end of the year. It is only recently that these verses have been given due attention: R. Urbánek, "Mařík Rvačka jako protihusitský satirik," *ČSPSČ*, LXIII (1955), 1–23; F. M. Bartoš, "Z politické literatury doby husitské. 1. Protihusitský veršovec Jakub Trch," *SbH*, V (1957), 23–25. Trch seems a likelier author than Rvačka but until more arguments are in, the verses are best regarded as anonymous.

the Blood and thus profane what is holy." The author named two of the expelled priests, Vojslav of Miličín and Master Wenceslas Višně, and added that there were "very many others." Since an independent source, in the "Old Czech Annalists," says that Master Višně was in fact replaced by Mníšek,[79] we can hardly resist tying all of the anonymous author's data together by inferring that not only Mníšek but the others in Olešák's group were obtruded into the vacated Rožmberk parishes. Furthermore, since Čapek had probably been among those ordained at Lipnic; since in addition to him we can identify Koranda, Abraham, Lupus ("Vlk" in Czech), Pater, and Rohlík as future priests of Tabor; and—finally—since we know that most of the priests of Tabor had been ordained at Lipnic: we can infer that many of the priests newly ordained at Lipnic were taken under Čeněk's patronage and installed in various South Bohemian parishes on the Rožmberk domains.[80] No doubt there were more than the anonymous author named, and certainly some of the ones he did name had been priests long before the Lipnic episode—some of Olešák's group had no doubt, like Mníšek, been turned out of their parishes by the Catholic reaction;[81] but

[79] *OCA,* p. 23 f.

[80] See above, n. 63, for the Taborite connection, and n. 62 for Čapek. Koranda is well enough known not to require further identification; we do not, however, know when he was ordained. As for Abraham, see *OCA-R,* p. 27, *OCA,* p. 476; it would be tempting to add the texts in *Documenta,* pp. 184 f., 342 f. (cf. *FRB,* V, 569), which tell of a judicial process in 1408 against a Prague priest Nicholas, called Abraham, who held that preaching was permitted even to laymen, and who refused to swear an oath on the Gospel (but he would swear by the living God)—however, apart from the name there is no reason to think that this was the Abraham of 1417. More likely would be an identification with the Taborite priest Abraham mentioned as suspect of Pikartism, in Laurence, p. 495. For Lupus or Vlk, see *OCA-R,* p. 27, also Příbram's "Život kněží táborských," *KJBB,* p. 263. For Rohlík see *OCA-R,* p. 27, *OCA,* p. 479. Pater was probably the Taborite priest and military leader Frederick of Stražnice, who is called "páter němý" by Příbram, *loc. cit.;* he also appears frequently in other sources.

[81] Nicholas Mníšek had had a parish, from which he was ejected by the episcopal authorities sometime before 2 April 1417 (*Libri confirmationum,* VII, 223). He was evidently a man of high qualifications; manuscripts of liturgical, homiletical, and devotional works were written out by him, in one case, as he tells us, during his time of troubles between benefices (J. Truhlář, *Catalogus codicum manuscriptorum . . . in . . . Bibliotheca . . . universitatis Pragensis,* 2 vols. (Prague, 1905–1906), Nos. 1155, 1156, 1396). Jaroslav of Lazištĕ had been a priest of that parish since 1405, and had held another parish before that (*Libri confirmationum,* VI, 132, 141); on 2 August 1415 he appeared together with Nicholas of Hus and the latter's two stepsons as exercising a right of presentation (*Lib. conf.,* VII, 167)—perhaps he had a family connection with the future Taborite military leader (cf. *ibid.,* p. 177; also Nov. II, 186, n. 2). In 1416, as we have already seen, Jaroslav was active in radical anti-Romanist violence around Písek —perhaps it was at that time that he lost his own parish, although the *Lib. conf.* are silent on the matter. Sigismund of Chotišan resigned the parish there some time before

allowing for the suggestive rather than the definitive character of the author's data, we can form a reasonably clear idea of what was going on.

At the same time we cannot help observing the significance of the fact that Čeněk was extending his patronage not only to ordinary Hussites but to a number of highly radical ones. Jaroslav of Lazištĕ had been active in the Písek violence of 1416; Koranda's heretical extremism, as described in Christian of Prachatice's letter to him, had undoubtedly helped to provoke the antiradical declarations of January and February; no less than six out of the sixteen named would become priests of Tabor, and this is a conservative figure.[82] The Lord Čeněk of Vartemberk who in January had bitterly inveighed against the extremists was now in June the chief architect of their good fortune—to use the vocabulary of the anonymous author, his prudence had vanished, for it had suddenly consented to malevolent men. A more objective way to put it would be this: having decided that the only way to respond to the double challenge of Catholic reaction and intra-Hussite dissension was to create a national pan-Hussite establishment, the political leaders of the Hussite party could not avoid accepting the radicals and working with them; no doubt the leaders hoped that a regularization of the radicals' conditions of life would moderate their ideas enough that they could fit into the structure of formal Hussite unity, a unity based above all on the lay chalice and the cult of Hus. There were risks in this calculation but also advantages, for the new establishment, based on a newly strengthened and more militant alliance with the Hussite feudality, gave the movement as much protection as possible from the Council of Constance, from the

September 1414 (*Lib. conf.*, VII, 131), but nothing more is known about him. Olešák was probably the Paul of Oleš who became a Master of Arts in 1410 and took part in Hus's Quodlibet in 1411 (see B. Ryba, ed., *Magistri Iohannis Hus Quodlibet* (Prague, 1948), p. 207). An anti-Hussite parody of the first chapter of the Book of Matthew links several Hussite leaders in a chain of "begats"; in the second version, dating probably in 1415–1416, Olešák appears along with Čapek and Koranda, as well as a whole series of university masters and two of King Wenceslas's Hussite councillors, John Sádlo and Peter Zmrzlík (see the text in Nejedlý, III, 369–374, where the date 1419 is suggested; the names, however, are all of people who were prominent in Hussite action in 1415–1416—by 1419 there were other names, which would not have been omitted).

[82] Thus Petriolus may have been either the Peter the Tall or the Peter of Ústí who were members of the proto-Taborite group at Ústí-nad-Lužnicí in 1418–1419 (see above, chap. iv, n. 78)—more likely the second than the first, to judge from the names. And Vácha may have been the Vanček mentioned by Laurence of Březová, pp. 357 f., as a founder of Tabor (and/or the Vĕnĕk mentioned as a radical in *OCA*, pp. 471 f.). Otík may have been the renegade monk who became a parish priest, according to the anti-Hussite verses, "Vlka poznáš po srsti," ed. V. Nebeský, *ČČM*, XXVI (1852), ii, 76. Ambrose may have been the same as the later well-known leader of the pro-Taborite radical Hussites in Hradec Králové.

Bohemian hierarchy, and from King Wenceslas's disturbing flirtation with plans for Catholic restoration. As for the risks, the politicians' wisdom had surely not deserted them when they decided to sacrifice ideological purity in favor of normalizing the actual conditions under which the reform was pursued. The anti-radical declarations of the university still stood, as a public position and a guide to the more conservative elements; they no doubt served what a contemporary said was their purpose, to attract conservatives to the chalice,[83] but no one took them literally as a condition of Hussite unity. Although directed against much that Jakoubek and his party believed, their main target was not university radicalism but subversive Waldensianism, and the masters did not need the insights of modern religious sociology to teach them that the best way to dissolve a sect was to integrate it into a church.

But this would take time. Meanwhile, one result of the new establishment was that the Hussite party as a whole now included a large component of radicalism as an integral part of the united movement. Earlier anti-Hussite polemicists had almost routinely sought to discredit their enemy by inventing, exaggerating, or extrapolating various excesses,[84] but from mid-1417 on the whole movement could be readily attacked simply by listing the more or less extreme radical doctrines and practices of the left wing. During this period Abbot Stephen of Dolany, in Moravia, wrote his *Epistolae ad Hussitas*—completed in October 1417[85]—in order to convince Master Simon of Tišnov and no doubt other conservative masters of the heretical, subversive, and scandalous character of their movement. Always addressing himself to the masters, he painted the picture of outrage in relentless detail: there was preaching by unauthorized, uneducated men and even women;[86] the vestments, holy vessels, and rituals of the church were being rejected;[87] images were being smashed, profaned, and their cult denied;[88] masses were being said in Czech;[89] the Eucharist was being given in barns and to children;[90]

---

[83] *Invectiva contra Husitas*, Höfler, I, 626; this work, written in 1432, may have been composed by the same man who wrote the *Sermones ad Bohemos*—see Bartoš, "Jakub Trch," *SbH*, V (1957), 29.

[84] See, e.g., above, chap. iii, *ad* nn. 89, 119.

[85] According to the *explicit*—see the edition by B. Pez, *Thesaurus anecdotorum novissimus*, IV, ii (Augsburg, 1723). The allocution to Simon of Tišnov is on col. 515 f.

[86] *Ibid.*, col. 518 f.

[87] Col. 552.

[88] Col. 539 ff. The whole of Part Three is devoted to Hussite iconoclasm, which Stephen says was of recent origin: "pro hac re, quam recenter confingitis. . . ." (539).

[89] Coll. 556, 590.

[90] B. Pez, *Thesaurus anecdotorum novissimus*, col. 580 (for the use of barns). It is odd that Stephen does not refer to *infant* communion but only to communion taken by *pueri* (coll. 509, 656, 668), whom he once calls *pueri septennes* (col. 576).

all clerical possessions were under attack as illegitimate.[91] At the same time he attacked the Hussites' campaign against the regular clergy,[92] their utraquism,[93] their attachment to the memory of John Hus,[94] and—at great length —their collaboration with the secular powers to enforce their doctrines and expel or persecute the Catholic clergy.[95] Thus he put both radical and standard Hussite points into a single package of heresy, to be left at the door of the university: "You masters—not the king, not the nobles, not the common people, but you yourselves are the cause and occasion of this infamy." [96] We do not know how effective his work was—Simon of Tišnov did in fact return to the Roman church but the Hussite Master Sigismund of Jistebnice, who borrowed the treatise and kept it for three months, in 1418, did not; [97] but we cannot mistake the justice of his indictment according to his own terms.

Nor was he the only one to trace the anatomy of the newly integrated Hussite monster. At about the time that he was writing, an anonymous literary man, perhaps the same one who wrote the *Sermones ad Bohemos,* put together a long rhymed polemic in Czech, "Listen All of You, Old and Young," which drew up an even more damning bill of particulars.[98] The

[91] *Ibid.,* col. 569.

[92] Coll. 517, 557 ff.

[93] The whole of Part Five deals with this: utraquism was preached as *necessary* to salvation (e.g., col. 576), and daily communion was forced upon the people (coll. 556, 699).

[94] Col. 520 f.

[95] B. Pez, *Thesaurus anecdotorum novissimus,* coll. 642 (". . . excitatis et quotidie excitatis potentes saeculi, quorum gaudetis patrocinio, in catholicos Dei"); 517 ("Wikleffistae . . . aliena beneficia, expulsis legitimis possessoribus . . . , invasa . . . , Saecularis tuitionis fiducia possederunt injuriose, et damnabiliter possident hactenus"); 570 f.; 596 ("publice praedicastis et odiosissime affirmastis, quod Dominus Rex Wenceslaus, qui nequaquam vestras inanes et falsas exhortationes sequitur, si nullam aliam occasionem suae perditionis haberet, hoc solum sufficeret . . . , quod possessiones Ecclesiasticas non auferat Clero circum circa."); 670 ("has [*scil.,* prebends, parishes] non solum per fas juxta ritum ecclesiae libenter acquiritis; sed etiam per nefas istis diebus vestris statim sub manu potentium, expulsis legitimis rectoribus, diripitis praebendas et parochiales ecclesias, et damnabiliter possidetis."). The last of these passages certainly seems to reflect a new situation created by the Hussite offensive of the first half of 1417.

[96] *Ibid.,* col. 590.

[97] The information was written on the manuscript and is given in Pez's edition; cf. O. Odložilík, "Z počátků husitství na Moravě," *ČMM,* XLIX (1925), 64, for Sigismund's involvement in Moravian Hussitism.

[98] The poem, "Slyšte všickni staří i vy děti," has been published by V. Nebeský, "Verše na Husity," *ČČM,* XXVI (1852), i, 141–151; there is a new and better edition by F. Svejkovský, *Veršované skladby doby husitské* (Prague, 1963), pp. 102–115. For discussion see Pekař, I, 216; Urbánek, "Mařík Rvačka," pp. 10–15; Bartoš, "Jakub Trch," p. 25 f.

ideas and policies of the leading masters are bitterly attacked—their alliance
with the barons, secularization of church property, the cult of Hus, utraquism, the treatment of Peter of Uničov, the Lipnic ordinations, and so
forth.[99] But there are also extensive passages on the same radical points the
conservative masters themselves had attacked: rejection of the post-Biblical
institutes of the saints, the rejection of the cult of images and of the saints,
the rejection of various church blessings, holidays, and fasts, and the rejection
of prayers and offerings for the dead.[100] And the author also deals with other
points, some of which have already become familiar to us: the Hussites
opposed offerings to the priests on the occasion of receiving the sacraments;
they were opposed to pilgrimages, to bell-ringing, to lofty church buildings—
they said mass in barns and in fields; there was preaching by laymen and
women; they rejected the churching of women, the lighting of candles,
auricular confession, the hierarchy of bishops; they baptized in ordinary
water.[101] And, according to the author, these outrages were carried through
with open violence: "You go to preach with swords and gauntlets, urging
the people on to hack away with axes, knives, pikes, spears, and clubs"; [102]
the Hussites say that "He who will not hold with us must suffer in his goods
and his body," [103] and their slogan is "Stand up for God's Law and strike,
and him who will not hold with you, kill!" [104] One does not have to believe
all of this in order to accept some of it; we have already encountered radical
Hussite violence at Písek in 1416, and similar charges had been made by
others, including Peter of Uničov. If we make allowance for venom, mendacity, and irresponsible poetic license, not too much in this polemic falls
outside the range of Jakoubek's radicalism, and the same may be said for
Stephen of Dolany's work. It may even be significant that neither one
accuses the Hussites of rejecting Purgatory—only works for the dead, which
Jakoubek too wished to curtail in terms about as drastic as those appearing in
the polemical rhymes.[105] The Hussites who smashed images and the Hussites

---

[99] Lines 9 ff.; 363 f.; 395 ff.; 94 ff.; 185 ff.; 421 ff.

[100] Rejection of institutions of the saints, line 141 f.; of images, 259 ff.; of blessings,
276 ff.; of prayers for the dead, 283 ff.

[101] Rejection of offerings, lines 254 ff.; of pilgrimages, 266 f.; of bells, 268 f.; of church
buildings, 269. Mass in barns and fields, 272 f.; lay preaching, 373 ff.; rejection of
churching of women, 275; of candles, 274; of auricular confession, 303 f.; of the
hierarchy, 72. Baptism in ordinary water, 313 f.

[102] Lines 335–338.

[103] "Slyšte všickni staří i vy děti," line 26 f.

[104] Lines 355 f.

[105] *De purgatorio*, ed. Walch, *Monimenta medii aevi*, III, p. 19: "Postremo hoc
ponimus et protestamur, quod nullum ritum, nullam consuetudinem ex pompa plebis,
vel avaritia sacerdotum ortam volumus relevare aut quovis modo approbare, sed omnem

who worked with the barons were of two very different varieties, but as a result of the events of the first half of 1417, both could be classed together in the polemics of the second half.

THE UNION OF HUSSITE PARTIES

If this reconstruction is correct we will expect to find the realities of the new situation—the pan-Hussite establishment—reflected in some new ideological development allowing in principle for the coexistence of conservatives and radicals. Since no formula could fully satisfy both parties, we will expect also to find evidence of intra-Hussite polemics. Unfortunately, given the tendency of the university masters to focus on points of doctrine rather than practice, the debates within their ranks perhaps inevitably turned on what to us seems a secondary issue, that of infant communion. Lord Čeněk opposed it, and perhaps at his orders his chaplain, Peter Cendát, wrote a remarkably cogent treatise against it, in fact against Master Jakoubek.[106] Within the ranks of the masters John Jesenic and Simon of Tišnov also distinguished themselves as opponents of Jakoubek, who was kept busy as probably the only theoretician defending the novelty.[107] He even had his authorities painted on the walls of Bethlehem Chapel, where they joined other texts put

---

simoniam, avaritiam et pompam circa exequias mortuorum, sicut et alias deordinaciones intendimus detestari, reprobare et usque ad mortem contra talia agonizare." See also the passages from Jakoubek's postil of *ca.* 1414, in Nejedlý, IV, 122 f. Cf. Hus's vigorous passages, above, chap. iv, *ad* nn. 219, 221.

[106] Bartoš has drawn attention to it and suggested the date of 1417 ("Roztržka v husitské straně r. 1417," *Do čtyř art.*, p. 69); the treatise survives in MS IV H 17, fols. 192ʳ-204ᵛ. On fol. 202ʳ there is a reference to "quidam parvulorum communicator" who has written a tractate beginning "Notare necesse est de communione parvulorum post baptismum"; this is in fact the *incipit* of Jakoubek's section on infant communion in his *De quibusdam punctis* (*LČJ*, No. 70), MS VIII E 7, fol. 106ʳ. In passing, it may be observed that although the latter work survives in only one text, Jakoubek's autograph, which apart from all other considerations is written in so hideous a hand that it could not have been intended for circulation, Peter's refutation shows that part or all of Jakoubek's *responsum* was in fact circulated—a healthy reminder that the surviving sources are only a fraction of what once existed.

[107] See *LČJ*, Nos. 71, 72, 74, for the works of Jesenic and Simon and Jakoubek's replies; also Nos. 70, 73, 73a, 75, 76. For the significance of the controversy in general as causing a split among the university Hussites, see Laurence of Březová, pp. 334 f.: the extension of communion to infants, in confirmation of their baptism, was promulgated and practiced by "Magistro Jacobello de Misa . . . cum sibi aliquibus adherentibus magistris et sacerdotibus": "propter quam quidem infancium communionem scisma grave inter magistros et sacerdotes veritati dei et Magistro Johanni Hus adherentes in Praga et in regno Bohemie est exortum."

there by himself and by Hus.[108] Insofar as the doctrine and practice were logical extensions of the radical idea of utraquism as necessary to salvation, the controversy had an obvious significance, for the more conservative masters shrank from that extreme position. Moreover, a certain importance should be assigned to the fact that infant communion fitted in with the process of constructing a Hussite church, for by giving the Eucharist to infants along with baptism, the radicals were establishing that church on the same foundation as that of the Christian church itself—new members were henceforth born into it. In fact, as Peter Cendát pointed out, many of the texts that Jakoubek used to justify the association of the two sacraments went back to the time when the Christian church was recruited in part from the conversion of adults.[109] However, these considerations formed only part of what was obviously an enormous investment of emotion in infant communion, which continued to be a hotly disputed issue into 1419. Like the lay chalice itself, it stood for many things that were only accidentally related to it.

Over on the left, of course, the main issues were those created by the "Waldensian" doctrines—most characteristically the rejection of Purgatory, oaths, and killing, but also the absolute rejection of certain things, like images, ceremonies, cults, that Jakoubek's doctrine rejected in a more qualified way. Here the ideological struggle had already been fought out, between Jakoubek and Nicholas of Dresden, but there is much evidence that sectarian ideas continued to be cultivated within radical ranks. We know, for example, that after Nicholas's pupil, Bartholomew Rautenstock, was ordained at Lipnic, he was assigned to St. Mary's of the Lake in Prague, where he preached and otherwise ministered to a congregation of probably German Hussites.[110] But when he fell into the hands of the Inquisition in Germany some years later, he confessed to not believing in Purgatory, and such must

---

[108] *LČJ*, No. 76; the text, along with the others on the Bethlehem walls, has been edited from MSS by B. Ryba, *Betlemské texty* (Prague, 1951), pp. 141–162. Fragments of the wall-text were found in the excavation of the site in 1949.

[109] MS IV H 17, fol. 194ᵛ: ". . . claret quod primitiva ecclesia sacramentum baptismi non conferebat infantulis sed adultis." It is probably significant that in his tractate Peter Cendát did not even raise the question of whether the Primitive Church should be taken as a model—he soberly drew attention to the discrepancy just noted about baptism, and took for granted his main principle (fol. 204ʳ), "sacramenta ecclesiastica sunt percipienda secundum ritum et ordinem sancti matris ecclesie." Cf. also fol. 204ᵛ: "Si igitur volunt salvari, teneant unitatem et ritum forme tradite sacrosancte matris ecclesie." On 25 January 1417 the masters also invoked this authority—the radicals were urged to believe in accordance "cum sancta matre ecclesia" (*Documenta*, p. 655), a formula that vanished in the redaction of 7 February, which took account of Jakoubek's views.

[110] Döllinger, *Beiträge zur Sektengeschichte des Mittelalters*, II (Munich, 1890) 628 f.

have been his doctrine even at St. Mary's. Nor is it easy to imagine Wenceslas Koranda changing his mind on this matter between the time when Christian of Prachatice wrote him in January or February and the time when Čeněk got a parish for him in mid-June, or even after that time. In fact, various works datable in about 1418 show the existence of Hussites who embraced the full corpus of Waldensianist radicalism as we have seen it in the works of Nicholas of Dresden,[111] as well as some—and here the evidence is rather fragmentary—who adhered to views probably derived from actual popular heresy, of the Waldensian or Free Spirit type.[112]

It should also be noted in this connection that Prague Hussitism continued to be well supplied with pious females of the sort that had been so prominent in the religious movement of the previous century. These Beguines or *Begutae,* as the hostile sources call them,[113] seem to have played the same role that they did elsewhere in Europe, that of providing a hothouse in which the ideals of evangelical piety, nourished by female emotion, could flower into the most luxuriant forms of heretical extremism. When Master John of Jičín led the procession that carried the bodies of the three anti-indulgence martyrs of 1412 into Bethlehem Chapel, he was assisted by such pious women, one of whom wrapped the bodies in white cloths. Later on, in 1419–1420, when John of Jičín had become a Taborite chiliast prophet, he and his fellows remained in contact with the Beguines in Prague.[114] If we attach value to the admittedly late source that associates him with the Dresden masters,[115] we can imagine this most radical of all the masters sharing the Dresden doc-

---

[111] See the detailed discussion in *OC & N,* Introduction, *ad* nn. 146 (a *confessio heretica,* MS 4314, fols. 134ᵛ–135ʳ, MS XII F 30, fols. 40ᵛ–41ᵛ), 149 (the *Collecta et excerpta* used above in chap. i).

[112] See just below.

[113] There are several passages in Stephen of Dolany, *Epistolae ad Hussitas,* in B. Pez, *Thesaurus anecdotorum novissimus,* col. 533 f. ("Begutae vestrae"); 537 (a "Beguta" has written a Hussite work in Czech (cf. 520 f.)); 556 ("et adhuc nova et inaudita Ribaldia Missas in Boëmico Sermone cantatis et legitis juvantibus vos concantare Begutis et Rebeccis mulieribus"). Andrew of Brod, *Tractatus,* Höfler, II, 345, also refers to the "begutas et beghardos" seduced by utraquist propaganda. A malicious anti-Hussite song, "Stala se jest příhoda," tells of a Wyclifite woman who undertakes to teach her faith to a young man; he slips into her room, where she reveals two pear-shaped chapters of the Bible to him, and so on,—after which they sing *Te deum laudamus*—well, the song goes on: "You young men . . . who want to learn God's law, you should ask the Beguines ("máte sě k Bekyněm ptáti") and learn it from them" (ed. J. Feifalik, "Altčechische Leiche . . . ," *SKAW,* XXXIX (1862), 669–671; there is another song against the Hussite Beguines on pp. 671 f.). For the Beguine element in the Bohemian religious movement see above, chap. i.

[114] For the 1412 episode see Nov., II, 117 f.; for 1419–20 see Appendix 3, p. 540.

[115] *OCA,* p. 472 (see above, chap. iii, n. 28).

trines, working closely with like-minded Beguines, and thus developing an environment extremely hospitable to whatever vagrant germs of sectarian heresy were drifting about in Prague.

Nor was this left-wing activity confined to Prague. It was probably in 1418 that John of Jičín and other future Taborites formed a nest of extreme radicalism in South Bohemian Ústí-nad-Lužnicí, a town that thenceforward had to suffer the penalties of incessant religious controversy and actual fighting between right and left.[116] All of these data and conjectures are enough to suggest if not to prove that what has here been called the Hussite left was in fact a mosaic of the most diverse points of view.

Some of these points of view were quite extreme, going beyond Waldensianism; while their importance does not appear until the end of 1419, at which point they will be discussed below, it is worth bearing in mind that they did exist on the Hussite left from an early time.[117] In 1416 Jakoubek of Stříbro felt it necessary to refute those who held to the dietary restrictions of the Jewish Law, most notably in matters of ritual slaughter; the same error was refuted by John Příbram at least twice, possibly in 1418 or 1419, and certainly at the end of 1420. The idea itself was associated with the heresy of the Passagini, as early as the twelfth century, along with other, more clearly "evangelical" points not unlike those destined to become characteristic of German Waldensianism; how the Hussites had adopted it is unclear. Perhaps the German heretics around Jindřichův Hradec had passed it on. Then, in 1418, a number of probably Free-spirit Beghards (the "Picardi") came to Prague from northern France or Belgium; they distinguished themselves by their denial of a real presence in the Eucharist, although that was not their only error, and they passed their ideas on to the Czechs; John Želivský's sermons of 1419 are a prime source for the continued presence of "Pikart" heresy on the left. Other aspects of it are also attested in 1418: in a sermon preached on 16 October of that year, Jakoubek attacked "those who say

---

[116] *OCA*, pp. 471 f.; see above, chap. iv, n. 78.

[117] Detailed documentation will be offered at the appropriate points in subsequent chapters. Meanwhile some brief references can serve. Jakoubek's *De suffocatis* is listed in *LČJ*, No. 65; for Příbram's works see *LČP*, Nos. 5, 7, and cf. my "O traktátu Ad occurrendum homini insano," *ČsČH*, VIII (1960), 895–904. For the Passagini see *The Summa contra haereticos Ascribed to Praepositinus of Cremona*, edd. J. Garvin and J. Corbett (Notre Dame, Indiana, 1958), pp. xv, 143 ff. The *Picardi* of 1418 are mentioned in Laurence, p. 431; for references to the denial of a real presence see Želivský's sermons (*Dochovaná kázání z roku 1419*, I, ed. A. Molnár (Prague, 1953)), pp. 103, 127, 167 f., 173; also, MS V G 3, fol. 159ᵛ: "nunc multi dicunt, non est ibi corpus Cristi sed solum panis. Ecce maiores heretici!" Jakoubek's sermon of 16 October 1418 survives in MS 4937; for the relevant passage see below, chap. ix, n. 60. For Příbram's attack on the same ideas, see my article just cited.

that children are not to be baptized, because Christ's command, 'Unless you are reborn, etc.,' was spoken to the old man Nicodemus." John Příbram attacked the same complex of heresies in one of his treatises whose date is however unclear. Was this just another fruit of the Free Spirit plant already rooted in South Bohemia? Or was it all part of what the "Picardi" of 1418 had brought from the West? We do not know. Later, when political and social circumstances were favorable, the whole Free Spirit corpus would rise to actual dominance among the Taborites; meanwhile, in 1418, the heresies in question seem to have been much less important than the Waldensianist views that had emerged in 1415 and had come to pose a critical challenge to the national leadership.

Since religious beliefs are not verifiable propositions about facts they are usually very stubborn; they change, if at all, only when there is a change in the basic way of thinking and feeling of the people who hold them. In the second half of 1417 and through most of 1418 there were no great changes in the mode of existence of the various groups of Hussites and hence no reason for significant changes in their mode of thought; we thus have no reason to think that doctrinal disagreements on the Hussite left ceased to exist. Nevertheless we can conjecture that the normalization effected by the Hussites may have had a moderating influence on at least the expression of disagreement, to the point where a sort of formal unity became possible. The center of gravity of such a formal consensus would naturally rest in the doctrines of Jakoubek of Stříbro, midway as these were between the conservatives and the extremists, and sharing important traits of both. Here it is essential to understand that during this period Jakoubek was probably not at odds with those extreme radicals who would later become his opponents, as priests of Tabor or otherwise. A classic case would be that of John Čapek, whom we have seen in 1416 translating the mass into Czech with Jakoubek's approval, an approval that was deliberately repeated at the end of 1417.[118] Also, in 1417 Čapek wrote a Czech "Book on the Lord's Supper" that covered many of the points Jakoubek had made in his *De ceremoniis* about the possibility of a simplified ritual in certain cases—but Čapek followed Jakoubek in noting that the standard rite ought to be followed normally.[119] Still in 1417 he wrote

[118] In Jakoubek's reply to Jean Gerson; see above, chap. iii, n. 94, and see the next note.

[119] The "Knížky o večeři Páně," in which the meaning of the mass and of communion is explained to the laity, was attributed by Bartoš to Jakoubek (*LČJ*, No. 48), chiefly because the viewpoints and motifs of the work are identical with his. Recently, however, Bartoš has observed that in 1429 Master John Příbram quoted from this work and said it had been written by John Čapek, who in turn acknowledged his authorship —thus the "Knížky" must be attributed to Čapek ("Z politické literatury doby husitské. 2. Kněz Jan Čapek," *SbH*, V (1957), 32 f.). In the present context the beginning of the

a didactic Czech song, "Let Us Begin in the Name of the Lord," in which he again outlined a corpus of doctrines very like Jakoubek's in both their radicalism and their nonsectarian limitations: for example, he strongly criticized the cult of saints and of images, but did not deny the sanctity of the former or demand the abolition of the latter, and he even allowed for the authority of pope and bishop if these gave commands in accord with God's law.[120] Yet in the second half of 1417 Čapek was probably in South Bohemia, on his way to becoming a Taborite. John Želivský would be another such case; his sermons between 1416 and 1419 are very radical, but almost precisely in conformity with Jakoubek's views, even to a criticism of extremists who rejected all church fasts, and to the typically Jacobellan formula of prudence: "There are often truths that are of grave concern to many, and these truths should first be discussed in secret conferences."[121] However, in 1419 Želivský emerged as the fiercely militant leader of those Prague radicals who refused to follow the university masters, including Jakoubek, in bending under the pressure of royal reaction, and although he did not adhere to the Taborite faith in its integrity, he was Tabor's strongest ally in Prague.[122]

---

work is of considerable interest: "This book is written for the information and encouragement of the people in the year 1417, when communion of God's body and blood in both kinds has been flourishing in Bohemia among the laity—among virgins, widows, and pious wives, [and among the laity] of both sexes" (ed. F. Menčík, *Rozmanitosti,* I (1879), 86). The reference to utraquist prosperity in 1417 corresponds to the events of the first half of that year and their sequel, and the emphasis on pious women suggests that Čapek wrote his work primarily for the "Beguines" living around Bethlehem Chapel, where his master Jakoubek of Stříbro was preacher. And Bartoš is no doubt right (*op. cit.,* p. 36) when he supposes that the Czech mass was developed in this same situation—he shows that the "Knížky" includes portions of the Czech mass, which thus was in existence when the book was written.

[120] The song, "Ve jméno božie počněme," is published by Nejedlý, VI, 190–193, and discussed in IV, 235 ff. Like other Hussite songs by Čapek and others, it is a deliberate effort to spell out the doctrines of Hussitism for the laity to understand. Thus the third canto, defining the church as the community of the predestined, seems to be essentially a Czech reworking of what Hus had written in his *De ecclesia* (ed. S. H. Thomson (Boulder, Colorado, 1956), p. 3 f.). The parallels with Jakoubek of Stříbro's ideas, especially his strident insistence on denying a cult to saints and images, and on reserving all forms of cult to God alone, are too clear to need demonstration.

[121] Bartoš has identified an anonymous postil of 1416/1419 as probably by Želivský and has published excerpts from it—"Nová postila Jana Želivského?" *ČČM,* CI (1927), 135–148; he offers a fuller treatment in his *Dvě studie o husitských postilách, Rozpravy ČSAV, Řada SV,* LXV (1955), pp. 21–37, where the authorship of Želivský and his close adherence to Jakoubek's radicalism are demonstrated even more convincingly. The passage quoted here is on p. 29. The postil is extremely interesting, but since it includes sermons of various years, without individual dating, its usefulness will be clear only when it is edited.

[122] See the following chapter.

Thus to understand Jakoubek's position in 1417 we must carefully ignore what happened in later years, except to explain why many who were more disposed than he to sympathy with extremist lines of thought could nevertheless accept his leadership at that time. Undoubtedly his position was strengthened by the fact that with Nicholas of Dresden gone, there was no alternative source of radical theory available.

Thus the problems of Hussite diversity after the middle of 1417 inevitably found a more radical and hence more realistic solution that that represented by the masters' declarations earlier in the year. The solution took the form of a series of articles worked out at a synod, the background for which appears in the prologue to the articles themselves:

> In 1418 at the time of the Feast of St. Wenceslas [28 September] several meetings of masters, of other senior brethren, and of many priests were held in Prague, in order to remove dissensions in regard to certain points about which the diversity of views among the brethren was causing many diverse scandals and vain controversies, among the brethren, against the brethren, and even among the people. The brethren were pleased to remain in unanimous profession of these points, and to hold them in mutual concord, and to instruct and teach the other, simple people to hold them in the same manner. Therefore no one is to attempt, preach, or hold any novelty on his own initiative and authority, even if it seems useful to him, unless he first refer and demonstrate it to the community of the brethren, by treating of it, examining it, and supporting and confirming it with scriptural texts. If anyone does otherwise, and by his own presumption seeks to teach anything beyond these articles, or to hold contrary beliefs, or to attempt anything new without common agreement, then let every such person know that he falls liable to the dangers of his own temerity.[123]

This paragraph and the articles that follow it comprise a source so informative, so detailed, and to cap it all, dated, that it seems too good to be true; perhaps for this reason scholars have tried to cast doubt on its information, revise its dating, or avoid subjecting it to full exploitation.[124] Such diffidence is not entirely perverse but it cannot be satisfactorily justified either; since the sources fits the reconstruction that has been attempted here, it will be taken at

---

[123] *Documenta*, pp. 677–681.

[124] I have discussed the various views in my "Hussite Radicalism," p. 126, n. 4; the main challenge to the manuscript's own dating has come from Bartoš, who sets the synod in 1419, chiefly because he sees no reason why it should have been held in 1418. Most recently R. Kalivoda, *HI*, pp. 397 f., has agreed with Bartoš, for Bartoš's reasons, and Kejř, *Husitský právník*, pp. 121 f., has followed suit. There is of course nothing sacred about a date given in a manuscript, but, as argued in the present context, there is ample reason to believe that by September 1418 it was necessary and possible for various Hussite parties to arrive at agreement in principle.

face value and analyzed in some detail. The synod agreed on twenty-three articles that for the sake of convenience may be briefly summarized here:

(1) Infant communion is to be given, in both kinds. (2) No one is to hold that explicit statements of Holy Scripture constitute all that may be believed. (3) Purgatory is to be believed in. (4) Masses are to be said for the dead. (5) Prayers, alms, and other works are to be done for the dead. (6) The saints can help the elect on earth. (7) No one may say that oaths are never to be sworn. (8) No one may say that the death penalty is never to be inflicted. (9) A priest who sins mortally does not lose his power to perform valid sacraments. (10) Only a priest can make the sacrament of the Eucharist. (11) In auricular confession various works of penance are to be imposed if necessary; mere repentance is not always enough. (12) Extreme unction is to be given. (13) Spiritual and temporal authorities are to be obeyed, even if evil, in legitimate matters, but lovingly resisted in illicit ones. (14) Constitutions of the church not against the Law of God but helping it are to be obeyed. (15) The authority of the holy doctors of the Primitive Church is to be respected. (16) All ceremonies, customs, and rites of the church, helpful to the Law of God and to good morals among the faithful, are to be preserved, unless something better is found. (17) Consecration of water and benedictions of other things are legitimate. (18) The ritual of the mass is not to be changed without great necessity. (19) The Gospel and Epistles are to be sung in the vernacular, the other parts of the mass in Latin. (20) Images can be kept in churches. (21) Sunday, other feasts of Christ, of Mary, of the apostles, and of other saints are to be kept. (22) Church fasts are to be kept. (23) Evangelical priests may have necessities by divine and natural law, although not by civil possession.

Even this summary, which does little justice to the extremely careful, well-motivated, and often qualified formulations of the original, suggests the spirit of moderation that prevailed in the synod's conclusions. We can well believe the prologue's statement, that the participants represented various levels of leadership and various parties, and that they came to final agreement only after several meetings at which their differences of opinion were fought out. Inevitably the final formulations had a conservative tone, but they were certainly not dictated by the conservative masters; on the contrary, the general sense of the articles can be characterized as the program of Jakoubek of Stříbro, cast in its anti-Waldensian aspect.

Thus there is no ambiguity about the rejection of the key Waldensianist tenets. *Purgatorium est ponendum* (3), and a flat *Nemo audeat dicere* ("Let no one dare to say") introduces the articles against rejection of all oaths (7), rejection of the death penalty (8), and Donatism (9); similarly the possibility of laymen consecrating the Eucharist is tersely and flatly denied (10). On the other hand, Jakoubek won an equally unambiguous victory in the matter of infant communion (1), and an important if incomplete victory in the use of Czech for the Gospel and Epistle readings of the mass; the defense of Latin for the other parts, moreover, was by no means absolute: "because of certain diversities . . . that give occasion of scandal . . . it would be good [*bonum esset*] to leave off the vernacular and continue in Latin" (19). Contrasted with the passive periphrastic formulations of most of the other articles—to say nothing of the *Nemo audeat dicere* formulas just canvassed—this wording seems to recognize that in time, or with increasing sentiment in favor of the vernacular, the article could be revised. Then in a series of points Jakoubek's exaltation of the Primitive Church was given explicit recognition as a norm; on the one hand—against the Waldensianist extremists—it was insisted that the literal statements of the Bible were not the only norm (2), and on the other hand—against the conservatives—the basic authority was to be that of the "holy doctors of the Primitive Church" (15), an authority appealed to in several other articles (12, 17, 21, 22). The authority of the post-Primitive or Roman church was explicitly recognized only in the articles on church constitutions (14), ceremonies (16), and the rite of mass (18), but in all cases with Jakoubek's qualifications—the constitutions and ceremonies had to be positively helpful to Christ's Law and the rite of mass was not to be changed *unless* there were special necessity or cause. We have already seen how broadly Jakoubek could interpret these qualifications when he was not fighting those to the left of him.

In a similar sense other articles that seem anti-radical were pronounced with sufficient attention to the claims of the other side, so that they ended up by being downright permissive. Purgatory was to be kept but no one should have such confidence in it that he would neglect his striving for the good (3). There were to be prayers and works for the dead, but none of the contractual masses, prayers, and chantings that smacked more of simony than of aid for the defunct (5). The cult of saints was recognized, but with a strong warning that it not be inordinate or distract from the supreme attention due to Christ (6). Oaths might be sworn only in the most important matters, and then with great caution, for they were dangerous (7). Evil priests had sacramental power, unless there were some revelation to the contrary in a particular case, but they were to be shunned in favor of good priests (9). The consecrations and blessings of water and other things were kept, "but hope for salvation should not be placed in them, and beware diligently of the evils that may follow from them" (17). As for the tolerance of holy images, the whole article deserves to be quoted:

> 20. Church images can be kept in the church, but only if they are not in superfluity and not wantonly or falsely adorned, in such a way as to seduce the eyes of communicants from respect for the Lord's body, or as to distract

the mind or otherwise be an impediment. Moreover they cannot be given adoration or cult in any way, by sacrifice of candles, or kneeling, or other forms of cult that rather belong to the Divine Body. But they may be cultivated only for their bare signification of deeds done in Christ or by Christ, that the simple people may be able more readily to see such deeds through the images and thus be furthered in their devotion.

Here as often elsewhere in the articles, the synod accepted not only Jakoubek's ideas but some of his very phrases.[125] Furthermore, it is obvious that careful attention was paid to the matter of formulation—certain articles were couched in the passive periphrastic (3, 4, 5, 11, 12, 13, 14, 15, 16, 18, 21, 22), others preceded by *Nemo audeat dicere* or a similar phrase (2, 7, 8, 9, 10); but another group was explicitly permissive, the key verb—as in the article on images—being *possunt*. A Hussite congregation, conducting its religious life according to the synod, would have communion in both kinds given to both adults and infants, and a mass in which the Gospel and Epistle readings were in Czech, while other parts conceivably might be in Czech under conditions in which there was no scandal to be anticipated therefrom. Furthermore, it could eliminate virtually all consecrations and benedictions of water, salt, grain, eggs, and the like, the cult of saints, and holy images. Its priest would not only lack civil title to possessions, but if the congregation were so inclined he might be restricted to a very bare support in "necessities." The rich profusion of Romanist works for the dead could be practically eliminated—reduced merely to congregational prayers. It requires very little imagination to see that even beyond these matters, a radical congregation could in practice ignore a great deal of what the synod approved, without thereby offering the synodal agreement an open challenge; for example, who was to decide whether the custom of aspersion with holy water was helpful or not to the Law of God? Or who could check up on a priest who followed Jakoubek in deemphasizing auricular confession, or for that matter followed Nicholas of Dresden in not prescribing penitential works? [126]

Thus given the framework of formal Hussite unity created in the first half of 1417, the St. Wenceslas Synod must be interpreted as providing the formula for coexistence between conservatives and radicals within a single

---

[125] A detailed demonstration would be too lengthy and perhaps also superfluous. As examples I would note that the formula for administering communion to infants, in article 1, is clearly taken from Jakoubek's discussion of the same problem—e.g., in his *De quibusdam punctis,* MS VIII E 7, fol. 109ᵛ; also the article on clerical poverty (No. 23) corresponds closely to Jakoubek's formulations quoted above, chap. iv, n. 179; also the article on images (No. 20) corresponds to Jakoubek's treatments of this subject (see above, chap. iv, *ad* n. 145; Nejedlý, IV, 115, n. 82).

[126] Cf. *LČJ,* No. 53. In the *Querite,* MS IV G 15, fol. 134ʳ, Nicholas argues against those "qui grave pondus venientibus ad penitenciam ponunt."

movement. The issues that had been raised by the university's declarations against radicalism in January and February of 1417 were here resolved in a manner that can only be described as political. The few masters who held out against infant communion were defeated, as were the hard-core Waldensianists; between these two extremes there was a wide range from conservatives to militant radicals, from such a master as, say, Prokop of Plzeň [127] to such a left-wing preacher as John Želivský, and all of them could stand on the common ground of the synod. Those of either side who could not left the Hussite movement; probably at this time Master Simon of Tišnov [128] and Master John Jesenic [129] lost their capacity to lead even in university circles, and the Dresdener Bartholomew Rautenstock left his post at St. Mary's of the Lake, to which he had been assigned after Lipnic, and set out on his career as a Waldensian-style itinerant preacher.[130] But these losses could be

[127] J. Prokeš, *M. Prokop z Plzně* (Prague, 1927), pp. 36 f., speaks of Jakoubek's victory in the matter of infant communion and his partial victory in other points of the synod's decrees: "It seems probable to suppose that the success of the compromise between the University and Jakoubek's party in September 1418 was made possible above all by Prokop and Příbram, whose conservatism, which had not yet become too sharp, was capable of making [apart from infant communion] even other, albeit smaller concessions to Jakoubek's standpoint."

[128] We last find Simon among the Hussites in the autumn of 1417 (as Bartoš observes, *Do čtyř art.*, "Roztržka," p. 69), at which time he was extravagantly praised by the university for defending the Hussite idea of the church as the community of the predestined (*Documenta*, pp. 663 f.). Since his first *anti*-Hussite work dates from *ca.* autumn 1419 (Odložilík, "Z počátků husitství na Moravě," p. 130), we can guess that 1418 was his year of decision, although when he gave up utraquism is unclear. John Želivský's sermon for 19 November 1419 has a marginal note, "Sicut Symon Magus fecit Petro, sic nunc noster Symon wlt alte volare" (MS V G 3, fol. 210ʳ)—thus Simon of Tišnov may only then have passed into renegacy.

[129] For Jesenic's further appearances see the following chapters; he played no role of significance after this period (see Kejř, *Husitský právník*, pp. 123 ff.), but refused to go all the way back to Rome; a MS note informs us that "he died in the prison of the Lord of Rožmberk because he refused to abjure communion in both kinds" (quoted by Bartoš, *Do čtyř art.*, p. 84).

[130] Bartholomew's confessions include the following (Döllinger, II, 629): "Item. Zum See [i.e., St. Mary's of the Lake, in Prague] hat er Mess gehalten, der Ketzer Glauben gepredigt, Beicht gehört und die Leut gecommunicirt unter beeder Gestalt, das hat er ein Jahr getrieben, als er bekannt hat. Item. Darnach als ihn sein Gewissen ermahnt hat, dass solches nicht göttlich, und unrecht zum Priester geweiht worden sei [*scil.*, at Lipnic], habe er ein Weib in Beheim genommen, und sich mit ihr heraus gen Bernheim gezogen. . . ." We can be sure that Bartholomew's scruples did not turn on the uncanonical aspect of his ordination, but that—quite the contrary—he did not wish to play the role of regular priest in a regular Hussite church; like the other members of the Dresden School, he preferred missionary activity. The question of his attitude to the sacrament of holy orders is of course complicated by his marriage (if such it was)—

endured, and they were amply counterbalanced by the fact that the great majority of Hussite leaders had come to an agreement that gave the radicals enough room to live, but secured for the university the formal recognition of its leadership that alone could prevent open schism and preserve the benefits of the alliance with the nobility. The religious agreement was to be sure much more tenuous than the political one, but under circumstances of peace and order the claim staked out for the future might have succeeded, with the different religious parties either moving closer to each other in thought or calmly agreeing to disagree on the basis of what historians would then be able to call High and Low Hussitism. Unfortunately for the Hussites this did not happen; only a short time after the synod a new wave of national and international reaction nipped its program in the bud. But the lesson of 1417 and 1418 was not lost on either conservatives or radicals in years to come, and long after real unity had ceased to be even remotely possible, the ideal of unity remained as an important determinant of Hussite history.

---

conceivably he persuaded himself that the Lipnic business was a farce, so that he could get married with a good conscience—but this did not end his career as a missionary: at first he settled down with his woman, then, when she died, he began to move around again, but he must always have been a preacher of heresy.

VI

1419: FROM REFORMATION
TO REVOLUTION

REACTION AND RESISTANCE IN PRAGUE

KING WENCESLAS IV's first serious attempt at a Catholic restoration, in the latter part of 1416, had been frustrated chiefly by the militant action of the Hussites themselves, acting in collaboration with leading members of the nobility, but also attempting to neutralize the king through leading Hussite members of the royal court. By the second half of 1417 the author of the *Sermones ad Bohemos* could complain that the king seemed to be favoring the heresy—"Generose rex laudande, / hujus cladis detestandae / diceris esse tutor"—because of the evil influence of women (that is, Queen Sophia) and the foul activities of the royal council.[1] How far the king indeed went in this direction is shown not only by his evident failure to stop the Hussite establishment of 1417, but also by his willingness, on 9 June 1418, to grant the citizens of the Prague Old Town a privilege against their being cited to any ecclesiastical court outside the realm; such a citation had been issued against some of them in March.[2] The privilege went even further, referring to a long-established general principle that no one in the realm might be cited to any court outside of it—the very principle Hus had appealed to in 1413 and that the Hussite League had manifested in 1415; the king's present confirmation of this principle was now said to be at the advice of the nobles and of the royal council.[3] However, the

[1] *Documenta,* pp. 691 f.
[2] See above, chap. v, nn. 1, 2.
[3] Tomek, III, 622; cf. Bartoš, *Do čtyř art.,* note 102.

265

weakness that made Wenceslas susceptible to such advice also guaranteed that when stronger pressure would be exerted from the other side he would change his policy again, and it was no doubt in awareness of this fact that the Hussite leaders had combined their militant program with an incongruous request to the Council of Constance that it reconsider the matter of communion in both kinds. Responding in their own fashion, the Council's theologians simply wrote more anti-utraquist treatises, but their real mood was clearly expressed by Jean Gerson: "Rather than reason with the utraquists, this holy general council should invoke the aid of the secular arm." [4] This was more easily said than done because the arm in question—the Emperor Sigismund—had other things to do and was in any case justifiably reluctant to lead an invasion of Bohemia; but the logic of the situation could hardly avoid producing such a step, sooner or later. The election of Pope Martin V, on 11 November 1417, only made matters worse, and in the spring of 1418 the Pope and Council together sent King Wenceslas a list of twenty-four steps to be taken in order that Bohemia might be reconciled to the church; the formula, typically, was one of complete restoration of the *status quo ante,* including even the demand that Hus's followers publicly approve of his condemnation and execution. [5] Coupled with the renewal of judicial processes against those who had infringed the church's rights and possessions, [6] the demands left nothing undone that the church herself could possibly do. All that was lacking was force, and after the Council had been dissolved, on 22 April 1418, Martin entrusted Sigismund with full power to proceed against the Hussites. [7]

It was several months before the Emperor could act on this mandate, but by autumn he was preparing for intervention, with the help of a papal legate, Cardinal John Dominici. [8] Moving eastward from Bavaria toward Hungary, Sigismund was met at Passau by emissaries from his brother Wenceslas, who expressed his misgivings over the Emperor's political intentions, just as he had had reason to do several times in the past. Sigismund replied in an open letter, dated 4 December, urging his brother to proceed to the extermination of heresy, and threatening him in case of continued inaction with all the spiritual and military sanctions that the church was ready to apply—and

[4] Hardt, III, 771.

[5] The text in Höfler, II, 240–243.

[6] See above, chap. iv, n. 81 (the process refers to events of 1416 but the "monitorium" was issued in 1418); chap. v, nn. 1, 2.

[7] Tomek, III, 627 ff. (I follow this account in the next paragraph). Cf. *Documenta,* pp. 676 f.

[8] *Loc. cit.* As early as 11 July 1418 Sigismund signified his intention to go into Bohemia with an army of Czechs, Hungarians, and Germans, and end the Wyclifite heresy (*DRTA,* VII, 349).

which indeed, he wrote, would long ago have been applied had not Sigismund, anxious for Bohemia's welfare, repeatedly intervened to defer them.[9] Now working with the Catholic barons of Bohemia, he decreed a diet to be held on 9 February in Skalica, a town that was part of his realm but lay close to the Moravian border. In January, at Linz, he again received envoys from Wenceslas, who complained that he knew nothing of the heresy to which Sigismund had referred; the latter's reply, on 19 January, was to wonder that Wenceslas could be ignorant of what the whole world knew, and to demand that the king send envoys to the Skalica diet.[10] Since leading members of the Hussite League had also come to deal with Sigismund,[11] the diet was evidently planned as an opportunity to subject the whole Hussite problem to a systematic solution. At the same time, however, the Catholics were not prepared to negotiate, except possibly on the timetable for Catholic restoration, and if the diet actually took place—we have no further information about it—it could only have been the occasion for a renewal of the old ultimatums. And lest the latter be dismissed as bluff, the papal legate Bishop Ferdinand of Lucena (who had joined Cardinal John Dominici) proceeded on 20 February to publish a citation directing Queen Sophia to appear before him in the Moravian town of Hodonín: she had expelled and persecuted Catholic pastors, introduced and fostered Hussite ones, and had allowed her "councillors, officials, and subjects" to do so.[12] Since the legate went out of his way to observe that only the strongest efforts by Sigismund had kept the Council and the pope from proceeding against Sophia earlier, the citation can be understood as implying that such efforts were no longer being made; and since the charges were formulated so as to raise the question of why King Wenceslas was not being cited too, he must have realized that he would be next. If mere threats had caused him to decree a Catholic restoration in 1416, the same threats, now backed up by ecclesiastical action, with Sigismund on his borders dealing with the barons of the realm, could hardly fail to be effective.

Thus King Wenceslas decided, "moved by what the King of the Romans had written and by the Apostolic Legate,"[13] to reverse the Hussite gains of the last few years. Jesenic, still the cause of the interdict, was finally forced out of the city; the Hussite incumbents were removed from Prague's parish churches—all but Christian of Prachatice's St. Michael's had been occupied

[9] *Documenta*, pp. 682–684.

[10] Tomek, III, 629.

[11] Bartoš, *Do čtyř art.*, n. 78.

[12] The text in A. Neumann, *Nové prameny k dějinám husitství na Moravě* (ST, VI; Olomouc, 1930), pp. 48–50.

[13] *Anonymus de origine Taboritarum*, Höfler, I, 528.

illegally [14]—and the legitimate holders were restored. The latter then reconsecrated their altars, refused communion to Hussites who would not renounce the chalice or do penance for their errors, and refused to allow Hussite clergy to celebrate mass at even the side altars of the churches, even—we may guess —when the Hussites had legitimate title to these altars.[15] Such procedures naturally frightened the Hussites, and a delegation of leading citizens protested to the king, who on 25 February presented both parties with a sort of compromise: asserting that he had never kept anyone from attending or celebrating religious rites as he liked and where he liked, Wenceslas said that the Hussites might celebrate mass at whatever altars they could gain access to, including those in private homes; at the same time the monastery churches of the Mother of God of the Snows and of St. Ambrose, in the New Town, and of St. Benedict in the Old Town, were to be available to the Hussites for their public services. Commanding all to keep peace in this anomalous situation, the king promised to consider the whole problem, together with the barons and the university masters, at a diet to meet on 6 March—on which occasion the "papal letters of excommunication" would also be discussed.[16] (We know nothing further about this diet.) The following day, 26 February, saw the interdict removed, at least partially, and Catholic services finally resumed.[17] Similar restorations also took place in the provinces, at least where royal officials wielded power, but to what extent is not known.[18]

It will not be supposed that four years of Hussite development could be reversed by so abrupt a policy, but it is equally clear that the complex and delicate structure of the Hussite reformation could not survive the attack without serious dislocations. The unifying policy pursued by the party's leadership in 1417 and 1418 had as an essential component the absorption of radical priests into a national establishment that by its very existence would work against the disintegrating forces of sectarian extremism; only a long period of success could make this unity real. The new establishment, moreover, was nothing but a portion of the Catholic church-structure, torn away from its legitimate directors—there was no *new* Hussite church that could have maintained itself in competition with a re-Catholicized establishment. Thus submission to the royal decrees could only mean the end of the Hussite

---

[14] *Chronicon universitatis pragensis, FRB,* V, 580.

[15] See the text in Pekař, *Žižka,* IV, 192.

[16] Pekař, IV, 192 f.; cf. the *Chronicon Procopii,* Höfler, I, 73. It is not clear what the papal letters were—they imposed a "kletba," which can mean either excommunication or interdict, or perhaps some other sort of prohibition—see below, n. 28.

[17] *Anonymus,* Höfler, I, 528.

[18] See below, the section "From Mt. Tabor to the Defenestration."

church as an institution. At the same time, however, resistance, with or without the help of the Hussite feudality, could only mean revolution—certainly against the royal power, and probably against much more of the established order, for the logic of a revolutionary situation would have brought the left to power within the movement. Hence the Hussite leadership—the nobility, the more substantial burghers of Prague, the university masters—could hardly contemplate disobedience; resigned moreover to obeying, they might well comfort themselves with the thought that the king's new policy could be a passing episode in a reign characterized throughout by weakness and irresolution. And both resigned and comforted, they might consider that utraquist communion had not after all been forbidden, even though it had been limited to a barely tolerated existence in a few churches. No Hussite could honestly say as yet that resistance was necessary to defend the lay chalice.

On the other hand, there were many Hussites whose idea of reform went far beyond utraquism. To the radicals, whose strength had been registered by the St. Wenceslas Synod, utraquism took on its full significance as an epitome of moral, liturgical, cultic, and doctrinal reforms that could be carried through only if the Hussites had their own parish churches and freedom to agitate against the Catholics. For them the royal reaction meant a stifling oppression leading necessarily to total defeat; the reform as such could be saved only by resistance. In the provinces, at least where radicalism had been associated with sectarianism, and where the royal policy was applied without concessions, this resistance took the form first of secession from the established order, then warfare against it—as we shall see. In Prague, where both the motivations and possibilities for such a development were less ample, resistance expressed itself in mutinous agitation against the new situation and against those Hussites who accepted it. Here Master Jakoubek of Stříbro and his associates at the university were in a painful predicament, for it was no longer possible to combine religious radicalism with the program of a Hussite establishment—there was no room for a central position. Although Jakoubek could hardly have regarded obedience as an absolute virtue, he could not take a stand against all the forces of legitimacy—the king, the nobility, the university: his whole concept of reformation presupposed the leadership of the established powers of the realm. He therefore fell silent, the steady flow of ink that had for years been issuing from his pen dried up to almost nothing, and there is no evidence that he continued to preach, although of course he must have—perhaps he did not say anything worth writing down.[19] The one item more or less

[19] See *LČJ*: except for No. 75 (see note 20), the only work Bartoš assigns to 1419 is No. 76 ("most probably" in August 1419), but it could just as well have been written in

clearly datable in this period, a paragraph entitled "Response to the King, that Infant Communion Should not be Suppressed," [20] reveals the situation very well; this radical novelty was evidently not included in the king's toleration of utraquism, and Jakoubek therefore wrote (in Czech) to some of the Hussite lords, asking them to inform the king that infant communion and adult communion in both kinds were "one and the same thing" and, as God's own institution, "not harmful to anyone or against the king's honor." "And," he wrote, "although I am very unwilling to arouse the king's wrath, I must fear even more to anger God by suppressing and pushing aside his truth, so useful for human salvation." But infant communion was not permitted, and Jakoubek did not as far as we can tell come out openly to defy the crown. The same silence overtook other university masters—John Příbram, for example, who like Jakoubek resumed his literary productivity only in 1420, and then increasingly as an anti-Taborite.[21] Even the reliable Prague Hussite historian, Master Laurence of Březová, is oddly reticent about the royal reaction—which indeed he passes over in complete silence, even though he gives an account of certain events understandable only as part of the resistance to this reaction, and even though his chronicle itself probably originated as a response to a Catholic work that took the royal reaction as its point of departure.[22] It is also significant that after King Wenceslas's death, in August 1419, the official characterization of his policy toward Hussitism entirely ignored the last few months of reaction and mentioned only his toleration of utraquism.[23]

But while Jakoubek and Příbram, and no doubt others of their circle, chose political conservatism at the expense of religious radicalism when those two principles had become incompatible, there were other Hussites who made the opposite decision. The radicalism that had established itself among

---

connection with the victory of infant communion at the St. Wenceslas Synod of 1418 (which Bartoš dates in 1419). It will be understood that my judgement in the text is based on surviving works attributable to Jakoubek; new discoveries are always being made, and the picture may turn out to have been different.

[20] *LČJ*, No. 75; the text in Bartoš, *Do čtyř art.*, n. 101.

[21] *LČP*, pp. 62 ff.

[22] For the relationship between the Catholic *Anonymus de origine Taboritarum* (Höfler, I, 528–534) and Laurence's Chronicle see F. M. Bartoš, "Z husitského a bratrského dějepisectví. I. Ztracená kronika o husitské revoluci a vznik kroniky Vavřince z Březové," *SbH*, II (1954), 83 ff., esp. 90 f. Both the congregations on Mt. Tabor and the Prague Defenestration are treated in the *Anonymus* and explicitly related to the royal policy of reaction. Laurence treats them too (*FRB*, V, 344–346)— and in the case of the Mt. Tabor congregation he follows the *Anonymus* almost literally in places—but he does not mention the royal policy.

[23] In the demands that the Bohemian Estates sent to Sigismund, *AČ*, III, 206.

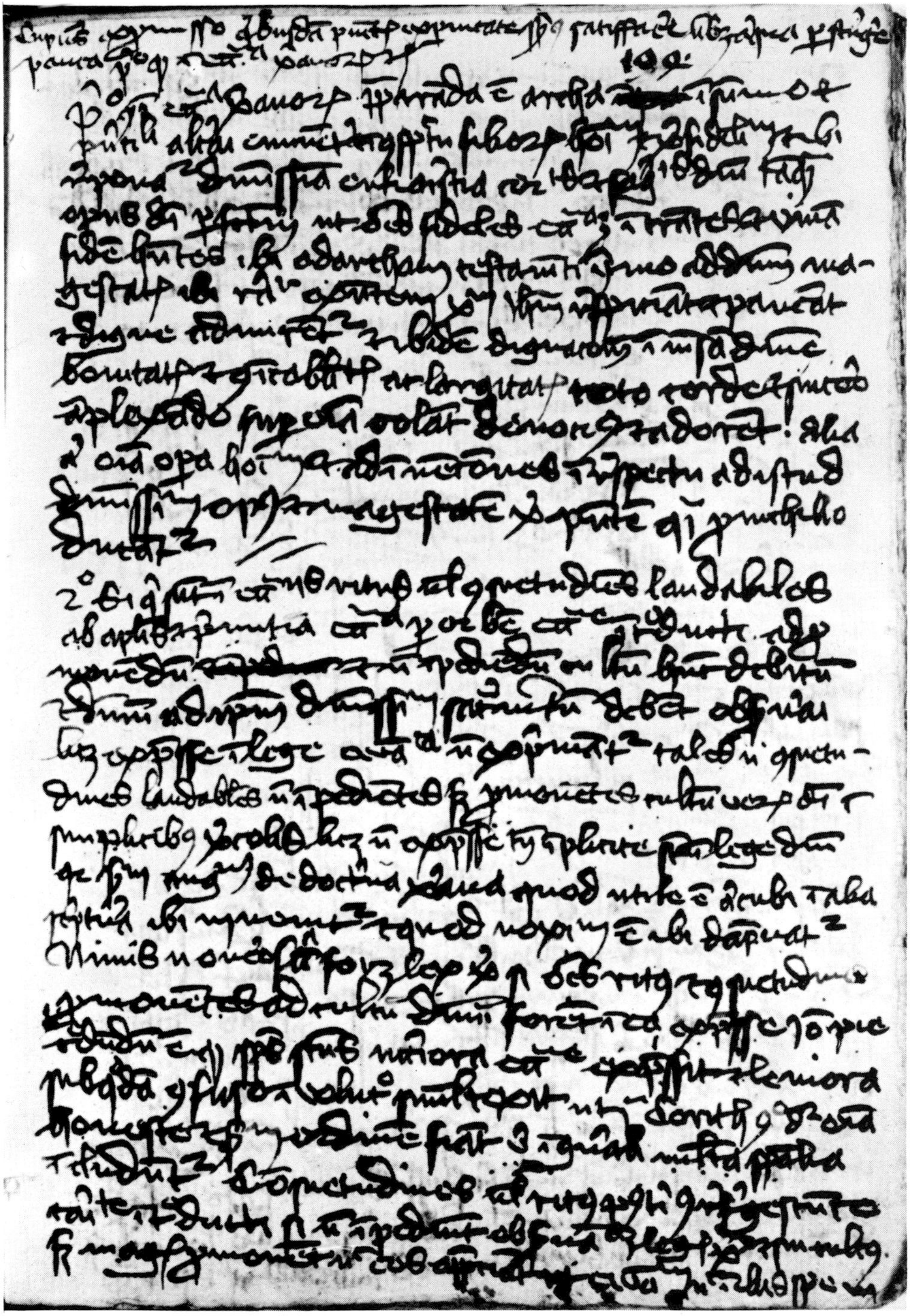

PLATE I. A page in the handwriting of Jakoubek of Stříbro (*De quibusdam punctis*, MS VIII E 7, fol. 104ʳ). (The Prague National and University Library.)

PLATES 2 AND 3. God on the cross *vs.* the suffering man. *Above:* Eleventh-century fresco of the Crucifixion, S. Angelo in Formis, Capua. *Right:* The Emaus Crucifixion, by a Bohemian Master before 1380 (the National Gallery, Prague). For the two conceptions of Christ, see page 20.

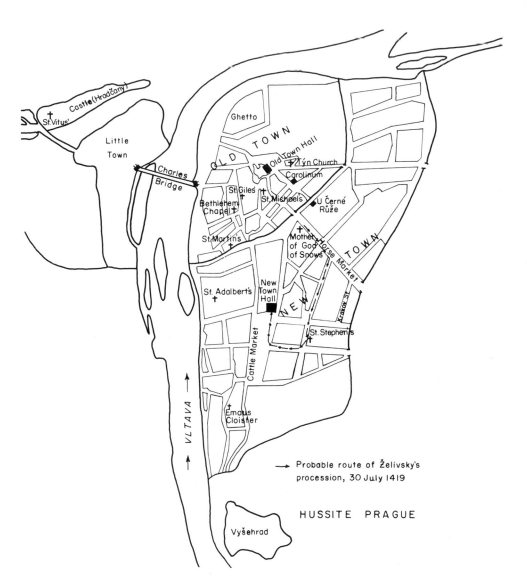

PLATE 12. Hussite Prague.

the petty craftsmen, workers, and floating paupers of Prague—particularly in the New Town, where these elements were more prominent[24]—was better able and more inclined to envisage the possibility of resistance to constituted authority than was the purely religious radicalism of university masters. In the spring of 1419, when the hitherto recognized leaders of Prague Hussitism had fallen silent, the leader of these popular elements, John Želivský, emerged as a leading preacher and agitator. He had been preaching for some years before, but entirely in the spirit of Jakoubek's program, and had no doubt been overshadowed by his master; with this inhibition removed, Želivský's remarkable political talents could find full scope, and his sermon outlines for the period from 16 April to 26 November 1419 survive to fill what would otherwise be a crippling gap in our sources.[25] It is unfortunate that we know so little about the man's origins: all that is certain is that some time after the beginning of the reform he left the Premonstratensian monastery of Želiv, in southeast Bohemia, and found his way to Prague where he preached an orthodox brand of radical Hussitism—quite militant but definitely not sectarian or extremist. By 1418 he was apparently serving as preacher and perhaps priest in the parish church of St. Stephen's; when the reaction of February 1419 expelled him from it, he moved to the monastery church of The Mother of God of the Snows, one of the three reserved for the Hussites by the king's decree. "Not particularly outstanding in intellectual quality," according to Laurence of Březová, his preaching was extremely eloquent and inspiring (according to the same source). From the spring of

[24] For the social composition of the lower elements of Prague's population see F. Graus, *Chudina městská v době předhusitské* (Prague, 1949); there is a useful discussion of this work by R. R. Betts, "The Social Revolution in Bohemia and Moravia in the Later Middle Age," *Past and Present*, II (1952), 24–31. Graus draws attention to the relatively large class of the "poor"—"those individuals living in the city who were unable to be independent producers and at the same time were forced by their economic condition to seek the source of their livelihood in a dependent position" (p. 33); he also argues that the position of this class was becoming worse in the period before the Hussite movement (pp. 70 ff.), and that the immediately superior class of petty artisans was also suffering steady pauperization (p. 131). He goes on to discuss the various efforts of the depressed classes to resist oppression (pp. 132 ff.), and he associates Hussite radicalism in Prague with this situation (pp. 147 ff.).

[25] The outlines are for sermons preached on the Sundays and certain holidays of the third and fourth parts of the church year, and are preserved uniquely in MSS IV F 23 (16 April to 16 July) and V G 3 (16 July to 26 November). Only the former has been edited, by A. Molnár, *Jan Želivský. Dochovaná kázání z roku 1419,* I (Prague, 1953); his introduction establishes the dating in 1419, and refers to the scholarly literature on the subject. Josef Pekař, *Žižka,* IV, 8–11, has argued that at least the sermons in V G 3 must be dated in 1418, but Molnár shows that the two collections are continuous, and since the first must be dated 1419, so must the second. See also below, n. 101.

1419 until his treacherous murder by the conservatives, on 9 March 1422, he exercised political leadership, at times even supreme rule over the capital and military control over the Hussite armies.[26]

Even the outlines of his sermons convey the atmosphere of tension in which the actual discourses—no doubt much meatier—were delivered. In fact, they reveal a situation of harsh repression amounting to persecution; although it is not clear what sort of persecution was being carried on, the themes of suffering and tribulation are so superabundantly represented that we cannot doubt the preacher's testimony.[27] It would appear that the Catholic authorities were resuming firm control over Prague's religious life, prohibiting any priest from celebrating mass or preaching without ecclesiastical licence, and enforcing their prohibitions with sentences of excommunication.[28] There is no evidence that Wenceslas's limited toleration of utraquism was being infringed,[29] but it seems clear that nothing but quiet, passive reception of the chalice was allowed. First and foremost among the forbid-

[26] For Želivský's career see Pekař, IV, 8 ff., and the treatment in Heymann, *passim*. Laurence's testimony is on p. 360 of his chronicle. See also A. Molnár, "Želivský, prédicateur de la révolution," *Communio Viatorum,* II (1959), 324–334.

[27] See Molnár's topical index to the sermons, *s.v.* "passio" (and even this extensive listing is not exhaustive). Želivský's own *explicit* to the first set of sermons reads: "Has collectas finivi . . . tempore mee magne persecucionis cum fratribus meis aliquibus" (Molnár, p. 244; cf. p. 8).

[28] On 17 April he complained (Molnár, p. 30) of "those who have walked about with bulls of the popes, who bear false witness, that no priest may dare to celebrate mass or preach without the license of a prelate." Cf. pp. 20, 29, 72, 166, 250.

[29] There is indeed one passage in the sermons that has been interpreted as indicating that utraquism was enjoying prosperity: ". . . [sunt] membra dyaboli, solum tempore prosperitatis predicantes vel sacramenta ministrantes, sicut patet de communione calicis: quando fuit persecucio, multi non fuerunt ausi ministrare, sed cum iam viderunt prosperitatem, quia prosperabantur in ecclesiis, cum introducebantur, primo inceperunt ministrare multi, qui in persecucione numquam ministrassent. Sic nunc de comunione parvulorum." (Molnár, p. 77, *ad* 30 April.) Pekař, IV, 9, has argued that this evidence of utraquist prosperity forces us to date the sermons in 1418 rather than 1419. But the Latin allows a different interpretation, particularly when we bear in mind the strong Czech influence on Želivský's Latinity (see Nejedlý, V, 33). If "cum iam viderunt" meant "now that they have seen," we would expect not the imperfect but the present indicative in the following verbs; in fact "iam" seems to be used in the sense of "already" and need not be translated—it intensifies the perfect aspect of "viderunt," which can indeed best be understood in the light of the Slavic perfective aspect, used for an action thought of as complete—both begun and ended. Thus the phrase would be translated, "when they saw," and the whole passage would present the following picture: (1) utraquism was at first persecuted (also the testimony of Laurence of Březová, p. 330), and many were afraid to practice it; (2) then it won control of the churches (evidently the reference is to the coup of November 1415) and many did practice it in their new churches; (3) now the situation is different—both 1 and 2 belong to the past, and now phase 1 is being repeated for *infant* communion.

den practices was infant communion, the propagators of which were being excommunicated,[30] but this was not all. Similarly proscribed was another radical achievement of the St. Wenceslas Synod of 1418, the use of Czech for the Gospel and Epistle in the mass,[31] and the vigorous, evangelical preaching that was so important in Hussite religious exercises was also banned.[32] Želivský's sermon outlines show us the main burden of such preaching: sharp criticism of clerical property-holding,[33] attacks on monastic orders,[34] scornful criticism of the clerical lassitude that led to neglect of evangelical preaching,[35] attacks on the evil consequences of the cult of saints,[36] and in general a sharply invidious comparison of Roman traditions and ordinances —especially the contemporary ones against the Hussites—with the standard of the gospels and the Primitive Church.[37] If we imagine the actual delivery

[30] That Wenceslas's policy was in fact hostile to infant communion is stated by an anonymous Prague University master writing in 1433: although, he says, Wenceslas gave his favor to utraquism, when infant communion was propagated "the king did not give such favor to this article (*Mon. conc. saec. XV,* I, 386). On 28 May, commenting on John 9:22—the Jews excluded Christ's followers from the synagogue, Želivský remarked: "Just as now, he who gives communion to children or sings new songs" (Molnár, p. 140; see also the preceding note, and p. 127).

[31] Thus in the sermon outline for 11 June 1419 (Molnár, p. 191): "The Dragon . . . seeks to devour the son of the mother church [cf. Rev. 12:4–6], that is, the fruit conceived by the study of Scripture, and to destroy it with the mandates of princes and prelates, by burning, destroying, and condemning all books of the Gospels and Epistles written in the mother-tongue. . . ." In the same passage Želivský uses an argument advanced earlier by Jakoubek of Stříbro: the Hebrews, Greeks, and Latins had been allowed to use their own languages for sacred purposes, therefore, and so on.

[32] See the many listings in Molnár's index, *s.v.* "predicacio."

[33] *Ibid., s.v.* "sacerdotes dotati," and there are more references still, including some against the clerical endowment in general.

[34] *Ibid., s.v.* "monachi."

[35] There are many passages; for example (p. 95), "the priests who do not have the Holy Spirit neither criticize abuses nor administer the sacraments where they fear to suffer in some way"; and (p. 104), "but now many priests do nothing because their life is evil and contrary to Christ."

[36] E.g.: (p. 94), "What then of the greedy, the proud, and the sensual—those who love their bodies that have been befouled by sin? They are not worthy to receive the Holy Spirit. Or what of those who love images, vestments, etc.? . . . What then of those who inordinately love relics of saints more than God?" And (p. 79), "O pious Christ, what great idols the princes have set up in Prague, in the form of endowed priests, and what great idols are in the churches, such as images, vestments!" And (p. 150), "[Christ] hates everyone who seeks the joys of the world and becomes an enemy of Christ's cross; such a man breaks the image of the living Son of God, but he honors dead images." And (p. 106), "Some wish others to pray for them and do not want to pray themselves, citing Jeremiah 37:3, 'Pray for us to the Lord our God.' But the Lord prohibits this."

[37] E.g.: (p. 16), "now many neglect Christ on account of traditions and mandates of men, and they do not go to sermons or to communion." (p. 62), "O how many now are faithless and hopeless, who neither know nor wish to know what Christ says! They say,

in Czech of these barely outlined Latin themes, we can understand why the king's policy pressed so heavily on a man like Želivský.

It is however clear that not all Hussites were of his sort. First of all there were downright renegades, men who "departed from the communion of the chalice," and who "in time of tribulation abandoned all good." [38] More important than these were the conservative Hussites who counseled obedience; "quasi amicabiliter," they advised: "Hold off for a while and everything will turn out well." [39] Rightly contemptuous of such timid counsel, the radical people, led no doubt by Želivský and his associates, took every opportunity to disobey the royal settlement and to manifest their mutinous spirit in provocative religious processions, during which they sang polemical songs against their enemies. [40] These included the obedient university masters, and we are fortunate in having the text of one splendidly abusive song that concentrates on them:

> You who become masters with false learning, have you studied so that you could get wealth by clever flattery? You dress in silks, laugh at the Law of God, and wallow in pleasures. The learning with which you deceive people is woeful blindness. If you had studied in order to spread the Truth of the heavenly Father you would abandon pride and care for nothing but God himself. But this one has studied how to buy a church or get prebends; that one attends to the craftiness that is called worldly wisdom, seeking benefices.

> They all praise the pope because they look for simoniacal wealth with him. . . . They oppose God . . . although many of them confess that [God's] Law commands all to drink God's blood and eat his body—but this is not commanded by the pope!

> They do not let the gospel be preached, read, or sung to the simple people. . . . They do not wish to talk about God, but only to run after wealth—Oh Judas clergy! [41]

'We do not understand the Truth and we do not know Scripture, but whatever our rulers [*seniores*] command, we are bound to obey them.'" (p. 117), "How then shall we stand with the ancient saints, who are the Primitive Church, when we are of . . . the faith of Antichrist, . . . and attend to human traditions?"

[38] Molnár, pp. 127, 151; cf. pp. 47, 56, 154, 176.

[39] Molnár, p. 127 (*ad* 25 May).

[40] The processions took place "festivis diebus" according to the *Chronicon Procopii* (Höfler, I, 73 f.), but Aeneas Sylvius (*Historia bohemica,* chap. xxxvi) says they took place every day—he doubtless exaggerates. The singing of "new" songs is mentioned in Želivský's sermons (above, n. 30), of Czech songs in the *Chron. Proc., loc. cit.* The program for reducing Bohemia to orthodoxy, sent to Wenceslas in the spring of 1418 by the Council and Pope, demands the prohibition of "cantilenae" against the Council and in favor of John Hus (Höfler, II, 242). For examples of songs presumably sung at this time see Nejedlý, VI, *passim.*

[41] The text in Nejedlý, VI, 181–183; see n. 45, below.

These sentiments are strikingly paralleled in Želivský's sermons, which frequently refer to the "false" and "perfidious" masters:

> The wise men of this world, the masters and prelates, exalted by the patrimony of the Crucified or by Constantine's dominion, or by the spoils of the poor, or by the heresy of simony, blush to preach the Kingdom of God to the people, but they magnify the Kingdom of the Antichrist, for they do not dare to open their mouths against the Devil . . . or to proclaim the Truth, for they, who are of delicate life, are not willing to suffer for the Word of God. Therefore they scorn preaching.[42]

And if we bear in mind not only this explicit association of the masters' perfidy with their possession of wealth, but also the very many other references in the sermons to the same themes,[43] we can again turn to the song just quoted for still further evidence of the mood of Želivský's party:

> If the masters had been really wise, they would have advised God to arrange things so: that the poor should never eat or drink, and should go naked, and sleep neither day nor night, but always work for the lords and render payments to them without stopping. And the lords, with the counsel of the priests, would become still harsher and would command that still more be given. And when they can get no more payments they make the poor man's body a beast of burden, making him do forced labor that has never been instituted by God or by anyone good. This is the anguish of the poor in all lands, and especially of the Czechs, on account of the arrogant clergy.

The same sarcastic figure, of the masters advising God for evil, appears in Želivský's sermon for 11 June, commenting on Romans 11:34 (For who hath known the mind of the Lord? or who hath been his counsellor?): "If our masters were his counsellors they would not admit that priests ought not to be endowed, or that the poor should preach against their arrogance." [44] Although Želivský was a religious enthusiast, not an outright social revolutionary, he took many opportunities to show his sympathy for the suffering of the poor, whose cause he clearly identified with that of Hussite radicalism.[45]

---

[42] Molnár, p. 181. In the sermons for the period 16 April to 16 July Želivský refers to the "magistri" fourteen times, always with disapproval and often in connection with "prelati" or "monachi."

[43] Mention has already been made of the criticism of "sacerdotes dotati"—Želivský attacks them dozens of times in the sermons under discussion. Their endowment is regarded as bad in itself, because it departs from Jesus's example and rule (e.g., p. 128), and as bad in its effect, which is to make the possessor unfit to receive the Holy Spirit and unwilling to suffer for the Truth (e.g., pp. 94, 95).

[44] Molnár, p. 192—"the poor" (*pauperes*) clearly means the poor priests.

[45] Molnár, p. 50: "In the Kingdom of Bohemia . . . in many places the peasants [*villani*] are now clamoring, oppressed and tormented by their persecutors." And there

But who were the false and perfidious masters? The texts just quoted suggest that they were the Catholics—the enemies of the reform—and it is true that Želivský does name two such, Mařík Rvačka of Prague and Stephen Páleč; but he also names the main leaders of the Hussite right: John Kardinál, John Jesenic, Simon of Tišnov.[46] And, according to him, it was the "magistri" in Prague who "gave poison" to Nicholas of Dresden.[47] The more radical masters—Jakoubek, Příbram, Prokop—are not named for evil, but neither is there any reference—with perhaps one exception[48]—to any good that they were doing. We can presume that as a result of the royal reaction, with the radical masters relatively silent, *the* masters were the conservatives, the leaders of the university corporation, who did not find obedience too difficult and counseled others to obey also. Thus they made themselves as odious in Želivský's eyes as the worst of the Catholic prelates; in fact, they were even more dangerous, for they continued to enjoy a certain prestige in Hussite ranks—hence, no doubt, the polemics against them by Želivský and others.

The radicals' processions just referred to were *ipso facto* mutinous, and since they proceeded in an atmosphere of anti-Catholic hatred they were often accompanied by violence, sometimes even bloodshed.[49] Here the movement came up against the town magistrates, who were royal officials; it is not

---

is an extraordinarily acute passage in the sermon for 19 November, MS V G 3, fol. 216ʳ, where, commenting on Mark 2:16 (the Pharisees said, "How is it that he eateth and drinketh with publicans and sinners?"), Želivský remarks: "Ecce magistri autem ignoraverunt quare sedit in mensa cum peccatoribus, sed vilani non ignoraverunt." That a Prague preacher should speak of *villani* in this way may be explained by reference to the close relationship between town and country in the Middle Ages (see, e.g., Graus, *Chudina městská*, pp. 39 f., for the probability that the poor of Prague worked on the land at harvest-time), and also perhaps by the contemporary idealization of the poor peasant (see V. Chaloupecký, *Selská otázka v husitství* (Bratislava, 1926), pp. 20 ff., for the Bohemian case). Thus I have associated the just-quoted song with Želivský's movement in Prague, rather than with rural radicalism (as Macek does, *Tábor*, I, 246–248), or with the Taborite hilltop congregations (*loc. cit.;* Nejedlý, IV, 260).

[46] Molnár, p. 20: "Nunc in partibus nostris exierunt falsi prophete ut Cardinalis cum suis et in Polonia Palecz, Marzyk, et qui seducunt in Bohemia a communione iuvenes et senes. . . ." And the passage from a later sermon quoted by Truhlář, *VČA*, VIII (1899), 288: "Gessenicz doctor, qui primus fuit contra comunionem calicis, sed in infirmitate fuit conversus, qui postmodum apostatavit iterum primus contra comunionem parvulorum, et Tyssnow Symon et alii eis adherentes."

[47] Molnár, p. 126 f.

[48] See below, *ad* n. 125. Příbram and Prokop were only relatively radical, in the matter of infant communion.

[49] See the *Chronicon Procopii*, Höfler, I, 72 f.; *Chronicon universitatis pragensis, FRB*, V, 580.

surprising to find these men vigorously criticized in Želivský's sermons,[50] but it is noteworthy that the preacher did not move on to outright attacks on the king. Instead, it would seem that radical policy sought to bring the king to relax the decisions he had made: sometime between March and July a large mass of Hussites confronted Wenceslas in Prague and, through one of his courtiers, the radical petty nobleman Nicholas of Hus, petitioned that freedom be granted for utraquism and for infant communion, and also, perhaps, that the Hussites be granted more churches.[51] The king could hardly agree, particularly since he regarded the démarche as a threat to his royal position; his response was to dismiss Nicholas of Hus from his court.[52] In fact, Wenceslas was following a course so repugnant to most of the people on whom his power depended that it could not possibly succeed, at least not without more skill and resolution than he could muster. Although the Hussites were not yet prepared to contemplate deposing him, as he feared, the radical wing of the movement refused to give up its religious demands. The turbulence in the streets of Prague continued, to prevent any normalization of the royal settlement, and John Želivský's sermons show that he began to balance his more or less sentimental adherence to Waldensianist pacifism[53] with an increasingly resolute acceptance of the need for physical violence.[54] Ultimately he would preside over the bloody revolt that is euphe-

[50] E.g., Molnár, pp. 150, 223, 240.

[51] Laurence, p. 345, says that the Hussites petitioned "pro libertacione communionis utriusque speciei tam ad adultos quam ad parvulos." Aeneas Sylvius, *Historia bohemica,* chap. xxxvi, says that the request was "sibi ut ampliores ecclesias elargiretur," a formulation perhaps best understood as complementing Laurence's.

[52] Laurence, p. 345.

[53] There are several expressions of Christian pacifism in Želivský's sermons (Molnár, pp. 62, 210, 220); his formulations are Waldensianist in tone and context—e.g. (p. 62), "Omnino nolite iurare, nolite occidere, nolite aurum possidere"—and remind one of the Waldensianist doctrines condemned by the St. Wenceslas Synod of 1418. But Želivský does not develop these points at all, and in the light of his doctrine generally, as well as of his whole career, we may guess that he simply repeated them as part of the noble cause represented by Nicholas of Dresden, whom Želivský esteemed and whose works he used. This last point deserves special study; as an example I would point to the sermon for 6 August, MS V G 3, fol. 38ᵛ, where Želivský quotes the antithesis worked out in Nicholas's *Tabule veteris et novi coloris,* III, §§1 and 2 (see the text in *OC & N*); I have also noted other cases.

[54] The theme appears especially in the sermons for July. E.g., Molnár, p. 237: "Misericordia sine iusticia est fatuitas et iusticia sine misericordia crudelitas." Page 238: "Quasi [Osee] diceret: . . . faciam vobis misericordiam, quia occidam [falsos prophetas] sicut tempore Helie." Page 249: "Compassio debet esse prudens, quia sepe contingit compati homini secundum corpus et per hoc animam destituunt ad graviora peccata." Page 245: "Infidelibus eciam veniunt passiones, sed non ad premium, sed ad dampnacionem." We can only guess what was actually said on these points in the actual preaching.

mistically called the Defenestration, but only after the limited and pragmatic disobedience of the Prague preacher had been reinforced and amplified by a more genuinely revolutionary program generated by the Hussite masses in the provinces. It was there that the emergence of the Taborite movement provided the means with which the stalemate in Prague could be broken.

FROM MT. TABOR TO THE DEFENESTRATION

The king's policy of reaction applied to the provinces as well as to Prague, no doubt with sharp variations from place to place, according to the varying dispositions of the burgraves and other magistrates charged with carrying it out.[55] Presumably outside of royal castle districts and royal towns the situation remained what it had been. For one place however, the most important one, we have detailed information, due to the exceptional nature of the radical response to the royal policy. This was the South Bohemian region of the Bechyně archdiaconate, around Ústí, Písek, and Bechyně castle, a region that we have already seen to have been a center of pre-Hussite sectarian heresy and a leading center of early Hussite extremism. It now emerged as the birthplace of a new and higher form of Hussite radicalism, the movement known as Tabor. Since the creation of new societal formations is not very common in history, we may here allow all the major sources to tell their own story:[56]

I

[Wenceslas ordered the restoration of the Catholic priests to their churches; divine services were resumed in the Prague church and in others. . . .] Seeing these developments, the Wyclifites began to think of how they might infringe this order so that their sect might not perish because of the king's

[55] Palacký, III, i, 288 speaks of a general repressive action in the provinces, wherever Hussite patrons did not prevent it, but he cites no evidence. One bit is offered by Želivský's sermon for 28 May (Molnár, pp. 139 f.); quoting the scriptural "Woe to the man from whom scandal comes!" (Matt. 18:7), he goes on: "So now [woe to] the temporal lords, who compel men on their domains to be scandalized, that they depart from Christ and adhere to the Antichrist."

[56] The paragraphs come from the following sources: I. *Anonymus de origine Taboritarum*, Höfler, I, 528 f. II. Laurence, pp. 344 f. III. *Ibid.*, pp. 400 f. (See above, n. 22, for these three.) IV-a. A historical passage in the Czech speech opening the Hussite Diet of 12 January 1426, and published by F. M. Bartoš, "Sněm husitské revoluce v Betlémské kapli," *JSH*, XVIII (1949), 99; Bartoš attributes it to Jakoubek of Stříbro. IV-b. From the *Chronicon causam sacerdotum Thaboriensium continens*, Höfler, II, 478; Bartoš, *op. cit.*, pp. 101 f., notes that the author, Tabor's Bishop Nicholas of Pelhřimov, writing in the 1430's, chose to follow IV-a very closely. I emphasize the more or less significant points of variation.

disfavor. About Eastertime [16 April] they congregated on a certain mountain about a half-mile or a little more from the castle called Bechyně, which
mountain they called Tabor, whence these sectaries have since been called
Taborites. It was on this mountain first, then next week on another mountain, and after ten or fourteen days again on another mountain, that they
celebrated their conventicles, continuously in this way. In a quarter of a year
their pestilential band grew in number to 50,000, not counting women and
children.

II

In the year 1419 evangelical priests, who were followers of Master John Hus
and who propagated communion in both kinds for the laity, and who at that
time were called Wyclifites or Hussites, began to frequent a certain mountain
near Bechyně castle, with the sacrament of the Eucharist and along with men
and women from various regions, cities, and towns of the kingdom of
Bohemia. They called this mountain Tabor, and there, particularly on feast-
days, they gave communion with the holy Eucharist to the laity, with great
reverence, for the enemies of that sort of communion [*scil.,* utraquist] would
not permit the laity to take communion in that way in the neighboring
churches.

III

In 1419 the priests and their vicars near the castle of Bechyně greatly abused
those taking communion in both kinds and drove them forcibly from their
churches as erring heretics. For this reason the priests with their flocks went
up to a large mountain, which boasted a large plateau, on which they set up
linen tents in the manner of a chapel. They performed divine services in
these tents and devoutly gave the venerable sacrament of the Eucharist to the
people coming there, without hindrance. When they had finished they struck
their tents and returned home, calling the mountain Tabor, so that those
coming there have been called Taborites.
When these things came to the ears of the adjacent cities, towns, and villages, the brethren priests of the vicinity, on a certain appointed feast day,
led their adherents with the venerable sacrament of the body of Christ to
Tabor, with sonorous voices, for the strengthening of the Truth there, as they
said, and for the consolation and comforting of the brothers and sisters who
were staying there [*ibidem existencium*].

IV-a

In the year 1419 there took place a congregation of *the laity* [*lidu obecného*]
on a certain mountain *and in an open place near the village of Chrástǎn in
the region of Písek and Bechyně, to which place* people came from many
other towns and regions *of Bohemia and Moravia,* to hear *and obey* the
Word of God and to take communion freely, with their children too, in the

glorious sacrament of the body and blood of Lord Jesus. There they recognized, through the gift of *the Holy Spirit* and of the Word of God, how far they had been led away and seduced by the foolish and deceitful clergy from the Christian faith *and from their salvation;* and they learned that the faithful priests could not preach the Scriptures *and the Christian doctrine* in the churches. And they did not wish to remain in that seduction.

IV-b

In the year 1419 there took place an congregation of the people on a certain mountain on which, *at certain and fixed times in that period,* there was held a concourse from many districts and towns, for the purpose of hearing the divine Word and for the free communion of the sacrament of the Eucharist, adults together with children. There, through the gift *and grace of God* and *the faithful preaching* of the Word of God *by the priests,* the laity [*populus simplex*] recognized their seduction by the false clergy from the true faith, *cult, order, and justice* of Christians, and when they saw how freedom was denied to faithful priests to spread the Word of God *and give communion to the people of God with the sacrament of the Eucharist according to the institution of Christ* [*scil.,* in both kinds], in the various parishes, they did not wish any longer to remain in that seduction.

In the light of these accounts the formation of the Taborite brotherhood seems extremely simple. The king's policy of Catholic restoration was implemented in the provinces, including the area around Bechyně castle—a royal castle occupied by Lord Henry Lefl of Lažany, who had been a friend of John Hus but who was also a royal councillor and therefore obliged to carry out his master's policy, at least to the extent of allowing the Catholic clergy to exclude Hussites from the churches.[57] It was nothing new for Hussites in such a position to form congregations outside the churches, for preaching and divine services, only this time they chose not some nondescript field but a mountain—actually a hill.[58] Since by this time there were large numbers of Hussites, whose sudden exclusion from the churches where utraquism had been established must have been felt as a severe shock, the movement took on an organized character, a massive dimension, that would not have been attainable in the first days of Hussite propaganda. Of course none of this merely happened, and we are fortunate in having the names of the men who were "the first inventors and organizers of the mountain meetings"—the

[57] For Lefl see Bartoš, *Čechy,* p. 379, and *passim.*

[58] Czech scholars have naturally sought to identify this hill, and there has been some controversy on the matter, which is not of importance here. See Macek, *Tábor,* I, 208, for a review of the literature, and a photograph of the leading candidate, a surprisingly paltry hill Nemějice.

priests Vaněk and Hromádka.[59] It is possible that both had been active in the center of radical Hussitism at Ústí, and quite probable that at just this time the city was re-Catholicized under Lord Ulrich of Ústí, the leading Catholic member of an otherwise Hussite family.[60] If similar events had taken place in the royal town of Písek, another center of Hussite radicalism, we can imagine that, as one of our sources (item IV-a) says, the congregation movement had a regional character from the very first; perhaps the environs of Bechyně castle were chosen because they fell about halfway between Písek and Ústí.[61] Or perhaps the implementation of reaction around Bechyně touched off the wider movement.

At the same time the mass congregations were not merely reasonable devices for providing utraquist communion. This theme certainly retained its extraordinary importance, particularly at the time of the first congregation "about Eastertime," for Easter was the occasion when even those who did not share the radicals' emphasis on frequent communion would nevertheless desire to take the Eucharist, as a matter of church law that had hardened into tradition. But we can be quite sure, in spite of the silence of the first three items quoted, that along with communion the very first congregations saw an equal emphasis on the stridently anti-Roman "evangelical" preaching favored by the radicals, preaching that taught the people to "recognize their seduction" by the Roman clergy. The congregations were in fact mass meetings, and could hardly have failed to generate the self-righteous hyper-tensive enthusiasm appropriate to those who have gathered together under persecution to defend God's Truth. The mood itself was no stranger to radical Hussitism, whose leading theoreticians, Jakoubek of Stříbro and Nicholas of Dresden, had seen themselves as the apostles of Christ's own Primitive Church, revived as the band of those obedient to God's Law, ready

[59] Laurence, p. 357.

[60] If Vaněk may be identified with the Věněk who was active as a radical earlier (see above, chap. iv, *ad* n. 78; both names are diminutives of Václav (Wenceslas)), the connection would be very instructive. For Hromádka see Bartoš, "Zakladatel Tábora," *JSH*, XXIII (1954), 44–48: he was Peter Hromádka of Jistebnice, probably ordained a priest in 1400 and given a chapel in Dolní Střimelice in 1413 (*Libri confirmationum*, VII, 100). In 1418 he resigned this post (*Lib. conf.*, VII, 265), one imagines under pressure, and perhaps went to Ústí as one of the Peters mentioned by the source quoted above, chap. iv, n. 78; cf. Tomek, IV, 30. Laurence calls him a "campanator" and in *OCA*, p. 35 he is called a "žák" (i.e., in Latin, *scolar*—a cleric in minor orders), even though he was in fact a priest: Bartoš therefore supposes that he functioned as sacristan, organist, schoolmaster. For the re-Catholicization of Ústí see below, chap. vii; for the lords of Ústí see *Documenta*, p. 697.

[61] This supposition of a regional character involves assuming that all the radical leaders of the region were in effective contact with each other, that they made joint plans; there are no sources to back this up, but it seems obvious.

to fight and suffer in the great confrontation with Antichrist. The sociological development of that ideology had been frustrated by Jakoubek himself, in the interests of national Hussite unity and a national Hussite establishment; it was only now, in the spring of 1419, that circumstances provided the powerful eschatological themes with an appropriate dimension of social existence so that the ideal and the real could resonate with each other.

This aspect of the congregations found its perfect denomination in the name of Mt. Tabor, the meaning of which is given in Matthew 28:16–20:

> Then the eleven disciples went away into Galilee, into a mountain where Jesus had appointed them. And when they saw him, they worshipped him: but some doubted. And Jesus came and spake unto them, saying, All power is given unto me in heaven and in earth. Go ye therefore and teach all nations, baptizing them in the name of the Father, and of the Son, and of the Holy Ghost: Teaching them to observe all things whatsoever I have commanded you: and, lo, I am with you always, even unto the end of the world.

Christian tradition, from at least the fourth century, had identified the mountain where Jesus was transfigured (Matt. 17:1–2; Mark 9:1; Luke 9:28–29) as Mt. Tabor, and the same identification was extended to the mountain referred to in the text just quoted; thus, preaching on this text on 21 April, five days after the first congregation, John Želivský commented:

> For the Lord had often said to the disciples that he would go before them into Galilee, where he appeared to them on Mt. Tabor, which is in Galilee, and where the disciples did not fear the Jews; for when Christ was in Judea he prayed on Mt. Olivet, in a garden, but when he was in Galilee, on Mt. Tabor.[62]

A divinely appointed mount of refuge from the "Jews," a place where the Primitive Church—Christ and his disciples—was revived after Jesus had died, a place where the law constituting that church was imposed in its classic form: all these traits were now applied to a South Bohemian hill, so

---

[62] Molnár, p. 43; cf. Aeneas Sylvius, *Historia bohemica,* chap. xl, and Pekař, *Žižka,* III, 36, n. 1. There are other passages in Hussite literature mentioning Mt. Tabor as the site of the transfiguration: John Příbram, "Eciam Moyses et Helias in monte Thabor cum Cristo apparebant" (*Contra articulos picardorum,* MS 4749, fol. 43ʳ; cf. *Ad occurrendum homini insano,* MS III G 26, fol. 253ʳ). And Jakoubek of Stříbro, *Výklad na Zjevenie,* ed. F. Šimek (Prague, 1933), II, 479. On the other hand, I know of no reference to the Mt. Tabor mentioned in Judges 4:6 ff. as the place where the Israelite host gathered in preparation for combat, and for this reason I disagree with Bartoš, *Do čtyř art.,* p. 31, n. 108, and Macek, *Tábor,* I, 209, who suppose the Taborites of 1419 had the Old Testament Mt. Tabor in mind. There is of course no reason to suppose they did not—the priests knew the Bible—but their explicit reference must have been to the New Testament.

ordinary otherwise that scholars are still not sure which hill it was. But the real hill was less important than the ideal mountain, conceived of in the Judeo-Christian tradition as the focal point of revelation, the physical locale of the encounter between God and man.[63] This idea, combined with the reality of mass secession from the established society, gave the Taborite movement its most characteristic qualities. Although modern Marxist scholars are right in emphasizing the element of actual and ideological class war in the Taborite congregations, which like all mass movements drew largely upon the numerous poor,[64] it would be wrong to think of Tabor as essentially but a higher form of class warfare: it was a religious congregation that had taken on social existence, and as such was a new formation. It could absorb and be nourished by everything that came into it from the outside, but it had its own irreducible pattern, its own laws of development, its own specific reality generating its own ideology.

Thus although the first congregation ended with all or most of the pilgrims returning home,[65] a group of permanent congregants very quickly took shape on Mt. Tabor and became the nucleus of mass congregations held repeatedly and attended by contingents from far and wide.[66] Nor may we doubt the testimony of one source (item I), that the series of congregations moved from mountain to mountain; we know that there were several sites for the congregations, some of them given new, biblical names: Mt. Horeb,

---

[63] See Amadeo Molnár, "Eschatologická naděje české reformace," *Od reformace k zítřku* (Prague: Kalich, 1956), p. 29: "Those who gathered on the mountain [in 1419] . . . were wholly in the grip of biblical eschatological symbolism in the very fact of a congregation on the mountains. In Scripture it is on mountains that the basic events of revelation occur. It is on a mountain that the Law is given, that Jesus prays, . . . that he preaches . . . , that he performs miracles . . . , that he summons the disciples . . . , that he sends them out to preach. . . . In the last book of the Bible a mountain is the scene of the events in which the glory of the messiah is manifested, when the elect gather around the Lamb who stands in power on Mt. Zion. . . . According-ing to the visions of the prophets the last, eschatological events occur on moun-tains. . . . Those who named their meeting-place Tabor gave to the mountain and the movement a name of rich biblical, unmistakably eschatological meaning." Certainly the Taborite songs connected with the mountain congregations support this view, with their long concatenations of biblical mountain-passages (see the texts in Nejedlý, VI, 183–187). The symbolism becomes even more strident in the chiliast documents—see the next chapter. For the more general mystique of the mountain as a focal point of the cosmos see Henri Frankfort, *The Birth of Civilization in the Near East* (Doubleday Anchor Books, 1956), pp. 56 f., and Mircea Eliade, *The Myth of the Eternal Return*, trans. W. Trask (New York: Pantheon Books, 1954), pp. 12–17.

[64] This is the basic theme of Macek's *Tábor, passim.* Robert Kalivoda, *Husitská ideologie*, speaks generally of the "peasant-plebeian" character of Tabor.

[65] Laurence, pp. 400 f.

[66] *Ibid.*, p. 401; see the paragraph III quoted above.

Mt. Olivet, and others.[67] Such a widespread movement could not fail to arouse the apprehensions of the established powers, and eventually, Laurence of Březová tells us, certain lords began to forbid their subjects to resort to Tabor "on pain of losing life and property, but the peasants [*rustici*] and their wives gave little or no heed to an order of this sort, preferring to abandon all that they possessed and not to miss going to Tabor on certain feast-days, drawn and attracted there as iron to a magnet."[68] Such peasants, obviously, would swell the numbers of the permanent communities on the mountains, communities that thus represented not merely secession but a kind of revolutionary defiance. Even today such mass assemblies would have an ominous character; in the Middle Ages, when "to convoke a multitude" was the exclusive prerogative of public power,[69] the Taborites seemed to represent a wholly anomalous tendency, one that Master Laurence of Březová could explain only by citing the testimony of "skilled astrologers," that a special influence that year of the heavens and the stars, including Saturn, had "inclined the minds of the common people to thus running about and rebelling against their superiors."[70]

Something has already been said of what went on at the first congregations, but it will be useful here to add the fuller evidence for the later meetings and for the movement as a whole in order to understand the enormous appeal that Taboritism clearly had for the religiously awakened people. Laurence of Březová gives us a description of the greatest of all the meetings, held on 22 July 1419:

> Their priests indeed exercised three kinds of offices there. The people having been divided into groups, the men by themselves and the women and children by themselves, the more learned and eloquent priests, from early morning on, fearlessly preached the Word of God and especially those things that concern the pride, avarice, and arrogance of the clergy. Other priests sat continually for the hearing of auricular confession. And the third group of priests, after divine rites had been performed, gave communion to the people in both the body and blood of Christ, from daybreak to noon. . . .

> All these things having been accomplished, as described, they go for bodily refreshment to a number of places prepared there on the mountain, and are

[67] See the map in Macek, *Tábor*, I, 223. For Mt. Olivet, renamed so by Nicholas of Hus see below, n. 84.

[68] Laurence, p. 402.

[69] Thomas Aquinas, *Summa Theologica*, II–II, Q. xl, art. 1, "Utrum bellare sit semper peccatum," says in his response, ". . . convocare multitudinem, quod in bellis oportet fieri, non pertinet ad privatam personam." He says it as a matter of course, as one of the reasons why only the legitimate powers might wage war.

[70] Laurence, p. 403.

convivial together in brotherly love, not to the extent of indulging desire or drunkenness, nor levity nor dissoluteness, but to the greater and stronger service of God. There all called each other brother and sister, and the rich divided the food that they had prepared for themselves with the poor. No drink that might cause drunkenness was permitted. Not only the elders but the children too refrained from indulging in any dancing, dicing, ball-games, or any other game of levity. Nor, finally, could there be found any arguments, theft, or playing of pipes or lutes, as was the custom at church dedication-festivals, but all were of one heart and one will, in the manner of the apostles, dealing with nothing except what pertained to the salvation of souls and to the reduction of the clergy to its original estate, that of the Primitive Church.[71]

One smells the miasma of Puritanism here, but the Hussites evidently liked it, and it is not hard to imagine how wonderful it must have been to common people to find a world where rich shared with poor and all were brothers—a world that had no doubt been deliberately fashioned to resurrect the brotherly, caritative communism of the Primitive Church in one of its happier moments, when "the multitude of them that believed were of one heart and of one soul: neither said any of them that ought of the things which he possessed was his own; but they had all things common, . . . and distribution was made unto every man according as he had need" (Acts 4:32 ff.). Even hostile observers conceded this to the Taborites—"meeting in peace, piety, love, and brotherly unity, they shared even eggs and crusts of bread with each other." [72] "They wished to live in imitation of the Primitive Church, and they held all things in common; they called each other Brother, and one provided what the other lacked." [73] Such fellowship, intensified by the conviction of righteousness and a relentless propaganda directed against the rich, powerful, sinful Catholic clergy, gave the common people something that belonged to them in a way the feudal order did not.[74] No wonder

---

[71] *Ibid.*, pp. 401 f. In the first paragraph "arrogance" translates "fastum," the reading of one manuscript; the other MSS have "statum"—that is, the "estate" of the clergy.

[72] Anonymous verses, ed. K. J. Erben, *Výbor z literatury české*, II, 251; also in *KJBB*, pp. 34 f.

[73] Aeneas Sylvius Piccolomini, letter to John Carvajal, 21 August 1451, ed. R. Wolkan, *Der Briefwechsel des Eneas Sylvius Piccolomini*, III, i, *FRA*, 2. Abt., LXVIII (1918), 26.

[74] This fact has been partly understood by modern scholars (e.g., Pekař, *Žižka*, I, 187), but it is fully appreciated and exploited as a key to understanding only in the monumental work of Josef Macek, *Tábor*, I and II. Although I regard his Marxism as too rigid and I sometimes have occasion to object to what I regard as a lack of due diffidence in his treatment of the sources, I can only be grateful for the brilliance with which he has used his own Communist standpoint as a basis for understanding the Taborites from the inside out, so to speak. I think he is mistaken in thinking of Tabor as *essentially* a phenomenon of class war, but class war was certainly a very important

that they exulted in their possession of it and urged others to join them; in the words of one of their polemical songs:

> Let us rejoice, having attained to recognition of the Law of God and having congregated in God's honor for festivals of the Glorious Lamb, innocent of all sins and sacrificed for us. Blessed they who will be drawn away and brought to this sacrifice, torn away from sins, obeying God in what he has said to his prophets and apostles. . . . [There follow biblical prototypes of pious congregations on mountains; then] . . . God orders evil pastors to rule their sheep and cease feeding themselves from them, for he wishes to free the sheep and take them out of their subjection and himself feed them on the mountains, . . . restoring and strengthening those who have gone under and been broken. . . . Therefore do not resist evil but go out to the mountain and here learn Truth; for so Christ commanded when he prophesied on the mountain and preached of the destruction of the temple, saying, "You who will be in Christendom [*sic*, for "Judea"], flee quickly to the mountains." . . . Have mercy on us, O Lord, for we await you in grief . . . , our lives are deeply wounded, bare of the Good—deign to save us! [75]

For those who sang this song and those who listened to it the grand plan of the conservative Hussite leadership, to make Hussitism the established religion of the established order, had become meaningless, and we should not be surprised to find early Tabor cultivating a sectarian faith corresponding to its posture of withdrawal from the social order. In fact, there is good reason to think that evangelical nonviolence of the Waldensian sort was accepted by the congregants,[76] and since we know that Tabor somewhat later embraced

---

component of the Taborite movement, and no one else has so fully shown the importance of this fact. I make this statement here because in the nature of things my footnote references to Macek are often critical.

[75] The text in Nejedlý, VI, 186 f.

[76] The just-quoted song, with its admonition, "do not resist evil but go out to the mountain," expresses the Taborite attitude in terms of an evangelical vocabulary. The hostile *Anonymus de origine Taboritarum* tells how as late as July 1419 the congregants declared their readiness to die for utraquism, "without resistance or any murmuring," their willingness "to be killed by others rather than themselves kill others" (Höfler, II, 528 f., 532). These passages justify us in applying to early Tabor the evidence for Waldensianist nonviolence in Hussite radical circles before 1419—in the works of Nicholas of Dresden, in the doctrines attacked at the St. Wenceslas Synod of 1418, and elsewhere. And later on, when Tabor took up an ideology of extreme violence, her critics compared this with her earlier pacifism: John Příbram in Höfler, II, 531; Jakoubek in Goll, *Quellen*, II, 60 (these items will be discussed in the next chapter); cf. the verses cited above, n. 72 ("now they walk hypocritically with staffs, but when they increase in numbers they will wage great war"), and *OCA*, p. 29 ("at that time they would not . . . do damage to people; and they walked only with staffs, like pilgrims").

the full range of the extreme radical doctrines condemned at the St. Wenceslas Synod of 1418,[77] we can suppose that the leading protagonists of those doctrines found a favorable environment for their work, even at the first congregations, although direct evidence here is lacking. On the other hand, common sense suggests that a movement drawing its membership and leadership from so many sources could not possibly have been unanimously in favor of any single doctrinal corpus, nor does it seem likely that all those who went to the mountains for the utraquist communion no longer available at home should have also accepted religious views of a clearly heretical character, views that went far beyond ordinary utraquism. The congregants who, according to Laurence of Březová, resorted to auricular confession before taking communion could not have been of a Waldensianist stamp. In fact, the priests were kept busy just propagating the basic principles of what may be called orthodox Hussite radicalism. According to one source, the main points preached on the mountains were these: (1) priests should not possess property or income by civil dominion; (2) tithes were not to be obligatory, and the clergy should be supported by freely given alms; (3) priests should abandon their legal possessions of all kinds, retaining only a limited right to live in their parish houses "with all title of civil dominion removed"; (4) "The New Testament is sufficient for salvation without the figures of the Old Testament and without customs of human invention"; (5) infants should be given utraquist communion after baptism; (6) the faithful should flee from "thieves and brigands"—that is, the Romanist clergy—and follow Christ, the true pastor.[78] Since our source here is Jakoubek of Stříbro we may feel somewhat uneasy about the precision with which these points correspond to his doctrine, even down to moderating the attack on clerical possessions in order to allow use of parish houses.[79] However, if we read all the sources that have been canvassed in these pages, we will find that these six points (and utraquism) include everything known to have been taken up at the congregations: attacks on the avarice and other vices of the Roman clergy, recognition of seduction by false preachers, fleeing from the evil ones, imitation of the Primitive Church in obedience to Christ's Law (the New Testament), infant communion. In other words, the congregations must have been led by men who belonged to the radical consensus that Jakoubek had defined against both right and left.

This view of the matter has been subjected to a vigorous attack by Josef Macek, who regards the congregations as predominantly composed of the

[77] See the following chapter.

[78] The points are given in the sources quoted above, as IV-a and IV-b; the point about infant communion is only in IV-a.

[79] See above, chap. iv, *ad* nn. 177–179.

rural "poor," [80] and as therefore expressing the ideology of the poor. The sources speak of utraquism, but to Macek "the chalice merely symbolized the smouldering resistance of the exploited," and the sources, none of them written by the poor, had a vested interest in covering up the class hatred that found expression on Mt. Tabor.[81] This last point is a kind of postulate: "we presuppose *the immanent existence of class hatred and rebellion* in the thinking of the exploited under feudalism." [82] For this reason Macek supposes that the true ideology of the congregations even in the spring of 1419 was the revolutionary, savagely violent chiliasm that came to the fore among the Taborites in the following winter.[83] In fact, if the poor had dominated the congregations, and if they had been motivated by pure class hatred, then certainly they would have led Tabor into chiliastic fanaticism; but for one thing, as we shall see, Tabor's chiliast phase *cannot* be dated earlier than the end of 1419, and for another, the mere fact that there were many poor people at Tabor does not mean that that element controlled the congregations. There are always more poor people than well-off ones, but the latter are usually the men who lead and prevail. Even if the poor had wanted to vent their immanent class hatred (which many of them were probably too unenlightened to feel), they could hardly have taken control away from the educated priests and preachers, the military men, and the propertied peasants —all of whom were on the hilltops.[84] Nothing is more clear from the actual

[80] Macek defines the rural poor as "subject people who were poor, propertyless, who worked for wages and occupied a dependent economic position"; these are distinguished from the "peasants" ("sedláci"), who were subject people with property (*Tábor*, I, 107).

[81] *Tábor*, I, 209: Laurence of Březová and others who emphasized the intense piety that prevailed at early Tabor offer testimony that is "hard to square with reality," for the reasons mentioned.

[82] J. Macek, "O třídním boji za feudalismu," *ČsČH*, V (1957), 297 (his emphasis).

[83] *Tábor*, I, 258 ff., and *passim* in both volumes.

[84] Few definite statements of any kind can be made about the congregants of the first few months, but there are some odd data that suggest a picture. The only priests definitely known to have been on hand were Vaněček and Hromádka, the organizers, but it is hard to imagine that the future leaders of Tabor were not there too—Koranda, Čapek, Nicholas of Pelhřimov, Markolt, Jičín. All of these were educated men. Then Laurence of Březová's words about peasants who were "willing to abandon all that they possessed" in order to go to Tabor shows that "the poor" were far from the only rural class taking part. As for petty noblemen, Macek himself supposes that several were there (*Tábor*, I, 215), but the only one we can reasonably say must have been was Nicholas of Hus: perhaps it was after he had been banished from the king's presence in Prague (Laurence, p. 345) that he went into the country and—as Aeneas Sylvius says (*Hist. boh.*, chap. xxxvi)—incited the "populares" more and more. The *OCA*, p. 28, inform us that in the period *before* King Wenceslas's death Nicholas had established a stronghold on Green Mountain, which he renamed Mt. Olivet, obviously in the Taborite spirit.

course of events in 1419 than that these men were in control, suppressing or deflecting the purely sectarian programs—Waldensianist, chiliastic—that no doubt were advanced by some. This is the only hypothesis that explains the passage of the Taborite movement from its original preoccupation with utraquist secession to its engagement, in the summer of 1419 and thereafter, in projects of national, political import.

Here we may return briefly to events in Prague, where the intransigent radicals led by Želivský were engaged in almost daily struggle against reaction. But now they were not alone: as the *Anonymus de origine Taboritarum* tells us, in a stereotyped but not therefore false formulation, the Taborite "conspiracy" had diverse heads but its tails were all tied together— that is, according to the context, the Prague movement had been brought into association with that of the provinces.[85] We have already seen Želivský explaining the meaning of Mt. Tabor, at just the right time, and even the Latin outlines of his sermons contain references to preaching on the mountains that were probably not accidental.[86] We may therefore believe the *Anonymus* when he tells us that King Wenceslas feared this many-headed conspiracy and therefore decided to take action against it: on 6 July he installed new, anti-Hussite councillors in the New Town of Prague; we are told that he planned similar action in the Old Town and Little Town.[87] The new regime acted with vigor: the parish schools, kept by the Hussites in spite of the restoration of the parish churches to the Catholics, were forcibly restored to the latter;[88] mass processions were forbidden;[89] some who took communion in both kinds were imprisoned.[90] In a note written on 10 July, Želivský referred to the time as that "of my great persecution, together with some of my brethren"; his sermons, never lacking in criticism of the magistrates, now begin to contain more such criticism, more indicative of persecution.[91] The powerful momentum of his agitation in Prague and the equally

[85] Höfler, I, 530. For the stereotype see H. Grundmann, "Der Typus des Ketzers in Mittelalterlicher Anschauung," *Kultur- und Universalgeschichte* (Goetz Festschrift; Leipzig and Berlin, 1927), p. 100; the image combines The Song of Solomon 2:15 with Judges 15:4.

[86] Thus one of the July sermons (Molnár, p. 243) complains: "Nunc volunt [principes et prelati] prohibere predicare in monte"; see also the index, *s.v.* "mons."

[87] *Anonymus,* Höfler, I, 530; for the date see Tomek, III, 635.

[88] *Anonymus, loc. cit.; Chronicon Procopii,* Höfler, I, 73 f.

[89] Aeneas Sylvius, *Hist. boh.,* chap. xxxvi; *Chron. univ. prag., FRB,* V, 580.

[90] *Chron. univ. prag.,* p. 580; *OCA-R,* p. 19: just before the Defenestration the Hussites demanded that the magistrates free those who had been imprisoned on account of communion in both kinds. This must have been a recent imprisonment, perhaps occasioned by violation of the king's original restrictions.

[91] For the note see Molnár, pp. 8 f. For the preaching against the magistrates see, e.g., p. 240.

powerful action of his allies in the provinces were thus met head-on by a royal counterblow that for once was clear and uncompromising.

But Wenceslas acted too late—"when he could he wouldn't; when he would he no longer could."[92] Several months of agitation and subversive action had prepared the Prague radicals of Želivský's following to meet force with force, while in the same period the escalating organization of the Taborites in the provinces had brought their mass movement to the point where it could be used as a genuinely political force. Its leaders, undoubtedly in constant touch with each other, now resolved to combine all their forces in the greatest demonstration of all, a nationwide congregation to be held at Mount Tabor on 22 July. The local Taborites were of course there, but this time they were joined by contingents from the regions around Plzeň in the west, Domažlice in the northwest, Hradec Králové in the northeast, from Moravia, and from Prague.[93] It is not known precisely who came, but it would be strange indeed if the tens of thousands reported by the sources did not include such leaders as Nicholas of Hus, Wenceslas Koranda from Plzeň, and John Želivský from Prague. And it is impossible to suppose that the leaders did not meet. In addition to the massive but not unusual religious actions reported by Laurence of Březová, there must have been high-level political conferences of the most serious sort, to decide on a program that might be realistically expected to put an end to the king's reactionary policy. The anti-Hussite magistrates recently installed in Prague by Wenceslas knew that the meeting would not be just an exercise in piety, and they therefore sent spies.[94] Laurence of Březová, who tendentiously insisted that the congregants "dealt with nothing except what pertained to the salvation of souls and to the reduction of the clergy to its original estate, that of the Primitive Church," portrayed the spies as slanderers who sought "to calumniate what was considered and done there, and to reveal these things to the enemies of the Truth." What they reported was, according to the same source, enough to make the king and the anti-Hussite barons afraid that the Hussites would elect a new king—perhaps Nicholas of Hus—and a new archbishop and make war on their enemies.[95] Here the *Anonymus de*

[92] *Anonymus*, Höfler, I, 530.

[93] *Ibid.*, p. 528, where the number of congregants is given as 50,000; Laurence, pp. 344 f., 401, gives the figure as more than 40,000. There is no way to check these figures. The places from which the congregants came are mentioned by Laurence, p. 402; on p. 344 he says only that they came "from various parts of the realm."

[94] *Anonymus*, p. 530.

[95] Laurence, p. 402: "rex Wenceslaus cum quibusdam inimicis veritatis baronibus ceperunt graviter ferre timentes, ne tanta populi multitudo regem et archiepiscopum, prout famabatur, pro defensa legis dei eligerent et sic eorum bona velut adversariorum per potenciam, cui resistere non valerent, invaderent ac depopularent." Also the anti-

origine Taboritarum is more precise: the spies reported that the Taborites planned to besiege the king in the royal castle of Nový Hrad at the end of September. But this account also says that the immediate result of the Taborite "conspiracy" was the event that occurred in Prague eight days later, the so-called Defenestration—in fact an insurrection of Želivský's party against the magistrates of the New Town.[96]

This is a hostile presentation but not necessarily a false one. On the contrary, it is supported by the logic of the situation as well as by the course of events to come. The leaders who presumably met at Mt. Tabor on 22 July were ardent radicals but they were not fanatics; they were at home in the world of political realities and they knew a good deal about their king and how he acted. The most reasonable way to change his policy of reaction would be to undertake limited action, to convince him that continuing the policy would cause him more trouble than reversing it, and the most reasonable kind of action would be a coup against the hated magistrates he had just installed. Of course responsible leaders must also plan for contingencies, and nothing is more likely than that the men at Mt. Tabor discussed the further steps that would have to be taken if their first one failed—nor need it be doubted that they were prepared to plan for the final step, actual war against the king and the establishment of a new government in church and state.[97] Such a revolution was in fact carried out a year later by the Taborites, as a last resort, and it caused political realignments that eventually brought Tabor to defeat; her leaders in July of 1419 must have been aware of the dangers and must have sought to avoid an irrevocable break with the legitimate order, but they could hardly have avoided contemplating the possibility. Thus although they made it known to the king that "they would

---

Hussite verses edited by Erben, *Výbor*, II, 252: "When those who were at Mt. Tabor informed King Wenceslas [of what they had learned], he said, 'Watch out for those people, they will cause great disturbance in the land; although now they hypocritically walk with staff, when they increase in number they will wage great war.'" Cf. Laurence's notice on p. 345, following his first account of the 22 July meeting: "Quam ob rem rex Bohemie Wenceslaus multum est turbatus, se de regali solio deici timens et expavescens, Nicolaumque de Hus in locum sui substitui suspicando." Aeneas Sylvius, *Hist. boh.*, chap. xxxvi, tells us that the king's situation "did not lack peril," and in view of later Taborite plans (see below) we may believe him.

[96] *Anonymus*, pp. 530 f. Here and for the rest of this section, the reader is referred to the more detailed account in my article, "The Prague Insurrection of 30 July 1419," *Medievalia et Humanistica*, XVII (1966), 106–126.

[97] Such is the testimony of Aeneas Sylvius, *Hist. boh.*, chap. xxxvi; as usual the information is conveyed in highly artistic rhetorical form—in this case via a surely invented speech by Koranda at the meeting; but perhaps we can accept the basic point, that something was said about deposing the king, and we can on this basis explain the more reliable sources cited above, n. 95. But cf. Bartoš, *HR*, I, 62 f.

rather be killed by others than kill others themselves," [98] the spies reported something else—a plan for actual revolution. What they apparently did not report, and therefore presumably did not know, was the immediate step that would be taken.

If John Želivský had indeed attended the meeting on Saturday, 22 July, he would have been back in Prague early next week, ready to plan a revolt for the coming Sunday, 30 July. Word was sent to his supporters to come to his church—the Mother of God of the Snows—under arms; at the same time the radical soldier John Žižka and perhaps others like him were drawn into the planning of an action that would require their special sort of leadership.[99] Finally, Želivský prepared a sermon calculated to bring his listeners to the needed pitch of tension and militancy. The *Anonymus* reports that "he vigorously incited the people to sedition in the city against the town council-lors and those who supported them," [100] but this may be a later inference; a better source is the sermon outline that Želivský probably wrote for the occasion and probably used.[101] There is much in it that has no evident relationship to the sedition that was to come, but was it only by chance that he quoted this passage from Ezekiel 6:3–5: "Behold, I, even I, will bring a sword upon you, and I will destroy your high places. And your altars shall be desolate, and your images shall be broken: and I will cast down your slain

[98] *Anonymus*, Höfler, I, p. 532.

[99] The more important sources are: Laurence, pp. 345 f.; *OCA-R*, p. 19; the chronicle of Bartošek of Drahonice, *FRB*, V, 591; the *Anonymus de orig. Tab.*, Höfler, I, 531 f.; *Chron. univ. prag.*, *FRB*, V. 580; *Chron. Proc.*, Höfler, I, 74, Aeneas Sylvius, *Hist. boh.*, chap. xxxvii; *OCA*, p. 25. The first three give John Žižka a leading role in the action; the next four mention only the leadership of Želivský; the last mentions no names. Pekař, *Žižka*, II, 92 ff., and III, 17, accepts the evidence for Žižka's participation, as does Heymann, p. 64; Macek, *Tábor*, I, 201, n. 122, is skeptical. That the people carried arms is reported by *OCA-R* (and *OCA*) the *Anonymus*, and Aeneas Sylvius.

[100] *Anon. de orig.*, p. 531. The testimony of the *Chron. Proc.*, p. 74, that at that time Želivský was preaching on Revelations was probably taken, sloppily, from Laurence's report (p. 360) on Želivský's preaching *ca.* March 1420. Still, the sermon Želivský probably wrote for 30 July did include a page of texts and commentaries from Revelations (MS V G 3, fol. 37ʳ), some of them quite savage, and he may have amplified these in the Czech delivery.

[101] See above, n. 25, for these outlines. Dated according to the order of pericopes in use in Bohemia at that time, the sermon outline on Mark 8:1–9 would have been scheduled for 30 July. In my article, "The Prague Insurrection," *ad* notes 62–65, I argue that Želivský did not use that outline, which he probably wrote before the Mt. Tabor meeting of 22 July; instead, he probably wrote a new outline after the meeting. I show that the outline on Matt. 7:15–21, the pericope for 6 August 1419, was certainly written before the Defenestration of 30 July (for one thing, because of the passage quoted below, n. 106), and I offer reasons for supposing that Želivský actually prepared this outline for use on the 30th. The text is in MS V G 3, fols. 33ʳ–42ᵛ.

men before your idols. And I will lay the dead carcases of the children of Israel before their idols; and I will scatter your bones round about your altars."? [102] Or Proverbs 7:26: "For she hath cast down many wounded: yea, many strong men have been slain by her."? [103] And there are more such: for example, Jeremiah 14:13–16, including the key words, "And the people . . . shall be cast out in the streets" (*erunt projecti in viis*); Revelation 19:20: "These both were cast alive into a lake of fire." [104] The Lamentations of Jeremiah over Jerusalem (Lam. 1:2–4)—

> She weepeth sore in the night, and her tears are on her cheeks. . . . All her friends have spurned her, they are become her enemies. Judah is gone into captivity because of affliction . . . all her persecutors overtook her between the straits. The ways of Zion do mourn, because none come to the solemn feasts: all her gates are desolate: her priests sigh, her virgins are afflicted, and she is in bitterness.

—these become Želivský's lament for Prague, when he adds, "Sic timendum est de civitate Pragensi!" [105] Of course there is no explicit line of argument in the sermon outline that could be construed as instructions to kill anyone, nor can we ever know just what Želivský actually said from the pulpit. But *if* he used his outline he would hardly have moderated its moods of violence and tension, and the recurrent images of men cast out, cast down, dying in the streets, must have had even more of an impact in the Czech, an impact that came from the images themselves, not from any logical sequence. In a similar sense we can appreciate the force of a long passage in which Želivský developed the theme of persecution of the righteous by the evil: the apostles and martyrs did not persecute, they were persecuted; the false prophets persecuted the true ones, not *vice versa*. Then: "the canons, parish priests, monks and nuns persecuted Master John Hus, but Hus did not persecute them," and finally: "And so the faithful community does not persecute the magistrates and councillors (*iudices et iuratos*), but these persecute the faithful Christians." [106] Logically this statement would imply that the faithful should bear up meekly under even more persecution, to imitate their pious models, but logic is for intellectuals, not for the masses; it is not hard to understand how the latter could listen to these words and be inflamed with desire for vengeance, in the first place against the government that had been put in office on the very anniversary day of John Hus's martyrdom.

[102] MS V G 3, fol. 38ʳ.
[103] *Ibid.*, fol. 35ʳ.
[104] *Ibid.*, fols. 36ʳ, 37ʳ.
[105] *Ibid.*, fol. 35ᵛ.
[106] *Ibid.*, fol. 39ʳ: "Sicut non persequitur communitas fidelis iudices et iuratos, sed iudices et iurati persecuntur fideles cristianos."

The sermon ended about 8:30 in the morning,[107] and the people moved out of the church in the kind of procession that had become familiar in the streets of the New Town, but which had recently been prohibited. As usual, Želivský marched at the head, carrying the body of Christ in a monstrance. Since the immediate effect on him of the royal reaction had been to deprive him of his pulpit in the church of St. Stephen, he led the procession there; it was a brief march, of about a quarter of an hour. The Catholic priest was inside, celebrating mass, and had locked the doors, but the Hussites broke them down and took over the church for a utraquist service. Then the crowd, newly fortified, moved out and marched on the New Town Hall, a walk of not more than ten minutes; they arrived at about 9:30. Ordinarily, perhaps, the magistrates would not have been conducting business on a Sunday, and at 9:30 would have been at mass; but at this time four of them, including the burgomaster, were in the Hall, actually a tower, wearing their chains of office and conferring with leading anti-Hussite burghers. This was probably a quickly convened meeting, prompted by reports of what had been going on at the Mother of God of the Snows, and the magistrates had barely had time to send for reinforcements to the Subchamberlain, John of Bechyně, at the Prague Castle across the river. But the troops had not yet come, the Hussite mob was in the square below the tower, and the magistrates were summoned to release the men they had previously imprisoned for having promoted the cause of communion in both kinds. Understandably, but unwisely, the magistrates decided to stall for time by engaging the Hussites in talk, about which we know little, except that instead of a promise to release the prisoners there was bickering and language that the Hussites could regard as insulting. Did the radicals, looking up at their enemies in the tower, suddenly hear the echoes of Želivský's sermon, with its scenario of the total war between Christ and Antichrist, its imagery of sinful men being cast down to destruction in the streets? Perhaps some of them did, and were brought to such a point of fury that they stormed into the Town Hall—led by Žižka?—assaulted those inside, and threw about thirteen of them out of the window. Those not previously killed or killed by the fall were finished off by the Hussites below, with Želivský standing by, holding up his monstrance and urging his followers on.[108]

[107] For this and what follows, see the analysis of the sources in my "Prague Insurrection," §2.

[108] The Prague Hussite, Master Laurence of Březová, who detested Želivský, joins the Catholic sources in registering horror: the magistrates were "enormiter deiecti et atrociter mactati et interfecti" (p. 345). It is the *Anonymus,* p. 531, who tells us that while the slaughter was going on, "dictus Johannes . . . non recessit cum corpore Christi, continue incitans populum ad istud immane facinus consumandum." This seems reasonable enough to me, as I imagine the situation, but otherwise there is no

While the actual murders may have been unforeseen, the coup itself—the forcible occupation of the Town Hall and the organization of power—was well managed. At once the raging mob was brought under strict control—the bodies of the magistrates were not even looted of their valuable chains of office—and when John of Bechyně finally arrived, at the head of about three hundred mounted soldiers, the Hussite force was so formidable that he withdrew without fighting. Meanwhile the call went out for all residents of the New Town to rally at the Town Hall under arms—those refusing had to flee the city—and a militia was organized under four captains, who also took control of the town insignia, including the seal.[109] Somewhat later the people elected a new set of magistrates who of course were Hussites, but interestingly enough they were men of substance, not even adherents of the extreme radicalism represented by Želivský. In other words, whatever may be said about the "Defenestration" itself, the political action was limited by political calculations. It was therefore possible for the moderate Hussite magistrates controlling the Old Town to associate themselves with the coup in the New Town and, with the help of pro-Hussite members of the royal court, to bring King Wenceslas to the point of accepting the *fait accompli*. At first, naturally enough, he flew into a violent rage, but then agreed to an arrangement whereby the New Town "humbled itself" to the king and in exchange received royal confirmation of its new magistrates. Reaction was dead in Prague; without direction from the crown it would soon be rolled back in the provinces as well, and the pre-February situation would be restored, under conditions of extreme Hussite militance. At least this is the way things must have looked in early August to the leaders of the Taborite-radical coalition. In his sermon for 13 August Želivský, who two weeks earlier had lamented over Prague in the words of Jeremiah, gave exultant expression to the new mood of victory:

> Oh would that Prague now, at this time, might be the model for all the faithful—not only in Moravia, but in Hungary, Poland and Austria! [110]

If he did not mention Bohemia, it must have been because he did not think of the triumph in Prague otherwise than as a triumph of Bohemian Hussitism.

Wenceslas, however, spoiled these prospects by succumbing to an apoplec-

---

reason to believe it and those who wish to rescue Želivský from the indictment are free to choose other, less explicit sources.

[109] Laurence, p. 346.

[110] MS V G 3, fol. 46ᵛ: "O utinam nunc tempore isto Praga civitas esset forma omnibus credentibus, non solum in Moravia sed in Ungaria, Polonia, Austria, etc.!"

tic stroke, at Nový Hrad on 16 August.[111] Everything was now once again
open to change, as the claims of the Emperor Sigismund, Wenceslas's half-
brother, could hardly be rejected without a revolution that few Hussites were
prepared to undertake. In fact, all of the forces in the realm would have to
fight their way to a new equilibrium; now, however, one of those forces was
a highly organized, militant, national union of radicals, a factor that neither
the Catholics nor the conservative Hussites would be able to ignore.

THE STRUGGLE FOR NATIONAL LEADERSHIP

The Defenestration had opened two lines of action to the radicals, and it
is instructive to see how they rejected one of them—a New Town-Taborite
revolution—in favor of the other—formal submission to the king, in alliance
with the conservative leadership. We can only speculate where this line
would have led them had the king not died; when he did, however, both
parties had to face the problem of securing the reform in some relationship
to the Emperor Sigismund, who was now the legitimate claimant to the
Bohemian Crown. Naturally there were different approaches to this problem, which was inevitably more painful to the conservative elements than to
the radicals, most of whom were prepared to face the fact that Sigismund
could never be a Hussite king. The university masters, for reasons discussed
in the preceding chapter, were literally unable to imagine defying the
legitimate authorities that could alone give sanction to the reformation; the
Prague burghers were perhaps more flexible, but they too found it hard to
conceive of life without a king. The Hussite nobility were themselves
incarnations of legitimate authority and were no doubt well aware of what a
revolt might mean to their own position, while the important class of royal
officials, burgraves, councillors, and the like were entirely dependent on their
relationship to the royal person. All of these groups faced the task of
reconciling their Hussitism with their royalism, under conditions that made
such a reconciliation far more difficult than it had been even in the most
reactionary periods of Wenceslas's reign.

Their program for the future was probably worked out at a diet held
sometime in August or September; there is little direct evidence that such a
diet met, but it is likely that some sort of meeting was held to consider the
conditions under which Sigismund would be accepted as king.[112] Two texts

---

[111] For interesting details about the king's poor health see *HR*, I, 64, n. 51. There is
no reason to believe the charge in the *Anonymus*, p. 533, that Wenceslas was smothered
by his favorites.

[112] A reliable memorandum composed in 1433 uses the phrase, "concilio communitatum celebrato," without clear indication of just when it happened (*Mon. conc. saec. XV*,

of these conditions survive, one in German, the other in Czech, with the latter containing some additional articles especially expressive of the interests of the Prague burghers; on the whole, however, the matter seems to have been handled under baronial leadership, as was natural.[113] In general, the tendency of the demands was toward a national church, subject to Rome but protected from all Roman intervention except that permitted by the Estates. No papal provisions, bulls, interdicts, or other decrees were to have effect in Bohemia without the consent of the king, the royal council, and the barons. No citations outside the realm were to be allowed. No foreigners were to be put in ecclesiastical offices if capable Czechs were available. The arbiter in questions of faith was to be the university, which was to be allowed to grant its degrees again, and to which obedience was to be compulsory. Within this framework the adherents of communion in one kind should celebrate or assist at mass beside the utraquists, neither party hereticating the other; the Catholic bishops were to ordain utraquist and orthodox candidates indiscriminately;[114] Sigismund was to lead the magnates and Estates of the realm in seeking the pope's consent to utraquism or at least his permission to appeal to a future council. On the other hand, within this national church the principles of reform were to prevail: the Word of God was to be freely preached; the sacraments were to be administered without charge; the clergy was not to hold secular office or dominion; the clergy was to be supported by the voluntary gifts of the people; the Czech language was to be allowed for the Gospel and Epistle in the mass. All in all these demands can be

---

I, 387). That "communitatum" means "of the Estates" rather than "of the communities" is pointed out by I. Hlaváček, "Husitské sněmy," *SbH*, IV (1956), 76. Tomek, IV, 8, suggests the diet met before the end of August; Pekař, *Žižka*, III, 19, guesses the first two weeks of September; Macek, *Tábor*, I, 224, accepts both possibilities; Bartoš, "Prvý sněm husitské revoluce," *JSH*, XX (1951), 81–87, and now also *HR*, I, 70 ff., argues that there was no diet, only a meeting of a Hussite League of towns, headed by Prague and joined by the Taborite congregations. His reinterpretation of the evidence seems to me too drastic to be safe; I offer more particular arguments as necessary, below.

[113] The German redaction is preserved in *Eberhard Windeckes Denkwürdigkeiten zur Geschichte des Zeitalters Kaiser Sigmunds*, ed. W. Altmann (Berlin, 1893), pp. 121–124; the Czech version is in *AČ*, III, 206–208. Windecke says the articles were sent to Sigismund by the Bohemian barons "alsbalde konig Wenclaus . . . starp" (p. 121); elsewhere, however, he says that Sigismund received news of Wenceslas's death on St. Michael's Day (29 September) (p. 109). The latter dating may be a confused reference to another Bohemian mission; there were several of them at this time (see *AČ*, III, 209; also Pekař, *Žižka*, IV, 26). Bartoš (as in n. 112) rejects the general view, that the articles in Windecke were formulated by the barons, in favor of the hypothesis that they came from Prague and the (conjectured) league of towns.

[114] *AČ*, III, 207, §12: "That worthy men be accepted for ordination without simony and without newly-invented oaths and renunciations;" cf. Windecke, p. 123.

characterized as a revival of the baronial program of 5 September 1415, amplified by the program of 1417, and enriched by the innovations sanctioned by the St. Wenceslas Synod of 1418.

But there were also secular demands. No foreigners were to be put in civil offices if capable Czechs were available; the Czech language was to be used in judicial proceedings; the Czechs were to have the "first voice" everywhere in the realm. The king was not to take escheats if any kin were alive; he was to protect the legal rights of widows and orphans; he was not to use the treasury of the Bohemian Crown for non-Bohemian projects. Prague for its part added demands that the recently destroyed brothels not be reestablished, that the recent rebellious actions "not be remembered for evil," that the king confirm the acts of the Prague magistrates since the death of Wenceslas (see below). There were other miscellaneous points, and of course the general demand, that the king confirm the liberties and rights of the land and of the towns. New in all this were the pronounced insistence on the privileges of the Czech nationality, a perhaps increased awareness of privilege on the part of the nobility, and, strikingly, the prominence of Prague alongside the barons. In itself the whole set of demands was realistic enough, reflecting real interests and possibilities within the realm; but in relationship to Sigismund and to the Roman church the demands had a wildly fantastic character that is in itself instructive—it shows how far the more conservative Hussites were from the correct appraisal of the situation that alone could insure their survival. Here the radicals were in a much better position.

Immediately after Wenceslas's death the radical mob in Prague had begun to resume direct action in the spirit of July. They attacked various churches and monasteries, destroyed the brothels, and kept the city in turmoil into the month of September.[115] In the provinces, too, the radical Hussites attacked, smashed, and burned monasteries, persecuted the monks and, in a number of Hussite towns, repeated the actions of their allies in Prague.[116] The congrega-

---

[115] For details see Tomek, IV, 2 ff., 10; Macek, *Tábor,* I, 222–224; Heymann, pp. 68–70. According to the *Chron. univ. prag.,* p. 581, the brothels were destroyed ("omnia lupanaria anihilata sunt") on 19 August. Želivský's sermon for 27 August notes: "plus accusant coram regibus et clientibus pro asseribus depictis quam pro aliquo puncto evangelico, sed non instant, quod destrueretur hampayss [Czech for "brothel"], sed aliqui dicunt, quia male factum est, quod destructus est Krakow [i.e., the red-light street in Prague]" (MS V G 3, fol. 69ʳ). The dates here confirm the dating of the sermons set forth above, n. 101; B. Auštěcká, *Jan Želivský jako politik* (Prague, 1925), p. 69, n. 73, quotes the passage, but because she dates the sermon on 13 August, assumes there were perhaps two destructive actions.

[116] The Dominican monastery in Písek was destroyed and burnt by the Hussites on 20 August (Laurence, p. 347), with some of the monks taken prisoner. Perhaps the attack on the Dominican monastery in New Plzeň, attested for 1419 (Höfler, I, 50), occurred at the same time. Cf. the *Anonymus,* Höfler, I, 529 f.

tion movement continued; its mode of existence must have tended to extend the influence of sectarianism toward the point where the Taborites would lose interest in moderation and be ready to do away with all the rites, ceremonies, institutions, cults, and practices of the orthodox faith, except for communion and preaching, to reject any belief in Purgatory, any images in the church, and any vestiges of a clerical endowment.[117] But all this is only supposition based on what came later; as far as the sources for the summer and autumn of 1419 go, we cannot see any tendency of the Taborite movement to lapse into sectarianism—whatever may have been its religious belief, its leaders evidently kept it committed to large-scale organized political action. It may be significant that the center of the movement seems to have shifted, from South Bohemian Mt. Tabor to the West Bohemian region of Plzeň, where Wenceslas Koranda was the outstanding leader and perhaps had been for the past year or so. We have already seen him as a fervent evangelical radical in Prague, as a Waldensianist sectarian in the provinces, as a beneficiary of the Hussite establishment of 1417; now we find him playing what was to be his most characteristic role—not that of a theoretician but that of a political, even military leader. As the challenge to the radical movement became increasingly serious, and as the nobility inclined more and more to try to stop the congregations by force,[118] the leadership of men like Koranda must have won more and more support.

Thus the next direct evidence for an important congregation after the Mt. Tabor one of 22 July comes from a hilltop in the Plzeň region, at Bzí Hora, on 17 September—a meeting that must have been dominated by Koranda.[119] It issued a manifesto defining its aspirations in a political sense, and laid down a plan for further action:

> We declare in this letter, publicly and to all, that our meeting on the mountains and in the fields is for no other purpose than for freely hearing

[117] See Laurence, pp. 403 ff. For the congregations after Wenceslas's death, see the *Chronicon veteris collegiati,* Höfler, I, 79, where Bechyně, Plzeň, and Beránek are mentioned. Anti-Hussite rhymes composed right after Wenceslas's death address the Taborites with the question, "And what are you doing on that Mt. Tabor—God knows!" (J. Feifalik, "Untersuchungen über altböhmische Vers- und Reimkunst," *SKAW,* XXXIX (1862), 341). In early November the *OCA,* pp. 29 f., refers to a community of the brethren from Ústí Sezimovo—obviously the same community that had been formed by the Mt. Tabor congregations and which had never been dissolved.

[118] See Laurence's testimony, above, *ad* n. 68; also *OCA,* pp. 28 ff.

[119] Since he is known to have been a prominent leader at the congregations that the Bzí Hora meeting organized, and since Bzí Hora was in the Plzeň area (I follow Tomek, IV, 10, and *HR,* I, 70, n. 65, rather than Pekař, *Žižka,* IV, 22, and Macek, *Tábor,* I, 208, n. 223, who suppose it to have been in South Bohemia), which was Koranda's home ground, the conclusion is inescapable.

the faithful and salutary message based on the Law of God, and for the necessary communion of the most worthy sacrament of the divine body and blood of our Lord and Savior Jesus Christ, in memory of his martyrdom and our redemption, and for fortification, preservation, and confirmation in a salutary life. Accordingly all of us, with one will, ask the dear Lord God that we may be of one Law, one faith, one heart, and one soul. First we ask God that we be purged of all that is evil and damaging to the soul, and developed in all that is good. We also ask God, now that we have recognized the cunning and damaging seduction of our souls by false and hypocritical prophets, guided by Antichrist against the Law of God, that we may beware of them and diligently be on our guard against them, so that they may no longer deceive and mislead us away from the old and true faith of Lord Jesus and of the apostles. For we now clearly see the great abomination standing in the holy place, as prophesied by the prophet Daniel: the ridicule, blasphemy, suppression, and repudiation of all of God's Truth, and the enormous glorification of all Antichristian hypocritical evil, under the name of holiness and benevolence. . . .

[There follow biblical passages, especially I Macc. 2:50–64, urging courageous defense of God's Truth.]

And so, dearest ones, we ask and beg you for God and your salvation, to join us all on Saturday [30 September] . . . in gathering at The Crosses [*Na Křížkách*], on the fields, on the Benešov road on the mountain that is behind Ládvy as you go toward Prague, for godly unity in behalf of the freedom of the Law of God and for the salutary benefit and honorable welfare of the whole realm, in order that offenses and manifest scandals and dissensions may be ended and removed, with the help of God, the king, the lords, knights, squires, and the whole Christian community.[120]

The religious element in this manifesto is clearly a reprise of old hilltop themes, including the idea of living in a crucial moment of decision, the abomination of desolation standing in the holy place, the recognition of seduction by the Romanist clergy, a certain exaltedly penitential fervor, utraquism. The mood is apocalyptic but not yet chiliastic; any doubts about this can be resolved by a glance at the last sentence, which summons the faithful not to total war or total withdrawal, but to ordinary political action, possibly involving force but still within the framework of the existing political and social order.[121] But how could the situation in mid-September seem dominated by the Antichrist? Had the great radical victory of late July been so thoroughly nullified? Obviously yes; otherwise the congregants of

---

[120] *AČ*, III, 205 f., reprinted in *KJBB*, pp. 43–45.

[121] Macek draws attention to the manifesto's recognition that force might be necessary —this comes through especially in the biblical quotations that I have not translated— but there is a difference between practical, political force and chiliast orgiastic violence —hence Macek is wrong in regarding the manifesto as a chiliast document (*Tábor*, I, 218 f., 380).

Bzí Hora would have to be regarded as hysterics. But who then were the reactionaries, and what had they been doing?

The answer emerges from a study of the sources for the great political action to which the Bzí Hora manifesto was a summons, the meeting of 30 September at The Crosses. Contingents came from all the radical centers of the realm, including Prague, and consummated the usual religious actions; the sermons stressed the duty of the people to love one another in God and to act vigorously in behalf of Christ's Truth.[122] Then on the night of that same day the congregants moved on to Prague, where they were received with great ceremony and lodged in the monastery of St. Ambrose; the Praguers supplied rations. At this point the direct narrative sources suddenly fade away, and we are left wondering why the congregants went to Prague and what they did there. The Bzí Hora manifesto, to be sure, had stated that the purpose of the congregation at The Crosses was "in order that offenses and manifest scandals and dissensions may be ended and removed" by joint action of all elements of society, including "the whole Christian community" —that is, the common people, led by their priests. But what were the offenses, scandals, and dissensions? Here we may cite a very instructive passage from a sermon that John Želivský wrote shortly after the congregants arrived in Prague:

> Now parish priests and masters have met with monks and nuns against Christ: formerly they were not in agreement about doctrine, as in the matter of lay communion [in both kinds], but now they are in agreement against infant communion. Similarly some of our party, before they had churches, attacked them vigorously because of their many ceremonies and their incomes, but now they are themselves in agreement with them in virtually all things, except that they sometimes give the chalice on certain occasions.[123]

The passage is certainly unambiguous; it tells us that by early October there had emerged a union of Catholics and conservative Hussites—the latter no doubt led by those who had fought against infant communion, chief of whom was John Jesenic.[124] The union evidently involved an agreement to

[122] Laurence, p. 348; *OCA*, pp. 28 f.

[123] Quoted by Auštěcká, *Jan Želivský*, p. 70; the text in MS V G 3, fol. 149ᵛ—the sermon scheduled for 15 October.

[124] See above, n. 46, and chap. v, nn. 128, 129. A list of articles in Czech, similar in reference to those of the St. Wenceslas Synod of 1418, but entirely lacking in any concessions to radicalism or even Hussitism, survive, undated, and are printed in *AČ*, VI, 37 f.; they have a prefatory note saying that all were accepted by Jesenic and the other masters who had led Hus's party, except for the matter of communion in both kinds. Various scholars have proposed various dates, but never with any serious attempt at proof (see Kejř, *Husitský právník*, pp. 121 f.); in the same spirit I would suggest that the articles might well fit into the situation now under discussion.

disagree about the chalice, but otherwise the basis of union was clearly nonreligious, and we can safely infer that it was political. It must have been based on the program sent to Sigismund by the alliance of Prague and the barons some weeks earlier, and it must have provided, in the spirit of that program, that both sides would coexist in peace until Sigismund could come, take over the realm, and procure a papal reconsideration of utraquism. Furthermore, the foundations for the union must have been laid in the first part of September, for the abomination of desolation mentioned in the Bzí Hora manifesto of 17 September can hardly have been anything but this Hussite-Catholic rapprochement. Thus although the program sent to Sigismund was far from being a betrayal of Hussitism—it provided for several radical reforms, even if it did not include infant communion—it may have paved the way for such a betrayal, a union of the university masters with the "rich and noble" of the world, a union that included an attempt to stop Želivský by confronting him with the authority of the masters. "The ones who preach the truth and attack the endowment they do not call masters any more," as he observed, possibly referring to Jakoubek and his party.[125] And indeed the policy of maintaining the *status quo* could only have led to the result it had produced at the beginning of the year: within the university, leadership came to the conservatives. And when Laurence of Březová tells us that after King Wenceslas's death Želivský had frequent conflicts with Master Christian of Prachatice "de ritibus ecclesie," [126] we can fit this information into the present context, when Želivský complained that "the Prague masters are doing what the ones at Constance did, in regard to ceremonies, oaths, killing—they cite no scriptural authority but only the multitude of masters." [127] As we shall see, Christian's church was to suffer most from the radicals' attacks at this time, and the reason may well have been their resentment of his "betrayal."

Thus it may be inferred that the radicals came to Prague after their meeting at The Crosses in order to struggle against the unfavorable constel-

---

[125] MS V G 3, fol. 149ᵛ: "Sic hodierna die eandem veritatem quam Cristus docuit spirituales persecuntur et docti, et congregantur in multitudine divites, elati, famosi, a mundo honorati, volentes iustos et pauperes opprimere. Cum dicunt, tamen omnes magistri sunt contrarii huic veritati. Iam istos non dicunt magistros qui veritatem predicant vel dotacionem impediunt." I date the sermon 15 October. Cf. the similar passage for 13 August, on fol. 51ᵛ.

[126] Laurence, p. 520.

[127] MS V G 3, fol. 149ᵛ: "Sic iam faciunt magistri Pragenses sicut in Constancia, nullam quasi scripturam ex lege aducentes, ut de ceremoniis, de iuramento, de occisione, sed solum allegant multitudinem magistrorum, sed non allegant veritatem. Unde vere imitatores sunt patrum suorum, sicut de Constancia scripserunt, quia tot et tot fuerunt. Et sic predicant mendaciter contra veritatem, confidentes in multitudine nequam."

lation that had come into being in connection with the negotiations with Sigismund, and it may also be inferred that the new situation had been recognizable for at least a month before. It is not surprising, then, to find that the congregants came to the capital with an *alternate* political program, their own, which had emerged from the congregation movement as early as the month of July. Here we are provided with a very explicit statement:[128]

> When King Wenceslas had died, there rose up a congregation of many thousand men and women of both the lay and clerical estates. They came to Prague, not, however, with any considerable arms [129] but in a kind of peaceful manner, and, their ranks swelled by large numbers of people, sought as it were by arousing sedition to set up for themselves a bishop and a secular prince, intending to simply cut themselves off from the Roman church. But others, although much fewer in number, dissuaded them from this and insisted on securing a hearing [*scil.,* for utraquism], in pursuit of which they compacted to such effect that the other plan came to nothing.

Two programs thus stood face to face, the one seeking to solve the problem of Hussite security by setting up an independent national church-state, the other seeking above all else a hearing before the pope, who could solve the religious problem by either accepting Hussitism for Europe as a whole or at least agreeing to tolerate it in Bohemia. Of course the latter possibility left no room for anything going *beyond* utraquism, while the radical program was —as argued above—associated with sectarian doctrines that could not possibly coexist with the Hussitism of the non-Taborite elements. We know of no outright doctrinal showdown between the two sides at this time, but none was necessary: the conflicting positions could come to an adequate encounter over the single issue of whether or not to entrust the future of the reform to the negotiations between the barons and Sigismund.

In any case, the understandable resistance of the Prague leaders to the radical program was reinforced by the pressures exerted from Sigismund's side. Involved in wars with the Turks and Venetians, the Emperor made the mistake of not dealing with the Bohemian problem at once; when he finally did, he had no answer for the Bohemian missions sent to him but an instruction to keep the peace, to maintain the religious *status quo* as it had been under Wenceslas, and to await his arrival, at which time he would hold a national synod and diet whose decisions would be referred to the pope.[130] The message must have sounded encouraging to Hussite conservatives and

---

[128] In *Mon. conc. saec. XV,* I, 387.

[129] Exactly the same point is made in *OCA,* pp. 28 f.

[130] In *Mon. conc. saec. XV,* I, 387. The passage comes right after the one just quoted, and begins with the word "interim"—hence Sigismund's message came at about the time of the congregation at The Crosses and the meeting in Prague. Sigismund also sent instructions to the other political entities of the realm—see, e.g., *UB,* I, 26 f.

to those who might perhaps have formed an alliance with the radicals. At the same time the promises were reinforced by detailed and vigorous threats. The queen and the barons, who now constituted a royalist party including both Hussites and Catholics loyal to the principle of legitimacy above all else, communicated the Emperor's message to the city of Prague in the form of a sharp summons, given added weight by the fact that Sigismund had named Queen Sophia regent.[131] The emperor, they said, would confirm the rights and liberties of all estates, but he insisted on obedience, and in particular on an immediate cessation of turbulence, of church-smashing, and of unauthorized congregations in Prague and in the other Hussite towns; the monks and nuns who had been expelled from their convents were to be restored, and the Prague burghers who had had to flee the city during the previous violence were to be allowed to return. Various usurpations of royal authority by the magistrates of Prague were to be stopped.[132] When the Emperor came to Bohemia he would consider the question of utraquism "with the bishops, prelates, masters, priests, barons, and towns"; meanwhile both forms of communion were to coexist in peace. If the Praguers refused to obey these orders, the Queen and the barons would, according to Sigismund's instructions, use the royal treasury to finance suppression of disorders—"if you do not do what we command, . . . we will make you do it!" The summons then closed with a sharp reproach: although the Praguers had compacted among themselves to promote what was good and honorable for the land and for Sigismund—the reference is obviously to the meeting out of which

[131] *AČ*, III, 209 f. The summons is undated; Palacký suggested the beginning of 1420 (*loc. cit.*) but in his *Dějiny* corrected this to the second half of October and certainly before the turbulent events of early November (III, i, n. 393). I date it in the first days of October, for the following reasons. (1) The summons refers to acts of violence and rebellion that are obviously those that took place in Prague and various provincial centers after the death of Wenceslas—"destruction of churches and cloisters, smashing of images and altars, illegitimate congregations." (2) Moreover, as is to be seen from the summary I give of the text, the barons issuing the summons seem to have been reacting to the great meeting in Prague in early October. (3) The summons also includes a threat to use the royal treasure to force obedience, evidently by hiring troops, and this step was taken on 17 October (below). (4) The summons charges the Praguers with acts of which the magistrates, at least, were not guilty after the first week of October—the acts all belong to the period between Wenceslas's death and the meeting in Prague after the congregation at The Crosses. (5) The summons gives the first news that Queen Sophia had been appointed regent; the Old Town of Prague, adhering to the royalist union on 6 October, referred to her as regent, not just as queen ("regina et gubernatrice nostra ac regni Boemiae," *UB*, I, 2). (6) The summons was probably communicating Sigismund's message that came at about the time of the early October meeting in Prague (above, n. 130).

[132] The magistrates had usurped the royal right of appointing superior judges and controlling customs collections (Tomek, IV, 8).

had come Prague's contribution to the demands sent to Sigismund a month earlier [133]—they had in fact been guilty of acts of violence against the church, they had engaged in congregations without the "knowledge and will" of the regent barons, and they "sought to elect a bishop."

It seems highly probable that this summons, which after all included attractive promises, played an important part in persuading the Prague burghers to dissociate themselves from the radical congregants and to adhere to the party of legitimacy. As we have already learned, the radical program "came to nothing." Laurence of Březová, the spokesman for Prague Hussitism, who wrote in a time when the shameful folly of Prague's decision had become clear, covers the discussions between the congregants and the Praguers in one of his extraordinarily suggestive silences. After describing how the congregants had come to Prague, solemnly welcomed by the light of numerous torches and the clangor of bells, and how they had then been lodged and provisioned by the Praguers, he proceeds thus:

> Finally however the Praguers, in particular the magistrates [*seniores*], concluded a truce [*treugas pacis*] for a certain period with the royalists holding the Prague castle and the Vyšehrad, and all the newly arrived outsiders [*omnes extranei seu adveni*] . . . went home.[134]

Our other main source, the narrative of 1433, confirms this: "and thus [*scil.,* by Sigismund's message] the parties were pacified and made a truce among themselves, waiting for the king." [135] Thus the congregation at The Crosses only helped to precipitate the reactionary coalition that it had been designed to frustrate; the Taborites and Želivský's party had failed.[136]

[133] One of Prague's demands was that "His Grace would praise and confirm all the acts and decisions of the magistrates after the death of King Wenceslas, which are for the general good of the land or of the city, and which are not against the honor and right of His Grace" (*AČ*, III, 208). The summons says, "Remember how you have compacted among yourselves to promote what would be good and honorable for His Grace . . . and hence for the land" (*AČ*, III, 210).

[134] Laurence, p. 348. See Seibt, *Hussitica*, pp. 136 ff., for a different understanding of *seniores,* as a kind of senate.

[135] *Mon. conc. saec. XV*, I, 387.

[136] The speech at the Prague Diet of 1426 (see above, n. 56) says that after the Crossroads meeting, the congregants went to Prague and there all the Estates [*obce*] agreed to a program, that which is generally known as the Four Articles of Prague, which are given. Nicholas of Pelhřimov's Latin version of this is virtually identical (Höfler, II, 479 f.). Tomek, IV, 12 f., accepts this account, as does Bartoš, "Sněm husitské revoluce," p. 102, n. 12. I regard it as a tendentious distortion that simply omits all the internal conflict between the Hussite parties from 30 September to the spring of 1420, when the Prague-Tabor alliance was reestablished. Both Jakoubek in 1426 and Nicholas of Pelhřimov in the 1430's had obvious motives to gloss over the embarrassing period, which was dominated by ideas and tendencies that neither approved of.

It may be supposed that predictions of what would happen had been brought by the Prague contingent to The Crosses, and perhaps it was in a mood of pessimistic caution that the priests at the congregation, before moving on to Prague, set a day for another meeting, to be held on 10 November in the capital itself.[137] Thus the failure of early October did not have to be taken as final, and the radical contingents left Prague in a stormy spirit, smashing images in churches and monasteries of the town, and devoting particular attention to the Church of St. Michael in the Old Town,[138] whose rector was Christian of Prachatice, no doubt one of the leaders in bringing Prague to make peace with the royalists. Violence continued to dominate the events of October, even after the magistrates of the Old Town formally adhered to the royalist union on 6 October, allegedly to advance the Law of God, to secure its freedom, to safeguard the realm, and to cleanse the Czech nation of the charge of heresy; in fact it was merely to keep the peace.[139] Želivský's party remained intransigent, and it included many of the people in both Prague towns as well as the magistrates of the New Town; it was therefore necessary for Lord Čeněk of Vartemberk, leader of the royalist union, to proceed with the plan for repression, on 17 October, by hiring German and other non-Czech mercenaries to maintain order and to garrison a number of places in the Little Town, across the river from the two major towns.[140]

We can imagine that this military rule clamped down on *all* religious agitation, but particularly on the propagandizing of anything beyond what the Estates had agreed upon after Wenceslas's death; thus the advocacy (and practice) of infant communion must have been forbidden. And Želivský's October sermon outlines show him reacting to just this. On 22 October he attacked towns that opposed the Law of God; in the latter part of the month he complained that the secular lords and the magistrates were setting up evil officials, and he asserted that God would not allow those giving communion to infants to be handed over to the torturers.[141] Later he was even more explicit: "our masters . . . have made their own will supersede the clear scriptural authority for communion of infants"; they "suffocate those taking communion in both kinds, those giving communion to infants after baptism, and those preaching against the endowment of the church." [142]

---

[137] *OCA*, p. 29.

[138] Laurence, p. 348.

[139] The text of the Old Town's adherence in *UB*, I, 2; a less euphemistic picture of the royalist union, including the names of the Catholic barons, is given in Lord Ulrich of Rožmberk's adherence, *AČ*, III, 208 f.

[140] Laurence, p. 348.

[141] See Auštěcká, *Jan Želivský*, pp. 23 f., 71.

[142] *Ibid.*, pp. 70 f.

Mutinous to begin with, the Prague radicals must have responded powerfully to preaching of this sort, and their courage must have been heightened by the awareness that early November would again see many hundreds of their Taborite allies streaming into the capital from the provinces. Tension and the spirit of resistance were soon replaced by outright fighting, and on 25 October the forces of the New Town, now including John Žižka, attacked and took the fortress of the Vyšehrad, just south of the city.[143] The two parties had become two military concentrations, the royalists dominating the Prague Castle and under it the Little Town, on the left bank of the Vltava, the New Town dominating the right bank through its control of the Vyšehrad. The Old Town was caught in between, in a symbolic situation.

It comes as no surprise to learn that the congregation of early November was rather different from previous assemblies. The royalist nobility, now in a state of military preparedness throughout the realm,[144] determined to prevent the radicals from reaching Prague, and the radicals for their part took care to arm themselves as best they could.[145] The Plzeň group, led by Koranda, joined with other West Bohemian contingents in the march to Prague and succeeded in getting through safely. The radicals from the South, identified as the group from Ústí, and identical with the community that earlier in the year had formed around Mt. Tabor, were unable to avoid an encounter with the royalist feudality, near Živhošť—the first real battle of the Hussite revolution—and they suffered heavy losses. News of the event reached Prague on 4 November at about two o'clock in the afternoon, when a group of radical priests led by Ambrose of Hradec Králové promptly summoned the people to arms by ringing the great bells of the city; the excited crowd, composed of men from both the Old and New Towns, decided to strike a counterblow by attacking the royalist positions across the river.[146] The armed forces, led by Nicholas of Hus, crossed the bridge and joined battle with the royalist garrisons of the Little Town; at the price of some losses the Hussites drove the enemy out of their strongholds, and although the following days saw a continuation of the fighting, the royalist forces were unable to regain what they had lost. In the midst of "the night of tribulation and anguish, the night of grief and sorrow," as Laurence of Březová called it, Queen Sophia fled from the Prague Castle, accompanied by Lord Ulrich of Rožmberk.

After such open warfare, which absorbed the "community" if not the magistrates of the Old Town as well as that of the New, Prague found

[143] Laurence, pp. 348 f.

[144] *OCA*, p. 29; cf. Tomek, IV, 14 f.

[145] *OCA*, pp. 29 f.; Laurence, pp. 349 f. See the account of Heymann, pp. 83 ff.

[146] See Heymann's strategic interpretation of this move, pp. 83 f.; I do not agree with it.

herself squarely in the camp of revolution. The royalists increased their efforts to build up an army; Prague's former allies of the royalist union— barons both Hussite and Catholic, and various Catholic towns—sent her formal letters of defiance on 6 November and thereafter,[147] and at the same time the masses of provincial congregants entered the city, where they reinforced the now thoroughly mobilized power of the radical population. Once again, however, the great surge of strength on the left produced its counterpart on the right, and the Prague magistrates began negotiations with the royalists in the Castle. In the remarkable absence of any information about the radical program of November, or about the radical-conservative confrontations that must have taken place, we must assume that the issues at that time were exactly what they had been a month earlier, and that exactly the same considerations that had moved the Prague *seniores* to join the royalist union on 6 October now—reinforced by the even more critical situation—led them to seek another accommodation. Želivský's radicalism was suppressed,[148] and on 13 November the magistrates of both Prague towns made a truce with the Queen and barons, to run until 24 April 1420: Prague would give up the Vyšehrad castle and would refrain from destroying images, churches, and monasteries, while the royalists promised to defend utraquism and the freedom of the Law of God in Prague and throughout Bohemia.[149] This should have put an end to the royalists' persecution of Hussites in various parts of the realm, but in fact it did not, and of course there was no provision for more than mere utraquism. As Želivský put it, the "false masters" were "now joining with the magnates to attack the

---

[147] *AČ*, IV, 375 ff.; cf. Tomek, IV, 19-21.

[148] Many passages could be cited from his sermons for November, but I here offer only examples, from the outline for 19 November. Thus, MS V G 3, fol. 218[r]: speaking evidently of his timid fellow-travelers, he wrote, "nunc dicunt, Scimus quia verum est quod predicatur, sed propter seniores non audemus facere." And it must have been with deliberation that he recalled the canon of Hussite martyrs—the three youths in Prague, the two in Olomouc, and the two in Constance (fol. 211[v]). The theme of the sermon, "abeuntes pharisaei consilium inierunt" (Matt. 22:15), was of course tailor-made for his purpose (fol. 209[r]): "Sic hodie nostri pharisei abierunt ab quibusdam veritatem predicantibus, in consilium, non ut informarent caritative sed ut caperent deceptive et traderent potestati presidis." Finally, just as Pilate knew Jesus had been betrayed by those who hated him, "Ut nunc spero quia rex Hungarie [*scil.*, Sigismund] iam scit quia Magister Johannes Hus [*MS:* Joh. id.] traditus. . . . Et nunc nostri pharizei sedent in iudiciis tradentes fideles" (fol. 209[v]). The "pharizei" are merely a term for the "magistri" (e.g., fol. 210[r], "pharizei et magistri . . ."): thus we have a clear reflection of the situation, in which the masters and magistrates were lining up with the royalists to persecute the radicals—just as Hus and the others had been persecuted.

[149] Laurence, pp. 350 f.; for a German text of the truce, see *UB.* I. 11 f.

just," in the matter of infant communion and other points.[150] There is indeed little favorable to say about the truce.[151] It was cowardly in that it marked a retreat from necessary warfare, foolish in that it placed reliance on Sigismund's promise to procure a hearing, and disastrous in that it prevented a political unification of the Hussite parties. The responsible leaders of the national movement had their own reasons for shying away from the political revolution and religious schism that Tabor had come to stand for, but it is impossible to see how, in mid-November, they could have thought there was any other course open to them. Events would soon discredit their policy; meanwhile the Taborites left Prague for their local centers, where they had to solve their own problems outside the framework of national and genuinely political action, and under a persecution of unremitting intensity. Naturally enough, the social, political, and religious development of Taboritism now entered a new stage.

[150] MS V G 3, Fol. 211ʳ: ". . . nunc cum magnatis conveniunt accusantes iustos"; the whole sermon teems with such complaints.

[151] Alone among scholars Bartoš has advanced a quite different view, most recently in *HR*, I, 76; it is based on his peculiar interpretation of the whole sequence of events in the autumn. He supposes that all the Hussites of Prague and the provinces formed a union, under Prague's leadership; this union produced the list of demands sent to Sigismund and the agreement of the St. Wenceslas Synod (which Bartoš redates to 1419). The consensus was based on the conservatives' renunciation of their opposition to infant communion, and on the Taborites' renunciation of their program to elect a king and bishop, as well as other things. The truce of 13 November, then, was not an act of treachery by Prague against the radicals, but a clever move to buy time *and* to release the forces of the provincial Hussites from their need to defend Prague—these forces could now turn to self-defense at home. The alliance remained unbroken. Against this view are some important sources, including Želivský's sermons (which Bartoš does not use); also the course of events, which clearly shows the most extreme split between Prague and the Taborites after 13 November; finally what I regard as the testimony of common sense.

VII

CHILIASM AND THE FOUNDING
OF TABOR, 1419–1420

ADVENTISM AND THE NEW CONGREGATIONS

THE FAILURE of the Taborites' national program was followed by a return of the provincial contingents to their respective home grounds; their bitter disappointment with the Prague leadership can easily be imagined.[1] As it turned out, moreover, the temporary peace bought by Prague was balanced by an intensified effort of the royalists to exterminate Hussitism in the provinces; immediately after his account of the November truce and the Taborite exodus from Prague, Laurence of Březová offers the following information:

> In these times therefore the faithful Czechs, both clergy and laity, who favored communion in both kinds and devotedly promoted it, and who grieved at the unjust death of Master John Hus . . . suffered very great difficulties, tribulations, anguish, and torment throughout the Kingdom of Bohemia, at the hands of the enemies and blasphemers of the Truth, who grievously afflicted them by plundering their property, by subjecting them to harsh captivity, to hunger and thirst, and by slaughtering their bodies. For these enemies of the Truth hunted down priests and laymen who ardently supported the chalice in various parts of the realm and brought them to the men of Kutná Hora, to whom they sold some for money. The Kutná Horans —Germans and cruel persecutors and enemies of the Czechs, especially of those loving the Truth of Christ—afflicted them with various blasphemies

[1] Before leaving, "the Taborites plundered the Malá Strana and caused great damage to the houses in which they were staying, by the destruction of buildings" (Laurence, p. 351).

and diverse punishments, and inhumanly threw them—some alive, some first decapitated—into deep mine shafts, especially into the mine shaft near the church of St. Martin near the Kouřim gate, which shaft the Kutná Horans called "Tabor" . . . . In a short time more than 1600 utraquists were killed by them and thrown into the shafts, the executioners often being exhausted by the fatigue of slaughter.[2]

Such persecution was not new to the Taborites, who had after all fought a pitched battle at Živhošť against the same royalists in early November, but it now struck them much harder, both physically and psychologically. Before the truce, royalist attacks were merely obstacles in the path of a great mass movement, imbued with hope and surging rapidly toward the crest of its power; now the separate Taborite congregations and the individual Taborite priests and laymen, dispersed throughout the country, the memory of failure fresh in their minds, had to face nothing less than an organized extermination machine operated by those opposed to them in class, nationality, and religion. Moreover, they stood alone in their peril, for Prague was spending the months following the truce in renewed pursuit of Sigismund's favor, and so far from offering help to the brethren of the provinces, was busily dismantling her own defenses as a sign of good faith.[3] Nobody could save the Taborites but the Taborites themselves; the only question was how they could do it.

The answer appears in Laurence's chronicle, in an entry just after that for 9 January 1420:

> During this time certain Taborite priests were preaching to the people a new coming of Christ, in which all evil men and enemies of the Truth would perish and be exterminated, while the good would be preserved in five cities. For this reason certain cities in which communion in both kinds could freely be given refused to enter into any agreement with the enemy, and especially the city of Plzeň.

> For these Taborite priests in the district of Bechyně and elsewhere were deceiving the people in a remarkable way with their preaching, advancing many erroneous doctrines contrary to the Christian faith, by falsely interpreting the prophetical books according to their own heads and by despising the Catholic doctrines of the holy doctors. They urged that all those desiring to be saved from the wrath of Almighty God, which in their view was about to be visited on the whole globe, should leave their cities, castles, villages, and towns, as Lot left Sodom, and should go to the five cities of refuge. These are

---

[2] Laurence, pp. 351 f. Cf. also the immediately following accounts of the murder of the priest John Nakvasa and the Kutná Horans' attack on the Hussites of Kouřim, both *ad* November. In January the Kouřim captives were killed (p. 355).

[3] *Ibid.*, pp. 353 ff.; cf. Heymann, pp. 105 ff.

the names of the five: Plzeň, which they called the City of the Sun, Žatec, Louny, Slaný, and Klatovy. For Almighty God wished to destroy the whole world, saving only those who had taken refuge in the five cities. They alleged in support of this doctrine prophetical texts falsely and erroneously understood, and they sent letters containing this material through the Kingdom of Bohemia. And many simple folk, accepting these frivolous doctrines as true, and having zeal, as the Apostle says, but not acting through knowledge, sold their property, taking even a low price, and flocked to these priests from various parts of the Kingdom of Bohemia and the Margravate of Moravia, with their wives and children, and they threw their money at the feet of the priests.[4]

Thus the reaction of some Taborites to the threat of annihilation was a renewal of the old message: congregate and find salvation among the faithful brethren! The feeling of eschatological crisis, always present in Taboritism—and indeed in Hussitism generally, as well as in the pre-Hussite Bohemian reform movement—now solidified into an adventist vision that illuminated the current crisis and also encouraged people to join the movement. The power of this appeal does not come through in Laurence's hostile and unbelieving summary, but specimens of the adventist letters he mentions have fortunately survived and they retain enough of their strength to allow us to appreciate their impact.[5] "The time of greatest suffering, prophesied by Christ in his scriptures, the apostles in their letters, the prophets, and St. John in the Apocalypse, is now at hand; it has begun; it stands at the gates! And in this time the Lord God commands His elect to flee from the midst of the evil ones, through Isaiah 51:[6] 'Go out from their midst, my people,' so that each may save his soul from the wrath of God and be spared His blows. And so that your heart may not perhaps soften, and that you may not stand in fear of the dreadful sound that will be heard on earth. And through St. John, Rev. 18 [4], the Lord says: 'Go out of it my people, so that you may not share in their sins; for their sins have reached the heavens.'"

These words of the anonymous Taborite prophet remind us of the Bzí Hora manifesto of the previous September,[7] with its, "we now clearly see the great abomination standing in the holy place." At the same time we are

---

[4] Laurence, pp. 355 f. What I distinguish as the second paragraph seems to be a more hostile recapitulation and amplification of the first, and may have been a later addition.

[5] *Archiv český*, VI, 43 f. (in Czech). Here, and in what follows, the presentation of "adventism" corresponds at many points with what Kalivoda calls "fatalistic chiliasm" (*HI*, pp. 324 ff.).

[6] Actually 52:11; cf. verse 12: "The God of Israel will congregate you." The actual quotations from the Bible are embedded in a matrix of biblical words and phrases throughout this and similar adventist appeals.

[7] *Archiv český*, III, 205 f. See above, chap. vi, and compare the discussion in *HI*, pp. 322 f.

struck by the radical difference between the two messages: the Bzí Hora congregants were determined to end "the enormous glorification of all Antichristian hypocritical evil" by the united effort of all Hussite forces, but the adventist letter reflects a situation in which such a prospectus was no longer possible: the evil were in possession of the world and could not be dislodged or reformed—only God could end their sinfulness and he was about to do so; the good could escape the secular catastrophe only by withdrawing physically. "But where are God's elect to flee? To fortified cities that the Lord God has provided in the time of greatest suffering. . . . And there are five of these cities, which will not enter into agreements with the Antichrist or surrender to him." Here the prophet refers to Isaiah 19:18: "On that day there will be five cities in the land of Egypt speaking the language of Canaan": "that day" is the day of Christ's advent; "Egypt" designates "all those who oppress the sons of God and force them away from God's Truth"; the "language of Canaan" is the language that speaks of the Promised Land. (The same text from Isaiah provides the name of one of the cities, "the City of the Sun," and the Taborite prophet mentions this, although he does not name Plzeň or indeed any other Bohemian city.) The letter closes with threats and polemics that bring the whole message down to earth:

> The lion has gone forth from his lair and the heathen pillager has arisen, that is, against God and His Law; just as the King of Hungary [*scil.,* Sigismund] . . . has gone forth from his city, that is, from Hungary, in order to lay waste your land. Your cities will be wiped out and remain without inhabitants. Therefore, knowing these things, give diligent heed to the Lord God Himself and do not be tardy; He is at the gates. . . . Do not let yourselves be turned here and there by unbelieving seducers who say, "This will not happen in our time"; it has already been fulfilled, and God knows when it will happen. . . . Therefore if you are faithful do not scorn holy prophecies. For the Lord God says through the prophet Amos in chapter 9 [10]: "All the sinners of my people will die on the sword who say, 'The evil approaches but it will not come on us' "—like those who say now: "It will not be in our time nor in the time of our children."

Since Sigismund actually left Hungary shortly before mid-December, arriving in Moravian Brno on the fifteenth, we may date this letter roughly in the latter half of December—a date that agrees perfectly with Laurence's entry in his chronicle—and we can suppose that at the very time when the Prague representatives were meekly accepting the most humiliating treatment from Sigismund at his Christmas Diet,[8] the militant radicals of the provinces were excitedly listening to the adventist message just discussed.

[8] See the following chapter.

The "unbelieving seducers" referred to by the Taborite prophet were of course the Prague masters and their followers, who now found themselves on the wrong side of the Christ-Antichrist antithesis. Most of the surviving anti-adventist literature came from the pen of Jakoubek of Stříbro, the Prague master who was closest to enjoying a national, pan-Hussite prestige; letters of guidance to his supporters, resolutions of controversial questions, and polemics against adventist prophets were produced by him in sufficient quantity to ensure the survival of a number of items. Since they all seem to fall into the early adventist period—one indeed is dated, on 22 January 1420 —and since their ideas are interrelated, they may be discussed as a group.[9] Perhaps their most striking feature is Jakoubek's acceptance of the terrifying vision of things to come, the "imminent perils of the Antichrist:" "there will be many tribulations suffered by the elect, to their salvation, and by the evil to their damnation."[10] But when will these perils come? "They are coming at a time and place known and determined not by me or by any man, but by God."[11] One prophecy, pronounced by the Taborite, Master John of Jičín, had fixed the time in Carnival, or just before, between 10 and 14 February; Jakoubek notes, with confident skepticism, that events will show if there is any validity to this prediction;[12] "hold out for a while," he wrote, "and soon the truth or falsity of their prophecies will appear."[13]

Of course Jakoubek had good reason to fear coming tribulations: Prague's capitulation to Sigismund at his Christmas Diet had inaugurated a period of great reactionary resurgence in Prague, with Catholic priests and émigré burghers—mostly Germans—returning to boast of their rosy future under

---

[9] They include the following items: (1) A letter to apparently nonadventist priests, dated 22 January (1420), edited by Bartoš, "Do čtyř art.," p. 97. (2) A letter responding to questions sent by an anonymous "frater," who had reported on adventist propaganda, and who had evidently asked for guidance on behalf of others as well as himself. The text in Appendix 3, No. 1. (3) A letter responding to the Taborite Master John Jičín, who had written an attack on the letter just noted. The text in Appendix 3, No. 6. (4) A response by Masters Jakoubek and Christian of Prachatice to four questions concerning adventism; the text in Appendix 3, No. 7. (5) A similar response to two of the same questions; it is dated 17 February 1420 and is anonymous, but so close to item 4 that Jakoubek's authorship seems likely. The text in Bartoš, "Do čtyř art.," pp. 97–100. (6) The tractate "Noverint universi," in Appendix 3, No. 3. (7) The tractate "Audio cum contra percussores," in Appendix 3, No. 4. (8) The brief "Item prophecias legis dei," in Appendix 3, No. 5. Items 2, 3, 4, 6, and 7 of the present list have been published in part by Goll, *Quellen*, II, 51 ff., and since his edition has always been used, I refer to it in the footnotes when possible.

[10] Bartoš, *"Do čtyř art.,"* p. 97; Goll, II, 58.

[11] Goll, II, 58.

[12] Goll, II, 60, 58.

[13] Bartoš, *loc. cit.*

Sigismund; at the same time the Emperor had replaced Hussite castellans and burgraves throughout Bohemia with Catholics, thus showing that the policy of royalism, with its basis in Hussite-Catholic coexistence, meant very little to him.[14] Although the ultimate anti-Hussite measures were not to come until March, Jakoubek and his associates could surmise that nothing good was in store for them. But the answer to tribulation was not flight or resistance, but an evangelical life. "It would be well for evangelical priests to live evangelically, and thus teach the people and destroy sin among them, and relinquish their presumptions";[15] "urge the people," he wrote, "not to leave their places of residence but to stay home and do salutary penance; then whatever happens it will be well with them."[16] The adventists preached, "Flee from the midst of Babylon" [Jer. 51:6], and they interpreted Babylon in a physical sense, to mean all sinful people and all the appurtenances of their sinful lives, "from the pope to the lowest priest opposed to the truths of the Law of God, . . . from the greatest evil king following this world to the least of the unfaithful laymen";[17] but Jakoubek held that Babylon, as well as flight from Babylon, and also the five cities, were to be interpreted spiritually: Christ's faithful will be saved no matter where they live.[18] Since from the Taborite point of view the whole "outside" world was joined in opposition to the true faith, the vision of Revelation 18:2—"She has fallen, she has fallen, Babylon the Great"—meant simply that the entire old order, with its social organization, its institutions, its great buildings, and its material possessions, would fall;[19] Jakoubek, however, doggedly maintained that even the worst calamities did not annul the sure path to salvation taught by Jesus, the path of virtue and humble suffering. The fact that this idea, central to the native tradition of Hussitism, had to be defended against the Taborites shows us better than any other evidence what had happened to the national reformation as a result of adventist preaching and, of course, the situation that had evoked it.

A second adventist letter replies to the Prague arguments just discussed.[20] Repeating the basic prophecies already noted, it insists that "in this time Christ gives the special command to his faithful, to flee not only from sins, but also from the midst of evil, hostile, and insincere people." "Do not say then: 'What, are we to flee before God? Wherever the just man dies, there

[14] Laurence, pp. 354 f.
[15] Goll, II, 58.
[16] Bartoš, *loc. cit.*
[17] This is John of Jičín's interpretation, Goll, II, 59.
[18] Goll, II, 58.
[19] Goll, II, 59.
[20] *Archiv český*, VI, 41–43 (in Czech).

he dies well.' That is sometimes the truth but not always." Lot was, after all, ordered to flee from Sodom, even though he was a good man. It is the false prophets who say "that a man need only flee from sins for Christ to be merciful to him"; these false prophets are the university masters and the nobles, whose falsity appears in the fact that "they have seemed to be something, but they are nothing"; one senses the true extent of the loss of authority suffered by the masters and Hussite nobility. The prudent counsel of men like Jakoubek: "Do not leave your property, they are deceiving you," is aptly met by the scriptural text [Matt. 19:29]: "Whoever leaves home, brothers, sisters, father or mother, or land and field for my name, will win a hundred times more and will obtain eternal life." Here we see what indeed we can also see from the whole corpus of the polemic: no amount of common sense and no assertion of ordinary morality can obscure the fact that the Taborite prophets, in the agony of their situation, had caught an authentic strain of the Christian tradition—or perhaps in this case more correctly, the Judeo-Christian tradition. Some of their Biblical texts were twisted rather violently, but most actually meant what the adventists said they meant, namely that in certain critical moments even the most virtuous normality falls far short of the total commitment demanded by God, and that in the light of such a total commitment, the ordinary life of the world, whether lived well or badly, is radically meaningless. In this sense the *religious* appeal of adventism was very much in the tradition of the whole previous congregation movement:

> [Christ's] disciples asked him, . . . "Where, O Lord?" And he said: "Where the Body will be, there the eagles will gather." Therefore brothers and sisters, where you know Christ's Body to be given with all the pieces of God's Truths, there gather in the time of vengeance and greatest suffering. . . . It is necessary to congregate without delay, to fast and weep for your own sins and those of others, to pray day and night to the Lord God, crying out to Him that He should please to save you in the times of greatest suffering. And also to fit yourselves, with God's Word, for good examples and counsels, and particularly in order to fill yourselves with the precious food and drink of Lord Jesus Christ. . . .

Perhaps indeed it was at this time that the people sang:

> Faithful ones, rejoice in God! Give him honor and praise, that he has pleased to preserve us and graciously liberate us from the evil Antichrist and his cunning army. . . .

> Take no heed of the faithless ones and do not follow them, for Satan draws them in his train, away from endurance. . . . Many will excuse themselves and depart from the feast, some to look at their villages, others to try out their oxen, and still others to embrace women. To such Christ has promised

that . . . they will be deprived of the eternal feast [Luke 14:16–24]. Therefore fear this and let us endure with him to the end, always keeping in mind
the reward that Christ will give to the one who stays with him to the end
and does not leave him on account of some suffering, or some whim, or booty
of some sort. [The faithful must not grumble.] . . . Give us [the strength]
not to look back as Lot's wife did. . . . And Christ mentioned her when he
spoke of his coming and commanded flight to the mountains; he said: Who
is then on the roof, let him not come down, and who is in the fields, let him
not look back. Remember Lot's wife, that faithless daughter, who looked at
her home.

Lord Christ, make us have strong faith in you so that we may conquer,
firmly staying with you, O living and most worthy Bread, until we come into
heaven, joyfully singing Amen, rejoicing with the Lord God, and ruling with
him forever.

But the idea in the song is so close to the heart of the whole congregation
movement that it might have been sung, for all we know, continuously since
the spring of 1419.[21]

There was, however, an important difference in the effect of the new
congregations, as against the old. The adventists themselves point it out to
us:

> But where are God's elect to flee? To fortified cities. . . .
> Christ says: flee to the mountains, that is, to the faithful people. . . .
> In that time those places [of refuge] cannot be in a village or elsewhere on
> account of the strong and dreadful Antichrist, but in fortified cities, of which
> St. Isaiah names five. . . .[22]

From now on, in fact, "mountain" seems to designate a Taborite community, no matter where it was located.[23] But the shift was not merely one of

---

[21] "Věrní se v bohu radujte," Nejedlý, VI, 183–185; cf. IV, 258–270. Nejedlý associates
it with the early congregations of 1419, and Josef Macek, *Tábor*, I, 381, accepts this
dating; although I regard it as much closer to the spirit of 1420, I should not venture to
exclude the earlier date, particularly since the present argument requires only the
supposition that the song, however early its origin, continued to be sung in the
adventist period. The striking parallels in thought and to some extent in words between
this song and Peter Chelčický's *O boji duchovním,* ed. K. Krofta (Prague: Otto, 1911),
pp. 116 f., 130, and *passim,* suggest that the song was not merely an adventist
confection, for Chelčický rejected adventism, but that it gave voice to the deepest
sentiments of the whole Taborite movement.

[22] *Archiv český,* VI, 41 ff.

[23] Cf. the formulation, "physical mountains or Tabor," in a chiliast "article" evidently
dating from the period after the foundation of Tabor (the text in *KJBB,* p. 58), and cf.
Příbram's formulation: "They preached and ordained, in the city of Písek, to those
people who had fled to them on the mountains" (*ibid.,* p. 265). Both passages reflect the
actual passage from congregations on mountains to congregations in cities.

place; the new congregations were actually new communities, organized for defense and therefore for combat. As such they raised misgivings even among those who, like Jakoubek, were prepared to concede that in times of imminent persecution and tribulation, the faithful "might withdraw to a place where there is not such great tribulation," in order to preserve themselves against the temptation of apostasy. "I dare not," Jakoubek wrote, "blame the common people [*simplicem populum*] for congregating *in articulo necessitatis,* for the good of their salvation and in Christ Jesus." [24]

But he did not mean to sanction the accompanying warfare. "The faithful common people who do not have what is needed for salvation in their own homes may go out and seek those things elsewhere, even if it means losing their temporal goods—I do not reprove this, in fact I approve it. But I do *not* praise, I rather reprove those who with raging cruelty and without charity attack their neighbors, kill them, or plunder their neighbors' goods." [25] Even the early hilltop congregations had provoked deep suspicion in some quarters; now, however, the representatives of legitimacy were faced by entirely new communities consciously and avowedly set up as antitheses to the established society, and dedicated to the immediate task of organizing their own defense by developing military power. The medieval mind was accustomed to a distribution of military power, but only within a framework of legitimately distributed right and privilege, a framework that had no place for the new communities, which for their part rejected it as "Babylon." And even in the fifteenth century, the phenomenon of mass withdrawal from towns and villages was regarded as *ipso facto* subversive; the peasant who gave up his land, burnt his house, and in some cases left his family, in order to flee to "the mountains," was behaving in a way for which there was no precedent. [26] And when that peasant claimed the right to wield arms, his

---

[24] The passage is in Goll, *Quellen,* II, 60; it includes the phrase "non audeo reprobare." Macek, *Tábor,* II, 164, translates it in the exact opposite sense, as "I do not dare to approve" ("Neodvažuji se . . . schvalovati"), an error that leads him to infer a split between Jakoubek and the other masters, who did sanction pious and necessary congregations. But there was no split.

[25] MS O 13, fol. 36ᵛ (in Appendix 3): "Simplicem autem et fidelem populum non habentem in propriis domiciliis necessaria ad salutem exire extra et alibi illa querere usque ad amissionem temporalium, non reprobo sed plus approbo. Sed si qui zelo crudelitatis sine caritate invadunt proximos et illos occidunt vel bona eorum dirripiunt, non laudo sed magis reprobo."

[26] We have already seen that some nobles forbade their peasants to frequent Mt. Tabor in 1419, and that the peasants disobeyed; Laurence, as noted above, provided an astrological explanation for this "rebellion" (p. 403). In 1420, of course, the flight to the Taborites had an even more clearly political and social character, augmented by the ideology of adventism or chiliasm; again Laurence informs us: "Some would call their neighbors together and say, 'Remove your homes from mine, because I want to burn it

behavior was more than anomalous, it was revolutionary. Jakoubek's anti-adventist polemic reflects the unwholesome situation. We have already noted his trenchant question to Master John Jičín: "Did you [priests] not formerly preach against killing, and how then has everything now come to be turned into its opposite?" Jakoubek comments on this "opposite":

> The common people [*communis populus*—perhaps "the laity"], urged on by the priests, are taking up carnal and secular arms against the enemy. . . . There is in this the danger of homicide and bloodshed, and hatreds are thereby generated which bring about a falling away from charity and a neglect of spiritual arms. . . . Against this hear the safe counsel of the Apostle, Rom. 12 [19]: "Beloved ones, do not defend yourselves.". . . The evangelical priest, therefore, should persuade people to fight an evangelical battle in God's cause, according to the evangelical and catholic sense, with spiritual arms, on the model of the primitive church of Christ's apostles.
>
> It is said that the people, impelled by your preaching and your perilous interpretations of Scripture, are taking up carnal military arms, abandoning the customary labor of their hands and living in idleness from the plundering of their neighbors' substance; they kill and shed blood. . . . Many trustworthy people are complaining about you, . . . calling you bloody priests [*sacerdotes sanguineos*], from whom, they say, none of the faithful should take the divine sacraments.[27]

For his part, Jakoubek was no pacifist: the way of Christian suffering was the safe way to fight, but there existed another way, dangerous but legitimate:

> However I concede that wars can legitimately be fought by the higher secular powers [*a sublimioribus potestatibus secularibus*], to whom, as it is said in Romans 13, is given the sword, for the punishment of the evil. Let the subject people beware lest they usurp that sword from the higher powers inordinately and against the Lord, without having any certain special revelation. The higher powers can legitimately fight, but in so doing there is a great danger to their souls.[28]

But this doctrine merely emphasized the illegitimacy, as well as the moral danger, of the military activities of the Taborite congregations. How can we

---

right away and take refuge on Mt. Tabor or in the five cities, to save my soul.' And when they burned their own homes the whole village would then catch fire and burn" (p. 426). John Příbram's "Story of the Priests of Tabor" also tells how the people would abandon their families, homes, and property—throwing their possessions away in the market-place or giving them away to any and all—in the conviction that the old world would be physically destroyed ("Život kněží táborských," *KJBB*, p. 264).

[27] Goll, II, 58, 60.
[28] Goll, II, 58.

account for Tabor's readiness to fight, in the face of the evangelical imperative so deeply rooted in the Hussite tradition and, in an even more extreme
form, in Tabor's own background?

It is of course easy to point to so-called realities. Even before 1420 there had
been sporadic outbreaks of anti-Catholic violence among the radicals, and the
battle of Živhošť in early November 1419 had seen the Taborites fighting for
their lives, with physical weapons; now, when the threat of extermination
was brutally real, why should the Taborites not take up arms in their own
defense? [29] Such reasoning ignores the reality of the alternatives to war:
evangelical suffering or a simple lapse into indifference, a withdrawal from
the struggle at the price of submission to the royalists. The urgency of
adventist propaganda attests to the existence of such indifference—we will
never know how many people, disposed to radicalism, did *not* join the
Taborite communities. We will never know how many of the Taborites of
1419 stopped being Taborites in 1420. Adventist literature also reveals the
presence of doubts about the legitimacy of warfare: "many are now ag-
grieved," the Taborite prophet wrote, "against Christ's commands, supposing
that it is not necessary to carry on a regular fight with a physical sword
against evils and abominations, against errors and heresy." [30] How could
such doubts be answered, when Tabor's own early adherence to Waldensianist nonviolence supported distrust of the "physical sword"? One answer was
provided by adventism itself: the Taborite prophet explained that "Christ
has said [Matt. 24:6; Mark 13:7], 'Do not complain when you hear battles
and struggles; these things must be'; as the holy prophets have prophesied."
There follow passages from Isaiah [30:32] and Revelation [17:14], both of
which certainly justify the battles of the elect against their persecutors in the
time of decision—a time, the prophet observes, that "Christ makes known by
conflicts, by many scandals, by the spread of evil, by many oppressions, by
destruction, by abomination in the holy place—that is, sins, idols . . . and

---

[29] Macek, *Tábor*, II, 162, heaps scorn on those historians who have regarded the
theoretical discussion about the legitimacy of warfare as decisive in guiding practice,
and he points to the history of violent outbreaks and actual fighting that had
characterized the radical movement even before 1420. Much of his argument can be
accepted without cavil, but he seems to underestimate the effect of the university's
opinion—and especially Jakoubek's opinion—on many radical priests and lay leaders of
the countryside, and through them on the common people. Nor does he seem to do full
justice to both the passivity and Waldensian pacifism present among many members of
the Taborite movement even in the winter of 1419–1420, as shown by the adventist
arguments against such tendencies. Macek dates the struggle against both passivity and
pacifism in the spring of 1419 (*Tábor*, I, 212 f.), along with adventism and chiliasm—a
dating that I believe is incorrect.

[30] *Archiv český*, VI, 41.

other disorders abominable to God, by torments, by imprisonment, and primarily by the killing of God's elect."[31] To this we may add another explanation of the shift from pacifism to war: Waldensianist pacifism was a part of the general sectarian rejection of the established order's claims to be a Christian order; Taborite adventist violence preserved this rejection, indeed lifted it to a higher level, at which rejection of the established order implied not merely spiritual withdrawal, but physical withdrawal, and the physical struggle thereby made possible.

The new development is brilliantly illuminated by one of the provincial radicals who refused to go along with it, Peter Chelčický, a layman who may well have been the most original thinker of Hussite Bohemia. In his *On Spiritual Battle,* written perhaps in the summer of 1420, he reviewed the development of Taboritism as he understood it:

> . . . to our great shame and sorrow, we must acknowledge how our brethren have been cleverly seduced by Satan, and how they have departed from Holy Scriptures in strange and unheard-of ideas and acts. When Satan first came to them it was not with an open face, as the Devil, but in the shining garb of voluntary poverty, which Christ commanded priests to hold to, and in the zealous work of preaching to and serving the people and in giving them the Body and Holy Blood of God. And all of this flourished to the point that a great many people flocked to them. Then the Devil came to them clothed in other garb, in the prophets and the Old Testament, and from these they sought to confect an imminent Day of Judgement, saying that they were angels who had to eliminate all scandals from Christ's Kingdom, and that they were to judge the world. And so they committed many killings and impoverished many people, but they did not judge the world according to their words, for the predicted time has elapsed with which they terrified the people, telling them strange things which they collected from many prophets.[32]

That even the first congregations, with their concentration on poverty, preaching, and utraquist communion, were the work of Satan was a judgement no doubt determined by subsequent events, but these events were not accidental. We do not know exactly when Chelčický realized what was happening, but his general conviction that few men could avoid the snares of the Devil, that the world as such could never really be Christian, suggests that the very success of the congregations—"many people flocked to them"—

---

[31] *Loc. cit.*

[32] *O boji duchovním,* ed. Krofta, pp. 27 f. See below, chap. ix in the section titled "The Problem of a Taborite Society," for Chelčický's relationship to early Taboritism, and further discussion of the works cited here. Kalivoda, *HI,* p. 329, interprets the origin of Taborite violence very much as Chelčický did.

constituted their fundamental fault. By reaching outside of the narrow limits within which sectarian ideals of perfection could be safely pursued, the congregations degenerated morally to the point where their reaction to persecution, in the winter of 1419–1420, was not the Christian suffering of the New Testament but the self-conscious violence of the Old. In condemning this violence, Chelčický does not simply repeat the Prague denunciations of unauthorized warfare—about which more will be said below; he rather speaks with the voice of original Taborite pacifism and nonviolence. *All* power is unChristian:

> If power were supposed to be administered through Christ's faith by means of battles and punishments, and try to benefit Christ's faith thereby, then why would Christ have abolished the Jewish Law and established a different, spiritual one? If he had wanted people to cut each other up, to hang, drown, and burn each other, and otherwise pour out human blood for his Law, then that Old Law could also have stood unchanged, with the same bloody deeds as before.
>
> . . . there is a grave confusion in the faith when the fullness of Christ's faith is ascribed to power—so that what power does, in ordinary nations that are outside the faith and the Law of God—so that this originally pagan affair becomes Christ's affair. . . .
>
> It is Christ's injunction that every man turn his other cheek to the one who strikes him in the face [Matt. 5:39; Luke 6:29], and the Apostle's injunction that he not defend himself against wrong [II Tim. 2:3]. But if power's official duty is to help the man in this situation by defending him so that no wrong be done him, then he will not be able to fulfill Christ's words in the manner of his defense. . . . And this is the pagan way and the way of this world, which is not fit to come under the yoke of Christ. . . .[33]

Although these formulations date from a period later than that of early adventism, they express ideas undoubtedly in the minds of many radicals during the winter of 1419–1420; that they did not prevail was due in part to adventist propaganda, in greater part to the objective development of Taboritism. The political program developed by the leaders of the Taborite congregations in 1419 had not only led to a great expansion of the movement, it had destroyed the mood of pious withdrawal, without which ideas and sentiments of nonviolence could hardly flourish. The new congregations of the winter marked a retreat from that political program, in favor of a new sectarianism, but here, too, nonviolence failed to resonate with reality. Great

[33] The quoted paragraphs are taken from Chelčický's treatise on the relationship between secular power and Christianity, *"On the Triple Division of Society"* (*O trojím lidu*), ed. K. Krofta, *op. cit.,* pp. 145, 158, 165 f. The work probably dates from around 1424. See my translation of the whole work (cited below, chap. ix, n. 17), pp. 139, 146, 151.

masses of people were concentrated in the Taborite towns, cut off from the stabilizing routine of everyday life, lacking any regular means of support, and imbued with the conviction that everything outside their communities was foredoomed to total destruction. Such a situation could hardly fail to generate violence of the most hysterical kind, to say nothing of the plundering criticized by Jakoubek but objectively necessary if the "elect" were not to starve to death. Thus Jakoubek's orthodox theory of legitimate warfare and Chelčický's sectarian theory of Christian renunciation of power, both of which would have denied the new communities the right to fight, were met by a new, adventist theory of warfare sanctioned by the requirements of the Day of Wrath.

That this interplay of ideas was not merely epiphenomenal, that a real contest for the Hussite mind was going on, appears from one of the most interesting surviving sources datable in this period, a rescript issued by the Masters Jakoubek and Christian of Prachatice.[34] Two preachers, the priests Nicholas and Wenceslas, had faced each other as opponents before a large number of people, and had finally agreed to refer the questions at issue between them to the decision of the two Prague masters, whose "salubrious" instruction would be accepted as final. The questions were these: (1) whether the secular lords were required to defend the evangelical Truth with the sword of their power; (2) whether, if the secular lords were unwilling to do so, the "faithful subject communities" might carry on such a defense, even "killing the enemy physically"; (3) whether the faithful might and ought to congregate in time of persecution; (4) "whether a woman of the faithful might leave her husband for the sake of Christ and his Gospel, if the husband were not of the faithful and forbade her to hear the word of God and take holy communion." Various scholars have tried to identify the Nicholas and Wenceslas in question, always by guesswork; the most popular solution has been Nicholas of Pelhřimov, the future Bishop of Tabor, and Wenceslas Koranda, the leader of Plzeň radicalism, with Nicholas holding the more moderate position on each question.[35] Such guesses are pointless, because the currently known sources do not contain the information needed to arrive at certainty or even probability; indeed they have been worse than pointless, for they have prompted scholars to identify the priests as Taborites, although the context suggests something very different. It is clear, if we

---

[34] Goll, II, 51–53.

[35] This was Goll's solution (II, 48); it was subsequently accepted by K. Hoch, "Husité a válka," *Česká mysl,* VIII (1907), 207; and by N. Jastrebov, *Etjudy o Petře Chelčickom i jego vremeni, Zapiski istoriko-filologičeskago fakultěta imperatorskago S-Peterburgskago Universiteta,* LXXXIX (St. Petersburg, 1908), 56; Macek, *Tábor,* I, 381, regards it as probable. Pekař, *Žižka,* I, 242, and Bartoš, *Do čtyř art.,* p. 87, n. 36, point to the lack of any real evidence for Goll's solution.

accept the words of the rescript as truthful, that a large number of people in the provinces [36] were assembled to hear one preacher assert the affirmative of the four questions, the other the negative. Thus one was a Taborite adventist, but the other was a non-Taborite, for otherwise he could not possibly have maintained the negative on the third and fourth questions—if he had, he would have been rejecting not merely the adventist congregations but the whole Taborite movement of 1419. Thus also, the "large number of people" could not have been a Taborite congregation, for it is all but impossible to imagine such a congregation, filled with ideas of Judgement Day and their own flight from Babylon, entertaining an opponent of the first principles of their being. Nor can we imagine such a congregation, or its preachers, sending these questions to Prague—Babylon!—for authoritative decision. Most likely it was a congregation of as yet uncommitted Hussites, whom the Taborite preacher was attempting to convince; the questions concerned not the past actions of the people but their future actions: should they leave their homes, join one of the Taborite communities, and prepare to fight? The value of the document is that it shows us, better than other adventist and anti-adventist polemics, just what questions were most important during the period.

The decisions rendered by the masters are also instructive, for they reflect an agreement between a radical and a conservative member of the university, Jakoubek and Christian of Prachatice; moreover we are told that "the advice of many masters had been requested." Although hardly to be dated much before or after January 1420,[37] the rescript in fact shows a distinct development beyond certain ideas also expressed by Jakoubek in that month, and this indication is all the more significant because otherwise the correspondence between Jakoubek's letters and the text of the rescript is very close. Thus, as we might expect, the first question is quickly disposed of by a reference to Romans 13:4—the classical text for a Christian justification of legitimate secular power, and so used by Jakoubek on various occasions.[38] The third point is also solved in Jakoubek's way:

[36] There is no way of determining where the addressees were, but Prague must be ruled out, partly because the very complex of questions is associated with the situation in the provinces, partly because the form of a rescript suggests communication at a distance.

[37] Goll, II, 49 suggests a date in November; Bartoš, *Do čtyř art.*, p. 82, points to January; Macek, *Tábor*, I, 381 f., suggests a date sometime around the beginning of 1420. Goll is certainly wrong, the other two probably right; for reasons indicated in the text, I should think the latter part of January, or even early February, more probable than an earlier date.

[38] E.g., Goll, II, 58. Cf. Jakoubek's Postil of 1420 on Matt. 24, cited by Bartoš, "Příspěvky k dějinám Václava IV.," *VČA*, LI (1942), 102 f.: "potestas coactiva est

. . . that Christ's faithful should actually congregate in certain cities, understood materially, five in number as it is said—this does not seem to us to form
a general rule, necessary to salvation for communities. For a law does not
make men confused, but this principle would confuse men, if it expressly
obliged them to go to five actual cities and yet did not express or determine
which cities these should be. In that case the faithful would be very confused
and dubious, not knowing to which cities they should flee, and the priests
ought to be especially careful not to lead the people into such confusion, just
as they should take care not to preach to the people in a presumptuous spirit
that a horrible disaster is about to visit the people, assigning a time for it on
their own authority and criminally keeping the people in a state of suspense,
without themselves having had any certain divine revelation about this.
Nevertheless, it is permitted to Christians to take flight in time of persecution, prudently and according to Christ's example, when . . . it will probably be of greater benefit to the church that they flee than that they remain
and occasion the killing of ministers of the church, without any benefit to
their souls.[39]

Here as elsewhere, Jakoubek disapproved of the general adventist principle
of flight, even while allowing the actual flight of the Hussite faithful—it was
no doubt a sufficient concession to serve the needs of the time. It is also
evident that the adventist preacher had urged flight to the five cities, but had
not named them—this conforms perfectly to the existing adventist letters. In
any case, since flight was permitted, the fourth question could be solved in
the affirmative, albeit with Jakoubek's usual obliqueness in dealing with
adventism—he wished to reject its general principle but at the same time
give an acceptable answer, on the basis of his own theoretical framework.

The second question marks the greatest deviation from Jakoubek's other,
presumably earlier, writings of the time. First we find a long defense of the
evangelical principle of suffering persecution, entirely similar to Jakoubek's
arguments already discussed. Then there follows a statement of the principle
"that the authority for fighting and the planning of war pertains to princes
and secular powers; . . . it is not permitted to just anyone from among the
people to stir up war." We are now launched on a discussion of the "dubious
and difficult way" of fighting—that is, actually fighting with material arms—

---

fundata Rom. xiii et I Petri ii." There were of course vast numbers of Old Testament
authorities for the legitimacy of war, but these were "imperfect," because "the Old Law
was very imperfect, in relation to the New Law of grace and love" (Appendix 3,
No. 4; Goll, II, 55). Fortunately for the hard-pressed Hussite masters, Jesus Christ
himself on one occasion provided a "figure" for legitimate use of force: when he drove
the money-changers from the temple with the "flagellum" of physical power (John
2:15)—see the rescript of 17 February 1420, Bartoš, *Do čtyř art.,* p. 98.

[39] Goll, II, 53.

and we find the classic scholastic definition of the requirements for a just war—a just claim, a valid authorization, an upright intention, with the second interpreted, also classically, to require the "authority of the prince." [40] So far, there is nothing unusual in the treatment of the question. But then the masters go on to elaborate nothing less than a right to revolution, obscured by qualifications but still unmistakable:

> . . . we concede that secular lords can resist God and his Law so much that their power may be removed by God himself, and it would then be permitted to the communities, admitted to this work by God, to defend the evangelical Truth, in a practical and not fantastic way [*realiter et non fantastice*]. But there must always be preserved the proper order, consonant with the Law of Christ, as this is indicated by divine instinct, certain revelation, or reliable evidence. Moreover, care must be taken that no one assert, forwardly and too precipitately, that the lords have been deprived of their power just because they have refused to go along with every vagrant breeze [cf. Eph. 4:14]. And further, communities can and should defend the Truth by helping their lords. It is neither safe nor just that the common people take on a task that does not belong to them, particularly when they have lords in whom there is no defect so evident, notable, or incorrigible, that the only way justice can be secured is for the people themselves to engage in a task that is not only difficult but full of perils and snares.

The principle here is based on Wyclif's doctrine, that mortal sin incapacitates a man for holding "dominion"—a doctrine that Wyclif himself had taken from Fitz Ralph,[41] but which fulfills its revolutionary implication only in the circumstances of Hussite Bohemia. For the rest, we can only be amazed at the masters' effort to limit the principle they had enunciated. In a period when the royalist barons were rounding up the faithful for shipment to the Germans who operated the Kutná Hora extermination center, when Sigismund had demonstrated his hatred of the Prague utraquists and his intention to destroy Hussite power in the realm, when the provincial Hussites were suffering daily persecution at the hands of the Catholic feudality, in this period the masters were concerned primarily not to encourage the faithful to defend themselves, not to excoriate the hostile lords, but to ensure that no lord be regarded as an enemy of the faith if he had shown even the slightest

---

[40] The requirements appear in Aquinas' *Summa theologica*, II-II, Q. xl, and Wyclif's *De civili dominio*, ed. Loserth, II (London, 1900), pp. 240 ff. Cf. Hoch, "Husité a válka," pp. 138 ff. Jastrebov, *Etjudy o Petře Chelčickom*, pp. 92 ff., shows, with parallel citations, that the masters were following Wyclif. See now Seibt, *Hussitica*, chap. ii.

[41] See R. R. Betts, "Richard Fitz Ralph, Archbishop of Armagh, and the Doctrine of Dominion," *Essays in British and Irish History in Honour of James Eadie Todd* (London, 1949), 46–60. And see above, chap. i, the section on "The Contribution of John Wyclif."

sign of corrigibility. One sees how thoroughly the Prague masters were committed to legitimacy, and how hesitatingly they legitimized the military action of the faithful commoners. Today, when revolutions and new political formations are accepted as a matter of course, we are apt to overlook the incredible obstacles, psychological as well as practical, in the way of the Taborite pioneers of a new society. In fact, the masters' pronouncement, itself a remarkable document in medieval history, helps us to understand why the Taborite revolution should have initially taken the form of adventism.

In any event, the university masters were now on record as approving the physical defense of the Truth; along with the agreement of the masters to at least some form of congregation of the faithful, this fact reveals that the political thinking of Prague in January was different from what it had been in November. We may attribute the change to disillusionment with Sigismund and to the impossibility of ignoring the changes introduced into the Bohemian political landscape by the adventists. Of course the latter would not be satisfied by mere militancy, but not all radicals were adventists, and it is likely that the basic questions concerning the legitimacy of congregating and fighting for the Truth were submitted to the university a number of times, perhaps in the hope of getting better answers. In addition to the rescript just discussed, there is another, dated 17 February 1420,[42] and it may be presumed that these two, each surviving in only one known manuscript, are mere fragments of what must have been a very extensive literature.

Particularly interesting is the fact that while the first rescript was requested by a group of the faithful, presumably commoners, the second was a reply to questions sent by a "noble lord, an outstanding proponent of the Law of God," who had evidently accused the masters of betraying the Truth by their cowardly silence.[43] Such a lord could not have been an adherent of the royalist party; the scholarly conjecture that identifies him as the Taborite Lord Břeněk of Ryzmburk seems probable.[44] It is of course possible to imagine a non-Taborite lord, disturbed by the events of the winter, and determined to get authoritative answers to the two questions noted in the rescript—whether it was legitimate for the faithful to congregate, and for the secular estate to fight, for the honor of God, the edification of the church, and the promotion of the evangelical Truth—but the possibility is exceed-

---

[42] Ed. Bartoš, *Do čtyř art.*, pp. 97–100.

[43] Protesting the difficulty of solving such weighty questions in a brief letter, the masters declare that they will nevertheless make the attempt, "ne tamen prodicione agnite veritatis ob liberam eius pronuncciacionem ac suspicione carnalis timoris a vobis, prout scribitis, arguamur" (Bartoš, *op. cit.*, p. 97).

[44] See the summary of opinions in Macek, *Tábor*, I, 382.

ingly slight; only a Taborite lord could have expressed any doubt about the legitimacy of warfare in general, not to mention warfare in behalf of the Truth. On the other hand, the only two Taborite lords we know of, Lords Břeněk of Ryzmburk and Valkoun of Adlar, had been fighting, with material swords, for a good while before 17 February; both were members of the Plzeň group of Hussites, who were noted for their refusal to come to terms with the enemy after the truce of 13 November 1419. Hence we may guess that the request for the masters' opinion was not prompted by a sincere desire to be informed, but rather by the intention to provoke the masters into a more resolute statement than any issued thus far. If these fragile speculations are correct, then the noble lord was disappointed. The two questions are answered entirely in the spirit of the previous pronouncement, except that since the troublesome question of the *communities'* right to wage war is not included, the whole tone of the rescript seems rather conservative. In fact, the masters take this occasion, probably a few weeks after their earlier rescript, to warn that their sanctioning of physical warfare should not be taken as a license to destroy monasteries, churches, altars, and parish houses, "as some now are presumed to be doing," and that by their approval of the congregation of the faithful they do not mean to offer the occasion for rapine, plunder, homicide, or destruction of churches and houses of the clergy. And although the scriptural authorities here cited for pious congregations show the latter to have taken place not only in synagogues, temples, or other appropriate enclosures, but also in deserted places and on mountains, the masters urge that it would be better for the Hussite faithful to congregate in churches, for hearing the word of God and taking the Eucharist, rather than "in fields or on deserted mountains, and especially where scandal . . . or danger may be probably feared."

If we take this rescript as marking the end of the first period of the new Taboritism and Prague's reaction to it—as we shall see, a new period began only a few days after the rescript was issued—we can sum up the doctrinal or ideological aspects of the situation thus: the effect of adventism was to create a new world, separate from the old, and a new ideology that, although authentically Christian, had nothing in common with even the most radical variety of official Hussite scholasticism. The Prague ideologues—the university masters—never came even close to sanctioning this ideology, but in points of practice they extended their own thinking so as to provide a sanction for the new phenomena—the congregations of the radicals in permanent communities, and the defensive warfare that these communities carried on even without the leadership of legitimate secular powers. Although the hard core of adventist preachers and congregants were probably indifferent to the attitude of the Prague masters,[45] there were many radicals, perhaps even some Taborites, who cared enough about the principle of university leadership to elicit the statements that tended to bridge the gap between Prague and the countryside in the winter of 1419–1420. Once again a national framework had been reconstituted, far more precariously than ever before, but still effectively enough to make a continuing ideological struggle both necessary and possible.

THE FOUNDING OF TABOR

In the light of the interplay just analyzed, the course of events during the period following the November truce may now be examined. With the dispersal of the great national Taborite concentration, the leaders of the party had to rebuild their movement in the various local centers of radicalism, under the difficult conditions that have been described. Laurence of Březová's entry for the beginnings of adventism has already been quoted; from it we learn that the preeminent center of resistance, among the five cities that "refused to enter into any agreement with the enemy," was Plzeň, the "City of the Sun." The same source also identifies the originators of adventist propaganda as the "Taborite priests in the district of Bechyně and elsewhere"; thus we are prepared to find, along with West Bohemian Plzeň, a South Bohemian center of resistance—not the old Mt. Tabor or any of the other holy mountains of 1419, but a fortified city. And this is just what we do find. Attacking the adventist claim that the faithful could find salvation only by joining the Taborite communities, Jakoubek of Stříbro observed that "the just man who refuses to consent to evil . . . will be saved either in Prague, or in Písek, or in Plzeň"; "a man's salvation is not to be hoped for solely on the grounds of his being in Plzeň or Písck." [46] This evidence can be dated roughly in January 1420, along with Jakoubek's other anti-adventist writings, in which, as we have seen, notice is taken of the fact that the adventists had spoken of five cities but had not named thcm. Thus we can envisage a still inchoate situation, with two well-established cities of concentration, but with the possibility that the masses who would heed the adventist message might

[45] See, e.g., Jakoubek's reproaches to Master John Jičín: "Why are you silent . . . ? . . . Why do you not write to the Prague masters and magistrates, to purge yourself?" (Goll, II, 60). The adventist letters already discussed show a similar attitude: the opposition of the masters is mentioned only to be refuted, and this not in order to change the masters' minds, but merely in order to persuade the people to ignore the anti-adventist propaganda.

[46] Goll, II, 58.

gather in other centers as well. Indeed, we can push the reconstruction even further. When Wenceslas Koranda led his contingent back home to the Plzeň region, he must have found the hostile elements still in control of the city. But soon many radicals began to join his group, including the Lords Břeněk of Ryzmburk and Valkoun of Adlar, John Žižka, and other military men, and it was possible for them to take control of Plzeň and expel the royalists. Exactly when this happened we do not know; Laurence enters the information for the month of January, just after his paragraph on adventism, and we may assume that he meant to indicate a meaningful sequence.[47] The military leaders put the city in a defensive posture, refusing to deal with the enemy, and the priests, led by Koranda, organized the destruction of the city's monasteries and churches. The mood was, of course, one of intense adventist expectation. Adventist prophecy had brought most of the new arrivals to the community; once there, they could listen to the preaching of Koranda who assured them that "one day we'll get up and find all the others lying dead, with their noses sticking up in the air, and on that day there will be more houses in Plzeň than evil people still alive." [48] Such encouragement was needed, for the "City of the Sun" had to face the hostile forces of Lord Bohuslav of Švamberk and then a siege carried on with great zeal by the royalist authorities of the realm. Jakoubek indeed pointed to the Plzeň case as an argument against the adventist message; the preachers had said that the faithful would perish if they remained in "Sodom," but "this is obviously false, for many who have left their towns and villages to go to Plzeň or elsewhere are perishing, but if they had stayed home they would not have perished.[49] It is easy to imagine the tension generated by this persecution, supplemented as it was by the hostility of many citizens still in Plzeň; the town had in truth become a beleaguered fortress, ruled by the faithful, and we may suppose that within its walls were concentrated all of the more resolute radicals of the west—those who had been involved in the early extremism of that region, who had taken part in the Taborite congregations, and who had followed Koranda to Prague in October and November.

South Bohemia also boasted its fortress of the faith, Písek. Evidently less prominent at the time than Plzeň, which had attracted the most brilliant collection of leaders in the radical movement, Písek's existence as a city of refuge is not attested by Laurence's chronicle; the evidence provided by

---

[47] Laurence, p. 356; the information about the establishment of the Hussite radicals in Plzeň begins: "Hiis, sicut premittitur, currentibus. . . ."

[48] Příbram, "The Story of the Priests of Tabor," p. 266.

[49] MS O 13, fol. 32ʳ (Appendix 3, in this volume): "multi exeuntes de oppidis et villis Plznam vel alias pereunt, quod si domi mansissent non perissent." See also Laurence, p. 356.

Jakoubek, however, is quite enough to convince us that the adventists who were urging the people of South Bohemia to take refuge in a fortified city were actually telling them to gather in Písek, and a document of 10 February, naming the centers of "Wyclifite" resistance in Bohemia, includes Písek as the only South Bohemian city on the list.[50] On the basis of this evidence we can safely refer still another source to this period; Master John Příbram, writing in 1429 and trying to reconstruct the historical development of Taborite chiliasm, began by telling how the adventist preachers had persuaded many people to leave their homes and join the Taborite communities, and then he continued his account with the following:

> The Taborite priests, . . . not satisfied with having deceived such a great number of people in so ugly a way in regard to their souls, their faith, and their property, immediately thought up another disgraceful deception. They preached and ordained, in the city of Písek, to those people who had fled to them on the mountains,[51] that all the brethren should pool absolutely everything, and for this purpose the priests set up one or two chests, which the community almost filled up for them. The administrator for the chest was the disreputable Matthew Louda of Písek,[52] and he and the other officials of the chest, along with the priests, did not lose anything thereby.[53]

It will be recalled that Laurence of Březová also notes that the people "threw their money at the feet of the priests" in the Bechyně region; he and Příbram must have been talking about the same set of events, and we may guess that after the Taborite exodus from Prague in November, the first place of congregation for those South Bohemians still loyal to the Taborite ideal was some hill in the Bechyně region—perhaps Mt. Tabor—but that the whole group soon transferred itself to Písek, for practical reasons. Ústí-nad-Lužnicí, which would have been the natural urban center for South Bohemian radicalism, was in the hands of the enemy,[54] and Písek, with its tradition of

---

[50] *UB*, I, 16.

[51] The Czech phrasing is difficult: "tomu zběhlému lidu k sobě na hory v městě Piesetským kázali a ustavili. . . ."

[52] F. M. Bartoš has argued that Louda was with Žižka in Plzeň (introduction to *Staré letopisy české z Vratislavského rukopisu,* ed. F. Šimek (Prague, 1937), p. vii), but the argument seems to me to be based on too many combinations to be cogent. For Louda's career see Macek, *Tábor,* II, 78 f.

[53] "Story of the Priests of Tabor," pp. 264 f.

[54] It was not recaptured until 21 February; see below. The Old Czech Annalists (*OCA,* pp. 29 f.) identify the South Bohemian congregants of early November 1419 as "those from Ústí," but this need not mean that they had possession of the town—perhaps they were "those from *around* Ústí," a speculation supported by Laurence of Březová's identification of the same group as those who were coming to Prague "de Thabor" (Laurence, p. 349): i.e., Mt. Tabor, for the city of Tabor had not yet been founded.

extremism, provided a satisfactory alternative. The common chests, like everything else connected with Taboritism, must have had their origins in several
sources: the practical problem of distributing limited resources to an abnor-
mally large number of people, the tradition of brotherly sharing connected
with the earlier hilltop congregations, the example of the primitive Christians
recorded in Acts 2:44-45, and, quite possibly, a feeling that those leaving
Babylon to become members of the elect ought to enter the new world
stripped of what they had brought from the old—a kind of ritual renunciation, parallel to that of monasticism. It may also be noted that the resources
of the chests probably included not only what had been brought by the congregants, but also what had been confiscated from the non-Taborites in Písek;
the latter also suffered a confiscation of their houses and land, which thus fell
into the hands of the new regime.[55] As for Příbram's charge that Louda and
his associates were not entirely honest in their administration of the common
funds, we can only observe that no other sources either confirm or deny the
accusation, and that it seems highly unlikely in a period characterized by so
high a degree of fanatical idealism.

Plzeň and Písek were not the only cities in rebellion against the legitimate
authorities. On 10 February 1420 Sigismund addressed a letter to the prelates,
the feudality, and the town magistrates of the Žatec region, declaring his
determination to restore the religious order that had prevailed in the days of
Charles IV, and commanding the addressees to renounce "Wyclifism," to
give no aid or counsel to "those of Plzeň, Písek, Hradec Králové, or other
towns . . . where they have their congregations," to neither join these congregations themselves nor allow others to do so; those who refused to obey
should be punished by the local authorities, or if these were unable to act, by
the royalist officials of the realm. The punishment was to be death and
confiscation of property. Similar letters were written to all officials, barons,
and town magistrates of the realm: all Wyclifites, Hussites, and utraquists
were to be restrained, persecuted, exterminated; one report of these letters
names not only the three towns mentioned in the letter of 10 February, but
also the town of Klatovy, in the Plzeň district.[56] That only the letter to the
Žatec region survives is no doubt an accident, and we wonder why the list of
Wyclifite centers did not include Žatec itself, Louny, and Slaný, which at
some point in the period of adventism were named, along with Plzeň and
Klatovy, as composing the five cities of refuge.[57] In any case, it is clear that

[55] See J. Macek, "K počátkům táborství v Písku," *JSH,* XXII (1953), 116.

[56] *UB,* I, 15–17; Laurence, p. 357; *UB,* I, 24.

[57] Laurence, p. 356; *OCA-R,* p. 27. It is impossible to say what significance the list of
five Bohemian cities had, but it is interesting to follow the problem through the sources.
One explanation is offered by Josef Macek, *Tábor,* I, 216 f., who refers the list, along

apart from Plzeň and Písek, there were other towns defending "God's Truth," and that some, like Hradec Králové, were not part of the Taborite movement proper. Furthermore, as we have seen, even the official Hussitism of Prague had begun to sanction defense of the truth. Still, it is clear enough that the distinctive nature of the two Taborite centers remained, and that the radicalism focused in other areas had not made the transition from the old world to the new; such towns as Hradec Králové and Žatec nourished a Hussite movement that was to prove very different from that of Prague, and indeed unshakably loyal to Tabor, but it was still not the same as the new Taboritism.[58] Perhaps these radical towns may be regarded, along with the quietest group led by Peter Chelčický, as so many divergent developments out of the great congregations of 1419; South Bohemian Taboritism was only another such particularization of the protoplasmic movement.

The situation just outlined did not remain stable. We have already seen that the Plzeň Taborites were living in a state of siege, and that in early

---

with other phenomena of adventism, to 1419, and explains the "cities of refuge" not as successors to the hilltop congregations but as parallels. Noting the towns in which there had been outbreaks of anti-ecclesiastical violence, Macek concludes: "The congregations on the hilltops served to concentrate the people where it was impossible to count on the support and sympathy of the surrounding towns; but in towns where the burghers and the poor had struck out against the ecclesiastical hierarchy and had shaken the position of the patricians, it was not necessary to take refuge 'on the hilltops'; there the country people had an opportunity to concentrate themselves in the towns." Overlooking at this point the explicit evidence of the adventist sources, to the effect that congregation in fortified towns had to *replace* congregation in the open, Macek comments that "up to now no scholar has put the question of how the pilgrimages to the mountains were related to the five cities." But he does not cite any evidence to persuade us to reject the evidence of the adventist sources themselves: the five cities *alone* were supposed to survive the Day of Wrath; hence they could not be parallel, in adventist theory, to the hilltop congregations, either in 1419 or 1420. And, as noted, the sources all refer to 1420. Furthermore, we have already seen the explicit testimony of Jakoubek, writing about January 1420, that those who preached the doctrine of the five cities did not say which cities these were (Goll, II, 53), and in fact no surviving adventist literature does name the five. Hence the naming must have come, at the very earliest, in the latter part of January. On the other hand, it could hardly have been in vogue after Plzeň—"The City of the Sun," chief of the five—had been surrendered, hence after about 20 March 1420. Why the list did not include Písek is unclear—perhaps it reflected local divisions among the Taborites.

[58] Heymann, pp. 131 f., offers a good characterization of the priest Ambrose, leader of the Hradec Králové radicals, and of his movement. Macek, *Tábor*, II, 227, makes the keen observation that the twelve Taborite demands presented to Prague on 5 August 1420 (see below), may be taken as evidence that Hradec Králové, Žatec, Louny, and Slaný did not adhere to the chiliastic prospectus or program—the twelve demands, made in the name of *all* the provincial radicals in Prague, did not include the characteristic chiliast program.

February King Sigismund had summoned all the powers of Bohemia to battle against the Hussites. Presumably even greater efforts by the royalists were now made, and it seems likely that sometime in mid-February Písek fell, and her Taborite community was forced to flee.[59] Since the menace of the enemy combined with the cold of winter to make protracted existence in the open unthinkable, the band of the elect had to find another city of refuge; it is not surprising that they turned to Ústí-nad-Lužnicí. Their leaders were the priests Vaněček and Hromádka (whom we have already met as the organizers of the hilltop congregations a year before), together with the priests John of Smolín and John of Bydlín, and Lord Procop of Ústí, the Hussite nephew of the royalist Lord Ulrich of Ústí, who held the city.[60] The Taborites, joined by local peasants, spent the period of Carnival hiding out in the woods and conspiring with their supporters within the city; then just before dawn on Ash Wednesday, 21 February, when the Catholics of Ústí were sleeping off the effects of the previous night's revels, the brethren struck. Ústí was captured, the Catholics either fled or were driven out, and the Taborites took over their property; in succeeding days the radicals of the vicinity, perhaps including those who had been forced to leave Písek but had not taken part in the capture of Ústí, flocked to the new city of refuge. We may conjecture that the regime of the common chests was immediately set up. However, Ústí was not to enjoy a long life as a Taborite city; it was evidently not easily defensible, and the brethren decided to take over a much stronger site, the nearby abandoned fortress of Hradiště.[61] The move from

[59] The royalist army that moved against John Žižka and fought the Battle of Sudoměř against him, on 25 March 1420 (see below), had previously moved into Písek ("do Pieska"), according to *OCA-R*, p. 26. In April "the city of Písek surrendered to the Taborites" (*Chron. vet. collegiati Prag.*, Höfler, I, 80). It would seem clear that Písek fell to the royalists some time before 25 March. F. M. Bartoš's arguments to the contrary (*JSH*, XXII (1953), 98 f.) are based on the hypothesis that the two sources noted offer not solid information, but only inferences based on Laurence of Březová's statement, that the royalists who moved against Žižka were gathered in the Písek *region* ("in districtu Piescensi," Laurence, p. 359); Bartoš also notes that Peter Chelčický, writing in 1421, tells how the Písek people defended themselves by shutting themselves in their walls and burning their suburbs (*O boji duchovním*, ed. Krofta, p. 76). I agree with Macek ("K počátkům táborství v Písku," *JSH*, XXII (1953), 115, n. 13) that the text from Chelčický is not specific enough to permit its use in the present context, and that Bartoš's other arguments are not cogent. The date of Písek's fall cannot be established, however, and my guess of mid-February is based primarily on the consideration that the capture of Ústí may be best understood as an effort to provide an alternative to Písek, which had been the city of refuge at least until 10 February.

[60] Laurence, p. 357; *Chron. vet. Colleg. Prag.*, Höfler, I, 79.

[61] Hradiště had been a town, with a fortress; in 1277 the town was destroyed, but the fortress was reoccupied; in 1420, however, the place seems to have been entirely abandoned (Laurence, p. 357; *OCA-R*, p. 25; R. Cikhart, "Pět set let města Tábora,"

Ústí began shortly after that town had been captured, and Hromádka, evidently still worried about the problem of defense, sent word to Žižka in Plzeň, informing him of what had been done and asking for help.[62] Žižka first sent one of his lieutenants, Chval of Machovice, with a contingent of fighters, and then decided, doubtless after taking counsel with the other Plzeň leaders, to transfer the whole Taborite community of Plzeň to the new settlement. A truce was concluded with the royalists providing for safe passage out of Plzeň and for continued freedom of utraquist communion within the city; thereupon, about 23 March, the brethren left the City of the Sun and set out for South Bohemia. On the way, however, they were attacked by a contingent of royalist barons, and on 25 March the two sides fought the severe battle of Sudoměř, which ended in a victory for Žižka but cost the lives of many Taborites, including Lord Břeněk of Ryzmburk; some Taborite prisoners, moreover, were transported to Kutná Hora. The survivors then continued on to Hradiště. A few days later, on 30 March, Ústí, now entirely abandoned, was burnt.

Now all the Taborites were concentrated in one fortress, which had the disadvantage of providing no urban conveniences, not even houses, but the great merit of being a new settlement. It was given the name of Tabor—thus once again the powerful meaning of the "mountain," in this case the old Mt. Tabor, was transferred to a city and the community of the elect within it.[63] The whole action in fact strikes us as the magnificent culmination of Taborite adventism: all the elect were in one group, uncontaminated by any carryovers from Babylon, and in a position to defy the encircling world— history offers no better example of the embodiment of an idea in reality. All of the attractive force of the new Taboritism, and much of the old, were inherited by the city of Tabor, to which Hussites from all over the realm now came, and in which the common chests were set up as the foundation of a new economic order, that of communism.[64] "Just as at Tabor there is nothing mine and nothing yours, but everything in the community is

---

JSH, X (1937), Příloha, pp. 4 f.). The best description of Tabor's site remains that of Aeneas Sylvius Piccolomini, in his letter of 21 August 1451 to Cardinal John Carvajal, ed. R. Wolkan, *Der Briefwechsel des Eneas Sylvius Piccolomini*, III, i, *FRA*, 2. Abt., LXVIII (1918), 23 ff. Macek, *Tábor*, II, 13 ff., offers an excellent discussion, based on recent archaeological investigations, and including a map and photographs of reconstructed models.

[62] *OCA-R*, p. 25. The rest of this paragraph is intended as a convenient summary of events to be treated in more detail in the next chapter.

[63] Laurence, pp. 357 f., first refers to Hradiště as a "castrum," but then as a "mons," "quem montem Thabor vocitant"—thus the city of Tabor was in fact Mt. Tabor. Needless to say, the fact that Hradiště was on a hill helped the identification.

[64] *OCA-R*, p. 27.

possessed equally, so everything should always be in common for all, and no one may have anything privately; if he does, he sins mortally" [65]—the actual regime of caritative sharing thus generated a universal ideal, which became an article of faith. At the same time, the population was organized into four military and political divisions, and while the work of fortification was carried on day and night at a feverish speed,[66] the military contingents, each operating autonomously under its own leader, began to make Tabor master of the surrounding countryside, imposing its overlordship on peasant villages, many of which indeed ceased to exist when their inhabitants went to Tabor, and reducing the fortresses of the feudality, one after the other.[67] With the liberation of Písek and other South Bohemian towns from royalist control,[68] Tabor emerged as the center of a confederation of Taborite communities, eventually dominating a large part of the South.

CHILIASM

An idea that is fully realized loses its dynamism. The founding of Tabor left only one element of adventism unfulfilled, the Day of Wrath; everything else—the flight from Babylon, the concentration of the elect, the defense against the forces of Antichrist—all these had been accomplished. At least one predicted time for the Day of Wrath, between 10 and 14 February, had come and gone, with no destruction of Babylon; other days might be set for the future,[69] but soon even the most fanatical Taborite would suspect that such days were not to be relied upon. Furthermore, the practical arrangements connected with adventism—the common chests, the confiscation of property, simple plundering—were hardly enough to support the growing population of Tabor and her associated cities, particularly since the mass of

[65] One of the Taborite articles in Czech, *KJBB*, p. 59.

[66] Laurence, p. 363; the organization was very simple, providing only the germs of a political system: "Thaborite de Hradisst electis ac erectis sibi quator capitaneis, ad quos respectum haberent. . . ." The four were Nicholas of Hus, John Žižka, Zbyněk of Buchov, and Chval of Řepice. Cf. also Macek, *Tábor*, II, 16.

[67] Macek, *Tábor*, II, 136 ff. and *passim;* I, 263 ff., 343 ff.

[68] See note 59 above.

[69] Aeneas Sylvius, *Historia bohemica,* chap. xlii, mentions the date as Pentecost (26 May), but on what evidence we do not know—perhaps it was the guess of one prophet. In fact the date of 10–14 February may have been similarly restricted in its acceptance; in general, the movement expected the catastrophe sometime in 1420. Cf. John Příbram's *Contra articulos picardorum,* MS Vienna Nationalbibliothek 4749, fol. 66ʳ, where the predicted event is dated "in anno presenti qui est annus domini M CCCC XX"; writing at the end of that year, Příbram could observe that "experience shows" the falsity of the prediction: "asserunt nudum et purum falsum, quod patet in anno isto ad experienciam ocularem." Cf. also Macek, *Tábor*, II, 54.

the people lived as fighters, not workers, and hence were largely unproductive. Indeed, the needs of the large army, lacking for the most part in any weapons except peasant flails and pitchforks, must have been a heavy burden.[70] Finally, now that Tabor was founded and organized, under capable, aggressive leaders like John Žižka, Nicholas of Hus, Zbyněk of Buchov, and Chval of Řepice, the city functioned not only as a center of refuge but as a headquarters for conquering armies; the adventist program of congregating and fighting in self-defense, always waiting for the day of divine intervention, could not fully illuminate the new situation.

This situation indeed had two sharply distinct components. On the one hand, the everyday rhythm of life, steadily augmented as the new city took on physical substance, required a religious dimension of its own—some kind of reformed church radical enough to correspond to the sentiments of the people, but stable enough to form part of an ordered society. On the other hand, the adventist enthusiasm of the previous period, and the savagely aggressive posture of Tabor vis-à-vis the surrounding society, naturally generated their own religious requirements, hardly reconcilable with those of normality. The first variety of Taborite religion was provided by Tabor's heritage from the previous period, when Waldensianist sectarianism had constituted the extreme left wing of the Hussite spectrum of doctrine; the nature of that faith has already been described in various places above, but it will be useful to repeat the description, according to our most explicit source, Laurence of Březová's treatise on Taboritism, included in his chronicle as an *excursus*, after the events of mid-August 1420. After a very sympathetic discussion of the hilltop congregations of 1419, Laurence tells how the Devil corrupted the movement in the period after the death of Wenceslas IV,[71] and prompted "very many" Taborite priests to reject the doctrines of the Church Fathers and of the Church tradition, and to interpret Scripture on their own, according to the principle that everything necessary to the salvation of man here on earth is sufficiently expressed in the New Testament; any interpretation necessary to understand the New Testament can be drawn from the Old, for the two Laws expound each other. Hence these priests expounded

---

[70] Heymann, pp. 97–101, has an excellent discussion of early Tabor's problems of armament and military organization. The interrogations of prisoners captured by the men of Lord Ulrich of Rožmberk in South Bohemia show that for years after the foundation of Tabor, bands of the brethren were actively engaged in petty plundering, of money, food, and armaments, and in the making of false money—some of what is uniformly described as brigandage in the interrogators' records was no doubt part of the battle for the faith, but a good deal must have been motivated, simply, by the need to eke out Tabor's still insufficient resources (*Popravčí kniha panův z Rožmberka,* ed. F. Mareš (Prague, 1878), pp. 25–52, covering the period from 1420 to 1429).

[71] Laurence, p. 403.

the following doctrines, "scandalously and pertinaciously promulgated among the common people in 1420": [72] the writings of the doctors are not to be accepted; university education is vain and heathen; "rites and traditions of human invention are to be abolished and destroyed as traditions of the Antichrist"; the chrism, holy water, consecrated chalices, corporals, chasubles, canonical hours, traditional church chant, the traditional rite of mass, traditional baptism, special priestly vestments and tonsures, all festivals except Sundays, all fasts, auricular confessions, prayers to the saints, holy images—all were rejected; priests might neither possess property nor enjoy it as their own; there is no Purgatory after death, and there should be no prayers or works for the dead; the physical appurtenances of the traditional religion—missals and other liturgical books, cult objects, rich vestments, paintings and statues—were to be destroyed. Therefore, Laurence, continues:

> The priests of the Taborites, fleeing human traditions, walked about with beards and unshaven heads, in grey clothing. They did not read the canonical hours, and, without chasubles, corporals, or special chalices, they performed divine rites under the heavens or in houses, not on a holy altar, but on any sort of table covered with a linen cloth. Nor did they observe the rite of the mass by saying the collects with the canon; but all at once the priests would kneel with the brethren, place their heads on the ground . . . and pray the Lord's Prayer; then the one who was to make the sacrament of the altar got up and said in a loud and intelligible voice, in the vernacular, no more than the words of consecration over the hosts and the wine. And so he made the Body of Christ, not in round hosts according to the form of the Church, but in hosts cut or torn with the hands in any which way. And he made the precious Blood of the Lord from wine, not in a chalice, but in any tin, iron, clay, or wooden vessel. As soon as this was done he administered the sacrament of the Eucharist to the priests and common people who were standing by.[73]

It does not surprise us then that the Taborites also held that the Eucharist was not to be elevated or reserved for the following day [74]—with everything centered on the *act* of communion, all elaboration and adornment having been stripped away, the cult of the Eucharist as a thing in itself could have little appeal. Indeed, the whole religious attitude reflected in these Taborite doctrines, as well as the practice of the Taborite service, harmonizes perfectly with what we may visualize the town of Tabor to have been—a rough

[72] *Ibid.,* p. 405.

[73] *Ibid.,* pp. 406 f.

[74] *Ibid.,* p. 405; this is not to be interpreted as part of the subsequent "Pikart" denial of a Real Presence in the Eucharist (see below), but only as a logical consequence of the Taborite service, which, as we shall see, coexisted with an acceptance of a kind of Real Presence.

encampment where an embroidered chasuble would have been as out of place as a Taborite priest would have been in a choir stall of St. Vitus' Cathedral. Other details also bring to mind images of the ardent simplicity of the new community: baptism in streams or with water brought from anywhere, confession of mortal sins in public, with the sinner asking forgiveness of the brothers and sisters, if he had sinned against any of them, and the people praying for the sinner.[75] It is Laurence's remark that the Taborites 'with the Waldensians" denied the existence of Purgatory [76] which reminds us of the fact that the marvelous suitability of the religious faith to the circumstances of Taborite life was no accident, that the faith had helped to create the life, and that one original inspiration of that faith, despite its similarity in many points to the radicalism of Prague, was Waldensianist sectarianism. By 1420, of course, such usual elements of Waldensianism as refusal to swear oaths, and the rejection of all killing and of all secular power, had virtually disappeared from sight, but the rejection of Purgatory is a reliable tracer, allowing us to see that although Waldensianism had been modified by Tabor's own development, it still stood at the heart of the new faith.

But the year 1420 also saw the propagation of a different faith among the Taborite brethren, the faith of chiliasm, or millenarianism, which also harmonized with certain aspects of Taborite reality, and which also had its doctrinal roots in a pre-Hussite, or non-Hussite sectarianism, that of the Brethren of the Free Spirit. Thus in one sense, chiliasm can be understood as the logical product of both the doctrines and the societal formations generated by adventism; it was in this sense that Master John Příbram reconstructed Tabor's stages of development.[77] First the priests of Tabor preached that Judgement Day would come in the year 1420; the whole world would be destroyed, except for the five cities, to which the faithful must flee. At first, according to this account, those taking flight simply abandoned their

[75] *Ibid.*, p. 410.

[76] Laurence, p. 411: "Item purgatorium animarum esse post hanc vitam cum Valdensibus negabant." The rationale is characteristically Waldensian: ". . . asserentes, solum duas, inferni videlicet et regni celestis, fore vias, eo quod in mortali peccato descendentes per viam inferni ad eternam deducantur dampnacionem, venialia autem habentibus, hos deus hic in via ante diem mortis tribulacionibus aut quibuscunque dolorum vexacionibus torquet et purgat sufficienter. . . ." Cf. the "articuli Valdensium," ed. Holinka, *Sektářství*, p. 176: "Item negant purgatorium. Item credunt tantummodo duas vias post mortem esse cuiuslibet hominis. . . ." And cf. the heretical, evidently Waldensian, articles in Döllinger, II, 614: "Sie sprechen ez sull auch kain fegfiure seyn, dann wann der mensch hye in armut sey, daz sull sein fegfiure sein." Similar, absolutely convincing parallels, could also be cited for the other Taborite articles, but further demonstration hardly seems necessary.

[77] "The Story of the Priests of Tabor," *KJBB*, pp. 263–266.

property or gave it away; then the priests conceived the idea of the common chests, and commanded the people to bring their property with them and put it into the chests. This obviously was the stage of adventism; it is noteworthy that *none* of the sources for this phenomenon—and no known source datable in the early period has been ignored—mentions a millennium that would succeed the Day of Wrath. In the next stage, however, according to Příbram, the millennium did make its appearance, as a kind of political necessity:

> The people, thus seduced, saw how they had evidently been deceived and how they had been deprived of their property. And seeing that nothing had come or was coming of the things that their prophets had prophesied, and suffering hunger, misery, and want, they began to grumble and complain greatly against the prophets. At this point the false seducers thought up a new lie somehow to console the people, and they said that the whole Christian church was to be reformed in such a way that all the sinners and evil people were to perish completely, and that only God's elect were to remain on the earth—those who had fled to the mountains. And they said that the elect of God would rule in the world for a thousand years with Christ, visibly and tangibly. And they preached that the elect of God who fled to the mountains would themselves possess all the goods of the destroyed evil ones and rule freely over all their estates and villages. And they said, "You will have such an abundance of everything that silver, gold, and money will only be a nuisance to you." They also said and preached to the people, "Now you will not pay rents to your lords any more, nor be subject to them, but will freely and undisturbedly possess their villages, fish-ponds, meadows, forests, and all their domains."

The beginning of this stage can be dated fairly closely. To judge from Příbram's reference to the people's disillusionment, it would seem that the *terminus a quo* must have been 14 February, when the predicted end of the world did not come to pass. But since elsewhere in the same work Příbram says that Wenceslas Koranda preached millenarian doctrines in Plzeň—that there would be no need for written books, but that all would be taught by God—and since Koranda left Plzeň with Žižka, about 23 March, we may take this date as the *terminus ante quem*.[78] For the rest, we will hardly be mistaken if we refer the flourishing of the second stage—millenarianism—primarily to the first several months of the city of Tabor. In this period of February and March we may also date the maturity of still another stage of development, which amplified but did not supersede the second:

[78] The text in Appendix 3, No. 2, may well mark this period; it contains the essence of chiliasm with only a mention of adventism and no reference to warfare. For Koranda's preaching, see *KJBB*, pp. 275 f.

Then the seducers, wanting to bring the people to that freedom and some-how to substantiate their lies, began to preach enormous cruelty, unheard-of violence, and injustice to man. They said that now was the time of venge-ance, the time of destruction of all sinners and the time of God's wrath . . . in which all the evil and sinful ones were to perish by sudden death, on one day. . . . And when this did not happen and God did not bring about what they had preached, then they themselves knew how to bring it about, and again thought up new and most evil cruelties, . . . that all the sinners were to be killed by the afflictions described in Ecclesiasticus [39:35-36]. . . . And again those cruel beasts, the Taborite priests, wanting to excite and work up the people so that they would not shrink from these afflictions, preached that it was no longer the time of mercy but the time of vengeance, so that the people should strike and kill all sinners. . . . And they called us and others who admonished them to be merciful, damaging hypocrites. . . .

To Josef Macek this whole picture of the stages of Taborite ideological development seems artificial, "an attempt *ex post* to bring some sort of inner meaning to the exposition of Taborite errors." [79] For in Macek's view there were no stages: as the militant ideology of the poor, chiliasm was substan-tially present at the very beginnings of Taboritism; it expressed not the needs of the moment, but the basic attitude of the poor to those who exploited them.[80] But even within the framework of a Marxist interpretation, it would be possible to reject Macek's opinion, for there is nothing either artificial or "idealist" about the notion that an ideology can have stages of development to correspond to the stages in the development of the social matrix. If we imagine an individual peasant living in his village, and then imagine the same peasant taking part in one of the temporary congregations on Mt. Tabor in early 1419, and finally giving up everything to move to the new community of Tabor in March of 1420—if we imagine all this, as we have every right to do, then we will hardly suppose that the thinking of that peasant was the same at each of the three stages in his life. When we think of masses rather than individuals, the case becomes even stronger—the new communities formed in the winter of 1419-1420 were not stable societies, they were essentially mass movements, with a character determined not by the social provenience of their members—who in fact came from all classes—but rather by the realities of the movement itself. These new social formations had no ties to the established society; except for the distinction between priest and layman, every member had the same social quality as every other

[79] Macek, *Tábor*, II, 45. Kalivoda, *HI*, pp. 336 ff., distinguishes between fatalistic and revolutionary chiliasm in a way that corresponds to the distinction I make; neither of us has copied from the other—we both use Příbram.
[80] Macek, *Tábor*, II, pp. 43-135, and I, 206 ff.

member, for all were equally members and nothing else. Practical needs, of course, caused the creation of primitive social, economic, and political institutions, in which individuals of varying abilities and backgrounds could occupy distinctive positions; but as long as the movement stayed in motion, it tended to prevent distinctions from hardening, and to keep the institutions at the level of practical arrangements, rather than let them develop to the point of forming an articulated social structure. In the light of these considerations, Příbram's reconstruction of Taborite ideological development seems eminently sound; at each point where the forces of disillusionment or despair threatened to bring the movement to a halt, the leaders provided new dynamic force in the shape of a further ideological development. Of course it would be unrealistic to suppose that the priests held periodic meetings to decide on the new doctrines to be preached the next day—Příbram's implication of conscious demagoguery is too crude to be acceptable—but if we bear in mind that the priests had many different opinions and inclinations, we can reasonably suppose that on any given occasion those whose ideas resonated with the need of the moment came to the fore as ideological leaders enjoying the support of the masses. In this sense Macek's interpretation can be accepted; for, as already seen, the Hussite Left had absorbed a full complement of Free Spirit and other extreme doctrines as early as 1418—each corpus would have its hour in the rapid succession of events. It was only later, when Tabor sought to halt her own development, that she began to regulate preaching, so as to prevent her priests from expounding Scripture *ad hoc*.[81]

Thus Příbram's account, valuable as it is, provides only a partial explanation of Taborite chiliasm. We would now like to know which priests were responsible for the new developments, and where they got their ideas; we would also like to know more about the substance of these ideas, and their relationship to adventism and the actual situation. All these desires can be fulfilled, in one way or another. At the beginning of his "The Story of the Priests of Tabor," from which we have taken the survey of the stages of Taborite development, John Příbram clearly states that all the Taborite priests, of whom he names twenty-six, preached that Judgement Day would come in 1420;[82] in discussing the other Taborite doctrines, Příbram attributes them variously to either "the Taborite priests," or "they," or to particular individuals. Since he was writing almost ten years later, in 1429, and since his main goal was to discredit the whole Taborite leadership, his effort to identify all of the priests with the basic errors may be regarded with suspicion. Perhaps it would be reasonable to suppose that in the first stage, adventism, almost all the priests of the Taborite movement were indeed

---

[81] Laurence, p. 438; Höfler, II, 482 f.
[82] "The Story of the Priests of Tabor," *KJBB*, pp. 262 f.

swept up in varying degrees by the enthusiastic prophecies. But as we shall see, by September 1420, at the latest, a substantial part of the Taborite clergy had rejected chiliasm for all practical purposes, and it must be presumed that this situation had begun to develop even in the spring. Here again Laurence of Březová provides more solid guidance; after a full account of Tabor's Waldensianist heresies, he passes on to the chiliast doctrines that were "added" to them: "They proclaimed to the people that the Kingdom of Christ would be renovated now in our time." [83] "The chief author, publicizer, and defender of these doctrines," he writes, "was a young priest from Moravia, of unusually fine intellect and extraordinarily good memory, whose name was Martin"—that is, Martin Húska; ". . . his chief helpers were Master John Jičín, Markolt, a bachelor of arts, Koranda, and other priests of Tabor. . . . All of these looked to a certain Wenceslas, a tavern-keeper in Prague, who had a surprisingly good knowledge of the Bible, expounding the New Testament by the Old, and vice versa." The doctrines in question are those both of chiliasm and adventism,[84] and we recognize in Jičín and Koranda the leading prophets of the Day of Wrath; both evidently continued to enjoy prominence as millenarians. Markolt was with Koranda in Plzeň,[85] and since his activity at this time is otherwise unattested, he may perhaps be regarded as simply a follower of his colleague's lead. Now it is a very striking fact that toward the end of 1420, when Tabor was divided by a struggle between a party of order and the hard core of the chiliast movement, the "Pikarts," none of the three, Jičín, Koranda, or Markolt, joined the latter group; [86] Martin, however, was its leader. Thus Laurence's statement, that Martin was the "chief author, publisher, and defender" of chiliasm, is borne out by the course of events; the path followed by Martin's "chief helpers," however, suggests that even in the beginning there were significant variations in the quality of commitment to, and understanding of, the chiliast corpus of doctrine. These variations cannot be explained in any positive way, nor does a study of the "hard core" chiliasts offer any illumination, except for the very tentative generalization that while at the beginning of the movement, chiliasm attracted a number of priests with university educations, these all seem to have deserted the cause when it reached its

[83] Laurence, p. 413.

[84] The two are mixed together without regard for logical distinctions or chronological stages. Thus the active warfare of the faithful against the evil, with the command to burn or otherwise destroy all cities, etc., precedes the original adventist doctrine that all cities, etc., outside of the five cities of refuge will be destroyed like Sodom—hence by God, not the faithful (Laurence, pp. 413 f.). More will be said about this below.

[85] Laurence, p. 360.

[86] *OCA*, p. 476.

"Pikart" stage.[87] But it would be unsafe to build too heavily on this point. More important than the individuals who espoused them were the doctrines of chiliasm. Surviving chiliast literature, accounts by observers, and what seems to have been a systematic collection of chiliast "articles" by the movement's opponents, all combine to provide a fairly clear and evidently complete picture [88] which can be systematically reconstructed into a logical

[87] The university-educated Taborites were Master John Jičín, the Bachelors of Arts Markolt and Nicholas of Pelhřimov, and a number of priests who had almost certainly been associated with the university and its reform-movement, but who had not received degrees: the only two more or less definitely known to fall into the category were Koranda and Čapek (see chap. iv above). None of these five ranged themselves with the Pikart sect that was expelled from Tabor.

[88] The sources may be most usefully classified as follows:

I. Chiliast literature. (1) A Latin tractate reproduced by Laurence, pp. 417–424. (2) A Latin tractate printed by Bartoš, _Do čtyř art._, pp. 102–111. (3) A chiliast letter, in Czech, printed by Bartoš, _op. cit._, pp. 96 f.

II. Descriptions of chiliast doctrines and practice in the narrative sources. (1) Laurence, pp. 424–428. (2) _OCA_, pp. 478 f. (3) _OCA-R_, pp. 27–29. (4) "Ein Chronicon breve saec. XV," ed. A. Horčička, _MVGDB_, XXXVII (1899), 465.

III. Lists of chiliast (and adventist) articles. (1) Articles 1–42 of a list of 91 (plus 3) Taborite articles, in Czech; ed. in _Archiv český_, III, 218 ff., and by Josef Macek, _KJBB_, pp. 57–61. (2) A Latin version of these articles, used by Laurence of Březová in his treatise on Tabor, _ad_ August 1420, pp. 413–416. (3) What seems to be a later redaction, in Latin, of a text related to (1) or (2), and composed for the purpose of attacking the Taborites; it survives in the following forms: (a) articles 1–34 of a list of 72 articles read off by the Prague masters at the Prague-Tabor confrontation of 10 December 1420; Laurence, pp. 454–458; (b) articles 25–57 of a list of 76 Taborite articles refuted by John Příbram in his _Contra articulos picardorum;_ the articles without the refutations have been published by Döllinger, II, 694–699, and F. Procházka, _Miscellaneen der Böhmische und Mährische Litteratur_ (Prague, 1784), pp. 284–291; for manuscripts see F. M. Bartoš, _Literární činnost . . . M. Jana Příbrama_ (Prague, 1928), pp. 64 f. (4) John Příbram's discussion and refutation of chiliast articles in his "The Story of the Priests of Tabor" ("Život kněží táborských"), ed. Macek, _KJBB_, pp. 262–276; this text corresponds more or less to (1), (2), and (3), but it has much more circumstantial information. (5) Jakoubek of Stříbro, _Vyklad na Zjevenie Sv. Jana,_ ed. F. Šimek, I (Prague, 1932), pp. 526 f., articles 7, 9, 10, 11, 12, 14, 16, and various articles on p. 528. (6) Taborite doctrines collected by Bishop Andrew of Escobar, ed. F. M. Bartoš, "Španělský biskup proti Táboru a Praze," _JSH,_ XI (1938), 69 f.; there are two sets of articles, of which the second is drawn, quite obviously, from item I (1), above—the two correspond verbally. The first set may have come from III (1) or (2), above, but here the correspondence is not close enough to prove anything. (7) A set of seven articles, with refutations, "Contra scripta de adventu Cristi," in MS O 13, fols. 34^r–35^v; these seem related to III (3)b, above; the text is published in Appendix 3 of the present volume.

The dating of the items in III is rather difficult. (1), (2), (3), and (7) certainly originated in 1420, but we cannot say just when; (1) and (2) are obviously closer to the original sources than (3), as shown in part by their respective wording, in part by the

sequence. To begin with, chiliasm establishes its relation to adventism. Essentially, the latter held that the Day of Judgement and the end of the world, both expected by all Christians, were going to come in the immediate, predictable future; this assertion and its practical implications formed the target for the anti-adventist polemics of Jakoubek and his associates. The chiliasts, however, held that the Coming of the Lord would mean not the end of the world, but only the end of the present age—the word "seculum," interpreted by the Prague masters in the orthodox sense, as meaning the world, was explicitly defined by the chiliasts as meaning the age.[89] The present age would be ended, but a new age would follow—the "regnum reparatum" of Christ, in which all would possess the Holy Spirit fully.[90] Some held, following Revelation 20:4, that the new age would last for a thousand years; others found ways to avoid this limit, and predicted an eternal life for the renovated kingdom.[91]

According to this scheme the transition from the present age to the next one involved *two* advents: first Christ would come secretly, "like a thief in the night," [92] then he would come openly; it was the first coming, according to chiliasm, that had been predicted by the adventists, and this coming had already taken place. Thus the manifest supernatural events anticipated by the Taborite communities in the winter of 1419–1420—events that did not take place—were not to be expected; Christ *had* come, the prophecies *had* been fulfilled, but the signs of his coming were human catastrophes. The first, secret advent had ushered in a period in which the faithful, the Taborite brethren, were called upon to destroy the enemies of Christ's Law

---

perfect logical order that characterizes (3) but not the others. (4) is explicitly dated 1429, but Příbram was doubtless working from a list compiled earlier, perhaps (3)(b), with glosses. (5) may be dated in 1421; (6) sometime before September 1422 (Bartoš, "Španělský biskup," p. 67). For discussions of these lists see Bartoš, *Do čtyř art.,* pp. 94–96; Macek, *Tábor,* I, 383 f.; Macek, "Táborské chiliastické články," *Sborník historický,* I (1953), 53–64; R. Kalivoda, "Vytvoření revoluční ideologie selskople-bejského Tábora," *Filosofický časopis,* V (1957), 821–876.

[89] Item I(1), Laurence, p. 418. For the Prague refutation see Laurence, p. 456 (item III(3)(a)): Döllinger, II, 697 (item III(3)(b)).

[90] Jakoubek, *Výklad,* ed. Šimek, p. 527 (Item III(5)).

[91] Příbram, "The Story of the Priests of Tabor," p. 265 (item III(4)), speaks of a thousand years, but the author of item I(2) writes: "Sed quam diu durabit hoc regnum, quid queritur, cum in evangelio dicitur: 'et regnabit in domo Jacob in eternum'? [Luke 1:33]" (p. 108). In another passage he says that all in the New Kingdom will be a "regale sacerdocium," then adds: "Quodsi post resurreccionem tantum omnes essent reges et scientes [*Sic pro* "sacerdotes"?], tunc tantum ad mille annos esset et non plus" (p. 111); I do not understand the passage, unless perhaps as an argument against the thousand-year limit, but at least it shows that the question was on the author's mind.

[92] Item I(2), p. 105; Item III(2), p. 413.

by fire and sword.[93] In this period, a time of punishment, vengeance, and retribution, Christ was "not to be imitated in his gentleness and mercy, but in zeal, in rage, and in just retribution"; he who refused to shed the blood of the enemy was accursed—he was rather required "to wash and sanctify his hands in their blood." Not even priests were exempt from this command.[94] The enemy were defined, simply, as those who did not flee to join the Taborites, for the obligation to take flight and congregate was if anything even greater than it had been before.[95]

But where the adventist prophet had interpreted the image, "where the body will be, there the eagles will gather" [Matt. 24:28; Luke 17:37], as referring to the Eucharist, which could be enjoyed in both kinds in the Taborite congregations,[96] the chiliasts interpreted the body as referring to the Taborite brethren:

> The Taborite brethren in this time of punishment are angels sent to lead the faithful out of all cities, villages, and castles to the mountains, like Lot from among the men of Sodom. And the brethren, together with those adhering to them, are that body to which, wherever it may be, the eagles will gather, and concerning whom it has also been said: "Every place that your foot strikes is yours and will remain yours" [Deut. 11:24]. For they are an army sent by God through the whole world to remove all scandals from the kingdom of Christ, which is the Church Militant, and to expel the evil ones from the midst of the just, and to take vengeance and visit afflictions on the nations of the enemies of the Law of Christ and against their cities, villages, and fortified places.[97]

The difference between these two concepts of "the body," that is, the Body of Christ, contains the whole significance of the transition from adventism to chiliasm. Traditional medieval thought also worked with both concepts—the real Body was in the Eucharist, the figurative Body (*corpus mysticum*) was Christian society, the Church Militant [98]—but the chiliast formulation was distinctively sectarian, for it made the Taborite brethren not merely the virtuous members of a *corpus permixtum,* but the *only* members of the Church Militant; all others had no status as Christians, and hence they and all of their works had no title to life. These ideas were "the new and most evil cruelties" that Příbram says were thought up by "those cruel beasts, the

---

[93] Item III(2), p. 413 f.; item III(4), pp. 266–270.
[94] Item I(1), p. 423; I(2), p. 111; III(2), p. 414.
[95] It was a mortal sin not to take flight: III(2), p. 414.
[96] *Archiv český,* VI, 43.
[97] Item III(2), p. 414.
[98] See, most conveniently, Ernst Kantorowicz, *The King's Two Bodies* (Princeton, 1957), pp. 193 ff., with full references to the literature.

Taborite priests," in order to bring their people to the point where they would not hesitate to execute the dreadful sentence.

It is also Příbram who tells us how this ideology of total, nihilistic violence actually came into being. In tractates "more full of blood than a fish-pond is of water," the Taborite priest John Čapek provided the "prime foundation" in doctrine for chiliast warfare.[99] He developed the idea of the time of vengeance, he specified the various kinds of violence to be done to the enemy —"according to the will of the Holy Spirit" [100]—and he insisted on the need for absolute, universal killing and destruction in the world outside the congregations of the elect: all sinners were to be killed, all buildings were to be destroyed, every last physical entity of the old world had to be wiped out of existence. Since the only way to destroy nonmaterial institutions was to kill the people making them up, Čapek also wrote that "all people in high ranks were to be brought down, chopped down like pieces of wood." In theory everyone was to be given the opportunity to support the Taborites in "the freeing of every truth, the increase of the glory of God, the securing of human salvation, and the destruction of sins," [101] but in fact the furor of destruction that gripped the Taborite armies caused them on several occasions to slaughter not only stubborn royalists and Catholics but even utraquists, even those who promised to do whatever the brethren wished.[102] The new violence was indeed religious violence, orgiastic and ritualistic as well as practical in character, for its purpose was to purge the world in preparation for the "consummation of the age," and its sanction lay in the new situation created by Christ's secret coming, which had annihilated all traditional guides to behavior.

Eventually, "in a few years," [103] the work would be done, the time of transition would be over, and Christ would come openly, to complete the work of destruction by the annihilation of the evil:

> At the end of this consummation of the age, Christ will descend from heaven and openly come in his own person to take up his kingdom in this world, and he will be seen by the actual eye. And he will prepare a great banquet and supper of the lamb as a nuptial feast for his spouse, the church, here on the physical mountains [cf. Apoc. 19:7–9]. And Christ the king will enter to look on those at the table, and he will send into outer darkness all those not wearing wedding garments [cf. Matt. 22:11–13]. And just as in the time of

[99] Item III(4), pp. 268, 282. Excerpts from the tracts are on pp. 268 f.

[100] This appears in a part of "The Story of the Priests of Tabor" (Item III(4)) not published by Macek, but quoted in Nejedlý, IV, 245 f., n. 40.

[101] Items III(4), pp. 269 f.; III(3)(a), pp. 455 f.; III(1), p. 59.

[102] Item II(1), *passim*.

[103] Item III(2), p. 416; III(1), p. 60.

Noah all who were outside the ark were swallowed up in the waters of the
flood, so then all the evil ones, who will have remained outside the mountains, will be swallowed up in one moment, and thus Christ will purge all
scandals from his kingdom.

In this manifest advent Christ will come in the clouds of heaven and in great
majesty, with his angels, and all who have died in Christ will rise up bodily
and come with him in the front ranks, to judge the living and the dead. Next
all the elect still alive at this time will at once be rushed from the ends of the
earth, bodily, to join those in the clouds and to meet Christ in the air, as the
Apostle says. And they said that this would happen soon, in a few years, so
that some of us now living would see the saints of God resurgent, and among
them Master John Hus. . . .[104]

These images are explicit enough, but they take on their full meaning when
we reflect that the Roman church also used the scriptural figures of Noah's
ark and the nuptial feast to refer to itself and its economy of salvation, and
that official Hussitism, following Wyclif, used the idea of the community of
the elect, past, present, and future, to define the true Church, in opposition to
Rome's effort to attribute the immaculate and infallible traits of the mystical
Body of Christ to its own, human institution, a *corpus permixtum*. Chiliasm
presented itself as a combination of both lines of thought: the renovated
kingdom would be the complete community of the elect—the perfect and
immaculate mystical Body of Christ—but it would be an actual community,
the reunion on earth of all the generations of those predestined to salvation.
Hence, as the chiliasts believed, "the congregation and liberation of the sons
of God"[105] would not only equal the primitive church in glory but would
surpass it.[106] "All kings, princes, and prelates of the church will cease to be";
"all kingdoms under the heavens will be given to the sons of God";[107] Christ
himself would rule over his elect,[108] who would possess the Holy Spirit

---

[104] Item III(2), pp. 415 f.; cf. III(1), p. 60. Příbram (item III(4)) adds that Lord
Břeněk of Ryzmburk, as well as John Hus, would rejoin the elect, as indeed would "our
other dead who are known to be God's elect."

[105] Item I(2), p. 106.

[106] Item I(1), pp. 420, 423 f. See Kalivoda's discussion, *HI*, pp. 353 ff. Here as
elsewhere in this chapter, I merely refer to his work; a systematic discussion would be
unfeasible because I agree with most of what he says. Our disagreements come chiefly
from the difference in our methods. As a philosopher he meditates on the inner
meaning of ideas; as a historian I am concerned with the proper arrangement of source-
data, and such meditations as I carry on are anchillary to this purpose.

[107] Item III(2), p. 415.

[108] Items I(2), p. 107; III(1), p. 60; III(4), pp. 270 f. The doctrine, that "solus
dominus regnabit et regnum tradetur populo terre" (III(1)), implied, as the Prague
masters noted, that no human king should be chosen by the Hussites. Whether this was

fully,[109] and would live a life of perfect happiness and joy:

> The elect . . . will be brought back to the state of innocence of Adam in Paradise, like Enoch and Elijah, and they will be without any hunger or thirst, or any other spiritual or physical pain. And in holy marriage and with immaculate marriage-bed they will carnally generate sons and grandchildren here on earth and on the mountains, without pain or trouble and without any original sin. Then there will be no need for baptism by water because they will be baptized in the Holy Spirit, nor will there be the tangible sacrament of the holy Eucharist, because they will be fed in a new angelic mode—not in memory of Christ's passion, but of his victory.
>
> In this renovated kingdom there will be no sin, no scandal, no abomination, no falsehood, but all will be the chosen sons of God, and all the suffering of Christ and of his limbs will cease. . . . Women will give birth to their children without pain and without original sin, . . . and children born in that kingdom, if they are of the kingdom, will never die, because death will no longer be.[110]

With this prospectus in mind, we will not suppose that chiliasm and Tabor's traditional Waldensianist faith were aspects of the same doctrinal corpus. Waldensianism applied to this world-age, chiliasm to the utterly different new age, and on point after point the two stood in patent contradiction. For one thing, since the chiliasts preached that "Paul's institution of gathering in church" would not be followed—there would be no churches [111] —the whole Taborite reform of the church service would be meaningless. The very epitome of Hussitism, utraquist communion, would also become meaningless, for the Eucharist was a memorial of Christ's suffering and would naturally give way, in the age of his triumphant return, to a new kind of holy meal. And the Law of God—above all, the New Testament, which the Taborites had said contained everything needed for salvation [112]—would, according to the chiliasts, "be voided in this world of the renovated kingdom and would cease as to act and execution." [113] It was Martin Húska who

---

a deliberate device of the chiliasts to prevent the setting up of a power that might interfere with them (so Příbram interprets it, III(4), p. 271), may be doubted; the doctrine emerged from a context of fanatic exaltation, not political cunning. Compare article 6 and its refutation, in Appendix 3, No. 2.

[109] Item III(5), p. 527; cf. III(3), p. 28: "So great an abundance of the Holy Spirit will come into the hearts of the faithful that one will not have to teach another, but all will be taught of God." And cf. III(2), p. 416: ". . . they will be baptized in the Holy Spirit," instead of in water.

[110] III(2), pp. 415 f.

[111] *Ibid.*, p. 416.

[112] See above, chap. vi, and Laurence, p. 403.

[113] III(2), p. 416. And see Appendix 3, No. 2.

pronounced this doctrine, which he justified rather logically by saying that in the new age "the Law of Grace would be evacuated and fulfilled just as the text, 'Lo, a virgin shall conceive' [Isa. 7:14], has been evacuated." [114] In other words, just as the New Testament evacuated the Old, by fulfilling it, so the new dispensation of the renovated kingdom would evacuate the New Testament, by fulfilling its promises. As John Příbram later noted, in refuting various chiliast predictions:

> If it were true, that there would be no sin in the renovated kingdom, then there would be no penance, because no sin; no merit, because no resistance [to sin]; no sacraments, because no wounds [of the soul]; indeed the Lord's Prayer would cease, for they would not have to pray, "Forgive us our debts as we forgive our debtors theirs, and lead us not into temptation, but free us from evil." Nor is this all: the greater part of the Old and New Law, if not all, would cease, on the basis of this most perfidious opinion, along with almost all the scriptures teaching us to pray, to repent, to give alms, to fast, and to do the works of mercy. [115]

And:

> If women give birth without pain, then also without sin, for all pain is from sin; thus original sin will cease, and so will baptism, and, consequently, Christianity. [116]

---

[114] John Příbram, *Contra articulos picardorum,* MS Vienna Nat. bib., 4749, fol. 78ᵛ: "Quod lex gracie quoad sensus suos scriptos in multis passibus in contrarium predictis opinionibus [*scil.,* the ideas of chiliasm] sonantibus, ut est de persecucionibus, scandalis, injuriis fidelium, fraudibus, rixis, mendaciis, explebitur, evacuabitur, et cessabit, et hoc in regno sic reparato ecclesie militantis: Est heresis, quia non preteribit generacio hec hominum malorum iniquorum, secundum Chrysostomum, qui punient bonos, donec omnia fiant que fienda sunt mundo; propter quod lex restringens talia erit eis ex fide necessaria. Et hunc articulum confinxit Abyron, ideo quia fortibus argumentibus [sic] compressus, evadebat scripturas multas, dicens eas in adventu predicto evacuari et expleri sicut et illa est evacuata: Ecce virgo concipiet, etc." "Abyron" was Příbram's remarkably apt name for Martin Húska, or Loquis; in refuting the first of the "articuli picardorum," the denial of a Real Presence in the Eucharist, Příbram refers generally to the rebellious defenders of this article, and adds: "de quibus est Martinus Loquis infelix sacerdos, qui Abiron, id est Magister Iniquus aut Magister Inutilis, dicitur; aut Chore, qui 'Clamans' interpretatur. Ipse enim sediciose insurrexit adversus Moysen et prophetas" (fol. 42ʳ). The reference is to Num. 16, the rebellion of Korah, Dathan, Abiram, and On against Moses and Aaron, a rebellion that could be taken as a precise prototype of the chiliast-Pikart rebellion, for the leaders said to Moses and Aaron (Num. 16:3): "Sufficiat vobis quia omnis multitudo sanctorum est, et in ipsis est Dominus. Cur elevamini super populum Domini?" (More will be said of this in the discussion of Martin's Pikartism, in chap. ix).

[115] *Contra artic. pic.,* fol. 66ʳ–66ᵛ. Cf. Appendix 3, No. 2.

[116] *Ibid.,* fol. 79ʳ.

This is exactly true, and Příbram's brilliance as a heresy hunter is nowhere better displayed than in these passages, where he not only catches the very essence of the chiliast faith, but also indicates the logical implications of that faith as demonstrated by subsequent events.[117]

The new, non-Christian religion of the chiliasts, as we have seen, operated with a tripartite division of human history: the Old Law, the New Law, the age of the renovated kingdom. Just as the second had superseded the first, so the third would supersede the second. Knowledge of the third period, however, was won by scriptural interpretation—not the classic, traditional system of patristic and medieval glosses, but a peculiar system of interpreting the New Law by the Old, and vice versa, so as to generate a third body of wisdom. This technique was learned by Martin Húska and his friends from Wenceslas the tavern-keeper in Prague,[118] and in fact it does appear recognizably, and at least once explicitly, in surviving chiliast writings.[119] At this point we can say, without fear of error, that the technique was nothing more or less than that developed by Joachim of Flora at the end of the twelfth

---

[117] See chap. ix.

[118] Laurence, p. 413.

[119] The method is defined in the first paragraph of the chiliast treatise published by Bartoš (Item I(2), above, n. 88), p. 102: ". . . ne videamur in religione angelorum Christi fideles decipere, ambulantes frustra inflati carnis sensu, teneamus super omnia capud, i.e., evangelium Jesu Christi, et totum corpus predicacionis per nexus coniunccionesque legis et prophetarum (*Bartoš:* prophetas) subministremus, ut possit crescere in augmentum divine coniuncionis." And the method does seem to have been carried out. Similarly, the chiliast treatise preserved by Laurence of Březová (item I(1)) demonstrates the method perfectly, but the fact can be appreciated only by those who read the whole work and catch the force of the massive accumulation of quotations, now from the Old Testament, now from the New. Here I shall cite only one or two examples. Thus the author's first postulate reads: (p. 417) "I suppose first that the following authorities are true. *Revelation 10:7:* 'In the days of the seventh angel, when he will have begun to sound his horn, there will be consummated the mystery of God, and He has told the good news of it through His servants the prophets.' *Daniel 12:7:* 'When the dispersion of the band of the holy people [*manus populi sancti*] will have been completed, then all these things will be completed.'" Thus the Old Testament provides the circumstantial detail that allows the chiliast prophet to make the New Testament prophecy actual. Again: "The Day of the Lord I call the day of punishment [*ulcionis*], concerning which it is written in *Isaiah 63:4:* 'The day of punishment has come in my heart, the year of my retribution [Vulgate: *redemptionis*] has come.' And *61:1,2:* 'The Holy Spirit [Vulgate: *spiritus Domini*] has sent me to announce a year of favor and a day of retribution [Vulgate: *ultionis*]. Also concerning this, *Luke 4:18,19.* And *I Thessalonians 5:2:* 'This day will come like a thief in the night.' And *I Corinthians 3:13:* 'And it will appear in fire.' And how a secession [from the faith] will come first is predicted by the Apostle, *II Thessalonians 2:3,* and in *Zachariah 14:2.*" This is much more than a mere heaping together of quotations drawn indiscriminately from both Testaments.

century,[120] and handed down in successive generations of Joachite tradition. By the fifteenth century, the strongest representative of this tradition was the sect of the Brethren of the Free Spirit, which also, as an actual and heretical sect, constituted the form of Joachitism most likely to have influenced the Hussites. Here, as in all questions of heretical influences, we will not expect to find rigorous proofs but if we can show a reasonable amount of evidence that Free Spirit sectarianism was present in pre-Hussite and Hussite Bohemia, if we can show that Free Spirit sectarianism elsewhere in Europe included doctrines closely and fully corresponding to those of Taborite chiliasm, and if, finally, we can show that there is good evidence that non-Bohemian sectaries of the Free Spirit came to Hussite Bohemia—then we may feel that a strong enough case has been made. The alternative would be to find some other pathway of Joachite influence, an unlikely prospect, or to suppose that Martin Húska or Wenceslas the tavern-keeper independently reinvented the Joachite technique of exegesis and the Joachite scheme of three world-ages; few will regard this as in any way likely.[121]

First we may consider the possibility that a Joachite sect—some variety of the Brethren of the Free Spirit—was in existence in Bohemia before the outbreak of Taborite chiliasm. There is an explicit statement in the Old Czech Annalists that seems to mean just that; after a digression on Taborite chiliasm, followed by a brief description of Plzeň's resistance to the royalists, the writer says:

> And so from these things there arose in Bohemia Czechs of a strange, base, and deluded faith, which they had formerly learnt from German heretics, whom the Czechs had burnt many years before [in 1393]. . . . These German heretics had reared their heads not far from Jindřichův Hradec

---

[120] See H. Grundmann, *Studien über Joachim von Floris. Beiträge zur Kulturgeschichte des Mittelalters und der Renaissance,* XXXII (Leipzig: Teubner, 1927), pp. 42–48 and *passim,* esp. p. 61: "spiritalis intelligentia ex littera utriusque testamenti procedit"; pp. 104 f.

[121] Macek, *Tábor,* II, 128–130, considers the possibility that Joachim's chiliasm may have influenced that of the Taborites, but he rejects it because Joachim did not attack the Church or the Papacy, and because Joachim assigned a central place in the Third Age to a monastic order—the Taborites, Macek notes, were passionately opposed to monks. Although recognizing that Taborite chiliasm was not, as a system of doctrines, unlike the chiliasm of various post-Joachim thinkers and groups (p. 134), Macek insists that the former was more perfect as a socio-political phenomenon—here I agree—and that it was developed independently, albeit in terms of general medieval ideas, as the ideology of the Bohemian poor. Cf. the criticism of this and related ideas by another Communist historian, Ernst Werner, in his "Die nachrichten über die böhmischen 'Adamiten' in religionshistorischer Sicht," *Circumcellionen und Adamiten* (Berlin, 1959), pp. 74 ff. On the basis of this and other criticism, Macek has modified his views (*ČsČH,* XII (1964), 860–863).

[Neuhaus], in the village of Stradim, where they had their meetings and committed ignoble and ugly sins.[122]

The writer then describes the destinies of the Pikart-Adamites in 1421—hence of the hard-core chiliasts. His evidence seems credible enough, but it has not received much attention from modern scholars; yet it is strikingly supplemented by another source, a report about a group of German heretics brought to light in Augsburg in 1393. Their doctrines formed a full corpus of Waldensianism, but "some of them believed that their sect would remain until a future judgement, secretly until the advent of Elijah and Enoch, then openly; and all generations were to be congregated with that sect."[123] If these doctrines, so perfectly similar to those we have noted for Taborite chiliasm, existed among heretics in Augsburg in 1393, it is hardly possible to doubt the explicit statement of the Czech chronicler that they existed among German heretics in South Bohemia in that same year. Indeed, if we pursue this line of hypothetical reconstruction, we might very reasonably suppose that the Bohemian heretics in question were, like the Augsburg group, basically Waldensian in belief, and hence part of the Waldensian background of Taboritism, as discussed in chapter 4, but that along with their Waldensianism some entertained ideas of a millennium, on earth—presumably as a kind of inspirational myth, in which form millennial ideas would not have been incompatible with Waldensianism.[124] On the other hand, they may have been, simply, Brethren of the Free Spirit. In any case, other evidence shows that the doctrines of the Free Spirit were known in Bohemia by the early fifteenth century.[125]

None of these hypotheses can be checked; they cannot be ignored, but they must be kept in a kind of special compartment, for possible future use. Less problematical is the theory that Taborite chiliasm derived from the doctrines of Free Spirit immigrants, during the Hussite period. With the flourishing of the Bohemian reform movement in the early fifteenth century, foreign heretics of various kinds began to gravitate to the realm, attracted by what they regarded as favorable conditions, and this movement continued throughout the Hussite period. In 1418, according to Laurence of Březová,[126] a group of forty "Picardi," with their wives and children, came to Prague, saying that they had been expelled by their prelates "because of the Law of God," and that "they had heard that Bohemia offered the greatest freedom

[122] *OCA-R*, p. 29.

[123] Döllinger, II, 364.

[124] Compare, for example, the present Seventh-Day Adventists, who believe in an imminent Judgement but meanwhile lead lives of an ordinary sort.

[125] See above, chap. i, n. 58; cf. chap. ii, n. 120.

[126] Laurence, p. 431.

for the evangelical truth." They were very well received by the Praguers as well as by Queen Sophia and members of Wenceslas' court. "Rarely, however, did they attend divine services, nor were they observed to take communion in both kinds, nor did they have their own priest with them, but only a 'vir latinus' who read to them in their own language." Some died, others left, and the original group faded away, but not before they had passed their heresy on to a number of Czechs. This heresy, known in Hussite Bohemia as "Pikartism," had as its characteristic doctrine the denial of a Real Presence in the Eucharist; it emerged onto the Hussite scene in August 1420. Among the Taborites, however, Pikartism also included the doctrines of chiliasm and of the Free Spirit, as we shall see, and the chief Pikart was also the chief chiliast, Martin Húska. Here there are two possibilities. Martin himself may have added the chiliast-Free Spirit element to the Pikart eucharistic doctrine, in which case the "Picardi" of 1418 would not be of much interest to us in the present context. On the other hand, the "Picardi" may have been a sect of the Free Spirit, whose eucharistic heresy was only a part of a much broader complex that included chiliasm. There are many considerations to support this hypothesis. For one thing, chiliasm included a rejection of the Eucharist—the memorial of Christ's passion would not exist in the new age; indeed it would be pointless for the faithful to take Christ in the sacrament when he was present with them in person, and when they in any case enjoyed full possession of the Holy Spirit—as Příbram pointed out, "nulla sacramenta quia nulla vulnera." [127] Furthermore, the most probable interpretation of the name "Picardi" is that it was a form of "Beghardi," [128] which in turn was a name frequently designating the Brethren of the Free Spirit throughout Europe.

Here we may profitably make a detour and examine the classic definition

---

[127] *Contra articulos picardorum,* fol. 66ᵛ.

[128] Berthold of Regensburg (d. 1272) mentions heretical "Pikardi" in his sermons: A. Schönbach, "Studien zur Geschichte der altdeutschen Predigt," *Sitzungsberichte der phil.-hist. Klasse der kaiserlichen Akademie der Wissenschaften,* CXLVII (Vienna, 1904), 81, 107. Herbert Grundmann, who points to these passages in his *Religiöse Bewegungen im Mittelalter* (Berlin, 1935), p. 393, n. 83, supposes the term to be a form of "Beghardi." The latter did in fact vary in ways that point to "Picardi"—see, e.g., "frater bycharus" in the statement of John of Brno (Wattenbach, p. 533; see below, n. 130). Following J. Dobrowský's identification of the two names (in 1788), F. Palacký repeated the point in his "O stycích a poměru sekty Waldenské k někdějším sektám v Čechách," originally published in 1868, then republished in *Radhost,* II (Prague, 1872), 453; Palacký, however, thought that the name was merely abusive, and that the heretics in question were Waldensians. Among moderns, R. Holinka, "Počátky táborského pikartství," *Bratislava,* VI (1932), 191, regards the "Picardi" as Beghards; F. M. Bartoš seems to reject any derivation of the name except that from the province of Picardie (see below): "Puer Bohemus," *VKČSN* (1923), p. 7, n. 16.

of the Free Spirit Beghards by the Council of Vienne, in 1311.[129] The sect, we
are told, believed (1) "that man in his present life can acquire such a degree
of perfection as to render him wholly sinless"; (2) that in this condition "a
man can freely grant his body whatever he likes"; (3) that "those who are in
this degree of perfection and in this spirit of liberty are not subject to human
obedience . . . for, as they assert, where the spirit of the Lord is, there is
liberty" [II Cor. 3:17]; (4) that man can attain the same perfection of
beatitude in the present as he will obtain in the blessed life to come; (5) that
"every intelligent nature is naturally blessed in itself"; (6) that the perfect
soul does not need to practice acts of virtue; (7) that "the carnal act is not a
sin, since nature inclines one to it"; (8) that the members of the sect "should
not stand up when the Body of Jesus Christ is elevated, nor show reverence
to it," for "it would be a mark of imperfection in them if from the purity and
loftiness of their contemplation they descended so far as to occupy their
minds with the sacrament of the Eucharist or the passion of Christ's humanity." As we have seen, the chiliasts held ideas corresponding to the first, third,
fourth, and eighth of these doctrines; the hard core of chiliasts, in their last
stage of existence in Hussite Bohemia, as the Adamites, expressed doctrines
corresponding to all eight, and we may assume that the Beghard doctrines
not found in the first stage of chiliasm were either lurking under the surface
or were added as a result of contact with the Czech disciples of the "Picardi"
of 1418: these points will be more fully discussed below.

What is missing from the Council of Vienne's formulation is the idea of
the alternation between the present age and the renovated kingdom—the
characteristically Joachite doctrine—but even this is implicit in ordinary
Beghardism. To take an outstandingly valuable example, John of Brno
(Brünn)—a Moravian who, interestingly, encountered a sectary of the Free
Spirit in Moravia, and then went to Cologne to join the sect himself—offered
the following description of the Cologne Beghards in the first half of the
fourteenth century.[130] The new member was received into a kind of novitiate
in which the emphasis was on absolute, Christlike poverty and humility: he
had to sell all his goods and turn the proceeds over to the sect, and when he
first appeared before the brethren he was stripped of his clothing. He was
then sent out to beg, with a companion to whom he owed absolute obedience; he was also required to spend time in church, praying, and to wash
the feet of wayfarers. Thus the first stage of Beghardism was a life of harsh

---

[129] The decree may be found in the Clementines, V, iii, 3, ed. E. Friedberg, *Corpus
iuris canonici,* II (Leipzig, 1881), col. 1183 f.

[130] The text is edited by W. Wattenbach, "Über die Secte der Brüder vom freien
Geiste," *Sitzungsberichte der kön. preuss. Akademie der Wissenschaften* (Berlin, 1887),
pp. 529–537.

asceticism, unquestioning obedience, and hence humility, and of evangelical poverty: this picture is amplified by a number of other sources too.[131] After completing his discipline, according to John's account, the Beghard passed to the highest degree of liberty; having killed his own sinful nature, he was "transmuted totally and physically so as to be made one with God, and God was totally and physically with him." Thus his one requirement was "to allow the divine nature and truth to work in him"—this was the highest liberty and it involved absolute indulgence of the promptings of the presumably new nature: he could, for example, take money from anyone, deceive anyone, have sexual intercourse with anyone, at any time he wished. The only danger was that he might submit to some restraint and hence "fall away from the freedom of the spirit, from the perpetual to the temporal." Thus: "They say that those who are in true liberty cannot be commanded by anyone, or excommunicated, or forbidden anything; neither the pope nor an archbishop nor anyone alive has authority over them, for they are free and do not come under the jurisdiction of any man; therefore they do not heed any statutes or mandates of the Church." In his new condition, the Beghard, who had begun by imitating "the poverty of Christ on the cross," was actually superior to Christ, at least in regard to the latter's earthly existence.[132]

Thus Beghardism, like chiliasm, implies that Christianity is superseded; the only basic difference is that the secular alternation of chiliasm is realized, among the Beghards, only within the individual members of the sect—otherwise the citizen of the renovated kingdom and the perfected Beghard can be thought of as living the same kind of life. In fact, chiliasm can be thought of as an expansion and a secularization of Beghardism. The fact becomes very clear when we once again take up the problem of the "Picardi" of 1418, and consider their probable provenience and doctrines. Laurence does not tell us where they came from, although his tantalizing reference to a "vir latinus" who read to them in their own language suggests that that language was not German, for if it had been he would have said so.[133] The renegade

---

[131] Cf. *ibid.,* pp. 524–526.

[132] Thus: "Post hec me instruxit de austeritate ordinis in hunc modum: 'Verus observator paupertatis nichil habet proprium, set debet esse vacuus ab omnibus rebus temporalibus, sicut Christus in cruce'" (p. 530). Cf. the interrogation of John Hartmann in Erfurt, 1367 (*ibid.,* p. 541): "Interrogatus an Christus fuisset liber spiritu, respondit quod non, quod probavit per ewangelium, quia Christus in passione sua dixit: 'Pater, si possibile est, transseat a me calix iste; non tamen sicut ego volo set sicut tu.' Et addidit quod Christus in die parascheves, postquam mortuus fuit in cruce, tunc primo veram libertatem fuerit assecutus, propter quod et feria sexta a vulgaribus dicitur fritag."

[133] H. Haupt, "Waldensertum und Inquisition im südöstlichen Deutschland," *Deutsche Zeitschrift für Geschichtswissenschaft,* II (1890), 397, also observes that the Picards' language was evidently foreign in Prague; German, of course, was not. He also

utraquist, John Papoušek of Soběslav, is more explicit; listing several groups of foreign heretics who came to Hussite Bohemia, he refers to "alii de Picardia"; it was probably on the basis of Papoušek's information that Aeneas Sylvius Piccolomini derived the Pikart Adamites from a "Picardus quidam ex Gallia Belgica." [134] Thus alongside of "Picardi"-"Beghardi" we have "Picardi"-"de Picardia"—and we cannot say whether or not the two derivations are mutually exclusive. In any case, once pointed in the direction of "Gallia Belgica", scholars have found rich evidence to suggest that the "Picardi" actually did come from there. At least one denizen of that region, the Tournai citizen Gilles Mersault, was in Prague as late (or as early) as 1420, and he returned to conduct active Hussite propaganda in his home town; [135] although the evidence of Free Spirit doctrine in his writings is not great—he might much more aptly be called a Waldensian, or simply a radical Hussite of the Taborite stamp [136]—still the fact of lively contact on the level of sectarian heresy between Hussite Bohemia and Tournai is very significant. On the basis of his analysis of the evidence bearing on heresy and inquisition in this general area, F. M. Bartoš concludes that the "Picardi" of 1418 may well have come from Lille and Tournai, after an inquisition in that year; the argument, although not conclusive, is rather persuasive.[137]

But the real treasure of "Gallia Belgica" lies elsewhere, in the record of an

conjectures, probably wrongly, that the "Picardi" were fugitive English Lollards; they could not have been true Beghards, Haupt argues, because they had wives and children. The latter point is well taken, but, as will be seen, Free Spirit groups, often called Beghards, did not separate men from women, quite the reverse, and it would be remarkable if there were no children.

[134] Papoušek in Höfler, III, 159; *Historia bohemica*, ch. xli; for the link with Papoušek see my "Pius Aeneas among the Taborites," *Church History*, XXVIII (1959), 291.

[135] F. M. Bartoš, "Manifesty města Prahy z doby husitské," *Sborník příspěvků k dějinám hlav. města Prahy*, VII (1932), 269 f., with the text of Mersault's manifesto of 1423 on pp. 290–302. The tracts published by Bartoš in "Puer Bohemus," *VKČSN* (1923), pp. 8–52, may also be by Mersault.

[136] This is against Bartoš, who writes that "all the characteristic traits of the brothers and sisters of the Free Spirit" can be found in the "Puer Bohemus" tractates (p. 6); I find none of them. The same is true of Mersault's manifesto of 1423: there are apocalyptic passages—the Roman church is the church of the Antichrist; the faithful should flee Babylon—i.e., the Roman church, which will be destroyed (pp. 295–298); and there is a summons to physical struggle against Babylon; these ideas, however, are identical with those of Tabor, whose other doctrines are also faithfully reflected in the manifesto, and there is no reason to suppose that Mersault had not derived them from Tabor, during his stay in Bohemia. What we do not find are the Free-Spirit doctrines of a New Age, a renovated kingdom, and so on.

[137] F. M. Bartoš, "Picardi a Pikarti," *ČČM*, CI (1927), 225–250; for the conclusions see pp. 227, 229. In *HR*, I, 122, Bartoš identifies Gilles Mersault as the "vir latinus" who led the *Picardi* of 1418.

inquisition of 1411, conducted by the famous Pierre D'Ailly, Bishop of Cam-
brai, and concerned with the members, the practices, and the doctrines of a
Brussels sect known as the "homines intelligentiae"—we may supply: *"spiritualis* intelligentiae." [138] Here we need not try to reconstruct the full corpus
of the sect's ideas, nor try to get at the truth about its way of life—which evidently assigned a prominent place to ritualistic sex play; the doctrines that
interest us are primarily the following:

> They say (1) that the time of the Old Law was the time of the Father, and
> the time of the New Law that of the Son; the present time is that of the Holy
> Spirit, which they call the time of Elijah. (2) In this time the Scriptures will
> be reconciled [or, in another version, "removed"], so that (3) those things
> that were previously regarded as true are now refuted—even the catholic
> truths that they had used to preach, concerning poverty, continence, and
> obedience. The opposite of these truths, they say, is [to be] preached in this
> time of the Holy Spirit. (4) [They say] that the preachings and doctrines of
> the ancient saints and doctors will cease, and new ones will supervene, and
> (5) that the meaning of Scripture will be more clearly revealed than it has
> been up to now, and (6) that the Holy Spirit will illuminate the human
> mind more clearly than it has done up to now, even (7) in the apostles, who
> had only the outer shell. And they say (8) that the time is at hand in which
> the Law of the Holy Spirit and of spiritual liberty will be revealed, and (9)
> then the present Law will cease.[139]

The substantive and at times almost verbal correspondence between these
doctrines and those of the chiliasts cannot be mistaken.[140] And if we turn our
attention to the last stage of Taborite chiliasm, Adamitism, the correspondence is even more exact and covers an even greater range.[141] Thus, on the
legitimate assumption that the victims of the Brussels inquisition of 1411
were only one group of those holding these doctrines in the general area of
South Belgium and North France, and on the probable assumption that the
"Picardi" of 1418 had come from this region, we can assume that the latter
group were in fact Beghards, cultivating a fusion of Joachite and Free Spirit

---

[138] The text is published by P. Fredericq, *Corpus documentorum inquisitionis haereti-
cae pravitatis Neerlandicae,* I (Ghent: J. Vuylsteke, 1889), 269 ff.; cf. n. 120 above.
Copies of the revocation of William of Hindernissen, a leader of the sect, survive in
Bohemian codices—MS C 40, fol. 294ᵛ, and another text printed by E. Werner,
*Nachrichten über spätmittelalterliche Ketzer aus tschechoslovakischen Archiven und
Bibliotheken.*

[139] Fredericq, pp. 272, 274, 276, 277; the mosaic was originally put together, for
comparison with Taborite chiliasm, by R. Holinka, *Sektářství,* pp. 169 f.

[140] See the comparison with Taborite chiliast doctrines in Holinka, *loc. cit.,* and
thence in my "Chiliasm and the Hussite Revolution," *Church History,* XXVI (1957),
69, n. 79.

[141] See the discussion in chap. ix, below.

ideas that needed only minor adaptations to become the ideology of Taborite chiliasm. In fact, although Laurence of Březová does not try to convict these "Picardi" of more than eucharistic heresy, common sense suggests that there was a good deal more than that, for people would not risk their lives, or indeed form a sect, merely for the sake of a deviant interpretation of the presence of God in the Eucharist—since there is no evidence of any presence at all, opinions about the matter can derive only from a prior disposition of ideas and attitudes. Furthermore, there is evidence, in John Příbram's treatise, *Contra articulos Picardorum,* that the "Picardi' were responsible for more than just the eucharistic articles under attack.[142] Finally, there is a certain amount of less direct, but still solid, evidence to relate the "Picardi" to ideas of the Free Spirit.[143]

If we now direct our attention back to the new community of Tabor, we can define both its reformational and revolutionary aspects with some precision. On the one side stood what we may call, somewhat prematurely, the Taborite church: a form of worship according to evangelical ideals, and an imitation of the Primitive Church, both in the spirit of Waldensianism; a clergy devoted to preaching and moral reform, and very close to the people in its way of life and social function. On the other side stood the chiliasm of Martin Húska and his associates: a body of ideas that entirely devalued the existing order, along with even the most radically reformed religion of that order; a body of fantasy that promised the people an entirely new life, free from all suffering, a life of perfect peace, happiness, and power, in the very technical sense a life of blessedness on earth. But these fantasies were hopes for the future; their practical consequence was chiefly the total war preached by the chiliast priests and in part practiced by the Taborite armies. Meanwhile, the contradiction between Waldensianist reform and Free Spirit chiliasm remained. Such contradictions are not necessarily intolerable over a short period of time because most people can comfortably entertain incompatible ideas simply by not thinking them through, but rather using this or that idea *ud hoc* to illuminate this or that practical problem. Furthermore, the contradiction between imitation of the suffering Jesus and imitation of Christ the Lord was resolved in Beghardism by a system of two stages:

[142] In his preface Příbram declares that he is refuting the "perfidissima dogma tot articulorum quadam subita tempestate per perfidissimos picardos advenas et alios errectorum" (MS Vienna Nat. bib., 4749, fol. 37ᵛ); the list includes chiliast and Waldensianist heresies as well as eucharistic ones, and it may be that Příbram assigned the Picards responsibility for more than just the last group. The fourth article, "Quod Ihesus Christus non sit verus deus et homo," is explicitly called "heresis picardica" (fol. 47ʳ); it may well correspond to the doctrine that Jesus did not possess the freedom of the Spirit—see above, n. 132, and the discussion of Adamitism in chap. ix.

[143] See chap. ix, below.

first the initiate purged his nature by the former path, then he entered into the total freedom of the latter. Logically the same alternation could contain the two branches of Taboritism, the evangelical discipline of the present being regarded as a qualification for enjoyment of the future; chiliast literature shows strong indications of such a way of thinking.[144] But the special feature of Tabor, that which distinguished it from all the sectarian heresies that influenced it, was its existence as a *society*—founded by adventism, animated by chiliasm, but actually supplying basic human needs in a practical, effective manner, just as other societies did. The Waldensianist religion—the Taborite church—was not in fact an initiation, it was a necessary component of the new society, and it necessarily generated loyalties and commitments that could not be turned on and off for the sake of future hopes. Hence the doctrinal contradictions between the two religions were made irreconcilable by their social contradictions, for the one developed in the direction of institutionalization, while the other could survive only by constantly keeping the present fluid, amorphous, in order to keep men's minds and hearts centered in the future. In the early spring of 1420 these contradictions were probably not more than implicit or inchoate; the course of events would bring them to a head and create the preconditions for a final resolution.

[144] E.g., Item I(2) (see n. 88): "nullus regnum intrare poterit, nisi prius ab omni sorde purificatus" (Bartoš, *Do čtyř art.*, p. 108); also: "et de apostolis in figura in actibus apostolorum legitur: 'alienus se illis coniungere non audebat'" (p. 108)—the reference is to Acts 5:13: thus the primitive church, so highly exalted in Waldensianist Taborite thought, is accepted as a figure of the renovated kingdom. See also Item I(1): "Inmaculati, hoc est sacerdotes, qui non sunt possessionati, et ab omni pulvere cupiditatis excussi sedentes cum deo ministrant iam nunc Christo" (Laurence, p. 419)—here the ideal of a priesthood living in evangelical poverty is closely related to the ideal of chiliasm: the priests who have given up everything will find their reward when they judge the world—indeed, they are already finding it, for the period is that of Christ's secret advent, when the Taborites were themselves doing the work of vengeance, spurred on by their propertyless priests.

VIII

TABOR AND PRAGUE: MARCH
TO SEPTEMBER, 1420

A S THE WINTER OF 1420 approached its end, the prospects for
Hussite success could not have seemed encouraging. The national
movement centered in Prague was committed to a policy of ap-
peasement and retreat, ready to forego any development of the reformation if
only the Roman church would show some sign of considering the toleration
of utraquism. The more resolute radicals of the provinces were now Hussitism's best hope, but the great national Taborite movement of 1419 was
dispersed into a number of local centers of resistance—Hradec Králové,
Žatec, Louny, Slaný, Klatovy, Písek, Plzeň, and the newly founded town of
Tabor. While fighting for their lives, they could hardly find either the
capacity or the desire to promote the grand design of 1419: national Hussite
unity under radical leadership. Indeed, the founding of Tabor can be understood as in large measure a monument to the failure of the earlier program
of the Taborite congregations. It was of course something else as well—a
bastion of the radical reformation and revolution—but how long could it and
the other radical centers survive without a union of their forces?

This was the situation at the beginning of March; by the end of the month
it had been entirely transformed, thanks to the failure of Prague's policy to
prevent the crusade that both pope and emperor had long been threatening.
What followed was the great epic of Hussite self-defense, when all joined
forces to fight off Sigismund and his crusaders. By autumn of the year
Sigismund's defeat was an accomplished fact, and the Hussites could begin
to consolidate and extend their power throughout Bohemia and into Moravia. The story is a familiar one and need not be retold here in any detail; less
familiar is the significance of this period for the structural and ideological

361

development of the Hussite reformation, which at this time, under the pressure of these events, passed from childhood into maturity. In March one could still think in terms of national unity; by September it was fairly clear that Hussite Bohemia would develop as a spectrum of religious communities, realizing in their coexistence the full range of possibilities that in other revolutions, most notably the French, would appear as successive stages of the classic cycle. It is this development that will be traced out in what follows.

Much of the credit for what happened belongs to Sigismund, or at least to his stupidity. The truce of 13 November 1419 had in effect created an alliance between the Romanist adherents of Sigismund and the Hussite conservatives —the Prague bourgeoisie, the university masters, and the utraquist nobility. In Moravian Brno, at the end of December, the alliance was consummated. The Bohemian Estates had been summoned there by Sigismund, to meet as a Diet; they came and swore obedience to him, Hussites and Romanists alike. Prague's representatives were also there, and although they indulged in a demonstrative act of utraquist communion, they nevertheless knelt before the Emperor, recognized him as king, and asked his forgiveness of the mutinous acts that had taken place in the capital. On his insistence, they promised to dismantle their defensive barricades and fortifications, and to guarantee the security of the Catholic religious who would return to the city. Then, Sigismund said, the Praguers would be restored to his grace, and he promised that then the problem of utraquism would be settled. On this fragile foundation Prague hoped to erect a structure of religious reform combined with political legitimacy in Bohemia; she further hoped to stabilize that structure by securing, through Sigismund's mediation, papal recognition of the reform—specifically, of utraquism.[1] When the Prague envoys returned home the city was at once put into its submissive posture, to the great rejoicing of the Catholics—the German émigrés and the Romanist clergy, who returned full of hope for a complete restoration.[2] In fact, it is hard to see how Hussitism could have escaped liquidation, if only Sigismund had moved directly from Brno to Prague: secure in the capital, supported by the Estates, served by the royal burgraves of castles and towns throughout the realm, he could have crushed the centers of radical rebellion one by one. Then the pope would surely have condemned utraquism, and Sigismund would have enforced this decree against his powerless subjects.

[1] The basic account is by Laurence, pp. 353 ff., but Sigismund's promises and Prague's hopes are added in a later, anonymous review of the proceedings, UB, II, 526. Both these sources give Prague's side; an apology for Sigismund may be found in Pekař, III, 39 ff. For a full-scale narrative in English of the course of events analyzed in the present chapter, see Heymann, pp. 105 ff.

[2] Laurence, pp. 354 ff.

That these were in fact his intentions is clear from his other dispositions at Brno. Queen Sophia having relinquished her position as nominal head of the royalist regency, Sigismund confirmed the utraquist Lord Čeněk of Vartemberk in his actual headship, as Supreme Burgrave of the Prague Castle, but at the same time he flanked Čeněk by two Catholic barons, Lords Henry of Elsterberk, as Steward, and Wenceslas of Dubá, as Chamberlain. These two had charge of the royal castles and towns, respectively; furthermore, they were to proceed to Bohemia and organize the war against the rebels—the "Wyclifites"—while Čeněk was kept at Sigismund's court until April. Furthermore, the Emperor replaced all the pro-Hussite royal officials and burgraves with Catholic ones.[3] These acts, together with direct reports and the evidence of Sigismund's letters, directing the anti-Wyclifite campaign,[4] show that he gave the highest priority to the reduction of the provincial radicals, whose main center, in Plzeň, now came under the heaviest attack.[5] Powerless to do more than watch, the Hussites of Prague could contemplate the future only with profound depression,[6] no doubt intensified by the realization that they were silent partners in the extermination of their brethren. It was a time when the extravagant agitation of the chiliasts, directed against both Sigismund the Antichrist and perfidious Prague, the city of "Babylon," did full justice to reality,[7] while the more rational Prague literature, barely conceding the right of self-defense and laying greatest stress upon the Christian duty of patient submission, served as a document of the capital's impotence.[8] "Whether in Prague or in Písek or in Plzeň, the just man who dies not consenting to evil . . . will be saved." And as for physical safety, "Many who have left their towns and villages to go to Plzeň or elsewhere are perishing, but if they had stayed home they would not have perished." [9] This was the best Jakoubek could offer at this time, and he stood on the extreme left wing, so to speak, of Prague's conservative leadership. In their own way, these statements are among the best witnesses to the success of Sigismund's politics.

But the Emperor was still not satisfied, and when he had concluded his affairs at Brno, at the very end of 1419, he moved on not to Prague but to Wrocław in Silesia, one of the Bohemian crown lands. As early as September 1419 he had summoned an imperial Diet to meet him there, to make

[3] *Loc. cit.*
[4] See above, chap. vii, *ad* note 56.
[5] Laurence, p. 356.
[6] *Ibid.,* p. 354.
[7] See above, chap. vii, the section on "Adventism and the New Congregations."
[8] Chapter vii, *ad* note 9.
[9] Below, Appendix, 3, p. 520.

preparations for a great military expedition.[10] He had a number of other matters to attend to in Wrocław, and the military expedition had perhaps been intended originally for his Turkish campaigns, but now the Hussite problem had supervened. On 21 January the Strassburg envoys wrote home that Sigismund had told them he intended to march from Wrocław to Prague, to punish the Hussites for their heresy (or "faithlessness"?—*umbe den ungelouben*), but that if the latter would voluntarily submit to him, he would not do it. The same report tells of the large force that he planned to lead against the Turks.[11] Perhaps he was dissimulating, or perhaps his mind was still not made up, but by mid-February there was no question of what he intended. Ordering his Bohemian officials to increase their efforts to exterminate the Wyclifites, he also asked Pope Martin V for a crusade; the Bull "Omnium plasmatoris domini" was in fact issued on 1 March.[12] Soon after, Sigismund and the papal legate, Bishop Ferdinand of Lucena, evidently his chief adviser in religious matters at this time, clarified the meaning of the new line. A Prague merchant John Krása was in Wrocław, no doubt trusting to the terms of the Brno agreement to ensure his safety, and he was rash enough to make known his adherence to the Hussite cause. He was arrested, brought before Bishop Ferdinand for interrogation, and finally required to declare his belief in these articles: (1) The Council of Constance had been legitimately congregated in the Holy Spirit; (2) whatever it had approved was right and had to be believed, whatever it had condemned was justly condemned; (3) the Council had justly and holily condemned John Hus and Jerome of Prague; (4) it had justly condemned communion in both kinds. Krása refused, was condemned to death, and on 15 March the sentence was carried out, with Sigismund's consent.[13] Two days later the Crusade Bull was publicly read out in the city; it called for the extermination of Wyclifites, Hussites, and other heretics—the realm of Bohemia was not named.[14]

What is strange about all of these transactions is their primitive, crude approach to a situation whose extreme delicacy had been correctly understood by the Emperor since he had heard of his brother's death. The judicious mixture of threats and promises that had twice averted a revolution in the autumn of 1419 and had brought Prague to her knees at the end of December, the sophisticated, deceitful policy that would almost certainly

[10] Macek, II, 151, with references to the sources. Heymann's statement, p. 105, that the Wrocław Diet was summoned only in December, must be corrected.

[11] *Deutsche Reichstagsakten*, VII, 408.

[12] The text in *UB*, I, 17–20.

[13] Laurence, p. 358.

[14] Laurence, p. 359; cf. Palacký, III, i, 355, n. 425.

have proven successful in the long run—these lines now gave way to nothing more or less than the old program of the Council of Constance. That body had repeatedly urged a solution of the Hussite problem by force, by the extermination of the heretics, and had, in its treatment of Hus and Jerome, shown the way; the Council had also refused even to consider debating the Hussite program, and had demanded nothing less than total renunciation of it as the price of reconciliation with the Church. In fact, the articles that Krása was asked to accept were essentially those formulated by the Council as the basis for the reduction of the Bohemians, at least as early as 1418,[15] at a time when not only that body but also the Emperor Sigismund and the pope were talking of a great military expedition against the heretics.[16] There was nothing unreasonable about this approach, but it was impractical without overwhelming force to back it up. The divided Hussites, their nation now garrisoned by royalists and Catholics, did not seem very powerful, but their weakness was the result of a policy that was now being reversed: every Hussite would now have to resist, unless he were prepared to accept the articles that Krása had refused; moreover, every patriotic Czech would feel at least some inclination to fight off the invading hordes of largely German crusaders. Sigismund himself well understood the danger of such a crusade for the independence and integrity of the realm, and it is hard to imagine how he could possibly have persuaded himself that his new policy was the right one.[17]

[15] The text in Höfler, II, 240–243. In MS 4937, fols. 2ʳ–6ᵛ, there is a "Forma inquisicionis concilii constanciensis cum responsionibus," and since it has not, to my knowledge, been either published or used, I quote some of its relevant passages: [fol. 2ʳ] ". . . interrogetur utrum credat, teneat, et asserat quod sacrum concilium generale . . . quale fuit in civitate Constanciensi universalem ecclesiam representet, et quod decreta, statuta, et ordinaciones ipsius concilii a cristifidelibus sunt inviolabiliter observande et observanda." [Fol. 5ʳ] "Item interrogetur si credit quod condempnaciones Magistrorum Johannis Wikleff et Johannis Hus et Jeronimi de Praga, facte de personis eorum et de doctrina per sacrum generale concilium constanciense, sunt iuste et sancte et a quolibet katholico pro iustis et sanctis tenende, credende, et asserende." There is more in this vein and much more besides. The "iuste et sancte" formula appears in Laurence's account of what Krása was asked to accept (p. 358), and there are also other verbal similarities.

[16] See above, chap. vi, *ad* notes 5–9. A generally reliable account written in 1433 actually refers to the Crusade as "cruciatam, in concilio Constanciensi . . . erectam" (*Mon. conc. saec. XV,* I, 387).

[17] As early as March 1416 Sigismund wrote the Hussite barons that if they were not careful they would bring down a crusade on themselves, "and the realm would then suffer permanent damage" (*Documenta,* p. 611). And in a letter to the Catholic barons, written at the same time, he spelled out the point: "your neighbors do not exactly wish the Bohemian Crown well, and it would not take much to make them join in destroying you" (*Documenta,* p. 620). And see Heymann, pp. 141–143, for an account

Its first, inevitable result was to discredit the architects of Prague's previous policy and, correspondingly, to strengthen the position of those Praguers who had always favored militant action in alliance with the radicals of the provinces. We know little or nothing about what Želivský's party had been doing between its great defeat in November and the crisis of March, but it would be reasonable to assume that it saw the disastrous situation in much the same way that the Taborite chiliasts did. At any rate Želivský now emerged, sometime about March 1420, as a Prague equivalent of a chiliast prophet; preaching a cycle of sermons on the Apocalypse, and drawing a great multitude of listeners, he applied the Manichaean imagery of that book to current realities, with Sigismund identified as the Red Dragon who would fight against God's angels in the last days (Rev. 12). Other preachers joined him in agitation, to the point that "many of the faithful were eager to throw their lives and property into the balance, for the sake of communion in both kinds." [18] No doubt prepared by continuous agitation in January and February, this militant mood must have become dominant as soon as the Praguers learnt of Krása's execution and of the proclamation of a crusade against them. The time had in fact come to undo the damage that had resulted from the victory of conservatism in the autumn, to recreate the great national movement of the left, to extend the radical reform and to defend it, arms in hand, against all enemies.

Perhaps the first task was to improve the Hussite military position in the areas where actual fighting had been going on, above all in Plzeň, where the Taborites were now very hard-pressed by a full-scale siege. The South Bohemians who had founded Tabor had asked Žižka for support, and he had sent them a contingent under Chval of Machovice, but it now seemed doubtful that the Plzeň bastion itself could be maintained. Having been created in the first place by those who refused to accept the November truce, it had been worth the price of its defense throughout the winter; the creation of the much stronger position of Tabor, and the imminent passage of Prague to a posture of self-defense, had created a new situation in which Plzeň had become a source of weakness. Hence its defenders, although committed in principle to a policy of no truce with the enemy, now entered into negotiations, "at the advice of certain men sent to them by the Praguers." [19] The source here is Laurence of Březová, who may fairly be called a Prague

---

of how such considerations came into play in Sigismund's camp during the siege of Prague, in July 1420. By the beginning of February 1420 Bishop John Železný was in Wrocław, and he may have helped persuade Sigismund to pursue this dangerous policy (*HR*, I, 8).

[18] Laurence, p. 360.

[19] *Ibid.*, p. 359. For the course of events, see Heymann, pp. 90–94.

apologist; he perhaps exaggerated the role of these envoys in the matter, but he would hardly have invented it. At the same time it seems clear enough that the Plzeň Taborites would have needed no advice about the facts of their situation, nor would they have welcomed guidance from the conservative party of the capital. The only reasonable supposition would be that the envoys had been sent by Želivský's party to inform the Plzeň defenders of changes that were going on or were about to take place in Prague, changes that would make the continued defense of Plzeň unessential.[20] Thus an agreement was in fact made, and the whole body of Plzeň Taborites, led by John Žižka, Lord Břeněk of Ryzmburk, Lord Valkoun of Adlar, and the priests Wenceslas Koranda and Markolt of Zbraslavice, moved out of the city under a truce. In spite of this they had to fight the very hard battle of Sudoměř, in which Lord Břeněk was killed, but the main body got through to Tabor, arriving on 25 March. At once the South Bohemian town became the strongest Hussite power in the land, its people organized as a standing army—or rather as four armies, led by the captains Nicholas of Hus, John Žižka, Zbyněk of Buchov, and Chval of Machovice. These at once set about imposing Taborite hegemony over as wide an area of South Bohemia as possible: towns, fortresses, monasteries, and villages of the enemy were conquered; victims were slaughtered, booty was often burnt, quarter was rarely given. It was the total warfare called for by chiliast military doctrine, a combination of the savage élan of a jacquerie with the organization and discipline of a *levée en masse*. Parallel if less spectacular efforts were made at the same time in the other provincial centers of resistance, the royalists powerless to stop all but a few of them.[21] It was a time when all the work of the previous five years suddenly revealed the basic success that underlay its apparently inconclusive character, for the faith that had been preached with such ardor, spread with such stubbornness, organized with such diligence, now stood forth as a liberating ideal that could summon up popular energies never before seen, a national possession that thousands of men, women, and even children were ready to die for.[22]

[20] See below, n. 24; also *HR,* I, 83.

[21] The best account of Tabor's campaigns is in Macek, *Tábor,* II, 136 ff.; for the other centers see pp. 19 ff. The ability of the other radical groups to come as armies to the defense of Prague suggests that they had been militarily active all along; see also the proofs cited above, chap. vii, *ad* notes 56, 57. Furthermore, their armies too were active in the burning and destruction of churches and monasteries—see Laurence, pp. 365, 372.

[22] The recording of martyrdoms was important in the Middle Ages, and Laurence's chronicle has a number of examples of the *passio* genre. None is more moving than the story of the martyrdom of the otherwise unknown parish priest of Arnoštovice, one Wenceslas, and his vicar, together with three peasants and four children, aged 7, 8, 10,

It remained, however, for Prague to draw these powerful forces into a national coalition. Thanks to Želivský and his associates she was able to do so. It was their propaganda that had forced the Praguers to realize that "King Sigismund of Hungary planned nothing good for them," and it was largely as a result of Želivský's instigation that the whole Prague Hussite community—the Old Town as well as the New—met at the Old Town Hall on 3 April to pledge total mutual support in defense of the chalice. This was a new political formation, a Hussite Union, and its first business was to set up a military organization—four captains in each of the Prague towns, with forty subordinate leaders under each group of four. These captains had full authority to take all measures necessary for defense of the Hussite cause; in other words, they constituted a new government, practically superseding the regular magistrates who had been the chief architects of the policy of submission. These magistrates were not however deposed but only required to swear loyalty to the Hussite Union.[23] One of them, from the Old Town, lost no time notifying the Mintmaster, Nicholas of Jemniště, one of Sigismund's chief agents in the realm, that "because of the union of the two Prague towns the city will not remain true to the King, unless Nicholas come quickly." At the same time the Magistrate (*judex*) of the Old Town went around showing some sort of letter and announcing, "Good news from our lord the King—he has given up the crusade!"[24] But the Hussites were

---

and 11 (pp. 385 f.). All were arrested on 6 July 1420 by the forces of the Duke of Austria, who was marching to aid Sigismund before Prague. They were interrogated, tortured, and urged to recant their utraquism. They refused and were set on a pile of wood, which was then burnt. All died, Wenceslas encouraging the rest and holding the children in his embrace and all singing hymns. Enough such episodes have been recorded to make a regular Hussite martyrology, but there must have been many unrecorded cases of heroic suffering and idealistic dedication. The Hussite cause had indeed become everything in Bohemia, imposing its polarization of values on even the daily life of the smallest village.

[23] Laurence, p. 361.

[24] *UB*, I, 24. The source is an anonymous, undated report, evidently written in Prague, and addressed, "Honorabilis D[omine] Johannes!"; it was transmitted by one Nicholas the Butcher, who had also been given other information, to transmit orally. Josef Pekař supposed that the addressee was John Želivský, the sender one of his confidants, and he dated it "perhaps from the end of March to the beginning of April" (Pekař, *Žižka*, IV, 33). While this would be close enough for most purposes, it is still worth trying to define the date more precisely. The report has four items of information, one, as noted, to the effect that Sigismund was said to have given up the Crusade —hence the report must have been written at least several days after the news of the Crusade, proclaimed in Wrocław on 17 March, had reached Prague. But it also relays a report that Sigismund had commanded that "all Wyclifites of whatever estate" be killed —if force were not possible, then they should be tricked by false promises—and that this should be done in Plzeň, Hradec Králové, Písek, Klatovy, and other places. Thus the

not fooled, even though some members of the union may have continued to cultivate the old hope that Sigismund might still become king of a utraquist nation. For when the union took the step of issuing a manifesto to the realm, denouncing the Crusade, there was no mention of Sigismund as its leader or as the Hussites' enemy. Instead, the emphasis was on showing how the Crusade had grown out of the policy followed by the Council of Constance and then by the pope, and the main danger was shown as coming from those who would make up the invading armies—"our natural-born enemies, the Germans," who planned for the Czechs the same fate they had inflicted upon the Polabian Slavs. Against this threat Prague summoned all faithful Czechs to defend the Hussite—and national—cause, formulated now in what would eventually, after some permutations, become known as the Four Articles of Prague:

1. We stand for the ministering of the body and blood of the Lord to the laity in both kinds, for . . . this was Christ's institution and . . . that of the first apostles and of the holy Primitive Church . . . , as the Council of Constance admitted to us.

2. We stand for the proper and free preaching of the word of God and of his every truth.

3. All priests, from the pope on down, should give up their pomp, avarice, and improper lordship in superfluity over temporal goods, and they should live as models for us.

4. We stand for the purgation of and cessation from all public mortal sins, by each in his own person; and for the cleansing of the Bohemian realm and nation from false and evil slander; and in this connection, for the common good of our land.

To secure these aims a Diet was summoned to meet in Prague, and all the communities of the realm were requested to send two or more of their

---

news of Plzeň's surrender, which was arranged *ca.* 20 March, had not yet reached either Sigismund or the author of our report, who would certainly have remarked on it. Thus the report can hardly have been written more than a few days before or after 25 March. But as we have seen, it also mentions that "concordia unionis facta est inter communitatem novae et majoris [*scil.,* antiquae] civitatis Pragensis," and the only such agreement known after the events of autumn 1419 was that of 3 April. What the report shows, then, is what ordinary common sense would also suggest, that the public agreement of 3 April had been preceded by discussions and a preliminary agreement—at least a week before. All of this confirms my conjecture about the import of the "advice" given to the Plzeň Taborites by the envoys from Prague. And for a bonus: if indeed the addressee was Želivský, then the report shows that he was not in Prague, where the report was written; perhaps he was among the Praguers who had gone to Plzeň! Such possibilities cannot be pressed too hard, but it would be equally unjustified to ignore them.

leading men to attend, "for the greater welfare and benefit of our whole Fatherland and realm of Bohemia." [25]

The Diet seems to have met, although there is no direct report of it; its main achievement was to mark the extension of the Hussite Union to include the utraquist feudality, led by Lord Čeněk of Vartemberk, just back from Wrocław, and his former ward, Lord Ulrich of Rožmberk. A new manifesto of 20 April, no doubt emanating from the Diet, improved upon the previous one by declaring Sigismund to be not king but "great and cruel enemy of the Bohemian realm and nationality"—a charge backed up by ten specifications, ranging from the Crusade itself, through the execution of John Krása and the organization of the Kutná Hora extermination center, to such nonreligious matters as Sigismund's alienation of certain Bohemian crown lands. Included were his responsibility for the burning of John Hus and, in the first place, his slandering of the realm by the charge of heresy. The manifesto called on all to refuse obedience to him and his officials, and it ended by repeating the earlier formulation of the Four Articles, with only the last one altered, by removal of the part about mortal sins. Added was a declaration of willingness to be corrected by Biblical proofs, a sign, no doubt, of the enduring desire of the university masters for a confrontation, a hearing at which their program could be urged on the Roman church. But in fact, the manifesto was a formal defiance of the Emperor, a renunciation of his authority, and when the November truce ran out, on 23 April, the policy responsible for it had already been abandoned.[26]

The manifesto must have been accompanied by practical preparations for the defense of Prague by the united forces of Bohemian Hussitism, a necessary step but one that could not fail to revive all the internal conflicts of the previous autumn, with the Hussite feudality on one side, the radicals on the other, and the Prague masters and bourgeoisie in the middle. The conflicts were grounded in conflicting class interests and religious viewpoints, but they actually developed as a contest for control of the nation, a political struggle. From the point of view of Prague conservatism, still the dominant force in the city, the problem was how to use the provincial radicals without accepting their program—that is, without surrendering Prague to a radical

[25] The text in *AČ*, III, 212 f. For its association with the 3 April meeting see Bartoš, *Do čtyř art.*, pp. 72 f.; *HR*, I, 88; and see below, n. 32. Cf. Seibt, *Hussitica*, pp. 134 f.

[26] The Czech text in *AČ*, III, 211 f. The text was sent to the various communities of the realm, in various languages, as a request by Čeněk that they renounce their obedience to Sigismund; for adverse reactions to it by Sigismund and by the town of Kadaň see *UB*, I, 25–27. It also circulated outside the realm: on 13 May the Nürnberg town council sent a copy of it to Ulm (*UB*, I, 29 f.).

regime. From the radicals' point of view the problem was more difficult: how to liquidate the power of the feudality, the Prague bourgeoisie, and the university masters in order to create a national society on radical principles. These were the issues in October and November of 1419 and they re-emerged, unaltered, in the spring of 1420, never forgotten even in the most crucial moments of military exigency. For when the provincial contingents rallied to the defense of the capital they came just as they had in the previous autumn, as whole communities, both men and women—it was in fact the last of the great congregations. But for several months these men and women had been accustomed to thinking of Prague as Babylon, the perfidious city that had bought her peace at the price of terrible suffering by those whom she now asked to save her. And Babylon was quite ready to try again, even after the arrival, on 30 April, of the first of the provincial contingents, the "Horebites" of the Hradec Králové region, led by their priest Ambrose. What happened, according to Laurence of Březová, was that the total warfare currently carried on by the Taborites in South Bohemia—their burnings, smashings, and killings—caused Čeněk of Vartemberk and the other nobles to become "dejected," to regret that they had ever defied Sigismund.[27] Čeněk had in fact used his position to get control of the Prague Castle away from Sigismund's supporters; now he resolved to deliver it back to them, as part of a more ambitious plan to reconcile Prague with Sigismund and to reconstitute the program of the November truce and the Brno submission. He performed his treachery on 7 May, and in spite of the protests of Želivský's party, Prague sent her envoys to Sigismund, then staying at Kutná Hora, to hear his terms. Had he been willing to promise protection for utraquism and a generally gracious disposition toward his Hussite subjects, he would have been received with open arms; instead, he insisted on total, unconditional submission, dismantling of all defenses, and disarmament—once in Prague, he said, he would decide on what sort of grace to grant.[28] It must have been with heavy hearts that the Prague conservatives heard their envoys' report, for now even they could see that there was no alternative to a coalition with the left despite all of its risks, including the alienation of the feudality. Prague thereupon sent envoys to

[27] Laurence, pp. 364 f.; cf. Pekař, III, 43; IV, 29 f.

[28] Laurence, pp. 365–369. It should be noted that Čeněk insisted, in his negotiations with Sigismund's agents, on permission for his continued practice of communion in both kinds. That is, he was thinking in terms of the pre-Wrocław distinction between conservative utraquists, who were loyal to Sigismund, and radical utraquists—the Taborites and others—who were not. But it would be fifteen years before Sigismund was ready to make that distinction once again.

Tabor with the urgent request to put aside all other concerns and hasten to Prague, to defend the truth of God's Law.[29] The Taborites did just that, arriving on 20 May. Four days later the communities of Žatec, Louny, and Slaný came.

Among the first acts of the Taborites in Prague was an apparently spontaneous attack on sinful luxury: burghers who wore decorative mustaches, and their wives who wore the usual superfluous millinery of the patrician female, suddenly found themselves confronted by outraged Taborite men and women, who cut these things off. At the same time, some of the church and monastery buildings were forcibly deprived of their ornamental pomposities, and at least one monastery was destroyed.[30] None of this seems very fundamental, some of it in fact seems trivial, but these acts must be understood as nothing less than first engagements in the war against Babylon. They point directly to a more obviously important action taken on 27 May, when the new coalition of forces in Prague carried out a kind of radical coup.[31] Now, finally, the councillors of both Old and New Towns were deposed, and others were chosen, by a new community consisting of the Praguers and their provincial allies. They based their union on mutual agreement to stand as one against Sigismund or any other enemy of God's Law and the chalice, and they took as their program the Four Articles, this time with the punishment of public mortal sins in a prominent place. Such things as Sunday drinking in taverns and excessive ornamentation in dress were the sins in question, and although they cannot arouse much indignation in an enlightened mind today, they evidently marked out the precise line along which the conservative and radical concepts of reform faced each other in opposition. There were of course many other issues, notably doctrinal ones, dividing Waldensianist and chiliastic Taborites from other radicals, but these were not now in order, nor would they be as long as the old hope of a national radical union remained alive. The main issue now, apart from that of anti-Roman militancy, was whether the existing society would be regenerated in a Christian sense by the rigorous and complete application of those moral norms that all Hussites agreed on in principle. And the Four Articles that had been originally produced by the radical-conservative union

---

[29] Laurence, p. 369. It is impossible to say if this was a second request—urgent in tone because the Taborites had not responded to a first, which would have been sent them after the Diet of 20 April. If not, then the Taborites must have been deliberately omitted from the request that had brought the Horebites to Prague on 30 April; this is the view of Macek, *Tábor*, II, 174 f.

[30] Laurence, pp. 371 ff.

[31] *Ibid.*, pp. 374 f.

of 3 April could be made to embody this issue with sufficient clarity, for each of them could be given a specifically radical content.[32] Utraquism was

[32] The Four Articles do not represent a stage in the development of Hussite ideology, but only a program which the Hussite parties could agree to accept as stating their common aims, chiefly for the purposes of external propaganda. Hence an analysis of the Articles themselves, of their origin, and of their variant redactions, is unnecessary here. Heymann, pp. 148–163, offers a convenient discussion of their content; for origins and development see Bartoš, *Do čtyř art.,* pp. 69–73, and his *Manifesty města Prahy z doby husitské,* offprint from *Sborník příspěvků k dějinám hlav. města Prahy,* VII (Prague, 1932), 253 ff.; cf. also Macek, *Tábor,* II, 219 ff., for a good discussion of their ideological signifiance. In the present context it is necessary only to draw attention to certain key points at which it is possible to glimpse the differences between a conservative and a radical understanding of the Articles. This can best be done by comparing two texts: (1) that used by the papal legate, Bishop Ferdinand of Lucena, in his letter to the Praguers in early July (*UB,* I, 33–37), and (2) a text dating from the second half of July, after Prague's victory had been assured by the Battle of Vítkov Hill (Bartoš, *Manifesty,* pp. 282–285). The first, according to Ferdinand, was copied from the text "cujusdam cedulae, quae a vobis dicitur prodiisse"—it is the Latin version of the Czech text cited above, note 25 (see my English translation, above), and, as Bartoš argues (*Do čtyř art.,* pp. 72 f.), its relatively conservative formulations can best be explained as the product of the 3 April meeting, at which the provincial radicals were not present. Thus utraquist communion is "communi populo ministranda," while in the second text the formulation is, "omnibus Christi fidelibus, nullo peccato mortali indispositis, libere ministretur"; the difference is not great, to be sure, but the second seems more drastic and it allows more clearly for infant communion—a point that can be better understood by comparing still another text, a German version of *ca.* 1 July (*Manifesty,* p. 275), which reads, "allen gelaubigen kristen, *die das begern* und nicht haben hindernisse der tötlichen sunden" (my emphasis). The article on free preaching of the word of God does not differ significantly in the two texts; both use the limiting word, "ordinata/ordinate." On the third article, however, the differences are important: the first says, "quod sacerdotes, a papa incipiendo, suam pompam, avaritiam et *inordinatam* dominationem *in superfluitate* bonorum temporalium *dimittentes,* nobis sic exemplariter vivant sicut . . . Christus ipsis praecepit . . . ," while the second reads, "quod dominium seculare super diviciis et bonis temporalibus, quod contra preceptum Christi clerus acceptavit in preiudicium sui officii et dampnum brachii secularis, ab ipso aufferatur et tollatur, et ipse clerus ad regulam evangelicam et vitam apostolicam . . . reducatur. . . ." Thus a demand that the clergy give up excess pomp and wealth is replaced by the strictly Wyclifite program of secularization of *all* the clergy's civil dominion over property. (The exact degree of rigor of the "vita apostolica" is another question, which we can pass over here.) As for the fourth article, the first text joins several points (see the English translation, *ad* n. 25 above), with only this for mortal sins: "pro expurgatione et desistentia omnium publicorum peccatorum mortalium, quilibet in sua persona. . . ." But the second text states: "quod omnia peccata mortalia et specialiter publica alieque deordinaciones legi dei contrarie in quolibet statu rite et racionabiliter *per eos, ad quos spectat,* prohibeantur et destruantur. Que qui agunt, digni sunt morte, non solum, qui ea faciunt, sed qui consenciunt facientibus. . . ." Again a desire is converted into a legal prescription, and the long list of such sins that follows, ranging

common to all, but the radicals insisted on infant communion along with it.[33] The second and third articles, in their radical form, called for reduction of the clergy to an apostolic life, not just removal of superfluous possessions; a prime motive for this was to free the clergy to preach the word of God, not just within the routine of the ordinary church service but continually, as a means of religio-political agitation. As for the "public mortal sins," the radicals had in mind not merely a repression of excesses by authorized officials but rather what amounted, in practice, to a revolution in the life of society, with the popular leaders entitled to clean up every evil they could find.

These points become clearer later on, but they are present from the first as the program of the political formation that had been attempted in the autumn of 1419 and was now being realized in the action of 27 May 1420. Under the pressure of military necessity the radical communities of all Bohemia were able to combine into a new religious and political organism, one that could reasonably hope to take over the national movement and reduce the conservatives to a minority opposition, within the framework of united Hussitism. Given the actual power and prestige of the conservative elements—the feudality, the bourgeoisie, the university masters—the chances of radical success were not great, but in favor of the left was the obvious fact that the right had shown itself entirely incapable of leadership in the most urgent of all matters, defense of the Hussite realm. Here it is instructive that the meeting of 27 May also provided that the priests in Prague should conduct a house-to-house visitation of all non-Hussites in the city, to offer them the choice between taking communion in both kinds or getting out. The measure seems obvious enough in a city facing a crusade; what is

---

from fornication to contractual masses for the dead, makes the article's intention perfectly clear. The words I have emphasized are usually regarded as a moderating element (e.g., by Macek, *Tábor,* II, 220), but they may perhaps also be seen as an attempt to give the law effect, by specifying who must execute it. In any case the article is very strong and almost certainly represents the particular wishes of the provincial radicals—here it may be recalled that the text produced by the Diet of 20 April, at which the Hussite feudality took the lead, omitted all mention of mortal sins from the fourth article. But if the above comparison shows that the "official" redaction was more radical than the first one, it also shows that elements of moderation were either preserved or added, and it must be born in mind that the official redaction was *not* the direct product of the union of 27 May, but rather something developed out of that union by the theologians; as Laurence says (p. 374), after his very brief and general summary of what that union agreed on, "Ex quibus quidem articulis quatuor articuli principales, pro quibus Pragenses cum sibi adherentibus instabant, sunt postea elliciti et ad formam debitam . . . redacti."

[33] This is the testimony of a historical account written in 1433, in *Mon. conc. saec. XV,* I, 386; cf Bartoš, *Do čtyř art.,* pp. 70 f.

remarkable is that many chose to leave—that is, the previous regime had not taken the elementary precaution of purging its own camp of likely traitors.

The narrative of the war in which Prague defended herself from the crusading armies has often been told and need not be repeated here. It is however important that the decisive battle, on Vítkov Hill, 14 July, was won by Žižka and the Taborites, and it is both instructive and wryly amusing to observe the role played by the Four Articles in the strenuous months of June and July. From the very first, as early as April, this program had been used as a statement of principles for the non-Hussite world—that is, as a means of propaganda. But the text that would become official was one developed in connection with the meeting of 27 May, a text explicating each article in considerable detail, notably in the specification of the public sins to be eradicated, and providing each article with a weighty dossier of scriptural, patristic, and even medieval authorities. This statement, translated into a number of languages, was distributed to the various units of Sigismund's army and sent to a number of towns and communities in Bohemia's orbit of interest.[34] Of course no text, however specific, is proof against interpretation, and the main body of Prague University masters saw the Four Articles as a protocol for discussion, for the "hearing" that they never tired of seeking. Even during the siege they pursued this aim, and in fact actually procured a meeting at which they debated the articles with their opposite numbers in the Crusaders' camp. What is more, agreement was reached on everything but utraquism—that is, the masters were prepared to castrate every article but that—and it was finally the refusal of the Catholics to debate this point further that frustrated the whole effort.[35]

After the victory of Vítkov Hill the siege was given up, the Crusade collapsed, and Sigismund withdrew; his only achievement had been his coronation in Prague's Cathedral, across the river from the city that rejected him. Prague was safe, thanks to her radical allies, but there were still royalist strongpoints around her, most notably the Hradčany and the Vyšehrad, and the realm itself was still a battleground. The radical communities from the provinces could remain in Prague only at considerable risk to their home bases, but the risk was hardly worth taking unless they could fulfill their national program by converting Prague into one of themselves. The program of 27 May still stood, but it had not been carried through in practice. The time had come to force the issue, and that is what the Taborites and other

[34] The several surviving texts are discussed by Bartoš in the two works cited above, n. 32. They fall into two main groups, one sent out in early July, the other sent out after the Battle of Vítkov Hill, and there is evidence that the copies did in fact reach their destinations.

[35] See the account in Heymann, pp. 161 f.

radical communities did, by formulating their demands in twelve articles which were then presented to the Prague community. Unless the latter consented to these points, maintained and defended them, the Taborites would leave:

These are the articles: We the whole community of the Taborites and others staying in the city [*Nos Thaboritarum et omnis advenarum communitas*] offer you, the Prague community, the following articles:

1. That the written instrument between you and us be kept and observed in its integrity by both sides.

2. That the articles to which the captains, councillors, and the community have agreed, and which have long been proclaimed by preachers and sermons, be held and observed under the published penalties.

3. That there be no toleration without punishment of evident sinners, adulterers and adulteresses, fornicators and fornicatresses, whoremasters and madames, ruffians and prostitutes whether open or hidden, idlers of either sex, thieves, and all enemies, blasphemers, and detractors of God, of whatever order or status.

4. That under fixed penalties there not be allowed any drinking in taverns of any drink, nor its sale on the street.

5. That they not wear or permit to be worn prideful clothing, costly to an ungodly degree of excess, such as garments dyed purple, fringed, painted, embroidered with silver, tufted, slashed; also silver girdles, nets, and all ornaments or adornments disposed for pride.

6. That it be provided in the crafts and in the market that there should be no deceptions, stolen goods, usury, oaths, useless or vain things, tricks or falsehoods; and this under any fit punishment.

7. That pagan and German laws not in agreement with the law of God be removed and that government, judgements, and the disposition of everything be according to divine law.

8. That priests be required to lead exemplary lives, in accordance with the divine ordinance and in imitation of the prophets and apostles.

9. That the university masters be regularly subject to divine law, like other faithful Christians, and that they compose their writings according to the will of God, and deposit them in the Town Hall, so that they may be examined according to God's Law.

10. That all priests' incomes be converted to the common good, that usurious incomes on houses, commodities, or whatever else be destroyed, and that all other usurious contracts be destroyed, and that the priests be supported by the voluntary contributions of the faithful [*et sacerdotes ut ex fide serventur*].

11. That they expel enemies of God's truth from their midst, and not receive

fugitives or banned people, for such have not kept faith with God or the Praguers, and therefore should enjoy no credit, by any favor.

12. That they destroy and demolish heretical monasteries, unnecessary churches and altars, images kept openly or secretly, prideful chasubles, gold and silver chalices, and every antichristian institution, every idolatrous and simoniacal depravity, which is not of God, the heavenly Father.

Dear Brothers, it is for this that we have exposed ourselves to peril of goods, property, and life, wishing to fulfill the divine will; for many of our brethren have already shed their blood for the above-written truths and have exposed their lives to danger. We do not intend to relinquish them under any circumstances, with God's help, and we wish the same for you. And we shall help you and we intend to help you as long as we endure, if you do not neglect them.[36]

Laurence of Březová, who preserves these articles in his chronicle, also provides our only account of the context in which they figured. He first notes that on 5 August the Taborite priests and captains presented the articles to the "Prague community," with the request that they be accepted—otherwise the Taborites would leave. The New Town at once consented, "without having taken due counsel with the masters." But the Old Town did act with the masters and asked for time to deliberate; then Master Peter Payne, in the presence of the town magistrates, read off the articles one by one, to determine how or whether each might be accepted without violating the consciences of the community. Then Laurence gives the list, as translated above. A paragraph follows telling how the Taborites, in the next few days, indulged in more destruction of churches, image-smashing, and even drunkenness. Then Laurence begins a new entry: *"Item,* in spite of the fact that everything was being done as the Taborites wished, they repeatedly made as if to leave [*iteratis vicibus se recedere fingunt*]." "Therefore," he writes, on Sunday, 18 August, the priests, at the instigation of some members of the community, announced from their pulpits that there would be a meeting at the Town Hall after lunch, to deal with some difficult matters; but the *seniores* of the community knew nothing of this. The meeting was run by Želivský, who brought about nothing less than a replacement of the town magistrates by new ones, chosen by him and the community "because the deposed councillors refused to go along with the Taborites on many points; and so the pro-Taborite priests chose . . . councillors virtually all of whom did agree with the Taborites." Their hope was that the Taborites would then agree to remain in Prague, but only four days later, on 22 August, "the Taborites withdrew from Prague, for no other reason than that the masters

---

[36] Laurence, pp. 397–400; this is also the source for the next paragraph.

continued to write treatises against their rites [*nisi quia magistri eorum ritibus scripturis resistebant*]."

Except for the last statement, which rather gratuitously lets the cat out of the bag, we have here one of Laurence's little masterpieces of tendentiously elliptical narrative. On his account the twelve articles, which did not concern rites, were not decisive, nor was the question of the composition of Prague's government; in fact it would seem, according to Laurence, that the Taborites fooled their best friends in Prague, including Želivský, by pretending that these things were at issue. But the real controversy was one between the university masters and the Taborite priests over rites—that is, the forms of religious observance—and yet other sources do not suggest that this issue was decisive, nor are the writings of either side known to survive.[37] It is all painfully obscure, and perhaps the best way to begin the necessary reconstruction will be to consider what distortion can be expected from Laurence in this matter. For this is not the first time that he has been wilfully opaque —in fact, at every point in his chronicle where the national, political program of the Taborites is in question, Laurence telescopes, generalizes, omits—in a word, he suppresses the truth. He does this in connection with the first Taborite congregations in the spring of 1419; he does it again when dealing with the great congregation of 22 July 1419 and the subsequent Prague insurrection of 30 July; he similarly maintains total silence about the politicking that went on after the death of King Wenceslas, and this silence becomes downright thunderous when he succeeds in noting the two great national congregations in Prague, in the autumn of 1419, without telling us what these assemblies wanted, how they tried to get it, or why they failed. His account of events in the spring and early summer of 1420 is somewhat better, but here, too, it is fairly obvious that he includes only a minimum of the intra-Hussite politicking that must have gone on. It would not be too simple to say that Laurence represents the cause of the Prague masters, as seen from the viewpoint of a disciple of Jakoubek of Stříbro; the provincial radicals of 1415–1418 do not appear at all, and the Taborites are allowed to figure in only two roles: either they are fervent adherents of common-Hussite doctrines or they are fanatical subverters of civilized order—vandals, murderers, mutineers, heretics. In general, the second role follows the first, and Laurence provides plenty of doctrinal explanation or at least illustration; but there is also a certain amount of mixing, to suit the requirements of his context.[38]

[37] That there was indeed a conflict over rites is implied by a later statement by Tabor's bishop (quoted below, chap. ix, n. 75), who also says, however, that the conflict did *not* result in an exchange of writings.

[38] For Laurence's silences see the account of the several episodes in the previous chapters, *passim*. His particular viewpoint is still subject to discussion. Thus Jaroslav

One of the presuppositions of the above analysis is that Laurence does not number actual mendacity among his historiographical sins—this is, at any rate, the opinion of almost every modern scholar who has used him, even those who accuse him of tendentiousness.[39] Thus there is no reason to doubt that he has given a true text of the Taborites' twelve points—in other words, that the break between Tabor and Prague really did involve these points in some way. Nor need the evidence of the twelve articles themselves be doubted. Thus points 1 and 2 seem clearly to recall the compact of 27 May and the Four Articles adopted as a common program at that time. And points 3, 4, 5, 6, 8, and 10 elucidate the two articles providing for the destruction of public mortal sins and for the reduction of the clergy to an apostolic life.[40] For the rest, points 7, 11, and 12 seem to push the radical demands further along the same line: the legal constitution of the city was to be transformed into something based on the divine law—that is, Želivský was to have full power to set up an evangelical dictatorship;[41] the solid

---

Goll in his introduction to his edition, *FRB*, V, p. xxxv, writes, "Laurence of Březová belonged to the party of the more moderate Calixtines, and thus to the resolute enemies of the Taborites and of the other radical parties." But I think it would be truer to say, with Bartoš, that Laurence generally manifests the outlook of Jakoubek, to whose party he certainly belonged in the 1420's—as opposed to the more conservative party of John Příbram and Prokop of Plzeň (see, e.g., Bartoš's "Z politické literatury doby husitské," *SbH*, V (1957), 51). The problem is complicated by the fact that in 1420 itself, Laurence expressed an extremely radical outlook in his verse compositions—thus Rudolf Urbánek can write, of *this* Laurence, "The Prague for which Laurence speaks is essentially the Prague of Želivský" ("Satirická skládání Budyšínského rukopisu M. Vavřince z Březové z r. 1420 v rámci ostatní jeho činnosti literární," *VKČSN* (1951), No. III, p. 27). Thus we must distinguish between the Laurence of 1420 and the Laurence of later years, and it was the latter who wrote the "Hussite Chronicle" (cf. Macek, *Tábor*, II, 200, n. 81). Finally, I would reject the view of Pekař, that Laurence's silences about events among the provincial radicals were due to his "Prague horizon" (Pekař, *Žižka*, I, 61); for not only does he in fact include many items about events outside of Prague, but his most painful silences are about actions that did take place in Prague.

[39] This "communis opinio" is so evident as not to require proof; almost everyone accepts the verdict of J. Goll, *op. cit.*, p. xxxiv: "The data in Laurence's chronicle are, with some few exceptions, correct."

[40] See, e.g., Macek, *Tábor*, II, 227 f., and Heymann, pp. 166 f. And compare the details in the official texts of the Four Articles, for example, in Laurence, p. 394.

[41] Article 7 raises a number of questions; Macek, *Tábor*, II, 228 f., calls it the most important of the list and holds that it meant a demand for "the complete abolition of feudal law and of the whole legal and administrative system of the towns." He also suggests that it was directed against the "German Law" that regulated the conditions of agrarian lordship. He may be right, but it would also be reasonable to interpret the article as a kind of vague desire for change, so that Bohemia's public life might be based on the Bible, as the reform program had always demanded. Whether this potentially revolutionary desire was thought of in specific terms is unclear; for a change in legal

citizens who had supported Sigismund and Romanism were not to be allowed to resume their leading roles; the external apparatus of the Roman religion was to be destroyed, so that Prague might replace that religion by something quite different—the kind of simple congregational worship evolved by the radicals.[42] However, these demands added up to much more than observance of the Four Articles: either the Taborites were now asking more or the compact of 27 May actually did include a Prague commitment to assume the shape of a radically reformed society. In either case, the great obstacle would have been the university masters, most of whom were strongly opposed to anything more than a pruning and cleaning of the Romanist religion, and all of whom, certainly, were outraged at the thought that anyone but themselves would dare to decide what was true in these matters. Hence the reason for point 9, which boils down to a demand that the masters answer for their opinions to the radical political leadership of Prague—that is, to John Želivský.

All of this brings us much closer to Laurence's explanation, that the real issue was a conflict between the masters and the Taborites over "rites." The difficulty here is that neither Laurence's chronicle of events nor Jakoubek of Stříbro's sermons for the period give any positive testimony to the existence of a special Taborite ritual until *after* the departure from Prague, in fact not until about October.[43] But both the silence and the testimony can be accounted for on various grounds, and certainly Laurence's *treatise* on Tabor, inserted into his chronicle, shows the simplified ritual as it was practiced by the Taborites in Prague.[44] Moreover, common sense suggests

---

principles did not necessarily mean a change in the laws themselves, which could be thought of as implementing the Law of God (see, e.g., my "Wyclifism as Ideology of Revolution, *Church History,* XXXII (1963), 66).

[42] It should be borne in mind that Tabor's own policy was to destroy precious vestments, gold and silver monstrances, chalices, and similar items in the churches of the towns, monasteries, and castles that she conquered: see Lawrence, pp. 363 f.

[43] Thus Bartoš, "Studie o Žižkovi a jeho době," *ČČM,* XCVIII (1924), 100 ff., has argued that Jakoubek's postil for this period shows him actually approving of such Taborite practices as destruction of churches and of images, and that it would therefore be wrong to suppose that there was a split between the Taborites and any but the extreme right wing of the Prague masters in August. Jakoubek's first mention of the Taborites' simplified liturgy comes in October of 1420, when he attacked it in his sermons; since he was a close observer of events, and reacted to them in his preaching, his silence must be taken as evidence that the Taborite liturgy was not in practice in August, as Laurence suggests.

[44] See the passage quoted above, chap. vii, *ad* n. 73; cf. below, chap. x, the section "From the Meeting of 10 December 1420 to the Murder of Želivský, 9 March 1422." In any case it is clear that the situation in October was different from that in August, for the program of all-Hussite unity had been replaced by the actual independent develop-

that the Taborites of August 1420 could hardly have been less radical in liturgical matters than had been the radicals of 1416–1418, when the most drastic reforms had been at issue within the Hussite movement. In 1419–1420 the whole direction of development was toward extremism, not away from it. But this consideration raises another point that Laurence does *not* mention: after the history of November 1419–April 1420, with Prague conservatism first betraying the left, then depending on the left for its salvation, is it conceivable that the triumphant radicals, reunited in Prague, should have forgotten their national program of 1419, when they had demanded schism from Rome and election of a Hussite bishop and a Hussite prince? Even the conservative leadership recognized that the repudiation of Sigismund made it necessary to find a new king, and they at once set about doing so; a first mission was sent to King Władysław of Poland in April and another was sent in July; the second one probably had the support of most of the radical communities—we know that John Žižka committed the Taborites to it, even though Nicholas of Hus, no doubt representing the views of a sizable group on the left, was opposed to choosing anyone but a native Czech as prince.[45] Laurence gives this information only by the way, and in a later context; he says not a word about the extensive discussions that must have preceded the enterprise. Thus if he also says not a word about a radical demand for the election of a bishop, it does not mean that there was no such demand. There must have been one, and even the most sober inferences from the Taborites' twelve points of 5 August point in the same direction. For these points in general, and point 12 in particular, amount to a declaration of war on the Roman system. If Prague had in fact carried through not only a complete disendowment of the clergy but also a systematic program of destruction of "superfluous" churches, monasteries, and altars as well as paintings and statues, she would have had to say goodbye, once and for all, to her inveterate hopes for a hearing by Rome. In other words, on this line of reconstruction, there was indeed a controversy over "rites" but it was part of a wider controversy in which the radicals, led by the Taborites, demanded not only a reform of the liturgy, not only a drastic enforcement of puritan morality on the body of Prague society, but the creation of a new church to be the national religious organization of Hussite Bohemia. This organization would of course preclude reunion with Rome, but it would also put an end to the religious authority claimed by the university; it would be a radical

---

ment of the various communities. Thus Jakoubek in October was reacting to a potential schism between Tabor and Prague, and Laurence reported the liturgical aspects of that schism in his account of events in the autumn; but the theoretical controversies of the summer would not have called for public comment.

[45] Laurence, p. 447.

church, expressing the religious consensus of the communities that made it up. Naturally the masters would have none of it and, evidently, they had a strong enough following to stand up to both the Taborites and Želivský. Hence the collapse of the Taborite initiative and hence the Taborites' departure from Prague—because "the masters continued to write treatises against their rites."

These hypotheses are advanced as the most reasonable explanation of a crucial event reported very confusingly by Laurence of Březová. But their basic assumption, that it is impossible to imagine that there were no discussions about setting up an independent Hussite church, finds its needed positive support in an odd text that records precisely such discussions between the masters and the Taborites. It is undated, but the situation it presupposes did not exist after 1420 or before 1419; I agree with F. M. Bartoš, its discoverer, that 1420 is the more probable date.[46] The text includes a Taborite theoretical statement to justify election of a bishop, on the grounds of the practice of the Primitive Church and on the basis of a radical rejection of Roman institutions: "The promotion of bishops customary in this modern age did not exist in the Primitive Church, but was . . . introduced by the satraps of Antichrist. . . . Furthermore, as the Evangelical Doctor [that is, Wyclif] says, the church would be better off if there were no pope or no person of the sects introduced by Satan, . . . and he says that it is a fiction of the Devil that without such men priests cannot be ordained."[47] The Taborites go on to define the positive reasons why a bishop should be elected:

1. Because of necessity, so that the salutary truths instituted by our labor and suffering [cf. the last paragraph of the Twelve Articles, above!] may progress further.

2. Because of the lack of good and catholic bishops, and the lack of priests.

3. Because of the carelessness of the laity about the things that concern their salvation.

4. In order to give direction and order to the clergy.

5. In order to exclude Antichrist's usurpation of priestly ordinations, and the sanctification of many other things; and because of the detestation of the simoniacal heresy.

[46] The text is printed and discussed by Bartoš in an appendix to his *Do čtyř art.*, pp. 75–78; there he argues for dating it in 1419. But in his later "Myšlenka svrchovanosti lidu v husitské revoluci," *Husitství a cizina* (Prague, 1931), pp. 164–166, he changes to 1420: the discussion "belongs to July and August of 1420, and it throws . . . light on the problem of why the Taborites left Prague. . . ." See also *HR*, I, 105.

[47] These ideas of Wyclif had long been cultivated on the Hussite left; see, e.g., the discussion by Nicholas of Dresden, *Consuetudo et ritus primitive ecclesie et moderne* (*ca.* 1412), in *OC & N*, pp. 66–72.

6. In order to weaken the cult of the Beast and the acceptance of his mark.

7. For the free progress of the divine law.

The Prague masters unanimously refused to consent: "At this time and in these circumstances, given the indisposition of the people and the divisions that are current, it is neither permitted nor expedient for the communities to elect a bishop or bishops without the customary mode of consecration." The reasons were then set forth: "First, the reason of the law [*scil.,* the Bible], for the Apostle and Timothy were bishops when they ordained priests. Second, because it cannot be found in the histories. Third, because it is against the canons. Fourth, because it is against reason, according to St. Jerome. . . . Fifth, because many improper things [*inconveniencia*] would follow therefrom."

To be sure, these texts register not a discussion but a confrontation between two alien points of view, essentially the same ones that were expressed in the ideological conflict between the Prague masters and the adventists. Whether there were in fact real discussions, just how the particular question of rites was involved, whether Želivský was wholeheartedly in favor of the Taborite view, what was the relationship between this contest and the political reorganization of Prague—these and other related questions can hardly be answered, even by hypotheses. For our purpose it is enough to know that Tabor did advance her national political program in the summer of 1420, and that once again she failed to carry it through. It was her last attempt. From now on she would solve the problems of Hussite reformation in her own way, among her own members and subjects. And we will not be surprised to learn that one of her first acts was to elect a bishop.

IX

THE DEFINITION OF
TABORITE SOCIETY

FROM its first beginnings in 1419, on the hilltops of South Bohemia,
the Taborite movement had carried the promise of a social and political
revolution. The radical and indeed sectarian religious doctrines of the
Taborites could not be realized or safeguarded without a regeneration of the
social order, nor could the thousands of self-uprooted men and women fail to
transform their conglomerate existence into a polity, a societal structure. This
implicit tendency toward self-definition in societal terms was, however,
countered by another impulse, derived from the pre-Taborite history of
Hussitism and Hussite radicalism: early Tabor was aware of itself only as a
section of a national movement, and its first leaders were priests and petty
noblemen whose aim was to make Tabor's program that of the Hussite
nation. In the periods when this enterprise was actively pursued, the sectarian political and social attitudes of Tabor's heresy—or heresies—had to give
way before ideas of a more orthodox political cast, positive ideas about how
to use power in an institutional framework based on the long-established
facts of political and social life. There could be no question of defining or
even localizing the Taborite movement which, in these periods, embraced all
the communities and contingents of provincial radicals. But the national
enterprise failed twice, first in November of 1419, then again at the end of
August, 1420. Both of these failures opened the way to what may be called
Taborite particularism, the tendency for Tabor to take the shape of a definite
society, occupying a definite area and composed of members who belonged
to the society not merely because they shared its ideas but because they were
subject to the society's institutions and norms.

The period of chiliast predominance, in the winter of 1419–1420, saw this sort of development. The prophets insisted that to be a Taborite meant joining one of the radical communities "on the hilltops" or in the "five cities of refuge"—outside of these there was no salvation. The brethren were organized into armies, under captains (and no doubt other regular officers); possessions and plunder were pooled under a definite regime of communist consumption; priests and prophets exercised the function of social leadership, even if only charismatic. But merely to name these inchoate forms of organization is to indicate their instability; in actual fact the Taborite communities were still parts of a movement whose structures, norms, and ideas remained fluid. When the Taborites again entered the arena of national political action, to defend Bohemia against Sigismund's crusade, they did so as a movement in the most evident sense: it was not just armies that went to Prague from Tabor, Hradec Králové, Žatec, Louny, and Slaný, but whole communities of men and women. Once again, however, these communities failed to win power in the nation; when they returned home they left behind the hope of Hussite unity and—more to the present point—any possibility of defining themselves merely as parties within a national political spectrum. Incidentally, too, they moved out of the original Taborite condition into a new situation of local, autonomous development: henceforth "Tabor" meant only the town of that name and the other towns and villages that were joined to it by definite ties of alliance, federation, or subjection. Žatec, Louny, and Slaný were close to Tabor in thought and feeling, Hradec Králové somewhat less so, but their subsequent development was independent. For this reason, and also because the sources for their history are relatively poor, they will be discussed only occasionally in the following pages; in any case, the creative development of the Hussite Revolution from now on was almost entirely the work of the Taborites.

THE PROBLEM OF A TABORITE SOCIETY

The sources for the inner life of Tabor in the autumn of 1420 are neither detailed nor abundant, and it will be useful to quote the best items of information in full—they are two paragraphs preserved in one manuscript of Laurence of Březová's chronicle:

> In (September) of 1420 the Taborites in Hradiště [i.e., the town of Tabor], not wishing to be without a spiritual leader, agreed to elect Nicholas of Pelhřimov, a priest and bachelor of arts, to be their bishop or elder [*in episcopum suum seu in seniorem*]. All their priests were to be guided by him, nor might any preach the word of God to the people unless with the consent of this bishop. Furthermore he, together with the other priests, was to dispense

the funds of the community, faithfully, according to what he deemed to be the need of each of the brethren. . . .

Also, in the same year, in spite of the fact that during the summer the priests of Tabor had publicly taught that peasants and rent-payers would no longer be obliged to pay their lords rents or any other exactions—because every exploiter would cease to be in this renovated realm: nevertheless, at about the time of St. Gall's Day [16 October], they very strictly exacted all the rents customarily due to the lords from all the peasants, including those who had joined the Taborites.[1]

Taken together, these paragraphs indicate and suggest a fundamental change in the Taborite community, a change that can be characterized as a process of consolidation, of establishment. One aspect of the process was economic: months of energetic warfare and raiding[2] had created the beginnings of what would shortly become a vast Taborite lordship, comparable to those of the barons and monasteries at whose expense Tabor's domains were being won. St. Gall's Day was one of the regular times when peasants paid their rents, and that was when Tabor's peasants paid theirs, to help support what would otherwise have been a completely unviable urban agglomeration.[3] In fact, the picture was even grimmer: sources that are only slightly later report that the Taborites collected not only the customary rents but also extra payments, the forced contributions called "holdy" in Czech.[4] At the same time, Tabor must have begun, even as early as the autumn of 1420, to develop the craft-industries and local trade that would very shortly give her all the typical traits of a medieval town, serving as the nucleus of a town-and-country complex based on a division of economic labor.[5] The

---

[1] Laurence, p. 438.

[2] See Macek, *Tábor*, II, 136 ff., esp. 145 f., for an analysis of both the major and minor actions; the petty raids are best known from the interrogations of captured participants, in the *Popravčí kniha Pánův z Rožmberka*, ed. F. Mareš (Prague, 1878), *passim*.

[3] But cf. Macek's argument, *Tábor*, II, 295–298, to the effect that Tabor did not yet have a lordship over peasant villages in the autumn of 1420; I do not find his argument convincing (see my "Chiliasm," n. 88), nor—most recently—does Bartoš, *HR*, I, 123, n. 11.

[4] Höfler, II, 484 f. (a Taborite resolve to stop the common Hussite practice of "exactio censuum holdy vulgariter vocatorum" from even Hussite peasants, especially when the latter had been compelled to make such payments to the enemy). Cf. Příbram, *Život kněží táborských*, *KJBB*, p. 266; also Příbram, "De condicionibus iusti belli" (*LČP*, No. 10), MS D 47, fol. 88ʳ: the Taborites "genus agricolencium . . . iniustissimis taliis, tributis, et exaccionibus triplicatis vel quadruplicatis in anno oneraverunt. . . ." The nature of these payments is defined by Otto Brunner, *Land und Herrschaft* (4th ed.; Wien-Wiesbaden, 1959), pp. 86 ff.; he gives the Latin form "holdae," German, "Huldi-gungen." See also H. Toman, *Husitské válečnictví* (Prague, 1898), pp. 62 ff.

[5] For this development in general, see Macek, *Tábor*, I, 263 ff. The guess that it began as early as 1420 is mine, based on the impossibility of imagining the opposite.

difference was that the economic structure of this complex was only the foundation for a political lordship that can be called, without much confusion, a city-state.

It is in the light of this pattern of development that the election of a bishop can be understood. Nicholas of Pelhřimov was born about 1385, earned the bachelor's degree in arts in 1409, and in 1411 became one of the first students in the "Lithuanian" College founded by Queen Jadwiga and associated with John Hus's Bethlehem Chapel. On 22 December 1414 he was ordained priest, and at about the same time received the parish church in Kondrac-pod-Blaníkem, in South Bohemia.[6] Nothing certain is known about his activities in the years of reformation and incipient revolution—one can only guess that he must have been a leading utraquist and radical, and that in 1419 he must have been a leading Taborite priest;[7] if we may believe John Příbram's testimony of 1429, Nicholas was one of the chiliasts of 1419–1420.[8] If so, his election as "senior" would seem more understandable than it otherwise does, and it would be possible to accept another of Příbram's statements, that Martin Húska, the leading Taborite chiliast, was the "ordainer" (*ordinator*) of Nicholas.[9] There is indeed some evidence that Nicholas—whether or not he was still a chiliast in September of 1420—used his office of leadership to organize some sort of militant action, at least among the Taborite clergy: one of the questions put to a Taborite captive, Slivka the Potter, by the torturers of Lord Ulrich of Rožmberk on 3 September 1420 was "whether the priest Biskupec [= *Episcopus,* Nicholas's cognomen or title] and his crew were sending letters around to their clergy and what plots they were making";[10] Slivka said he

---

[6] The data are collected by Bartoš, "Mikuláš z Pelhřimova," *Světci a kacíři* (Prague, 1949), pp. 175 ff.; he also refers to J. Dobiáš, *Dějiny Pelhřimova,* I (1927), 379, and II (1936), 36, 87, for some other data and conjectures, including the suggestion that Nicholas's cognomen, "Biskupec," may not have been derived from his episcopal office among the Taborites, as usually supposed, but from his father Peter, who may have been the Peter Biskup attested as Pelhřimov councillor in 1430–32. See below, n. 10.

[7] The fact that he does not appear in the sources listing radical priests in the period 1416–1418 would suggest that he stayed in his parish until early 1419, when he may have been among the victims of the king's reactionary policy. But cf. Bartoš, *HR,* I, 114.

[8] Příbram, *Život, KJBB,* pp. 262 f.

[9] The statement appears in Příbram's *Processus cause* (*LČP,* No. 31), written in the 1440's. The section listing the beliefs of Martin Húska begins, "Sequitur tractatus sacerdotis Martinkonis haeretici ordinatoris Nicolai episcopi . . ." (Höfler, II, 828). I have checked the manuscript (MS D 49, fol. 189ᵛ), and found Höfler's reading correct.

[10] Mareš, *Popravčí kniha,* p. 26. Since Nicholas was the only Taborite known as Biskupec, the entry no doubt refers to him; it may be proof, as I suggest in the text, that

did not know, but at least his interrogators were worried. On the other hand, what we know of Nicholas's functions suggests that his role must have been to moderate rather than to incite, for otherwise there would have been no need for an official to guide the clergy and regulate their preaching. The record of Rožmberk interrogations testifies to the kind of preaching in question—it names Taborite priests, otherwise unknown, who seem to have functioned as ideological commissars with small bands of Taborite plunderers, raiders, and warriors, inciting them to violence, no doubt by expounding the more bloody passages of the Old Testament.[11] Later the leaders of the Taborite church would prohibit this kind of preaching; in September of 1420 they may have been more concerned to organize and discipline it. Nicholas would hardly have been elected if he had stood merely for conservatism; he was the leader not of a right-wing faction but of the whole Taborite clergy, and his episcopate must be understood as part of a general Taborite movement toward stabilization and organization.[12]

His economic functions had a similar significance. The common funds had originally been those of the whole community, and although priestly management was present from the first, the one early case that we know

---

he had been chosen bishop even before 3 September. On the other hand, "Biskupec" may have been merely a personal cognomen (note 6, above).

[11] For examples see the *Popravčí kniha,* p. 32 and esp. p. 25: Slivka the Potter "confessed that the priests Michael, Procop, and Peter drove him and others to acts of arson, saying, 'If you don't do the burning, you'll be burned yourselves!'; and the priests themselves burned and wrecked homes and cloisters in Vodňany." Later on the Taborite clergy legislated against the "excesses" of some priests whose method of bible-preaching encouraged cruelty, and who either themselves committed acts of violence or excused others (Höfler, II, 482 f.).

[12] At one time Bartoš conjectured that Nicholas's election was the work of the right wing, impelled by Žižka, and that it was possible because the radical Wenceslas Koranda had fallen into enemy hands on 8 September ("Studie o Žižkovi a jeho době," *ČČM,* XCVIII (1924), 102–105). Most recently, in *HR,* I, 114, he conjectures that the election was carried out by a synod of the Taborite clergy at Klatovy, that it was done by lot, and that Nicholas was elected to serve as spokesman and ideologue, because of his university education. Only the last point seems likely to me. Macek, *Tábor,* II, 49, 294, defines Nicholas as a man of the center (as does Palacký, III, ii, 18), fluctuating between the Taborite right and left, but his admittedly tentative formulations are not convincing, chiefly because the crystallization of Taborite parties probably did not come until after Nicholas's election. The erection of the episcopal office itself, perhaps including the function of consecrating new priests (Příbram, *Život, KJBB,* p. 282; *KJBB,* p. 64; but cf. Laurence, p. 461, No. 64), was sufficiently radical to enlist the support of all Taborites; moreover, it was a schismatic step vis-à-vis Prague—thus the opposite policy from that pursued by Nicholas when he did take up an antisubversive program. Finally, all the evidence we have shows that Koranda supported Nicholas's leadership (below).

about shows the funds being administered by a layman.[13] But now the community had other sources of income more regular and no doubt more abundant than the funds—namely, the payments made by the peasantry— and the needs of Taborite society as a whole, above all the needs of her armies, must have been met by some ordinary system of secular management. At the same time individual Taborites were acquiring property—perhaps not so much in Tabor, which was still more of an encampment than a city, as in such Taborite towns as Písek.[14] What then was the function of the common funds? Probably they were in the process of becoming *church* funds. In its amorphous beginnings the Taborite movement did not have a church, only a number of priests and prophets working as individuals; but when the brethren proceeded to establish their movement as a society, then the religious function was inevitably institutionalized within the social order, as an organized church. Since the Hussite radicals rejected the idea of a property-owning church and held to the Waldensian ideal of apostolic poverty, along with the Wyclifite ideal of a clergy supported by "alms," the new Taborite church could hardly be provided for otherwise than by the gifts of the faithful. But these could not be merely haphazard individual donations: the community as a whole supplied funds for the maintenance of the clergy as a whole; Nicholas of Pelhřimov evidently had the function of

[13] The Taborite congregants originally "threw their money at the feet of the priests" (Laurence, p. 356); this was undoubtedly the beginning of the common funds. The priests went on to regularize the institution in chiliast Písek, in the winter of 1419–1420, but the supervisor of the funds was the political and military leader Matthew Louda of Chlumčany (Příbram, *Život, KJBB*, pp. 264 f.).

[14] J. Macek, "K počátkům táborství v Písku," *JSH*, XXII (1953), 113–117, shows how the revolutionary regime in Písek, led by priests, military captains, and administrators of the common funds, gave way after 1421 to a "normal" town government, with the property confiscated from the hostile burghers passing into the hands of those who were on the town council in 1422/1424, as well of other Taborites. But Písek could not have existed even in 1420 and 1421 without a normalization based on division of social and economic functions, and individuals must have even then begun to acquire property. It should be understood that even in the heyday of chiliast enthusiasm there was room for non-chiliast calculation—thus, e.g., MS XIV D 14 (Truhlář, *Codices latini*, 2522), containing ordinary medieval theological works, has a note indicating that it had been brought to Tabor from the Dominican cloister at Ústí-nad-Lužnicí when the latter place was destroyed, in March 1420. This seems to have been Tabor's normal way of building a library: see M. Kolář, "Hlídka rukopisů táborských," *Sborník . . . Koláře* (Tabor, 1924), p. 193—Kolář found sixteen surviving codices of Catholic provenience brought to Tabor from destroyed cloisters. Strict conformity to chiliast principles must always have been limited by common sense, particularly as 1420 progressed. Thus the elevation of communism to an article of Taborite faith (above, chap. vii, *ad* n. 65), no doubt formulated in the first half of 1420, disappeared from the lists of Taborite doctrines drawn up at the end of the year (below, *ad* n. 78, n. 80).

allocating shares and also—one guesses—using the available resources for the support of those laymen who had no other income. Thus the common funds of the originally communist community became the economic base of the new society's church—in a regularized manner that turned out to be remarkably practical, lasting as long as Tabor retained her independence.[15]

All of these developments were taking the Taborite brethren very far from the great days of their sectarian beginnings, and the sociologically inevitable process just outlined must have presented itself to many as a degeneration. It was not a matter of strictly religious doctrine, for almost the whole corpus of Waldensianist belief remained at the heart of Tabor's faith; at issue were those doctrines that had an explicitly social content. The most obvious differences—to be discussed in the following section—were those between the champions of the new Taborite establishment and the prophets of chiliasm, who had made an absolute commitment to the ideal of a regenerated humanity, to be free not only of pain and sorrow but also of the social and political discipline appropriate to man's sinful condition. To be sure, the great days of such prophecy were over, and the chiliasts must have become accustomed to imperfect reality; perhaps they did not at first object to the organization of a Taborite society and church, but the course of Tabor's development could only make the contradiction more intense. Politically less important but theoretically more profound was a quite different contradiction which came to a head very soon, as a crisis among those who were not inspired by chiliasm so much as by Waldensianism and the evangelical tradition of the Czech reform. Neither the heresy nor the more or less orthodox reform movement had ever developed a positive theory of Christian political power—to the contrary, power was associated with the societal establishment that made evangelical renewal necessary. Killing, prohibited by Jesus, was the *raison d'être* of the secular sword, pursuing the ideal of a Christian society, while the religion of that society had been evolved in countless compromises, expediential calculations, and routinizations—all made necessary by the fact that society included not only the fervid Christians but also the tepid and bad ones. The Waldensian sect, persecuted by Christian society, had developed a hostile attitude to society as such, which they regarded as anti-Christian: they rejected its estates, its this-worldly values, its characteristic religious forms, its learning and art, *and* they rejected its use of power to establish, run, and defend the state, by punishing criminals and waging war. We have already seen what happened when this constellation of sectarian attitudes penetrated the Hussite movement, and it is well to recall here that even the evangelical pacifism of the Waldensians had been taken over by the radicals who would later become the leaders of

---

[15] See my "Pius Aeneas among the Taborites," *Church History,* XXVIII (1959), 290 f.

Tabor.[16] Chiliasm and its equally sectarian ideology of total war must have permanently wiped out the pacifistic notions of many—but not of all; in any event, the specifically pacifist ideas were only particular formulations of a more basic attitude that could not so easily be changed. It would have been strange indeed if Tabor's resolve—to become a complete society, with a government wielding power, and to continue her military activity—had not aroused doubts among a still sectarian minority and also among the leaders of the enterprise.

Although the political significance of such doubts can only be guessed at, their existence and profundity are documented rather well in the works of Peter Chelčický, a member of the South Bohemian gentry who seems to have been part of the early Taborite movement.[17] As such he shared not only the Taborites' belief in Waldensianist religious doctrines but also their commitment to the sectarian political attitudes that included rejection of state power as *per se* unchristian. At the same time, for reasons that remain obscure, he went to Prague along with the other provincial radicals when the capital was threatened by Sigismund's crusade; perhaps Peter had been touched by the chiliast justification of warfare, perhaps his doubts had been shaken by the Prague masters' scholastic legitimation of fighting in defense of religion, or perhaps he went simply because the whole community was going. In any event, the defense of Prague did not set his mind at rest, and he began to speak against the Hussite war effort—not merely against the actual fighting but also against the very idea that adherents of an evangelical religion might use political power for allegedly Christian purposes. Since our knowledge of this episode in his life comes entirely from a passage in one of his own works, addressed to Master John Rokycana in the mid-1430's, it will be best to quote the text in full;[18] it begins with a historical critique of Christian power, then goes on to the events in Prague:

> It seemed to John Hus as though Christians were not henceforth obliged to follow the apostles and the Holy Primitive Church in suffering, because now kings have entered the church. But the Primitive Church followed the apostles for three hundred and twenty years in suffering and in great tribulations among the pagans, not using secular power but suffering from

[16] See above, chap. vi, n. 76.

[17] See my "Peter Chelčický: Treatises on Christianity and the Social Order," *Studies in Medieval and Renaissance History*, I, ed. Wm. Bowsky (Lincoln, Nebraska, 1964), 107 ff., for a summary of the data on Chelčický's life and career, with references to the Czech scholarly literature.

[18] The *Replika proti Rokycanovi* is printed by K. Černý, in *LF*, XXV (1898); the quoted paragraphs on p. 394; there is a German translation of the passage quoted here in Goll, *Quellen*, II, 89 f. For bibliography see E. Petrů, *Soupis díla Petra Chelčického* (Prague, 1957), pp. 61 f.

the pagan powers—up to Constantine. And when he, after many cruelties, wanted to glorify himself in Christ, he pushed himself into the Christian community along with his pagan lordship. And the poor priest [*scil.,* Silvester] who had hid before him in caves and forests received honor and imperial lordship from him and thus fell away from the faith. Hence when this evil came to pass, a voice was heard saying, "Today poison has been poured into the Holy Church"—as though the faith were to cease on account of these two rich lords, the secular and the spiritual, and as though suffering would be eliminated; for the secular lord would bear on his sword the spiritual lord's tribulations. . . . Then the doctors set about to serve the secular lords by collecting texts from the Old and New Testaments, to set the lord and his sword securely under Christ's faith, as the apostle and vicar of divinity. And they counseled the secular power . . . to serve God with pious harshness, so that at times whole regions have lain in ashes and many thousands of people have been killed after this harsh service. So from the time that the church and her doctors drank the poison, from that time the doctors have always declared that the church has two swords, and as the church has abandoned the commands of Christ and has stopped following him, she has become bloody and she renders evil for evil.

And so it was with your master Jakoubek when he sought to hereticate me on account of secular power [*kdyz mie gest kacerzowal pro moc*], in his chamber at Bethlehem Chapel. I said to him then: if that secular power is truly based in the faith, as you say, then are there scriptural authorities for its acts—its fighting and other cruelties? He said no, but that the ancient saints have justified it [*starzí swietí tak prawie*].

And then when the king [Sigismund] had departed from Prague, after many people had been killed on both sides, Jakoubek excused the killers, saying, "I cannot reproach their consciences with these killings, for the knightly estate would then be defamed." That man of great humility [*muz welike tichosti*], that figure of holiness—where did he drink this doctrine? [There follows the answer: passages from Gregory, Augustine, and others, to the effect that authorized killing does not violate the commandment, "Thou shalt not kill."]

The sectarian exploitation, in the first of these paragraphs, of the Sylvester legend and the Donation of Constantine is not original or even peculiar, but it is noteworthy that in another place Peter gives the legend in a specifically Waldensian form: "At first Sylvester and Peter Waldo [*Waldensky*] hid before Constantine in the forests and caves."[19] Whether he discussed this particular notion with Jakoubek in July of 1420 cannot be said, but if he has

---

[19] *LF,* XXV (1898), 455. Bartoš argues against the interpretation of this passage as indicating Peter's Waldensianism: "Chelčický a Valdenští," *JSH,* XVI (1947), 36 f., because the Berne chronicler, Konrad Justinger, who was no Waldensian, used the legend in the same form. But the form *is* of Waldensian inspiration, and it is uncommon enough to warrant notice.

reported his actual conversation correctly, then he did raise the general issue of whether or not the explicit precepts of the New Testament might be "interpreted"—that is, negated—by the doctors of the post-Primitive Church. And since he clearly rejected the argument that power—always understood as implying the right to kill—might be legitimately used by an authorized group within a Christian society—that is, by the knightly estate, he must even then have been prepared to refute not merely the use of violence by Christians but also the very idea of a Christian society based on such power. In his attitude to the "doctors" he disagreed with Jakoubek but entirely agreed with the Taborites—the Fathers were to be believed only insofar as they were in accord with Scripture;[20] on the other hand, the Taborites had been using power for at least a half year, and they were among the most militant defenders of Prague.

Of course the Taborites had not thus far claimed that their warfare was in conformity to the Sermon on the Mount or to the teachings of the Primitive Church. In practical terms they had been fighting for survival and for the establishment of a secure basis of power; these aims had also provided their motives, which were no doubt intensified, as Dr. Macek has argued, by the class hatred of the poor, their eagerness to settle accounts with the nobility.[21] As for theory, the only one they had was that of chiliasm, and specifically the "bloody" tractates of John Čapek, which justified total war on the basis of the coming new era, in which the old morality would be superseded.[22] But this theory hardly applied to the defense of Prague, and it had nothing to offer those who were beginning to construct a permanent society in this world, at Tabor. Even without Peter Chelčický the leading priests of Tabor would have had to consider this problem, and it is impossible to imagine that the man who had argued over power with Jakoubek did not also, and even earlier, carry on the same argument with his own brethren. There is no explicit evidence to this effect, but Chelčický's treatise *On Spiritual Warfare,* certainly among the earliest of his works, can best be dated and understood as a document of just such an argument.[23] For,

[20] See in general my discussion in the following chapter; for particular *loci* on Tabor's and Prague's differing attitudes to the doctors see, e.g., *Documenta,* p. 656; Laurence, p. 403; Nicholas of Pelhřimov, in Höfler, II, 599 ff.

[21] Macek, *Tábor,* II, 43 ff., *passim;* and see the passage quoted above, chap. vi, *ad* n. 82. According to John Příbram the ideology of total warfare developed by the Taborite Čapek (above, chap. vii, *ad* n. 99) was clearly directed against the nobility; cf. also the reference to this in Příbram's "Cum ab inicio" (*LČP,* No. 24), MS D 47, fol. 2ʳ: Čapek and his associates interpreted the Biblical "preclarior nacio . . . exterminata est" (Sap. xviii, 12) as: "preclarior nacio, subaudi nobilium, est exterminanda."

[22] See the preceding note.

[23] Kaminsky, "Peter Chelčický," p. 117; cf. Macek, *Tábor,* I, 385: the first half of 1421 seems to him convincing, but the second half of 1420 would also be possible.

among other things, it is clearly addressed to the Taborites and it reveals that
the latter had attempted to justify their military action by the classic text of
Romans 13:1–7: "The powers that be are ordained of God," and, "He
beareth not the sword in vain." These passages had done duty for centuries
of Christian compromise, and they had been richly exploited in the Prague
literature *de bello* of the previous winter; [24] the Taborites perhaps thought
that they could make use of them without further ado.[25] If so, Chelčický's
definitive refutation must have given them second thoughts, for he had only
to remark that Paul was writing not of Christian power but of pagan,
Roman power, and that this very sword had put Paul to death. "Take the
sword of the spirit"—that was the word of life; not "he beareth not the
sword in vain." [26] At the same time, here as in the discussion with Jakoubek,
the question of warfare was treated as part of a more general problem, that
of Christian society—so profoundly, indeed, that Chelčický's treatise may be
read as an attack on the whole line of development that Tabor was taking.

Himself a member of at least the early Taborite movement, Chelčický
shared with Tabor's priests the conviction that a total reformation was not
only necessary but in process; it was not a question of working out the
relationship between a religious reform and the existing order, as with the
Praguers, but rather of determining the shape of a completely open future.
One aspect of this situation was expressed by Tabor's ideology and practice
of total war; hence Chelčický appropriately cast his treatise *On Spiritual
Warfare* in the form of a commentary on Ephesians 6:10–20:

> Finally, my brethren, be strong in the Lord, and in the power of his might.
> Put on the whole armour of God, that ye may be able to stand against the
> wiles of the devil. For we wrestle not against flesh and blood, but against
> principalities, against powers, against the rulers of the darkness of this world,
> against spiritual wickedness in high places. Wherefore take unto you the
> whole armour of God, that ye may be able to withstand in the evil day, and
> having done all, to stand . . . , your loins girt about with truth . . . and
> your feet shod with the preparation of the gospel of peace. . . . Take . . .
> the sword of the Spirit, which is the word of God: Praying always with all
> prayer and supplication in the Spirit. . . .

Total spiritual warfare is thus set up as the analogue of Tabor's total physical
war, and the point is made explicit several times by reference to actualities—
thus, for example, just as Taborite Písek had prepared for a siege by laying
waste its suburbs, so the true Christian could withstand the siege of the Devil

[24] Above, chap. vii, *ad* n. 28 and *passim*.
[25] Kaminsky, "Peter Chelčický," p. 119; *O boji duchovním,* ed. Krofta (Prague,
1911), pp. 128 f.
[26] *Loc. cit.*

only by completely disengaging himself from worldly interests.[27] And Chelčický pushed this view into a kind of crisis theology every bit as terrifying as that of the chiliasts—the true Christian had to forsake everything, even his closest family ties, in order to be Christ's disciple.[28] "Therefore," Chelčický wrote, "let us not follow desire, or custom, or law, or man, and let us not come to terms with this world." [29]

But what did this mean in practice? The chiliast response, so close to Chelčický's in some respects, had been proved wrong, partly because the present age had not visibly ended, partly because the effect of chiliasm had been to push the faithful into acts of violence and cruelty that clearly violated the teachings of Jesus.[30] The moral residue of Free Spirit chiliasm, moreover, was equally to be condemned, and Chelčický criticized those who held that "it was not necessary to fight against the flesh, but only to live freely, enjoying one's own body in its desires"; [31] for "no man's evil passes away, and even though he thinks something of the sort about himself or others, he will not thereby make it so." [32] Chelčický's formula was less intoxicating: the morality of the Christian religion was that of the New Testament, particularly of those passages that expounded "the contempt of the world and of physical life, and the vanity of this world's praise"—that is, humility, suffering, love, and faith.[33] These simple teachings had been obscured by false preaching, carried on by "blind teachers" who lacked the gifts of the Holy Spirit; they might know the letter of the Bible, but to worse than no avail.[34] It was up to the individual—layman or priest—to seek the gifts of the Spirit by piety and prayer, and when he had a knowledge of the pure faith he would do best to "preserve it, not indeed speaking out very much about it, but suffering with it." [35] In other words, Peter was calling for the formation of a sect *within* Hussite Bohemia and even within the Taborite domain. The great dream of social reformation, the hope that the objective norms of Christian morality could be established by power for the whole of society, was dismissed by Chelčický as just another of the Devil's snares. It was good to have destroyed the abuses of Romanism,[36] but these were only some of the

---

[27] Krofta, *O boji duchovním*, pp. 76 ff.; pp. 96 f.: Žižka is a clever warrior but Satan is cleverer.
[28] *Ibid.*, pp. 81 f.
[29] *Ibid.*, p. 114.
[30] Above, chap. vii, *ad* n. 32.
[31] Krofta, *O boji duchovním*, pp. 8 f.
[32] *Ibid.*, p. 10.
[33] *Ibid.*, pp. 123–125.
[34] *Ibid.*, pp. 42 f., 133 f.
[35] *Ibid.*, p. 106.
[36] "Holy masses, beautiful singing, lofty churches," and "many other honorable things

Devil's trappings; as soon as they were torn off "he assumed other clothing, still more respectable; thus he has poured much heresy into Bohemia, taking on the guise of blameless lives, virtuous acts, many scriptural texts. . . ." [37] It was Satan who had seduced the chiliast priests by first coming to them "in the shining garb of voluntary poverty . . . and in the zealous work of preaching to and serving the people, and in giving them the Body and Holy Blood of God" [38]—thus even utraquism might be a trap. And it was the same Satan who stirred up men's hearts—and here Chelčický must have had the Taborites in mind—"to take on what was above their power . . . and impose laws on all things, without setting themselves under the Law of Truth." [39] That is, the true Christian had to renounce power; he might obey it, in licit things, but he was not allowed to use it.

Had these ideas not corresponded to at least some of those in the minds of the leading priests of Tabor, Chelčický would probably not have written his work or made himself troublesome in other ways. But in fact he was addressing himself to troubled men who were conscientious enough to take him seriously. When Nicholas of Pelhřimov was elected bishop, he made his seat at Písek rather than at Tabor, and it must have been on his invitation that Chelčický came to the former town, to discuss the basic problem of whether there could be a Christian authorization for political power. [40] We do not know much about this meeting, but it is hard to avoid supposing that Peter's presence was due to the critique that has just been discussed. The meeting was probably held in September or October of 1420, just at the time when the problems he had raised were most pressing. What is certain is that the Taborite priests, arguing against Chelčický, sought "to confirm power to themselves, as it were through faith," by taking over the common scholastic argument, drawn in this case from Wyclif's *Dialogus,* that the Church Militant was divided into three parts—the temporal lords or powers, as the vicars of Christ's deity; the clergy as the vicars of his human nature; and the commons. In this scheme the function of secular power was quite Christian —it was to defend the Law of God and the Christian people. [41] No doubt other arguments were also used, including Romans 13, but this Wyclifite theory must have been a novelty in Taborite argumentation, for there is no mention of it in Chelčický's *On Spiritual Warfare.* However, it was not new

in which the service of God was performed," were disguises of the Devil (Krofta, pp. 25 f.). As for the monks, "hell is shut up in those cloister walls" (p. 26).

[37] *Ibid.,* p. 29.

[38] *Ibid.,* p. 27 (and see above, chap. vii, *ad* n. 32).

[39] Krofta, *O boji duchovním,* pp. 42 f.

[40] See the discussion in the appendix to my "Peter Chelčický," pp. 174–177.

[41] *Ibid.,* p. 150; Wyclif, *Dialogus,* ed. A. W. Pollard (London, 1886), pp. 2 f.

to Prague—Jakoubek had indeed translated the *Dialogus*—nor did it offer anything but the most commonplace scholastic rationalization of the *status quo*. It is remarkable that the priests of Tabor felt entitled to use it; this fact shows that in point of basic Christian sociology there was no fundamental difference between Tabor, Prague, and Roman Catholic Europe—or at least there was no difference in the thinking of Tabor's party of order. More than any other datum, this information about the Písek encounter illuminates the meaning of Tabor's establishment as a society. It remains only to note that Chelčický was not convinced; he and those who were to become the Chelčice brethren remained aloof from the new Tabor—in contact with its leaders but otherwise outside of its history.

THE TABORITE PARTY OF ORDER

If the controversy between the Taborite leaders and Peter Chelčický can be understood as one between Christian church and Christian sect, the struggle between the party of order and the Free Spirit sectarians can best be defined, in comparable sociological terms, as one between a society and a movement. Obscure in its beginnings, the struggle eventually appears, according to the sources, as an issue of religious theory and practice, provoked by the "Pikarts" and centering around the question of the presence of Christ in the Eucharist. Some historians have indeed treated the intra-Taborite dissensions in this light.[42] But in fact the Pikart denial of a real presence was only part of a much more substantial corpus of religious and social ideas; moreover the corpus itself was only a new phase of development of Free Spirit chiliasm—or perhaps only the latter's new mode of existence in the period of waning tension that set in with the establishment of Taborite society, from September on. The Communist historians Josef Macek and Robert Kalivoda have therefore been able to argue very strongly that the struggle in question was essentially one of classes, the Pikarts figuring as the party of the "poor" or of "peasant-plebeian" Tabor, and asserting—against the "bourgeois opposition"—the original chiliast program of social revolution, the ideal of a new order of freedom, communist equality, and brotherhood.[43] Most of the Taborites were of course poor or plebeian in origin, and it is both reasonable and to a limited degree demonstrable that the issue of whether the revolution should be ended or continued did shape up as a class issue; but the data here are so scanty, the exceptions so important, as to make the class interpretation more a matter of *a priori* construction than of

[42] This is true in varying degrees of Palacký, III, ii, 12 f.; Pekař, *Žižka*, I, 49; III, 93; Sedlák, *TTE*, 2 ff.; Heymann, pp. 210 ff.; Bartoš, *HR*, I, 122 ff.

[43] Macek, *Tábor*, II, 103 ff.; Kalivoda, *HI*, pp. 358 ff.

scholarly inference. To put the point more precisely, there is no evidence at all to show that preexisting class interests *generated* the ideas in question, and there is no adequate evidence to show that the struggle between a relatively conservative and a relatively radical Taborite faction actually polarized Tabor in a manner corresponding to its class composition—which is, in any case, not precisely known.[44] What we do know are the doctrines at issue, some of the circumstances in which the struggle was pursued, and some of the lines of continuity between this phase of Tabor's existence and previous ones; from all of this it is possible to infer what the struggle meant in social terms—not class terms. Hence the terminology of the present discussion, which defines the parties in terms of the development of Taborite society as a whole, and therefore speaks of a Free Spirit sectarian movement on the one hand, a party of order on the other.

By December at the latest, the two parties had separated beyond any possibility of reconciliation. So fundamental a break must have been well prepared in the months before, and it would be reasonable to suppose that in September, when Tabor began to consolidate and establish itself as a society, there were diverging ideas of how this enterprise should be carried through. Some, following the lead of Peter Chelčický, must have rejected it altogether,

---

[44] The problem of defining classes and their interests is of course taken more seriously in the Communist world than among "bourgeois" historians. Thus there is a certain scholarly issue deemed to be at stake in the precise definition of the revolutionary element: František Graus and Josef Macek define the group as "the poor" of both town and country—those lacking property and dependent on wage-labor. Robert Kalivoda follows the older formulation of Engels and speaks of a "peasant-plebeian fraction," of which the poor formed a part. The whole discussion is rather scholastic, and to the present writer it seems clear that Kalivoda's construction is actually derived from his analysis of the programs—i.e., doctrines—in question. Graus and Macek, on the other hand, attempt to define the poor in terms of economic statistics, and only then to associate the programs with the social group. See, for a clear summary, with references to the literature, Kalivoda, *HI*, pp. 446 f. (notes 166 and 167). The present approach is not very different from Kalivoda's, except in vocabulary and in results: where Kalivoda sees the doctrinal conflicts at Tabor as indicating a struggle between peasant-plebeian and bourgeois-opposition fractions (terms taken from Engels, who knew little about the Hussites), I adopt a less ambitious terminology, explained in the text just below. As for Macek's concept of the poor, it is based on extraordinarily diligent, extensive, and even brilliant analysis of much source material, but in the end it only shows that in 1420 most of the Taborites were of rural provenience, and—rather less conclusively—that of these most belonged to "the poor" (*Tábor*, I, 263 ff., esp. 338 ff.); in time, he shows, the proportion of artisans and propertied peasants increased. His inferences from data are not always convincing, but one could accept them all and still wonder why the mere preponderance of the poor should be taken as proof that chiliast-Pikart ideology derived from the poor's class outlook, or that the chiliast-Pikart movement was essentially a class phenomenon.

thereby either ceasing to be Taborites or condemning themselves to merely passive participation in the new society. Others, certainly the majority, must have held to the ideas of chiliasm, retaining the fantastic prophecies as a kind of transcendent framework of aspiration while they gave more practical effect to such secondary doctrines as those of total warfare against Antichrist and of the plenipotential capacity of the elect to rule themselves without reference to king, nobles, or any existing institutional authorities. As late as August, the Taborites in Prague were still led by men who thought in terms of reconstituting the state and church in Bohemia—not by destroying them but by taking them over as institutions of national Hussitism. When this project finally failed, and Tabor was faced with the need to set up her own church and state, she must have drawn self-confidence from the chiliast assertion that "the Taborite brethren, together with those adhering to them, are that body to which, wherever it may be, the eagles will gather." [45] That is, the Taborites were the Body of Christ, hence the true Church—a belief that was not only a sufficient but indeed a necessary prerequisite for the founding of an independent church-state corpus; the community of the elect was coextensive with the actual body of Taborites. In context a revolutionary idea, it nevertheless pointed the way toward the orthodox sociology of Prague or Roman Europe, which also tended to define the actual societal body as the "ecclesia," the *corpus Christi mysticum.*[46] It was against exactly this sort of sociology that Peter Chelčický reacted, for example in his treatise *On the Holy Church,* in which he criticized the definition of the church as a body of estates: membership in such an estate did not give evidence of membership in the Holy Church, for the estates could also exist among the pagans, while Christians could belong to this or that estate and still be limbs of the Devil.[47] On this point the sectarianism of the Free Spirit, unlike that of the Waldensians, was compatible with Tabor's establishment as a society.

But what of the other chiliast ideas—those visions of regeneration that would tend to make any society seem useless or positively evil? By September 1420 these ideas were fully developed, nor had they been refuted by any Taborite leaders; on the contrary, they were accepted by virtually all Taborites as valid.[48] The very near future would show that they were incompat-

---

[45] Laurence, p. 414; see above, chap. vii, *ad* n. 96 ff.

[46] Above, chap. vii, n. 98.

[47] See the text in my translation, "Peter Chelčický," pp. 168–173.

[48] This would seem to have been the view of Laurence of Březová, whose treatise on Tabor, including the chiliast ideas, was evidently designed to characterize Tabor as a whole; its insertion in his chronicle *ad* late August 1420 must have been designed to date the characterization. As late as 10 December 1420, no Taborite was willing to repudiate the chiliast ideas charged against them by the Prague Masters (below, *ad* note

ible with a Taborite establishment—that indeed the establishment's bishop
would become, by virtue of his position, a leading persecutor of those who
held to the Free Spirit vision. Yet the leader of the chiliasts, Martin Húska,
who was venerated as an angel of God by many of the Taborites, must have
at least accepted the election of a bishop; as we have seen, one source actually
says he was the "ordainer" of Nicholas of Pelhřimov. Perhaps the most likely
guess would be that Martin's own leadership was so entirely charismatic, his
program so idealistic, as to take him out of any strictly political competition
among the Taborite priests. Perhaps he understood that Tabor could not
help taking on the lineaments of a polity, a social order, so he decided to
work within that framework to achieve his own goals. Everything we know
about him suggests that his chiliasm was not some lunatic or doctrinaire
fantasy, but a hope for human happiness—and that *this* was all that mattered
to him. His words to Peter Chelčický, reported by the latter, must stand as
the key to every aspect of his life and thought:

> But Martin was not humble or at all willing to suffer for Christ. . . . And
> he declared to us his belief that there will be a new Kingdom of the Saints on
> earth, and that the good will no longer suffer. And he said, "If Christians
> were always to have to suffer so, I would not want to be a servant of God."
> That is what he said! [49]

This was a religious hope, involving a belief in the working of God upon
men, but there is evidence that the belief functioned essentially as the basis
for an optimistic view of what men might themselves become, by changes in
their living and thinking. The Joachite prophecy of a new world-age always
contained this sort of realistic program, in the sectarianism of the Free Spirit
Beghards and in the works of Joachim himself; [50] although it naturally was

---

78, ff.). Of course people can "accept" ideas without actually believing them, and one
must allow for almost infinite variations in this respect—the key question would be to
what extent the consequences of the ideas were or could be acted out. This is the
sociological issue of "false consciousness."

[49] Chelčický, *Replika proti Mikuláši Biskupcovi*, ed. J. Annenkov and V. Jagić.
*Sočinenija Petra Chelčickago, Otdělenija russkago jazyka i slovesnosti, Imperatorskaja
Akademija Nauk* (St. Petersburg, 1893), pp. 464 f.

[50] Although Joachim developed a scheme that might be considered abstract or even
fantastic, he based it on a sense of the real nature of men and institutions; for
individuals the passage to the new age would be one of self-perfection, the good being
transmuted into better, while institutions would cease when their functions were over:
"a tempore illo . . . omittent homines zelari pro illis institutionibus, que facte sunt pro
tempore et ad tempus . . . unde et nonnulla cum tempore commutanda censue-
runt. . . ." For all this see H. Grundmann, *Studien über Joachim von Floris* (Leipzig,
1927), pp. 112 f., and *passim*. A similar generalization about Beghard teachings would
be open to many exceptions, but it is clear that some Beghard groups based their

not much emphasized in adventist or chiliast prophecy, nor in the anti-chiliast collections of "errors," traces of it can nevertheless be found. Thus, as we have already seen,[51] Martin did not simply ignore the disciplinary norms of the New Testament—as Chelčický's report might suggest—but he held that the Law of Grace "would cease as to act and execution" by being *fulfilled;* that is, men would internalize those norms, take on the evangelical virtues, and then would not need the Law. The point is put quite explicitly in an anonymous chiliast treatise, which stipulates that the glories of the new secular age would appear "only after all the sufferings of Christ [that is, of the Christian people] . . . shall have been completed, and not before"; at the same time, the treatise defines the "consummation" of the present age thus: "When there takes place a very remarkable change in men, then the age is consummated. The consummation of the age, therefore, I call the commutation of the good into better and the extermination of the evil."[52] Martin Húska may have been the author of these lines, but even if he was not, they could hardly have been written by anyone except one of his close associates.[53] If, in September 1420, Martin was indeed thinking along these lines, then he might well have accepted the establishment of Taborite society as a relatively useful thing—as the most practical way of enforcing the "evangelical Law," and thereby preparing the Taborites for their "commutation" into something better.

Of course the hoped-for change would not be automatic; it would have to be worked for by the leaders of Free Spirit sectarianism, who would thereby become an oppositional party within the new Taborite polity. And indeed that is just what they became, under the name of "Pikarts." In the chronicle of Laurence of Březová, the doctrinal content of Pikartism appears as a "dudum absconditus error" denying the real presence of Christ in the Eucharist; he inserts a discussion of it into his account of the events of late

---

concept of spiritual liberty on a prior perfection of human nature, through discipline: see the discussion above, chap. vii, *ad* notes 131 and 132; also Ernest McDonnell, *The Beguines and Beghards in Medieval Culture* (New Brunswick: Rutgers University Press, 1954), pp. 496 ff.

[51] Above, chap. vii, *ad* notes 113, 114.

[52] Laurence, pp. 417 f.

[53] Laurence, p. 413, characterizes Martin Húska as the "principalis auctor, publicator et defensor" of chiliast doctrines, and this only shortly before he inserts the tractate in question. Bartoš, "Z dějin chiliasmu r. 1420," *Do čtyř art.,* p. 93, suggests that the work may have been written by Húska in the summer of 1420, as a defense of chiliasm against the Prague masters; this last point may be doubted. Kalivoda's dating of the treatise in what he calls the period of "fatalistic" chiliasm, before mid-February 1420, seems to me entirely without foundation; indeed it is contradicted by Kalivoda's own analysis of the content, as representing a "higher stage" of chiliast development (*HI,* pp. 417, 327).

August/early September 1420, and clearly means to indicate thereby that the error emerged at that time—"eo tempore." [54] Its source, he says, was in a group of foreigners, *Picardi,* who came to Prague in 1418, were well received, and made Czech converts, including the petty nobleman Sigmund of Řepan, whose estate lay in the region of Žatec.[55] In the summer of 1420, according to Laurence, the heresy emerged chiefly in the regions of Žatec, Plzeň, and Prague. Something has already been said of these *Picardi* in the discussion of Taborite chiliasm, above—to the effect that the *Picardi* of 1418 must have cultivated many "errors" apart from the single eucharistic one that Laurence assigns to them, that *Picardi* meant *Beghardi,* and that the sect, which may *also* have come from Picardy, was one of the Free Spirit. At the same time, however, it is important not to mistake the key point that Laurence wishes to make. A long treatise on the history and ideas of the Taborites, inserted right after the account of the latter's departure from Prague (22 August) and the subsequent siege of Mt. Blaník (23 August), gives a full account of first the Waldensianist, then the chiliast doctrines of Tabor; it does not, however, mention the Pikart eucharistic doctrines, even though these were part of a comprehensive list of Taborite articles that Laurence certainly used when composing his work, at least a few years after 1420.[56] After the treatise on Tabor there follows a substantial paragraph on some abortive dealings between the Emperor Sigismund, the Praguers, and the Hussites of Hradec Králové, and only then does Laurence insert the short discussion of Pikartism and its origins. Furthermore, as just noted, he explicitly locates the first centers of Pikartism around Prague, Žatec, and Plzeň; he says nothing of any infection of the Taborites proper by the new heresy at this time. But in writing of subsequent events, Laurence does report information that shows Pikartism as part of Tabor's corpus of beliefs, about December 1420 and thereafter.[57] And the chief propagator of Pikartism among the Taborites was

[54] Laurence, pp. 429–431.

[55] The data on him are collected by Macek, *Tábor,* II, 324 f.

[56] For the dating of Laurence's chronicle see above, chap. vi, n. 22, a reference to Bartoš's most recent dating, in 1422. Pekař, *Žižka,* I, 221 f., argues that Laurence wrote closely after the events he describes, hence in 1420–1421, and that the treatise on Tabor was written not long before the end of 1420. No one has argued that Laurence wrote the treatise on Tabor before he knew about Pikartism, but even this possibility would not undermine the present argument. I assume that when Laurence wrote the treatise, perhaps at the end of 1420 or perhaps later, he knew of the seventy-two articles of Taborite doctrine presented by the masters on 10 December (Laurence, pp. 454 ff.), articles that included the basic Pikart doctrines. I also suppose that he knew of an earlier and even fuller list of articles, preserved for us in a Czech form (above, chap. vii, n. 88, item III,(1)), for he gives the Waldensianist and chiliastic articles of this list in his (Latin) treatise on Tabor—but he does *not* give the Pikart articles of this list.

[57] Laurence, pp. 459 f.

Martin Húska, who, according to later testimony offered by Peter Chelčický, was somehow associated with Sigmund of Řepan in developing the theory of Pikart eucharistic doctrine.[58] We thus have a clear picture of Martin, who had previously been the leading prophet of chiliasm, pioneering a new heresy among the Taborites in the very period of Tabor's initial establishment as a society. In fact, Taborite Pikartism can be defined as the opposition to Taborite orthodoxy in both secular and religious matters; as we shall see, it was an opposition based essentially on the sectarianism of the Free Spirit.

This reconstruction poses certain problems, among them the difficulty of imagining the chiliast Martin suddenly adopting a new heresy and using it for his own purposes, in conjunction with the Free Spirit content of his chiliast aspirations. It would be more reasonable to suppose that the Pikart eucharistic heresy had always been part of the chiliast corpus, and this is the interpretation given by Josef Macek:

> It seems to me quite illogical to assert, as previous historiography has done, that Pikartism was only the last and latest stage traversed by the chiliasts' temerity. I rather suppose that Pikartism (i.e., the doctrine denying the real presence of Christ in the sacrament of the altar) may have been an inseparable part of the attack of some chiliast priests against the old order and its authorities and dogmas. That polemical anti-Pikart literature makes its appearance only in 1420 and 1421 may be explained either by the fragmentary condition of the sources or, more probably, by the final settling of accounts with the chiliasts. In 1420–1421, when the chiliast priests were being pushed aside, the attack against them made use of the most effective propaganda to discredit them. Pikartism was a convenient name with which to smear the priests that the bourgeois opposition wished to get rid of. Therefore "the most monstrous heresy"—Pikartism—was spoken of when the chiliasts were being slaughtered.[59]

Unfortunately this interpretation also seems questionable, for it requires us to suppose that those who attacked the chiliasts before the autumn of 1420 refrained from remarking upon a eucharistic heresy that, if present, could not have failed to horrify—above all in Hussite Bohemia, with its emphasis on eucharistic devotion.[60] And why would Laurence of Březová, writing

---

[58] Chelčický, *Replika proti Biskupcovi*, p. 458: "Martinek prorok taborsky, a Zygmund z Řepan ten rozom wedu na šestu kapitolu swateho Jana . . ." ("Martin, the Taborite prophet, and Sigmund of Řepan apply this understanding to the sixth chapter of St. John").

[59] *Tábor*, I, 379 f.

[60] This statement would be invalid if John Příbram's treatise, *Ad occurrendum homini insano* (*LČP*, No. 7), were to be dated according to the scribal *explicit* in one copy, which has the date 17 April 1419. Jan Sedlák, who first studied the work, accepted this date as the *terminus ante quem* of the treatise; hence Pikartism would have been in

well after the liquidation of the Pikarts, have been so deliberate in distin guishing between stages of Taborite heresy? Indeed, at the risk of sounding naive, one might wonder whether the Hussite chronicler would have carefully constructed a false picture in order to serve merely propagandistic needs. In general, Laurence is misleading when he omits, not when he supplies information. For these reasons Macek's view can be accepted only with fundamental qualifications: it is reasonable to suppose that Martin Húska's Pikartism had its roots in his Free Spirit chiliasm, but it was not just the same thing with a new name; it was rather a different stage, actually a regressive one, in the life of the Free Spirit sect, determined by fundamental changes in the sociology of that sect at Tabor. Tabor had been an extremely plastic movement dominated by chiliast ideology; she was now, however, rapidly becoming a stable society incapable of resonating to chiliast prophecies, a society in which the Free Spirit was an oppositional minority. This was the usual mode of existence of Free Spirit sectarianism

---

existence, as a Taborite doctrine maintained by Martin Húska (supposedly the "homo insanus"), during 1418: *TTE*, pp. 7 f. But Bartoš, *LČP*, No. 7, argued that this early date conflicts with the sense of the other evidence about the origins of Taborite Pikartism, and he supposed that the scribe's XIX was an error for XXIX—hence the copy would have been written in 1429, and the treatise itself would have been composed *ca.* March 1421, along with Jakoubek's comparable treatise—both as replies to Tabor's request for help in refuting Pikartism (below, *ad* n. 127). Pekař took a similar view, although more tentatively (*Žižka*, I, 49, n. 1). Macek, however, insists that the earlier date would be perfectly likely, for the reasons given in the paragraph quoted from his work, just above, and that we must therefore accept the clear date given in the scribal *explicit* as determinative. In my "O traktátu Ad occurrendum homini insano," *ČsČH*, VIII (1960), 895–904, I analyze the treatise and consider the problem of its dating; I show that it contains much more than Sedlák has indicated, that the "homo insanus" was a layman and therefore not Martin Húska, and that the internal and external evidence for Bartoš's dating is extremely strong, even though nothing makes the earlier dating actually impossible. In fact I can even add an item to support an early date: Jakoubek of Stříbro's sermon for 16 October 1418, MS 4937, fol. 23ᵛ, refers disapprovingly to "quidam qui dicunt quod parvuli non sint baptisandi, eo quod Cristus dicens, Nisi quis renatus etc., locutus est ad senem Nicodemum; ideo parvuli non sint baptisandi sed senes"; this is the same idea, with the same justification, that Příbram attacks in *Ad occurrendum* (my article, p. 897). In other words, it must be conceded that the heretical ideas of Pikartism and even other sectarian formations were present on the Hussite left several years before the emergence of Tabor (see above, chap. v, n. 117). But I think the paltriness and character of the attacks on them show that although they were present, they were not of central importance; in 1420, when they *were* important, the attacks became more vigorous and were more directly concentrated on them. Hence I continue to disagree with Macek on the dating of *Ad occurrendum*, despite his renewed insistence on accepting the scribal *explicit* (J. Macek, "Chiliasmus ve světových dějinách," *ČsČH*, XII (1964), 860–863).

elsewhere in Europe, hence it may not have been an accident that the Pikarts of 1420 resembled the *Picardi* or Beghards of 1418.

On this basis, Martin's Pikartism would have to be understood in the light of his chiliast hopes, which implied a radical transformation of the basic Christian sacraments:

> Those elect still living will be brought back to the state of innocence of Adam in Paradise, like Enoch and Elijah, and they will be without any hunger or thirst, or any other spiritual or physical pain. And in holy marriage and with immaculate marriage-bed they will carnally generate sons and grandchildren here on earth and on the mountains, without pain or trouble, and without any original sin. Then there will be no need for baptism with water because they will be baptized in the Holy Spirit, nor will there be the tangible sacrament of the holy Eucharist, because they will be fed in a new angelic mode—not in memory of Christ's passion, but of his victory.[61]

The nature of the "new angelic mode" may be at least partly glimpsed in another chiliast prophecy:

> At the end of this consummation of the age, Christ will descend from heaven and openly come in his own person to take up his kingdom in this world, and he will be seen by the actual eye. And he will prepare a great banquet and supper of the lamb as a nuptial feast for his spouse the Church, here on the physical mountains.[62]

At the same time, this very definite visualization of the future did not exhaust the eucharistic content of chiliasm, and a more spiritual and practical understanding of the sacrament appears in a chiliast letter, undated and anonymous, but hardly attributable to anyone but Martin Húska or a close associate:

> May the grace of the almighty Father, our heavenly God, be granted to you, that it may be faithfully received by you, as befits saints . . . ! And give him honor and praise, the homage of bowing down, prayer and thanks, for all time, awaiting the Lord in sobriety and in holiness of life, knowing that the Lord already stands at the gate. . . . Let us be very vigilant, for we do not know what hour the third angel will blow his trumpet. And at once the sun

---

[61] Laurence, p. 416. Cf. the anonymous chiliast treatise published by Bartoš, "Z dějin chiliasmu r. 1420," *Do čtyř art.,* pp. 110 f., the section "De remanencia sacramentorum": "Remanebunt autem omnia saluti necessaria sacramenta, sed vanitati ultra non erunt subiecta. . . . Unum tantum comedent et bibent modo novo in exultacione. . . . gaudebunt et exultabunt usque in sempiternum in hiis novis, que creantur. Iam enim non facient hoc ad memoriam passionis Christi, ut facere consueverant, sed ob memoriam victorie Christi. . . ."

[62] Laurence, p. 415.

will blaze, the clouds will disappear, the darkness will vanish, blood will flow from wood, and he will reign who is not expected by those living on earth. . . . Therefore let us be ready for the Lord's coming, that we may go with him to the wedding.

And who is ready? Only he who remains in Christ and Christ in him. And he is in Christ who eats him. But to eat Christ's body is livingly to believe in him, and to drink his blood is to shed it with him for his Father. And he takes Christ's body who disseminates his gifts, and he eats his body who livingly listens to his word. And in this way we shall all be Christ's body. . . .

And through this eating the just will shine like the sun in the kingdom of their Father, when he comes in clouds with his glory and great power, and sends as representatives his glorious angels to sweep out all scandals from his inheritance. And then evil will be abashed, lies will perish, injustice will disappear, every sin will vanish; and faith will flower, justice will grow, paradise will open to us, benevolence will be multiplied, and perfect love will abound.

But before this for a short time the living waters will cease to flow . . . , the sun will darken, the moon will turn to blood, and the stars will fall from the heavens. [There follow more apocalyptic horrors.]

I write these things to you as to adults, able to eat all foods, and not as to those who live on milk. . . . And we admonish you, for the sake of the sublime Father, to beware of idols, do not bow down to any visible thing, but only to the Father . . . who cannot be contained by any human eye or heart or mind. . . . And I admonish you to beware of false and lying priests, for they are the dragon's tail that strikes the stars from the heavens. . . . And unless God shorten those days, they would lead even God's elect into error [Matt. 24:22–24]. . . .

I admonish you in the name of God, to make this letter known to the whole community.[63]

Here we have the all-important context, lacking in the previously quoted lists of "errors," and we see how the spiritualized interpretation of the Eucharist functions in an otherwise predominantly chiliast prophecy. The faithful—the elect—must form a definite group, living in readiness for the great moment; they must be *the* Church, Christ's body, and they make themselves it by the communion of eating—not in the sacramental sense but in the practical sense of believing in Christ, suffering with Christ, preaching Christ, and listening to such preaching. There is nothing *ipso facto* heretical about such a spiritualization of the sacrament of communion—it draws from both Biblical and patristic authorities[64]—but it could become heretical when

---

[63] Published by Bartoš, "Z dějin chiliasmu," pp. 96 f.; it is in Czech.

[64] Thus, e.g., John 6:56: "He that eateth my flesh, and drinketh my blood, dwelleth in

opposed to the more properly sacramental concept of the Eucharist. And the chiliast doctrine of a transformation of the sacraments certainly pointed the way to such a development, if only by encouraging its adherents to look for alternatives to the orthodox religion. One would like to be able to fix the pattern of doctrinal relationships more precisely, but in the present condition of our sources, the above reconstruction probably goes as far as would be justified.

It is thus most fortunate that the actual content of Martin's Pikartism is relatively well reported, and it is even possible to trace its main phases of development. As late as 10 December 1420, when all the Taborite priests faced the Prague masters in what the latter had planned as an ideological showdown, Martin Húska could still play the role of a leader, at the expense of Nicholas of Pelhřimov's official status. By the end of January 1421, however, Martin was undergoing persecution, attempting to rally his followers at Tabor, and trying desperately to win over to his views the Písek Taborites—hence those led most directly by Bishop Nicholas. He failed, and in short order was deprived of all power among the Taborites; his followers were expelled, hunted down, and killed, while he himself eventually suffered the same fate of martyrdom. Against this historical background, very rapid in development but marked by very sharp turning points, the permutations of Pikartism can be understood. Since there is no evidence of an actual Pikart sect among the Taborites before the end of 1420, the Pikart doctrines attested at the meeting of 10 December must be understood as the content of Martin's propaganda, carried on with varying success in the several Taborite communities—probably most successfully at Tabor, as we shall see. These doctrines were:

1. In the bread and wine of the eucharistic sacrament, there is not contained the presence of the true God and man, in a sacramental form.

2. The true God and man is not to be adored in the sacrament of the Eucharist with the cult of worship [*cultu latrie*].

3. Before the sacrament of the Eucharist the knee is not to be bent, nor other signs of divine worship shown.

---

me, and I in him," together with Augustine's explication of this passage in its converse sense: "Quid est Christum manducare? Non est hoc solum in sacramento corpus ejus accipere . . . , sed in ipso manere, et habere ipsum in se manentem." And this is defined as "spiritualis manducatio," distinguished from "sacramentalis" and defined as believing: "Credere enim in eum, hoc est comedere panem et vinum. Qui credit in eum, manducat eum" (all this in Peter Lombard's *Sententiarum libri quatuor,* IV, dist. xi, *MPL,* 192, col. 858). Cf. also the passage from Cyprian quoted by Nicholas of Dresden, *Apologia,* Hardt, III, 622 f.: "Gravior nunc et ferocior pugna imminet, ad quam fide incorrupta et virtute robusta parare se debeant milites Christi, considerantes, se quotidie calicem sanguinis Christi bibere, ut possint et ipsi pro Christo sanguinem fundere."

4. The whole Christ, with both his flesh and his blood, is not in the sacrament of Christ's body in either the species of bread or that of wine.

5. The sacrament of the Eucharist neither may nor should be reserved for the next day, for the use of the faithful or for the practice of the divine cult.

6. The sacrament of the Eucharist may not be elevated in the holy mass, according to the rite of the Primitive Church.

7. The body and blood of Christ are taken sacramentally in any food just as well as in the sacrament of the Eucharist, as long as the man is in a state of grace.

8. It is neither fitting nor permitted ever to celebrate more than one mass a day in any parish.

9. A layman may take the sacrament of the Eucharist as many times as he likes in any one day.[65]

Although constructed in order to show the Pikart doctrines as so many discrete heresies, these articles give a clear enough picture of what was at issue. The first, which proved capable of being endlessly discussed, was a denial of the real presence of Christ in the Eucharist; numbers two, three, five, and six were direct practical consequences of this denial. Number four, with its echoes of the old utraquist controversy, would seem to be a deliberate and artificial extrapolation, while numbers eight and nine are not clearly relevant in their preserved form—in a sense they even contradict each other, if eight be understood in association with five. Number seven, however, was closely associated with number one in a very special sense: in fact it *was* number one, put in positive form. That is, the denial of a real presence was not a mere issue of eucharistic doctrine, it was rather the anti-sacramental edge of a belief that Christ was with his saints in their actual meals, each of which, in this sense, was the "nuptial feast" or "great banquet and supper of the lamb" that the chiliasts looked forward to. But as we have seen, the eating of Christ at such dinners was conceived of spiritually—the faithful imitated Christ, identified themselves with him, and thus became one with him. Such must have been the content of Taborite Pikartism in the autumn of 1420.

At the same time there is no evidence that the Pikarts existed at that time as a definite sect, organized around communion-banquets; in fact there is reason to think that this practical development of the theory came later, and that at first the Pikarts may have tried to work out a mode of nonsubversive existence within the new Taborite polity. Thus, for example, the chiliast

---

[65] Laurence, pp. 459 f.; I have renumbered the paragraphs. It will be useful to quote the Latin of No. 1: "Item quod in sacramento eukaristie panis et vini non sit verus deus et homo contentive, sacramentaliter et presencialiter."

treatise referred to above [66] can be most reasonably understood as Martin Húska's attempt to define his beliefs, to defend them, and to justify them on the basis of Scripture—an attempt that in itself suggests a new phase of rationalization and codification, replacing the first stage of purely creative prophecy.[67] And the treatise, despite its resolute defense of the whole chiliast program, ends on a note of accommodation. After proving his final point, that "the glory of the new house [that is, the new age, the new kingdom of Christ] will be greater than that of the first [that is, the Primitive Church]," and that this will happen after all of Christ's sufferings have been consummated, the author goes on to say:

> The Apostle declares this in a figure, saying (I Cor. 12:21-26), "The head cannot say to the feet, . . ." up to, "if one of the members has honor done to it, let the others rejoice." I do not deny that this figure also has this meaning: that he understands it of the body in which there are also dignities of status, in which body the more contemptible should be established to give judgement. And in such a body let honor be given him to whom it is due. Nevertheless he also understands it as applying to these new saints, calling them the feet, who will receive this land too as a legacy, whence it is written . . . , "the kingdom that is under the whole heaven will be given to the people of the saints" (Daniel 7:27 [and cf. Daniel 7:18,22]).[68]

It cannot be doubted that the author has brought in the passage from Corinthians only because his opponents were using it in a sense contrary to the chiliast prospectus. Now we know, from Peter Chelčický's treatises *On the Holy Church* and *On the Triple Division of Society,* that the Taborites were using precisely this text as a scriptural justification for the scholastic-Wyclifite sociology that divided the Church Militant into the three estates of fighters, workers, and prayers.[69] However, Chelčický also tells us that the theory in question was presented to him at Písek, at a meeting that can best be dated in September or October of 1420. The chiliast treatise suggests that the Taborite party of order was advancing the orthodox scholastic sociology against both the sectarianism of Chelčický and that of the Free Spirit chiliasts, and that at least one spokesman for the latter was prepared to accept the theory as applicable to Tabor at large—"the body in which there are also dignities of status"—while insisting that "the saints" were also entitled to interpret Paul's words as a promise of their own future lordship

[66] Above, *ad* notes 52 and 53.

[67] Above, chap. vii, n. 119. It is instructive to compare the chiliast treatise in Laurence's chronicle with that published by Bartoš, which makes many, perhaps most, of the same points, but entirely lacks the rigorous, highly articulated form.

[68] Laurence, pp. 423 f.

[69] See the translated texts in my "Peter Chelčický," pp. 155 ff., 171 ff.

over the earth. Meanwhile the Pikarts would exist within Tabor as an extreme left-wing party, working to radicalize the whole.

On this basis we can best understand one of the important *Taborite* developments in the autumn, the assertion that the Roman rite of mass and vestments, even in a chastened form as used by the Praguers, were not merely superfluous but damnable. Tabor's extreme simplification of the mass, to the point where it became a congregational communion service, also involved a rejection of "ornates"—the special vestments of the officiating priest—and of gold or silver chalices and patens. The simplified rite had existed for some time, and had been practiced in Prague during the Taborites' stay there; [70] in fact, it was one of the points of controversy involved in the Taborites' decision to leave the capital at the end of August. But the issue came up again, as though it were something new, in November of 1420, after the Prague forces had won the battle for the Vyšehrad fortress with only minor support from a small Taborite contingent led by Nicholas of Hus.[71] The victory reinforced the power of the more conservative Prague leadership, which at the same time reached a peak of militant self-assertion that was never equaled before or after: Prague was the head and heart of the realm, the mother of cities, the leading estate in political affairs.[72] Thus on 14 November she joined her baronial allies to plan a new and more powerful mission to offer the Bohemian crown to the King of Poland; when Nicholas of Hus rejected this project in the name of the Taborites, "who had never wanted to elect anyone but a Bohemian as king," he was shown the Taborite seal that Žižka had attached to the credentials for the earlier mission sent to Poland in August.[73] And the same Prague meeting proceeded to take measures against Tabor's religious radicalism:

[70] See above, chap. vii, *ad* notes 71–75; chap. viii, *ad* notes 41 ff.

[71] The military and political background of the events treated in the present chapter is narrated by Heymann, pp. 164 ff.; his sound account makes it unnecessary for me to repeat the details here.

[72] Prague's extraordinary exaltation in her own eyes at this time is best represented by the political verses of the Bautzen manuscript, ed. J. Daňhelka, *Husitské skladby budyšínského rukopisu* (Prague, 1952); they are now attributed generally to Laurence of Březová; see Macek, *Tábor*, II, 200, where stress is placed on the radicalizing effect of the Taborite alliance. But Prague's spokesmen seemed to take special pride in the Vyšehrad victory, won with only minor Taborite help: Jakoubek and Příbram both boasted of it in their anti-Pikart treatises (see the quotations in my "O traktátu Ad occurrendum," p. 903), Příbram with special emphasis—Prague was Jerusalem, "super quam invocatum est nomen fortissimi dei"; she was the "matrem civitatum in Israhel" (MS. 4749, fol. 71ᵛ). The extreme political consequences of this consciousness, including the idea of Prague's legal right to a major role in choosing a king, are analyzed by Ferdinand Seibt, "Communitas Primogenita. Zur Prager Hegemonialpolitik in der hussitischen Revolution," *Historisches Jahrbuch*, LXXXI (1962), 80–100, esp. 92 ff.

[73] Laurence, pp. 447 f., the source also for what follows.

It was agreed that no one in the future should attempt to sow any novelties among the people, unless he were well able to show that these innovations were founded in Scripture, or could clearly prove them by infallible reason. Nor might he publish that innovation without first presenting it to four masters chosen by the community, and getting their approval—and if they did not consent, then he might not offer it to the people. Second, it was agreed upon that the rite hitherto kept in the mass, with ornates and chalice, should be observed by all the priests of Prague, only without excess or luxuriousness.

Soon after, first the Old Town then the New proceeded to depose the pro-Taborite magistrates who had been installed in August, and they chose new ones. Thus very suddenly Prague gave up her orientation toward the left in favor of a renewed alliance with the barons, around the key point of reconstituting the monarchy on the basis of the Polish candidacy. The measures taken to restrain religious innovation and to prevent a drastic reform of the basically Roman liturgy can be understood as merely the religious aspect of the political realignment, a declaration by Prague conservatism that it would no longer tolerate Taborite agitation in the capital.

The response of at least some of the Taborites was to counterattack. After his defeat on all points at the meeting of 14 November, Nicholas of Hus had left Prague to join the Taborite forces in the field; on receiving the news of the antiradical coup in the capital, he and his forces began a new operation, the siege of Říčany fortress, and demanded that Prague honor her military alliance with Tabor by sending help. This was done, against the strong opposition of the baronial leaders, but on 24 November, when the Prague forces arrived at Říčany and their priests began to celebrate mass, some of the Taborite men and women ran up and cried, "What are you doing with those sheets on? Take them off and conform to Christ and his apostles when you say mass, or we'll do it for you!" In fact, the leaders on both sides agreed to leave the other alone, with the understanding that the religious differences would be discussed at a future date. Nicholas of Hus was not satisfied and he rode off to Prague to make another attempt at gaining a foothold in the capital, but again to no avail. All that had been accomplished was to create a crisis among the Hussite allies; while this might, in other circumstances, have been enough to serve Nicholas's ends, it in fact caused their defeat. The conservative party in Prague was evidently quite strong, Prague's alliance with the Hussite barons was of fundamental import, and Tabor herself had developed strong inclinations toward a settlement. She had just concluded an armistice with Lord Ulrich of Rožmberk (18 November), and thus violated one of the prime rules of chiliast warfare, not to treat with the enemy;[74] moreover, she had acquired baronial allies of her own, most notably Lords

[74] Macek, *Tábor*, II, 256 ff.; the text in Heymann, pp. 485 ff.

Ulrich Vavák of Jindřichův Hradec and Peter Zmrzlík of Svojšín. On 29 November these and other Taborite lords came to Prague to promote a settlement between the parties. And it turned out that John Žižka also favored Hussite unity; at least he was prepared to deal with the Praguers in a reasonable manner, while Nicholas of Hus would not even accept a Prague invitation to dinner. Thus in this whole sequence of events we can see two political tendencies among the Taborites: one turbulent and subversive, the other moderate, anxious to preserve the alliance with Prague; there was no clear issue of *religious* import between the two factions, but rather a decisive difference in attitude toward the non-Taborite world. The moderates were interested in justifying certain reforms that had been carried through *within* the Taborite community, and they were prepared to argue with the Praguers about disputed matters.[75] The subversives, however, wanted the reformation and revolution to continue, even if this meant fighting the conservative Hussites. In fact, the subversives were prepared to provoke controversy, to keep interparty relationships unsettled, and in general to create an atmosphere of ill will and turbulence in order to prevent the kind of agreement to disagree that would, in effect, have meant renouncing any hope of really regenerating—that is, revolutionizing—the society of Bohemia. Thus although there is no reason to associate Nicholas of Hus with the ideas of Pikartism, his intransigent political line would seem to have corresponded to the sectarian idea of total reformation, and the pugnacious Taborites who were so eager to rip the chasubles off the backs of the priests of Prague were probably those sectarians who still saw the world in terms of chiliast antitheses.[76]

However, it was the politically minded leaders who won out. After the siege of Říčany had been brought to a successful end and the allied armies had returned to Prague, a meeting was arranged between the Prague and Taborite communities, on 8 December, in the monastery church of St. Ambrose; no priests or women were allowed to take part, so as to maintain a

---

[75] Thus at the meeting that took place on 10 December, Nicholas of Pelhřimov concluded his presentation of the case for Tabor's liturgical reforms by saying: "Hee . . . sunt scripture solide et raciones inviolabiles, contra quas magistri, *quamvis dudum affectavimus,* nullam adhuc dederunt scripturam" (Laurence, p. 464; my emphasis).

[76] To Josef Macek Nicholas of Hus was "the leader of the Taborite poor, undeviatingly pursuing the fulfillment and realization of the chiliast program" (*Tábor,* II, 290). Bartoš, *HR,* I, 117, notes that there is no support for this view in the sources, that Nicholas's character remains obscure, and that it is hard to decide where he helped and where he hurt the revolution. The scholarly disagreement on these points could indeed be pursued throughout the modern literature—see, e.g., Heymann, pp. 197 f.—but in the present context the points made in the text are sufficient.

reasonable atmosphere, and the more militant Taborites were prevented from associating themselves with their radical sympathizers among the Praguers. These precautions did prevent disruption, in fact, they seem to have prevented any action at all, and the meeting broke up on a note of quiet frustration.[77] But the leaders on both sides did not let the matter rest; they agreed to entrust Lord Ulrich Vavák with a kind of *ad hoc* leadership, and he summoned a meeting between the clergy of both parties, to take place on the afternoon of 10 December, in the Charles College, or Carolinum. The Prague magistrates even invited the leading Taborites to dinner, before the meeting, and all except Nicholas of Hus accepted; Nicholas hinted that he feared for his life in the Town Hall, and he rode out of the city with some of his followers. At the same time the Taborite priests had their own reasons to be dissatisfied with the arrangements, for many of them had once been the students of the masters whom they were now supposed to debate. Thus they refused to meet in the Carolinum, and the encounter could take place only after a new site had been agreed upon, the house of Lord Peter Zmrzlík, in the Old Town. There it was that all assembled—the masters, the priests of both sides, the magistrates, the barons, the military leaders, and no doubt others too—in order to discuss or hear discussed the key issue of the day, whether mass should be celebrated *in ornato* or not.[78]

But those who hoped for an expeditious settlement were disappointed, for the conservative element among the Prague masters were as doctrinaire in their own way as the sectarian party of Tabor, and they seized upon the opportunity to deliver a full-scale attack on *all* of Tabor's radical deviations. The barons asked in vain that the issue of rites be taken up; instead, Master Procop of Plzeň, then rector of the university, said, "We have here a list of certain articles damaging to the whole realm, and we would like these to be heard first; then the current issues may be taken up." Procop handed the list to Master Peter of Mladoňovice, who mounted a bench and read the articles out, first in Latin then in Czech. It must have taken a long time, for there were seventy-two articles, covering every doctrine that had ever been promulgated by anyone among the Taborites: the Waldensianist corpus, the chiliast corpus, the Pikart corpus, and a few others. After he had finished, Peter said: "Let all of you know that by these articles we do not accuse anyone by name of holding them, but you should flee from any brother or priests who would

---

[77] Laurence, p. 452: "frustrati fuerunt Thaborite sua intencione non potentes facere scissuram in communitate, quam sperabant, et igitur modicis propositis et auditis ad hospicia propria pacifice redierunt." Laurence says nothing about any other results that the meeting may have achieved, and it is not clear why Heymann supposes (p. 192) that agreement was reached on several points, with only the question of vestments remaining unsolved.

[78] Laurence, pp. 453 ff., for the whole course of the meeting.

dogmatize them and stubbornly defend them, for any such man is either a heretic or in error." In the language of the time, the Prague masters were "hereticating" the Taborites, putting them outside the pale within which discussion might be carried on; the masters would not indeed *discuss* the articles, and they were willing to give a copy of the list to the Taborites only if the latter committed themselves to defend the articles.[79] The procedure was that of a *provocacio* to scholastic disputation, but also that of a judicial process, in which the two parties would have contended before a panel of arbitrators, and it is not impossible that the masters hoped for such a contest. Indeed, it may be that Laurence of Březová has given a misleading account of the nature of the meeting, which may have been called in consequence of a legal complaint filed in the Town Hall by Master John Příbram against the Taborite priests, on account of the latters' errors, seventy-six of which Příbram listed and said he would prove.[80] If this information be true, then Příbram's action can best be associated with the Prague decisions of 14 November and the subsequent conservative seizure of power;[81] the sharp

[79] *Loc. cit.;* cf. Macek, *Tábor,* II, 284.

[80] F. Prochazka, *Miscellaneen der Böhmische und Mährische Literatur* (Prague, 1784), gives a text of the seventy-six errors from a manuscript copied in the early 17th century (now in the National Museum in Prague; I have not examined it), which included prefatory remarks in Czech, summarized in German by Prochazka: they associate the articles with a meeting held on account of a "gerichtliche Anklage" that Příbram had lodged in the Town Hall against the Taborite priests, on account of their errors; Příbram showed the seventy-six errors and promised to prove them. There were twenty-one Taborite priests present; they conferred, and Martin Húska, in the name of all, said that the Taborites held and taught all the articles, except for some that would also be acceptable if a word were changed. Bohuslav Balbin, *Epitome rerum Bohemicarum* (Prague, 1677), pp. 443 f., offers this information: "Hoc itidem Anno 1420 (dies in M.S. meo codice additus non est) *facta est maxima congregatio* (verba Codicis recito) *omnium Sacerdotum in Praga in Domo Zmrzliķonis,* in eo conventu cum alia multa adversus Sigismundum acta, tum praecipue Magistrorum Universitatis Pragensis ac sacerdotum Hussiticorum adversus Taboriticos sacerdotes accusationes auditae; praecipuus accusator M. Joannes de Przibram, isque LXXVI articulos (qui in M.S. meo recitantur) haereticos, et doctrinae SS. Patrum et veteri Ecclesiae contrarios attulit, quos Taboritae docerent; neque Taboritae inficiari poterant, imo ultro ipsi professi sunt eorum a se defensionem susceptam."

[81] The data given by Prochazka and Balbin pose problems no matter how one interprets them. It is possible that the information refers to the 10 December meeting; if so, Laurence must be corrected: Příbram, whom he does not mention, played a leading role as accuser, and there were seventy-six articles, not seventy-two; moreover the meeting came to certain decisions against Sigismund. Příbram's legal complaint would have been lodged in the Town Hall sometime before the meeting. But perhaps the complaint was made before or in connection with the Prague meeting of 14 November, which did take action against Sigismund, which did pass decrees against Taboritism, and which did involve the university masters—it set up a four-man committee of

conflicts that then occurred between Praguers and Taborites could then be readily explained without blaming everything on Nicholas of Hus, and the rather strange procedure of the masters at the Zmrzlík meeting would not be strange at all. For even though the articles were not on the agenda, they would have been pending as a charge, to be cleared up before any real discussion would be possible. Furthermore, the charge had a certain point. The list of seventy-six articles survives, along with Příbram's refutations, as a treatise, *Contra articulos picardorum;* although the errors cover all of Taborite doctrine, they are presented as primarily the work of the *Picardi* and of their Czech disciples—the Pikarts, and above all Martin Húska.[82] Thus the masters' action would in reality have been a challenge to the leaders of Tabor's party of order to reconcile themselves with Prague by purging their ranks of the Pikarts, their minds of Pikartism and indeed of all sectarian error.

In this light the events of the meeting compose a very clear picture. After Peter of Mladoňovice had finished reading the articles, and had made the disclaimer quoted above, Chval of Machovice, one of the Taborite military captains, said flatly, " I hold all those articles," and another of the captains, John Roháč of Dubá, burst out: "In Constance they imposed forty heretical articles on us, and you are imposing more than seventy!" Since Chval could not in fact have held all seventy-two articles, some of which were mutually exclusive and many of which were given in a perverse form, and since the military man could hardly have occupied himself with doctrinal subtleties, his declaration must be understood as a direct reply to the real intention of the masters: he was saying to Master Peter, "You want to force us into a defensive posture and you want to set us against each other—well, our answer is to present a united front, each of us publicly committing himself to

---

masters to censor doctrines. This hypothesis would explain many things, and it would fit in with Příbram's immediately subsequent role in setting Prague against Tabor; it would be reasonable then to explain the seventy-two articles of 10 December as a selection, for public use, from the seventy-six articles of Příbram's accusation, and it would be reasonable to explain Příbram's absence from Laurence's account as due to his position as one of the parties in the contest.

[82] The treatise has already been used in the discussion of chiliasm, above, chap. vii (see note 88); see *LČP,* No. 5, and see below, n. 95. For the stylization of the treatise as an attack against the Pikarts—even though all of Tabor's errors were included—see above, chap. vii, n. 142. The only Taborite priest named by Příbram is Martin Húska (above, chap. vii, n. 114), who is not only associated with a Free Spirit error of general import, but also singled out as the particular author of the first error ("Quod panis sacramentalis non est verum corpus Cristi . . ."). Thus, MS 4749, fol. 38[r], "Queritur abhuiusmodi heretico"; fol. 38[v], "hoc grossus hereticus"; fol. 39[r], "iste rudis hereticus"; Martin is actually named on fol. 42[r] (chap. vii, n. 114). Otherwise, Příbram refers to his targets in the third person plural, or as "Taborites" (e.g., fol. 65[r]).

the beliefs of the rest." Similarly, Roháč must have meant that the real issue was not the content of the several articles but the attempt of the masters to hereticate Tabor—a declaration comparable to the by now classic Czech complaint that the Council of Constance had defamed Bohemia by its accusations of heresy against Hus and the Hussites. But this line of flat defiance could not be pursued, probably because it would have implied, logically, a breaking-off of the whole discussion. It was therefore up to the priests of Tabor to take the floor. The first to speak, possibly after a brief conference of all,[83] was Martin Húska, who said, "Except for a few articles which are given venomously, we hold all of them"; then "the same was said by their bishop [that is, Nicholas of Pelhřimov] and brother Markolt of Zbraslavice." When the masters declared their willingness to prove the falsity of the articles against any defenders, Martin again spoke, "in the name of all the Taborites"; he asked for a copy of the list—to be told, however, that a copy would be given only if someone would undertake to defend the articles. No one could have mistaken this exchange for a final formulation in any sense, and it is therefore most instructive to read, in Laurence's account:

> When these exchanges had taken place, Nicholas, bachelor of arts and priest of Tabor, who had been elected bishop by them, stood on a bench holding in his hand a small sextern [i.e., a booklet], and he said these or similar words: "Now you have heard the masters, so hear us too. We came to this meeting thinking that it was to deal only with the rite of mass, whether it were better to consecrate the Lord's Supper and administer it to the people in vestments [*in ornato*] or without them. But the masters have cited many articles against us, which we hope to be true, excepting only what is venomous in them. But turning from these for the present, we say and hold that the priests of Tabor do better to consecrate the Lord's Supper and offer it to the people without the vestments of the [Roman] church than the Praguers in doing this in vestments. . . .[84]

Nicholas developed his arguments in systematic form, but as he was proceeding to the patristic dossier, saying "also, the holy doctors . . . ," Martin Húska and other priests did not allow him to continue, but said, "Leave off for now!" Nicholas accordingly finished by a brief criticism of the Praguers for not punishing mortal sins vigorously enough and for "having not yet wholly renounced the endowment of Constantine and the emperors into the hands of the secular lords." In other words, Nicholas ended by a counter-charge, that the Praguers had failed to live up to two of the four articles accepted by all as a common Hussite program.

The inferences to be drawn from all this are clear enough, chiefly because

[83] See above, n. 80.
[84] Laurence, p. 463.

Laurence has carefully constructed his account to make them clear, but there is no reason to doubt him. The rite of mass, which was Nicholas's chief concern in this period, was a particular issue that could be debated with Prague on the basis of common Hussite principles, while Martin's Free Spirit chiliasm and Pikartism implied either the complete liquidation of what Prague actually was, or a total break with the capital and the national Hussite coalition. Hence it was in Martin's interest to frustrate discussion and break up the meeting; this was also the desire of those, like Chval and Roháč, who shared Martin's spirit if not all of his doctrines. But they failed, and Nicholas of Pelhřimov, who had been forced to yield leadership to Martin and to submit to his disruptive intervention, nevertheless prevailed and got what he had long sought,[85] a debate about vestments. For after he had finished his discourse, Master Jakoubek took his turn on the bench and read a refutation; it was then agreed that both sides would deliver their present and future treatises to Lord Ulrich Vavák, and finally the meeting was dissolved—*terminus est dissolutus.* As we shall see, the exchange of written opinions and arguments continued, as an ideological reflex of what became the basic mode of Prague-Tabor coexistence: genuine agreement was out of the question, but the posture of doctrinal disputation made possible a good deal of practical collaboration. Thus the seventy-odd articles never became a protocol for debate, the list was never formally defended by anyone, and the Free Spirit "errors" were simply left out of the debate despite Příbram's occasional efforts to bring them in.[86] In fact, Prague's actual posture vis-à-vis Tabor, in the coming months, can be characterized as a compromise between the tendencies of Příbram and Jakoubek,[87] while

---

[85] See n. 75, above.

[86] In his *Ad occurrendum homini insano* (above, n. 60), which includes not only the Pikart eucharistic doctrines but also the Free Spirit doctrine, "quod sanctorum parentum filii concipiuntur sine peccato originali mortali, sed concipiuntur in peccato veniali," as well the denial of infant baptism and of baptism by water; it also attacks the "orthodox" Taborite rejection of the Roman rite of mass and vestments (MS. 4937, fols. 156ʳ, 159ʳ, 159ᵛ, 152ᵛ). In his *De ritibus misse, ca.* January 1421, he also made a special point of associating Tabor's liturgical reforms with the Pikart menace (Höfler, II, 541 f.).

[87] The events and texts just canvassed show that the right wing of the masters—Příbram, Peter of Mladoňovice, Procop of Plzeň—sought to avoid a limited debate on rites by pushing their total heretication of Tabor to the front; Jakoubek, on the other hand, was willing to debate rites at Zmrzlík's house and—to judge from his general posture—even before, although the other masters perhaps prevented him (above, n. 75). Later on he would wryly recall his constant readiness to discuss, and the suspicions to which he laid himself open thereby: "Et multi deridentes me narrant me dicere: Nescio cuius spiritus sunt [*scil.,* Thaborite] (Luke 9:55). Fateor, quod timui, ne veritati contradicerem, volui prius probare spiritus et postquam cognovi errores esse et spiritum

Tabor's posture was entirely that of her party of order, its clergy headed by Nicholas of Pelhřimov and its secular power led by John Žižka, whose silence at the Zmrzlík meeting was—as Heymann has observed—"more eloquent than many words would have been." [88] As for Martin Húska, he never again appeared as a leading priest of the whole Taborite community, but only as the leader of a disruptive sect, the object of persecution by the party of order.

THE LIQUIDATION OF THE PIKARTS AND ADAMITES

The exchange of doctrinal treatises about the rite of mass that had begun at the meeting of 10 December was continued in the following weeks, in accordance with the decision taken on that occasion. Since the subject was treated on both sides in considerable depth, the polemic amounted to a full-scale controversy over the meaning of the Hussite reform, with the actual differences between Prague and Tabor presented in systematic, rational form, by Nicholas of Pelhřimov on the one side, John Příbram and Jakoubek on the other. The substance of this exchange will be considered in detail in the next chapter; what it came down to was that Prague believed in imitating the Primitive Church, along with such post-Primitive accretions as were not in conflict with the norm, but rather useful in promoting piety, while Tabor, on the other hand, held that both the liturgical and doctrinal accretions were superfluous and, in general, harmful. At the same time there was also some disagreement, unfortunately never expressed with adequate clarity, over the definition of the Primitive Church, with Prague including the age of the Fathers, Tabor idealizing the church "whose rectors were the apostles." [89] These were serious differences, capable in fact of nourishing over twenty years of polemical action, but they were eminently debatable: Prague and Tabor were antagonists in the debate, but they stood on the same platform. Those who did not, the Free Spirit sectarians, were thus the enemies of both, and in this sense Prague and Tabor could even become allies against the Pikarts, to carry through what tradition almost forces us to call the Hussite Thermidor. At the same time Tabor remained a revolutionary society; her military activity did not slacken, and she opposed any attempt to moderate the reformation in order to please the barons, as Prague

---

mendacii, contradixi. Unde post hec sepius conveni cum eis, non quod eis vellem consentire, sed si forte potuissem eos retrahere ad me et ad pristinam concordiam spiritus et veritatis" (*Apologia, ST*, II, 163; *LČJ*, No. 101).

[88] Heymann, p. 196.

[89] See my "The Religion of Hussite Tabor," in *The Czechoslovak Contribution to World Culture*, ed. M. Rechcigl (The Hague, 1964), pp. 214 f.

was doing. On 3 January 1421 Wenceslas Koranda came to Prague to deliver Bishop Nicholas's treatise on rites, and in a sharply propagandistic sermon that he preached to his radical partisans in the city—especially the "begute," who thought he was an angel—he declared Tabor's intention to keep her radically simplified rites. He also reproached the masters for "repaying the sufferings of the Taborites" with compromises designed to keep the Hussite barons Hussite, and he threw the list of seventy-two "errors" back in the masters' faces: "The big shots [*homines altos*] who defend 'ornates' with irrelevant writings, and by falsifying the writings of the brethren—the Taborites will deal with such men just as they would with others of false faith who falsified writings, as they had done previously on behalf of images and holy water." [90] Shortly afterward, on 20 January, in the town of Soběslav, "the Taborites publicly proclaimed that if they found any priest officiating *in ornato,* they would burn him along with his 'ornates.' " [91] This was not a declaration of war against Prague, but it was a warning that within Tabor's domain there would be no tolerance of nonconformity.[92] On this basis the limited Prague-Tabor rapprochement took place.

Nor could the consolidation of Tabor tolerate the nonconformity of the Pikarts. If, as argued in the preceding section, a certain reasonable coexistence had been possible during the autumn, the logic of reality would sooner or later have set the two parties at war no matter what limited concessions each would have offered. Nicholas of Pelhřimov, with his seat in Písek, could for a time afford to watch the development of Martin Húska's movement in Tabor itself without precipitating a crisis—but only for a time; as he presumably began to work himself into his office of leadership—as indeed he created that office out of its potentialities—he must have realized that the Taborite reformation he headed could not be secure as long as there was a rival leader, offering a rival faith and way of life. On the other hand, Martin Húska could not have left the meeting at Zmrzlík's house without a clear understanding of the defeat he had suffered there—without a realization that only a bold stroke could change a situation that worked inexorably against him. Apart from these factors, there was also the pressure exerted by the

---

[90] Laurence, p. 468. The last allusion is unclear.

[91] Laurence, p. 470. Cf. also p. 427: Merely utraquist priests were taken from their churches and brought to Tabor, with the result that the people under Tabor's sway had to have recourse to Taborite priests.

[92] Bartoš, *HR*, I, 124 f., regards the action as the work of Martin Húska, who sought thereby to destroy the Prague-Tabor agreements worked out on 10 December. But it is most unlikely that Martin had anything to do with the attack on "ornates" at this time; he had gone far beyond this issue, and in any case Bartoš's interpretation goes beyond the source. Tabor was still free to impose uniformity in her own domain.

most powerful of Tabor's political and military leaders. Nicholas of Hus might have favored the subversives, but on 24 December he died of complications following a broken leg, suffered on his ride away from Prague two weeks before. Chval of Machovice, John Roháč, and perhaps other captains and lesser leaders might have supported Martin, but it is perhaps more likely that their religious radicalism was too general and nondoctrinaire to make them Pikarts; in any case, they were not the principal leaders of Tabor. On the other side, moreover, was a man they must have venerated, John Žižka, whose religious views were to be sure violent, but whose mind was too coarse to appreciate the fundamental values of the religion he espoused; at any rate, he was a soldier and a statesman who did appreciate the overriding importance of authority and stability within Tabor, and national unity within Bohemia.[93] During this period he was working very closely with the barons allied to Tabor, chiefly Lord Peter Zmrzlík and Lord Ulrich Vavák, both of whom had shown their line of thought in connection with the meeting of 10 December—they had indeed arranged it, to prevent priestly altercations from ruining the Hussite cause. Exactly how all of these factors interacted is unknown, but the course of events shows that the net result of what must have been bitter political struggle among the Taborites was an irresistible drive toward Taborite orthodoxy.

The first datum we have in this connection is Laurence of Březová's report that on 29 January "the priest, Brother Martin, called Loquis, the chief sower of all the errors of the Taborites," was captured and imprisoned by Lord Ulrich Vavák, "because not content with the many errors with which he had infected the people, he vomited forth a new error and heresy concerning the venerable sacrament [of the Eucharist], namely that the laity should themselves take the hosts that the priests had consecrated, and divide them up among themselves, for Christ said, 'Take this, and divide it among yourselves.' "[94] It is hard to believe that only this new error caused Vavák to take such a drastic measure, nor is it likely that he acted without some sort of understanding with other leaders of the party of order. On the other hand, it is true that Martin's new "error" was indeed new, in a significant sense; it was included in the seventy-six articles of Příbram's *Contra articulos picardorum*, but it was *not* included among the seventy-two errors read out in

---

[93] This view is the generally accepted one, although each scholar has his own concept of Žižka as believer and as political figure. See, e.g., Heymann, pp. 453 ff.; Macek, *Tábor*, II, 369 (Žižka was "the leader and spokesman of the Hussite bourgeois opposition"); Bartoš, *HR*, I, 126. Josef Pekař is virtually the only authority to regard Žižka as a religious fanatic of the most extreme sort (e.g., *Žižka*, III, 228).

[94] Laurence, pp. 470 f.; cf. Luke 22:17, where the words refer to the wine of the chalice!

Zmrzlík's house on 10 December.[95] Moreover, in a letter written from prison to his Taborite opponents—perhaps to the Písek community [96]—Martin said that he "had come to understand that the bread of the Lord's body was being given in a very improper way," and that he wanted to show the people the right way, the way of Christ's institution.[97] At the same time he wrote that he had not as yet spoken out in public about his new insights because he wanted to talk them over with the priests, but his imprisonment had supervened.[98] The most reasonable way to combine all of this information would be to suppose that Martin had indeed not "published" his new ideas

[95] Two articles in Příbram's list are relevant: No. 9, "Quod omnes fideles, non soli sacerdotes, possunt conficere sacramentum corporis et sanguinis Christi," and No. 10, "Quod omnes fideles licite possunt et debent more apostolorum ad manus accipere eucharistiae sacramentum" (MS. 4749, fols. 54ʳ, 57ʳ; also in Döllinger, *Beiträge*, II, 692). If, as indicated by the material in note 80 above, the seventy-two articles of 10 December were essentially a formulation of Příbram's dossier, then one would have to guess that the discrepancies between the two lists (Nos. 1, 2, 3, 5, 9, and 10 of Příbram are not in Laurence, while the latter's 35 and 36 are not in Příbram) were the result of some calculation by the Prague masters. Perhaps, as Krofta suggests, they left out articles that they knew were held exclusively by Martin and his followers ("O některých spisech M. Jana z Příbrama," *ČČM*, LXXIII (1899), 212)—or, as I would guess, articles that Martin had not yet promulgated or acted upon. It would be simpler if we could date Příbram's treatise after 10 December, and Bartoš does in fact regard this possibility as open (*LČP*, No. 5), but since the masters on 10 December stated their readiness to prove the heretical character of the seventy-two articles, they must have had their extensive proofs in hand—that is, they must have had Příbram's treatise, which refutes each article at length, and predominantly on the basis of Scripture, because that was all the Taborites would recognize (MS. 4749, fol. 37ʳ: Příbram says he will refute the articles "non argumentorum subtilitate, quia hanc rudes isti ut venenum fastidiunt nec raciones audire volunt, sed scripture sacre nuda et simplici firmitate").

[96] The Czech text is preserved in one manuscript of Laurence of Březová's chronicle, p. 495. Martin urges the addressees to see that they have been deceived by priests—hence they were a group of laity; he also writes to them: "I have always loved you, even though now you do not love me"—hence they were not his followers. The community of Písek would meet both these requirements.

[97] *Loc. cit.* Emending an untranslatable "tebe" to "sebe," we could add an important Free Spirit hope to this statement, for Martin goes on to say that once the people knew Christ's institution, "they could keep it and draw help from it and make themselves better [see above, *ad* n. 52], and await the future with confidence; but now they can expect only terrible vengeance." (I change "polepšili tebe" to "polepšili sebe.")

[98] *Loc. cit.* All of this is obviously of the greatest importance for a historical reconstruction of the Pikart crisis, and it confirms Laurence's report on the reasons for Martin's imprisonment. Kalivoda, however, rejects Laurence's information, because the "new" error was already included in Příbram's *Contra articulos picardorum*, and then goes on, consistently, to remark, "Martin's letter from prison unfortunately contains nothing that would allow us to judge what Martin's views were at this time" (*HI*, p. 458).

among his opponents—those to whom he wrote his letter—but that he had declared the new doctrine to his followers, and had even begun to implement it by organizing eucharistic suppers at which the laity did take the consecrated foods in their own hands. In other words, some time between 10 December 1420 and 29 January 1421, the Pikart opposition had taken on the character of a separate sect, leading a religious life outside that of the Taborite establishment. This would explain why Martin was imprisoned: he had passed from mere opposition to outright subversion.[99]

The inner life of Martin's sect was centered in the communion banquet, the nature of which can be inferred from Martin's writings, as preserved in fragmentary form by John Příbram and Peter Chelčický;[100] furthermore, it would be reasonable to suppose that the preceding and succeeding stages of the sect—chiliasm and Adamitism, respectively—can throw light on the ideas and practices of its middle period, at least insofar as the picture thus constructed turns out to be self-consistent. To begin with, Martin developed his eucharistic ideas in the form of an exegesis of the gospel of John, chapter six, apparently in collaboration with the Pikart layman Sigmund of Řepan.[101] Jesus had said (John 6:53), "Except you eat the flesh of the Son of man and drink his blood, you shall not have life in you," a passage that Hussite utraquism interpreted literally, but which was more usually understood in connection with related passages of the chapter, in a spiritual sense.[102] It was in this non-Hussite sense that Martin and Sigmund understood it, no doubt in accord with the teachings of the Free Spirit Beghards. Thus in the quoted passage, and in the similar one of John 6:56—"Who eats my flesh and drinks my blood remains in me and I in him"—the flesh was to be understood as bread (John 6:51: "The bread that I give is my flesh, for the life of the world") but neither was to be understood physically. For the prologue to the gospel says (John 1:14), "The word has been made flesh and has dwelt in us," and Jesus also said (John 6:27), "Do not work for the food that perishes, but for that which endures unto eternal life." This was the food of the spirit, according to John 6:62–63: "But what if you see the Son of Man ascending to where he was before? It is the spirit that gives life; the flesh is of no use at

[99] Macek, *Tábor,* II, 303, rejects not only the religious reason for Martin's imprisonment but any reason having to do with a presumed change in Martin's activities or role; the time had simply come to liquidate the revolutionary party.

[100] Příbram, *Život, KJBB,* pp. 290–294; and in Latin, in Höfler, II, 828–830 (see n. 9, above). Chelčický, *Replika proti Biskupcovi,* pp. 457–459.

[101] Chelčický, *Rep. Bisk.,* p. 458. What follows below is taken from Chelčický's account, except where otherwise indicated; the other sources agree perfectly with it. The quotations from John are cited according to the King James verse-numbers, but translated in accordance with the Czech source, itself based on the Vulgate.

[102] See above, Chap. III, *ad* n. 107, and *passim.*

all. The words that I have spoken to you are spirit and life." [103] Thus the true meaning of John 6:53 was that eating Christ's flesh was a function of the soul, a function carried out, to be sure, through the body: "the soul that does God's works is fed by them as the body is with bread; therefore these deeds of the word of God are called bread, for they feed the one who follows them, and they are called the flesh, for they are done in the flesh, being one with the body." Hence the exegesis: "Unless you eat the flesh of the Son of Man— that is, unless you do the deeds that the Son of Man did in the flesh, to the extent of your power; and unless you drink his blood—that is, unless you know the power and reason of his deeds," you will not have life in you; but if you do, you "will be one with the Father and the Son, just as the Son is one with the Father."

To become one with God and Christ, by doing Christ's deeds—this meant more than just the practice of evangelical virtue. In the chiliast letter quoted above (*ad* note 63), a similar program of behavior and understanding—"he takes Christ's body who disseminates his gifts, and he eats his body who livingly listens to his word"—was explicitly designed to fit the faithful for a real transformation of their human nature: they would thereby become "ready for the Lord's coming, that we may go with him to the wedding"; and "through this eating the just will shine like the sun in the kingdom of their Father, when he comes in clouds with his glory. . . ." A similar juxtaposition can be found in Martin's letter from prison, which begins with the hope that God will enlighten the addressees so that "they may see the kingdom of heaven," and goes on with the declaration that Martin "does not intend to go against any of the Lord's deeds, to the day of his death." In fact, before he was burnt to death, on 21 August 1421, Martin confessed his faith in words that included his steadfast belief: "it is enough for the salvation of each of the faithful that he live the life of Jesus Christ, according to what is written in the gospels and epistles, without the invented glosses of the doctors." [104] But this path to holiness was not understood in the usual "evangelical" sense, as the path of suffering and tribulation; we know this from Martin's declaration to Chelčický, quoted above (*ad* note 49), as well as from other sources. For one thing, the Christ with whom the faithful would be united was the Holy Spirit:

> Christ left the faithful and the apostles, and sits on the right hand of the Father. And Christ is the Holy Spirit, of whom Scriptures say, "And I shall

[103] This passage comes from Jakoubek's anti-Pikart treatise, *Jhesus Cristus dominus et salvator* (*LČJ*, No. 84), MS. 4944, fol. 252ʳ; it is my assumption that he refers to Martin's exegesis.

[104] The text is published in *JSH*, I (1928), 8; Příbram's condensed Latin version (Höfler, II, 829) identifies the occasion on which it was made.

give you another Comforter" [cf. John 14:16; 16:7]—that is, another, spiritual one. And so now, just as Christ gives himself spiritually and is with us
until the end of the world, so he is also in the foods of the Lord's Supper.[105]

This is the positive form of what the Hussites regarded as the most scandalous Pikart tenet, the denial of a real presence: "Since Christ ascended to
heaven in his body and sits on the right hand of the Father, he is not here in
the sacrament and does not give his holy body according to a real presence;
but his faithful only enjoy his holy body in a certain spiritual way, now in
the sacrament." [106] Thus Christ's spiritual presence in the Eucharist was in
fact the presence of the Holy Spirit; to become one with Christ was to
receive the Holy Spirit; to do the deeds of Christ was to act so as to prepare
oneself for this spiritual regeneration.

The best explicit testimony of this aspect of Martin's teaching comes from
Chelčický's discussion of the treatise on John 6:

> Next Martin speaks much of good deeds, and says that the Lord's Supper is
> founded on love, of which the Lord spoke to the disciples and which he
> showed them in visible deeds, washing their feet and leaving them an
> example, that they should wash each other's feet. . . . And Martin speaks
> much more of love and of deeds, founding the Lord's Supper on them.
> And . . . he says: the apostles kept to the manner of the Lord's Supper that
> they had seen in the desert from Jesus, when he fed the people twice, and
> when he ordered the people to be seated by hundreds, and each hundred
> divided into fifties; and thus they seated the people, and . . . they took and
> gave to the people. . . . And he further prescribes the order of the Lord's
> Supper: that the Christians should meet on the holy day, be diligent in the
> word of God, and, for perfection in love, eat what they want, and so to speak
> have a banquet. And he could not ever find a better manner of holding the
> Lord's Supper than that: by meeting in love on the holy day, being diligent
> in the word of God, feasting and filling themselves up . . . , and not
> growing thin on the little piece of bread of the popish and heretical supper.[107]

This description is amply confirmed by Martin's own testimony, in treatises
that he addressed as letters to the community of Písek and other Taborite
towns. They must have been written in December through February, 1420
and 1421, when he was fighting to justify his movement and win over the
non-Pikarts; hence they are primarily critical in orientation, refuting the
various elements of orthodox eucharistic theory and practice.[108] Christ's

---

[105] Příbram, *Život, KJBB*, p. 291.
[106] According to Jakoubek, *op. cit.*
[107] *Rep. Bisk.*, pp. 457 f.
[108] Other dates have been suggested—e.g., Macek, *Tábor*, II, 110: the spring of 1420; it
is all a matter of one's general understanding of Pikartism. See, most recently, Bartoš,
HR, I, 125. It is Příbram who defines the addressees (*KJBB*, pp. 290, 294).

physical body is in heaven, therefore not in the Eucharist, and the priests' attempt to bring it there is mere sorcery, while the adoration of the consecrated host is mere idolatry. Still worse is the ritualization of the Lord's Supper in the form of the mass, in which the priests give little bits of bread and little sips of wine to the faithful: every evil has proceeded from this—the chilling of love, the killings, plundering, burning. This was the popish mass, and it was a popish invention to set up altars, church buildings, holy images, for the rite of the Lord's Supper.[109] As a chiliast Martin had preached that in the new era "Paul's institution of gathering in the church will not be observed," [110] probably in reference to I Cor. 11:17-34, Paul's criticism of the Corinthians' habit of taking the Eucharist in connection with a meal; as a Pikart he held to the same basic ideal, that of a religious life not institutionalized into a discrete department of the community's activities, but identical with the true communal life of the faithful. To meet in the warmth of a small group around the supper table, to hear of Jesus' examples of love, and to perform acts of loving kindness for each other—all of this could for a time transform ordinary men and women into something better—"the commutation of the good into better" that the chiliast prophet had defined as the practical content of the "consummation of the age." [111] In this practical sense the Pikart banquet was a realization, highly restricted and sectarian in form, of the chiliast vision of a new age, in which the elect would be made sinless and even deified by the Holy Spirit. That these banquets developed into occasions of sex-play—a point to be treated below—may be taken in the present context as perhaps the best evidence of the Pikarts' tremendous effort to *will* themselves into the enjoyment of the Free Spirit hopes that had nourished them for a whole year.

If Martin's program can indeed be understood in this way, then one can understand why he had become intolerable to the Taborite establishment— but also why he still had many followers among the people and clergy, and why he apparently continued to enjoy the respect, even affection, of some who were on the other side. Appealing from prison to his Taborite opponents for at least the grace of a hearing, he was able to win enough support to secure his release—"*ad preces Thaboritarum.*" [112] But he seems to have continued his Pikart agitation, probably in Tabor itself, to the point where more than four hundred of the brethren were infected, according to one report.[113] "Martin's party began to hear sermons secretly, in taverns, and to

---

[109] Příbram, *Život, KJBB,* p. 293; Höfler, II, 829.
[110] Laurence, p. 416.
[111] See above, *ad* n. 52.
[112] Laurence, p. 493.
[113] *Ibid.,* p. 474 (see below, *ad* n. 127).

follow strange and unheard-of customs among themselves"—this from another report.[114] Among the customs must have been the Pikart love-feasts, but there was no doubt more to the sect than these. In his letter from prison Martin had claimed to have discovered new truths not only about the Lord's Supper, but also about baptism and preaching; while the new idea of preaching can best be related to the love-feasts, the new baptism would seem to have been a consequence of the Pikarts' belief in their own regeneration to holiness—the children of holy parents would be conceived and born without sin, and hence would need no baptism.[115] New members of the sect, on the other hand, would, and some form of adult baptism was probably practiced.[116] For the rest, it may be supposed that all of the chiliast prophecies that could be realized subjectively or within the sect were in fact realized, on the basis of the fundamental conviction—attested, to be sure, for a later phase of the sect's development—that "the Holy Church has already been reformed"—that is, renewed, regenerated—in the members of the sect.[117] The "Thy kingdom come" of the Lord's Prayer (Matt. 6:10) had already been related by a chiliast prophet to the declaration of the seventh angel of Apocalypse (Rev. 11:15): "The kingdom of this world has become the kingdom of our Lord Jesus Christ," with the latter understood as a real, perceptible change, in contrast to the evangelical formulation (Luke 17:21), "The kingdom of God is within you." [118] Now all of this was coming to pass. The chiliast prophet had written "we do not know what hour the third angel will blow his trumpet" (Rev. 8:10)—that is, to sound the signal for the purging of the Church by death and destruction; [119] but the Pikarts believed —or would soon believe—that the seventh angel had already emptied his bowl.[120] In Rev. 16:17 this event is also connected with the execution of God's vengeance (by themselves, the Pikarts believed), but it marks a fulfillment, and is followed by a loud voice saying "It is all over!" The sectaries of the Free Spirit were now one with God, and their form of the Lord's Prayer

---

[114] *OCA*, p. 476; reprinted by F. Svejkovský, *Veršované skladby doby husitské* (Prague, 1963), p. 161.

[115] See the references in n. 60, above; also n. 86; also Jakoubek, *Výklad na Zjevenie sv. Jana,* ed. F. Šimek (Prague, 1932), I, 526.

[116] Above, n. 60; also Jakoubek, *loc. cit.*

[117] Laurence, p. 518. This is the list of "Adamite" doctrines, as of 21 October 1421; but the Adamites were the Pikarts who had been expelled from Tabor. In his postil on Apocalypse of 1420–1421, Jakoubek speaks against those who said the eucharist was not the body of Christ; instead, they said, "We are the body of Christ" (*Výklad,* I, 596; cf. *infra,* n. 146).

[118] The treatise published by Bartoš, "Z dějin chiliasmu," *Do čtyř art.,* pp. 107 f.

[119] Above, *ad* n. 63.

[120] Laurence, p. 518.

began, "Our Father who art in us."[121] This final stage of the sect could not have come to be unless its characteristic traits had already been cultivated among the Pikarts at Tabor, no doubt within the closed circle of the sect.

As far as the other Taborites were concerned, however, the Pikarts were notable chiefly for their attacks on the cult of the Eucharist: they declared that the true body of Christ was not in the host, they refused to kneel to the host, they threw the consecrated wafers out of monstrances and pyxes, and stamped on them. In the city of Tabor, more than four hundred belonged to the Pikart group, and there were constant conflicts between them and the others, as well as theoretical controversies between the theologians of the two sides.[122] It is not clear exactly what Martin Húska's role was at this time, for although he was accused of responsibility for the heresy, the chief Pikart spokesman in the city of Tabor seems to have been the priest Peter Kániš, whose confession of faith contains the basic Pikart elements already discussed.[123] The "dead" bread and wine, he said, only signified the living food and drink—the body and blood of Christ; the bread and wine fed the bodies of the faithful, but their souls were fed spiritually, in the act of taking the sacrament with the right understanding of its meaning: "And the faithful soul, in this action, receives many good things from the beloved Jesus Christ, like many precious foods and drinks, which are known by none except those who have them and spiritually enjoy them."

Against this denial of an objective presence of Christ in the Eucharist, Bishop Nicholas of Pelhřimov wrote a defense of the real presence, which is

---

[121] *Ibid.*, p. 517. The precise parallelism of these and other Adamite doctrines with those of the sects of the Free Spirit elsewhere in Europe has been shown, in verbal confrontation, by Holinka, pp. 168 f.

[122] Laurence, p. 474; also *OCA*, p. 476 (Svejkovský, *Veršované skladby*, p. 161): "In this year 1420 there were great divisions among the priests at Tabor, and uproar among the people. On one side were Master Jičín, Philip, the priest Procop the Shaven, Chřenovský, Stephen Pacovský, and Abraham. On the other were the preacher Martínek Húska of Moravia, Peter Kániš, John of Bydlín, Bartoš, Nicholas the Blind, and Tršáček; they began to call the body of God an idol and a butterfly, and began to bring forth many desecrations against the holy sacrament; and they always sought to stamp it down and to kill priests. So they argued with each other, and Martínek was called a Pikart, for his party began to hear sermons secretly, in taverns, and to follow strange and unheard-of customs among themselves." It is noteworthy that neither Nicholas of Pelhřimov nor Wenceslas Koranda is named on either side; perhaps the reference is to the priests of the city of Tabor alone.

[123] The confession is published by A. Frinta, "Vyznání víry . . . Petra Kányše," *JSH*, I (1928), 6–8. For Peter's leading position see the testimony of Rokycana (more than twenty years later), in Z. Nejedlý, *Prameny k synodám strany pražské a táborské* (Prague, 1900), p. 150: ". . . quidam sacerdos Petrus dictus Caniss in civitate Thabor cum sibi adherentibus contra sacramentum altaris . . . consurrexerant. . . ."

chiefly valuable for providing still more information about Kániš's doctrine.[124] Thus we learn that Kániš had not only taken up the standard repertory of arguments against a real presence—there would be many Christs, Christ's physical body cannot be in two places at the same time, and so on [125]—but that he also stood for the positive content of Pikartism, as developed by Martin Húska—"The bread that I give is my flesh, for the life of the world" referred "to the virtues of Christ's body, which the individual man should take on." [126] Needless to say, the man who proclaimed these ideas at Tabor did not change his mind because Nicholas had written a tractate at Písek; what happened was that in the final contest at Tabor the party of order prevailed, and the Pikarts were expelled. The details are obscure, but the event must have followed Nicholas's tractate and also a letter sent to Prague by Nicholas and Master John of Jičín, at the end of February—it arrived in the capital on 28 February.[127] The letter describes the actions of the Pikarts in the city of Tabor, asks Masters Jakoubek and John Příbram for help in refuting the heresy, and warns the Praguers not to let the errors in question infect their own people. A year earlier Jičín had been among the most enthusiastic adventists and as such had received his own letter of refutation from Master Jakoubek; [128] now he appeared as a pillar of the party of order, on his way to an even more conservative position.[129] As for Nicholas, the turn to Prague must have been most unpalatable, but he must have regarded it as the inevitable price to be paid for the consolidation of the Taborite church under his own authority. Eventually he and other leading Taborite priests would themselves adopt eucharistic doctrines of an unorthodox sort, and Nicholas's tractate against Kániš would return to haunt him; but the needs of the time had to be served, the scholar had to yield to the statesman, and the Taborite clergy had to be brought into line with the policies of the men who had power.[130] Thus it would not be too

[124] Fragments are quoted by Rokycana, in Nejedlý, *op. cit., passim.*

[125] *Ibid.,* p. 152. See R. Holinka, "Počátky táborského pikartství," *Bratislava,* VI (1932), 194, for these and other arguments used by the Cathari and others outside Bohemia.

[126] Nejedlý, *op. cit.,* pp. 150 f.

[127] Laurence of Březová reports its arrival and contents, p. 474.

[128] See above, chap. vii, *ad* n. 12 ff.

[129] According to Příbram, *Život, KJBB,* p. 301, Jičín later wrote an orthodox tractate against Nicholas of Pelhřimov's quasi-Pikartism; Nicholas then "roused his gang against him" and wrote a treatise in his own defense.

[130] In 1443 John Rokycana attacked Nicholas's eucharistic heresies in a treatise *De existencia corporis Christi in sacramento* (*LČR,* No. 22), ed. Nejedlý, *Prameny k synodám,* pp. 116–153; he reproached Nicholas with having changed his ideas, after he had refuted Kániš: in 1443 Nicholas stood for the very doctrines he had written against in 1421. Nicholas replied that all of his eucharistic writings expounded the same

much to say that the campaign against the Pikarts was a consummation of the ambiguous alliance with Prague that had had its inception in the debate on rites at the house of Peter Zmrzlík.

The expulsion of the hard-core Pikarts from Tabor, to the number of two or three hundred,[131] was a step leading to their extermination. Most of them had no doubt shared in the great epic of Hussite striving, suffering, and success, but now they were no longer Hussites. Politically, moreover, they stood for both a rejection of Tabor's societal establishment and a negation of the national Hussite enterprise, which by 1421 had taken the form of a military and political coalition to set up a Hussite polity in Bohemia and to defend and extend the Hussites' power against the Catholics. Establishing themselves around the fortress of Příběnice, a few miles from Tabor, the Pikarts must have continued their contacts with their Taborite sympathizers; while at the same time developing their sectarian religion into forms of full spiritual liberty that previously had had to be restrained. From this time on the Pikarts are known in historiography as Adamites, who worked up the key themes of chiliast prophecy, Free Spirit liberation, and the Pikart love-feast into a higher stage that included ritual nudism and sexual emancipation.[132] Laurence of Březová reports:

---

doctrines, and he added: "quilibet prudens potest intelligere habita notitia terminorum, ad quam sententiam et ad quem finem mei tractatuli et praedicationes in materia sacramenti tendebant temporibus retroactis." This is the statesman's language of non-communication; I interpret it to mean: "If you recall the political situation you will understand why I had to attack Kániš at that time; inevitably, my arguments emphasized the real presence because I was, after all, attacking a Pikart." In fact Nicholas always did say he believed in a real presence, but he defined real in the sense of sacramental, i.e., figurative—at least when he was not attacking Pikarts.

[131] Laurence, p. 475, says the "fidelior pars" of the Taborites expelled "ultra ducentos utriusque sexus" of the Pikarts. *OCA*, p. 476 (Svejkovský, *Veršované skladby*, p. 161), says only that about three hundred Pikarts, including women and children, moved out from Tabor.

[132] The main sources are Laurence, p. 475 and, for a somewhat later time, pp. 517 ff.; *OCA*, pp. 476-478; *OCA-R*, pp. 29-31 (but a good part of the material on sex and nudism is drawn from Laurence, pp. 517 ff.); Aeneas Sylvius, *Historia Bohemica*, ch. xli; Jakoubek, *Výklad*, I, 526 f. Macek, *Tábor*, II, 321 ff., rejects all these sources as hostile slanders; more recently he concedes that there may have been individual cases of nudism and promiscuity (*ČsČH*, XII (1964), 862). See my "Free Spirit in the Hussite Revolution," pp. 181 f.; also the passages from Chelčický translated in my "Peter Chelčický," pp. 135 f. Kalivoda, *HI*, pp. 450 ff., offers a long discussion of the problem, but it is not clear what he concludes: possibly that the sources are unreliable but not necessarily all false, and that sexual freedom is not so dreadful anyway. Perhaps the best systematic treatment is that by Ernst Werner, "Die Nachrichten über die böhmischen 'Adamiten' in religionshistorischer Sicht," *Circumcellionen und Adamiten* (Berlin, 1959), pp. 73-134; he draws in a great deal of relevant non-Hussite material, and

Wandering through forests and hills, some of them fell into such insanity that men and women threw off their clothes and went nude, saying that clothes had been adopted because of the sin of the first parents, but that they were in a state of innocence. From the same madness they supposed that they were not sinning if one of the brethren had intercourse with one of the sisters, and if the woman conceived, she said she had conceived of the Holy Spirit.[133]

The sources never impute this sort of thing to Martin Húska, nor does it sound like him; one is therefore inclined to believe the report that he accepted an invitation to return from Příběnice to Tabor to argue his doctrines, and that the result was his public recantation in Tabor's church.[134] Perhaps this spectacular event was what made possible a Taborite expedition against the Příběnice group, some of whom were burnt to death. Their spiritual leader now was Peter Kániš, whose confession of faith, already referred to, was apparently issued as a manifesto for his brethren, perhaps to inform them that he, unlike Martin, had not recanted.[135] They also had other leaders, new men and indeed women, of simple origin, whose otherwise unknown names—like those of Rohan the blacksmith, Mary, Nicholas whom they called Moses, someone called Adam—survive to remind the historian of the extraordinary vivacity of the movement. It was Rohan who provided military leadership for those who survived the first Taborite attack and moved to a new seat, again not very far from Tabor. There, about 20 April, they were attacked by no less a force than John Žižka and his ally Lord Ulrich Vavák, and after bitter fighting were defeated.[136] Žižka brought the captives to Klokoty, in sight of the city of Tabor, and exhorted them to change their minds; then he burnt fifty of them, including Peter Kániš and another priest, and left the Taborites to burn twenty-five more.[137] It is noteworthy that at the same time the Praguers burnt their own Pikart, an otherwise unknown layman.[138] However, the sect was still not exterminated,

---

convincingly relates Adamite sexuality to the Free Spirit ideas of emancipation and renewal. In this regard one can profitably study the remarkable psychological interpretation of Free Spirit eroticism by Wilhelm Fränger, *The Millennium of Hieronymus Bosch* (trans. Wilkins and Kaiser; Chicago, 1951). The Adamites may yet turn out to be patron saints of the twentieth-century sexual revolution.

[133] Laurence, p. 475.

[134] *OCA*, p. 476; the report is rejected by Macek, *Tábor*, II, 321.

[135] The confession of faith begins, "Let my confession of faith . . . be known to all the faithful at Příběnice." (Ed. Frinta, "Vyznání víry," p. 6).

[136] *OCA-R*, p. 29. The best reconstruction of the details of the anti-Pikart campaigns is provided by Macek, *Tábor*, II, 337 ff.

[137] Laurence, pp. 475 f.

[138] *Ibid.*, p. 479.

and survivors fled to a nearby forest, around Bernatice, where still more were burnt, and then to the fortress of Ostrov, further to the south.[139] Their mutual love balanced by a totally nihilistic attitude to everything and everyone outside the group, they alternated their sex-play with expeditions to murder and pillage in the vicinity. For reasons that are not clear they were allowed to live on for several months, but on 21 October, after very fierce fighting, they were destroyed by Žižka and some baronial troops. Many Adamites were killed in battle, and all the prisoners were burnt, except one man spared to give an account of the sect's doctrines. Žižka sent this report to Prague.[140]

Among the victims of this extended and extensive terror was Martin Húska, who had disappeared from view after his recantation, in March or April. If he had dissociated himself from Adamitism, he remained nonetheless a Pikart, and perhaps it was his intention to propagate his sect outside the Taborite lordship, perhaps in his native Moravia. His name next appears when, on his way to Moravia with a companion, the priest Procop One-eyed, he was taken prisoner in Chrudim by the Hussite baron Lord Diviš Bořek.[141] After finding that Martin still believed that Christ's body was not in the Eucharist, Diviš struck him with his fist and prepared to burn him, but then yielded to the request of the priest Ambrose of Hradec Králové, that Martin and Procop be handed over to him. Ambrose took them to Hradec and spent two weeks trying to convert them, without success; he then washed his hands of the dirty problem by delivering them to Archbishop Conrad, in Roudnice, on 22 June. Conrad had adhered to the Four Articles, including utraquism, in April, much to the rejoicing of the Hussite right, but his chief desire seems to have been to keep his office and estates, and to avoid trouble; he therefore merely kept his prisoners in isolated confinement for eight weeks, without himself taking any measures to dispose of them. John Žižka suggested that the Praguers bring the Pikarts to the capital and burn them in the Old Town square, but the magistrates were afraid that Martin's sympathizers in Prague would make trouble; therefore they sent one of the town councillors and a professional torturer to Roudnice to extract information about Martin's teachers and followers. Hot irons were applied to the two prisoners, eventually perforating their flesh and piercing into their abdomens, but they kept silent; finally, when exhorted to return to "the unity of

---

[139] Macek, *Tábor,* II, 349.

[140] *OCA,* p. 478 (Svejkovský, *Veršované skladby,* pp. 162 f.); Laurence, pp. 517–519. The last item is exceptionally valuable, for it is one of the few noninquisitional reports of Free Spirit doctrines and practices. Filled with circumstantial details and proper names, it is clearly no pastiche of stereotypes, even though it was extracted by an enemy.

[141] Laurence, pp. 493–495, the source for this whole paragraph.

the church," they smilingly replied: "Not we but you are in error, seduced by the erring clergy into kneeling before a created thing—the bread of the sacrament." It only remained to burn both Martin and Procop, and this was done on 21 August; when he was urged to ask the onlookers to pray for them, Martin said, "Let those who need their prayers ask for them; we do not."

Neither Martin's death nor that of the Adamites, who had learned at least their Pikartism from him,[142] ended the Free Spirit movement in Bohemia. Alleged Pikarts—that is, people accused of various kinds of disrespect to the Eucharist—continued to be sought out and persecuted in Prague and no doubt elsewhere, and polemics against the heresy multiplied. A kind of Pikartism without Free Spirit sectarian content was in time adopted by the Taborites as their official doctrine, and such a man as Wenceslas Koranda, who seems always to have stood with the party of order, soon felt himself able to proclaim his solidarity with Martin's faith and memory, although he did take care to keep out of Žižka's way.[143] As for the Adamites, their peculiar practices seem to have been kept up for at least several years—in the mid-1420's they were described as actual by Peter Chelčický.[144] But the great battle was over: Tabor's future would be decided by the party of order, the reformation would be institutionalized, and the revolution would be consolidated—that is, halted. Whether the Free Spirit party could have provided any viable alternative may be doubted, for neither the divine intervention they preached, nor the human regeneration they sought, was a practical possibility.[145] There is much ancient wisdom on this point, and it is unfortu-

---

[142] Martin's final confession of faith chiefly concerned the Eucharist, for that was the doctrinal point at issue, but it also included the Free Spirit hopes incorporated in his Pikartism (see note 104 above, for the texts). The first item in the corpus of Adamite doctrines sent to Prague by Žižka was that these heretics "had been seduced by the priest Martin Loquis about communion in the body and blood of Lord Jesus; for they call ordinary bread and every food the body of God." This singling out of Martin's responsibility for just one error must have been meaningful; on the other hand, the whole Free Spirit matrix of Adamitism was certainly derived from the chiliast-Pikart stage in which Martin was the chief leader.

[143] Příbram, *Život, KJBB*, p. 294: Koranda carried Martin's final confession in his wallet; he showed it to other Taborites and said, "Ah, it was bravely Martin died for this!" Příbram also tells how Žižka was offended by this cult of Martin's Pikartism; he called some Taborite priests Pikarts, and Koranda steered clear of him for two years (or Žižka steered clear of Koranda; cf. Pekař, *Žižka*, IV, 199). Cf. also Příbram, *Život*, p. 294: before his death, Martin said there were a dozen Taborite priests who believed as he did.

[144] See my "Peter Chelčický," pp. 135 ff.

[145] Robert Kalivoda, *HI*, p. 491 and *passim*, offers a different judgement: order and stability as such were not at issue between what I regard as the party of order and a

nately all true. It was pungently expressed about 1421 by Jakoubek of Stříbro, in words that Nicholas of Pelhřimov could take over intact about ten years later:

> We do not consider to be true that story which some tell, that a good age is coming, in which there will be no evil-doers, and that they will not suffer at all, but will be filled with ineffable joy. For all this will be in Heaven [*in patria*]; but the things that are to happen here are uncertain.[146]

sectarian, subversive movement; rather there were two class-positions, each capable of developing its own order and stability. On the basis of his secularizing interpretation of Adamite and other ideology, he indeed manages to make this latter seem more practical than it appears in my account—he can speak of the Adamites as protagonists of "the modern European revolution" (p. 389). But I disagree with his basic method and also with what I take to be his overly optimistic idea of what modern man is capable of becoming. I agree that what happened in Hussite Bohemia was the first case of a type of revolution that has been a key factor in the progress of the Western world, but in all cases of this revolution the ideals of total emancipation and perfectibility have played a double role—as sources of inspiration but also of disruption, threatening the gains of the revolution itself.

[146] Nicholas's statement appears in his postil on Revelation, MS. 4520, fol. 80ʳ (originally quoted by Bartoš, "Táborské bratrstvo let 1425–1426 na soudě svého biskupa Mikuláše z Pelhřimova," *ČSPSČ*, XXIX (1921), 111; I have compared the manuscript text). Bartoš has since altered his dating from 1425–1426 to *ca.* 1430 ("Kdy vznikl Biskupcův Výklad na Zjevení Janovo?" *ČSPSČ* (1959)), and in matters of this sort it is best to follow him. But the passage in question is only a Latin version of Jakoubek's Czech statement, *Výklad na Zjevenie Sv. Jana* [Postil on Apocalypse], ed. F. Šimek, I (Prague, 1932), 295 f.; for the dating of this work see *LČJ*, No. 99, and Šimek's introduction, p. xvii.

X

THE CAUSE OF THE
PRIESTS OF TABOR

NICHOLAS BISKUPEC of Pelhřimov was the first bishop of Tabor and also the last. Elected in 1420 at the age of about thirty-five, he was still on hand in 1452 when the independent life of the Taborite reformation was ended. In that year George of Poděbrady conquered the city, forced its inhabitants to become part of the national polity and the national Hussite church, and imprisoned the two leading recusants, Nicholas Biskupec and Wenceslas Koranda, both of whom died in captivity. To make sure that the germs of subversion would not survive to infect others, George tried to destroy Nicholas's written works and ordered the persecution of those who possessed them.[1] But he was too late. Nicholas had been a prolific

---

[1] F. M. Bartoš, "Konec Mikuláše Biskupce," *Křesťanská revue* (1961), No. 6, *Theologická příloha,* pp. 90–93, with references to the older literature; for background see F. Heymann, *George of Bohemia, King of Heretics* (Princeton, 1965), pp. 230 ff., 247 f., where, however, George's war against Nicholas's works and ideas is not discussed. The main source appears in the *Monumenta historica universitatis pragensis,* III (Prague, 1844), 56 f., a series of entries "De quibusdam studentibus, baccalariis et magistris captivatis per Rectorem," "ex mandato regiae majestatis." Although well enough known in the Czech literature, the passages pertaining to Nicholas Biskupec may be usefully quoted here: "[16 April 1461] mag. Nicolaus de Horzepnik ex mandatis regiae majestatis per Rectorem Universitatis est detentus et post carceribus mancipatus, quia suspectus fuit in materia fidei ex libellis sacerdotis baccalarii, Nicolai dicti Biskupecz, qui circa eum erant repositi . . . tractatuli venenosi et infectivi, quos idem mag. negavit se habere, sed quod fuissent combusti, et post sunt inventi, dum Rector Universitatis cum aliis ad hoc vocatis cameram ejus ex mandato regio est ingressus. . . ." Then: "Item post hoc in propinquo sacerdos Joannes bacc. dictus Morawek est detectus similibus conjecturis, quia commissarius erat praedicti Biskupzonis, in cujus cistula epistolae et tractatuli plurimi venenosi sunt reperti. . . ."

writer throughout his career; some of his works have certainly been lost but a great many survive, among them his unique masterpiece of *Geistesgeschichte,* the "Chronicle containing the cause of the priests of Tabor, and the attacks on it by the Prague masters." [2] Begun in 1435, a year after Tabor's defeat at the Battle of Lipany, the chronicle is really a systematic collection of material to document the whole course of the disputations between Prague and Tabor, from 1420 to 1444, with the works of both parties either given in full or summarized. Nicholas must have seen that the days of Taborite messianism were over, that his own generation of heroes was getting old; with no new one rising to take up the cause, he saw that the time had come to write the record. He remembered the experience of his youth, when he had followed John Hus, Jakoubek of Stříbro, and Nicholas of Dresden in their great dream of a church regenerated first in Bohemia, then in the world. This ideal of regeneration and reconstruction was the authentic message of Hussitism, and to Nicholas it was identical with the cause of the priests of Tabor, a cause that he would deliver to the judgement of future generations:

> He who bears witness to these things and who has written them down knows the truth about what has taken place between the two parties . . . since the time when Master John Hus, of holy memory, preached. . . . And let those who read or hear these words know that he has written . . . only what is true, so that anyone who looks at the record with an impartial eye can judge the truth of the cause of the priests of Tabor, on the one hand, . . . and on the other hand, of the attacks by the masters.[3]

This invitation was taken up in the age of the Reformation,[4] but rarely since that time. It is not easy to use lengthy statements of doctrine in a

---

[2] Of the Latin works, the "Taborite Confession" of 1431 has been published by Flacius Illyricus, *Confessio Valdensium* (Basel, 1568), and again by Balthasar Lydius, *Waldensia,* I (Rotterdam, 1616), 1–303; Lydius also published some lists of Taborite articles, doubtless composed by Nicholas. The two orations at the Council of Basel, one defending the Prague Article on punishment of mortal sins, the other replying to the Catholic spokesman on this point, Aegidius Carlerius, have been edited by Bartoš, *Orationes,* Archivum Taboriense (Tabor, 1935), pp. 3–32, 36–82; for Carlerius's speeches see Mansi, XXIX, 868–972, XXX, 388–456. The *Cronica causam sacerdotum thaboriensium continens et magistrorum pragensium ejusdem impugnationes* has been published by Höfler, II, 475–820; the last part has been very usefully supplemented by Z. Nejedlý, *Prameny k synodám strany pražské a táborské v létech 1441–1444* (Prague, 1900). The major Latin works still in manuscript are the Postil on Apocalypse (*ca.* 1430), and a Postil on the Harmony of the Gospels (*ca.* 1435–1439); both are very long.

[3] Höfler, II, 476 f.

[4] See the references to Flacius and Lydius in note 2, above; also my "The Religion of Hussite Tabor," *The Czechoslovak Contribution to World Culture,* ed. M. Rechcigl (The Hague, 1964), pp. 211 f.

historical account, nor can Nicholas's presentations be accepted at face value: the critical historian must have constant reference to the frequently unpublished survivals of texts that Nicholas omits or compresses, and the cause of the Prague masters must be treated more amply than he did. In the present context, moreover, this work of critical reconstruction need be carried only to the point at which Tabor's religious development was complete. By 1424 all of her doctrines had been defined and given official formulation as a norm within the Taborite brotherhood and as a document in the debate with Prague. There were still twenty years of controversy ahead, but the products of that period will be used only when necessary to explain the earlier texts. The problem here is not one of systematic theological analysis, but one of history; it is the problem of tracing the development of Tabor's religion as a response to attack by Prague and as an expression of the nature of Taborite society.

FROM THE MEETING OF 10 DECEMBER 1420 TO THE MURDER OF ŽELIVSKÝ, 9 MARCH 1422

In the course of 1420 a number of Hussite parties and programs had emerged to claim either power or the right to survival. By the end of the year there were two main contenders, each with its variations. The Taborites, dominated by the party of order, stood for a reconstruction of Bohemian society on the basis of religious radicalism; they wanted a Hussite king and a Hussite bishop, but neither official would have resembled his legitimate counterparts elsewhere in Europe, for the Bohemia that they would have presided over would have been a mosaic of reformed communities. The basic unit, as the history of the Taborite brotherhood shows, would have been the congregation, under the secular rule of feudal lords in the countryside or of magistrates in the towns; larger units could be formed by various kinds of association, including domination of the peasantry and gentry by the towns, in a kind of city-state. Priests would interest themselves in governmental policy, and secular magistrates would provide for the support of the clergy and also enforce religious discipline. In matters of rite and doctrine there would be considerable leeway; any uniformity would result not from the bishop's power but from a consensus to be achieved at synods of the clergy. Such a program involved acceptance of permanent schism with the Roman church. Implied by the sectarianism that flourished on the Hussite left after 1415, the radical program emerged in a well developed form among the Taborite congregants of 1419; then, after the chiliast episode, it reappeared as the subject of controversy between radicals and conservatives during the defense of Prague. By the last months of 1420 it had become the program of an independent Taborite society. Here as before, the politics of this program involved an alliance between the radicals of the countryside and those led by John Želivský in Prague.

Against the radical program there stood the stubborn opposition of a conservative coalition—most of the Hussite barons, most of the propertied burghers, most of the university masters, and of course the clergy and commoners who followed these leading elements. What the conservatives wanted was essentially the program of John Hus, whose closest friends and followers were in fact the leaders of university conservatism. Their main idea of reform was that of replacing the authority of the papacy and the papally-directed hierarchy over the Bohemian church with the authority of the university and of the legitimate political powers of the realm. At the same time the church's property would pass under the civil dominion of the secular powers; the regular clergy and superfluous secular clergy would be eliminated; the rites and practices of the church would be simplified and purified but usually not changed in substance. Based on an alliance between Prague and the barons, this program looked toward the establishment of a Hussite monarchy by bringing into Bohemia a member of the ruling dynasty of Poland-Lithuania, and by securing the allegiance of even the Catholic barons to the reconstituted state. They also sought to legitimize the Hussite church by reintroducing episcopal authority in the person of the legitimate Archbishop of Prague, Conrad, who in fact joined the Hussites on 21 April 1421 and gave utraquist communion with his own hands. The history of Europe a century later would show that a program of this sort necessarily implied schism with Rome, and the fact seems obvious in retrospect, but in the first part of the fifteenth century it was not obvious at all. The age of the Schism and of the councils was a time of very bold exploration in both theory and practice, and there were many men in all countries who felt that the patterns of authority and power in the church might indeed be modified. A good part of the program of conservative Hussitism had actually been put into practice in France in 1398 and more drastically still in 1407; fourteenth-century England had more than once seen the national and evangelical opposition to papalism working in alliance; the concilarists had gone far indeed to proclaim a Europe of local churches.[5] In none of these cases was

---

[5] The liberties of the Gallican Church are discussed systematically by V. Martin, *Les origines du gallicanisme,* I (Paris: Bloud & Gay, 1939), 29 ff.; the programs of 1398 and 1407 are treated on pp. 243–340. Haller, *Papsttum und Kirchenreform,* I, discusses both Gallicanism and its debt to English theory and practice in the fourteenth century; he also indicates some of its relationships to conciliarism, the national component of which was at least as important as its more abstract and universal theories.

church property actually secularized, but in 1455 Aeneas Sylvius Piccolomini could argue before the pope that the secularization effected in Bohemia should not constitute a bar to reunion of the Hussites with Rome.[6] In other words, it was possible for the conservative Hussites to hope for such reunion without sacrificing the reforms they had carried out; in fact such a hope was necessary if the reforms were to be legitimate. They were after all reforms of the church, and there was only one church—holy, Roman, apostolic, and catholic.

It was a peculiar feature of conservative Hussitism that it included utraquism—logically it should not have, but historical understanding can go only so far in rationalizing the past. For a few years after 1414 Jakoubek of Stříbro had managed to direct the Hussite reform away from the path laid out by John Hus; relying on the support of the radicals, he had succeeded in making the lay chalice a pan-Hussite tenet. His national leadership indeed rested on his special combination of radicalism and conservatism, and without him the movement would have quickly split into two warring camps. But his capacity to hold right and left together could not survive the hardening of the parties into two different societies—a fact that became clear rather slowly, as the Prague-Tabor opposition revealed its inner logic. In the Prague debates of August 1420 he stood with the other university masters in rejecting Tabor's demands, but he did not then insist on a formal condemnation of Taboritism—indeed, he gave his approval to the destruction of images, cloisters, and unnecessary churches; he did not condemn the violence with which Catholic priests were ousted and church property was expropriated; in general he tended to support all acts by which the cause was promoted.[7] In October, to be sure, he came out in his preaching against the Taborites' liturgical reforms, but in reasonable terms. The Taborites had argued for the norm of Christ's precepts and practice, and had asserted that "Christ officiated without the modern rite"; Jakoubek replied that Christians were obliged to imitate Christ's moral actions but not necessarily the others, like walking on water. His basic principle here was his old one; even practices not explicitly founded in the Bible should be retained, if they were not directly opposed to the divine law but rather promoted it and increased devotion.[8] The class of practices justified by this principle was larger now

[6] My "Pius Aeneas," p. 299.

[7] Bartoš, "Studie o Žižkovi a jeho době," *ČČM*, XCVIII (1924), 100 f. (see above, chap. viii, n. 43).

[8] Bartoš, *loc. cit.*, quotes this passage from a sermon that Jakoubek preached *ca.* October 1420: "Circa ritum misse, si aliqua sunt in legis divine promocionem sive in devocionis excitacionem et non sunt legi divine ex directo contraria nec eciam sunt explicite in lege fundata, talia non sunt a spiritu mendacii, sed veritatis, quia dicit Salvator: qui non est contra nos, nobiscum est. Sed arguunt: Christus sine ritu moderno

than it had been some years before, but Jakoubek could still feel, no doubt honestly, that it was not he but the Taborites who had moved away from the old unity.[9]

Considerable light is thrown on his views in this period by the work of a master who looked to him for leadership, the Prague historian Master Laurence of Březová. Laurence's chronicle, composed at least a year or two later, reflects its author's current hostility to both the Taborites and John Želivský, but his verse compositions of the second half of 1420, particularly the "Dispute between Prague and Kutná Hora," show a very different attitude.[10] In this work, written in November, Laurence personifies Prague and Kutná Hora, the capitals of Hussitism and Bohemian Catholicism, as women, one beautiful the other ugly; they conduct a dispute before Jesus Christ, in the course of which, Kutná Hora accuses Prague of responsibility for the destruction of images, churches, cloisters, organs; the prohibition of precious vestments and utensils in the mass; the killing of priests; the abrogation or modification of festivals and fasts—in short, the whole catalogue of radical reforms. In each case Prague responds with a defense, not a denial:

> Lord Jesus, judge of our disputations
> Served mass without these preparations,
> Nor enjoined them he indeed;
> And this the faithful all should heed.

> Churches and altars that I need
> Destroy I not, no indeed,
> Nor by me are they even damaged;
> Only the superfluous are ravaged.

> He who doesn't have a fish,
> Let him eat another dish.

> If counterfeiters may be killed,
> And brigands, men with murders filled,
> Then how much more is killing valid
> For men who preach a faith that's squalid.

---

officiavit. . . . In oppositum: si Christus est in omnibus imitandus, tunc et sacerdos communicantibus debet pedes lavare. Sed dicendum, quod non est in omnibus imitandus sic, quod in mari ambularet, sed in moralibus."

[9] Above, chap. ix, n. 87.

[10] The "Hádání Prahy s Kutnou Horou" has been published, along with related works, by J. Daňhelka, *Husitské skladby budyšínského rukopisu* (Prague, 1952); the passages I translate begin on lines 983, 1015, 1733, 1275, 2933. My doggerel reflects an opinion about the merits of the poetry that specialists do not share.

But in a curious fashion the defense is distinguished from absolute approval. When, for example, Prague is accused of having priests who wear beards, she replies that only some priests of her party do so. And when Christ pronounces his verdict at the end, his approval of Prague's cause is modified by his criticism of various unworthy Hussites, including some of the radicals:

> There are some among your clerks
> Infringing Scripture in their works;
> The views of the saints they refuse to share,
> And little for their order care.

Thus while Prague speaks for the whole Hussite cause and loyally defends the legitimacy of many radical practices, she is made to distinguish between not only good and bad, but between good, better, and best. This was the policy that had united the Hussite movement in 1418; it was clearly Jakoubek's policy in the autumn of 1420.

Since there were practical military reasons why Prague and Tabor should not fall into outright opposition, Jakoubek's flexible line could seem useful. But those masters who saw the situation more clearly knew that the immediate advantages of conciliation were not worth their price, which included renunciation of any hope that Bohemian Hussitism might find a legitimate king, secure the political allegiance of the Catholic barons of the realm, or win toleration from the Roman church. The only course that could secure these benefits would be the defeat and extermination of Taboritism and its allied groups. John Příbram saw this and responded by compiling his seventy-six "Pikart" articles, in fact the full corpus of what conservative Hussitism regarded as Tabor's heresies, whether in fact Pikart or Waldensian. The Taborite mass was included among these heresies and was therefore condemned in terms far more absolute than those of Jakoubek's rejection. Hence when the secular leaders of both sides arranged the meeting of 10 December, the conservative masters' tactic was to pronounce Příbram's heretication in advance of any discussion; realizing that the divided Taborites could not undertake to defend the articles condemned in the list, the masters hoped that Tabor's party of order would dissociate itself from at least some of the articles, and in so doing recognize the university's *magisterium,* or that at least the air could be cleared for anti-Taborite action. As it happened the tactic failed, but only temporarily, and the discussion that in fact took place between Jakoubek and Nicholas of Pelhřimov served merely to reveal the inadequacy of the former's policy in the new situation.

Jakoubek's position proceeded from his old distinction between the essentials and the accidentals of the mass, but this time he moderated it in a conservative sense. The essentials might not be changed, but the accidentals too should be kept insofar as they were not against the law of God but rather served to promote the faith. In general, he argued, the church's traditions should be kept unless there were reason for not doing so.[11] This position made a possible reform of the liturgy a matter for rational debate, and it was in a similar sense that Nicholas set forth his views at the meeting and then in an official text that Koranda delivered to the Old Town Hall on 3 January.[12] He repeated the argument that the Taborites had advanced some months earlier:[13] Christ had not officiated at the Last Supper in Roman-style vestments, but rather in his ordinary garments; nor had he used the many prayers and ceremonies that formed part of the Roman mass. His apostles had held to a similarly simple rite, adding only a few things, including the Lord's Prayer, and dropping a few, such as the washing of feet. "If we are priests of Christ," Nicholas wrote, "then we do not know whom we should follow other than Christ and his apostles."[14] The modern rite had been developed by popes and other men "who had declined very far from the life of Christ and the apostles"—and here Nicholas included the historical material, drawn from Jakoubek's *De ceremoniis* and from Nicholas of Dresden, to show how each item of the Roman rite had been decreed by this or that pope.[15] Thus it was safer to follow the Taborites in this matter; in fact, it was a grave sin to prefer the worse to the better, and those doing so were hypocrites.[16] Jakoubek reacted to this charge with bitterness, and Nicholas offered a conciliatory clarification: he did not regard the Prague mass itself as sinful or illicit, nor did he assert that Tabor's mass was mandatory—only

[11] Laurence, p. 464.

[12] Laurence, pp. 463 f., reports what Nicholas read out at the meeting, "in hec vel similia verba." Nicholas's chronicle contains the official text prepared for deposit in Prague's Old Town Hall (Höfler, II, 488–501); it must have been this text that Wenceslas Koranda delivered to Prague on 3 January, after he had presented its gist orally, in the form of a sermon (Laurence, pp. 466–469). The sermon is given by Laurence, again in "hec vel similia verba," and seems obviously based on the official text, although Koranda added some comment of his own. On the other hand, although the official text includes most of what Nicholas reportedly read out at the meeting, the phrasing and order are different—presumably the official text was a more ample redaction of the former one. Nor, finally, is there any certainty that the official text, preserved for us only in Nicholas's chronicle, was not somewhat improved by him when he came to compose the chronicle, fifteen years later; see note 18 below.

[13] Above, n. 8; cf. chap. ix, n. 75.

[14] Höfler, II, 491; for a similar formula see Nicholas of Dresden's *Apologia*, Hardt, III, 594.

[15] Höfler, II, 557–560 (Nicholas of Pelhřimov's response to the *De ritibus misse*); cf. Jakoubek's *De ceremoniis*, ST, II, 149 f., 154 ff.; cf. Nicholas of Dresden's *Puncta*, MS IV G 15, fol. 36ʳ. For the connection see Bartoš, *Husitství a cizina*, pp. 133 f.

[16] Höfler, II, 492 f.; cf. Laurence, pp. 463 f.

that it was permissible.[17] Delivering this treatise in Prague, Koranda went out of his way to say that the Taborites had no fundamental objection to some kind of special liturgical vestment, to be worn over the priest's clothes when he was officiating.[18] In part a concession to Želivský's party, which did not follow Tabor's rite,[19] this was also an invitation to the Praguers to accept the Taborite reform as legitimate, although different from their own.

All of this must have been very embarassing to Jakoubek, for Nicholas showed great talent in basing his case on the former's earlier positions, set forth in the period "when Master Jakoubek agreed with us in this matter." [20]

[17] Jakoubek, *Výklad na Zjevenie sv. Jana,* ed. F. Šimek (Prague, 1932), I, 103 f., a sermon that he preached, according to the editor, *ca.* 20 December 1420 (*ibid.,* p. xii). Here Jakoubek lashes out against those "who abuse others and have an exalted idea of themselves . . . , often branding as a grave sin what is not a sin"—"Just as now," he continues, "they suppose and say that to serve mass in ornates, albeit simple ones, is in itself a sin. And they imagine that they themselves are on the side of the good in this matter." Nicholas's clarification, Höfler, II, 488 ff., did not to be sure retract the charge of hypocrisy (below, n. 18).

[18] Laurence, p. 469: "Vel aliter dicimus, quod non contradicimus, quod in distinccionem habeatur vel teneatur aliquod signum moderatum, non ab antichristo institutum, in quo offerentes Christum a laycis distinguantur: in hoc volens, ut in superpelliciis divina ab omnibus peragerentur." The meaning here is not perfectly clear, and perhaps the last passage ("in hoc . . .") is Laurence's comment. But cf. Nicholas's official text, Höfler, II, 493: "nec adhuc aestimare debent [magistri] se posse hypocrisim eis objicienti effugere, quando audientes nuper ab uno ex fratribus nostris, quod aliquis possit aliquando ex certis circumstantiis in illis eorum vestimentis . . . missare, in hoc non peccando. . . ." If this referred to Koranda's concession, it must have been inserted afterward; on the other hand it may refer to an otherwise unknown incident, and Koranda may have touched on the point in the course of presenting the official text itself.

[19] Nejedlý, V, 39, characterizes Želivský's rite as a true mass, but simplified in décor and translated entirely into Czech. Bartoš, *Kniha Zdeňka Nejedlého* (Prague, 1915), pp. 17 f., argues that Želivský's party simply followed the Taborite rite. His evidence does not seem conclusive, however: part of it is drawn from Laurence of Březová's accounts of cooperation between Želivský and the Taborites, accounts that prove at most only the radicals' opposition to the liturgical Romanism of the conservative masters; the one clear evidence, a statement in Nicholas of Pelhřimov's Postil on Apocalypse, that some of the Praguers follow the Taborites in rituals, dates from *ca.* 1430 and is therefore irrelevant (for the text see Bartoš, "Táborské bratrstvo," *ČSPSČ,* XXIX (1921), 116; for the date, Bartoš, in *ČSPSČ,* LIX (1950), "Kdy vznikl . . . Výklad"). Moreover the Prague magistrates several times prohibited the Taborite rite in the city (Laurence, pp. 448, 477; see below, *ad* n. 77), and Želivský certainly accepted the decree of the Prague synod of 4–7 July 1421 on this matter (below, *ad* n. 68 ff.). It was only at the end of 1421 that his party declared in favor of the Taborite principle (Laurence, p. 530), to what practical effect we do not know.

[20] Höfler, II, 489.

He was referring above all to Jakoubek's *De ceremoniis* of about 1415, which on point after point contrasted the practice of Christ and the apostles with that of the modern church, and argued that the safest course was to follow what Jesus did or instituted for the Primitive Church to do. His arguments here have already been canvassed in chapter iv, but it is worth recalling that in the matter of rites and vestments Jakoubek then drew the conclusion that the Taborites were now asserting: since Jesus and the apostles had used neither the rites nor the vestments of the Roman church, modern priests did not have to use them either. He had, to be sure, added that ordinarily, apart from cases of necessity, the modern rite ought to be followed, but the thrust of his argumentation was in the opposite direction.[21] Perhaps Jakoubek now realized that his old theories would no longer do; in a sermon preached soon after the meeting of 10 December he shifted to Příbram's position: even the accidentals of the mass were apostolic ordinances—minor ones, to be sure, in contrast to the major ones ordaining the essentials—and the Taborites, who scandalized many by their innovations, should recall the millstone that ought to be tied to the neck of him who gave scandal.[22] Here too Nicholas could rake up the ashes and remember that Jakoubek "used to say in his sermons that it was better to let scandal arise than to give up the truth."[23] The fact was that the early Jakoubek, with his declaration of war against the Antichrist embodied in the Roman system, had become quite a burden to the Prague cause. Again and again the Taborites justified their sectarian ideas and practices by reference to what Jakoubek once had declared, and with the latter's prudent qualifications omitted; the result, he complained, was that the conservative masters and priests of Prague accused him of responsibility "for all the evils now current in the realm."[24]

It is not surprising, therefore, to find that Prague's position in the matter of rites was defended against Nicholas's treatise not by Jakoubek but by John Příbram. The younger man, once Jakoubek's follower in the struggle for infant communion, was rapidly emerging as—in his own boast—"the zealous persecutor of all heresies," a role that he would play for a long time to come. Of his original radicalism there remained only a violent temperament,

[21] Above, chap. iv, *ad* notes 148–159.

[22] His otherwise unknown sermon is referred to by the Taborite treatise, Höfler, II, 494 ff.

[23] *Loc. cit.*

[24] In the "Apologia contra Taboritas," ed. J. Sedlák, *ST*, II, 161–164, Jakoubek complains about the Taborites' invocation of his authority for reforms going beyond the limits he had set. "Nicholominus," he continues, "tamen odientes me sacerdotes [et] magistri dicunt, quod ego cum meis predicacionibus sum reus omnium malorum iam currencium in regno." Cf. *Výklad*, II, 633.

harnessed now to a veritable passion for solidarity with the universal church, which in due course he would not hesitate to call the Holy Roman Church.[25] Had it not been for him, the principle of two reformations advanced by Nicholas, which was also a principle of religious freedom, might have prevailed; the treatises of both parties, deposited in Prague's Old Town Hall, would have acquired a kind of legal solidity that might have done duty for the genuine agreement that by this time was out of the question. Instead Příbram committed his party to the tactic of heretication, by developing the relevant portions of his *Contra articulos picardorum* into an absolute condemnation of the Taborite liturgy; his new treatise, the *De ritibus misse,* was pronounced publicly at the University of Prague, and copies were then sent to the various communities of the realm. In other words, the university was no longer debating with the Taborites, it was asserting its claim to judge and condemn them. This was a renunciation of the program of the meeting of 10 December; as Nicholas of Pelhřimov complained, Příbram had published his condemnation "even though the issue and discussion between the parties had not yet been decided."[26]

---

[25] Příbram identified himself in his Apologia (*ca.* 1427), MS D 49, fol. 333[r]: "Ego vilissimus omnium hominum peccator, verumptamen omnium heresum et precipue Wyclefistice et pikardice heresis sollicitus persecutor." In the 1430's he wrote, in his *Cum ab inicio* (*LČP,* No. 24), MS D 47, fol. 39[v], that the faithful were obliged to accept the "punctum . . . de invariabili et firma adhesione et obediencia ecclesie sancte Romane." Cf. n. 39, below.

[26] The verbal correspondence between the two tractates was noted by K. Krofta, "O některých spisech M. Jana z Příbramě," *ČČM,* LXXIII (1899), 217, but he did not try to determine how they were related. The relevant sections of the *Contra articulos* are of course those dealing with rites and vestments (§§ 22–24; MS 4749, fols. 62[v]–66[r]). The verbal agreement is so extensive and obvious as not to require proof, but the occasional differences are instructive. Thus on fol. 65[r], proceeding with his proofs, Příbram writes: "Et ad idem sunt multa antiqua concilia ecclesie primitive, inter que unum allego, scilicet Concilium Tolletanum undecimum . . ."—there follows a presentation of one of that council's canons, and then, "Alia consilia dimitto," after which Příbram passes to a text from Wyclif. In the *De ritibus misse,* however, the other councils are not omitted— there is a whole section on them (Höfler, II, 520–523), including an identical presentation of the Toledo canon just mentioned. But the *Contra articulos* was written before the end of 1420 (Krofta, *op. cit.,* p. 210, according to a scribal *explicit* with that date), while the *De ritibus* was a reply to the Taborite treatise brought to Prague by Koranda on 3 January 1421 (note 12, above). It is possible that Příbram cited only one council in the earlier work because he had not yet finished his research, but it would seem more likely that he selected the one from a dossier that he had compiled, perhaps when the issue of rites came to the fore in the summer of 1420, and that he simply included more of the dossier, or perhaps all of it, in the *De ritibus.* The latter is listed in *LČP,* No. 6 (but cf. *LČJ,* No. 83; Bartoš's view that Příbram included or worked up a work by Jakoubek seems to me highly unlikely); the text is published as part of Nicholas's

To understand the issues at stake in this stage of the controversy it will be well to consider just what the Taborite liturgy was at this time. Our best description is provided by Laurence of Březová, at three points in his chronicle.[27] First the priests and brethren would kneel, their heads touching the ground, and pray the Lord's Prayer, in the vernacular; there were no preparatory prayers, as in the Roman rite. Then the officiating priest would rise, stand over the bread and wine (which were on an unconsecrated altar [28]), take the bread in his hand, and consecrate it by pronouncing the scriptural text, "After Jesus had eaten, he took bread, and blessed it, and broke it. . ." and so forth, including the formula, "This is my body, . . ."[29] All of this was in the vernacular, as was everything else. Then he similarly consecrated the wine. After this he broke the bread and took communion; then the other priests came up and took communion; finally the priests turned to the people and gave them communion, one priest handing out the bread, another administering the wine. But even in this early period the normal Taborite mass probably included Czech gospel-readings and a sermon before the actual consecration, with congregational singing of Psalms, the Ten Commandments, and the Creed; the songs written for this purpose still survive.[30] Moreover, the text used in the consecration seems to have either varied or developed, for other sources show the actual words of institution contained in more complex texts than the one recorded by Laurence.[31] The simple décor of the mass should also be noted: the priests wore no special vestments, were not tonsured, did not shave; the altar was unconsecrated and could be any table or other object, covered to be sure by a cloth; the bread was ordinary leavened bread, and the wine was not mixed

chronicle, Höfler, II, 502–545. Nicholas writes of the treatise that the masters "publice in universitate Pragensi pronuntiari [illum] fecerunt" (p. 502), and in his response (pp. 545–574) complains, "male a magistris de nobis scribitur per communitates, nondum decisione causa et discussione inter nos consumata, quod infundate et sine omni deductione posuissemus dicta nostra de ritu nostrae missationis" (p. 573).

[27] Laurence, pp. 406 (translated above, chap. vii, *ad* n. 73), 474, 530. See the exhaustive discussion in Nejedlý, IV, *passim*, and 213 ff., with references to almost all the sources.

[28] Nejedlý, IV, 210 f.

[29] The words quoted by Laurence, p. 530 (" 'dominus Jesus, postquam cenavit, accepit panem et benedixit, ac fregit' . . .") are not directly from any one biblical text; they combine elements of Matt. 26:26 ff. and I Cor. 11:23 ff. The present Roman missal has a somewhat different formula.

[30] Nejedlý, IV, 270 ff.

[31] *UB*, II, 522 f. (a combination of scriptural passages, used by the Taborites in Procop's time); *Mon. conc. saec. XV*, I, 259 (a description of the Taborite mass as celebrated in Basel, during the time of the Council; the formula seems to be that of the Roman missal).

with water; the vessels of the ritual were ordinary cups and plates.[32] The church was bare of statues, paintings, and other adornments; there were no side altars and no votive masses—only the one congregational service each day. It is clear that everyone was expected to attend and, unless prevented by serious indisposition, to take communion.

Laurence of Březová's descriptions convey a lively sense of the shock experienced by those who observed this rite for the first time, and there is other evidence, too, that more conservative Hussites, not to mention Catholics, were revolted by Tabor's rough simplicity.[33] Nor are accusations lacking that the simplified mass was worse than merely rough: John Příbram, for example, paints a stimulating picture of the Taborite priests practicing their odious rites on ordinary stones of the field, using as covering a bedsheet on which God knows what had taken place the night before, and using as vessels any old cups and plates.[34] But such charges may have been extrapolated on the basis of sentiment; Nicholas Biskupec, at any rate, denied them categorically: all the equipment of the mass was special and kept apart from ordinary use; even in the field, when serving with the army, the priests had a special wagon containing the cloths and vessels, the bread and wine, that would be used for mass.[35] But was it in fact a mass? It did, to be sure, preserve the four essentials—the proper material of bread and wine, a duly ordained priest, the correct words of institution, and the true intention of consecrating—but otherwise it differed so radically from the Roman rite that it hardly seemed a mass at all: this was the charge of Tabor's opponents, and in fact, as Zdeněk Nejedlý has observed, Tabor's rite was really something new.[36] More to the point would be John Příbram's characterization of the new rite as "schismatic"—that is, with respect to the rite of the universal church that included both Prague and Rome.[37]

It was in this sense that Příbram worked out his attack on the Taborite liturgy in his *De ritibus misse*. The treatise begins with the prime "supposi-

[32] Nejedlý, IV, 210 ff.

[33] See below, n. 171.

[34] *De ritibus misse,* Höfler, II, 510.

[35] Höfler, II, 566: ". . . in civitatibus, in quibus missamus, habemus utensilia specialiter distincta, et in exercitu campestri specialem currum distinctum, in quo haec deducebantur, et non constat nobis, quod unquam aliquis in fratribus nostris hoc, quod magistri in nos mendaciter testificantur, fecisset."

[36] Nejedlý, IV, 198.

[37] In the *De ritibus misse* Příbram wrote that the Taborite principle, applied in practice, was "inductivum schismatum errorumque multorum" (Höfler, II, 531). Ten years later, in 1430, he spoke of the "celebrationem schismaticam suarum missarum" (*Professio fidei,* in Cochlaeus, *Historiae Hussitarum libri XII* (Mainz, 1549), p. 544).

tion" that "Every institution of God or of the holy mother Church that does not destroy but rather aids the Law of God, and the following of which is not of itself a sin, is to be observed by the faithful." [38] While obviously close to Jakoubek's principle of conservation, cited above, this formula nevertheless contains an important difference, for while Jakoubek spoke of laudable customs, Příbram preferred to talk of institutions or statutes, thus setting aside the residue of his colleague's subversive past. There was still room for disobedience—and of course the utraquist Příbram *was* disobedient—but only in exceptional cases: the norm was obedience to the clerical institution and conformity to the catholic tradition. Later on Příbram would go even further: in the matter of utraquism he declared that he disobeyed only the will of the office-holder in the church, not the office itself.[39] But even in January 1421 he was close to a Romanism that was only slightly more liberal than that of the pope. Thus he began by finding the Roman rite prefigured in the Old Testament, on the basis of the traditional glosses and commentaries on the relevant passages. He contrasted his pious adherence to these glosses with the Taborites' *luciferina superbia;* they interpreted the Old Testament as they pleased, to justify their killing, plundering, and destruction of churches, but would not accept the "exposition of the holy, catholic, universal church." [40] In any event, the case for the Roman rite had other support as well: Příbram argued that Christ had after all had more than one set of clothes—the ordinary ones and the snowy white ones of his transfiguration—and that the apostles had instituted special vestments for the mass, as well as the various portions of the liturgy that Tabor rejected.[41] Here he appealed to the oral tradition that according to Augustine was of great import: the Greek church, founded directly by the apostles, still had liturgical vestments; the immediate disciples of the apostles, Saints Clement, Anacletus, and others, had decreed special vestments, utensils, and rites; St. Dionysius, Paul's immediate disciple, had described a rite of mass that

[38] Höfler, II, 503; see Nejedlý, V, 66 f., for the difference between Příbram's position and Jakoubek's.

[39] In the *Professio fidei* of 1430 (in Cochlaeus, *Historia Hussitarum libri XII,* pp. 525 f.) he defined his obedience so: "teneo et volo usque ad mortem meam esse humiliter subiectus et obediens ecclesiae sanctae Romanae, et eius summo Pontifici et legitimo, et omnibus aliis praepositis et praelatis meis, et hoc in omnibus licitis et honestis, Deo et legi eius non adversis. . . . Et hic notanter adjicio, quod semper subesse debeo omni tali officio et potestati, sed non semper praesidentis voluntati; semper officio, sed nunquam malo imperio." Here Cochlaeus has added a marginal note: "Misere torquet hunc Bohemum communio laicorum sub utraque specie."

[40] Höfler, II, 504 f.

[41] *Ibid.,* pp. 505 f.

corresponded to the modern one and was in fact that observed in Prague.[42] Furthermore, these apostolic rites were continued in the Roman church by the early popes and councils "long before the Donation of Constantine" which, of course, marked the end of the Primitive Church.[43] If subsequent popes specifically decreed this or that rite, they were merely implementing what had been instituted in primitive times; in any case, the church's statutes were to be obeyed, when not unreasonable.[44] As Příbram observed in a slightly later work, there had to be one standard rite; otherwise the door would be open to endless schisms and the ordinary uneducated priests would be hopelessly confused. Even if a few elements of the modern mass were added by post-Primitive popes, the observances were not therefore invalid, for even the worst men can do good things.[45] As for the Taborite liturgy, which claimed to follow Christ's institution in the Last Supper, it deviated from that model in no less than twelve ways—for example, in not taking place in the evening, in not having everyone seated, in not prescribing the washing of feet; nor indeed were all of Christ's other actions during his life imitated in their details.[46]

No less interesting than Příbram's main line of argument are the general tone of his work and his habit of going out of his way to make nasty little

---

[42] *Ibid.,* pp. 506 ff. For the rite of (Pseudo-) Dionysius see pp. 513 ff. and 534, where Příbram insists that the Praguers observed it, against Nicholas's charge that the Prague rite was not that of Dionysius (pp. 494 f.), but that of the Roman popes (p. 492); Nicholas then proved the last point by the historical dossier referred to above, n. 15. At this time Nicholas was rather noncommittal about the merits of Dionysius's rite—which seems to have been Příbram's "discovery" (Bartoš, *Kniha Zd. Nejedlého,* p. 11, n. 4); later Nicholas took some trouble to show that the Taborites *did* observe this rite (*loc. cit.;* Nejedlý, IV, 219 ff.).

[43] Höfler, II, 519.

[44] *Ibid.,* p. 537: "obediendum est statutis ecclesiae et doctrinis credendum in omnibus veris, licitis et honestis etiam sub poena aeternae damnationis; ut enim illi culpandi sunt, qui sub nomine et occasione calicis multa inutilia adhuc tenent [a reference to those to the right of even Příbram?], ita illi, qui sub eodem nomine calicis plurima fidei adversa et omnia ecclesiae statuta quantumcunque licita volunt abrogare;" cf. pp. 520, 531. On p. 533 he says that even if the Prague mass had been decreed by the post-Primitive popes, still "idem illud sic rationabile teneremur sub praecepto observare"; the "precept" was that of I Pet. 2:18.

[45] *Ad occurrendum homini insano* (see above, chap. ix, n. 60), MS 4937, fols. 152ᵛ-fol. 153ᵛ; in particular (fol. 153ʳ, sq.): "neque enim sequitur, si pape quosdam ritus addiderunt, quod ergo non sunt // observandi; cum pessimorum regum Israhel et Juda plurima facta nedum per populum Israhel sed per deum in construccione templi et sacrificiorum sunt laudata et in fine [m?] observata: cur ergo hic similiter non fieret, circumscriptis superfluis et ad[h]ibita modestia in talibus dirrectiva."

[46] Höfler, II, 540 f.

remarks about his opponents. He mocked them for having falsely predicted the end of the world and the salvation of only five cities; he recalled how they had passed so suddenly from pacifism to violence; he reproached them with their church-burning, killing, plundering; he accused the priests of encouraging and even participating in the savage warfare of their party.[47] The priests of Tabor were guilty of devilish pride, unheard-of stupidity, and innumerable acts of sacrilege; Nicholas's tractate was a bit of fluffy incompetence that could be blown away with one breath—"the spider thinks it can spin threads of iron!"—and indeed Příbram wonders whether the brethren had ever read the Law of Christ.[48] Nicholas had appealed to Jakoubek's *De ceremoniis,* but Příbram said this was not a tractate, only a repertory of authorities for and against, and that it was not meant for publication or circulation—the Taborites had, he said, gotten a copy by guile, through one of their brethren.[49] The first point here was not true, to judge by the surviving texts, and Nicholas had enough faith that his own text was standard to be willing to compare copies with Příbram.[50] In any case, Nicholas's argument also drew from other works of Jakoubek's early period, and he was certainly right in his view that the old Jakoubek had worked out the arguments for very extensive liturgical reforms that the masters were now set against.

Here it is of considerable interest that Příbram also makes an appeal to the good old days of Hussite unity: on several occasions, citing Origen, Chrysostom, and Matthew of Janov, he refers to the fact that the Taborites had once (*olim*) commended these teachers, and in one passage he is more specific: "A year ago [*ante annum*]" the priests of Tabor had declared their adherence to the *magisterium* of these three men in the most exalted terms.[51] Just a year ago would have been January 1420, at the height of the adventist fever, and the reference cannot be applied to that time; more likely Příbram had in mind the very important but woefully obscure discussions of October and Novem-

---

[47] Höfler, II, 531, 538, 541 f., 544.

[48] *Ibid.,* pp. 505, 510, 518, 532 ("the spider . . ."), 538.

[49] *Ibid.,* pp. 544 f.; see above, chap. iv, *ad* n. 235.

[50] Höfler, II, 572: ". . . parati sumus cum eis [*scil.,* magistris] ejus exemplaria auscultare."

[51] *Ibid.,* p. 519 ("Utinam igitur suscipiatur probatio tam docti et tam sancti viri [*scil.,* Chrysostom] a fratribus thaboriensibus olim valde commendati."); p. 531 ("Utinam saltim hunc mellifluum Mathiam [*scil.,* of Janov] testem suscipiant fratres thaborienses, et quem ante annum amplexu cordis et corporis una cum beato Chrysostomo et Origene sibi asseruerant in magistrum laudibus perfecte efferentes, non . . . hunc respuant"). In the *Contra articulos picardorum,* MS 4749, fol. 65ʳ, there is material corresponding verbally to that in Höfler, II, 519, including the passage quoted.

ber 1419, in Prague—a time when the Taborite political movement had not yet been captured by the sectarians (Waldensians, Pikarts) in its midst.[52] By the beginning of 1421, of course, the great heretical threat was the Pikartism of Martin Húska's party, and Příbram may have been warning the Taborite majority that the only alternative to this tendency was recognition of Prague's authority. Elsewhere in the *De ritibus misse* he suggests something of the sort more directly: the Taborites will be accursed if they convert the sacrament of the Eucharist into a meal—a direct imitation of the Last Supper; if they destroy the wonted reverence for that sacrament and to this end burn churches, destroy altars, holy vessels, and vestments; and all this to wipe out the distinction between layman and priest. But they will be blessed if they take the opposite tack.[53] A clear reference to the intra-Taborite struggle over Free Spirit sectarianism, the passage is also one of several in which Příbram condemns the Taborite liturgical reform by Pikartizing or hereticating it.[54] And the threat was clearly stated: if the Taborites succumb to Pikartism, there will be no more arguments with them—we supply: there will be war.

Although the *De ritibus misse* was met by a Taborite reply, there is no evidence that the latter was published or that the controversy continued.[55] On the other hand, Příbram's tactic of Pikartizing Tabor's party of order may well have contributed to the campaign that led to the isolation, expulsion, and extermination of the Pikart sect at Tabor. For even though the internal development of Taborite society required such a campaign, the Pikart problem might not have been solved so quickly or so ruthlessly if Nicholas Biskupec and his associates had not felt obliged to preserve at least the forms of Hussite unity. John Žižka, for one, would not tolerate anything less. His zeal in slaughtering the Pikarts has already been described, and even the non-Pikart priests had reason to fear him, for he was opposed to their liturgical reforms.[56] As long as these were kept a religious issue he did not try to interfere, but he would not tolerate their interference with the Hussite political and military enterprise. On 26 March a Taborite priest named

---

[52] See above, chap. vi, *ad* n. 123 ff. Pseudo-Chrysostom, Origen, and Matthew of Janov were indeed among the main authorities of the Hussite radicals, who perhaps used them against the conservatives in the arguments of autumn 1419.

[53] Höfler, II, 541 f.

[54] E.g., *ibid.*, pp. 531, 538; at the same time it is clear from pp. 540 f. that Příbram recognized the *non*-Pikart practice of Nicholas's party—he merely went on to imply that it might well lead to Pikartism.

[55] Höfler, II, 545–574.

[56] See the chronicle translated by Heymann, p. 9; also the *Chronicon veteris collegiati Pragensis,* Höfler, I, 88: Žižka's "Orphans," unlike the Taborites, celebrated mass in ornates.

Antoch preached that the Prague masters were one of "the horns of the Beast" on account of their stand on rites and vestments, and he, together with other priests, led a group of Taborites out of Prague, where the allied armies were assembled; Žižka rode after them and stopped them, raining blows on many of the priests.[57] In the light of this sort of tension we can understand why, at the end of February, Nicholas of Pelhřimov joined Master John Jičín to ask Jakoubek of Stříbro and John Příbram for help in refuting Pikartism, and to warn the Praguers to guard against the heresy in Prague itself. Jakoubek responded with a straightforward eucharistic treatise; Příbram, however, attacked not only Pikart eucharistic beliefs but also some of the basic Free Spirit heresies, and even threw in a refutation of the Taborite liturgy.[58] But the last section was not included in all copies of the work—perhaps a sign that Nicholas's tactic of generating areas of agreement was effective.

The pressures that he evidently felt at this time were, paradoxically, the result in part of Tabor's military achievements in her own behalf and in alliance with Prague. The winter and spring saw Hussite power extended over a major part of the realm, to the point where the Catholic powers recognized that continued war would do them no good. The time had come for the Hussites to press forward with their national plans. On 21 April the conservatives could draw added confidence from the conversion of Archbishop Conrad; there was no reason now why the estates of the realm could not join for their common benefit, without regard to religious differences. Thus the leaders of national Hussitism called for a diet, to meet in Čáslav on 3 June, and to include not only all the Hussite groups but also the Catholics.[59] The diet met with the Catholic barons in attendance and agreed on a far-reaching program of national reconstruction, including a repudiation of Sigismund as king, a renewal of the efforts to get a king from Poland, and the formation of a regency council that would include all the estates and control all national military resources—in view of the anticipated second crusade and in order to repress all dissension in the realm. When the council would need advice on religious matters, it was to turn to Master John Příbram and John Želivský; this was as bizarre a team as could be imagined, but one that represented what were obviously felt to be the two major Hussite groupings—those who looked to the university, and the coalition of radicals that included Želivský's following in Prague and the Taborite

---

[57] Laurence, pp. 477 f.

[58] See my "O traktátu Ad occurrendum homini insano," *ČsČH*, VIII (1960), 895–904, esp. n. 15a.

[59] For the Čáslav Diet see Heymann, pp. 220 ff., and the same author's "The National Assembly of Čáslav," *Medievalia et Humanistica*, VIII (1954), 32–55.

brotherhood in the country. The common program of both groups, the Four Articles of Prague, was now affirmed as a national program, with the support even of the Catholics, who promised—how sincerely we do not know—to hold and defend the Hussite program, unless and until the Hussite priests and university masters were convinced by scriptural proofs that the Four Articles were wrong.

All of this made removal of intra-Hussite dissension seem absolutely necessary, while at the same time suggesting that the time had come to unite Hussites and Catholics in the national church headed by Conrad. At Čáslav, therefore, the archbishop sent out a summons to all the clergy of his province, both Hussite and Catholic, to meet in Prague on St. Procop's Day, 4 July.[60] Since national unity under these conditions would have meant suppression of radicalism by a coalition of Catholics and conservative Hussites, the Taborite-Želivskian alliance determined on countermeasures.[61] On 30 June, Želivský brought his New Town followers into the streets, led them to the Old Town Hall, and succeeded in forcing the removal of the councillors of both towns. The two communities were merged and elected four captains; then on 2 July the communities elected fifteen councillors from each town, to work as a single body. The purpose of this coup was to promote the cause of religious radicalism, more specifically the body of beliefs and practices held by Želivský, shared in part by the Taborites, and derived from the program of Jakoubek of Stříbro. Hence Želivský tried to draw the latter and his considerable following into the radical alliance. At the same meeting that chose the new town councillors, Želivský proposed still further action:

> See, now you laity are joined as one; if you want us clergy also to be one, and not divide the people, you must expel Master Christian [of Prachatice], parish priest of St. Michael's, from his church, together with his priests. For they refuse to conform to our practice but still hold to their humbug [that is, according to Laurence of Březová's note, their rites]; they do not give communion to infants, nor do they sing mass in Czech, as is done in other churches.

[60] Laurence, p. 491.

[61] Heymann, pp. 241–243, explains Želivský's coup differently: the priest Ambrose, leader of the Hradec Králové radicals, had come to Prague and complained of the treachery of the barons; the charges led to controversies among the people of Prague; Želivský then seized his chance. My interpretation is based partly on my sense of the political situation, partly on the evidently close collaboration between Želivský and the Taborites at this time, as shown below. Thus I interpret Laurence's statement, pp. 495 f., that the coup was begun "ex occulto tractatu quorundam cum domino Johanne presbytero," as a reference to plans made by Želivský and the Taborites.

And the people, shouting their agreement, "commissioned Master Jakoubek and John Želivský to install other priests in place of the legitimate ones." [62] By this time, moreover, there were many Taborite priests in Prague for the synod. Some of them, including John Čapek, preached in the Týn Church against the policies of conservatism and attacked Prague's recognition of Archbishop Conrad as head of the Hussite church; the new town councillors not only did not stop this preaching but provided an allowance to support the visitors. [63] Two Taborite priests, named Procop and Phillip, were obtruded into the Church of St. Peter, *Na Poříčí,* and the existing rector was removed because he had served mass in ornates—no doubt excessively sumptuous ones. [64] Similar efforts were made in two other churches, including an unsuccessful attempt to install one William, a close associate of Želivský, into Christian's church of St. Michael. [65] Although on this point as on others, Jakoubek refused to play the role Želivský had allotted him, the radical coup did succeed in checking the conservative program.

Thus the synod turned out to be rather progressive after all. The Catholic clergy did not attend; nor did Conrad attend, for he delegated his presidency to Masters John Příbram and Procop of Plzeň, who then acknowledged reality by coöpting Jakoubek and Želivský. [66] The committee of four organized the synod into four sections—those of Prague, Hradec Králové, Žatec, and Tabor; each section was assigned the task of discussing a number of proposed articles, and when majority consent had been reached, Příbram read out the list, article by article, in the presence of clerics, magistrates, and members of both the lesser and higher nobility. He asked for consent to each item and in most cases received it, only the Taborites objecting to certain ones—"especially those prescribing ecclesiastical rites and observances." Otherwise they accepted the synod's decisions, which were clearly inspired by a desire to secure the kind of unity that consensus alone could provide. [67]

---

[62] Laurence, p. 497.

[63] Laurence, pp. 498 ff.; cf. p. 478.

[64] Laurence, p. 497, and p. 407, where it is said that some of the Praguers followed the Taborites in the matter of rites, and that the turnover in St. Peter's, among others, was due to women—*begute*—who refused to tolerate service in ornates. I do not think this was Želivský's position. The Procop in this episode is often identified as Procop the Shaven, but there is no evidence for this.

[65] Laurence, p. 497.

[66] The decrees of the synod are given in *UB,* I, 128–134, and in Laurence, pp. 499 ff., where there is more of the background. Nejedlý, V, 45 ff., brings out the progressive character of the synod.

[67] Apart from Laurence's statement, p. 500, that the Taborites's opposition was directed especially to the articles defining rites and observances, there is positive evidence that the Taborites accepted other articles—see notes 68 and 92, below.

Most of the articles dealt with clerical standards and discipline (every priest to have a Bible, no fornication, no selling of the sacraments, and so on); there was a repudiation of the clergy's exercise of civil dominion; there was a very strong version of the clergy's duty to wipe out public mortal sins. Moreover the reforms introduced by Jakoubek's adherents were safeguarded against reactionary attack:

> To avoid various perils, we declare that in connection with ecclesiastical rites, those things that have been reasonably and for certain causes omitted in the Prague communities should be held and regarded as definitely omitted, unless a more reasonable or useful cause should occur for resuming such a rite.

This certainly pleased Želivský and the Taborites, both of whom could also accept the doctrinal norms of the synod: the Bible, the standard creeds, and "all the decrees and reasonable . . . statutes of the apostles and of the Primitive Church." [68] But the Taborites, unlike Želivský, must have rejected the article concerning the rite of mass:

> The order and office of the holy mass are to be diligently observed in every rite and action [*gestu*] emanating from and exemplified by the Primitive Church, and approved and held by the saints of the Primitive Church; and in the usual vestments [*in habitu communi*] that some call the *orarium,* others call *ornamenta:* unless unavoidable necessity prevents, each and every officiant must observe these things, to the exclusion, however, of all superfluity and lavishness.

Even here, however, the Taborites might have given this article the kind of acceptance that a minority gives to the unpalatable decisions of a majority, with the understanding that they would nevertheless continue their own rites, perhaps under the cover of "necessity." In any case, although the synod, with Conrad's consent, chose its four presidents as a permanent body to govern the clergy, there could have been no thought that this Prague body would exercise jurisdiction over Tabor. The spirit of the synod was that of Jakoubek in his period of statesmanship, when he had sought to keep the movement together by providing elastic formulas of unity as covers for actual diversity.

Had he continued in this policy, all would have been well for the radical alliance. Unfortunately he now found so much to criticize on the left that his

---

[68] Thus Příbram, writing in 1429, could recall that at the St. Procop's Day synod in Prague, the Taborite priests "promised . . . to hold faithfully to the decrees of the apostles and all the decrees and institutions of the Council of Nicea and of all other councils of the Primitive Church" (*LČP,* No. 18; the text in K. Erben, *Výbor z literatry české,* II (Prague, 1868), 424).

position became practically indistinguishable from that of the right. Laurence of Březová, who can be regarded as Jakoubek's adherent, probably represents the latter's view of the radical alliance in the summer of 1421; all trace of objectivity disappears as he describes Želivský's coup and the concomitant actions of his party, and at every point he raises the charge of Pikartism. He surrounds the account of the coup with material bearing on the Pikart menace, sometimes out of chronological order; he constantly attaches the phrase, "suspect of Pikartism," to Želivský's councillors and to the priests obtruded into the various Prague churches; he inserts the text of a complaint by some Prague women, perhaps followers of Jakoubek, against Taborite priests and Pikarts, indiscriminately.[69] But in fact the situation was more complex than he indicates, both in Prague and among the Taborites. Genuine Pikartism certainly persisted in both places; according to the complaint just mentioned, certain Taborite priests had instructed some Prague women that the bread and wine after consecration were only blessed, not changed into Christ's body and blood, and the priests had told the women to perform the consecration of the Eucharist themselves.[70] But these priests did not belong to the Taborite majority. In a sermon preached about mid-June 1421, Jakoubek complained of Latin and Czech tractates blaspheming the Eucharist; at about the same time he associated the Taborite liturgy with the eucharistic heresy, as Příbram had done, but in reverse order. The apostles, he said, had ordained the praiseworthy and devotionally suitable rites of the mass, but now "some have gradually put aside that rite and thereby cleared a path for Antichrist, and they have caused even the faith in the Eucharist to be abandoned."[71] This was probably a correct explanation, although it could be put in more objective terms: the nature of Taborite society required a radical reform of the rite of mass, and this reform required a change in the concept of the Eucharist. But it was not a change to Pikartism. The Czech treatises Jakoubek objected to may have been Pikart, but the Latin ones certainly were not. The priests of Tabor had not been unaffected by the persecution of the Pikarts; they addressed themselves to the eucharistic problem in many treatises, and eventually worked out a position of their own: the consecrated bread and wine were not, as the Pikarts said, merely food that had been blessed, but rather the real body and blood of Christ, in a sacramental or figurative sense. Christ was in them by his real presence, but

---

[69] Laurence, pp. 493–499.

[70] Laurence, p. 498.

[71] Jakoubek, *Výklad,* II, 19, complains of the tractates blaspheming the Eucharist; according to Šimek's dating (I, xiv), the passage would fall into mid-June 1421. Jakoubek's remark about Tabor's rites is in *Výklad,* II, 21; for Příbram's suspicions see Höfler, II, 541 f.

not through either transsubstantiation or consubstantiation: the presence was sacramental, not substantial. At the same time it was real, and the Taborites accepted the decree of the St. Procop's Day synod to this effect.[72] The details of this new theory will be discussed in the following section; the point here is that while it was not Pikartism, it might very well seem to be so, to those lacking sympathy or a spirit of toleration. Moreover, many of the cultic observances associated with the Eucharist presupposed a substantial presence, and the Taborites therefore rejected those observances in a way hardly distinguishable from that of the true Pikarts. Thus while Laurence of Březová was hardly correct in Pikartizing the Želivskian-Taborite alliance, he may have been sincere; and perhaps it was this issue, fused with Tabor's liturgical reforms, that provoked Jakoubek to throw his lot in with the conservatives.

The political situation was similarly complex. Želivský's power lay in the New Town, where his following included many men of some substance but probably even more of the poor, who did not possess the town franchise, and hence were unable to vote or hold office.[73] In the Old Town his following was less. He could bring the crowd into the streets when necessary and force the removal of existing councillors and the choice of new ones more to his liking; sometimes, as on 2 July, he could introduce structural changes in the government. But he either could not or would not carry through a democratic revolution backed up by terror against the masters and propertied burghers; hence the new councillors were never quite reliable, and once the crowd had dispersed, the basic realities of Prague's social and political life tended to impose themselves on the magistrates. Insofar as Želivský tried to maintain his leadership between coups, his position was that of a tyrant, alienating even those who might have favored him on religious grounds. In the coup of 2 July, one of the men he chose to be councillor refused, because the election violated the legal order, and this—we are told—was the general attitude of the "mature and propertied." [74] Jakoubek, whom Želivský sought to capture as an ally, also refused, and not for religious reasons alone. The Romanizing practices preserved so imperturbably by Christian of Prachatice were as offensive to Jakoubek as to Želivský, but Christian had been the friend and patron of John Hus, the protector and material benefactor of Jakoubek himself; one put up with the quirks of such a man.[75] The Hussite university masters were colleagues who disagreed with each other on the

---

[72] See below, n. 92.

[73] F. Seibt, *Hussitica* (Köln: Böhlau, 1965), p. 142, offers an interesting discussion of Želivský's difficulties. See also above, chap. vi, n. 24.

[74] Laurence, p. 496.

[75] Bartoš, *HR*, I, 142 f.; F. Borecký, *Mistr Jakoubek ze Stříbra* (Prague, 1945), p. 9; Nejedlý, V, 63.

basis of a certain mutual understanding; Jakoubek had worked successfully in that milieu and no doubt hoped to do so in the future. Looking at Želivský and the Taborites, however, he now saw only subversion of sound order, perversion of true reform, a spirit of mutiny productive of endless error. In fact he saw Antichrist, the old enemy who had found permanent employment in Jakoubek's mind as the villain of every drama. Now Antichrist spoke through the mask of Želivský.

Thus the month of July saw the Želivskian-Taborite alliance in Prague subjected to increasing attack, from a coalition of conservatives with followers of Jakoubek. Želivský's absence from the city on a military expedition made the coalition's task easier, but the turmoil in the city became chronic, with neither side winning a permanent victory. Pressure was brought on the magistrates by various means, including the women's complaint mentioned above, to remove Taborite priests from Prague churches, and Procop and Phillip, who had been installed in St. Peter's, were the first to suffer: they were arrested.[76] There must have been a mass-meeting of protest shortly after, for the two priests were subsequently released. Then on 21 July the conservative-center coalition summoned a meeting of the "great community" —the citizens of both Prague towns meeting together—and, led by Jakoubek, they had a number of reactionary decrees passed, including the reimprisonment of Procop and Phillip, as well as the imprisonment of those laymen who headed the pro-Taborite movement. At the same time there were decrees against those practicing or preaching the Taborite reform of rites, and against those holding to Pikartism. Finally a corps of investigators was set up, fifty from each town, to search out Pikarts and priests who refused to obey the masters.[77]

Two days later the conservatives had the satisfaction of killing a Pikart. The investigators—one guesses it was they—had turned up a certain Wenceslas, a cobbler, who did not believe in the Real Presence and turned his back on the sacrament when it was brought to him; he was burnt to death. The next day, 24 July, the great community met again, but this time in a mood of revulsion, and in effect reversed the earlier decisions: no one now was to abuse another by calling him a Pikart; if he did, he would have to prove his charge or suffer the same punishment his victim would have undergone.[78] Presumably the prisoners were now set free, and the dominant

---

[76] Laurence, p. 499, gives an unclear account of the effect of the women's protest: the councillors did not like it, but at a later meeting of the community it found approval, the "sanior pars" leading the whole. There are no details about the subsequent antiradical actions.

[77] *AČ*, I, 204–205; *AČ*, III, 237–239; *LČJ*, No. 85.

[78] For the burning of Wenceslas see Laurence, pp. 475, 508. For the meeting of 24 July see *AČ*, I, 206.

sentiment in Prague was such as to make further Pikartizing very hard.
Žižka, however, was in the city at the time, recovering from injuries that had
cost him his one good eye, and he contributed to the campaign by asking the
magistrates to bring Martin Húska and Procop the One-Eyed from Conrad's
prison in Roudnice to Prague, to be burnt as an example. The magistrates
refused, fearing tumult from Martin's sympathizers, but they did send an
interrogator and a torturer to Roudnice to get information about Prague
Pikartism. After this effort had been made, Martin and Procop were burnt to
death, with Martin defiantly proclaiming that a dozen Taborite priests held
with him, and the event was indeed followed by new arrests in Prague of
suspected Pikarts—one Kašek, a resident of the New Town, and three priests
of Tabor, Procop the Shaven, Jira of Klatovy, and Abraham, the last guilty
of not allowing candles to be burnt before the Eucharist.[79] Again, however,
the real issue must be seen elsewhere than in Pikartism. Abraham's refusal
may have had a liturgical rather than a doctrinal import, or may have been
based on Tabor's non-Pikart eucharistic doctrines; the three priests may have
been offensive merely because they had been intruded into Prague churches.
Moreover, another source tells us explicitly that in the great party conflicts at
Tabor, at the end of 1420, both Procop and Abraham were opposed to
Martin Húska.[80] In any case, these arrests were not followed by executions,
and it is likely that the prisoners were quickly released.

But the turmoil went on, involving all the major issues of Hussite policy,
in a context that can only be outlined in these pages. Again and again
Želivský had to act to preserve or extend his control over the city, and to
oppose the political constellation that the conservatives were trying to put
together. He attacked the efforts to get a king from Poland-Lithuania, he
attacked the barons as a class, he attacked the Prague-conservative and
baronial efforts to work out a national order, he attacked the university
masters, particularly his old enemy Christian of Prachatice.[81] Příbram, as we
might expect, worked closely with the barons; Jakoubek carried on an
incessant campaign of propaganda and intrigue against the radicals, against
the magistrates put in by Želivský, and against the latter himself, whom he
accused of having caused all the turmoil and bloodshed, and of having
seduced the whole realm. The leading figure in the anti-Pikart campaign of
July, he continued to Pikartize everyone on the other side, no doubt more
and more recklessly.[82] He was now joined heart and soul with the other

[79] Laurence, pp. 493–495.
[80] Above, chap. ix, n. 122.
[81] Laurence, pp. 509 ff. See the account in Heymann, pp. 265 ff., 307 ff.
[82] This is according to "Priest William's Accusation" against Jakoubek and the other
masters, after the murder of William's leader, Želivský: AČ, III, 237–239 (also OCA-R,
pp. 43 f.) Jakoubek's sermons of the time also show a continuing preoccupation with
the Pikart menace (Výklad, I, lxxxi, sqq.).

masters, including the most reactionary, and on 12 November the whole group met in the Carolinum to defend their authority against Želivský and the Taborites in the city.[83] They insisted that the official directors of the clergy, set up by the synod of 4–7 July, actually function as such, with the power to prohibit the preaching of unapproved novelties, to prevent Taborite priests from working in the city without permission, to prevent priests from being installed in churches without the directors' approval; and no one was to defend those whom the directors condemned. In form an admonition to obey existing law, the action was clearly directed against Želivsky, as he declared; it is therefore highly instructive to see that the masters did *not* raise the issue of eucharistic heresy—Pikartism—but this time resorted to the issue of Purgatory, which all the Taborites indeed rejected. Exactly what the masters wanted from Želivský is not stated, but it must have been a declaration of belief in Purgatory and prayers for the dead; instead they got a quasi-Taborite response, Želivský and his followers saying that they knew of no scriptural proofs for such belief. Two days later they got something else: a radical counterattack that secured the removal of Příbram and Procop of Plzeň from the board of directors and their replacement by John Kardinál and Peter Payne, along with Jakoubek and Želivský.[84] Then somewhat later the radicals more or less openly stated their belief in the first principles of Tabor's doctrinal system, although they may not have used the blatantly Taborite language reported by Laurence of Březová:

> A congregation of the community met in the Town Hall and concluded . . . that no priest might dare to hold or publish those things without which the human race could be saved; also that all those things that Christ and his apostles did not teach should be abandoned and entirely abolished, for Christ in his New Law adequately set forth what was pertinent to salvation.[85]

Laurence then adds: "For this reason they sought to cancel all ecclesiastical rites"; in other words, if we can believe him, Želivský's party was henceforth indistinguishable from the Taborites in liturgical practice.[86] This was of course a flat rejection of the masters' authority—not just resistance but actual schism—and like the Taborites before them, the radicals accompanied their action with a demand that the masters be subject to the Town Hall. Specifically, in this case, the demand was that all the university's charters, liberties, privileges, and statutes be deposited in the Town Hall so that the

[83] Laurence, pp. 521 ff.
[84] *Ibid.,* pp. 523 f.
[85] *Ibid.,* p. 530.
[86] *Ibid.,* p. 531, and see above, n. 19.

people might look at them and decide if anything in them were contrary to God's Law and hence in need of correction. The decree was not carried through.

Here as previously, Želivský could win only a battle, never the war. And a month or so later power passed from his hands to the conservatives, who were not reluctant to do what he shrank from doing, murder the enemy. The details of the upset need not be described; they involved a drastic intervention by leaders of the allied Hussite armies in Prague's political life as well as the relentless agitation of Jakoubek of Stříbro.[87] By now the real reasons for his hatred of Želivský were unimportant, just as Jakoubek's general authority had become a thing of the past: he was now a bitter party leader who did not hesitate to upbraid the new town magistrates, elected in consequence of the conservative action just mentioned, with negligent tepidity in the face of Želivský's schismatic turbulence. "Be diligent! Stop him!" was what he said, thus giving the magistrates the support of John Hus's successor in the pulpit of Bethlehem Chapel. Two days later, on 9 March 1422, they acted. Inviting Želivský and some associates to the Town Hall, the magistrates at first pretended to be interested in his opinion of some military problems; then the militia rushed in, arrested the radicals, and led them off to be beheaded in the courtyard—Želivský and nine others. The outrage of his followers fired a fury of riot and revolution in which revenge was taken against both the magistrates and the masters, and the government of Prague passed once again to the left.[88] But soon after, on 17 May, the long-awaited prince from Poland-Lithuania, Sigmund Korybut, entered the city and inaugurated a new period of conservative ascendancy. Korybut had become a utraquist for the occasion, but his aim was to lead the way back to the Church; thus the conservative masters and barons had a prince who wanted exactly what they did. And although Korybut's first period of rule was rather short—he left at the end of the year—the integration of right-wing strength and hope that he achieved remained the pattern for Prague's future policy. The struggle with Tabor had been bitter enough in 1420-1421; now it would get even worse.

INTERNAL WAR AND SCHISM, 1422-1424

Nicholas of Pelhřimov's chronicle ends the first encounter between Tabor and Prague with his reply to Příbram's *De ritibus misse,* perhaps January or February of 1421; it then jumps to its second episode, the debates

---

[87] Heymann, pp. 310-315, with references to the sources, especially "Priest William's Accusation."

[88] Heymann, pp. 315 ff.; for Korybut see pp. 319 ff.

at Konopiště in the late spring of 1423. Since Laurence of Březová's chronicle ends in December of 1421, the story of the year or so preceding Konopiště can only be reconstructed, painfully and often dubiously, from a few bits of information and from the doctrinal sources. Similar difficulties attend the history of the next, and for our purposes last, disputation, in October and November of 1424, and it could be argued that in view of these problems narrative should yield to analysis, for the doctrinal sources are reasonably abundant. But in fact these sources cannot be properly understood apart from their sequence, nor can the extremely tendentious accounts offered by Nicholas be criticized and supplemented without due attention to the development in time and in detail of what he was concerned to present under the aspect of eternal verity. In short, the following reconstruction is necessary, but also very tentative, and it will be densely studded with the usual words indicating inference, conjecture, and pure guesswork.

Although the issue of rites and vestments retained its vitality, and indeed figured prominently at Konopiště, it had to share the stage first with the issue of the Eucharist, and then, in 1424, with virtually all of the other doctrinal and ritual differences between Tabor and Prague. As the Taborite church was consolidated the schism between the two societies became worse, not better, and it was reinforced by their political and military competition, as two power-centers each seeking to increase the extent of its dominion in the realm. In fact, they sometimes fought or came close to fighting real battles with each other, a circumstance that made religious debate at once more urgent and more hopeless. Furthermore in these years, and indeed up into 1427, the dominant figure among the Prague masters was John Příbram, working hand in hand with Korybut and the barons; his great aim, pursued with ever increasing self-consciousness, was to eliminate every element of Hussitism that would make reunion with Rome nonnegotiable. It is worth bearing this in mind, for his total war against Taboritism was only the first stage of a development that would lead him to a wholesale repudiation of Wyclif in 1426 and, by 1430, to a partial rejection of John Hus.[89] In fact his fall in 1427, followed by nine years of "exile" from Prague, was due to just this reckless fanaticism, which tended to cut the heart out of even the Prague reformation.

After the advent of Korybut had restored Prague to conservative leadership, it became both possible and necessary to define the orthodoxy of

---

[89] For the rejection of Wyclif, which also of course implied a rejection of Hus, see the notice to this effect in Nicholas's chronicle, Höfler, II, 593 ff.; also the listings in *LČP*, pp. 71 ff. In the *Professio fidei* of 1430, Příbram says he approves of the works of John Hus and Matthew of Janov only insofar as they are catholic (in Cochlaeus, *Historiae Hussitarum, libri XII*, p. 540).

Prague's church—or more precisely, the church subject to Archbishop Conrad—in opposition to Tabor and other radical communities. Korybut summoned a synod for this purpose, to meet at the end of May 1422, but it probably met sometime in the first half of June; the text of its decrees, differing sharply in subject matter and tendency from those of the preceding year's synod, clearly betrays the leading role that John Příbram must have played.[90] The seven sacraments, called "necessary and salubrious antidotes of souls," were defined in function and form in a completely orthodox sense, obviously against Taborite rejection or modification of them; the only exception, of course, was that the Eucharist was to be given in both kinds and to infants. Purgatory, the cult of saints, the Roman rite of mass, the traditional fasts—all were to be held. And there were prohibitions of the handling of liturgical vessels by the laity, of the burning of churches and altars (unless strictly necessary), of participation in warfare by priests. There were also some other decrees, in several cases similar to those of the synod of July 1421, but the most important one was undoubtedly that defining the divine presence in the Eucharist. Here the difference between the two synods was very marked, and it will be useful to quote both decrees:

[1421] Let all priests believe with most faithful heart, and confess with most sincere voice, that the whole lord Jesus Christ, true God and man, with his own body and blood, is with us in his real presence in the most divine sacrament of the Eucharist, under the form of bread and likewise under the form of wine. And let them announce to the people that this is to be faithfully held and believed by all.

[1422] It is to be held and believed that Christ, true God and true man, is in the visible sacrament of the Eucharist according to his own nature and corporeal substance, and according to his natural existence—the very same one in number that he took from the Virgin Mary and according to which he resides in heaven at the right hand of the Father.

And we say that all and singular tractates, writings, and pamphlets contrary to this orthodox formula and faith are to be condemned; and we declare to all Christian faithful that they have been condemned, and we demand that they flee from such writings, tractates, and pamphlets as from pestiferous ones, fermented by heretical pravity.[91]

---

[90] The text is given by F. Prochazka, *Miscellaneen aus der böhmischen und mährischen Litteratur* (Prague, 1784), pp. 315–324; the MS date is June 1426, but several dates in this MS are wrong, and Bartoš gives convincing reasons for correcting the date to 1422, in connection with Korybut's summons (*AČ*, I, 213): "K počátkům Petra Chelčického," *ČČM*, LXXXVIII (1914), 313 f.

[91] Laurence, pp. 501 f.; Prochazka, *op. cit.*, pp. 316 f.

The decree of 1421 makes two points: the whole Christ, body and blood, is in *each* of the elements; he is there "in his real presence." The latter was the key point; it excluded Pikartism but could accommodate all other doctrines; we know that the Taborites accepted it.[92] The formula of 1422, however, could cover only Příbram's transsubstantiation and Jakoubek's consubstantiation, but not the true Wyclifite doctrine that Jakoubek had once defended and which was being taken up by the Taborites. This consisted of three main points: (1) the bread remains bread; (2) the consecrated bread symbolically signifies the body of Christ; (3) the consecrated bread receives a new spiritual quality.[93] Jakoubek may not have understood Wyclif fully, or he may have merely taken Wyclif's remanence and combined it with a conservative insistence on a substantial presence that would justify retaining all of the traditional doctrine and cult associated with the Eucharist in the Janovian exaltation of that sacrament.[94] But Nicholas of Pelhřimov, who had defended the *real* presence against the Pikart Kániš in February 1421, did not believe in a *substantial* presence, nor did the other leading Taborite priests, except for Master John of Jičín. And it was one of the consequences of the anti-Pikart campaign that the priests of Tabor felt the need to define their doctrine with precision; there was evidently a lively interchange of both oral and written arguments, the latter running into the dozens.[95] Even in 1421 these little tractates were being produced, and they continued to circulate for some years; the Prague synod of June 1422 condemned all of them by defining the true eucharistic doctrine in terms of a substantial presence. In

[92] Apart from the fact that Laurence says the Taborites' objection to the synod's decrees centered on rites, there is the explicit statement of the arbiters of the religious controversy in 1444, that the Taborites were present at the St. Procop's Day synod of 1421 and, along with the other participants, agreed on the synod's eucharistic article (which is then given in Czech, in a text exactly like the Latin one of the synod): Nejedlý, *Prameny*, p. 109.

[93] I follow the analysis of Erhard Peschke, "Die Bedeutung Wiclefs für die Theologie der Böhmen," *Zeitschrift für Kirchengeschichte*, LIV (1935), 462–483, esp. 463 f.

[94] *Ibid.*, pp. 463, 467 f. A similar interpretation of Jakoubek's relation to Wyclif was offered by J. Sedlák, *ST*, II, 135; cf. also *TTE*, pp. 2 f. (Sedlák's "Jakoubkův traktát remanenční," *Hlídka*, XXIX (1912), 433–440, has not been available; cf. *LČJ*, No. 1).

[95] Příbram, *Život kněží táborských, KJBB*, p. 301, tells how Jičín wrote "a good and faithful tractate against Biskupec's erroneous one," how Nicholas then "roused his gang" against Jičín, and how the Prague masters approved of the latter's views, not Nicholas's. Příbram also wrote that he had heard or seen no less than ten or twenty Taborite eucharistic tractates, and that he possessed five or six of them (see, e.g., below, n. 138); in various of his works he lists them, names their authors, summarizes them, or excerpts them: see the discussion in Bartoš, "K počátkům Petra Chelčického," *ČČM*, LXXXVIII (1914), 150 f.; and see the comprehensive treatment by J. Sedlák, *TTE*, pp. 5–19. The personal relationships and informal talks out of which these tracts emerged are exemplified by Biskupec's dealings with Chelčický (below).

other words, while the synod of 1421 sought to include the Taborites, that of 1422 sought to exclude them.

Nicholas of Pelhřimov was accustomed to being condemned by Prague, and in the matter of the Eucharist he sought only the kind of mutual toleration that he had earlier proposed in regard to rites and vestments, except that in this case there would have to be a special mode of accommodation: the actual disagreements would have to be covered over by verbal ambiguities and equivocations so that both sides could agree on a single formula. Since the masters never accepted his invitation he found himself in the posture of a kind of hypocrite in his encounters with them.[96] But as Bishop of Tabor he had different concerns: the multitude of eucharistic pronouncements had to be brought into a single, well-developed, and well-argued doctrine, which would then have to win the acceptance of the turbulent priests. Accustomed to speaking out as the spirit moved them, and in many cases functioning not merely as priests but as prophets, political leaders, and even military leaders,[97] the priests nominally subject to Nicholas could not be ruled by him; at best he could lead them on the basis of their consensus. We can only imagine the extremely important but utterly untested conversations that he and his associates must have had with other Taborite priests, the conferences, debates, arguments, perhaps even negotiations, with Nicholas always trying to broaden the area of agreement and hence the basis of his support. In one case, however, we can turn from imagination to evidence. Peter Chelčický, who by this time had lost touch with the problems of Tabor's religious life, was nevertheless both geographically and spiritually close to his former brethren; at the same time, however, he had his contacts among the Prague masters. Sometime in 1422 or thereabouts, Nicholas and the priest Luke came to the town of Vodňany and sent for Chelčický; the three sat down on the dam of a fish-pond, and the Taborites asked Peter what he had heard about their eucharistic doctrine.[98]

[96] For the first encounter, at Konopiště, see below, ad nn. 123–125. Twenty years later nothing had changed: an exchange of 1443 reported by Rokycana was typical of the whole controversy: the masters asked the Taborites to accept the proposition that Christ was in the Eucharist "veritate . . . sui corporis et natura permanente," but "istam proposicionem simpliciter concedere noluerunt, quavis sophisticacione nitebantur evadere. . . . Sophisticabant enim sic: veritate sui corporis et natura permanente, sc. in celo, est in sacramento altaris, per gracias scilicet et dona" (*Tractatus de existentia corporis Christi in sacramento,* in Nejedlý, *Prameny,* pp. 125 f.). For the system according to which the Taborites' "sophistries" were formulated, see below, n. 99.

[97] See below, ad n. 159; also above, chap. ix, n. 11. Příbram's, *Život, KJBB,* pp. 262–309, although hostile, gives a good picture of the irrepressible priests of Tabor at work —exploring, arguing, writing, preaching, prophesying, politicking, and even fighting.

[98] Chelčický's *Replika proti Mikuláši Biskupcovi,* eds. J. Annenkov and V. Jagić, *Sočinenija Petra Chelčickago, Otdělenija russkago jazyka i slovesnosti, Imperatorskaja*

He reported that some people praised it, others condemned it. Nicholas then defended his doctrine: he did believe in the Eucharist, according to Scripture, and his concern was to rescue it from false interpretations of human origin. This sounded good to Peter, perhaps because he had not yet studied the matter and was therefore unduly impressed by Nicholas's faith in a *real* presence; at any rate, the conversations were not resumed for quite a while. Of course Chelčický was not a Taborite priest, and the meeting at Vodňany was probably not typical of Nicholas's politicking in his own party, but it does suggest something of the process by which public opinion in Tabor's domain was prepared for the promulgation of a standard doctrine. For this is what happened. Taking the true interpretation of Wyclif from the excerpts made by Peter Payne, the priest John Němec (or "Teutonicus"—he was evidently a German) of Žatec wrote a solid, cogent eucharistic tractate that the Taborites then accepted as theirs, probably some time in 1422.[99] "It is

---

Akademija Nauk (St. Petersburg, 1893), is almost the only source for this and subsequent episodes of the encounter, although excerpts from Nicholas's Czech treatise written for Chelčický survive in the works of Příbram and Rokycana. For a modern account see Goll, *Quellen*, II, 16–19, with relevant excerpts from the *Replika* translated into German on pp. 69–73, and Příbram's (Latin) excerpts from Nicholas's treatise on pp. 63 f.; cf. Nejedlý, *Prameny, passim*, for Rokycana's excerpts. My "Peter Chelčický: Treatises on Christianity and the Social Order," *Studies in Medieval and Renaissance History*, I (Lincoln, Nebraska, 1964), 131–136, goes over some of this material; the best study is still Bartoš's "K počátkům Petra Chelčického," *ČČM*, LXXXVIII (1914), 27–35, 149–160, 303–314.

[99] The text of his *Cum spiritus veritatis summe odiens mendacium* has been published by Sedlák, *TTE* (texts), pp. 1–20. The approximate date is given by the fact that Nicholas of Pelhřimov used it for his own work, *Ad . . . magnificacionem*, which was attacked by Příbram before the meetings at Konopiště, April/June, 1423. In his *Život, KJBB*, pp. 294 f., Příbram introduces excerpts from Němec's work with the statement that "The Taborites' senior priest and preacher, John Němec of Žatec wrote it, together with the priest Sigmund and with other Taborite priests, and they distributed it over almost the whole land." He ends the excerpts thus (p. 298): "Concluding this treatise or pamphlet, the priests of Tabor say, 'we intend, with the fear of God, to proclaim this understanding of the laudable sacrament among the people, nor is it our intention by this writing to affirm any of Antichrist's institutions.' " But the work was probably written by Němec alone, as Příbram says in his later work, the *Processus cause*, in a passage that also defines the relationship between Němec's work, his sources, and his followers (*LČP*, No. 31; the text in MS D 49, fol. 187ʳ, and in Höfler, II, 824): "Deinde secuntur articuli Johannis theotonici praedicatoris de Zacz viri inter omnes sacerdotes Taborienses in libris Wicleff plus provecti et eius doctrinis et sentenciis sollicicius applicati. Hic enim ab Anglico Petro libros ipsos studuit et postea episcopum et alios Taborienses sacerdotes tamquam magister heresium primarius docuit, scribens primus eis quendam tractatulum latine et vulgariter . . . , in quo secutus est sentencias Wicleff de verbo ad verbum, a quo perversus episcopus traxit pene omnes sentencias una cum verbis trium suorum tractatulorum, ut hoc ego reperi per proprium oculum."

significant," the German scholar Erhard Peschke remarks, "that the ideas of the Anglo-Saxon Wyclif were reproduced most objectively and faithfully by a German Taborite, John Teutonicus of Žatec. . . ." But Peschke also notes, without ethnic comment, that John actually worked up Wyclif's ideas into a more rigid system than Wyclif himself had produced.[100] Nicholas of Pelhřimov then used this treatise to compose his own, still more concise, *Ad sacramenti eucharistie in veritate magnificacionem,* and this was circulated among the communities.[101]

All of this merely put the finishing touches on the schism between Tabor and Prague, a schism made even deeper by the fact that John Žižka, who believed in special vestments and in his simple way probably believed in a substantial presence, and who was also willing to accept Korybut as prince of the realm, had sometime in 1422 broken with Tabor and begun to identify himself with the radical brotherhood of Hradec Králové.[102] It is not too surprising, then, to learn that in October 1422 the Taborite Lord Bohuslav of Švamberk tried to foment a radical coup in Prague, without success,[103] nor that in about early April 1423 a coalition of Prague and royalist forces, inspired by the university masters, began a siege of the castle Křiženec, which belonged to Tabor.[104] The siege made no headway, and when in a few weeks Lord Bohuslav brought up a Taborite army, the besiegers agreed to a truce, which provided for a meeting a few days later at the castle of Konopiště: the two parties would try to end their hostilities and, in particular, "they would try to find out if there were any way of obtaining unity between the priests of Tabor and the masters of Prague." The issue, we are told, was still that of vestments, although the eucharistic problem was also

---

Cf. also Příbram's *Professio fidei* of 1430, in Cochlaeus, *Historiae Hussitarum, libri XII,* p. 544. Bartoš has argued ("K počátkům . . . Chelčického," p. 311) that Němec's tractate was probably published officially by the Taborites (according to Příbram's testimony, above), and that this must have been at a synod, and that the only suitably dated synod we know about was that of Písek, in February 1422; but the evidence does not seem precise enough for this inference.

[100] Peschke, "Die Bedeutung Wiclefs," pp. 471 f. His *aperçu* was partly anticipated by Příbram (above, n. 99) and Chelčický (below, n. 101).

[101] For the relation between Nicholas and Němec, see above, n. 99; moreover in the *Replika proti Biskupcovi,* Peter Chelčický tells (pp. 421, 426) how Nicholas and Koranda praised Němec's doctrine and virtuous life to him, at Písek *ca.* 1424; he also remarks on the similarity between Němec's work and Nicholas's (p. 424). The Latin text of Nicholas's work is not known to survive; the Czech text has been published by V. Sokol, "Traktát Mikuláše z Pelhřimova: O zvelebení v pravdě svátosti těla a krve pána našeho Jezukrista," *JSH,* II (1929), Příloha, pp. 4–14.

[102] Heymann, pp. 354 ff.

[103] *Ibid.,* pp. 344–347.

[104] *Ibid.,* pp. 367–371; see Höfler, II, 574 f., almost the only source.

involved.[105] In due course both armies showed up at Konopiště, ready to go at each other, but thanks to calmer spirits from both sides it was agreed, after some discussion between the theologians, that the controversy over vestments would be arbitrated by a panel chosen from each party. The arbiters must have been laymen, who could appreciate at least the practical advantages of Tabor's thesis, that "ornates" were a custom of the church, not an obligation imposed by the Law of God; they therefore decreed that each side should celebrate mass in the manner of the other, to demonstrate acceptance of the principle of mutual toleration.[106] Procop the Shaven did in fact then officiate *in ornatu* but the Praguers refused to do the reverse, probably because Příbram was in control, and he of course held that vestments *were* obligatory. Hence there was nothing left but to schedule yet another full-dress disputation at which Příbram would try to prove his point—not to the priests of Tabor but to a panel of lay auditors from both sides. The new meeting was set for 24 June, in Konopiště Castle.

There were four auditors—or arbiters, as they were also called. Prague furnished Lord Smil Holický of Šternberk and the prominent burgher Simon "of the White Lion"; Tabor's two were the military captain Chval of Machovice and the captain of Písek, Matthew Louda of Chlumčany. For interpretation of difficult points of theology the board was supplied with Master Peter Payne from Prague and the priest John Čapek from Taborite Klatovy. On the Prague side John Příbram was the chief or only spokesman, but he was backed up by Masters Jakoubek, John Kardinál, John Rokycana, and the priests George, Albus, Vacha, and Jaroslav. Nicholas conducted Tabor's presentation, and his team included Master John Jičín and the priests Havel of Sušice, Markolt, Procop (the Shaven, no doubt), Chřenovský, Quirin (also known as Laurence the German of Reichenbach), and perhaps also Wenceslas Koranda.[107] Nicholas began by propounding Tabor's basic principle:

> The Taborites believe every truth promulgated as worthy of belief by the Lord Jesus Christ, by the holy prophets, and by the apostles; nor do they refuse to include here the statements of other saints in which Christ speaks and which are truly founded in the aforementioned truth. And, hoping in Christ the Lord, their head, they are prepared to suffer the dreadful pain of

[105] Höfler, II, 575–593, for the whole episode.

[106] *Ibid.*, p. 575; the formulation given was that the Praguers should officiate *sine superpelliciis,* which in context seems to mean simply without special vestments—i.e., including chasubles (the "ornates" proper). Heymann (p. 369), following Tomek, distinguishes between the ornates and the *superpellicia* or "surplices."

[107] All these names are given by Příbram in a kind of memorandum (*LČP,* No. 9), MS D 74, fol. 109ʳ. For Koranda's presumable presence see below, *ad* n. 127.

death rather than voluntarily to say or assert anything contrary to the will of Christ and his Primitive Church.

John Příbram had already had some experience with this norm and he would have much more—it allowed the Taborites to interpret Scripture as they wished, to use or not use the early and medieval doctors as they saw fit, and thus to evade the whole force of their opponents' arguments.[108] Hence the masters took care to set forth their norms, in the form of four suppositions, to which they asked Tabor's response: (1) Holy Scripture, in which all the faithful must believe, is contained in the Bible commonly used by Christians; (2) the faithful are similarly required to believe that St. Jerome's translation is entirely true to the original; (3) the books that are accepted without question by the catholic church as the books of Dionysius, Clement, Origen, Chrysostom, Augustine, Jerome, Ambrose, and Gregory, are indeed the books of those doctors; (4) when the Four Doctors (*scil.*, the last four just named) agree unanimously in any point of faith, or in any other point not contrary or harmful to the catholic faith, it is safer and more useful to believe their statements than the "new concepts" of the moderns. The Taborite reply was an assent so highly qualified as to be useless. In regard to point one they distinguished between the canonical and apocryphal books even though, as Příbram later pointed out, their doctrine of warfare had been based on the latter.[109] On the second point they noted Nicholas of Lyra's criticisms of Jerome's translation, as well as the latter's own invitation of critical judgement—but still, they said, they were willing to accept the Vulgate as conveying the truth of the Holy Spirit. On point three they expressed grave (and justified!) doubts about the authenticity of some of the books in question, noting in addition that the belief requested by Prague could not be a matter of faith, for the Primitive Church obviously did not have such belief, and that in any case, "we did not come here to argue about the books of the doctors." As for point four: "If in any point of faith the Four Doctors speak unanimously and erroneously, then they are unanimously in error, and this is highly possible. . . . We believe the Holy Doctors as they themselves want to be believed, that is, insofar as they base

---

[108] E.g., Höfler, II, 505; *Život, KJBB*, p. 274.

[109] *Cum ab inicio* (*LČP*, No. 24), MS D 47, fol. 2ᵛ: ". . . quedam dicta de libro Ecclesiastici . . . in summam auctoritatem assumserunt et per ea falsissime et abusive bella sua cruentissima aprobaverunt . . . [with references to chaps. xxix, xl]. . . ." And, fol. 3ʳ: "Quod autem talia sic allegando egerunt patet in communi predicacione eorum, et scripto de bellis Johannis Czapkonis presbiteri, armiductoris homicidarum et omnium predictorum scelerum primarii auctoris et suscitatoris, qui eciam in tractatulo eodem de bellis allegat illud Ecclesiastici xvii [11–12], 'unicuique mandavit deus de proximo suo'; dicens illum librum totum Ecclesiasticum esse scripturam sanctam a spiritu sancto editam. . . ." This sort of thing did not make Nicholas's job any easier.

themselves truly in Scripture; for an argument taken solely from their testimony is not enough—they could all be deceived." Furthermore, "if by revelation . . . of Scripture God should today grant a more potent understanding to someone, that man would be more to be believed than those Doctors"—a crucial point for Tabor's understanding of her place in history as a revival of the Primitive Church rather than, as in Jakoubek's current concept of the reformation, a necessarily inferior imitation.[110] Finally they declared, "We do not receive canonizations of the saints and their books as articles of faith, but rather according to our own judgement of belief." [111]

So much for the preliminaries. The next day it was the Taborites' turn to ask a question: did the masters really intend to persist in what they had publicly promulgated—in Příbram's *De ritibus misse*—namely, that their rites and vestments, those of the modern church, had had their origin with St. Peter, the other apostles, and their first holy disciples; and that in virtually all points it was the rite of Peter, James, Clement, Anacletus, Dionysius, and other martyrs, the custom, confirmed by the apostles' words, of the universal church? Jakoubek, at least, could not possibly have given more than a very reserved and qualified yes. According to Nicholas, this question threw the masters into confusion, from which they tried to escape, after much recrimination, by saying that "their rite of mass was apostolic." [112] Tabor then asked for proof; Prague offered essentially what had been written in *De ritibus misse*; Tabor then resumed what Nicholas had written in response to that work. The principles of both sides were just what they had been in 1420 and 1421, just as irreconcilable, and argument was just as fruitless. But Příbram had also raised another point that remained to be

[110] Jakoubek's view at this time was expressed in his Postil on Apocalypse, *Výklad,* II, 435: "Just as in an actual house the bigger stones are put in the foundation, to support the whole structure, and then above these are other stones—still big ones, and then on top there are the smaller stones: so in the Primitive Church were set as a foundation the saints who were stronger in faith, in life, in counsel, and in wisdom; after them others set themselves on them, to govern the church; and we, the last ones, are set as smaller stones on top of these earlier ones." In the great days of the utraquist revolt, Jakoubek too had believed in special revelations (above, chap. iii, *ad* n. 9), but in opposing the Taborites' revolutionary warfare, in early 1420, he observed that it could be justified only "ex certa revelacione," but "iam non sic solet communiter fieri, licet potest contingere, sed raro" (MS O 13, fol. 36ᵛ; in Appendix 3, No. 3).

[111] For all of this see Höfler, II, 577 f. The passage about the Four Doctors reads even better in Latin: "Si doctores quatuor in aliqua materia fidei unanimiter loquuntur erronee, tunc unanimiter errant, et hoc est valde possibile. . . ."

[112] As we have seen, Jakoubek had derived much of the modern mass merely from post-Primitive papal ordinances, which in this case, he said, happened to be praiseworthy. As for the masters' formula, "dicentes, ritum suum missandi esse apostolicum" (Höfler, II, 579), it may have been a euphemistic way of admitting that it was *papal*.

taken care of: the "fantasy," as Nicholas called it, that the faithful were required, under pain of eternal damnation, to obey not only the institutes of the Primitive Church but all the "statutes of the church, even of the malign and unreasonable one," as long as they were reasonable and not directly opposed to the Law of God.[113] This could be and was refuted in principle, but the Taborites proved their case by showing in detail how the Prague-Roman rite *was* opposed to the Law of God. The demonstration deserves some attention, for it constitutes perhaps the best single source for the nature of Tabor's religious life, and it shows, in an indirect way, what the Taborite reformation was about. What follows is a summary.[114]

The Prague rite restricts the Law of Christ by preventing priests from saying mass unless all the many prerequisites are on hand; hence the ministration of the sacrament is impeded. Moreover, since that rite consumes a lot of time in useless things, the people get bored, become indisposed to worthy reception of the Eucharist, and the priests do not have enough time left for adequate preaching. The Prague rite also includes a lot of dubious or even fictitious material in its readings, as well as much noisy chanting not founded in the Law of God; and both readings and chanting are done in a language that the people do not understand—all they do is say Amen. "It were better to speak five words that the people understood than to rumble out and barbarize ten thousand." Although the masters say that some of this Latin material consists of "occulta" that are not to be spoken to the people, and of "obscura" that many priests would not be able to expound, still, if these things are so obscure or occult, they should simply be omitted, as useless to the people. If they must be said, then let it be apart from the mass. Moving on, the Taborites objected that if the Prague rite were to be observed in the daily services, it would be necessary to have missals containing more than just the Sunday masses; but in fact there were very few such available, with the result that the priests would have to use the Sunday Gospel and Epistle readings for the whole week. In any case, the fixed order of Roman pericopes prevents the priests from expounding the Law "according to the needs of the people and of the time." Another objection: the Prague rite allows bad or unsuitable priests to function, for on the one hand it allows for the multiplication of masses beyond the needs of the congregation, and at the expense of the poor, and on the other hand it allows the unworthy man to

---

[113] Höfler, II, 585; the Taborites' refutation is a good example of Nicholas's dry humor: ". . . si quilibet sub aeterna damnatione esset obligatus ad tenendum et custodiendum omnia statuta legi Dei non repugnantia, tunc non cito aliquis possit salvari, cum non cito invenitur talis homo, qui haec omnia statuta nedum impleat sed cognoscat."

[114] Höfler, II, 579–584.

hide behind ceremonies. The Roman rite of Prague, moreover, was what had led to the abuse of communion in only one kind, for its multiplication of masses had obscured the true function of communion, and had encouraged the people to rest content with only the sight of the sacrament. With the multiplication of masses there are often several being celebrated at one time, at the various altars of a church, to the confusion of everyone. The Prague rite also "contains a multitude of signs that are occasions to many of false faith and superstition; indeed, the uneducated [*simplices*] priests even regard the signs as having magical power"—reference here was especially to the sign of the cross. Furthermore, the Prague rite provides for masses in honor of saints: these masses serve the greed of priests and lead the uneducated into idolatry, for they think that the masses are offered *to* the saints; but there is nothing in Scripture to justify even the mere invocation of saints. The masters also provide for masses for the souls of the dead in Purgatory; such masses had been instituted by Pope Pelagius in 568. They were not the practice of the Primitive Church, nor indeed is there any sound authority for the very existence of Purgatory, and the masses predicated on its existence are occasions of simony and false hopes.

These objections tell their own story about the sociology of Tabor's religion and liturgy. The consecration of the Eucharist was in fact the mass, but the purpose of this consecration was communion; moreover, the accompanying sermon expounding the Bible was of equal importance.[115] These congregational purposes determined the rite, which was stripped of what did not serve them. In traditional Roman thought the consecration and communion had another purpose, that of consummating a sacrifice; as Příbram put it:

> The sacrifice of the mass is principally made for the whole Church, which accumulates benefits thereby; nor should anyone deem it a small thing to be the mediator and arbiter between God and all the people on behalf of whom the most welcome sacrifice is to be offered to God the Father.[116]

This concept of the mass, which as a sacrifice could be offered to God even without a congregation's presence, had generated most of what the Taborites objected to: the precious vestments and vessels, the sumptuous decorations of the church, the Latin, the multiplication of lengthy prayers, the votive

[115] Thus, e.g., in John Němec's tractate, *TTE*, p. 14: Christ is present in the Eucharist *spiritually*, "et pro eo sancti dicunt, quod verbum dei et sacramentum istud sunt paris dignitatis" (a dictum of Augustine's).

[116] *Contra articulos picardorum*, MS 4749, fol. 60ᵛ: ". . . ecclesie tocius pro qua principaliter fit sacrificium beneficia cumulantur; non ergo hoc parum cuiquam videatur esse sequestrem et arbitrum inter deum et universum populum, pro quo sacrificium gratissimum est deo patri offerendum." Cf. Höfler, II, 527.

masses. Logically the Prague-Tabor controversy in this matter could be expressed as turning on the difference between the Eucharist as sacrifice and the Eucharist as communion. In fact, however, this clear definition was not formulated, although Nicholas probably had something of the sort in mind when he said that Christ's death was "the unique and sufficient sacrifice." [117] But there are few passages in the Prague literature comparable to the one just quoted from Příbram, for Hussite Prague, like Tabor, was primarily interested in the Eucharist as communion; this was the Janovian tradition that had led to utraquism in the first place. Secondarily Jakoubek and the others promoted another favorite practice of Matthew of Janov, the adoration of the consecrated host on the altar, between masses; the Taborites did not reject this outright, but they had little use for it.[118] In any case it is obvious that these differing notions of the *function* of the Eucharist were themselves effects of more general differences, and that they could hardly fail to nourish different conceptions of the *nature* of the Eucharist. The eucharistic schism, no less than the schism over rites and vestments, expressed the irreconcilability of two types of society. This fact also explains the absolute inability of Prague and Tabor to agree even on a norm of authority, for Příbram could justify Prague's religion only by appealing to the tradition that had produced it, while Nicholas of Pelhřimov, justifying what was in fact a novelty on the face of the earth, could ultimately accept nothing but "naked Scripture" [119]—that is, the supreme Christian authority, but interpreted with absolute freedom.

Having failed to come to any agreement on rites and vestments, the theologians of Prague and Tabor then moved on to the more recent problem of the Eucharist, which had become a public issue of controversy when John Příbram published a treatise, *Surge domine,* attacking Nicholas's *Ad mag-*

[117] Höfler, II, 581 f.: "in ecclesia primitiva . . . unus sacerdos conficiebat in omnium fidelium congregatione, . . . et alii praesentes in memoriam mortis Christi, quae est unica et sufficiens oblatio, sacramentum Eucharistiae ab illo sumebant."

[118] Jakoubek wrote in his treatise of 1428 on the real presence (*LČJ*, No. 90; text in Hardt, III, 920): "patet error impie dicentium, quod hoc sacramentum vel corpus Christi in sacramento solum esset nobis datum ad manducandum, et sanguis ejus ad bibendum, et non ad colendum sive adorandum." The priests of Tabor seem not to have arrived at unanimity on this point; some agitated vigorously against adoration, others, including Nicholas, did not refuse at least to kneel before the sacrament, on behalf of the Christ *represented* in it. Echoes of these controversies abound: Příbram, *Život, KJBB,* pp. 305, 306, 308 (the priest Quirin preached in Písek that he would rather pray and kneel to the Devil than to the Eucharist), and *passim;* Chelčický, *Replika proti Biskupcovi,* p. 433 (the Taborites of Nicholas's party allow Christians to pray to the sacrament with a "lower sort of praying," thinking, however, of Christ who was in heaven), and *passim;* Nejedlý, *Prameny,* pp. 50–52 and *passim.* See n. 174, below.

[119] Příbram's phrase, *Cum ab inicio,* MS D 47, fol. 1ʳ: "sola nuda lege. . . ."

nificacionem. Nicholas's account of the debates on this problem is both compressed and distorted, but it can be corrected or at least confronted by Příbram's memorandum covering the same event. First the masters proposed an eight-point formulation of eucharistic doctrine composed by Příbram; Nicholas implies that it was artfully phrased to obfuscate the issue and induce the Taborites to accept it.[120] There was much haggling over exactly how Christ was present in the Eucharist, the Taborites insisting that the formula specify that however he was there, it was not as though his actual body were there—corporeally, locally, or dimensionally—and as though the faithful could bite off here a nose, there an eye.[121] Some of these objections may have been taken into account in the version that survives:

1. Let all faithful Christians believe with faithful heart, and profess with sincere voice, that in the most divine sacrament of the Eucharist, under the form of bread and likewise under that of wine, the whole Lord Jesus Christ, true God and man, with his own body and blood, is with us in his real presence.

2. Christ is in the perceptible sacrament according to his natural corporeal substance, which he took from the Virgin Mary.

3. In the Eucharist, the visible consecrated host, there dwells corporeally the fullness of divinity.

4. The substance of the body of Christ is in the sacrament of the Eucharist in the quantity of body and in the quantity of substance, but it is not there dimensively.

5. The substance of the body of Christ is in the sacrament of the Eucharist to the extent that the substance is in the body itself.

6. The substance of the body of Christ is in the visible sacrament in the quantity that it is substance, and in the quantity that it is body; thus it is in the sacrament substantially and corporeally. But it is not there dimensionally or in a dimensive or extensive sense.

7. Christ, true God and man, is at one and the same time in many distant places and in communicants, according to his true, natural, and substantial body in which he resides in heaven; for he is in every duly consecrated host. But he is not there extensively or dimensively.

8. That same Christ, true God and man, who is believed in that venerable sacrament, is to be adored in it with kneeling and all honor due to Christ.[122]

---

[120] Nicholas in Höfler, II, 587. Příbram gives the text in his memorandum, MS D 74, fol. 108ʳ, and adds: "Istas quidem octo proposiciones, per me formatas et in termino exhibitas et conclusas, censeo simpliciter katholicas, fideles, et orthodoxas."

[121] Höfler, II, 587; cf. Příbram's version, n. 123 below.

[122] The text is printed in Höfler, II, 576, from Prochazka, *Miscellaneen,* p. 268; I have also consulted MS D 74.

The first of these articles is virtually identical with the formulation of the synod of 4–7 July 1421, which the Taborites had accepted; Příbram's obvious intention was to build on this area of agreement by defining the "real presence" of article one in terms of the substantial presence declared by the synod of June 1422. Here as elsewhere the Taborites were the innovators, hence the troublemakers, and the traditional doctrine of Příbram was what everyone, including the Taborite military leaders, had been used to believing; hence, perhaps, some pressure may have been exerted on Nicholas and the other priests to accept the eight points. Otherwise they would hardly have done it, and even so, when they signed, they added the reservation: "We concede these propositions in their true, primary, and principal catholic sense, saving the definition of terms."[123] Příbram mentions no such reservation, however; he says that the agreement was unanimous, that it was pronounced as true and binding by the arbiters, that the members of each side signed their names to copies, and that these were then exchanged between the parties as guarantees of permanent adherence. But this was not all. The Taborites had two articles of their own that, according to Nicholas, the masters had agreed to accept—it may well have been the price for Tabor's adherence to the eight points; the two were:

1. The sacramental bread, remaining bread in its nature, is sacramentally the body of Christ.

2. The sacramental bread, remaining bread in its nature, is not identically the body of Christ, that is, understanding identity in its material sense.[124]

Příbram also gives these articles but says nothing about any agreement to accept them; however, his discussion of them suggests what may have happened.[125] He first declares that they are not to be conceded in the

---

[123] Höfler, II, 587; Příbram writes, MS D 74, fol. 108ʳ: "Isti sunt articuli de corpore Cristi per magistros pragenses et sacerdotes taborienses post longam altercacionem in Conopist Castro unanimiter et concorditer conclusi, et per arbitros et auditores utriusque partis tunc presidentes et auscultantes pro katholicis et orthodoxis ab omnibus cristianis habendis et tenendis decreti, pronuncciati, et sub pene fidei et honoris ad tenendum et credendum demandati; et pro perpetua memoria mutua sibi ipsis proscripcione, et uniuscuiusque eorum et nominis sui subscripcione firmati et roborati, ita ut una pars omnium suorum nomina propriis manibus subscripta alteri parti tribueret et econtra, ut nulla fraus in perpetuum partis utriusque predictam fidem violare presumeret, cui propria subscripcio repugnaret."

[124] Höfler, II, 587, with a flat statement: "istud enim concesserunt magistri."

[125] Příbram, MS D 74, fol. 109ʳ: "Articuli duo taboriensium sacerdotum, quos ipsi ediderunt: [1] Panis sacramentalis in sua natura manens panis est sacramentaliter corpus Cristi. [2] Panis sacramentalis non est ydemptice corpus Cristi [cf. Höfler, II, 587]. Istas quidem proponens ad sensum taboriensium dico a nullo fideli esse concedendas, de quanto supponunt panem materialem remanere in sua natura post consecra-

Taborite sense—that is, in the sense that the material bread remains in its nature after the consecration. They can however be conceded in another sense, he says, which finds support in the doctors: that is, that the *species* of bread remains the species of bread and as such is sacramentally the body of Christ; similarly with the second, supplying "species" and referring to the natural, not sacramental, being of the bread. This sort of sophistry may have done service as an agreement, or perhaps, since Příbram was rejecting the remanence that Jakoubek accepted, the agreement may have been a matter of private understanding between Jakoubek and Nicholas.

These matters settled, the meeting proceeded to deal with Příbram's attack on Nicholas's eucharistic tractate, the thesis of which latter was "that Christ after his ascension to heaven is not here on earth substantially, corporeally, or dimensionally, in that body and in that magnitude in which he rose from the dead and ascended to heaven, the apostles seeing him do so." [126] Nicholas complained that Příbram had misunderstood a crucial turn of phrase, and that the attack had defamed him throughout the realm; he also charged that Příbram's *Surge domine* was itself full of bad things. Both sides—according to Nicholas—agreed to subject the two treatises to examination. *Ad magnificacionem* was turned over to Příbram and the Taborite Havel of Sušice, who made certain additions and then released the work for publication in the churches of both parties; Nicholas says the additions applied to just one passage, which he admitted was capable of being misunderstood. The *Surge domine* was entrusted to Jakoubek and the Taborite Wenceslas (Koranda?), but nothing was accomplished; Nicholas says that Jakoubek neglected the task. Příbram, on the other hand, says nothing about his own work's having been called into question, let alone being subject to correction, but he says that Nicholas's tractate was found erroneous in many passages, and that the necessary additional phrases were added by Havel in his own hand; but, he goes on, the Taborites continued to circulate the uncorrected text, in both Latin and Czech. And the same year, he says, Nicholas came to the Prague Town Hall and declared that except for that one dubious passage his work was all true. [127] A later source, from among the pro-Taborite Bohemian

---

cionem. Intelligendo vero per panem sacramentalem species panis sacramentalis utique, prout communiter doctores alii exponunt et capiunt, ut patet in tractatu speciali, tunc a sapiente possent ambe sustineri, ut sit sensus prime: Panis, id est species panis, sacramentalis in sua natura manens panis species, est sacramentaliter corpus Cristi, et conformiter dicendo de secunda, considerando ad esse naturale, non ad esse sacramentale."

[126] Höfler, II, 588; the Czech text, V. Sokol, "Traktát Mikuláše z Pelhřimova," is cited above, n. 101. The text of Příbram's *Surge domine* is in *TTE*, pp. 56–106, with some of the authorities left out.

[127] Příbram, *Život, KJBB*, pp. 300 f.

Brethren, informs us that a version of the surviving text—which in fact is not reconcilable with Příbram's doctrine, hence was not "corrected"—was written into the Old Town's books, but that Příbram had it torn out.[128] All that can be said with certainty about all of this is that the Konopiště meeting did produce a kind of agreement about the Eucharist, and that the result was probably more welcome to Prague than to Tabor.[129] But there was no agreement in substance, nor were the political and military conflicts between the two sides resolved in any permanent sense, although there was some sort of compact that failed to last very long: in September 1424, when Žižka made peace with Prague after leading an army against the city, he dourly prophesied that it would not last longer than the peace of Konopiště.[130] Unfortunately it is not clear what even this short-lived compact achieved.

With the failure of Prague and Tabor to restore order under Hussite auspices, the task was taken up by the barons, both Hussite and Catholic. At Kolín in September 1423, a meeting of both religious parties, including the Hussite towns but dominated by the nobility, decided to call a national diet to meet in Prague on St. Gall's Day, 16 October. At the same time it was decided that Hussite theologians would debate the Four Articles at Brno with spokesmen of European Catholicism. The St. Gall's Day diet pursued this last point and also set up a twelve-man baronial council, half Catholic and half Hussite, to govern the realm until a more regular settlement could be arranged.[131] None of this boded well for Tabor and her allies, nor were even the Praguers united in supporting the plan; apart from the New Town

---

[128] In Sokol's edition, p. 4.

[129] Thus in October/November 1424 the masters tried to hold the Taborites to the Konopiště formulations; see Appendix 2. More weighty perhaps is the admission of the priests of Tabor themselves (Nejedlý, *Prameny,* pp. 51 f.): In 1443, refuting various hostile reports about themselves, they took up the matter of Quirin's utterance in Písek, more than eighteen years earlier—he had said he would rather kneel to the Devil than to the Eucharist (above, n. 118), and the incident was never forgotten by his opponents. Now he conceded that he had said it, but only in the context of an attack on transsubstantiation—the Eucharist was not the substance of God, and the devil had at least been created by God as an angel. Of course "he did not mean thereby to dishonor the laudable sacrament or the Lord Christ, whom we believe in it in the sense that the Lord Christ has declared. For," the statement continues, "right after he had said what he did in his sermon, he went on to say how the Taborites had agreed with the Prague masters at Konopiště, that we are to bow down to, and give all due honor to, Lord Christ, true God and man, whom we believe in the sacrament." This is literally identical with the eighth point of the Konopiště formula, and the context suggests that the Taborites indeed agreed to the whole formula, no doubt with a tacit interpretation of the language into their own sense.

[130] Heymann, pp. 426 f.

[131] For these and the following events see Heymann, pp. 395 ff., and the slightly different account by Bartoš, *HR,* I, 187 ff.

radicals, Jakoubek's followers were reluctant to enter a conference under such unfavorable auspices. Hence the meeting never took place and the government of the realm failed to function. In 1424 there were new wars, with Žižka leading the Taborite-Horebite forces against both Catholics and the coalition of the barons with conservative Prague. On 7 June he soundly beat this coalition at the Battle of Malešov. Then on 29 June Prince Sigmund Korybut returned, having defied his uncle, Duke Witold of Lithvania; he was thus free to pursue his own policy, in recognition of reality. He suppressed the leaders of Prague conservatism, arresting John Příbram and four others who had led the city into rupture with Žižka; hence on 10 September, when Žižka marched against Prague, that city was under less conservative council-lors than those responsible for Malešov. They sent as their spokesman an adherent of Jakoubek's, Master John Rokycana, who persuaded Žižka to call off the attack and to make peace, on 14 September. It was on this occasion that Žižka prophesied that the peace would last no longer than that of Konopiště, and perhaps he was thinking of the fact that the changes in Prague were not really decisive, that the conservatives had suffered only a temporary check. Their spokesman Příbram indeed did not stay long in prison; he emerged to insist on what had always been his view of the situation: the troubles in the realm were the fault chiefly of the Taborites, whom he regarded as plunderers, brigands, and tyrants determined to pre-vent the establishment of a government that could repress their iniquity. And all of this barbarism came from the *sacerdotes barbati,* the bearded priests of Tabor.[132]

Still, the peace of 14 September did provide a basis for another attempt to arrange a general political and religious settlement. Prague's old policy was bankrupt; the Catholic barons and towns were unable to defend themselves; the Hussite barons could not impose their policy against Žižka's power. On the other side the Taborites were moving to solve the problem of pacification in their own way—by making separate settlements with their Catholic enemies which would not be mere truces but would deal with even the religious issues of the conflict. Hence the last week of September saw negotiations in Prague between all the Hussite groups (the Prague alliance,

---

[132] Příbram's views are set forth in greatest detail in his *De condicionibus iusti belli,* MS D 47, fols. 78ʳ-93ᵛ (*LČP,* No. 10). In *HR,* I, 190, n. 23, Bartoš associates this treatise, which Příbram wrote "requisitus per capitaneos," with the work of the St. Gall's Diet of October 1423 and the baronial council set up then to govern the realm. Earlier (*LČP,* No. 10) Bartoš had dated it only approximately, between 1423 and 1428. My own guess is that it may have been written in the first half of 1424, after the Taborites had frustrated the work of the St. Gall's Day diet. Seibt, *Hussitica,* pp. 38 ff. argues for a date in 1421, but his arguments are quite unacceptable (see my review of his book in *Speculum*); on the other hand Seibt's summary of the contents is useful.

Žižka's Horebite brotherhood, and the Taburite brotherhood) and the Catholics (barons, towns, and others).[133] By about the end of the month the negotiations produced the Agreement of Zdice, which contained a principle of religious freedom—laymen might have recourse to the priests of their choice—as well as providing guarantees of the *status quo* in power and property, mutual aid against the foreigner, and various decrees regulating the ordinary affairs of the land. The Catholic feudality, who had profited enormously from the collapse of the Church's autonomy, were secured in their economic gains; on the other hand, they had to accept certain Hussite principles: clerics of either party could travel freely in the domains of the other; tithes were not to be collected (the lords could use these revenues as they wished!); when both sides joined to maintain the peace, there was to be no gambling, prostitution, drunkenness, or cursing in the allied armies. Finally it was decided that there would be a hearing for the Four Articles before an all-Bohemian panel of lay arbiters, in March of 1425.[134] It must have been very soon after the Zdice Agreement that a Prague-Tabor meeting of theologians was scheduled, partly as an obviously desirable implementation of the peace, partly no doubt to prepare a common Hussite front for the March debates. The meeting was to take place on 16 October in the Prague Castle, under the same four auditors who had presided at Konopiště. On 11 October Žižka died, but the meeting took place, and what effect his disappearance may have had can only be guessed at.

The Prague masters came to the meeting with a list of more than twenty articles defining virtually all points at issue between the parties. Many of these articles were drawn from Příbram's synod of June 1422; he must have resumed his leading role, for in general the Prague doctrines expressed his thinking, allowing for the irreducible essence of the Hussite reform, but mostly concerned—particularly in the polemic with Tabor—to emphasize Prague's conformity to the Church's tradition. The articles produced much argument, which was only intensified when Příbram insisted on *his* definition of the sense of the eight eucharistic articles of Konopiště; no doubt he also upbraided the Taborites for not having kept to the agreement.[135] The outcome was that the meeting was adjourned, presumably to give the Taborites a chance to prepare their replies; they did so in a synod held at Klatovy on 11 November. Probably the first comprehensive definition of

---

[133] For this and what follows, the best modern treatment is Josef Macek's "Úmluvy zdické," *Acta Universitatis Carolinae, Philosophica et historica,* II (1958), 199–212.

[134] *Ibid.,* pp. 202–208; there were to be one hundred lay arbiters, half to be chosen by the Catholic party, half by the Hussites.

[135] Höfler, II, 590. The articles are given below in Appendix 2, which also includes the sources for the Taborite synod of Klatovy.

Taborite doctrine as a whole, the articles of the synod were declared binding on all the party's priests, and were circulated in Latin and Czech to all the communities. Thus prepared, the Taborites returned to Prague and the meeting was resumed in the Castle, on 23 November; it was then transferred to the Carolinum, in the Old Town, with the lay auditors now joined by many of the clergy and laity, as well as representatives of the various Hussite communities. It was no doubt felt, correctly, that this would be a definitive confrontation, on which would depend the whole future development of Hussitism and the prospects for peace in the realm. Had the masters wanted peace they would not of course have chosen to enlarge the scope of what had been a rather limited controversy, but, even so, a kind of mutual toleration could still have been worked out, for the Taborite responses to Prague's articles were clearly designed to hold forth just such a possibility. In substance they rejected Prague's doctrine and practice on most points, but not on all; in form they tended to suggest that the views of the two parties were only variants of a common reformed faith. Příbram in fact complained, later on, of precisely this crafty style of formulation, which cloaked error in reasonable-sounding words.[136] (For details of this confrontation, the reader is referred to Appendix 2, which includes both the Latin texts of both sets of articles and a summary of each in English.) And it may be supposed, in general, that although no formal agreement to disagree was reached— the sources would certainly have informed us of such—the net effect of the Taborite response was to produce a kind of stand-off, perhaps due to the laity's insistence on ending the squabbles.

But this did not suit Příbram, who "burst forth in words of defamation, in his usual way." [137] First he Pikartized the Taborites, charging that "the most evil Pikart heresy was coming forth from among the priests of Tabor present at the meeting"—that is, he accused them of fostering the kind of subversive Pikartism that all major Hussite parties had joined to stamp out. Referring no doubt to this occasion, he later wrote (in 1427): "Some time ago, before a great and distinguished audience, I did not fear to publicly read out and publish" the heresies contained in five or six Pikart tractates that he had in his possession. These included both the Taborite-orthodox tractates of Nicholas of Pelhřimov and John of Žatec, and the truly Pikart tractates of Martin Húska. But this attack did not succeed. Some of the other masters demurred at following their leader so far and onto such treacherous ground, and among the Taborites Procop the Shaven, who would soon move into Žižka's role as military leader, rose to say that he agreed with Příbram in rejecting some of the tractates—in fact he had personally burnt two or three of them.

[136] See Appendix 2, *ad* n. 8.
[137] Höfler, II, 590.

But the ones he had burnt were not the official ones, of Nicholas and John of Žatec; they were evidently those of Martin and perhaps other real Pikarts.[138] Foiled again, Příbram now shifted his ground and attacked the Taborite Markolt of Zbraslavice, whom he accused of holding that "evil priests do not validly consecrate the Eucharist"—that is, Donatism. Given time to prepare a reply, Markolt on the next day presented a very careful defense, distinguishing various irrelevant kinds of evil priests from those who had sinned against the faith; here he chose to deal only with those guilty of the simoniac heresy, and he could reasonably argue, as Nicholas of Dresden had done, that priests who had been ordained simoniacally had not been validly ordained, hence were not true priests, and *therefore* did not have sacramental powers. This was not the point that Příbram had had in mind, and he therefore regarded the defense as unsatisfactory,[139] but it seems to have been enough to satisfy the lay auditors, and Nicholas of Pelhřimov could write that Markolt "slipped out of the masters' grasp." [140] In any case, the audience did not come to a final decision on anything; it ended with each party holding to its own beliefs.[141] Příbram had failed to achieve his evident goal of rousing a national coalition against the heretical Taborites, but the priests of Tabor had also failed to carry their point, for neither now nor ever did the Prague masters accept the *principle* of two reformations. At most they and their adherents would accept the fact, when they had to; and episodes of genuine debate alternated with Příbram's style of heretication in the next few decades of the controversy, just as periods of military and political collaboration alternated

[138] This episode of the meeting was reconstructed by Bartoš, "K počátkům Petra Chelčického," p. 150. Příbram's declaration is in his *Apologia*, MS D 49, fol. 334ʳ: "Ecce plurima sunt alia testimonia realia, tractatuli quidem et scripta heretica repleta venerabilis sacramenti incredibili blasfemia, per sacerdotes et laicos conficta et per regnum universum volitancia . . . quorum tractatulos sex me habere et decem aut citra viginti me audisse reor aut vidisse, et modo quinque aut sex perniciosissimos erga me reor habere, quos pridem coram magno et inclito auditorio publice non pertimui legere et publicare, et hereses horrendissimas quas continent universis seriatim explicare." In his *Život, KJBB*, p. 304, Příbram tells of Procop's statement on this occasion, and adds, "we praised him for burning the tractates he did, but we do *not* praise him for not having burnt those of Biskupec and others, which are just as bad and even worse"—my inference in the text is based on the assumption that Biskupec's tracts were *not* just as bad, but that Biskupec and others merely happened to be the current enemies.

[139] *Život, KJBB*, p. 309.

[140] Höfler, II, 593. The text of Markolt's *questio*, "Utrum mali sacerdotes conficiunt," is on pp. 590–593; for the Czech version and its use by Chelčický, see F. Ryšánek, "P. Chelčického 'O jistém a nejistém očistci' a 'O zlých kněžích' s obranou Markoltovou," *Slovanský Sborník*, ed. M. Weingart (Prague, 1923), pp. 272–293.

[141] Höfler, II, 593: "Et sic illa . . . audientia . . . sine finali inter partes decisione est finita, utrisque circa sua opinata remanentibus."

with open warfare between Prague and Tabor. If the confrontation of November 1424 achieved anything positive, it was in the field of Tabor's own development, for now she had been prompted to define her deviant faith on virtually every point; her program henceforth did not change, and it provided the basis for the future work of her priests and above all her bishop, whose incessant and ever more powerful literary defenses of the Taborite cause were destined to free Tabor's reformation from the limitations and fluctuations of Bohemian history.

THE REFORMATION AS REVOLUTION

To identify the Hussite Revolution as, in the last analysis, the cause of the priests of Tabor is to assert a particular view not only of Hussite history but of the relationship between religion and society. It is the view that the historical meaning of religious ideas must be construed in terms of the situation in which those ideas were expressed, or, more specifically, that a given corpus of religious thought constitutes a view of the human situation as seen from a definite social standpoint. This interpretation allows and indeed makes necessary the use of a vocabulary that may seem anachronistic or reductionistic, since it applies to fifteenth-century religious history such modern political and sociological terms as conservative and radical, or right, left, and center, or even the more dubious word "ideology." Many who would not deny the interrelationship of the religious, social, and political spheres may still feel that the connections are too subtle to be grasped by such terms. Others may insist that religion is sui generis and must be studied as such, while on the opposite side there are those who see religious ideas as merely the masks worn by social interest in an age when the truth about society had not yet been discovered. Each of these approaches could lead to a different picture of Taboritism or Hussitism than the one presented here; nor need any one picture be taken as the only right one. In any case, historical theory is much less important than historical work, and perhaps the best way to defend the understanding of Taboritism that has been developed in the foregoing pages will be to present the evidence defining the nature of Tabor as a new religious society.

The identification of this society with revolution was first made (rather easily) by its Calixtine and Catholic opponents, who saw in Tabor only the subversion of all traditional law and order. The exaggerations of this view have often prompted modern scholars to provide a corrective. Thus it has been pointed out that after the elimination of the chiliast-Pikarts, Taborite society became more and more conformable to the established norms: there were peasants who paid rents, barons and lesser nobles who plied their military trades, urban classes not much different from those of other towns, and civil magistrates of the usual type.[142] Taborite theory, moreover, expressed these realities very quickly by embracing the common medieval idea of a triple division of society.[143] In other words there was no substitution of one ruling class for another, no reconstruction of the economic basis of society. But these sober correctives are themselves misleading: Tabor, and to varying degrees the other towns of her brotherhood, may have preserved the medieval economic forms of production and social forms of distribution, but these towns were obviously new sociopolitical formations and their religion was something that had not been seen before in European history. The new was more important than the old.

Whether a new settlement like Tabor, or the continuation of an old town under new auspices, the Taborite community had its origin as a congregation of people drawn from diverse places and social estates who joined the brethren in order to begin a new life. They thought of this life as a reconstitution of the Primitive Church, and if the priests of Tabor had been asked to define their cause in a phrase, they would probably have called it an imitation of the Primitive Church. But it was obvious even to contemporaries that this was inaccurate. Peter Chelčický pointed out that the Primitive Church had been a persecuted sect in a pagan world; it had not been an established society, dominating the world with the instruments of political and military power.[144] And John Příbram not only commented on the difference between the humble apostles and the lordly priests of Tabor,[145] he also noted in his attack on the Taborite liturgy that in at least twelve points the priests of Tabor did *not* follow Christ's rite of mass; nor was Nicholas of

---

[142] F. Bezold, *Zur Geschichte des Husitenthums* (Munich, 1874), pp. 65 f., notes that the Taborite towns kept their traditional magistrates and constitutions, with some new elements (the "captains," the role of the "community"); he also shows (pp. 71–74) how the Taborites continued to operate with the usual medieval estates, the nobility serving as military leaders. R. Urbánek, *Věk poděbradský, České dějiny*, III, i (Prague, 1914), 650 f., says Tabor remained unique and uncompromising only in religion. J. Pekař, *Žižka*, I, 169 ff., devotes a whole chapter to refuting "the error about Taborite democracy"; he contrasts the brief, partial, or theoretical manifestations of true social revolution with the actual persistance of the old social order and actual deterioration in the peasants' condition. Macek, *Tábor*, I, 263–314, offers the most exhaustive study of Tabor's social composition, 1420–1452; he contrasts the brief, early period of domination by the poor with the inexorable development of the usual classes of a typical "craft town." The present interpretation has most in common with Urbánek's *Lipany a konec polních vojsk* (Prague, 1934), pp. 9–80, which does justice to both the new and old elements of Taborite society.

[143] My "Peter Chelčický," pp. 125–127.

[144] Chelčický, "On the Triple Division of Society," *ibid.*, pp. 137–167.

[145] *Život, KJBB*, pp. 285–287.

Pelhřimov's response an adequate rebuttal.[146] Tabor in fact was not imitating the Primitive Church, she was proceeding as though she were that church. Both the chiliasts and the Pikarts had expressed their sectarian religion by claiming that they and they alone were the true church, the body of Christ;[147] what Tabor did was fuse this sectarian notion with her societal establishment: "They regard themselves," Příbram complained, "as the Holy Universal Church of all Christendom."[148] Just as the Donatists in Augustine's day had held that the one universal church was only in Africa, so the Taborites now claimed that it was only in Bohemia.[149] In matter-of-fact terms the claim was of course fantastic, but we must not forget that Tabor had been named after the mountain on which Jesus had appeared in glory, and that the eschatological tension in which Tabor had taken shape did not disappear with the ebbing of outright chiliasm. Nicholas of Pelhřimov never lost his faith in "God's vengeance and the secret coming of Christ,"[150] and it was a spirit soaked in the Apocalypse that saw the Taborite enterprise as not merely an imitation of the Primitive Church but a *repetition* of the days when Christ was on earth. Hence the priests of Tabor could claim the sovereign freedom that so shocked their opponents: Tabor's only norm was herself.

The form of this freedom was that of the city-state, the autonomous town, governing and drawing support from the peasants and squires of the countryside. The emergence of this form has always had spectacular cultural effects—in ancient Greece, in Renaissance Italy, and mutatis mutandis in Puritan New England. It constitutes a solution of the problems of social organization on the basis of the citizens' participation in the active life of the community, their identification with it; hence there is a minimal elaboration of those structures tending to favor tradition over innovation. The

---

[146] Höfler, II, 540 f. (the twelve points); 568–572 (the refutation). The principle of the refutation was this: "negabimus assumptum, quod videlicet omnes ritus debeamus observare, quos Christus observavit. Nam multi ritus a Christo et ab Apostolis pro tunc adhuc observabantur de lege veteri, ut patet de circumcisione corporali et aliis plurimis, quae jam non oportet observari. . . . Non enim voluit Christus, ut immitaremur eum praecise in illis omnibus circumstantiis, quas tunc fecit." But Nicholas' often sharp arguments do not always prove his distinction between the rite and the circumstances.

[147] For the chiliasts see above, chap. vii, *ad* n. 97 and *passim;* for the Pikarts, chap. ix, *ad* n. 117.

[148] *O poslušenství* (*LČP*, No. 14), MS 4314, fol. 149ʳ: "Ale sami sie magi za czierkwe s. obecznú wšeho krzestianstwa."

[149] *Ibid.:* "yako nyňýe rzkú že gest toliko w Čzechach."

[150] Postil on Apocalypse, MS 4520, fol. 244ᵛ; the context shows that Nicholas himself believed in these things, not that he was attacking the chiliasts' belief in them, as Bartoš supposed—"Táborské bratrstvo" (as in n. 146, chap. ix, above), p. 110, where the passage is quoted in Latin.

creation of the city-state polity in the towns of the Taborite brotherhood did not change the existing order of Bohemia as a whole, of course, still less that of Europe; it was not a revolution in the sense of the French Revolution. But the secession of the Taborite communities from the established order amounted to a revolution for the people of those communities, and that is the important point. It was not merely a case of free cities in rebellion against their lords, a common enough phenomenon, but of cities that recognized no lords and which generated a spiritual life unique to themselves, hence schismatic with respect to the rest of the world. "We disagree with the Roman Church in substantial matters of the faith, and we therefore do not intend to conform to Roman rites"—this was the defiant answer of the priests of Tabor to the Prague masters in 1424.[151] And Tabor's political thought tended to be equally schismatic, even though this branch of intellectual activity was not well-developed. In general, neither Tabor nor Prague showed much interest in the more sophisticated political theories of their age; the unreality of such theories made them useless to men actively engaged in transforming reality. Moreover the Wyclifite tradition of Hussitism, common to both the Prague masters and the priests of Tabor, operated with pre-papalist and pre-Hildebrandine concepts, very often with the modest figure of the two swords, each ordained by God to collaborate in the suppression of evil.[152] But when Tabor had to, she could go beyond the commonplaces and

---

[151] See Appendix 2.

[152] In his Postil on Apocalypse, MS 4520, fol. 227ʳ, Nicholas of Pelhřimov declared that the two swords were derived separately from God ("potestas secularis . . . habet a domino gladium"); the priests and magistrates should collaborate in punishing sinners: "status secularis audit spirituales viros, qui in malicia maturos et in operibus infructuosos demonstrant eis et publice quandoque denuncciant" (*ibid.*, and see Bartoš, "Táborské bratrstvo," p. 112). At the Council of Basel he developed the program in more detail (see my "The Religion of Hussite Tabor," pp. 219 f.). Peter Chelčický also testifies to the practice, in his own way: "Weak is the preaching of Christ's priest who, unable to bring some people into Christ's justice through Scripture, calls upon power and announces their adultery, drunkenness, and other sins in the church, forces power to punish them, and believes that in so doing he is successful in his preaching" (my "Peter Chelčický," p. 144). John Příbram had similar ideas about the collaboration of the two powers for reform, but he developed them *ad hoc* and hence rather inconsistently, at first exalting the spiritual power in almost hierocratic terms, then emphasizing the separation of powers, in his polemics against the power-wielding priests of Tabor. Thus, in the *Contra articulos picardorum*, MS 4749, fol. 70ʳ, he writes: "Quamvis autem Cristus iussit apostolos habere gladios duos, hoc est intelligendum, quod sacerdotes habent duplicem gladium, unum spiritualem verbi dei principaliter ipsis recomissum, quem Cristus non iussit reducere in vaginam; alium corporalem, non ut ipso soli percuciant, sed ut ipsum in manibus laycorum regant et secundum dei legem regulent et gubernent." Worked out in terms of current needs, this line of thought leads to a claim that the university masters should direct the lay powers in

give remarkably clear expression to her own conviction of sovereign freedom. Replying to the Prague articles of 1424, and trying to preserve as much of them as possible, the priests of Tabor at Klatovy repeatedly felt it necessary to assert the principle of popular sovereignty. Prague held that the waging of war and the killing of criminals should be done at the command of the legitimate powers; the Taborites added the reservation that if those powers were lacking or remiss, their place might be taken by the people or by anyone moved by the spirit of God.[153] A similar claim for the people was made by Nicholas of Pelhřimov at the Council of Basel: clerics were subject to secular jurisdiction, which could be exercised not only by princes or magistrates, but even by the "community of the faithful." Here and indeed elsewhere in his discourse he based his position on extensive excerpts from Marsilius of Padua's *Defensor Pacis,* one of the few moments in history when that celebrated work was made to fulfill the revolutionary promise that has so distinguished it in the eyes of modern scholars.[154]

---

religious matters: *fol. 82ʳ:* ". . . in potissimis officiis secularibus constituendi sunt magistri et veri doctores . . . ," and: ". . . magistri in spiritualibus debent esse directores." More passages could be cited. At the same time, he states that God gives the nation its king (fol. 76ᵛ). Later, when he wished to condemn the Taborites' defiance of legitimate authority and the Taborite priests' intervention in politics and warfare, he emphasized the last notion. Thus his *De condicionibus iusti belli* (*LČP,* No. 10; see above, note 132), MS D 47, fol. 83ʳ, states: "Secundum theologos . . . Rex est princeps vel dominus ydoneus, qui suum omne regnum vel principatum continue dat Ihesu Cristo et in veritate recognoscit quod quidquid sortitur laudis glorie vel lucri a suis subditis, quod hoc solum omnino habet a Cristo Ihesu. . . ." And *fol. 81ᵛ:* ". . . sicut totus ordo et regimen spiritualium pendet auctoritative et impermixte a pontificibus, sic tota machina seu policia secularium agendorum dependet capitaliter et impermixte a civiliter principantibus ulterius. Ex hiis patet quod in negociis secularibus sicuti in bellicis, auctoritas et potestas bellandi ordinacione divina pendet a principibus. Cui periculosa usurpacione a cunctis detrahitur quando potestas huiusmodi principum ab aliis precipue a sacerdotibus occupatur. Tali enim usurpacione vel officiorum permixtione // (fol. 82ʳ) religio cristiana vim patitur, ordo Cristi confunditur. . . ."

[153] Appendix 2.

[154] F. M. Bartoš, "Myšlenka svrchovanosti lidu v husitské revoluci" ("The Idea of Popular Sovereignty in the Hussite Revolution"), *Husitství a cizina* (Prague, 1931), pp. 157–163, and *passim.* The passages in question appear in Nicholas' speech at the Council, in *Orationes,* ed. Bartoš (Tabor, 1935), pp. 56, 58, 63 ("communitas fidelium quandoque possit iudicium ferre in contumaces aut aliter criminosos, eciam in sacerdotes"), 66 ("liquet aperte cunctos episcopos Romanos principi coactiva iurisdiccione subiectos"); the references to the *Defensor pacis* are noted on these pages. Nicholas cited it as a work of Ockham's; Bartoš conjectures that knowledge of the treatise may have come to the Hussites from England, where the false attribution was also made. Cf. E. F. Jacob, *Essays in the Conciliar Epoch* (2nd ed.; Manchester, 1953), pp. 41–42, for the use of Marsilius by Dietrich of Niem in 1410.

The freedom of the community was matched by that of the individual Taborite, no matter how he may have been bound by the obligations of the social system. At Tabor, the commoner was a participant in the higher culture of his community—in its religion. In church he did not merely observe a self-contained liturgical drama, he was an actor, singing the hymns that constituted the service and listening to liturgical formulas that were kept brief and were uttered in his own language. In the religious discussions endemic in the Taborite towns, the ordinary layman could speak; having listened to countless sermons expounding the text of the Bible, he would have considerable knowledge of that book; if, as was often the case, he knew how to read, he could study not only the Bible in Czech but also the current doctrinal positions of the priests, who regularly wrote in both Czech and Latin. Peter Chelčický was not typical, but his case suggests what a wealth of intellectual nourishment was available to the educated layman, and how significant the ideas of such a layman might be in the processes that formed Tabor's religion.[155] John Příbram, who tells us that the Taborites suppressed Latin schools, also reveals that they taught boys and girls in Czech; the result was a remarkably well-educated citizenry. "This perfidious genus of men has the single good quality of loving letters," observed Aeneas Sylvius Piccolomini, who also commented that "among the Taborites you will hardly find a woman who cannot demonstrate familiarity with the Old and New Testaments."[156] Such educated laymen could be found elsewhere in late-medieval Europe, but in the Taborite communities they lived not as separate groups of pietists, but as the ordinary citizens of the state.

While the religious aspect of the commoners' participation in public life had its own basis in religious thought, it must have been related to the fact that the common people formed an important part of the Taborite armies, which were at first almost entirely of peasant composition, and retained a popular character for many years into the twenties and thirties. They were in

---

[155] Much material may be found in Příbram's *Život, KJBB;* for example, the case of William the Soap-boiler, who pronounced eucharistic theories (p. 301). Urbánek, *Lipany,* pp. 36–47, treats the subject more amply.

[156] Příbram, *Život, KJBB,* p. 275, where he does not fail to suggest the worst in regard to the priests' teaching of girls; also p. 277: the Taborites "rejected all church singing" *but* they sang songs in Czech of their own composition. Rokycana, *De septem culpis Taboritarum,* MS D 88, fol. 265ᵛ, charged that the Taborite priests were bad Latinists ("quos videmus adeo diminutos, ut eciam neque gramatice congruum sciant proferre sermonem"); Nicholas of Pelhřimov must have taken special pleasure in reminding Rokycana of a grammatical rule that the latter had forgotten ("Quod relativum quod potest ad duo referri antecedentia, ad proximum refertur, si non cum priori magis sit accidentibus limitatum"—in Lydius, *Waldensia,* I, 193 f.). For Aeneas Sylvius's testimony, see my "Pius Aeneas," p. 290.

fact known as "the community working in the field of battle." [157] There were changes here, of course, and by about 1430 Nicholas of Pelhřimov could write scathingly about those who served in the army as warriors of God, proclaiming "I am faithful, yes I am," but who really sought only temporal gain. And he could hold up to scorn those who once, when poor, never wanted to stay home, saying "I never miss a campaign, I always turn out," but who, having become rich, neglected military duty along with other holy obligations.[158] But his strictures are actually good evidence for the continuing popular character of Taborite public life.

This same phenomenon meets us when we move to what may seem a different subject—the extraordinary public role of the Taborite priests. Procop the Shaven was the example par excellence of what such a priest might become—one of the greatest generals of his age. Others played more modest military roles, as organizers of local actions, as morale-builders who were assigned the definite function of urging the warriors on to fight well, or merely as what we would call chaplains. At home their functions were even more important, for not only did they daily expound the law—the Bible—in their sermons, they also denounced sinners and saw to it that such were punished by the civil magistrates.[159] In fact the magistrates could not afford to ignore the priests, the real leaders of the people. John Příbram provides the best testimony:

> There is hardly a town of their party where priests are not lords—nay, kings, exercising in fact all royal rights over the townsmen and the surrounding squires and peasants. They depose and install magistrates, expel whomever they wish from the towns, receive whomever they wish, take property away from whomever they wish and give it to whomever they wish, and they themselves have sat on councils that sentenced priests or others to death.

---

[157] H. Toman, *Husitské válečnictví za doby Žižkovy a Prokopovy* (Prague, 1898), pp. 96–104 and *passim,* for the composition of the Taborite armies. Also Urbánek, *Lipany,* pp. 48–80, and esp. pp. 69 ff., for the continuing prominence of commoners and for the standing armies ("polní vojska"). See also Heymann, p. 382.

[158] Postil on Apocalypse, MS 4520, fol. 284ʳ; in Bartoš, "Táborské bratrstvo," p. 113 (I have changed his text slightly, according to the manuscript): "Nostri exercitus fidelibus fictis repleti sunt, qui se eciam quidem blaspheme vocant fideles, dicentes: *sem wyerny, sem.* . . . Qui multi non bellarent pro veritate, si non sperarent se per bella multa temporalia acquirere. Sicut hoc iam de multis compertum est, quod quamdiu pauperes fuerunt, numquam vel raro domi in civitatibus quiescere voluerunt, dicentes: *yat' nykdy nezmeškam pole, wzdy tahnu.* Sed dum iam saturantur burse et pera vel sacculi florenis, statim occasione accepta sinistra iacet, ociatur, raro vel numquam ieiunat, convivia diligit, inebriatur, superba sibi vestimenta comparat, et uxorem ducit, iam delicatus et impingwatus."

[159] See above, n. 152.

Thus they have taken over such a position of power in the towns that the magistrates or communities can do nothing against their will.[160]

Very similar charges were also drawn up by John Rokycana, to prove that the priests of Tabor were systematically violating the third Prague article, against the civil dominion of the clergy.[161] In his own way Nicholas of Pelhřimov admitted the truth of these complaints:

> In our convocations we have decreed that no priest or cleric in major orders may, as a matter of common law, be involved in secular affairs [see Klatovy §16, for example]. . . . Nevertheless, if by divine permission the secular powers are inept or incorrigible, any priest moved by the spirit of God may duly and meritoriously arrange peace among laymen and bring them into harmony, lest the poor be despoiled through their conflict. In doing this the priest may not seek his own advantage. . . . And we suppose that among us there is no priest who would not gladly be relieved of cares of this sort, which interfere with his office.[162]

---

[160] *Život, KJBB*, p. 285.

[161] *De septem culpis taboritarum*, of 1431 (*LČR*, No. 3), MS D 88, fols. 259ʳ–264ʳ, attacking the "civil dominion" exercized by the priests of Tabor in both military and civil matters. Excerpts follow: *fol. 260ᵛ*: ". . . quidam dicunt, dominium civile est dominium racione cuius potest licite viator actus exercere seculares, clericis ex lege Cristi prohibitos. Quales actus sunt corporaliter bellare, causam sanguinis agitare, in corporibus homines tormentis aut captivitatibus affligere, contenciose possessiones repetere, gladio ipsas defendere. . . . Est eciam causa cur execucio iuris civilis sit clero prohibita, quia habet potestatem coactivam sibi quasi inseparabiliter annexam; alias non valeret." *Fol. 261ᵛ*: ". . . ut ad actus civilis dominii quosdam, quos quidam ex clero regni Boemie tempore hoc nostro, sede regia vacante, sunt amplexati, ipsos tangamus, libet ad eosdem condescendere." *Fol. 262ᵛ*: ". . . quid diceremus illis sacerdotibus qui istis temporibus uti sunt ausi in bellis corporalibus armis . . . ?" *Fol. 263ʳ*: ". . . quidam sacerdotes moderni inverecunde actibus civilis dominii se implicarunt, quia iudicia secularium negociorum pertractant." *Fol. 263ᵛ*: "Quid autem de hiis dicemus qui constituere procurant iudices et officiales seculares, capitaneos, purgravios, consules, decanos, atque per turmas centuriones . . . ?" *Fol. 264ʳ*: "Periculose ergo agunt sacerdotes moderni, qui de locacione et constitucione secularium officialium pro sue voluntatis implecione se intromittebant et hodierna die intromittunt. Sed quid dicemus et de illis sacerdotibus qui media sive consilia ad exequenda bella dant et in facto in medium proponunt, ut sunt machinarum bombardarum disposicio, acierum ad ssturmonem sive conflictum cum inimicis dirreccio, sagittariorum lanceatorum currium tritulatorum regulacio, et cetera." To show the practical disadvantages of such activities Rokycana quotes from Jakoubek; *fol. 265ʳ*: ". . . implicantur valde negociis secularibus, et vacare libris sanctorum non curant, eciam tot libros sanctorum originales non habent, in quibus invenirent qualiter puncta fidei nunc eis dubia de necessitate inevitabiliter ostenderetur ex scriptura."

[162] Höfler, II, 689 f.

But there could be no relief, whether desired or not. Free elections based on universal manhood suffrage constitute one form of democracy but by no means the only or even the most usual one; more important is the form of the leader acting with the people, in a sort of resonance that cannot be fixed in the routine of institutions. This was the real power in the Taborite towns, no matter what their civil constitution.

These remarks about the facts of Taborite society lead back to the point with which this discussion was begun—the sovereign freedom of the resurrected Primitive Church. But the anatomization of this freedom in social and political terms leads back to its religious dimension, and to the priests of Tabor, who in a sense personified it. Příbram, who was always the best recorder of Taborite atrocities, painted a memorable portrait of these priests and of their sovereign freedom, the *superba praesumptio Thaboritarum*:

> The priest of Tabor is pious and mild in appearance, but inside he is an impious tyrant; outside innocent and pure, but inside stinking and squalid with blood; outside submissive but inside elevated over all. He will suffer subordination to no one, but seeks to be over all; he presumes himself to be better, but does not believe that he is arrogant. He mixes into everything, turns away from those who are wiser, reordains what has been ordained, redoes what has been done—whatever he himself has not done or ordained, he deems improperly done and poorly ordained. He sits in judgement on the judges, prejudges what has been judged. Unbridled, unbending, precipitate, and bold, he rashly, impiously, and prophanely attacks all things holy and divine.[163]

When such men insisted on scripture alone as the law of society and the norm of truth,[164] they were really claiming the right to draw whatever lessons they wished from the Bible's infinitely varied reservoir. Hence, for example, they rejected the Roman missal: its prescribed order of lessons provided texts that might not be the right ones for a given situation. At first each priest preached with full freedom, although even then he must have determined his discourse according to his sense of what would have an effect on his lay followers; later a synod of the clergy laid down certain restrictive norms within the biblical framework, but not the patristic or scholastic

---

[163] *Professio fidei*, in Cochlaeus, *Historiae Hussitarum libri XII*, pp. 516 f.

[164] The basic Taborite position, as stated by Nicholas in the Confession of 1431, was "[scimus] legem ipsius [*scil.*, Christi] esse solam sufficientem ad regimen Ecclesie militantis" (Lydius, I, 94 f.). This was simply Wyclif's thesis (see my "Wyclifism as Ideology of Revolution," *Church History*, XXXII (1963), 66), which had been taken up by John Hus (*LČH*, p. 89, No. 82). This law was the whole Bible: "Christus Jesus . . . unam legem instituit, que est vetus et novum testamentum" (*Orationes*, ed. Bartoš (Tabor, 1935), p. 40); the Old Testament, however, was to be understood according to the sense of the New (e.g., Höfler, II, 482, 484).

norms that served to lock the present into the past.[165] Unlike Jakoubek, who saw the Primitive Church as an ideal that moderns should try to imitate but could never attain, the Taborites retained the hope of their chiliast days, that the Primitive Church, resurrected in themselves, would progress to a still higher stage of eschatological fulfillment. Individual inspiration, which Jakoubek regarded as extremely rare in modern times, was an important factor in Tabor's self-consciousness.[166]

John Příbram saw the implications of Taborite freedom in this respect: it was freedom to break out of the common civilization of Europe:

> They say that the whole Christian church should be content, in regard to all things to be believed, held, or acted upon, with only the naked Bible—the Old and New Laws—and that in its express assertions and manifest expressions. Thus whatever they do not find expressly stated in the Law, they reject and despise it all as unprovable and alien to the faith, as the vain invention of men. . . .

> This principle is undoubtedly the pestilential root and origin of all the errors and enormities currently produced by them. . . . And if this principle should establish itself in the hearts of men, it would allow thousands of the worst errors and heresies into the church. . . .

> How, I ask, can the thoughts of so many minds and so many men, with so many different opinions and desires, be brought to one understanding of the same gospel . . . unless they be restricted and regulated . . . by the golden boundaries that our holy Fathers have set? . . . But to reject the doctrines of such great saints . . . is to remove the repressor of all their presumptions, so that, infallibly, every sort of license will be given to every error, every path hitherto closed will be opened to all perversity, and in short order the world will rest on the worst errors and irremediable enormities. . . . Indeed their own case proves this, as experience now shows . . . : divided and diverse among themselves, . . . they have broken up their own unity into innumerable parts, . . . and it would be hard to find among them two men who agree with each other. . . .

> And how will the sacred order of the church be stabilized if each single nation can choose its own teachers as it likes, without testing, approval, or authorization by the church? Indeed, if this license be given to the world, in a short time doctrine will confound doctrine, nation will turn away from nation, and the common faith will stand in peril.[167]

---

[165] Appendix 2.

[166] See above, *ad* n. 110. In the Postil on Apocalypse, Nicholas of Pelhřimov once referred to the "statum ecclesie primitive, cuius rectores erant *et sunt* apostoli" (MS 4520, fol. 190ᵛ; my emphasis).

[167] *Cum ab inicio* (*LČP*, No. 24), MS D 47; the translated passages read as follows: *fol. 1ʳ*: ". . . dicentes quod tota cristianorum ecclesia, quoad omnia credenda tenenda et

With certain qualifications, this diagnosis and prognosis can be accepted as not only precise but profound. Aeneas Sylvius Piccolomini would make similar judgements after his visit to Tabor a decade or so later.[168] It only remains for the historian to suggest that the vicious license that destroyed the order of civilization was also the freedom with which an organized society created its own order and its own spiritual values.

Indeed what we find among the men and women of the Taborite communities is not license but the self-imposed discipline of spiritual aristocrats, ready to accept the obligations of their quest for perfection. There were of course exceptions and variations, increasingly numerous as time passed, as conditions became more settled, and as the ranks of the enthusiasts were infiltrated by the uncommitted. Some, we hear, avoided military service or served only for booty; they did not fast, they wore luxurious clothes, they got married.[169] Some tried to stay home during the long sermons, to which they might have to be driven by force.[170] But these were the cases that attracted the attention of critics; by and large, for the whole of Tabor's life, the laity not only provided funds to support their priests, they followed the priests'

agenda, debet esse contenta sola nuda lege veteri et nova dumtaxat in assercione eius expressa et in expressione eius manifesta, ita ut quicquid in legis expressione non reperiunt, totum hoc tamquam improbabile et alienum a fide dicunt, et tamquam vanam invencionem hominum abiciunt et contempnunt. . . ." *Fol. 1ᵛ:* ". . . hoc principium talium indubitanter est radix et origo pestilentica omnium errorum et enormitatum modo ab eis prodencium. . . . Revera si illud principium in cordibus hominum coallesceret, mille pessimis erroribus et heresibus in ecclesia locum daret. . . ." *Fol. 6ʳ-6ᵛ:* ". . . quomodo queso tot capitum // quot hominum in mundo tam varie senciencium atque dessiderancium ingenia ad unam intelligenciam in eodem ewangelio redigentur . . . , nisi videlicet hiis preclaris terminis, quos posuerunt sancti patres nostri, tamquam aureis limitibus, prestringantur et regulentur? . . . . Amotis et abiectis tantorum sanctorum doctrinis, . . . auferetur repressorium omnibus presumpcionibus, quo facto infallibiliter dabitur omnis licencia quibuslibet erroribus, omnis via hucusque preclusa patebit cunctis perversitatibus atque in brevi mundus ipse stabit pessimis heresibus et irremediabilibus enormitatibus. Quorum omnium detestanda inicia patule nunc elucent in talium . . . stulticia, prout omni ore facundius ocularis modo probat de eis rerum experiencia: . . . divisi et diversi a se facti, . . . ipsam propriam unitatem per innumeras partes inter se distinxerunt, mores et fidem inter se dilaceraverunt, ut difficile in eis inveniantur duo pariter qui sibi consentirent. . . . *Fol. 25ʳ:* "Advertant queso et discernant quomodo stabilietur sacratus ordo Ecclesie si una queque nacio pro libito capiat sibi doctores absque ecclesiastica probacione et approbante auctorisacione. Revera si mundo ista licencia dabitur, in decursu brevi temporis doctrina a doctrina confundetur, gens a gente avertetur, et fides communis periclitabitur."

[168] See my "Pius Aeneas among the Taborites," *Church History,* XXVIII (1959), 292 f.

[169] See above, n. 158.

[170] The report of Aeneas Sylvius, who also noted, however, that in general the Taborites "have no greater concern than to hear sermons"—and this in 1451 (my "Pius Aeneas," p. 290).

leadership not only in the doctrine and liturgy that made so few concessions to human frailty, but in a puritanical moralism that certainly had its tedious moments. Outside of the Taborite brotherhood, if we can believe John Rokycana, "almost everyone in Bohemia" hated Tabor's simple rites; and Nicholas Biskupec could concede that the carnal and worldly people naturally preferred the Whore of Apocalypse, with her golden cup,[171] but the reformed liturgy would not have come into being or have been continued unless the Taborites had in fact hated the Roman mass and everything that went with it. Nor was any hand lifted against the priests as they had sinners put in the stocks, as they abolished such presumably popular things as the cult of saints and holy images, the otiose Roman feast days, and the rather complex comforts of Purgatory and works for the dead. In eucharistic doctrine, to be sure, there was some tension between the people who still clung to faith in a substantial presence, and the priests who held to a merely sacramental one. Příbram gives some relevant examples,[172] and Peter Chelčický expatiates on the "unheard-of" situation—the priests offering the Eurcharist as one thing, the people taking it as another.[173] If Nicholas Biskupec and his colleagues agreed to permit an *adoratio vicaria,* adoration before the sacrament but directed to Christ in heaven, it was no doubt because the laity would not accept the abolition of all adoration.[174] But the

---

[171] Rokycana's charge and Nicholas's response are in Höfler, II, 698. Cf. the testimony of Aeneas Sylvius in 1455: the nobility preferred the Roman rite because it was more beautiful (my "Pius Aeneas among the Taborites," p. 299).

[172] *Život, KJBB,* pp. 301 ff.

[173] *Replika proti Biskupcovi,* p. 496: "you priests have one understanding of this sacrament and the lay people have another. . . . And this is an unheard-of thing, that the people seek salvation in one interpretation, but the priest ministers to the people in another, and dares not tell the people frankly what he thinks of that which he ministers to them." In a sense this charge was admitted by the Taborites: thus John Němec of Žatec wrote, *Cum spiritus veritatis . . . , TTE,* p. 7: "Et sic fidelis potest indifferenter sacramentum appellare nunc corpus Christi, nunc vero panem. . . . Et sic fidelis potest dicere infidelibus quandoque uno modo quandoque alio modo, secundum quod viderit ex hoc profectum."

[174] See above, n. 118. Nicholas's tractate *De non adorando Christo Ihesu in sacramento* has not survived in its full form, but excerpts from it are given by Rokycana (Nejedlý, *Prameny,* pp. 116–153 *passim*) and Příbram (Goll, *Quellen,* II, 62 f.), and an abridged version is published by Sedlák, *De adorare et colere, TTE,* pp. 51–55. According to Nicholas adoration proper, "adoracio latrie," is due to Christ only as God in heaven, which is where he is, but "adoracio reverencie" is fitting for things that signify God, and the Eucharist comes under this heading—it should be venerated "Sic dum fidelis viderit sacramentum, debet tamquam ex propinqua ymagine Christi suam pigriciam ad passionis Christi memoriam cum reverencia excitare et maxime dum hoc sacramentum manducat" (*TTE,* p. 53). "Sed quid est," wrote Rokycana (*Prameny,* p. 136), "nisi quod isti fratres . . . vocant aliquid adoracionem, quod non est adoracio, et Christum nuncupant, quid non est Christus."

concession shows rather the reciprocity between priests and people than any outright gulf.

How far the priests could go in leading the people away from the old consolations appears perhaps most clearly in Nicholas's attack on the cult of saints, preserved by the Prague masters:

> The masters wish to show the sufficiency of the saints, so that everyone may more freely and securely turn to them, for he has heard that they pay heed to our needs and have compassion for us and are solicitous for our welfare. . . . And the uneducated can draw no other conclusion from all of this than that *they are sure of their salvation* if they diligently serve the saints, pray to them, fast to them, burn incense to them, and on their feast-days take up no sickle, axe, or other instrument of servile labor. But it is all right to take up a cup of wine or beer! Such doctrines are very harmful and enticing to men.

> [The Virgin Mary is called] The Most Desirable Hope of Sinners, the Queen of Heaven, Omnipotent, Merciful; she gathers all, indiscriminately, under the protection of her cloak. . . . But such magnification of her makes it seem to the uneducated, even to the greatest sinners among them, that *no one will be damned,* because the Hope of Sinners rules in heaven and is diligent on behalf of her clients.[175]

He put the matter more systematically thus:

> From his hidden judgements God wishes to benefit some men and does not wish to benefit others; some he benefits without being asked, . . . some he hears because he sees their future conversion; . . . sometimes, moreover, he does not hear even his elect in their difficulties. And the saints are of no use in all these things, for they do not have God's knowledge of them. Therefore the function of interceding cannot well subsist in the saints, because they cannot have so great a knowledge of hearts, of predestination, and of the other differences among men, as God has.[176]

A similar logic applied to the sacraments. Prague regarded them as necessary means to salvation, but Tabor judged them to be only useful; they could not help the man foreknown to damnation, nor would one of the predestined faithful fail to be saved for want of a sacrament.[177] Many more such statements could be adduced, but always to the same point: salvation was not to be captured by ecclesiastical operations, the tension of religious striving was not to be dissipated by cultic observances. Like Nicholas of Dresden, whom he copied, Nicholas of Pelhřimov rejected Purgatory not least because it functioned essentially as a rationalization of the scheme of salvation—on

---

[175] Höfler, II, 675 (Lydius, *Waldensia,* I, 199); Lydius, I, 234.

[176] Höfler, II, 679 f. (Lydius, I, 205 ff.).

[177] Lydius, I, 117; Höfler, II, 602. And see the Prague and Klatovy articles in Appendix 2.

the one hand a comfort to the tepid Christians, on the other an assurance that no one was going to get away with anything by a last-minute repentance. "God may do as he likes," Nicholas declared, and as for the masters' argument that it would be unjust for the repentant bad man to go to heaven without first suffering, Nicholas scornfully remarked, "God is accused of injustice if he does not act according to their confections!" [178] In this way the faith of Tabor became a challenge to her people, an endless summons to religious dedication. Such a faith must have been uncomfortable, but also exciting; in an age of disorientation, with the traditional order unstable in fact and rejected in theory, the faith based on heroic pessimism no doubt seemed more relevant than the more pleasant faith of the tradition.

Enough has been said to show that Tabor's faith, the cause of her priests, was the specific ideology of Taborite society. The values of the Hussite reform could be developed to a certain extent within the old order represented in different degrees by Prague and the barons; if those values were to reveal their full potential in rejection of Romanism and in construction of a new spiritual world, they had to pass into a different society—the city-states of the Taborite brotherhood. To call the religion the ideology of the society does not of course exhaust the relationship between the social and spiritual spheres, but—as suggested in the present section, and indeed in the whole of this study—that relationship can be understood in general terms only when reconstructed in its particulars as a complex of interactions. For similar reasons one can only conjecture whether the Taborite religious system was essentially or only accidentally limited to the city-state polity. Tabor did try to win national power but failed, and her congregational reformation never had to prove its capacities for either national development or even local endurance. Unable to transform the old world, and unable to leave it physically behind, the Taborites perhaps inevitably succumbed to the national coalition headed by George of Poděbrady. Before they did, however, their bishop provided at least the record of their hopes and their achievements, the story of an experiment that would be repeated more than once, to the enrichment of our civilization.

[178] Höfler, II, 662–664 (Lydius, I, 177–179). For the parallels with Nicholas of Dresden's *De purgatorio,* see my discussion of this work in *OC & N* p. 22; the verbal correspondences are noted by J. Sedlák, *Mikuláš z Drážďan* (Brno, 1914), p. 45.

Appendix I

THE ANONYMOUS ANTI-UTRAQUIST TREATISE, *ESTOTE SINE OFFENSIONE* (HARDT, III, 658-762)

UNIQUELY broad, deep, and rich in its attack on the problem of utraquism, this treatise is potentially a first-rate source for the whole intellectual history of Hussitism in the period 1414–1415, more so even than the equally anonymous but more famous *Eloquenti viro* (Hardt, III, 338–391). In addition to the single manuscript text transcribed by Von der Hardt (probably VNB, 4945), six more in Bohemia and Moravia have been listed by Jan Sedlák: UP, I F 18; Cer. II. 387; Olomouc Capit. 519; Prague Capit. D 48 and D 65; Třeboň, A 11 (incomplete); no doubt several others could be found, and a critical collation of all would certainly yield valuable results. Meanwhile Sedlák is the only scholar who has discussed the work, rather briefly ("Počátkové kalicha" (1914), 78–80), dating it at the end of 1415 but leaving the question of authorship open. Bartoš does not discuss it at all. In what follows I offer some tentative conclusions, designed chiefly to support my own use of the work in chapter iii.

The treatise is divided into two main parts, the first labelled "General" (Hardt, III, 658–690), the second "Special" (689–762). Part Two is in turn divided into three special tractates: I (691–720), "Generalia momenta ac fundamenta pro explicanda doctrina communionis sub una"; II (719–742), "Proposita argumenta pro communione laicorum sub una specie"; III (741–762), "Quo examinata argumenta Jacobi de Misa, pro communione sub utraque allata." The titles are undoubtedly provided by Hardt—the work nowhere refers to Jakoubek—and it is not clear to what extent the major divisions appear in the manuscript, although Sedlák says that the chapters are there.

Part I begins with the statement that some men in Prague are asserting

that the laity should take communion in both kinds. Taking as his text I
Cor. 10:32, "Give none offense, neither . . . to the church of God," the
author sets up the problem as one of church authority, church discipline, and
ecclesiology. How can these upstarts presume to set themselves against the
accumulated wisdom of the Roman church? He correctly puts his finger on
the main point, the Hussite idea that the modern church should be reduced
to the estate of the Primitive Church, in particular to propertylessness (663).
From this he goes on to a general consideration of sectarian heresy, using the
anti-Waldensian treatise (about 1250) of Rainerius or perhaps of Pseudo-
Rainerius (1266-1270) (see the entries for both in A. Hugon and G. Gonnet,
Bibliografia valdese [Torre Pellice, 1953], Nos. 657, 665). He quotes a whole
conspectus of sectarian errors from this work, and thus lays the foundation
for his own presentation, which selects some of the errors for special attention and terse refutation. The picture he paints is unmistakably that of a
sectarian heresy of the Waldensian type, with emphasis on the points that—
obviously—corresponded to those that had been agitating Prague in the
period 1410-1414, and more particularly, 1412-1413. Here I in turn select
some of the more interesting ones:

> (676) Contra hos, qui dicunt, quod Principes et Domini seculares possunt
> sibi clerum subjicere in suis terris. . . .
> (677) Contra hos, qui dicunt, quod quilibet sacerdos tenetur praedicare
> . . . [et] qui dicunt quod quilibet sacerdos potest praedicare, ubi vult
> et quando vult, imo sine superiori consensu.
> (678) Contra hos qui dicunt, quod decimae sint purae eleemosynae.
> (680) Contra hos qui dicunt, quod nullus debet excommunicari nisi sit in
> mortali peccato. . . .
> (681) Contra hos, qui dicunt, quod excommunicato majori excommunica-
> tione participare non sit peccatum.
> (681) Contra hos qui dicunt, quod libri haereticorum possint legi, et libri
> Wicleff.
> (682) Contra hos, qui dicunt, quod antichristus non veniet, sed dudum
> venit: Quia Papam vocant antichristum et pingunt ipsum in pileo
> Papali et cum aquilae pedibus.
> (685) Contra illos, qui dicunt, quod indulgentiae nihil sunt. . . .

This last point is followed by a long disquisition on indulgences (685-690),
clearly oriented to the controversies of 1412. The author was evidently
someone quite familiar with those controversies, and the other points just
quoted also show that he was well aware of the struggle against the Forty-
five Articles of Wyclif, of Eppinge's discourse on excommunication, of
Jakoubek's identification of the pope with Antichrist, and of Nicholas of

Dresden's works in the same sense. The explicit reference to a painting of the pope wearing the tiara and equipped with an eagle's claws for feet shows that the author knew of—and had probably seen—the illustrations of the *Tabule,* where this picture went with Table IX (only the title, "Anticristus cum meretricibus," survives—see the edition in *OC & N*—but the picture was undoubtedly similar to that preserved in the later Czech version, of which the illustrations survive in two codices; the picture in question from the "Jena" codex, is reproduced in *SbH,* V (1957), after p. 80, with the false title (in Czech): "The Pope Hears Nuns' Confessions"—the tiara and claws are there).

Special Tractate I is similarly interesting, for it proceeds to its eucharistic subject via a series of chapters devoted to matters of ecclesiology. Again we are drawn back to the earlier period, now to the ecclesiological literature generated by the controversy that came to a head with the synod of 6 February 1413; in fact the work under discussion has frequent points of correspondence with that literature, particularly with Stephen of Páleč's *De ecclesia* and other allied works of 1413. Before getting to these, however, let us consider the following set of correspondences:

1. *Estote sine offensione* (697): "Interrogare quis poterit, utrum decreta Papae, seu *Decretum,* talis liber, Decretales, constitutiones et alia jura canonica, sint observanda? Et videtur, Quod non. Quia Decreta sunt humana inventio, Decretales sunt correctoria, et alia jura sunt propter quaestum inventa." [There follows a refutation.]

2. Páleč, *De ecclesia* (1413; Sedlák, *M. Jan Hus,* p. 292, n. 2): [The Hussites are "contemptores canonum"] . . . "Audent palam dicere: . . . Quid decreta et canones nisi litere private et antiqua coopertoria pape et humane tradiciones!"

3. Andrew of Brod, *De sumpcione* (1415; *loc. cit.*): "Memini me audisse ab adversario [*scil.,* Jakoubek] necnon ab eius in hac parte sociis: Quid decretum? Humana tradicio! Quid decretales epistole? Verius coopertoria pape!" [Cf. Hardt, III, 474.]

Even if we refrain from emending "correctoria" to "coopertoria," to make the first passage conform to the others, we still cannot escape the impression that the authors had all heard the same thing about the canon law from the Husiste radicals. The author of *Estote* must have belonged to the same circle of theologians that included Páleč and Andrew, and if we eliminate those of the circle who had died (Stanislav of Znojmo), or whose publications were different in tone (John Hildessen; see Sedlák, "Počátkové kalicha" (1914), 75), or who did not as far as we know publish anything to the point—then we can do no better than identify the author of *Estote* with either Andrew or

Stephen. The latter is more likely, for the following reasons: (1) Our treatise offers a discussion of the utraquist problem that differs in some important points from Andrew's: it carefully distinguishes the sacrifice from the sacrament (705 ff.); it does not deny the utraquism of the Primitive Church, as Andrew had tended to do, but rather argues that the customs of the Primitive Church were inferior to those of the modern church (713 ff.). (2) We have anti-utraquist treatises by Andrew of Brod but none by Stephen of Páleč. This point is not as silly as it may seem: it is inconceivable that Stephen would not have taken part in *the* polemic of the time, but no work thus far attributable to him (see the list drawn up by J. Fikrle, "Čechové na koncilu Kostnickém," *ČČH*, IX (1903), 428–431) corresponds to the anti-utraquist treatise of 1415 that we would expect. *Estote* would of course fill the bill nicely. (3) Finally, it may be observed that Stephen was an extraordinarily sharp and profound critic of Hussitism, while Andrew of Brod, though lively enough, rarely got below the surface of the obvious; *Estote,* in short, is too good to be by Andrew.

At this point the demonstration would require a careful comparison of *Estote* with the known ecclesiological works of Stephen of Páleč. This has not yet been feasible for me, and instead I offer only a few references to parallel treatments of the same points. Thus *Estote*'s refutation of the doctrine that a priest's sacramental power depends on his possession of the Holy Spirit (675) may be compared with Páleč's *De ecclesia,* as quoted by Sedlák, *M. Jan Hus,* p. 290, n. 5. Similarly, on the doctrine that only God can excommunicate (680; p. 291, n. 5); and on the assertion that a priest can preach wherever and whenever he likes, even without his superior's consent (677; p. 289*). Furthermore, *Estote*'s remarkable concept of the relationship between the Primitive and Roman churches (see above, chap. iii, *ad* nn. 64, 65) is much the same as Páleč's doctrine in the *De ecclesia* (pp. 266*–269*), that the Donation of Constantine was good and that the church's increase in riches and honors was good. Finally, if the treatise against Nicholas of Dresden's doctrine discussed above in chap. i, n. 137 (and see my introduction to *OC & N, ad* n. 149), was in fact the work of Stephen of Páleč, then it would provide support for attributing *Estote* to him. The two works are very similar in concept and even to some extent in composition: both use older anti-heretical authors (Benedict of Marseilles, Rainerius, respectively) to block out the image of heresy and to define heretical doctrines; both proceed by repetitions of "contra istos qui dicunt," and so on, both emphasize the questions of ecclesiology and ecclesiastical jurisdiction as at the root of all particular doctrines they refute, both praise the Donation of Constantine and the resulting enrichment of the church.

These hypotheses can be confirmed only by careful textual comparisons, which will in turn become feasible only when the works in question are edited, along with Stephen's earlier and later works. Meanwhile it may be suggested as a thesis worth study that the gap between Stephen's ecclesiological works of 1413 and his treatises against the Four Articles and other Hussite doctrines, written from 1420 on when he was a professor at Cracow, is suitably filled by *Estote sine offensione* in 1415 and the treatise against Nicholas of Dresden's doctrines in about 1417.

THE TABORITE SYNOD OF KLATOVY, 11 NOVEMBER 1424, AND RELATED PROBLEMS

NICHOLAS of Pelhřimov begins his chronicle with an inspirational prologue, then offers a brief and artful review of the congregation-movement of 1419, the Four Articles, and the common Hussite resolve—which included the approval of the Prague masters and other priests—to wage war in defense of the Law of God against the Crusade. But the wars that ensued, he notes, were not always fought by men with pure purposes, and many abuses—*deordinationes*—arose; here Nicholas passes to another section, the last before his coverage of the controversies over rites, and tells how the priests of Tabor sought to eliminate these abuses.[1] For this purpose they had several synods, one in Písek (21 to 24 February 1422), one in Tabor (23 to 30 April 1424), and one in Klatovy (about 11 November 1424). Many articles were promulgated against the abuses and, he says, he will insert some of them; nine follow, all rather long. The ninth deals with the Eucharist, the other eight with questions of warfare and clerical participation in it: the first four seem to state general principles, the second four to spell out certain applications of these.[2] But which articles came from which synods? Nicholas does not say. The problem of distribution has been taken up by several scholars, but it remains unsolved. The fact is that there are no other sources indicating what the Taborite priests did at the synods of Písek and Tabor, but a good deal of evidence variously proving or suggesting that all the articles, especially the first four and the last, came from the synod of Klatovy, which also promulgated many other articles.[3] Here the historical

---

[1] Höfler, II, 482–488.

[2] H. Toman, *Husitské válečnictví* (Prague, 1898), p. 49.

[3] Tomek, IV, 312 f., supposed that at Klatovy the Taborites accepted the Prague articles of 1424 on warfare and killing, and even developed them further, in practical terms—hence the first eight articles in Nicholas's listing. Toman, p. 50, rejected this

context is of essential importance: first there were the efforts in September of all Hussite parties to promote the pacification and organization of the realm, then in consequence the meeting between the Prague masters and the priests of Tabor about 16 October; here the masters presented their articles to the priests, and the meeting was adjourned, the Taborites returning home and then holding their own synod at Klatovy, on 11 November. The Prague meetings were resumed on 23 November. Since the points raised by the Prague articles covered all the points at issue between the two parties, the confrontation virtually defined the whole content of the doctrinal dispute thus far; at the same time it would be only a slight exaggeration to say that this definition can be taken as valid for the remaining twenty years of Prague-Tabor disputation. It will therefore be useful in this Appendix to present the texts in question—both the Prague articles, which survive and pose few problems, and the Taborite articles of Klatovy, which have to be assembled from various sources. Most of what follows represents a mere digest

---

view, which implied "that the basic articles [i.e., the first four] were the exclusive spiritual property of the Prague masters. . . ." This is the real issue of the scholarly controversy—in its origins it is the old Prague-Tabor controversy in modern dress. Toman went on to suggest that the triple division of Nicholas's articles (1-4, 5-8, 9) corresponded to a chronological sequence, that in a general sense it derived from the succession of the three synods he named, and that the correspondence between the Prague articles of 1424 and the Taborite articles 1-4 reflects their common derivation from a now lost non-partisan original (pp. 50, 55). Jaroslav Goll, "Dva příspěvky ke kritice Tomanova 'Husitského válečnictví,'" *ČČH*, V (1899), 151-158, refuted all these propositions: the first eight articles are tied together so logically that they must have originated at the same time; in regard to the first four, the Prague counterparts clearly, on textual grounds, have priority; any attempt to reconstruct the presumed common original will produce a text substantially identical with the Prague formulations. N. Jastrebov, *Etjudy o Petře Chelčickom i jego vremeni* (St. Petersburg, 1908), contributed a demonstration of the verbal derivation of some of the material in the articles from Wyclif (pp. 92-95), and then, in a special appendix (pp. 95-106), dealt with the problems raised by Toman, whose views he supported, chiefly by showing that our main source for the Klatovy synod, John Příbram, says nothing of any Taborite articles on war, but does give eucharistic articles that are much the same as the ninth Taborite article given by Nicholas. But F. M. Bartoš, "Ke konvokacím táborským r. 1422 a 1424," *ČČM*, LXXXVIII (1914), 307-311, showed that Příbram's list of Klatovy articles was incomplete, including only what served his anti-Taborite purposes. Thus, chiefly for want of real evidence, we cannot associate the Taborite articles 1-8 with any synod earlier than Klatovy, although, as Bartoš later observed ("Klatovská synoda táborských kněží z 11. listopadu r. 1424," *JSH*, VIII (1935), 9), Nicholas may have merely given the Klatovy formulations of articles that could have been adopted at the earlier synods, which he does, after all, mention (but I would regard this notion as too hypothetical to be useful). For the possible eucharistic activity of the Písek synod of 1422, see above, chap. x, n. 99.

of the work of F. M. Bartoš,[4] with the single advantage of being in English, but on a few points additional inferences will be offered.

We may begin with the Prague articles, known to scholars ever since F. Prochazka printed them in his *Miscellaneen aus der böhmischen und mährischen Literatur* (Prague, 1784), pp. 271–279; the relative rarity of this work justifies reprinting the text.[5]

1.] Primo et ante omnia credendum est, ac firmiter tenendum a cunctis Christi fidelibus, quod septem sacramenta ecclesiae universalis, videlicet baptisma, confirmatio, sacrosancta eucharistia, poenitentia, ordo, matrimonium, unctio sacra, sunt ex fide catholica ecclesiae necessaria ac salubria antidota animarum ab omnibus promovenda, et tenenda.

2.] Item, tenendum et credendum est, quod Christus verus Deus, et verus homo est in sacramento eucharistiae visibili, secundum suam propriam naturam et substantiam corpoream, et secundum eius naturalem existentiam, eandem penitus in numero, quam sumpsit de Beata Virgine Maria, et secundum quam residet in caelo, in dextera Patris.

Cum annexis octo propositionibus pridem et modo praedictis sacerdotibus per nos oblatis, et in ipsis unanimiter nobis et ipsis concordatis et unitis, et pacto gravissimo desuper utrinque firmatis et roboratis.

3.] Item tenendum est quod sacramentum baptismatis more ecclesiae exercendum est, cum exorcismis, cum patrinis, cum chrysmate et oleo sacro, ac cum trina immersione in aqua benedicta, dum ad ista adest congrua opportunitas loci, temporis, et personarum.

4.] Item tenendum, credendum et instandum est, quod baptizati a proprio episcopo iuxta formam et statuta ecclesiae primitivae cum chrysmate sunt confirmandi.

5.] Item tenendum et credendum est, quod pro remedio omnium lapsorum et labentium, et poenitere debentium, confessiones auriculares idoneo sacerdoti sunt exercendae et promovendae: et ipsa remedia salutaria, scilicet ieiunia, eleemosynae, et orationes et cetera opera satisfactionis, pro modo culpae sunt eis iniungenda.

6.] Item tenendum est et credendum, quod sacramentum ordinis duntaxat ab episcopo vel episcopis est conferendum.

7.] Item tenendum est quod sacramento ordinis soli duntaxat annexae sunt claves ecclesiae et potestas solvendi et conficiendi, et vasa sacra contrectandi, sic quod non alteri statui vel personae.

8.] Item tenendum est et credendum, quod sacramentum matrimonii, usque in finem saeculi libertatum ac libertandum, est exercendum legitime in

---

[4] In *ČČM*, LXXXVIII (1914), 307–313; *JSH*, VIII (1935), 4–10; *ČSPSČ*, XXIX (1921), 102–122 ("Táborské bratrstvo let 1425–1426 na soudě svého biskupa Mikuláše z Pelhřimova"). These will be cited below in abbreviated form.

[5] The text is printed here with a few corrections, made subsequently by Prochazka and by Toman, *op. cit.*, pp. 51–54, where there are also references to the manuscripts.

personis idoneis et capacibus, iuxta statuta sanctorum et ecclesiae catholicae, et regulas ad illa traditas et ordinatas, exclusis circa hoc erroribus et caeteris exorbitantiis, et signanter hoc errore, quod filia in annis discretionis, in aetate puellari existente, et absque consensu parentum cuipiam matrimonium vovente, sit divorcianda propter dissensum parentum vel propinquorum.

9.] Item credendum et tenendum est, quod sacramentum extremae unctionis poscentibus aegris et infirmis in oleo sacro, iuxta formam ecclesiae catholicae, est ministrandum et exercendum: et quod contemptores illius et aliorum sacramentorum sunt castigandi, iuxta censuras ecclesiasticas corrigendi.

10.] Item credendum est et fideliter tenendum, quod decem praecepta dominica et caetera puncta evangelica sunt a cunctis fidelibus sub obtentu salutis aeternae observanda, secundum sensum verum et legitimum quem spiritus sanctus in ipsis flagitat, et concors sanctorum sententia disserit et explanat, potissime attendendo ad matrem et magistram omnium nostrum, ecclesiam primitivam et praxes eius et exequutiones eorundem praeceptorum.

11.] Item tenendum est et firmiter observandum, quod in occisione reorum non est lex vetus in singulis suis iudiciariis sequenda et alleganda, nec ipsa occisio a quoquam in propria causa ac vindicta est exequenda, nec in quenquam nisi in eum qui aliter corrigi nullatenus valet, et magna compassione exercenda, nec unquam aliter nisi ubi urgente necessitate lex nova occidere licentiat, et per potestates legitimas suadet et auctorisat; ita tamen quod erga ipsam sedecim conditiones charitatis observentur, et ipsa legis naturae regula: Quod tibi non vis rationabiliter, ne alteri facias.

12.] Item tenendum est quod bella christiana non sunt a quoquam attemptanda et exercenda, nisi ubi et quando lex nova licentiat, et potestas legitima autorizat, et causa iusta impellit et necessitas: nec contra alios nisi in fidei destructores, et innocentum oppressores, et regionis aut reipublicae invasores et vastatores, et alios pertinaces et sceleratos legis domini transgressores, qui aliis modis levioribus nullatenus a sua pertinacia reduci possunt et coerceri. Hac regula in bellis potissime observata, quod hostem in impetu necessitas perimat non voluntas. Exclusa prorsus a bellantibus nocendi cupiditate, ulciscendi crudelitate, implacato atque implacabili animo, feritate rebellandi, libidine dominandi, res alienas invadendi et avare rapiendi, et si quae sunt similia, prout sancti doctores elucidant et explanant.

13.] Item credendum est et tenendum, quod in bellis quantumcunque iustis res alienae non solum non sunt avare invadendae, sed nec tangendae nocive nec concupiscendae, nec plebes fidelium et innocentum quomodolibet opprimendae, iuxta apostoli praeceptum aut documentum: mala non sunt facienda ut bona eveniant.

14.] Item tenendum est et diligenter observandum, quod ecclesias seu basilicas exurere sive destruere absque inevitabili et stricta necessitate, aut ipsas quomodolibet violare et contemptibiliter prophanare, altaria sacra subvertere, ac loca alia consecrata quovis modo polluere, est grande sacrilegium et nephas, a cunctis fidelibus execrandum.

15.] Item tenendum est et firmiter observandum, quod ecclesiae res et deo dedicatas, ut sunt ornamenta, pallae, vasa sacra, in ministerium domini deputata, et alia caetera eiusmodi auferre, absque inevitabili et pia necessitate, et illa in alios usus humanos convertere et commutare, est sacrilegium et prophanum.

16.] Item ex fide tenendum est et credendum, quod nullus sacerdos Christi aut aliis maioribus ordinibus insignitus debet aut potest corporaliter quenquam, etiam infidelem, de lege communi occidere aut vulnerare, aut quod minus est ad sensum apostoli, percutere, aut in persona propria bellare, acies bellorum dirigere et ad bellandum seu occidendum immaniter provocare, aut aliqua facilitate crudelitates exercere aut exercitatas a saecularibus et sacerdotibus prohibitas irrationabiliter excusare, seu verba aut proverbia crudelia ad invadendum acrius proferre et homines ad severitatem succendere et irritare.

17.] Item tenendum est et fideliter observandum, quod ritus et ordo sacrificandi seu missandi in gestu, signis et habitu seu vestimentis consuetis, puta in alba, humerali, orario, mappula, cinctorio et casula, more ecclesiae universalis tentus et observatus, in loco sacro, et tempore, ac aliis circumstantiis ad sacrificandum correquisitis: circumscriptis ab eisdem omni pompa, avaritia, et superbia, et aliis deordinationibus, a cunctis sacrificantibus est observandus, et absque inevitabili necessitate cum aliis officiis divinis, ad dei cultum per sanctos constitutis et deputatis, a Christi sacerdotibus non est praetermittendus, sed operetenus exequendus.

18.] Item tenendum est et ex fide scripturae credendum, quod sancti qui sunt in ecclesia triumphante fidelibus in ecclesia militante degentibus suis quotidianis orationibus et charitativis auxiliis et iuvaminibus pro capacitate uniuscuiusque suffragantur. Quos fideles possunt licenter et catholice pro sui indigentia exorare, et pro alio quovis iuvamine petere et postulare. Circa talia cultu latriae soli deo semper reservato.

19.] Item tenendum est et credendum, quod locus purgatorii animarum a corpore exutarum et salvandarum, non ad plenum hic in via per satisfactionis remedium purgatarum, post hanc vitam est ponendus: Quodque fideles hic in via talibus, propter vinculum charitatis et spiritus, possunt et debent ieiuniis et orationibus, et eleemosynis, et sanctis oblationibus pie suffragari, semotis omnibus avaris quaestibus et quaestuosis lucris, pactis, et commemorationibus, prohibitis a lege divina et patrum sanctorum constitutis, quos solent facere sacerdotes simoniaci et avari.

20.] Item tenendum est diligenter et firmiter observandum, quod sacerdotes evangelici et alii Christi fideles ipsam legem divinam, Moysi et prophetarum et evangeliorum, ut dicit sanctus Clemens, non secundum propriam ingenii virtutem vel intelligentiam debent legere, explanare, et alios docere. Quia multa verba in scripturis et prophetis possunt et solent trahi a praesumptuosis ad eum sensum, quem unusquisque praesumpserit, impertinenter prophanans, ad loca et tempora applicans; sed quod debent ex ipsis sacris scripturis sensum capere veritatis secundum veritatem a maioribus sibi traditam, scilicet a sanctis doctoribus ab ecclesia universali acceptatis: quibus est fideliter innitendum et ab eorum catholicis explanationibus non recedendum.

21.] Item tenendum est et firmiter observandum, pro unitate et societate catholica in nobis perpetua conservanda, et pace ecclesiae custodienda iuxta decretum Clementis: Omnes sacerdotes et alii Christi fideles subiecti tenentur episcopis etiam discolis, aliisque praepositis, in omnibus praeceptis licitis et honestis obedire: etiamsi ipsi aliter (quod absit) agant quam debeant, iuxta praeceptum domini qui dicit: Quae dicunt facite, quae autem faciunt, facere nolite. Et quod tales episcopi non leviter sunt arguendi, sed potius portandi, nisi in fide erraverint.

22.] Unctio extrema est unum de septem sacramentis, a cuius rationali ministratione usitata ab ecclesia cessare est periculum, et quia probatio totius istius articuli, quoad nostram partem, videtur stare in hoc, quod unctio extrema est sacramentum: superest hoc fundare. Pro quo fundando est notandum, quod Christi opera et apostolorum suorum fiebant principaliter propter salutem et sanitatem animae consequendam; unctio de qua fit mentio Mar. 6 cap. et Iac. 5. sic fiebat. Et per consequens est illius salutis praedictae, quam repraesentat, signum efficax, et sic verum sacramentum.

Item, pro eadem sententia habentur doctores plurimi, de quorum numero est Beatus Dionysius, sancti Pauli coaetaneus, Iohannes Chrysostomus, S. Beda, et caeteri sancti multi.

Item, usus ecclesiae, quae est praedestinatorum numerus, crescens a multis centenis annorum, facit satis notabiliter pro materia iam praetacta.

In Prochazka's manuscript these articles were preceded by a statement (in Czech) that he does not quote but only summarizes: the meeting at the Prague castle was arranged at the wish of all the communities of both parties; the articles would be faithfully kept, as an obligation of both sides. In fact the Taborites did not accept the articles, and Prochazka's text must have been merely a protocol, prepared so as to be ready for possible signing. Furthermore, it is possible that articles 20, 21, 22 were added later, perhaps after the first session had shown them to be necessary.[6] Otherwise the list represents what the masters were proposing to the Taborites, and the synod of Klatovy must have directed its labors to dealing with each of these articles; when the parties met again in Prague, on 23 November, they discussed them.[7]

About twenty years after these events John Příbram put together a number

---

[6] Bartoš, *ČČM* (1914), p. 310.

[7] The date of the second Prague meeting is given in a brief report discovered by Bartoš, *JSH* (1935), p. 10. Nicholas of Pelhřimov says only "in spatio aliquot septimanarum." He also says there had been a long argument over the Prague articles at the first meeting ("praehabita . . . longa concertatione"); at the second meeting a discussion was begun ("tractatum inter se incipientibus") but interrupted by Příbram—we do not know at what point (Höfler, II, 590 for all of this).

of doctrinal items he had collected, in order to show how heretical his opponents were; among these texts, following several batches of articles extracted from Taborite tractates, was a record of the Klatovy decrees, introduced thus:[8]

> . . . magis utile visum michi est particulares tractatulos eorum nunc obmittere, et quid in communi senserunt, condixerunt, et concilialiter instituerunt, hoc ad publicum offerre. Et quamvis plura concionabula heretica celebraverunt, tamen ex aliquibus certis convencionibus eorum articulos intendo nunc extrahere. Et primo ex congregacione Clatowiense secuntur isti articuli, ab arte quidem et ingenio diaboli miromodo ingeniati, et ne deprehendatur ad reprobacionem intencio eorum, fallaciter pall[i]ati et saltem unius verbi addicione colorati; et quod deterius est, hoc ingenio, ut et reprobacioni sapientum precaveant et ab alia parte populum plebeium a fide sacramenti detrahant et periculosissime inficiant.

The list of articles that follows is the basis for our knowledge of the Klatovy synod, but as Professor Bartoš has shown, the articles Příbram gives are only excerpts (as his preface would in any case suggest), nor are all the Klatovy decrees represented—here the basic premise is that each of the Prague decrees must have been answered by at least one Klatovy decree.[9] Fortunately a number of Příbram's defects can be remedied, by drawing on certain other sources. (1) Bartoš has discovered, in Nicholas of Pelhřimov's Postil on Apocalypse, what seem to be the more or less full texts of two Klatovy articles (Nos. 5 and 19, in the list below)—they contain more than Příbram gives, but they also include what he gives. (2) In his chronicle, Nicholas of Pelhřimov mentions the arguments that ensued when the masters presented their list of articles, but he says that he will not give the relevant texts now, he will give them later. And in fact he concludes the second part of the chronicle (*ad* 1436, but written in 1442) with what he calls an epilogue of everything covered thus far; it consists of 23 articles of the masters, each one followed by a Taborite counterpart, usually contrary. Of the 23 articles of the masters, 18 are more or less the same as those in the list of 1424. Of the Taborite articles, 2 are virtually identical with Příbram's Klatovy texts, and 3 others include Příbram's words but offer more; these five are Nos. 14 and 15, 4, 6, and 7, below.[10] In all seven cases noted thus far, the presumably full

[8] *Processus cause* (*LČP*, No. 31), MS D 49, fol. 191ᵛ; slightly less of this is printed by Bartoš, *JSH* (1935), p. 6.

[9] Bartoš, *ČČM* (1914), p. 309—this is an unsupported assertion, but the main point is the obvious one, that the Klatovy synod, coming as it did between the two Prague meetings, *must* have taken up all the Prague articles, for these constituted the agenda.

[10] The "Omnium quasi praecedentium epilogatio" is in Höfler, II, 711–724; for the date of composition see Nejedlý, *Prameny*, pp. 162 f. It is this text that Nicholas must have had in mind when he noted, in his report of the Prague meeting of *ca.* 16 October

articles clearly respond to their Prague counterparts, and in the five of these cases where Příbram has left something out, the omitted material is what does not serve his hereticating purpose—the material that makes the articles "fallaciter palliati et . . . colorati." (3) In some cases the Klatovy decrees actually conformed more or less to the Prague articles, particularly in the matter of warfare and killing; Příbram naturally does not include these, but they can be found, with great probability, in either the Epilogue or in the nine articles at the beginning of Nicholas' chronicle. It remains, however, uncertain to what extent Nicholas enhanced the virtuous aspects of these articles to make the priests of Tabor seem sweeter than they may in fact have been.

The list of Klatovy articles that follows includes the whole of what Příbram reports, supplemented wherever possible according to the methods indicated above—in such cases, Příbram's text is italicized, and a footnote gives the other sources used. The order is that of the Prague list; [11] Prague numbers for which a probable Taborite response cannot be found are provided with appropriate notes or clearly labelled texts drawn from other sources to present Tabor's doctrine. This procedure is justified by the fact that the Klatovy decrees were promulgated as binding on the Taborite clergy and were circulated, in Latin and Czech, to all communities; even in later years they were quoted as standard. [12]

1.] (No known response at Klatovy; see Epilogue, No. 2.)

2.] In materia sacramenti sepius ponenda est differencia inter panem communem, panem vivum de celo descendentem, et panem cene dominice quem

---

(Höfler, II, 590), "In qua . . . audientia, . . . oblatis per magistros certis articulis de septem sacramentis, ritu missandi, purgatorio et invocatione sanctorum, et super eisdem praehabita . . . longa concertatione modo tempore suo in posterum exprimendo et hic causa brevitatis praetermisso. . . ." Since this part of the Chronicle was completed in 1435, the Epilogue must have been composed by then, and only *inserted* later on. Jastrebov, *Etjudy o Petrě Chelčickom,* pp. 83–85, identifies the Taborite and Prague articles of the Epilogue as drawn from both the confrontation of 1424 and from the Prague synod of January 1432, with the Taborite response thereto (Lydius, *Waldensia,* I, 316–332); but he wrongly supposes that Příbram's text of the Klatovy articles was complete, and that additional material in the Epilogue articles (Nos. 4, 6, 7) shows a later modification of Taborite doctrine to conform to Prague.

[11] For convenience I give Příbram's sequence, as printed by Bartoš, *JSH* (1935), pp. 6 f., with the corresponding numbers of my arrangement (i.e., the Prague sequence), the latter italicized: 1–4, 2; 5–6, 17; 7–8, 3; 9, 4; 10, 5; 11, 6; 12, 7; 13, 14; 14, 15; 15, 9; 16–21, *given at the end;* 22, 18; 23, 19; 24, *at end.*

[12] Příbram's No. 24 lays down the Klatovy decrees as binding, and in his *Život, KJBB,* p. 304, Příbram says the texts were sent throughout the realm, in Latin and Czech versions. Nicholas's later use of some of these formulations, in his Postil and in the Epilogue, suggests that they had become standard.

monstrando frangimus, cavendo ne scriptura que convenit tantum pani vivo, celesti ac eterno, applicetur pani sacramentali, ne ex hoc populus in ydolatriam prolabatur, honorem soli Christo debitum pani [P(říbram): "soli pani"] sacramentali tribuendo; eciam ne scriptura sonans de pane sacramentali, ad panem communem retorqueatur [*P*, No. 1].

Item falsi sensus circa verba Christi dicentis: "Hoc est corpus meum, hic est sanguis meus," sunt populo declarandi, ut non panis ille corpori Christi ydemptificetur, nec Christus corporaliter, situaliter in pane illo affirmetur, vel per hec demonstrativa "hoc" et "hic" aliud quam panis et vinum demonstrari reputetur [*P*, No. 2].

Item locuciones grosse et termini, dicciones seu verba extra sacram scripturam, qui vel que sonant in ydemptificacionem, in exhortacionibus sunt vitanda, ut: "ministro corpus Christi et sanguinem," item: "preparo corpus et sanguinem Christi, benedico corpus et sanguinem Christi, porto corpus et sanguinem Christi, transeo cum corpore et sanguine Christi" [*P*, No. 3].

Item instruatur populus, ut a predictis cavens sibi locucionibus, non petat a sacerdote sibi Deum, corpus vel sanguinem Christi,[13] quamvis bene possit dicere: "Opto corpus et sanguinem Christi" [*P*, No. 4].[14]

3.] (No known response at Klatovy; see Epilogue, No. 3.[15] But there was a *general* Klatovy decree about the mode of administering the sacraments:)

Item ritus Romane ecclesie, a qua in substancialibus fidei discordamus, appreciare et eos tenere circa sacramentorum administracionem non intendimus [*P*, No. 7]. Item ad magistrorum improbaciones et deducciones sinistras talium ex scriptura, locuciones diversas, qui nec unum filum vel signum dicunt se velle obmittere, nullo modo eosdem volumus in toto reassumere vel in parte [*P*, No. 8].

4.] Item manuum imposicionem, quam nunc vocant confirmacionem, si episcopus canonice electus per se reservaverit, illam exerceat, ecclesie ad

[13] Thus Bartoš's text.

[14] This group of four articles actually forms a single, unified statement, much of which appears as such in article nine of the Taborite decrees listed by Nicholas (Höfler II, 487 f.), although there the article is enriched by material drawn from the *De non adorando* and elsewhere. What the actual Klatovy numbering was cannot be established.

[15] The third Taborite article in the Epilogue is very much to the point, and it is hard to imagine the Taborite response to Prague put differently; moreover it begins, ". . . tenemus, sicut et antea semper tenemus," and it has a reference to modern Roman practices that is not unlike the Klatovy text quoted here. But it is possible that the priests of Tabor could not agree on all points regarding baptism; Příbram, *Život, KJBB,* pp. 279 f., writes that on this matter "some of them have acted and believed badly, others worse"—he then describes how all the Roman ceremonies of baptism were omitted and water was not consecrated for the purpose. A report of the November discussion in Prague says that the Taborites "asseruerunt . . . quod omnes baptizati ex parte ecclesie Romane non sunt Christiani, asserentes ipsorum baptismum fore et esse lavacrum sathane" (in Bartoš, *JSH* (1935), p. 10).

profectum, cuius [*P:* "confirmaciones,"] *licet in apostolis sanctis habemus exemplum, nullibi tamen in scriptura invenimus de faciendo* ipsam *ex obligacione preceptum;* intencione tamen ac ritu apostolico factam, ceteris paribus, salubrem fore et utile confitemur.[16]

5.] Ad penitenciam hortamur et sic continue hortamur, ut eciam secundum formam ecclesie primitive confiteantur peccata, in necessariis sibi a prudentibus consilia requirentes; *formam* tamen *et obligacionem* [*P adds:* "penitencie seu confessionis"] *ab Innocencium III. introductam vitare volumus,* qua usi sunt communiter avari sacerdotes. Remedia eciam penitentibus iniungenda salubria profitemur.[17]

6.] *Non ex fide scripture sed ex* [*P:* "de"] *consuetudine habetur ecclesie, quod ordo a solis dumtaxat episcopis conferatur;* intelligendo episcopum plus sacramentalis auctoritatis essencialis habere ultra alios veros et simplices sacerdotes.[18]

7.] Item potestas solvendi atque ligandi et conficiendi data est a Christo apostolis et conceditur veris eorum sequacibus vicariis, non tamen ut pro sua utantur talibus voluntate; *vasa* vero *ecclesiastica contrectandi nullibi in scriptura* [*P:* "lege"] *aliis licencia denegatur* fidelibus, *exclusis tamen irreverencia et contemptu.*[19]

8.] (No known response at Klatovy, but the one made could hardly have been too different from the one in the Epilogue, No. 8:)

Item matrimonium exercendum legitime in personis idoneis et capacibus libere profitemur, nubere tamen volentibus lascivia, temeritas, parentum inobediencia, deordinaciones cetere precludantur.

9.] Item infirmi poscentes sunt oleo unccionis competenti inungendi, non autem oleo fetido aut a symoniacis sive quibuscumque hereticis benedicto [*P,* No. 15].

10.] (No known response at Klatovy; see Epilogue, No. 10.)

11.] Nec in condemnacione reorum nec in occisione lex vetus ut huiusmodi in singulis suis iudiciariis est exequenda, neque leges humane evangelio contrarie sequende sunt et allegande; nec ipsa occisio umquam in aliqua causa alicui infligenda, nisi si et in quantum urgente necessitate lex nova occidere et condemnare licenciat, et per potestates legitimas suadet et auctorisat, aut illa deficiente populus aut quicumque spiritu dei agitatus debite et meritorie eiusdem vicem suppleat, et sic, quod lex vetus de tanto in iudiciariis

---

[16] Epilogue, No. 4 (Höfler, II, 713).

[17] From Nicholas's Postil on Apocalypse, in *ČSPSČ* (1921), p. 105, where Klatovian orthodoxy on this point is asserted against priests who repel those wishing to confess and against laymen who do not repent of their sins (cf. MS 4520, fol. 167ʳ).

[18] Epilogue, No. 6 (p. 714).

[19] Epilogue, No. 7 (p. 715); this is a good example of how Příbram apparently excerpted only what suited his purpose, thereby obscuring the sense of the Taborite article as a complete response to the Prague formulation.

sit sequenda, de quanto eam Christus licenciat et ecclesia primitiva praxi declarat et ostendit, ita tamen, quod circa predicta sedecim condiciones charitatis observentur et ipsa legis nature regula: Quid tibi non vis, racionabiliter alteri ne feceris.[20]

12.] Bella christiana non sunt a quoquam attentanda et exercenda, nisi nova lege licenciante et potestate legitima auctorisante, aut ex illius defficiencia populo christiano aut quocumque alio spiritu dei agitato debite et meritorie vicem eiusdem supplente et causa iusta impellente; nec contra alios nisi in fidei destructores, innocentum oppressores, vel regionis et rei publice invasores et vastatores, vel alios pertinaces sceleratos legis dei transgressores, qui aliis modis lenioribus nullatenus a sua pertinacia reduci possunt et coerceri; hac regula in bellis potissime observata, quod hostem in impetu necessitas perimat, non voluntas, exclusa prorsus a bellantibus nocendi cupiditate, ulciscendi crudelitate, implacato atque implacabili animo invadendi et amore rapiendi, et si que sunt similia, prout sancti doctores in lege fideliter fundati elucidant et explanant.[21]

13.] In bellis quantumcumque iustis res aliene non solum non sunt avare invadende sed nec tangende nocive, nec concupiscende, nec plebes fidelium et innocentum quomodolibet opprimende, iuxta apostoli sentenciam: Mala non sunt facienda ut bona eveniant.[22]

14.] Item ecclesias divino cultui mancipatas exurere seu destruere prohibemus; speluncas vero latronum execratas et symonia infectas, in quibus legis domini praxis non exercetur fideliter, tractare ut tales prohibere nolumus [*P*, No. 13].

15.] Item res ecclesie quascumque furto vel sacrilegio aufferre interdicimus, sed in usus pauperum, [seu redempcionem captivorum,] aut in alios quoscumque convertere pios usus non intendimus prohibere [*P*, No. 14; cf. Epilogue, No. 19].

16.] Nullus sacerdos Christi aut aliis maioribus ordinibus insignitus debet aut potest corporaliter quemquam, eciam infidelem, de lege communi occidere aut vulnerare, aut quod minus est ad sensum apostoli, percutere aut in persona propria bellare, acies bellorum dirigere, ad bellandum aut occidendum immaniter provocare, aut aliqua facilitate crudelitates exercere, seu ex-

[20] Toman, *Husitské válečnictví,* p. 54; cf. Höfler, II, 484 and (Epilogue) 717. For the "sedecim condiciones caritatis" see Příbram's *De condicionibus iusti belli,* MS D 47, fols. 78ʳ–98ᵛ; the quoted phrase appears on fol. 78ᵛ.

[21] Toman, p. 53; cf. Höfler, II, 483.

[22] Toman, p. 53; cf. Höfler, II, 483 f. I have omitted a section defining the difficult mode of Christian killing (according to Wyclif), since it smells like a later improvement. The text in the Epilogue, No. 12 (p. 717), not only lacks this section but also lacks the conclusion, "iuxta . . . eveniant"—instead it forthrightly cites scriptural passages in the *opposite* sense, to *justify* plundering. Only a failure of nerve prevents me from supposing that this text, and not the one I have given, was the real Klatovy article.

ercitatas a secularibus et sacerdotibus prohibitas irracionabiliter excusare, seu verba aut proverbia crudelia proferre et homines ad severitatem succendere et irritare; bellis tamen iustis in causa dei licite potest interesse, bellantes ut iuste et sancte faciant exhortando.[23]

17.] (The Klatovy article is not known, but it must have been close or identical to the article in the Epilogue, No. 15, *q.v.;* some such is presupposed by the fragments given by Příbram: [24])

Item in ritu Clatovie concluso quiescimus, intendente[s] indispositos arcere, quantum nobis est possibile, a visione sacramenti [*P,* No. 5].

Item instruantur fideles, quod ritus introducti tales qui iam modernis usitantur temporibus, sunt preternecessarii ad salutem, quorum appreciacio, eorum multiplicacio et pro hiis contencio, ad eos obligacio seu cum eis dispensacio nimis est deceptoria et nociva [*P,* No. 6].

18.] Item de desiderando sanctorum suffragia in scriptura sacra nullibi habemus de hoc faciendo exemplum explicite vel preceptum [*P,* No. 22].

19.] *Purgatorium post hanc vitam esse* eodem modo *qualiter a sacerdotibus avaris promovebatur* in decepcionem salutis animarum *non concedimus; ad sensum tamen scripture apostolorum purgacionem animarum suo tempore fiendam* [*P:* "sumendam"] *non negamus.* Pocius vero quemlibet, ut in presenti vita sic vivat, ne postea purgacione alia indigeat, volumus admonere, ne super dubio innixus, decipiatur.[25]

20.] Sacerdotes evangelici et alii Christi fideles ipsam legem divinam et scripturam Moysis, prophetarum et evangelistarum non secundum propriam ingenii virtutem et intelligenciam debent legere, explanare et alios docere, aut impertinenter prophetas ad loca et tempora applicare, sed quod debent ex ipsis sacris scripturis sensum capere veritatis.[26]

---

[23] Toman, p. 52; Höfler, II, 483.

[24] It would seem that the Klatovy synod actually defined a certain rite and then referred to it ("in ritu Clatovie concluso"); to judge from the Epilogue, No. 15 (p. 719), this was the actual Taborite rite, supplemented by some points in the "rite of St. Dionysius," which included a dismissal of the catechumens before communion—this became "indispositos arcere" and so on (cf. Příbram's discussion, *De ritibus misse,* Höfler, II, 534, which refers to the Greek custom of having doors before the altar). Bartoš, *JSH* (1935), p. 8, supposes the reference here was to an earlier Klatovy synod, but this assumption is not necessary.

[25] From Nicholas' Postil on Apocalypse, in *ČSPSČ* (1921), p. 104. The last sentence picks up one of Jakoubek's ideas; see my discussion in *OC & N,* p. 24, and see the formulation of the St. Wenceslas Day Synod of 1418, *Documenta,* p. 678.

[26] Toman, pp. 51 f.; Höfler, II, 482. I have left out the section that immediately follows "veritatis": "cum diligencia perpendendo, ne parti scripture alicui contradicant, sensum vero elicitum solide fundent, vite doctrineque Christi et sanctorum apostolorum se diligenter conformantes . . ." and so on. This was no doubt what Nicholas and his party had in mind when they thought of the "sensum . . . veritatis," but it sounds like a later addition.

21.] (The Klatovy article is not known, but it must have been similar to that in the Epilogue, No. 23, *q.v.*)

22.] (No Klatovy response is known.)

The Prague articles of 1424 must have included at least two not preserved in Prochazka's MS, one on the celebration of feasts and holidays (see Epilogue, No. 17), and one on fasts (see Epilogue, No. 16). Příbram gives Taborite responses on each point, in two sets of three articles each; the numbering below is according to his list:

> 16. Item in festis apostolorum et aliorum, in cathologo legis nove positorum, fiant predicaciones ad ipsos imitandum, sed populus ad laborem moneatur.

> 17. Item festum incarnacionis Christi proximiori die dominico festivetur, Epiphania autem et Purificacio festiventur in loco suo, sed populus non prohibeatur a labore.

> 18. Item festum, quod prius corporis Christi dicebatur, non in loco proprio, ut prius, sed in Cena Domini diligencius memoretur.

> 19. Item si communitas ex necessitate vel aliis debitis circumstanciis exemplo Ninivitarum super ieiunacione consentit, talis ieiunacio a quolibet pro possibilitate cum diligencia observetur.

> 20. Item ieiunantes ex devocione feria sexta vel aliis diebus, dummodo iuste fit, approbamus, dissolutos hiis vel aliis diebus reprehendentes, libertatem lege Dei utentibus nullo modo precludentes.

> 21. Item vigilie sanctorum, a papis introducte, et alia ieiunia sanctis limitata, que sonant in Idolatriam, cassentur.

Finally, the Klatovy list ended with this article:

> 24. Item omnes unanimiter et concorditer conclusimus, ut omnes suprascriptos articulos fideliter teneamus et eos coram communitatibus singuli promoveamus. Quodsi postmodum aliquis ex nobis alicui displicuerit, per se non audeat retractare.

On the basis of this reconstruction of the Klatovy articles, with some added conjectures, the following summary of the Prague-Tabor confrontation of 1424 can be offered: [27]

> 1. *Prague:* The seven sacraments are necessary and salubrious antidotes of souls. *Tabor:* They are not absolutely necessary, but are useful and salubrious antidotes of souls, in the form in which they were held by the Primitive Church.

> 2. *Prague:* Christ is in the Eucharist according to his corporeal substance and

[27] Here I have drawn more freely from the Epilogue to supply Taborite articles not otherwise attested for the Klatovy synod, and I have included some more material from the articles in Höfler, II, 482–488. Thus the summary here is only generally valid for Tabor as of *ca.* 1424.

natural existence; and the eight articles of Konopiště are to be held. *Tabor:* Christ is not corporeally or locally in the consecrated bread, which is not identical with his body; his substantial body is the living, eternal, celestial bread, not the sacramental bread, which in turn is distinct from ordinary unconsecrated bread. The people are to be instructed not to confuse these three.

3. *Prague:* All the ceremonies usual in baptism are to be retained—godparents, exorcisms, chrism, holy water, and so on. *Tabor:* Only the necessary or useful forms taught by the Primitive Church need to be observed in baptism; we disagree with the Roman church in substantial matters of the faith, and we do not intend to esteem or keep her rites.

4. *Prague:* Those who have been baptized are to be confirmed by their own bishop, with chrism. *Tabor:* A duly elected bishop may reserve this act for himself, and indeed confirmation has its example with the apostles, although there is nothing in Scripture to make it obligatory. It can be useful.

5. *Prague:* Auricular confession and the useful works of satisfaction are to be practiced in connection with penance. *Tabor:* We urge penance, according to the form of the Primitive Church; let penitents take council if necessary with prudent men, and let proper remedies be enjoined. But we reject Innocent III's form (*scil.,* auricular confession) and its obligation—these are useful only to greedy priests.

6. *Prague:* Holy orders are to be conferred only by bishops. *Tabor:* This is only a custom of the church, not the faith of Scripture—at least when a bishop is understood as someone having greater sacramental authority than an ordinary priest.

7. *Prague:* Only priests have the power of the keys, of binding and loosing, of consecrating the Eucharist, and of handling sacred vessels. *Tabor:* This is true in regard to binding and loosing and consecrating, but nothing in Scripture prohibits the laity from handling sacred vessels.

8. *Prague:* Matrimony is to be practiced according to the statutes of the saints and the church; a girl who is of age and takes marriage vows without her parents' consent is not to be divorced because they object. *Tabor:* (The part about matrimony is accepted, but) disobedience to parents must be excluded.

9. *Prague:* The sick who ask for extreme unction are to receive it according to the form of the church. *Tabor:* Those asking for unction may receive it, but not with the special oil blessed by simoniacs.

10. *Prague:* The Ten Commandments and other evangelical points are to be observed according to the sense of the Holy Spirit, manifested by "the mother and teacher of us all, the Primitive Church." *Tabor:* Indeed the whole Christian Law—the aggregate of all the truths of the Bible—is to be kept.

11. *Prague:* In the matter of killing men guilty of crimes, the Old Testament is not to be followed in its particular judicial provisions; moreover, the killing

is to be done at the command of the legitimate powers, not by individuals in their own cause, and it should not be done at all except when the guilty man is otherwise incorrigible, and except in cases where the New Testament permits it; moreover it must be done with caritative spirit. *Tabor:* (Accepts Prague's article, in the same words, with these modifications:) The Old Testament as such is not to be followed here, but it is to be followed insofar as Christ and the Primitive Church permit and exemplify such practice. Human laws contrary to the gospel are not to be followed. The killing is to be done by the legitimate powers, but if they are lacking or remiss, then their place may be taken by the people or by anyone moved by the Spirit of God.

12. *Prague:* Wars are to be waged only insofar as and when the New Testament allows them, legitimate power authorizes them, a just cause impels them, and when they are necessary—that is, against those who would destroy the faith, who oppress the innocent, invade the commonwealth, or otherwise transgress the Law of God. The enemy is to be killed from necessity, not desire. And on the part of the fighters there must be no wish to hurt, no vengeful cruelty, no implacability, no savagery of rebellion, no lust to dominate or plunder—all this according to the holy doctors. *Tabor:* (Accepts the article and its wording, with these modifications:) The place of legitimate power may be taken by the people, and so on (as in 11). (The phrases about savagery of rebellion and lust to dominate are left out, and the point on plundering is weakened.) The holy doctors must be faithfully founded in the Law.

13. *Prague:* Even in just warfare the property of the enemy should not only not be plundered, it should not be damaged or desired; nor should the innocent common people be oppressed. *Tabor:* (The same.)

14. *Prague:* Churches and altars are not to be burnt, destroyed, or profaned, without strict necessity. *Tabor:* We prohibit burning or destruction of churches devoted to the divine cult, but we will not prohibit dens of thieves and simoniacs, in which the Law of God is not faithfully practiced, from being treated as what they are.

15. *Prague:* Holy vestments and vessels are not to be removed from churches or converted to lay use, without strict necessity. *Tabor:* These things are not to be stolen from churches, but we do not prohibit their conversion to pious use—for the poor, to redeem prisoners, and similar uses.

16. *Prague:* No priest or other cleric in major orders may himself take up arms, kill or even strike, direct battles, incite others to kill, excuse those who have fought with cruelty, or urge the army on. *Tabor:* (The same article, with the addition:) But they may be present at just battles, in the cause of God, urging the fighters to battle justly and holily.

17. *Prague:* The rites and vestments of the mass are to be kept in all respects according to the custom [*more*] of the universal church, but without pomp, pride, or other abuses; they may be omitted only in case of strict necessity.

Tabor: We hold to the substance of the mass, following the rite of St. Dionysius in moderate singing, in the vernacular, in reading from Scriptures, in edifying sermons, and in excluding the indisposed from even the sight of the sacrament. But the rites introduced in modern times are not necessary for salvation, and the faithful are to be told this. Furthermore harm has been done by the esteeming of these rites, by their multiplication, by their obligation, and by contention over them.

18. *Prague:* Saints in the Church Triumphant help the faithful in the Church Militant, according to the capacity of each of the faithful; and the latter may pray and ask for such help. *Tabor:* The saints do help the faithful on earth, who should ask God for a share in this help, but there is nothing in Scripture in the way of explicit example or precept obliging the faithful, as an article of faith, to invoke the aid or intercession of the saints.

19. *Prague:* There is Purgatory, for those who have not made full satisfaction on earth, and those in it can be helped by the faithful on earth, by prayers, alms, offerings to the saints—but without simoniac contractual commemorations. *Tabor:* We do not concede this kind of purgatory, promoted by greedy priests—but we do believe, according to the Epistles, that there will be a purgation of souls at some time. Let each one live this life so that he will not need further purgation later.

20. *Prague:* Priests and others of the faithful should not expound the Bible according to their own ideas, or presumptuously apply scriptural texts to particular places and occasions, as they see fit; rather should they follow the traditional interpretations of the holy doctors accepted by the universal church. *Tabor:* (The same basic text, but with modifications: nothing is said about the holy doctors—instead, probably, the Taborite norm was defined as conformity of scriptural interpretation to the life and doctrine of Christ and the apostles.)

21. *Prague:* Bishops and other authorities are to be obeyed, even when they are unreasonable [*discolis*], in all their licit precepts; nor are they lightly to be accused. *Tabor:* This applies (with some serious reservations) to bishops who have been canonically elected, not simoniacally intruded (evidently a reference to Archbishop Conrad).

22. (see above, 9)

(23) *Prague:* Feast-days of Jesus Christ, Mary, the apostles, the holy martyrs, and other ancient saints, are to be properly observed, with cessation from corporal labor and sinful pursuits; minor festivals can be reduced by unanimous consent of the clergy. *Tabor:* Feast-days of Christ and the apostles and other saints of the New Testament are to be kept (with some amalgamation of the Christ-festivals); on the Christ-festivals the people are not to be prohibited from working, and on the other festivals they are to be told to work—the observance is to take the form of sermons urging imitation of these saints.

(24) *Prague:* We will observe fasts on the vigils of the saints, and other fasts legitimately observed by the church, and we will enjoin such observance on the clergy subject to us. *Tabor:* If the community wishes to decree a fast for a particular purpose, let it be observed by all as far as possible. And we approve of voluntary pious fasting on Fridays or other days, disapprove of dissolute practices—but always according to the liberty of the Law of God. Vigils of the saints, however, and other fasts to the saints, have been introduced by the popes and smack of idolatry: let them be abolished.

Appendix III

THE TREATISES OF MS O 13 ON ADVENTISM, CHILIASM, AND WARFARE: THE LATIN TEXTS

IN HIS *Quellen und Untersuchungen zur Geschichte der Böhmischen Brüder,* II. *Peter Chelčický und seine Lehre* (Prague: Otto, 1882), pp. 51–60, Jaroslav Goll published five short texts (only one complete) bearing on the problems raised by Taborite adventism and warfare. He noted that the texts were taken from MS O 13 of the Prague Cathedral Chapter Library, but did not give the folio numbers. A. Podlaha's catalogue of this collection, *Soupis rukopisů knihovny metropolitní kapitoly pražské,* II (Prague, 1922), lists only three of Goll's items, on fols. 62ʳ–72ʳ; the others were not found by those using the codex since Goll's time. Access to this collection of manuscripts is now much freer than it had been, and in 1960 I was able to study the codex and find the missing items, apparently displaced by an early binder; they occupy fols. 26ʳ–26ᵛ, 32ʳ–38ʳ, which the catalogue includes in a listing of a commentary on a prophecy by Hildegard of Bingen. The texts have always been recognized as extremely important; since Goll's excerpts are too brief to do justice to the contents, and since he neglected some texts entirely, I here offer a complete edition of all the relevant items in the codex.

The listing that follows has been kept as brief as possible; indications of authorship, dating, and contents are usually given according to the generally received views, as set forth by Bartoš, *LČJ* and *LČP,* and Macek, *Tábor,* I, Appendix 4. These guides also refer to the scholarly literature. In editing the texts, known to survive only in MS O 13, I have put all editorial additions, emendations, and comments in square brackets. Obvious scribal errors are corrected in silence, as are Goll's occasional errors, except in cases where they affect the meaning; the passages printed or summarized by Goll are here included in bold-face parentheses.

517

THE TEXTS

1. A Letter to a Priest or Priests, refuting Adventist Prophecies, fols. 32^r–33^v. Extracts in Goll, II, 57–59; listings in Bartoš, *LČJ*, No. 79, and Macek, *Tábor*, I, p. 382, No. 8. The author was Jakoubek of Stříbro; in item 6b, of which he names himself as author, he refers to the present letter as his own. The date would be late January or early February. Note that the letter begins by using the second person singular, then drifts into the plural.

2. *Contra scripta de adventu Cristi etc.*, fols. 34^r–35^v. Not previously published or known to scholars, this text groups seven chiliast articles and provides refutations for each. The refutations correspond very closely to those in John Příbram's *Contra articulos picardorum* (*LČP*, No. 5), of late 1420 or early 1421; the present text is probably a much earlier work by the same author, reacting perhaps to the first chiliast agitation, in February or March of 1420.

3. *Noverint universi,* fols. 35^v–36^r. Extracts (only eight lines) in Goll, II, 55; listings in *LČJ*, No. 81, and Macek, pp. 382 f., No. 12—but these listings refer to Goll's conflation of *Noverint* with item 4; the true *Noverint* is virtually unknown to scholarship. The author was no doubt Jakoubek, the date probably January or February of 1420.

4. *Audio cum contra percussores,* fol. 37^r–37^v. Extracts in Goll, II, 55–56, as part of *Noverint universi;* in fact each of the two works is self-contained, propounding the same complex of ideas in different ways, and the present item begins with a distinctive capital letter, larger than that used for ordinary paragraph-beginnings. The listings noted for item 3 apply chiefly to this work; the author was no doubt Jakoubek, the date perhaps February 1420 (although Bartoš and Macek say the spring of that year).

5. *Item prophecias legis dei,* fols. 37^v–38^r. Perhaps an addendum to item 4, this text nevertheless deals with a different subject and can be treated as distinct; no part of it has been printed before. Authorship and dating as in item 4.

6a and 6b. Jakoubek of Stříbro, Letter to Master John of Jičín, fols. 62^v–64^r (6a), and fols. 64^r–68^v with a displaced portion on fol. 26^r–26^v (6b). Excerpts from 6b in Goll, II, 59–60; listings in *LČJ*, No. 80, and Macek, p. 382, No. 11. Jakoubek names himself as author in the text of 6b; the letter was probably written in the second half of February 1420. Bartoš regards 6a as an earlier draft of 6b; a case could be made for the view that 6b was the version for publication, 6a the letter written to Jičín. (The displaced portion of 6b has been reintegrated here according to the instructions at the top of fol. 26^r:

"Iste sexternus debet esse post tercium sexternum ante 1^m, ubi est: habens misticum poculum.")

7. Rescript of Masters Christian of Prachatice and Jakoubek of Stříbro, fols. 69^r–70^v. The full text in Goll, II, 51–53; listings in *LČJ*, No. 78, and Macek, pp. 381 f., No. 7. The authors are named in the text, but Jakoubek must have done the actual composition; the date is about January 1420. I reprint Goll's text, corrected from the manuscript, and with some changes in spelling, punctuation, and biblical citation.

8. *Bellandi materiam concernit infrascriptum,* fols. 70^v–72^r. Excerpts in Goll, II, 53–55; listings in *LČP*, No. 3, and Macek, p. 383, No. 13. The author was probably John Příbram; the date, spring or summer of 1420.

1. A Letter to a Priest or Priests, Refuting Adventist Prophecies.

[**fol. 32^r**] (Gracia et veritas per dominum Ihesum Cristum. Care in Cristo frater: Nolens omnino scripta et petita tua sub silencio pertransire, sed utcumque perstringens pro responso videtur michi) primum, (quod illud *Ieremie li* [6], Fugite de medio Babilonis, ut salvet unusquisque animam suam; similiter et illud *Isaie xix* [18], In die illa erunt quinque civitates in terra Egipti loquentes lingwa Canaan, etc., et alia dicta prophetarum similia), prout ad intencionem spiritus sancti nobis debent deservire, (non intelliguntur ad literam de materiali Babilone et corporalibus ac materialibus quinque civitatibus manu et arte hominum edificatis, nec de civitate solis materiali); sicut et illud ewangelicum in parabola salvatoris *Luce xix* [17–19], Euge serve bone et fidelis, quia in modico fidelis fuisti eris potestatem habens super x civitates; et alter venit dicens, domine mna tua fecit quinque mnas, et huic ait: Et tu esto super quinque civitates, etc. Illa parabola non intelligitur de materialibus civitatibus, sed archana sunt misteria ibi magna omnia saltim semotis carnalibus sensibus iudaisantibus. *Unde Origenes in quadam Omelia* [*scil., XXI*] *super Ieremiam dicit* [*MPG, 13, 534 f.*]: In Babilone est tunc anima quando confunditur, quando turbatur, quando pace deserta bella sustinet passionum, quando tumultus malicie circa eam fremit, tunc in Babilone est et ad istam animam sermo dirigitur dicens, Fugite de medio Babilonis ut salvet unusquisque animam. Donec enim quis in Babilone est, salvari non potest. *Et iterum dicit* [*ibid., 540*]: Si in alicuius corde non cecidit civitas confusionis, huic nondum Cristus advenit; veniente quippe eo Babilon ruere conswevit. Propter hoc ad oracionum presidia confugientes, petite ut veniat Ihesus in corda nostra et conterat Babilonem et faciat ruere omnem maliciam eius, ut reedificet pro hiis que subversa sunt, et pro Babilone que fuerit ante constructa in ipso principali nostri cordis,

Iherosolimam civitatem sanctam dei. *Et iterum idem dicit* [*ibid., 535 f.; non stricte*]: Fugite de medio Babilonis, non gradatim, non pede tepido, sed cum velocitate; id est, quicumque confusam habetis animam aut variorum viciorum passionem; ideo si adhuc in confusione sum mentis, in Babilone sum. Et precipit deus, non dicens exite sed fugite de medio Babilonis, id est, de corde malo fugere debere. Qui enim valde immersus est viciis, hic medius habitator Babilonis est. [*hic finis Origenis*] Ex quo patet quomodo et quid est intelligendum per civitatem Babilon. Et idem videtur patere per magnum [**fol. 32ᵛ**] et fidelem Augustinum, fere per totum librum *De civitate dei,* et idem est intelligendum de numero quinque civitatum *Isa. xix.* Archanum quid et misticum est ibi senciendum et non carnale et literale ad sensum Iudeorum.

(Ex quibus patet quod Cristi fideles) viventes secundum ewangelica precepta, integra fide, spe, et caritate, et in bona consciencia, malo nequaquam consencientes et sic usque in finem perseverantes, (in quacumque civitate) materiali, castro, opido, vel villa vel campo vel via vel silva, continuantes in hunc modum ad dei beneplacitum, quacumque morte preoccupati fuerint, (salvabuntur). Sicut scriptum est, Iustus quacumque morte preoccupatus fuerit, anima eius erit in refrigerio [*cf. Sap. iv, 7*]; et talis iustus ubicumque fuerit in loco materiali, habitat in spirituali Iherosolima extra spiritualem Babilon[em]. (Ergo sive in Praga sive in Pieska sive in Plzna, iustus malo non consenciens contra ewangelium, dum moritur salvabitur.)

Sed cum dicitur, Iustus quacumque morte et ubicumque mortuus fuerit, anima eius erit in refrigerio, obiciunt dicentes quod non sufficit, nam et Loth iustus erat in Sodomis, et tamen si non exisset de Sodoma perisset. Si tales volunt intelligere literaliter et corporaliter, tunc videtur esse falsum, cum tunc multi exeuntes de opidis et villis Plznam vel alias pereunt, quod si domi mansissent non perissent. Eciam cum iustus Loth exiret de Sodoma fecit hoc ex certitudine revelacionis, et nos ex fide scripture certitudinem habemus illius revelacionis. Sic autem non est hic, non enim tantam certitudinem fidei habent homines iusti ad exeundum sicut Loth de Sodoma. Vel si habent, ostendant illam certitudinem; si autem non habent, cur secundum suam propriam estimacionem dubio et incerto sic populum ad pericula magna exponunt?

Unde talis (iustus nec in Praga nec alibi) sic in iusticia perseverans (debet timere dampnacionem ex hoc solo quod in Praga manet vel alibi, sicut nec ex hoc solo speranda est salus alicui quod in Plzna vel in Pieska moratur. Et patet quod prophecia Isaie vel Ieremie ad sensum carnalem incertum, ut videtur, indebite applicatur, et in termino prefixo, in carnisprivio ut scribitis, prophecia talium sic implebitur vel non implebitur, patebit clarius veritas vel falsitas, ut eventus rei probabit. Fateor tamen, ut concipio, si non fallor, quod multe erunt tribulaciones electis ad salutem, reprobis ad dampnacionem, nam apropinquant loco et tempore non a me vel ab homine, sed a deo cognitis et prefinitis. [fol. 33ʳ] Ex istis ulterius timeo, ne nostri sacerdotes agitentur spiritu erroris secundum altitudinem sathane ad periculose scindendum et dementandum pauperculum et simplicem populum cristianum. Unde sicut olim Ieremias prophetabat populo Israhel quod transirent ad Babilonem et ibi manerent 70 annis), ut patet *Ier. xxvii et viii,* (alii autem prophetabant false quasi ex parte dei, quod deberent exire cicius filii Israhel de Babilone: sic unus spiritus prophetat quod rex Babilonis, id est rex Ungaris [*sic*]) etc. (veniet de cubili suo, id est de sua terra, et destruet Babilonem, id est Pragam; alius spiritus prophetavit et dixit, quod predictus rex nullomodo veni[re]t ad Boemiam sive ad Pragam. Cui ergo est credendum? Re vera est populum dei reddere perplexum: bonum esset igitur ewangelico sacerdoti ewangelice vivere et sic populum docere et peccata in populo destruere, dimissis talibus propriis presumpcionibus. De hoc autem quod communis populus arripit carnalia et secularia arma, concitatus per sacerdotes, ut scribitis, contra inimicos, ubi agitur periculum homicidii et effusionis sanguinis et odia generantur, per que exciditur a caritate obmittendo arma spiritualia,) de quibus (*Eph. vi* [*12–18*]: contra quod audiamus apostoli securum consilium *Rom. xii.*[*19*], Karissimi, non vosmet ipsos defendentes,) et *II Timoth. ii* [*11–12*]: Si comortui simus et convivemus; si sustinemus et conregnabimus. Quasi dicat, si vos posteriores fideles ad finem seculi in causa dei eritis comortui nobis, simul nobiscum convivetis; si nobiscum cum apostolis et primitiva ecclesia sustinebitis et compaciemini in eadem scilicet dei causa, in eodem spiritu sic cum spiritualibus armis, non curando carnalia arma—nam et alibi dicit Apostolus [*II Cor. x, 4*], Arma nostra non sunt carnalia—et cum tali mansuetudine sicut et nos cum tali proposito et voluntate et tali perseverancia usque in finem, tunc nobiscum conregnabitis post [*MS:* per] hanc mortalem vitam. Si autem aliter et non conformiter nobis sustinebitis inpacienter, cum armis carnalibus sine spiritualibus, cum odio et rapina sine vera caritate ad inimicos, non in eodem spiritu mansuctudinis, tunc sic non dico quod nobiscum regnabitis, id est non promitto vobis regnum pro illo, si sic paciemini. Sed si nobiscum sustinebitis, scilicet conformiter nobis in eodem spiritu mansuetudinis, etc. ut supra, tunc simul conregnabimus.

Et (patet quod via pugnandi in causa dei instar apostolorum et primitive ecclesie [fol. 33ᵛ] est secura via, sed via aliter pugnandi non conformiter primitive ecclesie, sed longe difformiter, cum alio spiritu et aliis armis,) etc. ut supra, (est periculosa. Sacerdotis ergo ewangelici est suadere pugnam in causa dei ewangelicam secundum ewangelicum et catholicum sensum cum armis spiritualibus instar primitive ecclesie Cristi apostolorum. Concedo tamen quod bella possunt licite fieri a sublimioribus potestatibus secularibus, ut dicitur *Rom. xiii,* [*1–6*], cui datus est gladius ad vindictam malorum. Caveat subditus populus, ne usurpet sibi illum gladium a sublimioribus potestatibus inordinate contra dominum, non habendo certam et specialem revelacionem. Potestates autem sublimiores possunt licite bellare, sed periculum ibi magnum animarum currit [*Goll:* currunt]. Ideo secundum apostolum [*cf. I. Cor. vi, 12; x, 22*] multa licent que non expediunt, et sacerdotes non oportet consulere ad omnia que licent fieri cum magnis periculis, sed debent suadere omnia que expediunt, ut prelia domini contra vicia cum armis spiritualibus agantur. Istis autem condicionibus adhibitis, potestates sublimiores licite possunt bellare: Primo quod sit causa dei, pro qua bellum committitur; 2° intencio recta; 3° instinctus divinus ad sic bellandum, quem olim David in causa dei bellando solebat habere; 4° quod tanta sit caritas pugnantis, quod velit parate cessare a preliando, adversario se volente reddere tamquam reum. Nullus tamen frontose presumat se habere instinctum divinum ad taliter bellandum ex collisione alicuius spiritus erroris et simulate fantasie, occasione cuius populum moneat ad insurgendum contra personam aliquam, inordinate eius sanguinem effundendo.

Et hec ad vestra scripta et quesita responderi sufficiat pro presenti, et si in istis aliquo modo essem devius, a quocumque volo corrigi et melius edoceri.)

2. *Contra scripta de adventu Cristi etc.*
[**fol. 34ʳ**] Contra scripta de adventu Cristi etc.

Quia iam in istis temporibus periculosis et novissimis aliqua [*MS iterum:* aliqua] emergunt de quodam adventu Cristi, et consumacione seculi, et novo regno hominum hic in via fiendo et infra breve tempus reparando, et circa hoc quedam inaudita et tocius fidei cristiane destructiva: ideo nos ad hoc obligati volumus et debemus omnes populos a talibus malis et perversis omnimodo declinandis premunire.

Primo quod in regno sic reparato et in illo seculo hic in via predicto, nullum erit peccatum, nullum scandalum, nulla abhominacio, nullum mendacium. Et sic ex illo sequitur quod tunc nullum erit originale peccatum, nec actuale, veniale vel mortale.

Istud autem est contra scripturas. Primo, quod originale [peccatum] erit, patet *Rom. v* [*12*]: Propterea sicut per unum hominem peccatum in hunc mundum intravit, et per peccatum mors, ita in omnes homines mors pertransiit in quo omnes peccaverunt. *Item ad Eph. ii* [*3*]: Et eramus natura filii ire. *Item Ps. l*[*7*]: Ecce enim in iniquitatibus conceptus sum, et in peccatis concepit me mater mea. *Item Ioh. iii* [*5*]: Nisi quis renatus fuerit ex aqua et spiritu sancto, non potest intrare in regnum dei. Sed de aliis peccatis actualibus patet quod dicitur *Ecc. vii* [*21*]: Non est enim homo iustus in terra, qui faciat bonum et non peccet. *Item Prov. xx* [*9*]: Quis potest dicere, mundum est cor meum. *Gallat. iii* [*22*]: Conclusit scriptura omnia sub peccato. *Item I Ioh. i* [*8*]: Si dixerimus quia peccatum non habemus, ipsi nos seducimus et veritas in nobis non est. *Item Ps. lii* [*4*], *et Rom. iii* [*12*]: Omnes declinaverunt, simul inutiles facti sunt. *Item* si nullum esset peccatum, sequitur quod baptismus periret et penitencia, quod est contra illud *Ioh.* [*iii, 5*]: Nisi quis, etc. Et contra illud *Luc. xiii* [*3,5*]: Nisi penitenciam egeritis omnes simul peribitis. *Item* sequitur quod nullus erit Cristianus, quia nullus baptisabitur, cessante baptismo. *Item* sequitur quod non orabunt illi homines, Pater noster; et, Dimitte nobis peccata nostra, etc. quod sequitur. *Item Mat. xviii* [*7*]: Necesse est ut veniant scandala.

Secundo, quod omnes passiones Cristi et membrorum eius in illo seculo et regno hominum supradicto cessabunt, et non erunt, sed omnes in hac consumacione seculi explebuntur.

Contra istud sunt plane scripture et multe, quia in tota biblia per omnia capitula, que promittunt nobis hic in via tribulaciones pro Cristo, angustias et passiones. *Item* contra hec **[fol. 34ᵛ]** dicitur *Mat. v* [*10,5,11*]: Beati qui persecucionem paciuntur, etc. Beati qui lugent. Beati estis cum vobis maledixerint homines propter me. *Act. xiv* [*21*]: Per multas tribulaciones oportet nos intrare in regnum dei. *I Tess. iii* [*3*]: Nemo moveatur in tribulacionibus hiis, scientes quia in hoc positi sumus. *Item ad Heb. ultimo* [*recte: x, 36*]: Paciencia nobis necessaria est. *Item Iac. primo* [*2*]: Omne gaudium existimate fratres, cum in varias temptaciones incederitis. *Item I. Pet. ii* [*21–22*]: Cristus passus est pro nobis relinquens exemplum ut sequamur vestigia eius, qui peccatum non fecit. *Item Mat. vii* [*13–14*]: Intrate per angustam portam, etc. Et: Quam angusta porta et via est que ducit ad vitam, etc. *Item II Tess. iii* [*recte: II Tim. iii, 12*]: Omnes qui pie volunt vivere in Cristo persecuciones pacientur.

Item iste punctus tollit penitenciam. *Item* tollit ieiunium. *Item* tollit sutores, pellifices, et omnes artifices. Si enim nichil paciemur, ad quid erunt artifices? *Item* cessabunt omnia opera misericordie. Contra quod dicitur *Deut. xv* [*11*]: Non deerunt pauperes in terra habitacionis tue. Idcirco ego precipio tibi ut aperias manum fratri tuo egeno et pauperi, qui tecum versatur in terra.

Tercio, quod gloria huius regni sic reparati in hac via ante resurreccionem mortuorum erit maior quam ecclesie primitive.

Contra, *Dan. ii* [*32,43*] *dicitur,* quod statue caput erat ex auro optimo; ubi post hoc declarat ultimum regnum mundi assimilatum ferro mixto teste ex luto, quod nunc in facto cernitur. *Item Apok.* [*i, 12–15*], quod vidit similem filio hominis etc., cuius pedes, id est ultimi sancti, similes sunt auricalco. *Item idem ibidem, ii* [*18*]. *Item* de tempore novissimo Cristus prophetavit dicens, Tunc habundabit iniquitas et refrigescet caritas [*Mat. xxiv, 12*].

Quarto, quod illud regnum et domus novissima in hac vita ante resurreccionem maioribus donis dotabitur quam domus prima.

Contra, dicitur de apostolis, Nam nos spiritus primicias habentes, intra nos ingemiscimus [*recte:* gemimus; *Rom. viii.23; cf. 22*]. *Item* dictum est discipulis superexcelenter, *Ioh. xvi* [*13*]: Cum autem venerit ille spiritus veritatis, docebit vos omnem veritatem. *Et infra:* Et que ventura sunt annunciabit vobis. *Item* Paulus dicit de se, *ad Eph. iii* [*3–5*]: Secundum revelacionem notum michi factum est sacramentum, sicut suprascripsi in brevi, prout potestis intelligere legentes prudenciam meam in ministerio Cristi, quod aliis generacionibus non est agnitum filiis hominum, sicuti nunc revelatum est sanctis apostolis eius et prophetis.

Quinto, quod sol humane intelligencie non lucebit hominibus in predicto regno, hoc est quod non docebit [**fol. 35ʳ**] unusquisque proximum suum, sed omnes erunt docibiles dei.

Contra, *Ier. iii* [*15*] *dicitur,* Dabo vobis pastores iuxta cor meum et pascent vos sciencia et doctrina. *Item Mat. ultimo* [*xxviii, 19*]: Docete omnes gentes. *Item* ex isto sequitur quod omne officium predicacionis iniunctum et mandatum a Cristo tamquam opus excellentissimum et potissimum sacerdotum cessabit, quod est contra multa precepta Cristi. *Item Deut. vi.* [*6–7*]: Eruntque verba hec que ego precipio tibi hodie in corde tuo, et narrabis ea filiis tuis.

Sexto, quod in illo seculo et regno hominum supradicto, cessabit exactor et quiescet tributum.

Ex quo sequitur quod nullus erit dominus secularis, quod est contra scripturam quamcumque, qua deus mandavit subditis superioribus suis obedire, et quibus dominium temporale approbavit, ut sunt iste scripture: Reddite que sunt cesaris cesari, et que dei deo [*Mat. xxii, 21; Mar. xii, 17; Luc. xx, 25*]. *Item Rom. xiii* [*1*]: Omnis anima potestatibus sublimioribus subdita sit. *Et infra* [*5*]: Ideoque necessitate subditi estote. *Idem ibidem* [*7*]: Cui honorem honorem, cui tributum tributum. *Item I Pet. ii* [*13–14*]: Subditi estote omni humane creature propter deum, sive regi quasi precelenti, sive ducibus quasi ab eo missis. *Item* cessaret oracio pro regibus que mandata est *I Thim. ii* [*1–3*]: Obsecro igitur primo omnium fieri obsecra-

ciones, oraciones, postulaciones, graciarum acciones pro omnibus hominibus, pro regibus et omnibus qui in sublimitate sunt constituti, ut quietam
et tranquillam vitam agamus in omni pietate et castitate. Hoc enim bonum
est et acceptum coram salvatore. *Ad Titum iii* [*1*]: Admone illos principibus et potestatibus subditos esse, deo obedire, ad omne opus bonum
paratos esse.

Septimo, periculosissime et infidelissime innuunt et dicunt quod lex gracie
perfectissima, post quam non erit alia hominis, sufficienter dirrectiva in hac
via, evacuabitur et cessabit quoad actum et execucionem.

Ex quo debent fideles scire quod sic opinantes reddunt totam legem
suspectam, ymmo quodlibet capitulum tocius legis periclitabitur in multis
punctis.

Contra, *I Pet. i* [*25*]: Verbum domini manet in eternum. Hoc est autem
verbum quod ewangelisatum est vobis. *Item Ps. cxviii* [*44*]: Et custodiam
legem tuam semper in seculum et in seculum seculi. *Luce xvi* [*17*]:
Facilius est celum et terram transire; *Mat. xxiv* [*14*]; *Luce xxi* [*33*]. *Item
ad Gall. i* [*8–9*]: Licet nos aut angelus de celo ewangelisaret vobis aliud
preterquam ewangelizam vobis, anathema sit, sicut predixi. Et nunc
iterum dico, Si quis [**fol. 35ᵛ**] vobis ewangelisaverit preter id quod acce-
pistis, anathema sit. *Iacobi i* [*25*]: Qui autem perspexerit in lege perfecte
libertatis et permanserit in ea, non auditor obliviosus factus, sed factor
operis, hic beatus in facto suo erit. *Item Iacobi ii* [*10*]: Qui autem totam
legem servaverit, offendat autem in uno, factus est omnium reus, etc.

3. *Noverint universi*

(Noverint universi modum et viam bellandi in causa dei duplicem.
Prima est quam habuit noster dux belli dominus Ihesus et sui apostoli
atque martires in hoc suum dominum imitantes, ceterique sancti ipsum
sequentes.) Qui modus bellandi Cristi et suorum nequaquam est sicut modus
humanus preliandi, nam non efficitur clarum divine virtutis opus si humanis
aminiculis fulciatur, quia non salvatur rex in multitudine virtutis sue [*cf.
Psa. xxxii, 16*]. Propterea dixit dominus ad Gedeon [*Iudic. vii, 2–3*]: Multus
est populus tecum. Non tradam Madian in manus eorum ne forte exultet
adversum me Israhel dicens, quia manus mea hec fecit. Propterea loquere
dicens, Qui timidus est et formidolosus corde, discedat ex preliis, bella
deserat, certamina virtutum forcium derelinquat. Sic hodie princeps milicie
nostre dominus noster Ihesus clamat ad milites suos in ewangelio dicens, Qui
timidus est ad bella non veniat. Hoc est quod in aliis verbis dicit, Qui non
tollit crucem suam et non sequitur me non est me dignus [*Mat. x, 38*]. Et
qui non oderit patrem suum et matrem suam, fratres et sorores, adhuc et

animam suam, non est me dignus [*Mat. x, 37; Luc. xiv, 26*]. Et iterum: Qui
non abrenuncciaverit omnibus que possidet non potest meus esse discipulus
[*Luc. xiv, 33*]; ubi evidenter ostendit timidos [*MS:* tumidos] et formidolosos
quos dominus Cristus de castris suis separat. Igitur procul sit a militibus
Cristi mundanus timor [*MS:* tumor], ut possint dicere: Si consistant adversum me castra, non timebit cor meum, etc. [*Psa. xxvi, 3*]. Solent in istis
castris sepe eciam mulieres vincere, quia non corporis robore sed fidei virtute
pugnatur, et unus militum Cristi ad hanc nos viam bellandi in causa dei
provocat, dicens *Hebr. xii* [*1–4*]: Ideoque et nos tantam habentes impositam
nubem testium, deponentes omne pondus et circumstans nos peccatum, per
pacienciam curramus ad propositum nobis certamen, aspicientes in auctorem
fidei nostre et consumatorem Ihesum, qui proposito sibi gaudio sustinuit
crucem, confusione contempta, atque in dextra dei sedis sedet. Recogitate
eum qui talem sustinuit a peccatoribus adversus semetipsum contradiccionem, ut non fatigemini animis vestris deficientes. Nondum enim usque ad
sanguinem restitistis adversus peccatum repugnantes.

Et Petrus sui belli capitaneus monet dei exercitum, *I Pet. ii* [*21–23*]:
Cristus passus est pro nobis, nobis relinquens exemplum ut sequamur [**fol.
36ʳ**] vestigia eius qui peccatum non fecit, etc., qui cum malediceretur non
maledicebat, cum pateretur non cominabatur, tradebat autem iudicanti se
iniuste, etc. *Et infra, cap. iv* [*1*]: Cristo in carne passo vos eadem cogitata-
cione armamini. *Rom. xii* [*19*]: Carissimi, non vosmetipsos defendentes. Et
dominus exercituum *Mat. v* [*38–44*] amonet, dicens: Audistis quia dictum
est antiquis, dentem pro dente, oculum pro oculo, etc. Ego autem dico vobis
non resistere malo, sed si quis [te] percusserit in dexteram maxillam, prebe
illi et alteram. Et qui vult tecum iudicio contendere et tunicam tuam tollere,
dimitte ei et palium. Et quicumque angariaverit te mille passus, etc. *Et infra:*
Ego autem dico, diligite inimicos vestros, benefacite hiis qui oderunt vos, etc.
Et ad hec sancta domini prelia magnus [miles(?)] Cristi prefatus Paulus,
exercitatus in illis bellis, provocat ad arma non carnalia sed spiritualia, dicens
[*cf. II Cor. x, 4*]: Nostra arma non sunt carnalia sed spiritualia. Que sint
autem illa exprimit *Eph. vi* [*14–17*]: State ergo induti lorica [*sic*] iusticie et
succincti lumbos vestros in veritate, sed et galeam salutis accipite et gladium
spiritus. Super omnia autem scutum fidei assumite in quo possitis iacula
maligni ignita extinguere; sed et calceati pedes in preparacione ewangelii
pacis. Hec est via regia Cristi et suorum sanctorum bellandi in causa Cristi;
igitur secure ambulate in ea. Sic Debora et Barat, *Iudicum v* [*2*], confortando
exercitum domini cecinerunt dicentes: Qui sponte obtulistis de Israhel animas ad periculum benedicite domino. *Et infra* [*8–9*]: Nova bella elegit
dominus et portas hostium ipse subvertit. Clipeus et hasta si apparuerunt (id
est non apparuerunt) in 40 millibus Israhel? Cor meum diligit principes

Israhel. Qui propria voluntate obtulistis vos discrimini, benedicite domino.

Et patet quod in ista via domini preliandi, nemo debet presumere de se nec de suis armis carnalibus neque in multitudine hominum, sed super omnia in potencia virtutis dei, secundum illud *Zach. iv* [6]: Non in exercitu nec in robore, sed in spiritu meo, dicit dominus exercituum. Quia ab ista via bellandi Cristi disperget dominus quadrigam ex Efraim et equum de Ihero-solimam, et dissipabitur arcus belli, etc., ut dicitur *Zacharie ix* [10]. Unde Cristi militibus non est recurrendum ad huius seculi arma et in eis sperare, iuxta illud *Isa. xxxi* [1]: Ve qui descendunt in Egiptum ad auxilium in equis sperantes, et habentes fiduciam super quadrigis quia multe sunt, et super equitibus quia prevalidi nimis, et non sunt confisi in sanctum Israhel et dominum non requisierunt. *Et infra* [3]: Egyptus non deus sed homo, et equi eorum caro et non spiritus, et dominus inclinabit manum suam et corruet auxiliator et cadet cui [*MS:* cum] prestatur auxilium, simulque omnes consumentur. Ideo ille David pugnator dei dicebat *in psalmo* [*xxxii, 16,18*]: Non salvatur rex per multam virtutem, et gigas non salvabitur in multitudine virtutis. Ecce oculi domini super metuentes eum et in eis qui sperant super misericordiam eius. *Et iterum* [fol. 36ʳ] [*Psa. xliii, 4-7*]: Nec enim in gladio suo possederunt terram, et brachium eorum non salvabit eos, sed dextra tua et brachium, et illuminacio vultus tui, quoniam complacuisti in eis. Tu es ipse rex meus et deus meus, qui das salutes Iacob; in te inimicos nostros ventilabimus, et in nomine tuo spernemus insurgentes in nos. Non enim in arcu [*MS:* artu] meo sperabo nec gladius meus salvabit me.

Aliter bella instruere sacerdotibus ewangelicis Cristi non est ita securum, iuxta illud *primi Machabeorum v* [67]: In die illa ceciderunt sacerdotes in bello, dum volunt fortiter facere, dum sine consilio exeunt in prelium, etc. Nec ista via regia et secura primitive ecclesie est nunc temporibus anticristi periculosis deserenda, sed securius a fidelibus amplectenda, et presertim ab ewangelicis sacerdotibus, cum *Apok. ii* [24] dicatur: Non mittam super vos aliud pondus—scilicet quam legis ewangelice. Hoc enim est ewangelium eternum quod non debet deseri usque in finem et donec veniat [*cf. Apoc. xiv, 6*].

(Secunda via in causa dei bellandi est in qua plus periculi salutis imminet, per quam sublimioribus postestatibus sive brachio seculari, cui datus est a deo gladius sive potestas illa secularis, licet armis materialibus pugnare in causa dei et defendere prudenter legem et ordinacionem Cristi, et ad vindictam malorum), ut dicitur *Rom. xiii* [*cf. 1-7; cf. I Pet. ii, 14*]. Hoc autem talibus licet istis condicionibus observatis: Primo quod sit causa dei pro qua bellum geritur. Secundo quod sit recta intencio, quia si oculus tuus fuerit simplex, totum corpus tuum lucidum erit [*Luc. xi, 34*]. Tercio quod sit instinctus divinus ad taliter proximo bellandum, quia ut dicitur *Rom. viii* [*14*]: Filii dei spiritu dei aguntur. Quarto quod tanta sit caritas pugnantis ad inimicos, quod velit parate cessare a prelio incepto cum inimici vellent converti ad dominum et amplecti veritatem et veritati non contradicere, iuxta illud *Mat. vii* [*12*]: Omnia quecumque vultis ut faciant vobis homines, facite illis. Que omnia raro concurrunt in bellis secularium. Ideo dico quod hec via licita est, sed plus habens periculi quam prima, cum ibi in bellis caritas ad inimicos periclitatur. Multa autem secundum Apostolum aliquando licent que tunc non expediunt [*I Cor. vi, 12; x, 22*], propter quod exempla bellorum patrum et regum sanctorum veteris testamenti non debent quomodolibet trahi pro confirmacione quorumcumque indifferenter bellorum, cum illa communiter bella fiebant ex certa revelacione, quod iam non sic solet communiter fieri, licet potest contingere, sed raro. Ecce quod non nego omnino hunc secundum modum bellandi in causa dei, qui licite possit fieri aliquibus auctoritatem habentibus, sed non ewangelicis sacerdotibus, quamvis prior via sit perfeccior et securior. Simplicem autem et fidelem populum non habentem in propriis domiciliis necessaria ad salutem exire extra et alibi illa querere usque ad amissionem temporalium, non reprobo sed plus approbo. Sed si qui zelo crudelitatis sine caritate invadunt proximos et illos occidunt vel bona eorum dirripiunt, non laudo sed magis reprobo. Etc.

4. *Audio cum contra percussores*

[**fol. 37ʳ**] (Audio cum contra percussores allegatur illud Apostoli [*Rom. xii, 19*]: Non vosmetipsos defendentes karissimi—dicunt enim se in peccatis excusando: Tamen nos non defendimus nos, sed legem dei. Attendunt Machabeos, quomodo ipsi pro lege veteri et in veteri pugnaverunt. Ideo movent [*aut:* monent] ut libri Machabeorum populo declarentur. Sed circa hoc pro responsione ad dicta eorum primo notari potest, quod lex vetus respectu nove legis gracie et amoris erat valde imperfecta, et sic eis erat inperfecta via bellandi in causa dei contra inimicos dei et suos), qua imperfecta via bellandi bellabant omnes fere una cum sacerdotibus, per grossam ac sensibilem armaturam nimis gravantem et distrahentem. (Que quidem via sic imperfecta adhuc est permissa et concessa potestatibus sublimioribus propter eorum imperfeccionem. Quia autem lex nova gracie est perfeccior multo amplius quam vetus, ita [*MS:* in] alia via ewangelica preliandi in causa dei [est] longe perfeccior, presertim sacerdotibus ewangelicis et cetero populo cristiano perfecciori et spirituali) iniuncta, consulta, sive demandata: scilicet resistendo contra peccatum et regnum peccati ac anticristi usque ad sanguinem, per pacienciam, fidem, et caritatem et constanciam ac perseveranciam usque ad finem, induendo sextuplicem armaturam spiritualem dei, de qua *ad Eph. vi* [*10–18*], sequendo in hoc dominum Ihesum Cristum et suos apostolos ac martires et alios sanctos veros Cristi milites per viam regiam et securam, iuxta illud *Mat. v* [*10*]: Beati qui persecucionem paciuntur propter iusticiam, quoniam ipsorum est regnum celorum. Et ad hanc secure sacerdotes ewangelici debent se ipsos et populum cristianum preparare et invitare.

(Ad primam autem viam imperfectam ubi plus imminet periculi, ubi caritas periclitatur sicut castitas in deliciis, non ita cautum sacerdotibus ewangelicis populum concitare, cum homines ex natura infecta proni sunt ad iram et sediciones, percussiones, atque ex hoc ad sanguinis effusiones, nec sic ad illam viam imperfectam veteris [*sic*] Machabeorum obligamur. Et non oportet quod sacerdos ewangelicus per gesta Machabeorum ad talia bella incerta et periculosa usque ad effusionem sanguinis concitet, nisi forte velit dicere populo quod illa carnalia bella fuerunt figura spiritualium preliorum sacerdotum Cristi et ecclesie sue legis futurorum [*sic*]), contra spiritualia nequicie in celestibus, contra potestates et terrores tenebrarum harum [*cf.* *Eph. vi, 12*]. Sic enim fieri potest, sed non corporaliter, sensibiliter, modo mundano—Paulo magno dicente, *Eph. vi* [*12*]: Non est nobis colluctacio adversus carnem et sanguinem, etc.

(Sed notandum est quod pars Cristi, cum preliatur prelia domini contra dei adversarios, id est contra peccatum et regnum diaboli, tunc ibi currit iniuria dei simul et iniuria nostra vel partis Cristi. Communiter multi ergo heu in causa dei pugnantes, sub pretextu cause dei et iniurie dei, nimis graviter ferunt iniurias proprias et inordinato zelo accenduntur) [**fol. 37ᵛ**] ad vindictam proprie iniurie sub pretextu cause dei et iniurie eius. Sic quod ipsimet sepe estimant de se et alii de eis quod ex bono zelo dei facerent et causam dei et eius iniuriam vindicarent, et sic non cognoscunt in se spiritum ipsos dementantem. (Sic ex tali zelo) prohibito, quasi in causa dei vindicando dei iniuriam, (Petrus servo pontificis amputavit auriculam et correptus est, quamvis corpus Cristi in eius vita mortali voluisset defendere. Sic, *Luce ix* [*54–56*], Iacobus et Iohannes adhuc inperfecti et fragiles, inordinato zelo accensi, contra gentem Samaritanorum dixerunt: Domine vis dicimus ut ignis descendat de celo et consumat illos? Et conversus Ihesus increpavit illos et dixit: Nescitis cuius spiritus estis. Filius hominis non venit animas perdere sed salvare. Ideo et hodie heu timeo faciunt qui sub pretextu cause et iniurie dei ex magno zelo inordinato, palliato, quasi dei zelo vindicant propriam iniuriam, et semetipsos defendentes dicunt: Tamen nosmetipsos non defendimus), sed causam et iniuriam dei—non cognoscentes in semetipsis spiritum sive zelum moventem arma ad vindictam, sub pretextu, proprie iniurie. Quibus bene dicit dominus Ihesus: Nescitis cuius spiritus estis. Filius hominis non venit animas perdere sed salvare. Ideo talibus qui non cognoscunt in se talem spiritum moventem sub pretextu valde colorato [*MS:* colorate] ad vindictam proprie iniurie, non est credendum dum dicunt: Tamen nosmetipsos non defendimus, sed Cristum. Sed in tali casu plus est Cristo credendum dicenti et scrutanti nostrum pravum cor inscrutabile: Nescitis vos cuius spiritus [estis]; quasi diceret: Ille spiritus et zelus quo sic movemini ad perdendum proximum sive ad effusionem sanguinis non est meus spiritus. In tali enim spiritu ad corda vestra non veni, ut sic perdatis vel occidatis, sed pocius pacienter et humiliter mecum in causa mea occisionem tolleretis in [?] die. [Et] subdit: Filius enim hominis non venit perdere sed salvare. Et patet quid ad talia est talibus respondendum.

5. *Item prophecias legis dei*

Item prophecias legis dei legere bonum est ad intelligendum; si quid intellexeritis certitudinaliter, potestis utiliter populo predicare. Que-[dam] sunt ibi archana, que autem non intelligitis nec ibi scitis certos sensus et securos invenire, eo quod prophecie sunt alti putei et profundi, clausi et signati, ex quibus nemo potest haurire aquas vivas sanas, nisi agnus de tribu Iuda habens clavem David apperuerit sibi hos puteos et dederit ei secundum sue condonacionis mensuram. Alias quilibet de se presumendo, secundum instinctus Sathane transfigurantis se in angelum lucis, multos sensus erroris in populum seminabit. Ideo humiliter et cum timore dei legatis prophecias; si quid certi recipietis, [fol. 38ʳ] potestis aliis dicere; quod autem non intelligitis, dicatis quod nescitis vel non intelligitis, et quantum potestis inquiratis ut intelligatis. Omnes enim heretici circa textus legis et prophetarum receperunt sibi magnam occasionem errandi. Nam sic dicitur *II Petri i* [*19–21*]: Et habemus firmiorem sermonem propheticum, cui benefacitis attendentes quasi lucerne lucenti in caliginoso loco donec dies illucescat et lucifer oriatur in cordibus vestris; hoc primum intelligentes quod omnis prophecia scripture propria interpretacione non fit. Non enim voluntate humana allata est aliquando prophecia, sed spiritu sancto inspirati locuti sunt sancti dei homines, etc.

6a. Master Jakoubek of Stříbro, Letter to Master John of Jičín (I)

[fol. 62ʳ] Gracia tibi et pax in mortuorum primogenito et principe regum terre. Frater karissime! Quia in tua epistola transmissa michi circa principium dicis quod in mea epistola, quam petitus et requisitus ad partes misi sacerdotibus, videntur multa poni contra dominum deum, prophetas eius, atque dominum Ihesum Cristum cum apostolis ipsius, et subdis consequenter in tua epistola quod ut videtur ego pono solummodo spiritualem Babilonem, animam quando confunditur, quando turbatur, quando pace deserta bella sustinet; et infra iuxta tuum conceptum misticas Babilonem, allegando confirmacionem illius misticacionis [*MS:* institucionis *?*] *Gen. xi, Ysa. xlvii,*

Daniel. xiii, Apok. xvii [*3*]: Vidi mulierem sedentem etc.: Ideo iam tangam prout deus dederit michi hiis scriptis sentenciam mee epistole priorem, et verba tua et sentenciam salutabo.

Ego dixi in meo scripto, quod videtur michi quod illud *Ierem. li* [*6*], Fugite de medio Babilonis etc., et illud *Isa. xix* [*18*], In die illa erunt quinque civitates in terra Egipti etc., non intelliguntur ad literam de materiali Babilone et corporalibus et materialibus quinque civitatibus, arte hominum edificatis, nec de civitate solis materiali [*cf. Isa. xix, 18:* . . . civitas solis vocabitur una], prout ad intencionem debent spiritus sancti nobis deservire. Tu vero tamquam bonus frater nomine dicis quod ego posui ut videtur solummodo spiritualem Babilonem, animam quando confunditur, quando turbatur, etc. Ecce frater quam stabilis es et constans: primo mittis [*sic, pro* mutas *?*] michi verba et elicis sentenciam ex meis verbis prout placet. Quomodo rogo tenet talis sequela: Illa dicta Ieremie et Isaie predicta non intelliguntur ut preassumitur prout ad intencionem spiritus sancti nobis debent deservire, igitur Babilon spiritualis aut spiritualiter intellecta solummodo est anima quando turbatur, quando confunditur, etc.—ac si sic argueres: Ista verba, Tu es qui venturus es an alium expectamus, prout secundum intelligenciam spiritus sancti debent deservire Iohanni, non intelliguntur de adventu Cristi in carnem [*sic*], cum prius Baptista sciverit Cristum incarnatum, igitur intelligi debent solum de Cristi adventu ad passionem sive mortem. Iam tu discute et delibera in tua consciencia, an valet talis sequela, et discas in posteris verba fratris tui et presertim sentenciam non mutare. Dicis enim quod videntur multa poni in mea epistola contra dominum, prophetas, atque Cristum et eius apostolos, sed dei gracia mediante, unum ex illis multis finaliter non ostendes, nisi per consequencias non valentes pro misticacione tua propria confirmanda. De Babilone allegas *Gen., Ys., Dan., et Apok,* ut preallegatum est, sed utinam verba textus in Gen., Isa., Dan., et Apok. aplicasses convenienter ad tuam propriam misticacionem, nec persaltando nec truncando, sed sensum misticum sensui literali applicando ubi saltem in predictis locis literalis et misticus non coincidunt, et consequenter probasses racione vel scriptura aut auctoritate quod ille sensus misticus esset acceptandus a viantibus tamquam fides prout tu intendis illam acceptandam, aut enim ut estimo non velles [**fol. 63ʳ**] populum tantum hortari et excitare ad sic fugiendum, occasione cuius fuge fiunt mirabilia, et utinam omnia bene. Si autem Babilon taliter intelligatur ut tu pretendis, responde ad interrogata secundum ordinem congruum et honestum.

Primo quero utrum manebo ubi aliquis conversatur sacerdos. Si dixeris sic: Contra: Ex tibi dubio ipse dampnabitur, et per consequens est prescitus infidelis; sed cum per te conversans infideli est in medio Babilonis aut in Babilone, igitur non licet michi cum tali conversari. Si vero dixeris quod licet michi cum talibus conversari sacerdotibus quos spero aut reputo bonos et fideles, peccata declinando secundum graciam concessam, gracias tibi reddo quod vere et sane sentencie appropinquas.

Secundo quero utrum manebo in aliquo regno tamquam subiectus alicui regi qui de facto est malus, dummodo idem rex habet aliquem servum infidelem in villa, opido, civitate vel castro in quo ego traho moram: quod non probatur, quia tunc non servo preceptum de fuga a Babilone iuxta te ut videtur. Et ut finaliter perstringam sentenciam in hac parte, quero ubi est illa civitas ubi non est aliqua domus sumptuosa, alta, ampla, vel sic de ceteris per te nominatis?

Frater mi karissime, de scripturis illis altissimis senciamus humiliter et discrete, nullum populum cristianum et saltem simplicem per sensum nostrum non bene fundatum reddendo perplexum. Perplexitas namque meo videre in fide scripture est ianua satis propinqua desperacioni. Insuper ubi intendis improbare similitudinem meam adductam de civitatibus memoratis in ewangelio *Luce xix* [*17*], et de illis quinque civitatibus de quibus facit *Isa.* [*xix, 18*] mencionem, similitudinem negas sed diversitatem non assignas quare non debeant ille civitates spiritualiter intelligi, de quibus loquitur Isaias sicut et ille de quibus facit mencionem Lucas. Si autem post hoc pro causa diversitatis dicere volueris quod illud Luce est parabola, aliud vero est prophecia, animadverte tunc Pauli verba [*cf. I Cor. x, 11*] ubi sic contingebant eis in figura, et destruetur tua sentencia. Fuga Cristi, suorum apostolorum, et aliorum sanctorum bene est nobis data in exemplum, quod quandoque licet fugere, sed Cristus sapiencior nobis non dixit determinate, specificando ad quas civitates quinque esset tempore persecucionis fugiendum, saltem materialiter intellectas, cum tunc nimium cristianismum onerasset [*MS:* honorasset] tempore fuge sue a presencia persecutorum, nam plura sunt regna cristianismi quam quinque. Onus ergo grave nimis esset quod [non] haberent nisi quinque civitates ad quas homines illorum regnorum tempore persecucionis inique fugerent.

Et utinam frater mi, tu in Cristi verbis et sentencia, tam literaliter quam spiritualiter intellectis, quievisses describendo materiam talis fuge, quia tunc non plus [*MS:* plus quam] quinque civitates materialiter intellectas publicasses, ad quas esset fugiendum quam 20. Non enim sequitur: Cristus fugit ab una civitate in aliam sicut eius apostoli, igitur ille quinque civitates de quibus loquitur Isaias non debent modo tempore gracie spiritualiter intelligi sed literaliter, sicut tu asseris. Et miror ex quo illa verba *Mt. xxiiii* [*16*], "Tunc qui in Iudea sunt, fugiant ad montes," tu [*MS:* tunc] misticas [**fol. 63ᵛ**] ad sensum spiritualem, per Iudeam intelligendo homines fideles qui dicunt se cristianos et non sunt; et tamen non libenter audis hoc tempore quod ille quinque civitates, de quibus prius, debent spiritualiter intelligi. Eciam satis periculose, frater mi, ut videtur, exponis hec verba *Mt. xxiiii* [*15*], "Cum videritis abhominacionem desolacionis que dicta est a Daniele propheta stante in loco sancto," etc.: Abhominacionem desolacionis, id est destruccionem abhominacionis, sicut est dotacio sacerdotum, spelunce latronum, etc. Quia ewangelista [*MS:* ewangelium] Matheus dicit, cum videritis illam abhominacionem stantem; tu vero glosas: cum videritis ipsam destructam. Quod simul staret et destrueretur, non bene sonat. Fateor tamen tecum, quod tempore persecucionis licet fideli fugam inire; quandoque vero non, nam mercenarius videns lupum venientem ex fuga laudem non reportat [*cf. Joh. x, 12–13*]. Sed non expedit ultra Cristi doctrinam frontose civitates specificare ad quas homines fugere tenerentur, presertim cum homo possit quandoque securius, salubrius, et melius quam in talibus specificatis preservari ab invasione persecutorum. Negare eciam ego nolo quod prophecie satis multe literaliter intelliguntur, cum practicata et executa tempore legis gracie, de quibus fit mencio in ewangelio, fuerunt in prophetis illis misterialiter et secrete demonstrata; sed absit quod ex isto quis dicat iam ita grosse intelligendas esse illas prophecias sicut litera historie prima facie pretendit. Nam tunc Messiam adhuc expectaret, cum *Isaias* [*vii, 14*] dicat, Ecce virgo concipiet et pariet filium, etc.

Ex quibus dictis patet quod nimis culpabiliter populum simplicem seducunt in magnum periculum animarum suarum, qui ultra Cristi doctrinam et suorum apostolorum vel quinque vel 10 specificant civitates ad quas homines recurrunt [*sic*], tamquam ad loca refugii tempore persecucionis. Sed illuc tunc videtur esse fugiendum ubi homo securius, melius, et deo placencius servire poterit ipsi omnipotenti domino dominorum, ad ecclesie edificacionem et sue anime salutem.

Ulterius, frater mi, advertas quod non solum insecure scripturas applicas, sed finaliter quasi in tuis scriptis fidem cristianorum blasfeme niteris inpugnare. Quid enim magis credi debet a quolibet viatore quam quod in quacumque civitate materiali, castro, opido, campo, via, villa, vel silva, Cristi fideles secundum ewangelica precepta viventes, fide integra, spe et caritate usque ad finem perseverantes, et in bona consciencia malo nequaquam consencientes, continuantes hunc modum ad dei beneplacitum, quacumque morte preoccupati fuerint, salvabuntur? In veritate, frater mi, huic principio fidei cristiane directe et explicite discredens, et eius oppositum tenens et firmiter asserens, est purus hereticus, si affuerit pertinacia, cum illud oppositum enervat fidem nostram ex integro et innuit deum posse peccare infidelissime, et posse esse iudicem iniustissimum. [**fol. 64ʳ**] Sed quid detestabilius? Et ergo quando tu velles illam veritatem fidei cristiane inpugnare, affirmans ex illa sequi contradiccionem, loqueris contra Cristum, non sane sed inintelligibiliter. Ab illo igitur errore male inchoato recedas et ad Ihesum convertaris, qui est via, veritas, et vita.

Quantum autem ad alia que in tua inseris epistola, de exitu a civitatibus materialibus ad alias, tempore persecucionis, sicut de Loth quamvis uxor eius periit, similiter de exeuntibus de Egipto ad mandatum domini, qui omnes perierunt, sicut prius dictum est: fateor servando lecciones [*MS:* lectores *?*] doctrine Cristi et suorum apostolorum, quod licet quandoque fugam inire de loco ad loca [*MS:* loco], sed nolo temerarie diffinire aut insecure loca ipsa. Nec recolo quod umquam dixissem aliquem falsum predicasse ex hoc quod consuluit aliquem sic fugerc ut premittitur [*MS:* pretermittitur], quamvis sibi casualiter aliquid periculi sive mors immineret tempore talis fuge. Approbare tamen nolo sinistram, insecuram, et infundabilem applicacionem scripturarum. Et patet ex hiis que iam dicta sunt, quid senciendum sit de sentencia epistole mee priori[s], et manifestatur in parte insecuritas specificacionis seu determinacionis civitatum ad quas homines recurrunt [*sic*] persecucionis tempore in hac via. Hiis igitur diligenter notatis, errores et pericula declinantes, viam securam et sanam ad beatitudinem tendentem [*MS:* -tes] curramus alacriter, quam beatitudinem nobis dignetur concedere qui semper regnat ubique. Amen.

6b. Master Jakoubek of Stříbro
to Master John of Jičín (II)

(Gracia tibi et pax in mortuorum primogenito et principe regum terre! Frater karissime! Quia in tua epistola michi transmissa circa principium dicis quod in mea epistola, quam petitus et requisitus ad partes misi sacerdotibus, videntur multa poni contra dominum deum, prophetas eius, atque dominum Ihesum Cristum, cum apostolis ipsius: unde circa istum punctum ego Magister Iacobus Magistro Iohanni Giczin respondendo protestor quod non intendi nec intendo per dei graciam aliquid dicere, predicare, per epistolas scribere, vel consulere, contra dominum deum) ac prophetas eius atque dominum Ihesum cum apostolis ipsius. Quod si umquam dixissem forte ex mea ignorancia, presumpcione, aut quomodolibet aliter, habeo pro non dicto. Et si in ista cartula quam nititur Magister Iohannes Giczin reprobare fuero fideliter et veraciter doctus, quod in aliquo essem devius, volo humiliter a quocumque corrigi et emendari.

(Secundo subiungit Giczin contra me sic: "Et primum posuisti ut videtur solummodo spiritualem Babilonem, animam quando confunditur, quando turbatur, quando pace deserta bella sustinet," etc. Et contra hoc subdit sua verba dicens: "Non solum anima peccatrix dicitur [fol. 64ʳ] esse spiritualiter Babilon, sed eciam prelati moderni viventes secundum hunc mundum, a maximo papa usque ad minimum sacerdotem adversantem veritatibus legis dei, dicuntur esse Babilon misterialiter. Et a maximo rege malo sectante hoc seculum usque ad minimum laicum infidelem, dicuntur Babilon."

Pro responsione ad istam obieccionem est notandum) et fide primum credendum est catholice, quod sicut anima racionalis et caro unus est homo personalis, ita deus et homo unus est Cristus, sic quod Cristus simul est deus et homo, et divisim deus et divisim est homo. Sicut vere dicitur, Cristus est homo et Cristus est deus, sic vere unus homo personalis coniunctim et divisim est simul anima racionalis et caro. Et idem personalis homo divisim est caro, quia substancia carnea, et idem homo est anima intellectiva, quia scilicet est substancia intellectiva racionalis et animalis. Et in scriptura sepe homines anime vocantur. Sic enim Cristus dictus est filius dei et hominis divisim et coniunctim, ymmo ipsum verbum caro factum est, quia substancia carnea, et ipsum verbum sive dominus est suus spiritus et intellectus: *Trenorum iv* [*20*]: Spiritus oris nostri cristus dominus captus est in peccatis nostris, etc. Sic enim Apostolus pluries videtur innuere quod eadem persona hominis est duplex homo, scilicet tam interior quam exterior, *II Cor. iv* [*16*]: Licet is qui foris est exterior homo corrumpatur, tamen is qui intus est renovatur. Et *Rom. vii* [*18*]: Scio enim quia non habitat in me, hoc est in carne mea, bonum. Ex quo patet quod quia se Apostolus dicebat carnem suam, ipse erat caro sua, et si erat caro tunc a forciori suus spiritus erat, sicut et iam vere est spiritus. Et si ipse fuit homo exterior animalis, quia caro, a forciori ipse fuit homo interior raptus in tercium celum, nesciens an in corpore tunc vel extra corpus fuit, etc.

Potest circa ista eciam notari quod plures homines sunt unus homo, tum quia participacione specie plures homines sunt unus homo, tum quia (omnes fideles aggregatim sunt una sponsa) et una (Cristi) columba. Tercio supponitur et notatur quod omnes fideles non solum sunt unus homo sed sunt unus spiritus et una caro et una anima, et quilibet divisim est anima [*MS:* omnia], ergo omnes simul sunt una anima, (unus spiritus, ac unum corpus, unaque Iherosolimam spiritualis). Ex adverso autem (omnes iniqui) et impii anticristi in malo, in spiritu Sathane coniuncti, (sunt una anima et Babilon) mater fornicacionum magna, (ut sunt prelati, papa, episcopi simoniaci, totusque clerus cupiditatis lepra contaminatus, et omnes iniqui [*Goll:* magni] reges, principes, potentes, divites huius seculi, capti amore Babilonis et seculi.)

Cum ergo dixi de Babilone [**fol. 26ʳ**] anime malivole, malis replete, patet quod cum omnes clerici, prelati cupidi et mali iuxta superius dicta sunt una anima malivola et Babilon spiritualis, mea epistola intelligenda est non solum de anima singulari hominis unius mali, sed et de omnibus animabus hominum malorum, que sunt Babilon spiritualis. Spero ergo quod in isto puncto non dixi quicquam contra dominum Ihesum Cristum, suos apostolos sive prophetas. Et per hec dicta potest responderi ad Magistri Iohannis Giczin obiecta sic contra me dicentis: non solum anima peccatrix dicitur esse spiritualiter Babilon, sed eciam prelati moderni, etc. Nec ego in mea epistola umquam assumpsi quod solum anima peccatrix diceretur Babilon, sed dixi: anima, etc.—sine illa exclusione, scilicet "solum"—primarie clerum simoniacum et secundarie corpus reliquum anticristi intelligendo, quia omnes sunt anima malivola, unus spiritus nequam, et caro sive corpus anticristi.

Quod si apposuissem *li* "solum," adhuc argumentum Giczin contra me non valeret, cum dicit ipse: non solum, etc.; cum adhuc non exclusissem clerum simoniacum aliosque impios, ut patet ex supradeclaratis diligenter intuenti, quomodo videlicet omnes mali dicuntur anima malivola, etc. Vide ergo frater quomodo stabilis es et constans: primo mutas michi verba et elicis sentenciam ex verbis meis prout placet. Quomodo rogo tenet talis sequela: illa dicta Ieremie et Isaie, puta de Babilone et quinque civitatibus, non intelliguntur ad literam de materiali Babilone et corporalibus ac materialibus quinque civitatibus, arte hominum edificatis, prout ad intencionem spiritus sancti nobis debent deservire; ergo Babilon spiritualis aut spiritualiter intellecta solummodo est anima quando turbatur, quando confunditur, etc. Ac si sic argueres: ista verba, "Tu es qui venturus es, an alium expectamus?" [*Mat. xi, 3*], prout secundum intencionem sancti spiritus debent deservire Iohanni, non intelliguntur de adventu Cristi in carne, cum prius Baptista scivit Cristum incarnatum; ergo intelligi debent solum de Cristi adventu ad passionem sive mortem. Iam tu discute et delibera in tua consciencia, an valeat talis sequela, et discas in posterum verba fratris tui et presertim sentenciam non mutare. Dicis enim quod videntur multa poni in mea epistola contra dominum, prophetas, atque Cristum et eius apostolos, sed dei gracia mediante, unum ex illis multis finaliter non ostendes, nisi per consequencias non valentes, etc.

(Secuntur verba Giczin: "Et non tantum," inquit, "illi prelati prefati, sed omnia edificia sumptuosa, alta, ampla, superba, dicuntur esse babilonica.) Eciam vestes preciose, superbe, [**fol. 26ʳ**] superflue, pompatice, coccinee, inaurate, dicuntur esse babilonice. Unde *Gen. xi* [*1-9*], *Isa. xlvii, Dan. xiii; Apok. xvii* [*3*]: Vidi mulierem sedentem super bestiam coccineam. *Et infra, etc.* [*4*]: Et mulier erat circumdata purpura et coccino et inaurata auro et lapide precioso et margaritis, etc." Hec verba eius, etc. Hic dico quod aliud est esse vel dici Babilon, et aliud dici vel esse babilonicum. Esse enim Babilon mistice de se malum est. Esse autem vel dici babilonicum est aliquid possessum a Babilone. Talia autem possunt esse multa que non sunt mala moraliter, ut olim Daniel, Ysmahel, Azarias, Ananias, et ceteri filii captivitatis, erant quodammodo babilonici, quia ad literam a Babilone materiali possessi; non tamen erant mali sed boni. Et licet Babilon cum rege suo abutebatur

Daniele, ipsum odiendo et incarcerando, ipse tamen ex hoc non fuit moraliter malus. Non ergo oportet omnia babilonica esse mala. Et dato quod
omnia babilonica essent mala, adhuc non esset contradiccio huic dicto: Quod
anima peccatrix que viciis turbatur dicitur Babilon. Si autem Babilon taliter
intelligatur ut tu pretendis, responde ad interrogacionem secundum ordinem
congruum et honestum.

Primo quero utrum manebo ubi aliquis conversatur sacerdos. Si dixeris sic:
Contra: Ex tibi dubio ipse damnabitur, et per consequens est prescitus
infidelis. Sed cum per te conversans cum infideli est in medio Babilonis aut
in Babilone, ergo non licet michi cum tali conversari. Si vero dixeris quod
licet michi cum talibus conversari sacerdotibus quos spero aut reputo bonos
et fideles, peccata declinando secundum graciam michi concessam, gracias
tibi reddo, quia vere et sane sentencie appropinquas. Secundo quero utrum
manebo in aliquo regno tamquam subiectus alicui regi qui de facto est
malus, dummodo idem rex habet aliquem servum infidelem in villa, opido,
civitate, vel castro, in quo ego traho moram; quod non probatur, quia tunc
non servo preceptum de fuga a Babilone iuxta te, ut videtur. Et ut finaliter
perstringam sentenciam in hac parte, quero: ubi est illa civitas ubi non est
aliqua domus sumptuosa, alta, ampla, vel sic de ceteris per te nominatis?

Item ex hoc quod illa mulier sedens super bestiam habet nomen scriptum:
"Misterium, Babilon, Magna Mater fornicacionum," tunc utique secundum
suam racionem principalem et primariam, qua nominatur esse talis, est ut sic
mistica et spiritualis. Ex quo in fronte habet scriptum nomen misticum, tunc
in misterio et sensu mistico ad principalem intencionem spiritus sancti,
secundum racionem suam primariam, Babilon nominatur, et est tota mistica
et spiritualis cum fronte et nomine, [fol. 65ʳ] habens misticum poculum,
misticam vestem coccineam, et habitacionem spiritualem. Et ut sic, secundum illam racionem propriam et primariam sui, non est materialis et sensi-
bilis, nam videtur repugnare eandem mulierem secundum suam primariam
racionem, ad principalem intencionem spiritus sancti, esse misticam, spiritualem, et sic inmaterialem et insensibilem, et esse secundum suam propriam
racionem materialem, sensibilem, et sic non esse misticam et spiritualem.
Videtur ergo sicut in Apokalypsi sic et in aliis prophetis, ubi mencio fit de
Babilone, quod intelligitur principaliter ad intencionem spiritus sancti de
mistica Babilone et spirituali, et ut sic immateriali et non sensibili. Rebus
siquidem materialibus et sensibilibus potest aliquis bene et male uti; racio
autem abutendi talibus est mala, sed non ipse res materiales et sensibiles se
solo sumpte sunt male, nisi forte dicatur quod talia materialia et sensibilia
sunt signa remota valde per accidens, per que notificari potest hec mistica
meretrix. Omnis denique creatura dei bona est, ut dicitur *I Tim. iv* [4]. Et
ad Titum i [15]: Omnia munda mundis, etc. Ergo boni, iusti, et sancti in

medio nacionis prave babilonice possunt bene et sancte uti illis quibus babilonici inique et inmunde abutuntur. Insuper quia iuxta salvatoris dictum, Omne quod intrat in os non coinquinat hominem [*Mat. xv, 11*]; ergo eadem racione, et quod vestit hominem vel exterius situat hominem non coinquinat hominem. De corde enim exeunt cogitaciones male, etc. Hec sunt que coinquinant hominem, et non exteriora sensibilia, saltim de per se; ergo illa mala que sunt ex corde procedencia habent racionem Babilonis, et non exteriora materialia bona et utilia, mundisque hominibus munda.

Ex quibus apparet, mi frater, quod in verbis scripture longe tibi usurpas alium remotum sensum a principali et primario sensu spiritus sancti; propter quod, karissime, de scripturis illis altissimis senciamus humiliter et discrete, nullum populum cristianum et saltim simplicem per sensum nostrum non bene fundatum reddendo perplexum. Perplexitas namque meo videre in fide scripture est ianua satis propinqua desperacioni, etc.

(Post hec Magister Iohannes dicit quod "illa iam dicta sunt simul casura tempore ulcionis. Ideo dicit Iohannes in *Apokalipsi xviii* [2]: Cecidit, cedidit Babilon magna, etc. Et ideo, ne participes sint Cristi fideles delictorum eius, et de plagis eorum ne accipiant, mandat dominus exire eisdem in diebus ulcionis) [fol. 65ʳ] de illa, dicens [*Apoc. xviii, 4*]: Exite de illa popule meus [*sic*], ne participes, etc. Ex quo textu habetur quod non solum mandat dominus spiritualiter exire de Babilone, subdens causas aliquas, quarum prima est ne sint participes delictorum alienorum; secundo, ne accipiant plagas infidelium, cum eis habitantes tempore vindicte; tercio, [*cf. Ier. li, 45–46*] ut salvet unusquisque animam suam ab ira furoris domini; quarto, ne molescat cor fidelium per multas oppressiones infidelium, seducciones, astucias, crudelitates, quia dicit salvator, Quoniam refrigescet caritas, etc. [*Mat. xxiv, 12*]; quinto, ne timeant auditum qui audietur in terra, ut est formido a potentibus huius seculi, blasfemie, obprobria, irrisiones, etc." Hec ille.

(Hic respondendo dico quia ut dictum est, ex quo scriptura principaliter mistice intelligit de mistica Babilone, tunc et de exitu) principalius intelligit de vita babilonica spirituali, ut videlicet proposito exeant, et voluntate malo non consenciendo. Et quamvis fragilibus caucius esset de medio malorum exire, et in consorcio iustorum ne seducerentur comorari, sicut scriptum est: Cum sancto sanctus eris [*Psa. xvii, 26*]; tamen fideles ab impiis vexati, si illos aufugiunt, in ippocritas incidunt seductores et astuciores, sub specie sive veste ovina sensus et errores contra fidem tenentes, ita quod nullibi inter homines istius temporis securitas invenitur. Et pro isto videtur sonare illud propheticum *Amos v* [*18–19*]: Dies domini ista, tenebre et non lux. Quomodo si fugiat vir a facie leonis et occurrat ei ursus, et ingrediatur domum et innitatur manu sua super parietem, et mordeat eum coluber. Et *Michee vii* [*5*]: Nolite credere amico, nolite confidere in duce, ab ea que dormit in sinu tuo custodi claustra oris tui. Et si iam est illud tempus de quo Cristus dixit, putas cum venerit filius hominis inveniet fidem super terram? Tunc rarus est de apostolica fide integra, et qui sunt fideles domini pauci. Ubi senciunt Babilonem, quomodo ergo extra eam possunt fugere secure, nisi forte extra hunc mundum babilonicum totum in maligno positum, ad sinum Abrahe et domum [*MS:* dm̄] Ihesu Cristi in celis [*?; MS:* ē alis] ? Ergo exitus corporalis et localis generaliter per omnes non videtur posse impleri. Misticus autem fit satis communiter et generaliter, quem sancti ecclesie primitive docent, et per consequens a fidelibus est amplectendus. Et si dicitur quia sicut Loth iustus exivit de Sodomis, sic nunc debent fugere fideles [**fol. 66ʳ**] de medio impiorum: sed contra hoc potest dici quia sicut Ioachim cum Susanna ambo iusti manserunt in Babilone, domino placentes, sic nunc (multi iusti in medio malorum habitantes salvantur dum tamen ex mistica et spirituali exeunt Babilone.) Si autem ut dicitis materialia edificia debent iam cadere per Babilonem designata, tunc et scriptura, "Ecce relinquetur vobis domus vestra deserta," *Mat. xxiii* [*38*], ad literam deberet intelligi de edificiis materialibus; que si deserta erunt, tunc non cadent, et tamen secundum aliam scripturam cadent. Et sic ad idem tempus cadent et erunt deserta, quod videtur repugnanciam claudere, que quidem repugnancia non esset si scripture predicte ad sensum spiritualem et misticum ad principalem intencionem spiritus sancti intelligerentur. Et cause ille exeundi de mistica spirituali Babilone eedem possunt poni sicut prime: prima videlicet, ne sint participes delictorum; secunda, ne paciantur cum infidelibus; tercia, ut salvet unusquisque animam suam; quarta, ne cor molescat, etc. Quia post completum exitum de Babilone mistica, confortatur et non molescit cor in tribulacionibus, nec timebit blasfemias et irrisiones, etc. Unde aliquando melius est aliquibus fidelibus pati persecucionem propter Cristum usque ad mortem, et non fugere, ut floreat martirium. Quid eciam prodesset materialis casus vel destruccio edificiorum, si tamen spiritualis et mistica Babilon non caderet?

De post subiungit Magister Iohannes Giczin plura, dicens enim hec verba contra me, etc.: "Eciam posuisti in epistola quod ille quinque civitates quas ponit Ysaias [*xix, 18*] ad diem illam, tempore maxime persecucionis, ad quas debent confugere fideles, intelliguntur spiritualiter, sicut et illud parabolicum *Luc. xix* [*17*]: Euge serve bone et fidelis; eris potestatem habens super decem civitates, etc. Negatur," inquit, "similitudo ibi, sed intelligitur literaliter ibi quinque civitates ad quas fideles debent confugere tempore oportuno, sicut et Cristus fecit tempore persecucionis, cum Ioseph et matre sua fugiens de loco ad locum corporaliter ante Herodem, *Mat. ii* [*14*]. Et in persecucione phariseorum fugit in civitatem Effrem [*Ioh. xi, 54*]. Et *Mat. x* [*23*] dicit: Cum persequitur vos in civitate ista, fugite in aliam. Simile est et illud *Mat. xxiv* [*16*]: Tunc qui in Iudea sunt, fugiant ad montes." Hec ille.

Frater karissime, similitudinem de quinque civitatibus, *Isaie xix* et *Luc.*
xix supramemoratis, negas, sed diversitatem sive **[fol. 66ᵛ]** causam raciona-
lem diversitatis non assignas, et hoc non est respondere sed subterfugere
quare ille civitates non debeant spiritualiter intelligi, de quibus Isaias loquitur, sicut et ille de quibus facit mencionem Lucas. Si autem post hoc pro
causa diversitatis dicere volueris quod illud Luce est parabola, aliud vero est
prophecia: animadverte Apostoli Pauli verba sic dicentis [*I Cor. x, 11*],
"Omnia contingebant eis in figura," et destruetur tua sentencia. Et quid dices
si erunt plures quam quinque, vel pauciores ad confugiendum civitates?
Fuga autem Cristi, suorum apostolorum, et aliorum sanctorum bene est
nobis data in exemplum, quod quandoque licet fugere, sed Cristus sapiencior
nobis non dixit determinate, specificando ad quas quinque civitates esset
tempore persecucionis fugiendum, saltem materialiter intellectas, cum tunc
nimium cristianismum onerasset tempore fuge sue a presencia persecutorum,
nam plura sunt regna cristianismi quam quinque. Onus ergo grave nimis
esset quod [non] haberent nisi quinque civitates ad quas homines illorum
regnorum tempore persecucionis confugerent. (Non) ergo (oportet, si
Cristus fugit in Egiptum cum Ioseph et matre, quod ergo nunc fideles
debeant in illam Egiptum descendere. Morale tamen fateor fidelibus fragilibus esse exemplum relinquendum, sic scilicet quod imminente persecucione
maxima et tribulacione, ne frangantur a fide et bono proposito, adherencia-
que veritatis, possunt cedere ad locum ubi non est tanta tribulacio. Nunc
vero aliqui ad consilium aliorum, de Praga exeuntes sine persecucionibus,
incidunt in tribulaciones et persecuciones et pericula corporum et animarum.
Adhuc siquidem electi dei in Praga tantam novissimam tribulacionem non
paciuntur, et futura non scitur [*sic*] pro certo. Et tamen vos scripsistis ad
Pragam ad sexum femineum, ut cito exeant de Praga, cum alibi occurrunt
[*sic*] impii et peccatores sicut in Praga. Insuper, ut michi scriptum est,
nominastis certum tempus carnisprivii inter festum Scolastice et Valentini,
puta quod tempore illo plaga horribilissima super malos debuisset venire.
Quare autem illa omnia in scripto vestro non notatis ad plenum, intencionem
vestram exprimendo, ut eo melius possemus nos funditus concipere? Quis
rogo potest cognoscere qui sunt predestinati et qui presciti, ut relinquendo
omnes prescitos exirent [*sic*] ad solos predestinatos?)

Et miror ex quo illa verba *Mat. xxiv* [*16*], "Tunc qui in Iudea sunt,
fugiant ad montes," tu misticas ad sensum spiritualem, per Iudeam intelligendo homines **[fol. 67ʳ]** fideles qui dicunt se cristianos et non sunt; et
tamen [non] libenter audis hoc tempore quod ille quinque civitates, de
quibus prius, debent spiritualiter intelligi. Et si ut vos vultis per montes
intelliguntur sensibiles et materiales montes, tunc eadem racione, sine racione
diversitatis, Iudea deberet intelligi gens iudaica circumcisionis. Eciam, si in

uno loco scripture per montes intelliguntur sensibiles et materiales montes, tunc et eadem racione in alio loco, presertim cum non est causa diversitatis, sensibiles montes sunt intelligendi. Et sic illud *Isaie xiii* [2]: Levate signum super montem caliginosum, etc.; et illud *Psa.* [*lxxxvi, 1*]: Fundamenta eius in montibus sanctis; et illud *Isaie ii* [2]: Et erit in novissimis diebus preparatus mons, etc.—deberet quodlibet eorum intelligi de sensi[bili]bus, corporalibus montibus. Sed hoc non bene stat. Ergo nec illud, "Tunc qui sunt in Iudea fugiant ad montes," ad literam est intelligendum; alias ex eadem racione posset videri quod Cristus in hoc adventu venire [*?; MS: exemere*] deberet in nubibus materialibus celi, eo quod scriptura dicit: Sic veniet quemadmodum vidistis eum, etc. [*Act. i, 11*]. Ita eciam populus fidelis deberet exire de materiali Egipto et transire per mare rubrum, sicut olim filii Israhel, sed quia hoc non oportet fieri, *Rom. vii* [*14*]: Scimus enim quia lex spiritualis est; et *Hebr. x* [*1*]: Umbram enim habens lex futurorum bonorum, non ipsam imaginem rerum. Unde Origenes super Leviticum, *Omelia 4*, dicit [*MPG, 12, 435*]: Si secundum divine legis fidem hec que locuntur [*recte: leguntur*] nobis, dominus locutus est ad Moisen, puto quod tamquam dei verba non debeant secundum capacitatem audiencium, sed secundum loquentis, scilicet prophete et dei, intelligi. Dominus, inquit, locutus est. Quis dominus? Apostolus tibi respondeat, et ab ipso disce quia dominus spiritus est. Si igitur et dominus et deus spiritus est, que [*MS: que quia*] spiritualiter loquitur, spiritualiter debemus audire. Ego adhuc et amplius dico, quia que dominus loquitur non spiritualia tantum, sed et spiritus credenda sunt, non meo sensu hec, sed de ewangeliis approbabo. Audi dominum ad discipulos suos dicentem: Verba que locutus sum vobis spiritus et vita sunt [*Ioh. vi, 64*]. Si ergo ipsius salvatoris voce didicimus quia verba que locutus est apostolis sunt spiritus et vita, nequaquam dubitare debemus quod eciam que per Moisen sive per alium prophetam loquitur spiritus et vita esse credenda sunt. Hec ille.

Item idem Origenes, super Genesim, *Omelia vii* [*MPG, 12, 202*], quomodo Agar Ysmahelis mater recepit utrem aque. Non enim habebat, [**fol. 67ᵛ**]. inquit, puteum aque vive, nec poterat puer Ysmahel de puteo aquam haurire. Isaac habebat puteos pro quibus et certamina patitur adversus philistinos; Ysmahel autem de utre bibit aquam, sed hic uter quasi uter deficit; ideo sitit et non invenit potum. *Et infra* [*ibid.*]: Uter legis litera est, de qua ille populus carnalis bibit. In multis enim defectum patitur sensus literalis, frequenter deficit et explicare se non potest. In multis defectum patitur historialis sive carnalis intelligencia. Ecclesia autem de ewangelicis et apostolicis fontibus bibit, qui numquam deficiunt, sed in plateis suis percurrunt, quia in latitudine spiritualis interpretacionis habundat spiritus et defluit, etc. [*hic finis Origenis*] Ex quibus patet quod qui continue in scripturis voluerit uti carnalibus sensibus, ut de quinque civitatibus, de Egipto, de meretrice mistica, et aliis, timeo ne tamquam uter Agar deficiat sibi sensus carnalis. Sed accedat pocius ad puteos misteriorum et spiritualis intelligencia habundabit sibi; quamvis etenim sensus carnales possunt currere aliquando, sunt tamen incerti et dubii plerumque, cum quibus dum quis, neglecto sensu spirituali ut manna abscondito, sepe se occupat supervacue, etc.

Quando autem dicit *Apok. xviii* [2], "Cecidit, cecidit Babilon magna," etc., non videtur hoc primarie intelligi de materiali edificiorum habitacione, quia textus dicit quod sic cadet quod adhuc in posterum remanebit. Casus autem et ruina materialis edificii non facit postea ipsum edificium remanere. Unde postquam dictum est, "Cecidit, cecidit Babilon," subditur postea, "et facta est habitacio demoniorum et custodia omnis spiritus inmundi." Cum ergo hoc totum simul proprie in edificiis materialibus non ita completur, videtur quod fidelis erigat se alcius ad sensum misticum, ut supra tactum [*MS:* tractum] est, etc. Eciam satis periculose, frater mi, ut videtur, exponis hec verba *Mat. xxiv* [*15*], "Cum videritis abhominacionem desolacionis que dicta est a Daniele propheta stantem in loco sancto" etc.: abhominacionem desolacionis, id est destruccionem desolacionis, sicut est dotacio sacerdotum, spelunce latronum, etc. Quia ewangelista Matheus dicit, "Cum videritis illam abhominacionem stantem"; tu vero glosas, "cum videritis ipsam destructam": quod simul staret et destrueretur non bene sonat.

Nolo eciam negare quod prophecie satis multe literaliter intelliguntur cum practicate et execute tempore suo fuerunt. Sed absit quod ex isto quis dicat iam ita grosse intelligendas esse illas prophecias, sicut litera historie prima facie pretendit. Nam tunc messiam adhuc expectaret, cum Isaias dicat [*vii, 14*]: Ecce virgo concipiet et pariet filium, etc. Ulterius, frater mi, ad- **[fol. 68ʳ]** vertas quod non [solum] insecure scripturas applicas, sed finaliter quasi in tuis scriptis fidem cristianorum niteris inpugnare. Quid enim magis debet credi a quolibet viatore, quam quod in quacumque civitate materiali, castro, opido, campo, via, villa, vel silva, Cristi fideles secundum ewangelica precepta viventes, fide integra, spe, et caritate usque ad finem perseverantes, et in bona consciencia malo nequaquam consencientes, continuantes hunc modum ad dei beneplacitum, quacumque morte preoccupati fuerint, salvabuntur? In veritate, frater mi, huic principio fidei cristiane directe et explicite discredens, et eius oppositum tenens et firmiter asserens, est purus hereticus, si affuerit pertinacia, cum illud enervat fidem nostram ex integro, et innuit deum posse peccare infidelissime, et posse esse iudicem iniustissimum; sed quid detestabilius! Et ergo quando tu velles illam veritatem fidei cristiane inpugnare, affirmans ex illa sequi contradiccionem, loqueris contra Cristum non sane sed inintelligibiliter. Ab illo ergo errore male inchoato recedas, et ad Ihesum convertaris, qui est via, veritas, et vita!

Sed cum Magister Iohannes contra me replicat dicens quod ex dictis meis sequatur contradiccio, nam ex prima parte Cristifideles vivunt secundum omnia precepta domini usque in finem, ergo implent omnia precepta ad salutem eis pertinencia, et quando ulterius arguitur, per consequens maxime tribulacionis fugient de medio infidelium ad certa loca: Respondetur quod hoc non oportet sequi, nam implendo omnia precepta exit spiritualiter de Babilone, corde, fide, et proposito, et non oportet de necessitate quod localiter ad locum exeat. Tum quia stat, aliquos fideles non posse exire localiter, cum infirmi vel captivi essent; tum quia stat, in casu tribulacionis ita in domino confortari, quod non oportet eos exire, fugiendo de medio malorum, sed quod melius esset ibi eis in medio impiorum occidi et subire martirium et salvari, quam fugiendo postea numquam talem occasionem martirii habere. Igitur dictum meum non implicat contradiccionem.

Et fateor quod sicut Loth per certam revelacionem angelicam exivit de Sodoma, et salvatus est in monte quoad vitam mortalem, sic nunc videtur michi, si fidelibus Cristi esset certa revelacio, sive per scripturam sive alio modo, fugere de uno loco ad alium, deberent fugere de illis locis periculosis ad loca tuciora. Omnis enim certificacio sive revelacio per scripturam legis, sive prophetarum aut apostolorum doctrinam, sive per verbum Cristi ewangelicum, est revelacio **[fol. 68ᵛ]** ewangelica. Cum omnes apostoli et prophete cum aliis sanctis eorum imitatoribus sunt angeli, et dominus noster Ihesus Cristus est angelus magni consilii: ideo si per doctrinam eorum et sensum illorum ad intencionem spiritus sancti primariam essemus certificati ad exeundum de certis locis ad alia tuciora, sub pena eterne dampnacionis omnes deberemus exire, certificati per revelacionem angelicam, sicut Loth in Sodomis. Et quia adhuc ad historiacum et carnalem sensum sic non sumus certificati sicut ad misticum sensum, sive de fuga Loth de Sodomis, sive de Iudea in montes, ergo non oportet nos sic carnaliter iam illa explere. Nec ego recollo quod umquam dixissem aliquem falsum predicasse, ex hoc quod consuluit aliquando sic fugere ut inmediate premissum est, quamvis sibi casualiter aliquid periculi sive mors immineret tempore talis fuge. Approbare tamen nolo sinistram, insecuram, et infundabilem applicacionem scripturarum.

Et patet ex dictis quomodo Magister Iohannes non probat quod talia dicta que ipse scribit, predicat, et docet, contra que iam replicavi, nunc ex precepto omnes fideles tenentur observare et explere. (De hoc autem quod populus ex vestris predicacionibus, ut dicitur, et periculosis scripture interpretacionibus, arripit arma bellica carnalia et relinquit consuetum laborem manuum suarum, et ociose vivit de substancia et rapina aliorum proximorum, et occidunt effunduntque sanguinem—Hec enim magna inconveniencia multi contra vos clamant qui sunt fide digni, cum ut spero sunt amorem dei pre oculis habentes, vocantes vos sacerdotes sanguineos, a quibus dicunt nemo fidelium deberet sacramenta divina percipere. Nonne prius predicastis contra occisionem [*MS:* occesiom], et quomodo iam res sit versa in oppositam qualitatem? Et puto quod hec non latent vos, quoniam multi simplices fideles et pusilli scandalisantur. Cur ergo hec sciendo dici de vobis tacetis? Cur te non excusas si reus non es? Cur non tollis scandala? Cur non scribis ad magistros et scabinos pragenses, pro tui expurgacione? Si autem es in aliquo reus, non queras excusaciones in peccatis, sed humiliter confiteri debes rei veritatem, in quo es reus et in quo non. Alias tacendo que tibi ascribuntur, videris approbare.) Non credimus ad quantum nos iam altitudo Sathane dementavit, ut saperemus et intelligeremus ac novissima provideremus, etc.; (verumtamen simplicem populum in articulo necessitatis congregari, in bono salutis et in Cristo Ihesu, non audeo reprobare.)

7. Rescript of Masters Christian of Prachatice and Jakoubek of Stříbro

[**fol. 69ʳ**] (Salus Cristi fidelibus ad quos pervenerint ista scripta. Quia inter discretos viros, Nicolaum parte ex una et Wen[ceslaum] parte ex altera, sacerdotes predicantes, orte sunt quedam materie litium in auditorio populo provocative, tandem predicti sacerdotes parte ex utraque coram multitudine populi super dictarum materiarum disceptacione sese ad nostram, videlicet Magistri Cristani de Prachaticz et Magistri Iacobi de Misa, informacionem evocarunt, et quicquid salubriter in materiis, in quibus habent controversias, eos docuerimus, accipere promiserunt. Nos igitur, consilio plurium magistrorum advocato, quatuor articulorum summarie sentenciam discucientes, ad tollendas contrarietates odiosas de medio, et ad caritatem inserendam in Cristi populo, per hec scripta taliter respondemus.

Ad primum articulum, cuius sentencia est: An domini seculares tenentur gladio materiali defendere legis veritatem, dicimus quod sic, quoniam dicit Apostolus [*Rom. xiii, 4*]: non sine causa gladium, scilicet dominus secularis, portat; sed [*I Pet. ii, 14*] ad laudem bonorum, vindictam vero malorum. Ideo enim et tributa accipiunt, ut inquietos corripiant, bonos exaltando, semper tamen caritate servata quoad deum et proximum, prout decet.

Ad secundum, cuius sentencia est hec: Si domini seculares ad tantum sint desides, quod nolunt veritatem gladio accepto defendere, an communitates fideles subiecte possint et debeant eam gladio defendere materiali, adversantes videlicet corporaliter perimendo,—taliter respondemus: Quia cum simus cristiani, Cristus autem nobis tamquam precessor et legifer noster dicit: Ego sum via [*Ioh. xiv, 6*]: securius est nobis per pacienciam veritatem cristianam protegere quam per accionem repercuciendo, quoniam dicit Cristus: In paciencia vestra possidebitis animas vestras [*Luc. xxi, 19*]. Ymmo

ad tantum pacienciam nobis verbo et opere exemplavit, eciam in causa dei
vel propria, quod discipulis volentibus ut ignis de celo descendat et Samari-
tanos nolentes hospitari dominum consumat, comminatorie ait: Nescitis,
cuius spiritus estis; filius hominis non venit animas perdere sed salvare [*Luc.
ix, 56*]. Et Petro volenti ewangelii conditorem gladio materiali defendere
dicebat: Converte gladium tuum in vaginam [*Ioh. xviii, 11*]. Quomodo
autem noster legifer Cristus coram Pilato velud agnus mansuetus stabat,
potestatem, quam desuper Pilato esse datam dicebat, pacienter usque ad
mortem crucis sustinendo, est Cristi fidelibus indubie manifestum. Hanc
viam securissimam, tutissimam apostoli sequebantur. Nam Petrus, qui se-
quebatur vestigia eius usque in patibulum crucis, in suis epistolis Cristi
fideles ammonet dicens: Cristus passus est pro nobis, nobis relinquens exemplum, ut sequamur vestigia eius [*I Pet. ii, 21*]. Sic alii apostoli et martires in
hoc mundo pressuras paciebantur sine repercussione et remurmuracione, et
hoc idem verbo et facto communitates fideles edocebant secundum illud
dictum ecclesie catholicum: Ceduntur gladiis more bidencium, non murmur
resonat, non querimonia, sed corde tacito mens bene conscia conservat
pacienciam. Grave autem et periculosum videtur consulere communitatibus
ad pugnandum corporaliter, et inter omnes artes ars ista pugnandi cum hoc,
quod servetur caritas, est difficilima, quam oportet quemlibet hominem
habere de necessitate salutis, iuxta illud Apostoli [*I Cor. xiii, 1*]: Si lingwis
hominum loquar et angelorum, etc. Eciam quia belli auctoritas atque consilium videtur esse penes principes et potestates seculares, secundum illud
Rom. xiii [*1*]: Omnis anima potestatibus sublimioribus subdita sit. Et ad
idem videtur esse Augustinus, libro contra Faustum [*in Decreto, XXIII. q.i,
c.4*]. Ex qua sentencia patet quod non cuilibet de populo licet bella suscitare.
Ymmo nulli cuius adest facultas habendi aliunde secundum legem divinam
vel humanam iusticie complementum.

Ad belli namque rectificacionem videntur tria esse necessaria, videlicet
iusta vendicacio, licita auctorisacio, et recta intencio. Ex primo patet quod
oportet bellantem esse in gracia et habere iusticiam, quia aliter non esset
vendicacio iusta. Ex secundo patet quod deficiente iuris suffragio, sic videlicet quod aliunde non posset haberi iusticie complementum, tunc ex auctoritate principis consulto domino esset bellandum. Ex tercio claret quod oportet
intencionem cuiuscumque bellantis purgari a putredine vane fame, a libidine
dominandi, et zelo propriam iniuriam vindicandi.

Ne tamen ignaris quibusdam videamur nimis disgredi a proposito, concedimus quod domini seculares possent tantum deo resistere et eius legi, quod
per ipsum deum potestate eorum ablata, liceret communitatibus a deo ad hoc
opus admissis realiter et non fantastice defendere ewangelicam veritatem—
servato tamen semper ordine debito et consono legi Cristi, divino instinctu

vel certa revelacione, sive evidencia non fallente ad hoc movente. Cavendum autem est, ne quis frontose et nimis precipitanter potestatem dominorum eis ablatam asserat, quia nolunt condescendere cuicumque indifferenter [**fol. 70ᵛ**] vento nimis levi [*cf. Eph. iv, 14*]. Possunt autem communitates veritatem defendere et debent suos dominos adiuvando. Securum autem non est neque iustum videtur, quod communis populus acceptet opus sibi impertinens, presertim ubi talis populus habet dominos in quibus non est defectus tam evidens et notabilis aut incorrigibilis, quod aliunde fieri non possit iusticie complementum, nisi ipse populus opus aggrederetur satis arduum, periculis et laqueis involutum. Et ergo, sicut supra dictum est, securior via in hac causa pugnandi Cristi et suorum sanctorum est amplectenda, via ambigua dimissa, hec est via paciencie, quam Cristus docuit et implevit. Hac enim via sancti induti virtute ex alto quondam ecclesiam edificaverunt, que facit diligere inimicos, et non solum non occidere sed nec irasci, ut patet *Mat. v* [*21–22*]. Sic enim ad hanc viam Apostolus hortatur communitates fideles dicens: Imitatores mei estote, fratres, sicut et ego Cristi [*I Cor. xi, 1*]! Qui provocans ad alia arma, *II Cor. x* [*4*], dicit: Arma, inquit, nostre milicie non sunt carnalia. Ex lege igitur Cristi patet, quod nemo pronus sit exhortari ad pugnam ambiguam et perplexam, sed tucius est crebrius prohibere, cuilibet sacerdoti ewangelico, quantum in eo est, tam periculosum modum pugnandi. Sic enim quodammodo esset cum Petro gladium in vaginam convertere. Quod securitatis est, teneant magis fideles, quod ambiguum et difficile pretermittant et declinent.

Ad tercium, cuius sentencia est: An fideles debeant et possint congregari tempore persecucionis—dicimus quod mistice et spiritualiter congregari tenentur fideles in domino Ihesu, sic videlicet quod eorum sit anima una et cor unum. Congregari vero corporaliter Cristi fideles ad certas civitates materialiter intellectas, sub quinario numero, ut dicitur, contentas, non videtur nobis cadere sub precepto generaliter pro communitatibus tamquam necessarium ad salutem, cum lex non reddit ad se homines perplexos. Hoc autem faceret, si expresse obligaret ad quinque civitates materiales, et tamen non exprimeret neque determinaret eas, que essent ille distincte. Tunc enim fideles valde essent perplexi et ambigui, nescientes ad quas deberent confugere; ad quam perplexitatem populum inducere sacerdotes debent sibi summe precavere, sicut debent cavere, ne presumptuoso spiritu populo predicent quod iam infra breve tempus ventura est plaga horribilissima super populo, private tempus assignando et populum [**fol. 70ᵛ**] culpabiliter tenentes in suspenso, nulla super hoc habita certa revelacione divina. Fugam tamen inire cristianis tempore persecucionis licet prudenter exemplo Cristi, quando scilicet ex fuga ipsorum, ut est verisimile, non sequetur fidei irrisio et iusticie depressio, sed probabiliter coniecturatur, quod alibi ex tali fuga maior sit utilitas ecclesie quam ex remansione, ex qua sequeretur occisio ministrorum ecclesie sine fructu salutifero animarum.

Ad quartam, cuius sentencia hec est: An mulier fidelis propter Cristum et eius ewangelium potest relinquere virum infidelem, si ei defenderet verbum dei audire et sacram suscipere communionem—taliter respondemus: Quod mulieri non licet consentire viro suo in malo contra salutem anime sue, et tali modo et forma ipsum relinquere, scilicet virum, licet sibi, videlicet in illicitis non consenciendo. Et ad tantum posset vir uxori sue irasci, quod liceret sibi volenti iram sedare mariti, ab eo localiter discedere ad tempus, circumscripta tamen omni simulacione in hac parte; que si affuerit, illum recessum inficiet undiquaque. Ex quo tamen recessu nullus sane mentis presumat asserere, quod vivente marito priori licet ipsi mulieri alteri viro matrimonialiter copulari, aut quod non teneatur curam habere filiorum, quos peperit viro suo. Hoc enim asserere pertinaciter esset heresis contradicens sentencie Cristi et sui Apostoli sancti Pauli.)

8. *Bellandi materiam concernit infrascriptum*

(Bellandi materiam concernit infrascriptum. Primo notanda sunt que bellum rectificant iustum. Prima enim condicio rectificans bellum iustum est iusta vendicacio, iuxta quam condicionem oportet bellantem esse in gracia et habere iusticiam ad damnum [*MS:* dum] vel iniuriam vindicandum, secundum iura divina vel humana in ipso fundata.) Aliter enim iniuste facit quicquid facit—*Mat. vii* [*18*]: Non potest arbor mala fructus bonos facere. Et quia debemus omnia in caritate facere, patet hec prima condicio. (Secunda est licita auctorizacio, propter quam condicionem patet quod nulli persone licet bellum suscitare, cui aliunde adest facultas habendi iusticie complementum. Sed quando deficit iuris suffragium, tunc ex auctoritate principis, consulto domino, est bellandum.) Vult ergo *Augustinus,* in epistola ad Bonifacium [*in Decreto, XXIII.q.i, c.3*], quod bellum debet esse necessitatis, ut deus liberet ab iniuratore et reservet in pace. [**fol. 71ʳ**] Bellum ergo non est per se bonum, sed mediare debet ad pacem. (Tercia condicio est intencio recta), que principaliter et finaliter rectificat bellum, iuxta illud *Mat. vi* [*22*]: Si oculus tuus fuerit simplex, totum corpus tuum lucidum erit. (Sine istis condicionibus non licet cuiquam proximum debellare, et per consequens oportet causam pro qua quis pugnat, aut saltem pugnare debeat, esse dei iusticiam et non bona temporalia. Nemo namque debet se bello exponere, quod est periculum mortis, nisi in causa qua mortuus foret martir. Necesse est ergo intencionem bellantis purgari a putredine vane fame, a libidine dominandi et zelo propriam iniuriam vindicandi, et ira culpabili, postposita autem [*MS:* a] cupiditate temporalia perquirendi); et indui intencionem divini honoris, intendendo ex utraque parte bonum virtutis, vindicacionem divine iniurie, et cum inturbata milicia habere intencionem merendi bona patrie.

(Ex qua sentencia patet ipsos insipientes esse et non habentes fidem vivacem caritate formatam, qui se mortis periculo exponunt in causa quam ignorant esse dei iusticiam, propter stipendia magna, ducti magis cupiditate insaciabili quam zelo iusticie, quorum merces temporalis, cum affuerit damnacio perpetua pro perpetrato facinore, eis non proficiet sed nocebit. Que enim maior stulticia, quam Boemum gentem suam debellare propriam, causa racionabili non habita, propter temporale commodum, quo quesito et obtento, et occiso suo proximo, sibi dominabitur aliena nacio, que si posset ipsam non solum bonis privaret fortune, sed ut verisimile est, evisceraret, misericordia postposita qualicumque. Adverte ergo, o gens boemica, tempestive, ne cecitate ducta tuam conculces culpabiliter et iniuste propriam nacionem! Si enim vix licet cristianum in iudicio bona sua repetere, quomodo, cum plus distat a lege Cristi, pugnare, ubi causa non subest racionabilis, sed stipendium solum, quia facile perpenditur, temporale.) *Luce* enim *vi* [*27*] scribitur: Diligite inimicos vestros, benefacite hiis qui oderunt vos, etc. Ibi bene nota! Ibi enim sunt verba magni concilii angeli, non ad pugnam infundabilem nacionis proprie ortancia, sed ipsam prohibencia, ut videtur. Supposita enim malicia proximi, debet cristianus sibi compati, cum de lege nova debet diligere sibi simile. *Ecccli. xiii* [*19*]: Omne animal diligit sibi simile. Firmiores eciam debent imbecilitatem infirmorum sustinere, et non sibi ipsis placere. [**fol. 71ᵛ**] *Ad Rom. xii* [*18*]: Si fieri potest quod ex vobis est, cum hominibus omnibus pacem habentes. Sic enim congeritur ignis dileccionis super arbitrium sementis, cum dileccio hominis dileccioni divine in omnibus conformatur.

(Nulli) enim (cristiano licet dubitare quin debuerit sub pena peccati mortalis servare mandata domini, numquam persequendo fratrem per se vel per alium, nisi propter caritatem fraternam, diligendo ipsum plus quam omne bonum fortune pro quo prosequitur. Scribitur namque *Mat. v* [*21*]: Audistis quia dictum est antiquis, non occides, etc. Ubi communiter in textu ira illicita erga fratrem est prohibita, sicut verbum derisorium, irracionabile, obprobriosum, contumeliosum, aut aliter irritativum, non sub quacumque pena, sed sub pena dampnacionis perpetue. Caritatem autem servare fraternam, preservando se ab ira lege dei prohibita, sub pena que premittitur, valde difficile [est] Boemis invadere saltem volentibus homines proprie nacionis, quia inter omnes artes videtur, quod cum arte bellandi stat de difficillimo observancia caritatis, quam tamen oportet omnem hominem habere de necessitate salutis. Et sic nemini licet suum fratrem invadere nisi propter amorem et commodum sic invasi, cum aliter ibi deesset intencio caritatis.) Sed quis scit utrum sic invasus, quem bellator intendit occidere, ex hinc decidet a caritate, et moriendo forte damnabitur peccato finalis impenitencie? Et quis vellet racionabiliter se ipsum taliter castigari? Inter alias quidem correcciones, ista videtur a scola Cristi maxime elongata, fratrem scilicet occidere propter stipendium temporale. Primum autem peccatum quod clamare dicitur ad deum ex scriptura est fratricidium, de quo *Gen. iv* [*10*] *et ix* [*6*]: Qui effuderit sanguinem alterius, sanguis illius effundetur. Et *Mat. vii* [*12*] scribitur: Quecumque vultis ut faciant vobis homines, ita et vos facite illis.

Si autem amor virtutis non moneret ad homicidium declinandum, timor tamen pene ad hoc aliceret, quia ut patet *Gen. iv* [*11*], maledixit deus Cain super terram, quia occidit fratrem suum Abel. Farao autem, quia voluit masculos hebreorum occidere, ut patet *Exodi primo* [*16*], occisus est, ut patet *Exo. xiv* [*28*]. Eciam Abimelech, qui fratres suos occidit, filios Gerobaal 70, ut patet *Iudicum ix* [*5*]. Qui postea miserabiliter interemptus est. Quid autem Achab et Gezabel reportarunt lucri ex morte Naboth, propter vineam suam, de qua materia scribitur *III Reg. xxi et xxii:* iudicet fidelis habens [**fol. 72ʳ**] scintillam fidei. Et ut estimatur quomodo consimile reportabunt volentes suam propriam invadere nacionem, ubi non subest, ut sepe premittitur, causa aliqua racionalis, propter stipendium satis transitorium et periculose adquestum.

Et ut satis singulariter condescendam, videtur quod sicut Ioab occidit Abner filium Ner, principem milicie, ut patet *II Reg. iii* [*27*]; Amasam, ut patet *II Reg. xx* [*10*]; et Absolonem filium David, ut liquet *II Reg. xviii* [*15*]; et omnes de intencione sinistra vel dolo, ut clare intuenti historiam evidet: (Sic Boemi, quibus non desunt inimicicie, quadam ut apparet cecitate moti, aliis inimicis ex hoc gaudentibus et finem expectantibus eis valde prosperum, proprios ut videtur culpabiliter et saltem imprudenter, velud talpe subterranee lucem odientes, volunt invadere indiscrete. Ad cuius nutum, consilium, aut mandatum faciunt hec, deus novit! Sed hoc ex scriptura cognosco, quod Ioab facinora perpetrans, Salomonis precepto ad altare occisus est, *III Reg. ii* [*31*]. Et indubitanter estimo, quod idem eveniet ipsis, qui se legis ewangelice pretendunt zelatores et tamen simplices nacionis proprie invadunt, pretermissis consiliis hominum discretorum, quales indubie habent in propria nacione! O magna cecitas, o grandis perversitas! Ubi est hec scriptura cordi impressa: Omnis qui odit fratrem suum, homicida est), *I Ioh. iii.* [*15*]? Item *Ioh. viii* [*44*]: dyabolus homicida fuit ab inicio. Item, quid accidit regi Ioram idolatre et fratres suos occidenti, patet *II Paral. xxi* [*13 ff.*]. Et ut finaliter sermones perstringam, modo non sufficit michi tempus enarrandi scripturas contra ingratitudinem ipsorum qui frontose et omni pretermissa racione nituntur proprios destruere, in magnum dedecus atque dampnum non iam perceptum a cecatis in penam peccati, sed revera gemebundum et irrecuperabile. Evidet ut dicitur ubi est fides huius scripture, scilicet: Sine offensione estote iudeis et gentibus et ecclesie dei, sicut et ego per omnia omnibus placeo, non querens quid michi est utile, sed multis, ut salvi fiant—*I Cor. x* [*32–33*]. Item, Imitatores mei estote, sicut et ego Cristi [*I Cor. xi, 1*]. *I Pet. ii* [*21*]: Cristus pro nobis passus est, nobis relinquens exemplum, ut sequamur eius vestigia, etc.

BIBLIOGRAPHY

The bibliography is intended primarily as a guide to those who may wish to read more. Hence the works in the more generally known languages have been separated from those in Czech, while the latter have been selected to form a conspectus of the current status of scholarship on the various aspects of Hussitism. Some of the items listed have not been cited in the footnotes of the present work, for one reason or another, and conversely the bibliography omits a number of works that have been cited—works not directly concerned with Hussitism and studies of minor or marginal points. The third section, listing editions and studies of primary sources, is offered only as a more or less convenient substitute for a full-scale critical analysis, which remains to be done. Those wishing more information are referred to the author's study of the narrative sources in his University of Chicago doctoral dissertation, "The Hussite Movement in History" (1952), available on microfilm.

WORKS IN MAJOR LANGUAGES

I. Background and Antecedents

Bartoš, František Michálek. "Hus, Lollardism and Devotio Moderna in the Fight for a National Bible," *Communio Viatorum*, III (Prague, 1960), 247–254.

Bernard, Paul. "Heresy in Fourteenth Century Austria," *Medievalia et Humanistica*, X (1956), 50–63.

Betts, R. R. "English and Czech Influences on the Hussite Movement," *Transactions of the Royal Historical Society*, XXXI (1939), 74–102.

———. "The Influence of Realist Philosophy on Jan Hus and His Predecessors in Bohemia," *Slavonic and East European Review*, Vol. XXIX, No. 73 (June, 1951), 402–419.

———. "The Regulae Veteris et Novi Testamenti of Matěj z Janova," *Journal of Theological Studies*, XXXII (1931), 344–351.

———. "Some Political Ideas of the Early Czech Reformers," *Slavonic and East European Review*, Vol. XXXI, No. 76 (1952), 20–35.

———. "The University of Prague: 1348," *Ibid.*, Vol. XXVII, No. 68 (1948), 57–66.

———. "The University of Prague: The First Sixty Years," *Prague Essays*, ed. R. W. Seton-Watson (Oxford, 1949), pp. 53–68.

Brandt, Miroslav. "Wyclifitism in Dalmatia in 1383," *Slavonic and East European Review,* XXXVI (1957), 58–68.

Haupt, Hermann. "Waldensertum und Inquisition im südöstlichen Deutschland," *Deutsche Zeitschrift für Geschichtswissenschaft,* I (1889), 285–330; III (1890), 337–411. Also repr. as a book (Freiburg: Mohr, 1890).

Kaminsky, Howard. "Wyclifism as Ideology of Revolution," *Church History,* XXXII (1963), 57–74.

Krofta, Kamil. "Bohemia in the Fourteenth Century," *Cambridge Medieval History,* VII (1932), 155–182.

Kybal, Vlastimil. "Étude sur les origines du mouvement hussite en Bohême. Matthias de Ianov," *Revue historique,* CIII (1910), 1–31.

Loserth, Johann. (Reviews of Haupt, "Waldensertum" and Preger, "Über das Verhältnis," in:) *Göttingische gelehrte Anzeiger* (1889), No. 12, pp. 475–504; (1891), No. 4, pp. 140–152.

——. "Beiträge zur Geschichte der Husitischen Bewegung, II. Der Magister Adalbertus Ranconis de Ericinio," *AÖG,* LVII (1879), 203–276 (texts on 248 ff.).

——. *Hus und Wyclif* (Munich and Berlin: R. Oldenburg, 1884; 2d ed., 1925). English translation by Evans: *Wycliffe and Huss* (London, 1884).

——. "Nachträgliche Bemerkungen zu dem Magister Adalbertus Ranconis de Ericinio," *MVGDB,* XVII (1879), 198–213.

——. "Zur Verpflanzung der Wiclifie nach Böhmen," *MVGDB,* XXII (1884), 220–225.

Molnár, Amadeo. "Cola di Rienzo, Petrarca e le origini della riforma hussita," *Protestantesimo,* XIX (Rome, 1964), 214–223.

——. "Le mouvement préhussite et la fin des temps," *Communio Viatorum,* I (Prague, 1958), 27–32.

——. "Les Vaudois et la Réforme tchèque," *Bolletino della Società di Studi Valdesi,* No. 103 (May, 1958), 37–51.

Naegle, August. "Der Prager Kanonikus Matthias von Janow auf Grund seiner jüngst zum ersten Male veröffentlichten *Regulae veteris et novi testamenti,*" *MVGDB,* XLVIII (1910), 1–17.

Novotný, Václav. "Les origines du mouvement hussite en Bohême," *Revue de l'histoire des religions,* I-IV (1929).

Odložilík, Otakar. "The Chapel of Bethlehem in Prague. Remarks on Its Foundation Charter," *Studien zur älteren Geschichte Osteuropas,* I, ed. G. Stökl (Graz-Köln: Böhlau, 1956), pp. 125–141.

——. "Wyclif and Bohemia," *VKČSN* (1935).

——. "Wycliffe's Influence on Central Europe," *The Slavonic Review* (1929).

Schlauch, Margaret. "A Polish Vernacular Eulogy of Wycliff," *Journal of Ecclesiastical History,* VIII (1957), 53–73.

Thomson, S. Harrison. "Learning at the Court of Charles IV," *Speculum,* XXV (1950), 1–20.

——. "Pre-Hussite Heresy in Bohemia," *English Historical Review,* XLVIII (1933), 23–42.

Werner, Ernst. "Ideologische Aspekte des deutsch-österreichischen Waldensertums im 14. Jahrhundert," *Studi medievali,* 3ª Serie, Vol. IV, No. i (1963), 217–237.

———. "Nachrichten über spätmittelalterliche Ketzer aus tschechoslovakischen Archiven und Bibliotheken," Beilage to *Wissenschaftliche Zeitschrift der Karl-Marx-Universität Leipzig,* XII (1963), 215–284.

Winter, Eduard. *Frühhumanismus. Seine Entwicklung in Böhmen* (Berlin: Akademie-Verlag, 1964).

II. John Hus

De Vooght, Paul. *L'Hérésie de Jean Huss.* Bibliothèque de la Revue d'histoire ecclésiastique, Fasc. 34 (Louvain, 1960).

———. *Hussiana. Ibid.,* Fasc. 35 (Louvain, 1960).

———. "Jean Huss et ses juges," *Das Konzil von Konstanz,* edd. A. Franzen and W. Müller (Freiburg: Herder, 1964), pp. 152–173.

Höfler, Constantin. *Magister Johannes Hus und der Abzug der deutschen Professoren und Studenten aus Prag 1409* (Prague: F. Tempsky, 1864).

Krofta, Kamil. "John Hus," *Cambridge Medieval History,* VIII (1936), 45–64.

Loserth, J. *Hus und Wiclif* [as above].

Lützow, F. *The Life and Times of Master John Hus* (London: J. M. Dent, 1909).

Matthaesius, F. "Der Auszug der deutschen Studenten aus Prag (1409)," *MVGDB,* LII (1914), 451–499; LIII (1915), 58–110.

Molnár, A. "Réflexion sur la notion de vérité dans la pensée de Jean Hus," *LF,* LXXXVIII (1965), 121–131.

———. "Les réponses de Jean Huss aux quarante-cinq articles," *Recherches de Théologie ancienne et médiévale,* XXXI (1964), 85–99.

Müller, K. "König Sigmunds Geleit für Hus," *Historisches Vierteljahrschrift,* I (1898), 41–86.

Schaff, David. *John Huss. His Life, Teachings, and Death* (New York: Scribners, 1915).

Seibt, Ferdinand. "Johannes Hus und der Abzug der deutschen Studenten aus Prag 1409," *Archiv für Kulturgeschichte,* XXXIX (1957), 63–80.

Spinka, Matthew. *Jan Hus and the Czech Reform* (Chicago, 1941).

———. *John Hus' Concept of the Church* (Princeton, N.J.: Princeton University Press, 1966).

Vischer, Melchior. *Jan Hus, sein Leben und seine Zeit.* 2 vols. (Frankfurt a.M.: Societätsverlag, 1940; 2d ed., 1958).

Workman, Herbert. *The Dawn of the Reformation.* II. *The Age of Huss* (London: C. H. Kelly, 1902).

III. Hussitism

Amann, Emil. "Jacobel et les débuts de la controverse utraquiste," *Miscellanea Fr. Ehrle,* I (Rome, 1924), 375–387.

Bartoš, F. M. "Picards et Pikarti," *Bulletin de l'histoire du Protestantisme français,* LXXXI (1932).

Bernard, Paul. "Jerome of Prague, Austria and the Hussites," *Church History*, XXVII (1958), 3–22.

Bernhardt, R. *Die Inanspruchnahme des deutschen Reiches durch die Hussitenfrage in den Jahren 1419–1423* (Halle, 1901).

Betts, R. R. "Jerome of Prague," *University of Birmingham Historical Journal*, I (1947), 51–91.

———. "The Place of the Czech Reform Movement in the History of Europe," *Slavonic and East European Review*, XXV (1947), 373–390.

———. "Social and Constitutional Development in Bohemia in the Hussite Period," *Past and Present*, No. 7 (1955), 37–54.

———. "The Social Revolution in Bohemia and Moravia in the Later Middle Ages," *Past and Present*, No. 2 (1952), 24–31.

Bezold, Friedrich von. *König Sigmund und die Reichskriege gegen den Hussiten.* 3 vols. (Munich: Ackermann, 1872–1875–1877).

———. *Zur Geschichte des Hussitenthums. Kulturhistorische Studien* (Munich: Ackermann, 1874).

Binder, S. *Die Hegemonie der Prager im Hussitenkrieg.* Prager Studien, VIII-IX (Prague, 1901–1903). [See "Goll" below.]

Böhmer, Heinrich. "Magister Peter von Dresden," *Neues Archiv für Sächsische Geschichte und Altertumskunde*, XXXVI (1915), 212–231.

Bretholz, B. "Die Übergabe Mährens an Herzog Albrecht V. von Österreich im Jahre 1423," *AÖG*, LXXX (1894), 249–349.

Brock, Peter. "Peter Chelčický, Forerunner of the Unity," Chap. I in *The Political and Social Doctrines of the Unity of Czech Brethren in the Fifteenth and Early Sixteenth Centuries* (The Hague: Mouton, 1957), pp. 25–69.

Denis, Ernest. *Huss et la guerre des Hussites* (Paris: Leroux, 1878; repr. 1930).

Girgensohn, Dieter. *Peter von Pulkau und die Wiedereinführung des Laienkelches* (Göttingen: Vandenhoeck and Ruprecht, 1964).

Goll, Jaroslav. "König Sigmund und Polen 1419–1436," *Mitteilungen des Instituts für österreichische Geschichte*, XV (1894), XVI (1895).

———. *Quellen und Untersuchungen zur Geschichte der Böhmischen Brüder. I. Der Verkehr der Brüder mit den Waldensern. II. Peter Chelčický und seine Lehre.* (Prague: Otto, 1878, 1882).

———. "Zur Geschichte des Hussitenkrieges," *VKČSN* (1901), 15 pp. [A critique of Binder, above.]

Grünhagen, C. *Die Hussitenkämpfe der Schlesier 1420–1435* (Breslau, 1872).

Haupt, H. "Husitische Propaganda in Deutschland," *Raumers Historisches Taschenbuch*, 6. Folge, VII (1888), 233–304.

———. "Johann von Drändorfs Verurteilung durch die Inquisition zu Heidelberg, 1425," *Zeitschrift für Geschichte des Oberrheins*, LIV (1900), 479–493.

Heymann, Frederick. "City Rebellions in 15th-Century Bohemia and Their Ideological and Sociological Background," *Slavonic and East European Review*, Vol. XL, No. 95 (1962), 324–340.

———. "The National Assembly of Čáslav," *Medievalia et Humanistica*, VIII (1954), 32–55.

———. *John Žižka and the Hussite Revolution* (Princeton, 1955).

————. "The Role of the Towns in the Bohemia of the Later Middle Ages," *Journal of World History*, II (1954), 326–346.

Hlaváček, Ivan. "Die Geschichte der Kanzlei König Wenzels IV. und ihre Beamten in den Jahren 1376–1419," *Historica*, V (Prague, 1963), 5–69.

Höfler, K. "Die Schlacht am Žižkaberg 1420," *SKAW*, XCV (1879), 899–912.

Jacob, E. F. "The Bohemians at the Council of Basel," *Prague Essays*, ed. R. W. Seton-Watson (Oxford, 1949), pp. 81–123.

Jastrebov, N. *Etjudy o Petre Chelčickom i jego vremeni*, I. *Zapiski ist.-fil. Fakulteta Imperatorskago S-P. Universiteta* (St. Petersburg, 1908). [All published.]

Kaminsky, Howard. "Chiliasm and the Hussite Revolution," *Church History*, XXVI (1957), 43–71.

————. "The Free Spirit in the Hussite Revolution," *Millennial Dreams in Action*, Supplement II of *Comparative Studies in Society and History*, ed. Sylvia Thrupp (The Hague: Mouton, 1962), pp. 166–186.

————. "Hussite Radicalism and the Origins of Tabor 1415–1418," *Medievalia et Humanistica*, X (1956), 102–130.

————. "Nicholas of Dresden and the Dresden School in Hussite Prague," Introduction to *Master Nicholas of Dresden, The Old Color and the New*, edd. Kaminsky et al., *Transactions of the American Philosophical Society*, N.S., Vol. 55, part 1 (Philadelphia, 1965), 5–28.

————. "Peter Chelčický's Place on the Hussite Left," Introduction to "Peter Chelčický: Treatises on Christianity and the Social Order," *Studies in Medieval and Renaissance History*, I, ed. W. Bowsky (Lincoln, Nebraska, 1964), 107–136.

————. "Pius Aeneas Among the Taborites," *Church History*, XXVIII (1959), 281–309.

————. "The Prague Insurrection of 30 July 1419," *Medievalia et Humanistica*, XVII (1966), 106–126.

————. "The Religion of Hussite Tabor," in *The Czechoslovak Contribution to World Culture*, ed. M. Rechcigl (The Hague: Mouton, 1964), pp. 210–223.

Kavka, F. "The Hussite Movement and the Czech Reformation," *Journal of World History*, V (1960), 830–856.

Köpstein, Horst. "Über den deutschen Hussiten Friedrich Reiser," *Zeitschrift für Geschichtswissenschaft*, VII (1959), 1068–1082.

————. "Über die Teilnahme von Deutschen an der hussitischen revolutionären Bewegung," *Ibid.*, XI (1963), 116–145.

Krofta, K. "L'aspect national et social du mouvement hussite," *Le Monde Slave*, V (1928).

————. "Bohemia in the Fifteenth Century," *Cambridge Medieval History*, VIII (1936), 65–115.

————. "La France et le mouvement religieux tchèque," *Le Monde Slave*, XII (1935), 161–185, 321–360.

Lippert, J. "Die Čechisirung der böhmischen Städte im XV. Jahrhunderte," *MVGDB*, V (1867), 174–195.

Loserth, J. "Beiträge zur Geschichte der husitischen Bewegung, IV. Die Streit-schriften und Unionsverhandlungen zw. den Katholiken und Husiten in den Jahren 1412 und 1413," *AÖG*, LXXV (1889), 287–413 (texts, pp. 333 ff.).

——. "Beiträge zur Geschichte der husitischen Bewegung, V. Gleichzeitige Berichte und Actenstücke zur Ausbreitung des Wiclifismus in Böhmen und Mähren von 1410 bis 1419," *AÖG*, LXXXII (1895), 327–418 (texts, pp. 348 ff.).

——. "Der Kirchen- und Klostersturm der Husiten und sein Ursprung," *Zeitschrift für Geschichte und Politik*, V (1888), 259–290.

——. "Die litterarischen Widersacher des Huss in Mähren. 1. Stephan von Dolein," *Zeitschrift des Vereins für Geschichte Mährens und Schlesiens*, I (1897), 1–16.

——. "Neuere Erscheinungen der Wiclif- und Huss-Literatur," *Ibid.*, XX (1916), 258–271.

——. "Simon von Tischnow. Ein Beitrag zur Geschichte des böhmischen Wiclifismus," *MVGDB*, XXVI (1888), 221–245.

——. "Über die Beziehungen zwischen englischen und böhmischen Wiclifiten in den beiden ersten Jarhzehnten des 15. Jahrhunderts," *Mitteilungen des Instituts für österreichische Geschichtsforschung*, XII (1891), 254–269.

——. "Über die Versuche wiclif-husitische Lehren nach Österreich, Polen, Un-garn und Croatien zu verpflanzen," *MVGDB*, XXIV (1886), 97–116.

——. "Die Wiclif'sche Abendmahlslehre und ihre Aufnahme in Böhmen," *MVGDB*, XXX (1892), 1–33.

——. "Wiclif's Buch 'Von der Kirche' (*De ecclesia*) und die Nachbildungen desselben in Böhmen," *MVGDB*, XXIV (1886), 381–418.

——. "Zur Geschichte des Wiclifismus in Mähren," *Zeitschrift des Vereins für Geschichte Mährens und Schlesiens*, XVII (1913), 190–205.

Lützow, F. *The Hussite Wars* (London: J. M. Dent, 1914).

Macek, Josef. *The Hussite Movement in Bohemia* (2d ed.; Prague: Orbis, 1958).

Martinů, Johann. *Die Waldesier und die husitische Reformation in Böhmen* (Vienna and Leipzig: H. Kirsch, 1910).

Molnár, Amadeo. "Apocalypse XII dans l'interprétation hussite," *Revue d'Histoire et de Philosophie Religieuses* (No. 1, 1965), 212–231.

——. "L'Evolution de la théologie hussite," *Ibid.* (No. 2, 1963), 133–171.

——. "Želivský, prédicateur de la révolution," *Communio viatorum*, II (1959), 324–334.

Müller, J. T. *Geschichte der böhmischen Brüder*, I. (Herrnhut, 1922).

——. "Magister Nikolaus von Dresden," *Zeitschrift für Brüdergeschichte*, IX (1915), 80–109.

Nejedlý, Zdeněk. "Das Verhältnis des hussitischen Gesanges zu der vorhussiti-schen Musik," *VKČSN* (1904).

Ozolin, A. I. "Gusity v Turně," *Učenyje zapiski instituta Slavjanoveděnija*, VI (Moscow, 1952), 330–340.

——. "Manifesty goroda Pragi v gody krest'janskoj vojny v Čechii," *Ibid.*, V (1952), 327–342.

Palacký, František. *Geschichte von Böhmen,* Vol. III, Nos. i–iii (Prague, 1845–1851–1854).

———. *Würdigung der alten böhmischen Geschichtschreiber* (Prague, 1830).

Peschke, Erhard. "Die Bedeutung Wiclefs für die Theologie der Böhmen," *Zeitschrift für Kirchengeschichte,* LIV (1935), 462–483.

Preger, Wilhelm. "Über das Verhältnis der Taboriten zu den Waldesiern des 14. Jahrhunderts," *Abhandlungen der königlichen Bayerischen Akademie der Wissenschaften,* hist. Cl., XVIII (1889), 1–111.

Schlesinger, L. "Saaz in der Husitenzeit bis zum Tode Žižkas," *MVGDB,* XXVII (1889), 97–153.

Schmidt, Valentin. "Südböhmen während der Hussitenkriege," *MVGDB,* XLVI (1908), 203–245, 326–356.

Schofield, A. "An English Version of Some Events in Bohemia During 1434," *Slavonic and East European Review,* Vol. XLVII, No. 99 (1964), 312–331.

Seibt, F. "Communitas Primogenita. Zur Prager Hegemonialpolitik in der hussitischen Revolution," *Historisches Jahrbuch,* LXXXI (1962), 80–100.

———. "Geistige Reformbewegungen zur Zeit des Konstanzer Konzils," *Vorträge und Forschungen,* IX (Konstanz, 1965), 31–46.

———. "Hus und die Hussiten in der tschechischen wissenschaftlichen Literatur seit 1945," *Zeitschrift für Ostforschung,* VII (1958), 566–590.

———. *Hussitica. Zur Struktur einer Revolution* (Cologne-Graz: Böhlau Verlag, 1965).

———. "Die hussitische Revolution," *Zwischen Frankfurt und Prag* (Munich, 1963), 75–102.

———. "Die Hussitenzeit als Kulturepoche," *Historische Zeitschrift,* CXCV (1962), 21–62.

Spinka, Matthew. "Peter Chelčický, the Spiritual Father of the Unitas Fratrum," *Church History,* XII (1943), 271–291.

Tomek, Václav. *Johann Žižka,* trans. V. Prochaska (Prague: Otto, 1882).

Töpfer, Bernhard. "Fragen der hussitischen revolutionären Bewegung," *Zeitschrift für Geschichtswissenschaft,* XI (1963), 146–167.

Uhlirz, Matthilde. "Der Genesis der vier Prager Artikel," *SKAW,* CLXXV (1914), Abh. III, 98 pp.

———. "Petrus von Dresden. Ein Beitrag zur Geschichte des Laienkelches," *Zeitschrift des Vereins für Geschichte Mährens und Schlesiens,* XVIII (1914), 227–238.

Vogl, K. *Petr Cheltschitzki, ein Profet an der Wende der Zeiten* (Zürich-Leipzig: Rotapfel, 1926).

Werner, Ernst. "Die Nachrichten über die böhmischen 'Adamiten' in religionshistorischer Sicht," *Circumcellionen und Adamiten,* by T. Büttner and E. Werner (Berlin: Akademie-Verlag, 1959), pp. 73–141.

———. "Popular Ideologies in Late Medieval Europe: Taborite Chiliasm and Its Antecedents," *Comparative Studies in Society and History,* II (1960), 81–100.

Wulf, Max von. "Hussitisches Kriegswesen," *Preussische Jahrbücher,* LXIX (1892), 673–689.

———. "Zahlen der hussitischen Heere," *MVGDB*, XXXI (1893), 92–99.
Zöllner, R. *Zur Vorgeschichte des Bauernkrieges* (Dresden, 1871).

WORKS IN CZECH

Auštecká, Božena. *Jan Želivský jako politik.* Husitský Archiv, II (Prague, 1925).
Bartoš, František M. *Čechy v době Husově 1378–1415.* České dějiny, II, 6 (Prague: Laichter, 1947).
———. "Chelčický a Valdenští," *JSH*, XVI (1947), 33–38.
———. *Co víme o Husovi nového* (Prague: Pokrok, 1946).
———. "Dantova Monarchie, Cola di Rienzo, Petrarka a počátky reformace a humanismu u nás," *VKČSN* (1951), No. 5, 22 pp.
———. *Do čtyř pražských artykulů. Z myšlenkových i ústavních zápasů let 1415–1420* (Prague, 1925). (Also in *Sborník příspěvků k dějinám hlavního města Prahy,* V (1932), 481–591; a 2d ed. (Prague, 1940) omits all the appendices.) Includes appendices: I, "Počátky táborství a pražské jeho ohnisko z let 1414–17"; II, "Roztržka v husitské straně r. 1417"; III, "Vznik pražských artikulů"; IV, "Z dějin chiliasmu r. 1420."
———. "Hus a Viklef," in *Husitství a cizina,* pp. 20–58.
———. "Hus jako student a profesor Karlovy university," *Acta Universitatis Carolinae,* Phil. et Hist., II (1958), 9–26.
———. *Husitská revoluce,* I. *Doba Žižkova 1415–1426.* České dějiny, II, 7 (Prague: ČSAV, 1965).
———. *Husitství a cizina* (Prague: Čin, 1931).
———. *Kniha Zd. Nejedlého o husitské písni a bohoslužbě* (Prague, 1915).
———. "K počátkům Petra Chelčického," *ČČM,* LXXXVIII (1914), 27–35, 149–160, 303–314.
———. "Miličovo obrácení," *Ze zápasů české reformace* (Prague: Kalich, 1959), pp. 7–17.
———. "Miličův Sermo de die novissimo," *Reformační sborník,* VIII (1946), 49–58.
———. "Myšlenka svrchovanosti lidu v husitské revoluce. Marsiliův *Defensor Pacis* v husitské literatuře," *ČČM,* CII (1928), 13–26. (Repr. *Husitství a cizina,* pp. 154–175).
———. "Německá kronika [*Flores temporum*] v duchovní výzbroji Táborů," *JSH,* XII (1939), 82–85.
———. "Pad Želivského," *JSH,* XXI (1952).
———. "Pikardi a Pikarti," *ČČM,* CI (1927), 225–250. (Repr. *Husitství a cizina,* pp. 176–208.)
———. "Počátky kalicha v Čechách," *ČČM,* XCVI (1922), 43–51, 157–173; XCVII (1923), 34–51. (Repr. *H. a ciz.,* pp. 59–112.)
———. "Příspěvky k dějinám Václava IV.," *VČA,* LI (1942), 67–104; LIII (1944), 75–108.
———. "Prvý sněm husitské revoluce," *JSH,* XX (1951), 81–87.
———. "Sněm husitské revoluce v betlémské kapli," *JSH,* XVIII (1949), 97–102.

———. "Studie k Husovi a jeho době. 1. Hus a Valdenství. 2. Hus ve sporech o Viklefa 1401–1408," *ČČM*, LXXXIX (1915), 1–8, 273–285.

———. "Studie o Žižkovi a jeho době," *ČČM*, XCVIII (1924), 1–15, 97–105, 209–221; XCIX (1925), 13–22, 242–257.

———. *Světci a kacíři* (Prague, 1949).

———. "Táboři a duchovní jejich otec," *JSH*, II (1929), 75–84.

———. "Táborské bratrstvo let 1425–1426 na soudě svého biskupa Mikuláše z Pelhřimova," *ČSPSČ*, XXIX (1921), 102–122.

———. "V předvečer Kutnohorského dekretu," *ČČM*, CII (1928), 97–113.

———. "Vznik a počátky táborství," *Husitství a cizina*, pp. 113–153. (Repr. of *Do čtyř art.*, Appendix I.)

———. "Vznik a osudy protestu proti Husovu upálení," *JSH*, XXII (1953), 50–60.

———. "Vznik Táborství a Valdenští," *JSH*, III (1930), 38–48.

———. "Zastupci Karlovy university na kostnickém koncile," *Sborník G. Friedricha* (Prague, 1931), pp. 1–8.

———. "Žižka a pikarti," *Kalich*, VIII (1924), 97–108.

———. "Z počátků Jednoty bratrské," *ČČM*, XCV (1921), 30–43, 127–139, 203–218.

———. "Z politické literatury doby husitské," *SbH*, V (1957), 21–67.

Betts, R. R. "Jeronym Pražský," *ČsČH*, V (1957), 199–226.

Borecký, Fr. *Mistr Jakoubek ze Stříbra* (Prague: Kalich, 1945).

Chaloupecký, Václav. *Selská otázka v husitství* (Bratislava, 1926).

———. "K dějinám Valdenských v Čechách před hnutím husitském," *ČČH*, XXXI (1925), 369–382.

Chytil, Karel. *Antikrist v naukách a umění středověku a husitské obrazné antithese.* Rozpravy České Akademie, Tř. I, No. 59 (Prague, 1918).

Dekret Kutnohorský a jeho místo v dějinách. Acta Universitatis Carolinae, Phil. et hist., 2 (Prague, 1959).

Eršil, Jaroslav. *Správní a finanční vztahy avignonského papežství k českým zemím ve třetí čtvrtině 14. století.* Rozpravy ČSAV, LXIX, Řada SV, No. 10 (1959).

Fikerle, J. "Čechové na koncilu kostnickém," *ČČH*, IX (1903), 413–428.

Goll, Jaroslav. *Čechy a Prusy ve středověku* (Prague: Bursík and Kohout, 1897).

———. *Petr Chelčický a Jednota bratrská v XV. století* (Prague, 1916).

Graus, František. *Městská chudina v době předhusitské* (Prague: Melantrich, 1949).

———. *Dějiny venkovského lidu v Čechách v době předhusitské,* II (Prague: ČSAV, 1957).

Hlaváček, Ivan. "Husitské sněmy," *SbH*, IV (1956), 71–109.

———. "Inkvisice v Čechách ve 30. letech 14. století," *ČsČH*, V (1957), 526–538.

Hoch, Karel, "Husité a válka," *Česká mysl,* VIII (1907), 131 ff., 193 ff., 285 ff., 375 ff., 439 ff.

Holinka, Rudolf. "Počátky táborského pikartství," *Bratislava,* VI (1932), 187–195.

————. *Sektářství v Čechách před revolucí husitskou. Sborník filos. fak. university Komenského v Bratislavě,* VI (1929), No. 3.

Kalivoda, Robert. *Husitská ideologie* (Prague: ČSAV, 1961).

————. "Vytvoření revoluční ideologie selsko-plebejského Tábora," *Filosofický časopis,* V (1957), 821–876.

Kaminsky, Howard. "K dějinám chiliastického Tábora. O traktátu Ad occurrendum homini insano," *ČsČH,* VIII (1960), 895–904.

Kejř, Jiří. "Boj o státní formu v husitském revolučním hnutí," *Právněhistorické studie,* II (1956), 130–171.

————. "Deklarace pražské university z 10. března 1417 o přijímání pod obojí a její historické pozadí," *SbH,* VIII (1961), 133–154.

————. *Dvě studie o husitském právnictví.* Rozpravy ČSAV, LXIV, Řada SV, No. 5 (1954).

————. *Husitský právník M. Jan z Jesenice* (Prague: ČSAV, 1965).

————. "O některých spisech M. Jana z Jesenice," *LF,* XI, n.s. (1963), 77–90.

————. "Quodlibet M. Prokopa z Kladrub z r. 1417," *Acta Universitatis Carolinae,* Phil. et Hist., II (1958), 27–48.

————. "Quodlibetní Questie Kodexu UK X E 24," *LF,* LXXVIII (1955), 216–221; LXXIX (1956), 63–70, 228–233.

————. *Stát, církev a společnost v disputacích na pražské universitě v době Husově a husitské.* Rozpravy ČSAV, LXXIV, Řada SV, No. 14 (1964).

————. "Sporné otázky v bádání o dekretu kutnohorském," *Acta Universitatis Carolinae,* Hist. Univ. Carol., III (1962), fasc. 1, pp. 83–121.

————. "Struktura a průběh disputace de quolibet na pražské universitě," *Ibid.,* I (1960), 17–45.

————. "Z disputací na pražské universitě v době Husově a husitské," *SbH,* VII (1960), 47–74.

Krofta, K. "Kurie a církevní správa zemí českých v době předhusitské," *ČČH,* X (1904), 15 ff., 125 ff., 249 ff., 373 ff.; XII (1906), 7 ff., 178 ff., 274 ff., 426 ff.; XIV (1908), 18 ff., 172 ff., 273 ff., 416 ff.

————. "Novější bádání o Husovi a hnutí husitském," *ČČH,* XXI (1915), 40–78, 121–160, 347–379.

————. "N. V. Jastrebova Studie o Petru Chelčickém a jeho době," *ČČH,* XV (1909), 59–72, 152–172.

Kybal, V. *M. Jan Hus, život a učení,* II. *Učení,* i–iii (Prague: Laichter, 1923–1926–1931).

————. "M. Matěj z Janova a M. Jakoubek ze Stříbra. Srovnávací kapitola o Antikristu," *ČČH,* XI (1905), 22–37.

————. *M. Matěj z Janova. Jeho život, spisy, a učení* (Prague: KČSN, 1905).

Macek, Josef. "Chiliasmus ve světových dějinách," *ČsČH,* XII (1964), 860–863.

————. "K ohlasu husitství v Německu," *ČsČH,* IV (1956), 189–207.

————., ed. *Mezinárodní ohlas husitství* (Prague: ČSAV, 1958).

————. "Národnostní otázka v husitském revolučním hnutí," *ČsČH,* III (1955), 4–29.

————. "K počátkům husitství v Písku," *JSH,* XX (1953), 113–128.

———. *Tábor v husitském revolučním hnutí.* 2 vols. (Prague: ČSAV, 1952–1955; vol. I, 2d ed., 1956).

———. "Táborské chiliastické články," *SbH,* I (1953), 53–64.

———. "Úmluvy zdické," *Acta Universitatis Carolinae,* Phil. et Hist., II (1958), 195–212.

Maleczyńska, Ewa. *Ruch husycki w Czechach i w Polsce* (Warsaw, 1959 [in Polish]).

Mendl, Bedřich. "Hospodářské a sociální poměry v městech pražských 1378–1434," *ČČH,* XXII (1916); XXIII (1917).

———. "Sociální krise měst ve století čtrnáctém," *ČČH,* XXX (1924), 35–73; XXXI (1925), 233–270, 533–565; XXXII (1926), 249–282.

Nechutová, Jana. "Traktát Mikuláše z Dráždan 'De imaginibus' a jeho vztah k Matěji z Janova," *Sborník prací filos. fak. Brněnské university,* E 9 (1964), pp. 149–161.

Nejedlý, Zdeněk. *Počátky husitského zpěvu* (Prague: KČSN, 1907); *Dějiny husitského zpěvu za válek husitských* (Prague: KČSN, 1913). These are now included in the reprint, in new format: *Dějiny husitského zpěvu,* 6 vols. (Prague: ČSAV, 1954–1956).

———. "Mládí Jana z Rokycan," *ČČM,* LXXIII (1899), 517–534.

Novotný, Václav. *Hus v Kostnici a česká šlechta* (Prague, 1915).

———. *M. Jan Hus, život a učení,* I. *Život a dílo,* i–ii (Prague: Laichter, 1919–1921).

———. *Náboženské hnutí české ve 14. and 15. stol.* (Prague: Otto [1915]).

———. "Několik příspěvků k poznání osoby a doby Žižkovy. IV. K otázce polské kandidatury na český trůn," *Sborník Žižkův,* ed. R. Urbánek (Prague, 1924), pp. 100–133.

Odložilík, Otakar. "Z počátků husitství na Moravě. Šimon z Tišnova a Jan Vavřincův z Račic," *ČMM,* XLIX (1925), 1–170.

Palacký, František. *Dějiny národu českého v Čechach a na Moravě,* III, i–ii (2d ed.; Prague: Tempský, 1870–1871).

Pekař, Josef. *Žižka a jeho doba.* 4 vols. (Prague: Vesmír, 1927–1928–1930–1933).

Prokeš, J. "K počátkům M. Jana Rokycany," *VKČSN* (1927).

———. "Kvodlibet Šimona z Tišnova r. 1416," *ČMM,* XLV (1921), 25 ff.

———. *M. Prokop z Plzně* (Prague, 1927).

Ryba, Bohumil. "Kvodlibet Šimona z Tišnova," *LF,* LXXII (1948), 177–186.

Schmidtová, Anežka. "Hus a Viklef," *LF,* LXXIX (1956), 219–227.

Sedláček, A. "Uvahy o osobách v stížných listech l. 1415 psaných," *ČČH,* XXIII (1917), 85–109, 310–352 (cf. also *ČSPSČ,* XXX).

Sedlák, Jan. "Husův pomocník v evangeliu," *ST,* I (1914), 362–377; II (1915), 302–316, 446–449; III, i [1919], 24–38.

———. *Mikuláš z Dráždan* (Brno, 1914).

———. *M. Jan Hus* (Prague: Dědictví sv. Prokopa, 1915).

———. "Počátkové kalicha," *ČKD,* LII (1911), 97–105, 244–250, 397–401, 496–501, 583–587, 703–708, 786–791; LIV (1913), 226–232, 275–278, 404–410, 465–470, 708–713; LV (1914), 75–84, 113–120, 315–322.

Šimák, J. "Bitva u Sudoměře," *Sborník Žižkův* (Prague, 1924), pp. 75–81.

Souček, Bohuslav. "Veritas super omnia. Z biblických studií a odkazu Mikuláše Biskupce z Pelhřimova," *Křesťanská revue* (1961), No. 6, *Theologická příloha*, pp. 73–90.

Svejkovský, Fr. "Z básnické činnosti Jana Čapka," *LF*, LXXXV (1962), 282–295.

Toman, Hugo. *Husitské válečnictví za doby Žižkovy a Prokopovy* (Prague: KČSN, 1898).

Tomek, Václav. *Dějepis města Prahy*, III, IV, V (Prague: F. Řiwnáč, 1875, 1899², 1881).

——. *Jan Žižka* (Prague: Otto, 1879).

Urbánek, Rudolf. *Lipany a konec polních vojsk* (Prague: Melantrich, 1934).

——. "Mařík Rvačka jako protihusitský satirík," *ČSPSČ*, LXIII (1955), 1–24.

——. "Počátky českého messianismu," *Českou minulostí*, edd. Odložilík *et al.* (Novotný Festschrift) (Prague, 1929).

——. "Český messianismus ve své době hrdinské," *Od pravěku k dnešku* (Pekař Festschrift) (Prague, 1930).

——. "Satirická skládání budyšínského rukopisu M. Vavřince z Březové z r. 1420 v ramci ostatní jeho činnosti literární," *VKČSN* (1951), III, 38 pp.

——. "Žižka a husitské válečnictví," *Sborník Žižkův*, ed. R. Urbánek (Prague: Vědecký Ústav Vojenský, 1924), pp. 20–74.

Vlk, Miloslav. "Obrazy v Betlémské kapli. Rozbor historických pramenů," *ČČM*, CXXX (1961), 151–168.

PRIMARY SOURCES

I. Catalogues

Bartoš, F. M. "Husitika a bohemika několika knihoven německých a švýcarských," *VKČSN* (1931), V, 92 pp.

——. *Literární činnost M. Jakoubka ze Stříbra* (Prague: Česká Akademie Věd a Umění, 1925).

——. *Literární činnost M. J. Husi* (Prague: ČAVU, 1948).

——. *Literární činnost M. Jana Rokycany, M. Jana Příbrama, M. Petra Payna* (Prague: ČAVU, 1928).

——. *Soupis rukopisů národního musea v Praze*. 2 vols. (Prague, 1926–1927).

Bartoš, F. M., and Spunar, P. *Soupis pramenů k literární činnosti M. Jana Husa a M. Jeronýma Pražského* (Prague: Historický ústav ČSAV, 1965).

Dokoupil, Vladislav. *Soupis rukopisů Mikulovské Dietrichsteinské Knihovny* (Prague, 1958).

Eršil, Jaroslav, and Pražák, Jiří. *Archiv Pražské Metropolitní Kapituly. I. Katalog listin a listů z doby předhusitské (–1419)* (Prague, 1956).

Petrů, Eduard. *Soupis díla Petra Chelčického* (Prague, 1957).

Podlaha, Ant. *Soupis rukopisů knihovny metropolitní kapitoly pražské*. 2 vols. (Prague: ČAVU, 1910–1922).

Prokeš, Jaroslav. *Husitika vatikánské knihovny v Římě* (Prague, 1928).

Truhlář, Josef. *Catalogus codicum manu scriptorum latinorum qui in C.R. bibliotheca publica atque universitatis pragensis asservantur.* 2 vols. (Prague: KČSN, 1905–1906).

Weber, J. *et al. Soupis rukopisů v Třeboni a v Českém Krumlově* (Prague: ČSAV, 1958).

II. *Sources: Editions, Translations, Studies*

Annenkov, J. S., and Jagić, V., edd. *Sočinenija Petra Cheľčickago.* . . . 2. *Replika protiv Biskupca. Sbornik otdělenija russkago jazyka i slovesnosti Imperatorskoj akademij nauk,* LXVI (St. Petersburg, 1893), 411–501.

Bartoš, F. M. "Chronicon veteris collegiati Pragensis," *ČČM,* XCVIII (1924), 260–267.

——. *Dvě studie o husitských postilách. Rozpravy ČSAV,* LXV, Řada SV, No. 4 (1955).

——. "Manifesty města Prahy z doby husitské," *Sborník příspěvků k dějinám hlavního města Prahy,* VII (1932), 253–309.

——. "Z musejních i jiných rukopisů Starých letopisů," *ČČM,* CII (1928), 208–228.

——. "Nová postila Jana Želivského?" *ČČM,* CI (1927), 135–148.

——. "Předvečer husitské revoluce v osvětlení pražského duchovního," *JSH,* VIII (1935), 43–49.

——. "Puer Bohemus. Dva projevy husitské propagandy," *VKČSN* (1922–23). (Partly superseded in "Manifesty," above.)

——. *Orationes quibus Nicolaus de Pelhřimov.. . . et Ulricus de Znojmo . . . articulos de peccatis publicis puniendis et libertate verbi dei in Concilio Basiliensi anno 1433 ineunte defenderunt.* Archivum Taboriense (Tabor, 1935).

——. *Petri Payne Anglici, positio, replica et propositio in concilio Basiliensi a. 1433 atque oratio ad Sigismundum regem a. 1429 Bratislaviae pronunciatae* (Tabor, 1949).

——. "Sborník husitského kazatele asi z r. 1415," *VČA,* LVII (1948).

——. "Španělský biskup proti Táboru a Praze," *JSH,* XI (1938), 67–70.

——. "K traktátovým cyklům J. Příbrama proti táborům a Paynovi," *LF,* XLI (1914), 112–121.

Bartoš, F. M., and Frinta, A. "Kněze Petra Kányše Vyznání víry a večeře Páně z r. 1421," *JSH,* I (1928), 2–12.

Bernt, A. "Ein deutsches Hussitenpaternoster aus dem Stifte Hohenfurt," *MVGDB,* XXXIX (1901), 320–322.

Černý, K. "Klasobraní po rukopisech," *LF,* XXV (1898), 259–280, 384–404, 453–478 (Chelčický's "Replika proti Rokycanovi" and other texts).

Daňhelka, J., ed. *Husitské pisně* (Prague, 1948).

——., ed. *Husitské skladby budyšínského rukopisu* (Prague: Orbis, 1952).

Döllinger, J. *Beiträge zur Sektengeschichte des Mittelalters,* II, *Dokumente vornehmlich zur Geschichte der Valdesier und Katharer* (Munich: C. H. Beck, 1890).

Emler, Josef, and Tingl, František, edd. *Libri confirmationum ad beneficia*

ecclesiastica pragensem per archidiocesim (1354–1436), 10 Bks. in 8 vols.
(Prague: E. Grégr, 1867–1874; Prague: B. Stýblo, 1868: Prague: Grégr, 1879;
Prague: I. Kober, 1865–1866; Prague: Grégr, 1883–1886–1889).

Erben, Karel, ed. *Mistra Jana Husi Sebrané spisy české*. 3 vols. (Prague: Tempský, 1865–1866–1868).

Flajšhans, V., and Kominková, M., edd. *Mag. Joannis Hus, Super IV Sententiarum* (Prague: J. Vilímek, 1905–1906).

Goll, Jaroslav, ed. *Fontes rerum Bohemicarum*, V (Prague: Nadání F. Palackého,
1893). (Includes the "Hussite Chronicle" of Laurence of Březová and the
"Chronicon Universitatis Pragensis," etc.)

Hardt, H. von der. *Rerum concilii oecumenici constantiensis*, III, IV [*Alias,
Magnum concilium constantiense*] (Frankfurt and Leipzig, 1698–1699).

Historia et monumenta Joannis Hus atque Hieronymi Pragensis. 2 vols. (Nuremberg: J. Montanus and U. Neuberus, 1715; 1st ed.: Nuremberg, 1558).

Höfler, Konstantin. *Geschichtschreiber der husitischen Bewegung in Böhmen*. 3
vols. *Fontes rerum Austriacarum, Erste Abtheilung*, II, VI, VII (Vienna,
1856–1865–1866).

Holinka, R., ed. *Traktáty Petra Chelčického. O trojím lidu, O církvi svaté*.
(Prague: Melantrich, 1940).

Jakoubek ze Stříbra. *Betlemská kázání z roku 1416* (Prague: Blahoslav, 1951).

Kaminsky, Howard; Bilderback, D.; Boba, I.; Rosenberg, P., eds. *Master Nicholas of Dresden, The Old Color and the New. Transactions of the American
Philosophical Society*, New Series, Vol. 55, Part 1 (Philadelphia, 1965).

Kaminsky, Howard, trans. "Peter Chelčický: Treatises on Christianity and the
Social Order," *Studies in Medieval and Renaissance History*, I, ed. W. Bowsky
(Lincoln, Nebraska: U. of Nebraska Press, 1964), 105–179. (Translations of *O
trojím lidu* and *O církvi svaté*, pp. 137–173.)

Klicman, L., ed. *Processus judiciarius contra Jeronimum de Praga habitus Vien-
nae a. 1410–1412* (Prague: Česká Akademie, 1898).

Krofta, K. "Zur Geschichte der husitischen Bewegung. Drei Bullen Papst Johanns
XXIII aus dem Jahre 1414," *Mitteilungen des Instituts für österreichische
Geschichtsforschung*, XXIII (1902), 598–610.

———. "O některých spisech M. Jana z Příbramě," *ČČM*, LXXIII (1899),
209–220.

———, ed. *Petr Chelčický: O boji duchovním a O trojím lidu* (Prague: J. Otto,
1911).

Kybal, Vlastimil, ed. *Matthiae de Janov dicti magister Parisiensis, Regulae veteris
et novi testamenti*. 4 vols. (Innsbrück and Prague: Wagner, 1908–1909–1911–
1913). Vol. 5 ed. O. Odložilík and V. Kybal (Prague, 1926).

Loserth, J. "Beiträge zur Geschichte der husitischen Bewegung, III. Der tractatus
de longevo schismate des Abtes Ludolf von Sagan," *AÖG*, LX (1880), 343–561
(text on 402 ff.).

———. "Urkunden und Traktate betreffend die Verbreitung des Wiclifismus in
Böhmen," *MVGDB*, XXV (1887), 329–346.

————. "Zur Geschichte der husitischen Bewegung," *MVGDB*, XXIX (1891), 290–296.

Lydius, Balthasar, ed. *Waldensia, id est conservatio verae ecclesiae,* 2 vols. (Rotterdam and Dordrecht: J. L. Berewout, 1616–1617). (Includes Taborite Confession of 1431.)

Macek, Josef, ed. *Ktož jsú boží bojovníci. Čtení o Táboře v husitském revolučním hnutí* (Prague: Melantrich, 1951).

Mansi, Joannes, ed. *Sacrorum conciliorum nova et amplissima collectio,* vols. 27–31 (Venice: A. Zatta, 1784–1798 [repr. Paris: H. Welter, 1903 ff.]).

Mareš, František, ed. *Popravčí kniha panův z Rožmberka.* Rozpravy KČSN, Řada 6., No. 9 (Prague, 1878).

Molnár, Amadeo, ed. *Jan Želivský. Dochovaná kázání z roku 1419.* I (Prague: ČSAV, 1953).

Nebeský, V. "Verše na Husity z rukopisu musejního," *ČČM,* XXVI (1852), 141–151. (Texts repr. Svejkovský, below.)

Nejedlý, Zdeněk, ed. *Prameny k synodám strany pražské a táborské v let. 1441–1444* (Prague: KČSN, 1900).

Neumann, Augustin. *Nové prameny k dějinám husitství na Moravě. ST,* Vol. VI (Olomouc: Matice Cyrilometodějská, 1930).

————. "Glossy v Drändorfově postile," *Hlídka,* XLI (1924), 457–465.

————. *Prameny k dějinám duchovenstva v době předhusitské a Husově. ST* [vol. V] (Olomouc: Matice Cyrilometodějská, 1926).

Novaček, J. "Sigismundi regis Bohemiae litterae donationum regalium," *VKČSN* (1903), No. I, 56 pp.

Novotný, Václav, ed. *M. Jana Husi, Korespondence a dokumenty* (Prague: Komise pro vydávání pramenů náboženského hnutí českého, 1920).

————. "Monitorium Patriarchy konstantinopolského Jana na uchvatitele církevního majetku v Čechách z r. 1418," *VČA,* XXIV (1915).

————. *Petri de Mladoňovice opera historica nec non aliae de M. Johanne Hus et M. Hieronymo Pragensi relationes et memoriae. Fontes rerum Bohemicarum,* VIII (Prague, 1932).

Palacký, František, ed. *Archiv český,* I–VI (Prague, 1840–1872).

————, ed. *Documenta Mag. Joannis Hus vitam, doctrinam, causam in constantiensi Concilio actam et controversias de religione in Bohemia annis 1403–1418 motas illustrantia* (Prague: F. Tempský, 1869).

————. *Die Geschichte des Hussitenthums und Prof. Constantin Höfler. Kritische Studien* (2d ed.; Prague: Tempský, 1868).

————, ed. *Staří letopisové čeští, 1378–1527. Scriptores rerum Bohemicarum,* III (Prague: KČSN, 1829).

————, ed. *Urkundliche Beiträge zur Geschichte des Hussitenkriegs vom Jahre 1419 an.* 2 vols. (Prague: Tempský, 1873).

Palacký, František, and Birk, E., edd. *Monumenta conciliorum generalium seculi decimi quinti. Concilium Basileense, Scriptorum.* I (Vienna: Officina typographica Aulae et Status, 1857).

Pez, Bernard. *Thesaurus anecdotorum novissimus.* IV, ii (Augsburg, 1723). (Stephen of Dolany's Anti-Hussite works.)

Piccolomini, Aeneas Sylvius. *Historia bohemica.* Many editions; I use *De Bohemorum . . . origine ac gestis historia* (Prague: J. G. Schneider, n. d. [1766]).

Ryba, Bohumil, ed. *Betlemské texty* (Prague: Orbis, 1951).

———, ed. *Magistri Iohannis Hus. Quodlibet. Disputationis . . . a. 1411 habitae Enchiridion* (Prague: Orbis, 1948).

Rynešová, B., ed. *Listář a listinář Oldřicha z Rožmberka, 1418–1462.* Vol. I, 1418–1437 (Prague: Ministerstvo školství, 1929).

Schaff, David, trans. *John Huss, De ecclesia. The Church* (New York: Scribners, 1915).

Schmidtová, A., ed. *Iohannes Hus, Magister Universitatis Carolinae, Positiones, Recommendationes, Sermones* (Prague: Státní pedagogické nakladatelství, 1958).

———, ed. *Magistri Iohannis Hus. Sermones de tempore qui Collecta dicuntur. Magistri Iohannis Hus Opera omnia,* VII (Prague: ČSAV, 1959).

Sedlák, Jan. "Jakoubkův traktát remanenční," *Hlídka,* XXIX (1912), 433–440.

———. *Studie a texty k náboženským dějinám českým,* I-III,i (Olomouc: Matice Cyrilometodějská, 1914–1915–1919).

———. *Táborské traktáty eucharistické* (Brno, 1918; repr. from *Hlídka*).

Siegl, K. "Briefe und Urkunden zur Geschichte der Hussitenkriege," *Zeitschrift des Vereins für Geschichte Mährens und Schlesiens,* XXII (1918), 15–73, 167–196; XXIII (1919), 1–38.

Sokol, V., ed. "Traktát Mikuláše z Pelhřimova: O zvelebení v pravdě svátosti těla a krve pána našeho Jezukrista," *JSH,* II (1929), *Příloha,* 14 pp.

Šimák, J. V. "Studie ke Starým letopisům českým," *VČA,* XXVII (1918), 171–185.

Šimek, František, ed. *Jakoubek ze Stříbra: Výklad na Zjevenie sv. Jana.* 2 vols. (Prague: Česká Akademie, 1932–1933).

———, ed. *Staré letopisy české z vratislavského rukopisu* (Prague: Historický spolek, 1937).

Spinka, Matthew, trans. "John Hus: On Simony," in *Advocates of Reform, Library of Christian Classics,* XIV (London: SCM Press, 1953), pp. 196–278.

———, trans. *John Hus at the Council of Constance.* Records of Civilization, Vol. 73 (New York: Columbia University Press, 1965).

Straka, J., ed. "Petra Chelčického Replika proti Mikuláše Biskupci táborskému," *JSH,* III (1930), *Příloha* (Tábor, 1930), 17–80.

Svejkovský, František, ed. *Veršované skladby doby husitské* (Prague: ČSAV, 1963).

Svoboda, M., ed. *Mistra Jakoubka ze Stříbra Překlad Viklefova Dialogu* (Prague: Česká Akademie, 1909).

Thomson, S. Harrison, ed. "Four Unpublished *Questiones* of John Hus," *Medievalia et Humanistica,* VII (1952), 71–88.

———, ed. *Magistri Iohannis Hus. Tractatus de Ecclesia* (Boulder, Colorado: U. of Colorado Press, 1956).

————, ed. *Mag. Johannis Hus. Tractatus responsivus* (Princeton, N.J.: Princeton U. Press, 1927).

Workman, H., and Pope, R., transs. *The Letters of John Hus* (London: Hodder & Stoughton, 1904).

INDEX

There are no general entries for Bohemia, Hussites, or Hussitism. Entries for Prague, Taborites, and Utraquism are selective. The names of medieval persons are listed under their places of origin or their cognomens, except when their first names seem obviously the ones under which they would be sought. Saints are listed under their respective names, but the saintly titles of churches and places are listed under *St.* Except for Prague and Tabor, Czech place-names are given in the Czech form, with the German name in parentheses when significantly different.